FAMILY
PSYCHOLOGY

FAMILY PSYCHOLOGY

THE ART OF THE SCIENCE

EDITED BY

WILLIAM M. PINSOF & JAY L. LEBOW

OXFORD
UNIVERSITY PRESS

2005

OXFORD
UNIVERSITY PRESS

Oxford University Press, Inc., publishes works that further
Oxford University's objective of excellence
in research, scholarship, and education.

Oxford   New York
Auckland   Cape Town   Dar es Salaam   Hong Kong   Karachi
Kuala Lumpur   Madrid   Melbourne   Mexico City   Nairobi
New Delhi   Shanghai   Taipei   Toronto

With offices in
Argentina   Austria   Brazil   Chile   Czech Republic   France   Greece
Guatemala   Hungary   Italy   Japan   Poland   Portugal   Singapore
South Korea   Switzerland   Thailand   Turkey   Ukraine   Vietnam

Published by Oxford University Press, Inc.
198 Madison Avenue, New York, New York 10016

www.oup.com

Oxford is a registered trademark of Oxford University Press

Library of Congress Cataloging-in-Publication Data

Family psychology : the art of the science / edited by William M. Pinsof and Jay Lebow.
p.   cm. — (Oxford series in clinical psychology)
Includes bibliographical references and index.
ISBN-13 978-0-19-513557-2
ISBN 0-19-513557-1
1. Family—Psychological aspects.   I. Pinsof, William M.   II. Lebow, Jay.   III. Title.
IV. Series.

HQ728.F3225 2005
306.85′019—dc22   2004017539

1 3 5 7 9 8 6 4 2

Printed in the United States of America
on acid-free paper

With love and hope,
we dedicate this book to our children,
Laura, Caitlin, and Ellen

Preface

This book has three sources. The first was the desire of Joan Bossert and Oxford University Press to publish a handbook of family psychology. The second derived from the twin goals of the Family Psychology Division (43) of the American Psychological Association to stimulate research in family psychology and to more closely integrate researchers into the division membership. The third and last source was our hope, as editors, to stimulate a self-reflective discourse within a leading group of family psychology researchers about the state of the art of family psychology research.

To address these multiple goals, with the consultation and support of the board of directors of Division 43, we came up with a two-phase plan. The first was to create a small, invitation-only conference, to which we would invite leading researchers in five distinct areas of family psychology. The second phase of the plan was to publish a book organized around the five areas, with chapters that elaborated the authors' conference presentations.

Between ourselves and with the directors of Division 43, we went back and forth about which areas to address. After a fair bit of wrangling, we agreed on three selection criteria. We wanted areas (a) with fairly well developed bodies of theory and research, (b) that had substantial fertile ground for new theory and research, and (c) that were of significant public health relevance. We eventually settled on the areas that define the book: depression, families and health, divorce and remarriage, marriage and marital intervention, and partner violence.

After we selected the areas, we struggled with how to determine leading researchers in each area. Because one of our major goals was to stimulate discourse in each area, we thought that it was a good idea to try to invite people who would be able to talk to each other—people who already had at least a minimal professional alliance. We settled on a group leader model, in which we invited one person to function as the leader in each area. The responsibilities of the leader were to determine, with our assistance, the list of invited presenters in their area and to chair the panel at the conference we were planning. We fortunately were able to recruit an august, distinguished, and helpful group of leaders: Nadine Kaslow in depression, Betsy Wood in families and health, James Bray in divorce and remarriage, John Gottman in marriage and marital intervention, and Amy Holtzworth-Munroe in partner violence.

In inviting each of the presenters in each area, we specifically asked that they not use their presentation at the conference and their subsequent chapter in the book as a forum to present their own work. We wanted each researcher to reflect on what they considered the major questions in their area, the research and theoretical dilemmas they had faced in their work, the choices they had made in regard to these dilemmas, and what they considered the major challenges for future research. We wanted them to think self-reflectively about their research, stepping out of their own work to reflect more broadly on their field.

With major financial support from Division 43 and additional support from Oxford University Press, The Family Institute at Northwestern University, and the Office of the Vice President for Research (Lydia Villa-Komaroff) at Northwestern University, we held the two-day conference at Northwestern's beautiful Allen Center alongside Lake Michigan in April 2002. An intensely stimulating two-day experience in which the invitees presented preliminary drafts of their book chapters to the other members of their section panel, as well as to all of the other invitees, the conference culminated the first phase of the process we had planned.

We hoped that the interaction and feedback from the conference would affect each invitee's book chapter. It was our plan that the interaction within each section panel and between the panel and the audience would impact each presenter's chapter for the book. We wanted the synergy of the conference to help the presentations/ chapters in each section/part inform each other and cohere.

After the conference we engaged in a dialogue with each author and each section leader about each chapter. We strove to help the authors look at the big issues and challenges in their research area and to explore how they had chosen to address them, exploring, if possible, alternative and future directions.

We also strove to make each part of the book a mini-manual for young researchers in that particular research area. Along these lines we asked the authors to aim their chapters at an imaginary advanced graduate student or postdoctoral fellow interested in building a research program in that research area.

Last, we wanted the authors, as much as possible, to address relevant domains from the scientific paradigm we articulate in the chapter at the beginning of the book. Unfortunately, this paradigm was implicit through the period of most of our communication with the authors, only becoming explicit as we finished the book. It particularly informed how we organized each part, treating the chapters that comprised a part as an integrated work addressing as many of the dimensions of the scientific paradigm as possible.

We want to thank all of the authors and section leaders (authors as well) for their wonderful contributions to the book and the art of the science. They did not just write chapters. They prepared their papers, attended the conference, and put up graciously with our editorial hassling and nagging. We also want to thank Joan

Bossert of Oxford University Press; the board of directors of APA Division 43, in particular past presidents Terry Patterson and Nadine Kaslow; and the Office of the Vice President for Research at Northwestern University, especially the vice president at the time of the conference, Lydia Villa-Komaroff. Last, we want to thank Jo Ann Casey at The Family Institute at Northwestern University. Without her invaluable administrative assistance with the conference and her tenacious and astute editorial assistance with the book, this entire project would not have been possible. Her competence, grace, and goodwill facilitated the entire process.

In the scientific tradition, we think of this book as the penultimate step of an experimental pilot project. As the principal investigators, we assembled teams of researchers focused on specific research areas to synergistically generate new knowledge about the conduct of research in their area of expertise and ultimately to create better research. Dear Reader, you are the last step in this experiment. May the book strengthen and inspire your work.

Contents

PART IV FAMILIES AND DEPRESSION

PART V FAMILIES AND HEALTH

Contributors

JOAN ROSENBAUM ASARNOW, Ph.D., Professor of Psychiatry and Biobehavioral Sciences, Neuropsychiatric Institute, University of California, Los Angeles, California

DAVID C. ATKINS, Ph.D., Assistant Professor of Psychology, Fuller Graduate School of Psychology, Pasadena, California

STEVEN R. H. BEACH, Ph.D., Professor, Institute for Behavioral Research, University of Georgia, Athens, Georgia

MARGRET E. BELL, B.A., M.A., Doctoral Candidate, Department of Counseling, Developmental, and Educational Psychology, Boston College, Boston, Massachusetts

MICHELE S. BERK, Ph.D., Assistant Researcher, Neuropsychiatric Institute, University of California, Los Angeles, California

GUILLERMO BERNAL, Ph.D., Professor of Psychology, Department of Psychology, and Director, University Center for Psychological Research, University of Puerto Rico, Río Piedras Campus, San Juan, Puerto Rico

SANFORD L. BRAVER, Ph.D., Professor of Psychology, Principal Investigator, Prevention Research Center, Department of Psychology, Arizona State University, Tempe, Arizona

JAMES H. BRAY, Ph.D., Associate Professor, Department of Family and Community Medicine, Baylor College of Medicine, Houston, Texas

BERNADETTE MARIE BULLOCK, Ph.D., Oregon Social Learning Center, Child and Family Center, University of Oregon, Eugene, Oregon

DEBORAH M. CAPALDI, Ph.D., Senior Scientist, Oregon Social Learning Center, Eugene, Oregon

ANTHONY L. CHAMBERS, Ph.D., Clinical and Research Fellow in Psychology, Harvard Medical School, and Massachusetts General Hospital, Boston, Massachusetts

ANDREW CHRISTENSEN, Ph.D., Professor of Psychology, University of California, Los Angeles, California

JEFFREY T. COOKSTON, Ph.D., Assistant Professor, San Francisco State University, San Francisco, California

BRIAN D. DOSS, Ph.D., Assistant Professor of Psychology, Texas A&M University, College Station, Texas

MARY ANN DUTTON, Ph.D., Professor, Department of Psychiatry, Georgetown University Medical Center, Washington, DC

IRENE EASLING, Dr.P.H., Department of Family and Community Medicine, Baylor College of Medicine, Houston, Texas

MAI EL-KHOURY, M.Phil., Doctoral Candidate, Department of Psychology, The George Washington University, Washington, DC

LAWRENCE FISHER, Ph.D., Professor, Department of Family and Community Medicine, University of California, San Francisco, California

MARION S. FORGATCH, Ph.D., Senior Scientist, Oregon Social Learning Center, Eugene, Oregon

JOHN GOTTMAN, Ph.D., Emeritus Professor of Psychology, University of Washington, and Executive Director, Relationship Research Institute, Seattle, Washington

WILLIAM A. GRIFFIN, Ph.D., Professor, Department of Family and Human Development, and Director, Marital Interaction Lab, Arizona State University, Tempe, Arizona

MAYA E. GUPTA, M.S., Institute for Behavioral Research, University of Georgia, Athens, Georgia

AMY HOLTZWORTH-MUNROE, Ph.D., Professor of Psychology, Indiana University, Bloomington, Indiana

SUSAN M. JOHNSON, Ed.D., Professor of Clinical Psychology, University of Ottawa, and Director, Ottawa Couple and Family Institute, Ottawa, Ontario, Canada

CLAUDIA A. JONES, B.S., Research Project Coordinator, Emory University School of Medicine, Atlanta, Georgia

ERNEST N. JOURILES, Ph.D., Professor of Psychology, Southern Methodist University, Dallas, Texas

NADINE J. KASLOW, Ph.D., Professor and Chief Psychologist, Emory University School of Medicine, Atlanta, Georgia

HYOUN K. KIM, Ph.D., Research Associate, Oregon Social Learning Center, Eugene, Oregon

GALENA H. KLINE, M.A., Center for Marital and Family Studies, University of Denver, Denver, Colorado

JAY L. LEBOW, Ph.D., Clinical Professor, Department of Psychology, Northwestern University and The Family Institute at Northwestern University, Evanston, Illinois

HOWARD J. MARKMAN, Ph.D., Professor of Psychology and Codirector of the Center for Marital and Family Studies, University of Denver, Denver, Colorado

RENEE MCDONALD, Ph.D., Associate Professor of Psychology, Southern Methodist University, Dallas, Texas

JEFFREY C. MEEHAN, A.B., Psychology, Harvard University, Cambridge, Massachusetts

BRUCE D. MILLER, M.D., Professor of Psychiatry and Pediatrics and Division Chief, Child and Adolescent Psychiatry, School of Medicine and Biomedical Sciences, State University of New York at Buffalo, Buffalo, New York

MEGAN MURPHY, B.A., Master's Candidate, Department of Social Work, Boston College, Boston, Massachusetts

K. DANIEL O'LEARY, Ph.D., Distinguished Professor and Director of Clinical Training, Department of Psychology, State University of New York, Stony Brook, New York

FRANCES PALIN, M.A., Doctoral Candidate, Clinical Psychology, Georgia State University, Atlanta, Georgia

JOÄN M. PATTERSON, Ph.D., Associate Professor, University of Minnesota, Minneapolis, Minnesota

WILLIAM M. PINSOF, Ph.D., President, The Family Institute at Northwestern University, and Director and Clinical Professor, Center for Applied Psychological and Family Studies, Department of Psychology, Northwestern University, Evanston, Illinois

SAMANTHA SIMMS PIPER, M.A., University of Denver, Denver, Colorado

JACQUELINE G. REA, M.A., University of Denver, Denver, Colorado

KIMBERLY RYAN, Ph.D., Assistant Professor of Psychology, New College of Florida, Sarasota, Florida

EMILY SÁEZ-SANTIAGO, Ph.D., Assistant Research Scientist, University of Puerto Rico, Río Piedras Campus, San Juan, Puerto Rico

IRWIN N. SANDLER, Ph.D., Regents Professor of Psychology and Director, Prevention Research Center, Arizona State University, Tempe, Arizona

JOANN WU SHORTT, Ph.D., Research Scientist, Oregon Social Learning Center, Eugene, Oregon

NANCY A. SKOPP, M.A., Doctoral Candidate, University of Houston, Houston, Texas

RACHEL SOMBERG, B.A., Doctoral Candidate, Department of Psychology, The George Washington University, Washington, DC

SCOTT M. STANLEY, Ph.D., Co-Director of the Center for Marital and Family Studies, University of Denver, Denver, Colorado

MARTHA C. TOMPSON, Ph.D., Assistant Professor, Boston University, Boston, Massachusetts

EDWARD M. VEGA, M.A., Graduate Student, State University of New York, Stony Brook, New York

ROBERT L. WEISS, Ph.D., Professor Emeritus of Psychology, University of Oregon, Eugene, Oregon

VALERIE E. WHIFFEN, Ph.D., Professor, School of Psychology, University of Ottawa, Ottawa, Ontario, Canada

JASON WILLIAMS, M.A., Doctoral Candidate, Arizona State University, Tempe, Arizona

MELVIN N. WILSON, Ph.D., Professor of Psychology, University of Virginia, Charlottesville, Virginia

BEATRICE L. WOOD, Ph.D., Associate Professor of Psychiatry and Pediatrics, State University of New York at Buffalo, Buffalo, New York, and President, Family Process Institute, Rochester, New York

LAKEESHA N. WOODS, M.A., Clinical Psychology Doctoral Student, University of Virginia, Charlottesville, Virginia

FAMILY
PSYCHOLOGY

A Scientific Paradigm for Family Psychology

William M. Pinsof and Jay L. Lebow

Psychology as a science is approximately 100 years old. *Family psychology* is now approaching its 25th birthday. It is a very young science that is just beginning to come into its own. In this chapter, we present a new scientific paradigm to facilitate and guide the development of family psychology as a science. This paradigm builds on prior work, particularly Pinsof's (1992) preliminary version of the foundations for a scientific paradigm for family psychology.

The science of family psychology has significantly evolved and expanded over the last quarter century. In doing so, it has faced the inevitable controversies and challenges that have characterized all domains within psychology. It has grown down, in the sense that it has focused increasingly on individual and biological systems. It has grown up and out, becoming more concerned with larger systems issues, such as culture, ethnicity, and politics. It has grown wiser with the development of new and more sophisticated methodologies for examining complex questions. We propose this scientific paradigm as a way to mark and underline the growth of family psychology, as well as a way to facilitate its further development and maturation. The field is well along the way in exploring certain dimensions of this paradigm, while in other dimensions the process of discovery has hardly begun.

The paradigm we present provides a framework from which to view research in family psychology. Our paradigm is descriptive in placing research in family psychology in the context of a matrix. Our paradigm is controversial, in that it attempts to resolve certain "hot" dilemmas, particularly dilemmas of theory and, to some extent, practice. It is prescriptive, in that it recommends courses of action. More specifically, it recommends the consistent and universal consideration of certain dimensions in the conduct of the science of family psychology. This does not mean that every study within family psychology should explicitly address every dimension of this paradigm, but rather that it is useful to locate each family psychology study within the intellectual space of this paradigm. This means understanding and acknowledging what is directly addressed in the research, as well as what is only addressed indirectly or not at all.

Our paradigm is an evolving phenomenon. If we write another chapter about it in 10 years' time, we are sure it will have grown and evolved. We hope and suspect that the core of the model will remain similar, but it will evolve to include new dimensions. As an evolving paradigm, it should not be taken, nor is it offered, as the final word. It is comprehensive, not definitive. We offer it as a useful guide to the development and improvement of our science.

Last, this paradigm has informed our planning and editing of this volume. As much as possible, we have tried to create and organize each of the five substantive parts of this book around the core dimensions of this paradigm. We have also urged the chapter authors to position their chapters within the intellectual context of this paradigm. We believe that each of the parts, taken as a whole, reflects the values, as well as the theoretical and methodological implications, of the new paradigm.

■ The Paradigm

Before presenting the new paradigm, two preliminary questions need to be addressed—what's a scientific paradigm and who needs it?

Defining a Scientific Paradigm and Science

Originally proposed in Kuhn's (1962) classic work on the philosophy of science, a scientific paradigm represents a set of ideas "that some particular scientific community acknowledges for a time as supplying the foundation for its further practice" (p. 10). "It defines the appropriate questions to be pursued, the ideal and acceptable methods for pursuing them, the criteria for evaluating the results of those methods and the legitimate theories in the light of which those results will be interpreted" (Pinsof, 1992, p. 432). More specifically, in the context of this volume, we delineate the scientific paradigm for family psychology through articulating a set of core theories and dimensions that are integral to this science.

Implicit in this chapter, and the book in which it appears, is the idea that family psychology is a science. What do we mean by science? Borrowing from Pinsof (1992), we view science as a set of rules for establishing truth. We elaborate this definition, particularly what we mean by "truth," below, in our discussion of epistemology. Thus, family psychology is a science dedicated to establishing the truth about families and the individuals within them. Furthermore, family psychology is a clinical science, in that it is concerned not only with discovering truth, but also with improving the health and well-being of individuals and the families in which they live. The interventions that constitute family psychology's tools for improving health and well-being (Liddle, Santisteban, Levant, & Bray, 2002) must be grounded in and informed by its quest for truth. That "grounding" and "informing" does not mean that clinical practice must be limited to the current state of "proven" or "empirically validated" knowledge. Families cannot wait for science to explicate the answers to all relevant questions. And even in its most comprehensive form, science will never be able to completely specify the complex clinical decision making in prevention and treatment programs. However, clinical practice should derive from, be consistent with, and ultimately be subject to the quest for truth. Without a firm foundation in science, clinical practice with families remains rooted in ever-changing opinion, hard to differentiate from the stuff of the latest expert on daytime television. In that world, the bold marketing of pseudoscience can be utilized to push incomplete or even wrongheaded understandings.

Who Needs a Scientific Paradigm?

A scientific paradigm is important at least for two reasons. The first is that it makes scientists aware of the basic and frequently assumed or "tacit" (Polanyi, 1964) assumptions that guide their work. It makes those assumptions explicit, clarifying them as it exposes them to conscious examination. Second, a scientific paradigm ideally facilitates the next stages of a science's development. It resolves problems and dilemmas that have constrained the growth of the science and it opens new doors—substantively and methodologically. Until now, family psychology has been functioning with an implicit paradigm. We believe it is time to formally articulate an explicit scientific paradigm for family psychology.

■ The Family Psychology Scientific Paradigm Matrix

The main dimensions of the scientific paradigm for family psychology are visually displayed in the 3×6 matrix on page 6. The paradigm consists of two major dimensions. The first, "Core Theories," embodied in the columns, represents the three core, underlying theories within the paradigm. The second dimension, "Domains of Inquiry," represented by the rows, specifies the major substantive domains that are considered in the conduct of the science of family psychology.

Core Theory Dimensions

The core theory dimensions of the paradigm encompass the underlying ontological, epistemological, and mechanical assumptions of the paradigm. As reflected in the matrix, the core theory dimensions cut across and underlie each of the domains of inquiry. This presentation of the core theory dimensions derives substantially from the underlying theoretical framework of Pinsof's (1995) integrative problem centered therapy.

Biopsychosocial Systems Theory.   A variant of general systems theory (Buckley, 1968; von Bertalanffy, 1968), biopsychosocial systems theory (BST) involves the application of general systems theory to biopsychosocial or human systems. The primary foci of BST are individuals, families, and the communities in which they reside. It views the behavior of individuals, families, and communities as a product of and stimulus to the interaction of biological, individual psychological, and social factors.

The Family Psychology Scientific Paradigm: Core Theories and Domains of Inquiry

Domains of Inquiry	Core Theories		
	Biopsychosocial Systems Theory	Epistemology	Causation
Personality psychopathology Development–life course focus Gender Diversity Politics Intervention/prevention			

BST is the ontological component of the underlying theory, in that it specifies a theory of being or nature. From the perspective of BST, nature consists of systems. Most fundamentally, BST specifies the organization and interrelatedness of biopsychosocial or human systems. It asserts that human systems are organized as interacting and mutually influencing sets of open systems. Each system has its own boundary and identity and can be viewed vertically as containing smaller subsystems and as itself a subsystem of a larger system. Thus a married couple constitutes a system itself, but consists of individual subsystems and is itself a subsystem of the nuclear and extended family.

Systems are characterized by nonsummativity—the whole is greater than the sum of the parts (Watzlawick, Jackson, & Beavin, 1967). A husband and wife are more than the sum of their individual characteristics. Their interrelatedness takes on a degree of wholeness that cannot be reduced to or explained by their individual characteristics. In addition to nonsummativity, the most basic defining characteristic of a system is that the parts of the system influence each other. Change in one sooner or later results in change in the other. Typically, this influence is mutual or bidirectional. Pragmatically, if one entity changes and another entity reacts in no discernable way over a reasonable period of time, it is safe to say that they are not part of the same system. Essentially, a system defines a sphere of mutual influence around a set of factors, variables, or entities.

The boundary of a human system is always and ineluctably ambiguous (Pinsof, 1995). With the pragmatic "change" criterion presented above, it may be difficult to ultimately discern whether in fact two or more entities are parts or subsystems of the same system. The reactive changes may not be discernable to the viewer or they may not occur in what constitutes a reasonable period of time. Thus, we can seldom if ever be completely sure about the elements of a system. As will be elaborated below, ultimately systems and BST are constructions that help us understand and impact nature.

Various implications of the BST component are reflected in the chapters in this volume. Some chapters explicitly articulate this viewpoint, such as those by Wood and Miller (ch. 20), Patterson (ch. 21), and Fisher (ch. 22) in part V, "Families and Health," whereas other chapters focus on specific aspects of this core theory.

We would particularly like to note the inclusion within recent family psychology research of, on the one hand, more microbiological systems and, on the other, of more macrosocial systems. These research initiatives have helped to move the field well beyond a simple, singular focus on nuclear families.

- *Including biological systems*   Most obviously, the chapters in part V reflect the focal inclusion of biological systems in family psychology. Furthermore, as each of the chapters in that part reflects, family psychology is particularly interested in the interaction between interpersonal, family variables and biological processes and disorders. Additionally, as reflected in the chapters in part IV, "Families and Depression," consideration of the genetic contribution to depression as well as the vegetative signs of depression place biological factors squarely in the purview of family psychology. Consistent with the research on schizophrenia, autism, and other *Diagnostic and Statistical Manual of Mental Disorders* (specifically, *DSM-IV-TR*) axis I disorders, research on depression has truly become a biopsychosocial endeavor.
- *Including larger systems*   Family psychology research has also grown by reaching up and out to larger social systems. For instance, in the chapters in part III, "Families in Divorce and Remarriage," a number of the programs that have been developed to support families going through these processes work with family members in larger groups and represent efforts to strengthen the community resources available to these families. Additionally, Markman et al.'s chapter 5 discusses the PREP (Prevention and Relationship Enhancement Program) divorce prevention program that has been widely adapted within military and religious organizations within the United States. Last, a number of the chapters in part II, "Partner Violence," address the interaction between broader social, legal, and political systems and efforts to scientifically investigate and treat partner violence.

Epistemology.   The epistemology core theory addresses "reality" and "truth" and how we can know them. This aspect of the paradigm derives from Pinsof's (1995) concept of interactive constructivism. This concept asserts that there is an independent (of humans) and objective reality, but that it is ultimately unknowable. Humans can construct cognitive representations of this reality that they share with each other and that constitute an intersubjective reality. Polanyi (1964) refers to these representations as "personal knowledge," the only type of knowledge to which humans have access. These representations "fit" objective reality more or less. They allow humans to systematically explore and manipulate aspects of objective reality.

Science represents a set of systematic rules for investigating and "mapping" this objective reality. It tests hypotheses about this objective reality that represent the "best" constructions available at the moment. A hypothesis is "true" insofar as there are no consistent data emerging from scientific investigations that indicate it is false. This notion of science has been aptly summarized by Kenneth Norris (1983) as "a set of rules that minimizes the likelihood of our lying to each other."

Scientific constructions or hypotheses are never definitive. They will be modified and ultimately replaced as new knowledge accumulates. In this sense, science is progressive. Its constructions "fit" objective reality better and permit greater understanding and manipulation.

On one hand, the concept of interactive constructivism avoids the simplistic reductionism of logical positivism and the notion of objective scientific knowledge. On the other hand, it avoids the nihilistic relativism of radical constructivism, which denies the existence of an objective reality and the notion of progressive science. Interactive constructivism asserts that we can know objective reality, but that our knowledge is always partial and incomplete. It also asserts that science, as a set of rules for investigating and knowing objective reality, is the only way to determine the truth as best we can know it.

There are several pragmatic implications to the interactive constructivist position and the notion of progressive, but partial or incomplete, scientific knowledge. Quantification does not necessarily imply objectivity. It is a tool to help us understand and manipulate reality, but it does not confer an inherent objectivity on the knowledge it generates. As a consequence, this paradigm incorporates both quantitative and qualitative methods. Neither has the corner on objective reality and both are scientific methods. They are not incompatible. On the contrary, within this paradigm, they exist in a circular, reiterative relationship to each other. They generate somewhat different, yet compatible types of knowledge that are complementary and mutually enriching.

The chapters in this book attest to the growing methodological sophistication of family psychology. We have developed an array of well-validated and sophisticated research methods. The quarter century of research in family psychology has seen an ever-increasing sophistication in research methods. In its beginnings, there were few methods well suited to the investigation of the kinds of questions of greatest interest and importance in family psychology. We now have a wide array of instruments to conduct that research. Additionally, we now have statistical techniques for data analysis, such as hierarchical linear modeling, to address the complexities of family life.

While we have seen continuous improvement in the methods of research in family psychology, we also note that this research has been dominated by a behavioral, objectivist paradigm that leans heavily in the direction of quantitative investigation. Rigorous qualitative research has hardly begun to emerge. For instance, in the more than 20 research programs represented by the chapters in this book, few have substantially integrated qualitative methods. Qualitative methods are particularly useful to develop research hypotheses, to explore and illuminate unanticipated and puzzling quantitative findings, and to add texture and meaning to predicted findings. Such uses of qualitative methods as Gottman and Levenson's oral history interview mark the beginnings of the kind of complementary qualitative research that we believe would be immensely useful for our field of endeavor. It is time for family psychology research to move beyond either/or dichotomies that juxtapose qualitative and quantitative methods toward a both/and stance that integrates knowledge from both perspectives.

The notion that our knowledge, albeit progressive, is ineluctably partial and incomplete argues for a stance of humility in regard to what we know about individuals, families, and communities and how to help them. The "truths" of today will be replaced by new and better knowledge as science progresses. This means that claims of certainty about what we know about families and change are inappropriate and that family psychologists need to remember that our discoveries and inventions, although useful and "true" for the moment, will fall by the wayside of scientific progress. Weiss (ch. 1 in this volume) illustrates this type of evolution of research on marriage by tracing the history and questioning the validity of the concept as well as the research on "marital satisfaction."

Causation

Every science embodies a theory or multiple theories of causation or influence. A theory of causation specifies how things affect each other. Our paradigm rests on a theory of differential causality (Pinsof, 1995). This theory incorporates and builds upon the concept of mutual causality—that parts of a system mutually affect each other. This concept of mutual causality has played a very important role in the evolution of theory and research in the field of family therapy. Early family therapists treated the family as the causal agent in disorders such as schizophrenia (Bateson, Jackson, Haley, & Weakland, 1956; Haley, 1963) and autism. Causation in these models was seen as linear and unidirectional. Subsequent research called these linear and nonmutual models into question. Slowly, it dawned on researchers that the individual with a serious disorder also influences the family and that the patterns researchers saw in these systems may be as much a reaction to the individual's disorder as a causal factor in the evolution of the disorder.

If this volume represented a clinical trial about whether the family and the individual affect one another mutually, that trial could be stopped since the findings so consistently point in this direction. Research in family psychology no longer needs to establish that there is such a relationship. For example, the chapters in the part on depression in this book indicate that there is a clear relationship between depression and marital and family functioning. Adult depression clearly affects marriages, parent-child relationships, and the mental health of children. Conversely, these impacted systems clearly affect depression. The correlations between relational and individual dysfunction are large and significant and occur in numerous disorders, including substance use, anxiety, and most disorders of childhood and adolescence. The questions that remain are principally concerned with the variables that mediate these relationships and the pathways of influence.

Despite the fact that the concept of mutual causality fits the emerging research data far better than linear and unidirectional causal theories, the concept of mutual causality remains problematic because it treats all causal relationships as equally important. From this vantage point, everything affects everything. Within the framework of mutual causality, the abused wife contributes as much to the variance in the violence in her marriage as her abusive husband, and family and genetic factors both contribute equally to the emergence of schizophrenia. We know that the research clearly does not support these equal contribution or equal effect models.

Differential causality adds to the basic concept of mutual causality the critical notion that all causal effects are not equal. Within a system or sphere of influence, the parts or factors contribute differentially to different processes and outcomes. In the language of statistical regression, different factors account for different amounts of the variance in the behavior of any particular variable. Thus, genetic factors appear to account for more of the variance in the emergence of schizophrenia than environmental factors. However, we also know that environmental factors, such as expressed emotion, play an important role in the ebb and flow of schizophrenic symptoms.

An additional implication of the concept of differential causality is that sometimes certain effects may be appropriately conceptualized as linear or unidirectional. For instance, the effect of an abusive parent on the child is generally considered greater than the effect of the abused child on the parent. What differential causality adds to the concept of linear causality in this context, however, is the idea that although the impact of the parent on the child is the primary or major determinant of the abuse, the child does contribute somewhat to the variance in the abuse.

Perhaps this concept is most relevant to and problematic in its application to politically controversial subjects like partner violence. As the chapters in part II attest, there is considerable controversy about the contribution of women to the phenomenon of partner violence. Some investigators and theorists in the field of partner violence attribute most, if not all, of the variance in the phenomenon to men (Holtzworth-Munroe & Meehan, ch. 7), while others (O'Leary & Vega, ch. 10) have examined the contribution of both partners. In identifying and assessing causal pathways in problems such as partner violence, it is essential to examine the contribution of each party, recognizing at the same time that some factors and parties may, in fact, contribute more to the variance of certain variables than others. For instance, based on the work of Holtzworth-Munroe and Meehan (ch. 7) and others, it appears clear that male factors contribute more to the variance in serious and dangerous partner violence than female factors. Female factors appear to account for a somewhat greater portion of the variance in low-level partner violence, such as pushing, shoving, and slapping. The perspective of differential causality is reflected by most of the theory and research presented in the chapters on the various subjects in this book, and hopefully it will inform future research, intervention, and policy on this subject.

■ Domains of Inquiry

The core theories presented above cut across and can be applied to all potential domains of inquiry or subject matter. The second axis of our paradigm specifies certain domains of inquiry. For simplicity's sake, we have highlighted six specific domains of inquiry that we believe need to be considered in most, if not all, programs of family psychological research. We do not view this list of domains as exhaustive or comprehensive. However, we believe that it highlights certain aspects of research in family psychology that are in the process of receiving greater emphasis and that we believe need to continue to be emphasized in the future.

Personality/Psychopathology

The first domain of inquiry is personality and psychopathology. Historically family therapy, and to some extent family psychology, rejected or attempted to minimize focusing on individuals and, concomitantly, on individual psychopathology. At one time in the eyes of the systemic world view, any focus on individual functioning was seen as incompatible with a systemic perspective. Even worse, focusing on individual psychopathology was seen as being co-opted by the medical model and abandoning critical aspects of systems theory, such as circular causality and "the identified" patient. Our paradigm views the study of the interaction of individual and family as an essential domain of family psychology and rejects the early systems theory viewpoint about individual personality and psychopathology on several grounds.

First, the individual is every bit as much a system as the family and can be viewed as being made up of various "smaller" biopsychosocial subsystems, as well as being a subsystem of larger biopsychosocial systems. System does not just mean "social system" or "family." We can conceptualize the individual in a variety of "normal" ways, ranging from examining a person's profile on quantifiable personality variables like the Big Five (e.g., extroversion, agreeableness, neuroticism) to viewing personality as a narrative or story (McAdams, 1993). In the latter vein, Sternberg (1998) has taken the notion of narratives from individual psychology into the domain of marriage, looking at couples' "love stories."

One of the areas in family psychology that has begun to integrate personality theory is research on partner violence. In fact, Holtzworth-Munroe and Meehan's typology of male batterers (ch. 7) is in essence a personality typology. Partner violence research has also invoked personality theory and research to debunk the myths of the "masochistic wife," consistently finding that, in contrast to which males batter, personality variables do not predict which women are likely to end up or stay in violent relationships. Despite such efforts, family psychology still has a long way to go in integrating modern personality theory. Normal personality variables have great potential as predictors of a variety of family processes and outcomes, such as parenting styles, parent/child "fit" or compatibility, spousal fit, and divorce.

The rejection of psychopathology by the early family therapists and family psychologists (e.g., Haley, 1963) was predicated on a dichotomous, either/or position that viewed the concept of individual psychopathology as fundamentally incompatible with a systemic perspective. In contrast, our paradigm views the concept of individual psychopathology and the systemic concepts in our core theory as compatible, and in fact, mutually enhancing. By acknowledging the existence and the importance of individual psychopathology, one does not have to buy "the medical model" (which, if the part in our book on families and health is any indication, in fact remains a straw man even in medicine). Modern medicine and family psychology have and will continue to acknowledge the mutual interaction between physical/mental illness and environmental factors over the life course.

Family psychology has more fully and rapidly integrated individual psychopathology than it has a focus on individual personality. This disparity derives at least in part from the fact that over the last 2 decades, the National Institute of Mental Health has refused to fund research that does not focus on a mental disorder of national significance. To get funding for their research on family processes, family researchers needed to link their research to some disorder. We believe and hope that this focus on individual personality and psychopathology will continue. The data on the comorbidity of family processes and individual psychopathology are very powerful. Snyder and Whisman (2004) report that at least 15% of distressed couples have one member with a mood disorder (compared to 7% of nondistressed couples) and 28% have one member with an anxiety disorder (compared to 15% of non-distressed couples).

Consistent with these data, we believe that the current trend within family psychology toward relational diagnosis, while very worthwhile, does not represent an alternative to the current individually focused nosology, but in fact represents a necessary complement. We do need a nosology of "abnormal" and dysfunctional interpersonal relationships, but this needs to be linked to our growing appreciation and integration of individual psychopathology.

Development/Life Course Focus

The second domain of inquiry is development–life course. Perhaps because developmental psychology was a well-developed discipline when family psychology began, a considerable body of work has already emerged that has begun to articulate the pathways of development over the life course in families. We believe that it is essential that family psychology continue to expand its focus on families and the individuals in them over the life course.

This assertion in our paradigm has three implications. The first and most obvious is that family psychologists need to focus on families with young children, families with adolescents, and families with older adults (and it goes without saying, on adults within families). In organizing this book, we attempted as much as possible to examine research in each of the five focal areas from a life course perspective, including chapters on individuals at different life stages.

The second implication is that we need to focus on the developmental trajectories of particular types of individuals as they develop within family systems. For example, the remarkable longitudinal research conducted over 2 decades described by Capaldi, Shortt, and Kim in chapter 6 reveals that conduct-disordered children have a much higher probability of engaging in partner violence in adulthood. More of this kind of longitudinal research is needed to help us better understand development. In a similar vein, a great deal of research, both cross-sectional and longitudinal, described by Whiffen in chapter 15 has clearly established that depressed parents have children at higher risk for a range of mental disorders. Research on the developmental trajectories of mentally disordered adults holds great promise for furthering the development of preventive interventions. Identifying the early markers and pathways of later disorders in essence specifies the primary targets of prevention programs (Pinsof & Hambright, 2002).

The third and most complex implication is the notion of looking at family systems as transgenerational phenomena with individuals simultaneously at all stages of the life course. Historically, there has been a quest to identify developmental stages of families akin to the developmental stages of individuals. The problem with this approach is that it is too focused on the nuclear family and obscures the fact that nuclear families are just subsystems of larger extended family systems. These larger family systems span at least 3 generations and usually have someone being born and someone dying of old age at the same time.

This focus to specify the development stages of families is understandable as a product of the American ideology of the isolated nuclear family (parents and children) of the middle decades of the 20th century. However, the increased speed, accessibility, and ubiquity, as well as the decreased cost of modern communication technologies have made it easier for the geographically distant generations within a family to be in touch. Additionally, other cultural models of family that view the family system as multigenerational have begun to enter and affect the mainstream Western cultural landscape. Family psychology needs to develop a more comprehensive theory and research methodology that truly incorporates a life course, transgenerational perspective. Our systemic lens needs to be wider, looking at family systems as living and transforming systems spread over 4 to 5 generations, with new individuals entering and exiting the system continually.

Gender

Another substantive domain of enormous importance is gender. Family psychology has made great strides to become a psychology that recognizes the differences between males and females. However, family psychology in its research and practice still leans substantially in the direction of being a psychology of female adults with children of both sexes. For instance, the literature on depression and marriage is still largely a literature on depressed, married women (see Whiffen, ch. 15 in this volume). And much of the extensive research on parent training is essentially a literature on training mothers.

As reflected in the part in this book on divorce and remarriage, there is a growing literature on fathers in divorced family systems that provides an antidote to the older literature which pictured divorced systems as fatherless. Braver and his colleagues (ch. 12) report research on a program to involve divorced and nonresident fathers more actively and centrally in the lives of their children. Wilson et al. (ch. 13) report research examining the factors that influence the involvement of nonresident African American fathers in the lives of their children.

By and large, the literature within psychology in general and family psychology in particular on internalizing disorders and family systems is a literature on females, whereas the literature on externalizing disorders and addictions is largely a literature on males. Family psychology also needs to play a leading role within psychology by promoting an understanding of males with internalizing disorders and, concomitantly, of females with externalizing disorders. We need studies of conduct-disordered girls as well as depressed and anxious boys. Furthermore, these investigations need to be developmentally informed, looking at these disorders and gender over the life course. This book was planned with such a consciousness about gender and we hope it will play a role in facilitating the development of a truly gender-informed or gendered family psychology.

Diversity

Family psychology, along with the whole of psychology, is beginning to seriously address diversity. External validity was once the Achilles heel of research in family psychology. Findings would be presented and conclusions drawn, only to be followed by the belated understanding that the subjects in the research were all middle-class White Americans. This major caveat severely truncated the validity of the findings from this research.

In planning this volume, we strove to address the major substantive areas with as much diversity as possible. Specifically, the chapters by Bernal and Sáez-Santiago (ch. 19), Wilson and colleagues (ch. 13), and Kaslow and colleagues (ch. 16) represent significant steps in that direction. These chapters emphasize the inclusion of racial and ethnic variables in the study of postdivorce families and families with depressed children and adolescents. Nonetheless, there remains an enormous diversity gap within the research, one most particularly about what makes for a good marriage and how to help marriages that are in trouble. Although researchers, theoreticians, and therapists have attempted to draw attention to the crisis in marriage in the African American community in the United States (Pinderhughes, 2003; Tucker & Mitchell-Kernan, 1995), there is still an appalling paucity of research addressing this complex problem.

Most typologies for marital and family systems have been developed, validated, and utilized with middle-class, primarily Caucasian populations. How these typologies perform and apply to African American, Latino, and Asian populations within the United States is still largely unknown. Furthermore, the extent to which our theories and methods apply to different racial and ethnic groups in other countries is an even greater void in our knowledge. Unfortunately, a major limitation of this book is the lack of international representation in the authorship.

Another frontier that remains largely uncharted in the domain of diversity is that of sexual orientation and gender identity. There is a very little research that illuminates couple and family processes in gay and lesbian couples and families (Laird & Green, 1996) and almost none about families and couples with transgender members. It is a striking reality that even the simplest information about gay, lesbian, and transgender couples, such as the relationship between relationship stability and health, has not been studied in the same way that it has been in heterosexual couples. One very salient result of this knowledge gap has been that in the highly politicized debates about gay and lesbian families, advocates of older views of family cite data for the importance of stable marriage for family life but are able to simply say they lack the data about whether such trends apply in gay and lesbian families. Such data are desperately needed to inform the public discourse about these matters (see the discussion of politics below).

Politics

This next domain, politics, is a recent addition to our paradigm. There is no dealing with issues in family psychology at the beginning of the 21st century without reference to politics. Within the United States, and increasingly throughout the world, behavioral science and particularly family psychology occur within an extraordinarily politicized arena. This politicization occurs in a least two ways. The first is that behavioral science data have become tools within the agendas of different political parties. The second is that different constituencies within society exert political and economic influence in regard to the questions and systems that research and intervention can legitimately address.

Perhaps nowhere more clearly than in the consideration of marriage can the political use of scientific data be seen. Within this political context, the reduced rate of marriage, the 50% divorce rate, the increase in nonmarital cohabitation, and the possibility of marriage for gay and lesbian couples are viewed by some on the political right as signs of societal decay and weakened families. This perspective typically asserts that marriage as the union of two heterosexual adults needs to be encouraged and strengthened, while other forms of family life, such as unions of gay partners and so-called single-parent families, need to be discouraged. However, the primary "science" that is used to justify this perspective is predicated upon a fundamental failure to preserve the elementary distinction between correlation and causation. For example, the fact that couples that cohabit prior to marrying have a higher incidence of divorce than couples that did not cohabit premaritally is used to suggest that cohabitation limits the success of marriage. The take-away message is if you don't want to get divorced, don't cohabit before you get married. This causal misinterpretation of correlational data also obscures the selection factor—that people who chose to cohabit before marriage have different values and beliefs than people who chose not to cohabit and that these beliefs and values may have more to do with their increased divorced rate than the fact that they cohabited before marriage.

A second type of politicization concerns the efforts of particular societal constituencies to define what constitutes "normal" or permissible science and practice within family psychology. This type of politicization of science and practice is nowhere more apparent than in research and practice in the domain of partner violence. Certain groups within contemporary American society have lobbied strongly to minimize or ignore the role of women as instigators or participants in partner violence, focusing solely on their role as victims of male aggression. The same groups have also tended to argue for a homogeneous or undifferentiated perspective on partner violence that does not distinguish different types of violence or different types of abusers. Politicization of the data about partner violence places pushing and shoving within the same global category of violence as punching with a fist or threatening a partner with a gun or a knife. The product is misleading headlines about the levels of partner violence, which orient the discussion of social policy in a very special territory.

The same constituencies have also tended to argue for a uniform approach to the treatment of partner violence that is predicated on separating the partners and treating them in separate individual or group (victim and abuser groups) contexts. In fact, this approach has become the standard and only accepted treatment approach for partner violence in many states. Conjoint treatment strategies are scorned.

The chapters in part II show the value of a more balanced data-based and nuanced approach to this complex problem. O'Leary and Vega (ch. 10) argue for a more differentiated approach to treating partner violence; Holtzworth-Munroe and Meehan (ch. 7) advocate a more differentiated model for typing and potentially treating male abusers; and Dutton et al. (ch. 8) examine women as both victims and participants in partner violence. Partner violence is a major social problem in most cultures at this time, but distorted views of the problem mislead and do not help in its resolution. At times, such solutions even result in the premature abandonment of what may prove to be the most helpful solutions to these problems (see, for example, the data of Stith, McCollum, Rosen, Locke, & Goldberg [in press]) on the efficacy of couple therapy for partner violence or the highly thoughtful feminist approach to such violence developed by Goldner and her colleagues (Goldner, Penn, Sheinberg, & Walker, 1990).

It also is important to call attention to a more subtle version of how politics impacts on the science of family psychology. Science is primarily driven by funding for research and these monies are differentially available to study various questions about family life. There are two ways that this profoundly affects knowledge. First, it is inevitable, given this, that we will know more about some kinds of families than others. As already has been noted, there simply are many more data available (and will be) about the beneficial impact of marriage on heterosexuals than on gay, lesbian, and transgender individuals, and, as long as funding priorities are as they are, this always will be the case. Concomitantly, the existence of more data about one family form than another has an inevitable effect on the shaping of social policy. Second, some categories of research fit more with funding priorities than others. So, in an example already described, it has become extremely hard to obtain support for studies of treatments for distressed marriages without tying those treatments to a diagnosable disorder in an individual. That marital distress has such a profound effect on individual functioning is trumped by an agenda that directs money toward the treatment of diagnosable disorders. (Here, the lack of relational diagnoses in the *DSM* comes to have a crucial impact on the development of the science.) The product of these trends is that some areas of research have developed far more slowly than they might have otherwise, leaving us with limited information about such vitally important subjects as the impact of marital therapy on distressed marriages.

Our paradigm advocates understanding the political context in which family psychology research and practice occurs, as well as guarding tenaciously against the political manipulation of scientific data and discourse. As mentioned at the beginning of this chapter, family psychology science and practice need to be aimed at uncovering the truth and practicing truthfully. We believe that the chapters in this book, by and large, reflect this paradigm.

However, our inclusion of the political domain should not be interpreted as an argument for scientific and therapeutic insensitivity to the special needs and concerns of particular groups within our society. The parents and family members of severely mentally ill patients created and have used the National Alliance for the Mentally Ill to push family psychology research and practice to understand and address the complex interaction of biopsychosocial systems in the development, emergence, and treatment of severe mental disorders, such as schizophrenia and bipolar disorder. Sensitivity and inclusiveness in regard to political constituencies makes for responsible science and practice. However, when these constituencies drive and dominate science and practice, the integrity of family psychology as a discipline is at risk.

Intervention/Prevention

The last domain of inquiry in our paradigm addresses the intervention/prevention aspect of any scientific initiative within family psychology, that is, the implications of the research for prevention and/or intervention. As an applied science that is simultaneously dedicated to improving life and discovering truth, family psychology research ultimately needs to impact practice—the vehicle through which family psychology strives to improve people's lives. Practice covers a spectrum that ranges from intervention to prevention. Intervention (tertiary prevention in public health terms) aims to ameliorate the symptoms of or cure current disorders. Prevention aims to prevent the emergence of disorders within at-risk populations (secondary prevention) or within the population in general (primary prevention). From a public health perspective, the work of family psychology typically pertains primarily to secondary or tertiary prevention, though efforts such as those of Markman and his colleagues in marriage preparation fall into the realm of primary prevention.

Clinical relevance represents an essential criterion that should be applied to any research study or program within family psychology. Much of the research within family psychology has focused either on understanding the etiology of disorders or on developing and testing treatments for particular disorders within specific populations. These studies derive from two research traditions. The first is an experimental psychopathology research paradigm that attempts to discern the unique characteristics of a population with a particular disorder or problem. The second tradition is a clinical trial paradigm that evaluates the efficacy of particular interventions for specific disorders within specific populations. Typically, both of these traditions have aimed toward a special kind of clinical relevance, aimed at understanding and treating specific disorders.

More recently, family psychologists have begun to integrate experimental psychopathology research with a developmental perspective, attempting to discern the developmental trajectories of people who develop disorders. For instance, Holtzworth-Munroe and Meehan (ch. 7) have begun to hypothesize about the developmental trajectories of the different types of batterers within their typology.

And Gottman and Ryan (ch. 3 in this volume) have focused much of their research on discerning the marker behaviors in couples' interaction that predict divorce.

This type of developmental and longitudinal research that attempts to discern the early markers for major problems and disorders holds great promise for enabling the development of preventive interventions. Pinsof and Hambright (2002) have attempted to lay out the pathway for the development of this kind of preventive intervention in a phase model for this research. First, the distinctive risk markers in a person's or a family's interaction that predict the emergence of the disorder or problem are identified. These markers then become the targets of the preventive intervention program, which then is tested for its efficacy and effectiveness. The chapter by Markman and his colleagues in this volume nicely illustrates the development and application of a preventive intervention program aimed at reducing risk for divorce in young couples. Many of the targeted behaviors in Markman et al.'s PREP program derive from the findings that emerged in the type of interaction research described above. We need to see much more of this kind of research leading to assessments of research prevention programs that have the potential to change pathological developmental trajectories before they become entrenched and pernicious.

Laudably, the field of family psychology is also beginning to direct more attention to the integration of process and outcome studies. The work of Susan Johnson and her colleagues (ch. 4 in this volume) and the recent work of John Gottman and his colleagues (ch. 3) are very good illustrations of the increasing focus within treatment research on the mechanisms of change and the little "outcomes" that make up the change process. There is a great deal to be learned from such process-outcome research that goes beyond simply whether treatments "work" and we need to see much more of this kind of research.

We also would like to see much more research on treatment effectiveness—the impact of treatments as practiced in real world rather than clinical trial settings. As yet, although there is a considerable body of research demonstrating the efficacy of couple and family therapies in clinical trial research (Sprenkle, 2002), there has been almost no effectiveness research in family psychology. Given the considerable skill sets needed to be a competent family therapist and the vicissitudes of working with families in community settings, it is especially important to investigate the impact of treatments offered in these real world settings.

■ Conclusions

We have delineated this scientific paradigm with two primary goals in mind. The first is to elaborate the underlying scientific perspective that guided us in creating and editing this book. The second is to facilitate the development of the science and practice of family psychology. By delineating core theories and the major domains they traverse, we hope to expand the horizons of family psychology. No study or research program can or should address every aspect of this paradigm. Our hope is that the paradigm can provide the richly textured ground against which the figure of family psychology can evolve and mature, perpetually becoming a more artful science.

■ References

Bateson, G., Jackson, D. D., Haley, J., & Weakland, J. (1956). Toward a theory of schizophrenia. *Behavioral Science, 1,* 251–264.

Buckley, W. (Ed.). (1968). *Modern systems research for the behavioral scientist.* Chicago: Aldine.

Goldner, V., Penn, P., Sheinberg, M., & Walker, G. (1990). Love and violence: Gender paradoxes in volatile attachments. *Family Process, 29,* 343–364.

Haley, J. (1963). *Strategies of psychotherapy.* New York: Grune & Stratton.

Kuhn, T. S. (1962). *The structure of scientific revolutions.* Chicago: University of Chicago Press.

Laird, J., & Green, R. J. (1996). Lesbians and gays in couples and families. New York: Jossey-Bass.

Liddle, H., Santisteban, D. A., Levant, R., & Bray, J. (Eds.). (2002). *Family psychology I: Science-based interventions.* Washington, DC: American Psychological Association.

McAdams, D. P. (1993). *The stories we live by: Personal myths and the making of the self.* New York: Guilford Press.

Norris, K. (1983). Comments during *Nova* program: Public Broadcasting System, October 11.

Pinderhughes, E. (2003). African American marriages in the 20th century. *Family Process, 41,* 269–282.

Pinsof, W. (1992). Toward a scientific paradigm for family psychology: The integrative process systems perspective. *Journal of Family Psychology, 5*(3, 4), 432–447.

Pinsof, W. (1995). *Integrative problem centered therapy. A synthesis of family, individual and biological therapies.* New York: Basic Books.

Pinsof, W. M., & Hambright, A. (2002). Toward prevention and clinical relevance: A preventive intervention model for family therapy research and practice. In H. Liddle, D. Santisteban, R. Levant, & J. Bray (Eds.), *Family psychology I: Science-based interventions.* Washington, DC: American Psychological Association.

Polanyi, M. (1964). *Personal knowledge: Towards a post-critical philosophy.* New York: Harper Torchbooks.

Snyder, D. K., & Whisman, M. A. (2004). Treating distressed couples with coexisting mental and physical disorders: Directions for clinical training and practice. *Journal of Marital and Family Therapy, 30*(1), 1–12.

Sprenkle, D. (2002). *Effectiveness research in marriage and family therapy.* Washington, DC: American Association of Marriage and Family Therapy.

Sternberg, R. J. (1998). *Love is a story: A new theory of relationships.* New York: Oxford University Press.

Stith, S. M., McCollum, E. E., Rosen, K., Locke, L., & Goldberg, P. (in press). *Domestic violence focused couple treatment.* In J. Lebow (Ed.), *Handbook of clinical family therapy.* New York: Wiley.

Tucker, M., & Mitchell-Kernan, C. (1995). Trends in African American family formation: A theoretical overview. In M. Tucker & C. Mitchell-Kernan (Eds.), *The decline of marriage among African Americans: Causes, consequences, and policy implications* (pp. 8–26). New York: Russell Sage.

Von Bertalanffy, L. (1968). *General systems theory: Foundations, development, applications.* New York: Braziller.

Watzlawick, P., Jackson, D., & Beavin, J. (1967). *Pragmatics of human communication.* New York: Norton.

PART I

MARRIAGE AND MARITAL INTERVENTION

Research on marriage and marital intervention undoubtedly constitutes one of the strongest and most vital areas of research within family psychology. Links with three other bodies of research also highlight the growing public health significance of this domain of research. New and old research on comorbidity demonstrates a strong and incontrovertible link between marital distress and depression and anxiety; the economic and psychosocial costs of divorce attest to the importance of research that can strengthen marriages and reduce the likelihood of divorce. Last, research on the impact of children's exposure to chronic marital conflict demonstrates the destructive effect of "bad" marriages on children's social, emotional, and academic well-being. This part showcases research initiatives and reflections aimed to better understand and strengthen marriage.

The five chapters here provide a cutting-edge perspective on the history of research on marriage and marital intervention, but even more significantly, they highlight important new challenges and pathways for future research. Robert L. Weiss's lead-off chapter provides a sorely needed critical examination of the concept of and research on marital satisfaction. Andrew Christensen, Brian D. Doss, and David C. Atkins critique the "holy grail" of empirically validated treatments, the new "gold standard" in treatment research. They present and exemplify the alternative of empirically validated principles as a remedy to some of the problems with empirically validated treatments. John Gottman and Kimberly Ryan critique the emphasis in marital therapy outcome research on big "O," global outcomes, and argue for a science of marital intervention that attempts to understand the impact of particular types of interventions on particular types of outcomes. Going well beyond standard behavioral and cognitive perspectives, Susan M. Johnson details and exemplifies the emergence and relevance of the study of emotion in marriage and couple therapy. Howard J. Markman and his colleagues tackle the enormously important and complex domain of preventive intervention—how to strengthen marriages early on in an effort to prevent distress and divorce.

A theme that cuts through these chapters is that research on marriage and marital intervention must become more specific and differentiated. The science of marriage and marital intervention research is entering a new stage in which it moves beyond global or molar impressions to a much more fine-grained understanding of what goes on in marriage and how family psychologists and family therapists can help maximize healthy processes. They embody the excitement and new energy in this vital research area and point the way ahead for the next research stage.

1

A Critical View of Marital Satisfaction

Robert L. Weiss

*Perhaps we should question the utility of assessing the state of intimate
relations by asking for global evaluations of levels of happiness. After all, a
global assessment of the relationship requires participants to construct a
simplified, relatively abstract construction of a unique relational history. It
may be theoretically useful to ascertain what other types of evaluative referents
may be made about intimate interaction. For example, why not ask
participants about relationship change, transformations, challenge, crises, or
growth as indicators of relational "health"?* Perhaps satisfaction has outlived
its usefulness for determining why and how relationships "work" or are
supposed to work.

—ERBERT AND DUCK, *1997, p. 210 (emphasis added)*

The title of the conference paper that gave rise to this chapter was "Don Quixote
Glimpses the Windmills of Marital Bliss." Then, as here, my concern was with
the theories and methods fashioned to understand that quintessential component
of marital quality, marital satisfaction, arguably a most important aspect of adult
intimacy, yet so elusive in its promise. "Marital bliss" is transitory and not as readily
accessed as "marital satisfaction," but it serves to call attention to the limitations of
the search itself. How can the methods of family science help us to understand
marital satisfaction as a respectable variable, the correlates of which lead to formulating testable basic research questions as well as facilitating all important preventative and ameliorative interventions that address adult intimacy? As with the
idealistic Don, are we also pursuing an elusive truth? The present journey in search of
marital satisfaction selects from among attractive ideas from the literature. I explore
how the construct of marital satisfaction has infiltrated the behavioral science
approach to adult intimacy, highlighting where necessary limiting assumptions.

The overarching issue, of course, is marital quality, which encompasses both
subjective and objective methods for defining and assessing satisfaction. In this
critique of marital satisfaction it will become obvious that a broadened view of
satisfaction, one that goes beyond subjective assessment, might be necessary for
understanding marital quality. The vastness of, and the continuing scholarly interest
in, this literature presents a challenge to anyone who would deign to mine it for
original ideas, new systematization, or new strategies for investigating satisfaction.
For example, Whisman (1997) reported finding over 2,500 citations to marital or
marriage satisfaction in the 30-year period from 1967 to 1997; the proliferation
continues unabated (see also Bradbury, Fincham, & Beach, 2000). Gottman (1982)
once observed that the goal of marital research is to understand satisfaction variance.
Implied in this simple but elegant statement is the belief that marital satisfaction

is the gateway to our knowledge of important information about couples, with relationship stability heading the list. Since my focus is largely conceptual I do not systematically address the very considerable literature on interventions for marital distress; I do, however, consider features of various interventions that, in my view, seem to inform the satisfaction construct. Again, the reader should be reminded that marital quality lurks in the background, giving way in this chapter to marital satisfaction.

■ How Satisfying Is "Satisfaction"?

Satisfaction is at once a subjective experience, a prevailing sentiment, and an attitude, all of which are based on intraindividual factors that influence the perceived quality of marital interactions; these in turn take place and develop within larger familial and social contexts. The evaluations of outsiders, in their roles of researchers and therapists, are also part of the mix in setting standards of satisfaction—boxes within boxes within boxes. Not surprisingly, the construct marital satisfaction serves many ends, as an ideal to be strived for in its own right, often equated with personal success, and as the dependent variable in empirical studies (e.g., the targeted goal of therapeutic and psychoeducational programs). In studies seeking correlates of levels of satisfaction it also serves as the independent variable. The same construct occupies different statuses depending on whether the focus is on conditions that result as a consequence of satisfaction or conditions that foster changes in satisfaction. Thus the pursuit of the correlates of satisfaction is often bidirectional—truly an all-purpose construct! Correlation does not establish unidirectional causation, although concomitance nevertheless whets the appetite for understanding.

The semantics of satisfaction are most interesting. Writers often relabel existing definitions of satisfaction by establishing correlations among newer and older self-report measures in order to demonstrate the construct validity of the new measures. Such correlational relabeling does not actually break new ground. The problem lies not in these efforts but rather in the nature of the beast. Although our search for understanding may not be entirely quixotic, marital satisfaction may just turn out to be more elusive than even we idealists dreamed.

A Protean Construct

Marital satisfaction (or, more generally, couples relationship satisfaction) is an odd construct not only because of its numerous accrued meanings but also because of its persistence in light of its total subjectivity. Only a spouse can report his or her degree of satisfaction. Can we overcome this subjectivity? The search for objectivity will always fold back on a simple fact: satisfaction is at base a statement made by the individual. This is incontrovertible. Just why or on what basis persons (or researchers, for that matter) make such statements is a fascinating epistemological problem (discussed below). *Beware, there really isn't any magic in measures of marital satisfaction:* persons answer questions about their contentment (or lack thereof) with the person they wake up next to each morning. Why should reported contentment matter? Reported unhappiness with one's marriage has all sorts of implications for one's behavior, cognitions, and health, as repeatedly shown in the literature. For example, Coyne et al. (2001) showed that reported marital satisfaction predicts the length of survival of men with congestive heart failure. This finding illustrates how self-reported marital satisfaction can serve as a proxy for the very correlates that might predict satisfaction. That is, spouses' reported satisfaction probably contains information about the quality of interactions in these families. Marital satisfaction is special just because its significance pervades so much of the fabric of our daily lives. Would this be true for other forms of satisfaction, such as job satisfaction? Satisfaction matters most when we invest our hopes, expectations, and efforts in people and situations that can exert fate control. In committed intimate relationships, each person acquires the power to move the other's comfort level up and down a scale of affective intensity. Having this power is as good a definition of fate control as any.

Can we overcome the inherent subjectivity of satisfaction by focusing on marital stability? After all, a relationship that ends cannot be said to be satisfactory. Unfortunately, marital stability as a measure is highly conditional since it is defined by negative instances, i.e., stability is equivalent to a marriage not yet ended in divorce or otherwise terminated. As such, stability can only be quantified as years in service. Survival analysis is one way to quantify the temporal trajectory before some defining event (e.g., in medicine, how long a patient survives before succumbing to a predictable outcome). In this manner stability is a proxy, albeit a static one, for satisfaction. But is it always a good proxy? Both Gottman (1993) and Fitzpatrick (1988) have independently developed marital typologies, based on various self-report and observational assessments, which describe couples who have stable relationships but were equally likely to be satisfied as unsatisfied. Davila and Bradbury (2001) have also shown the possible disconnect between satisfaction and stability using attachment as a person variable. Rogge and Bradbury (1999) found that communication and abuse differentially affect satisfaction and stability, respectively.

Marriages remain stable for various exogenous reasons (e.g., cultural prohibitions on termination, economic, religious, and legal, among others). For example, consider cultural traditions in which marital satisfaction is not a prominent factor. In arranged marriages the wisdom of the elders prevails and whether the partners are satisfied with their relationship is of little consequence to stability. In Western cultures marital satisfaction is a construction based on acceptance of voluntary, rather than obligatory, marriage formats (cf. also Berscheid & Lopes, 1997, pp. 139–141). Success in obligatory arrangements is defined by fulfilling prescribed roles (e.g., producing children, fulfilling gender-specific roles). For voluntary relationships, partners choose one another based largely on romantic notions of love. The success of the marriage is said to depend on the personal happiness of the individuals, not on the fulfillment of cultural expectations, the continuation of "love" (in some form). "Failure" means that one is no longer able to keep the commitment of love, either because one has chosen the wrong person or because one's needs are no longer being met. In any event, failure means "time to move on," since satisfaction has critically declined. In practice, however, there are always circumstances that interfere with a simple dissatisfaction-dissolution relation. Whether spouses' theories of their relationship failure(s) turn out to be a source of useful information (i.e., for understanding satisfaction) is yet to be determined.

Thus we arrive at an interesting point when considering satisfaction as an aspect of marital quality: satisfaction as a construct is always subjective, basically a self-report, yet one having considerable experiential and palpable significance for daily life. But satisfaction is not necessarily related to the scientifically (potentially) more acceptable (i.e., objective) concept of stability. In the broadest sense, the question we need to ask is what do we wish the construct of marital satisfaction to *do* for us? As with any scientific construct, it should play a role in basic research, leading to new knowledge by facilitating empirical investigations and fostering theory development. Marital satisfaction has an important role in applied work; knowledge about satisfaction certainly has implications for prevention of marital distress and interventions for so-called distressed relationships. Implied in my questioning of the construct is whether we can be successful in appropriating constructs based on folk experiences of daily life (e.g., marital happiness) and then be able to pursue them with the objectivity required for scientific discourse, namely, intersubjectivity? In what follows I explore conditions under which the construct of marital satisfaction has been useful and where it may be failing.

■ How Shall We Know Thee?

It is customary in the marital satisfaction literature of the past 2 decades to distinguish between connotations of satisfaction based on subjective versus objective information (e.g., Fincham & Bradbury, 1987; Norton, 1983; Sabatelli, 1988). Do descriptions of satisfaction denote relationship *adjustment* or spouses' *evaluation* of the quality of their experience? This distinction is important whenever the items of self-report measures of marital satisfaction reflect both the evaluative or quality aspect of a relationship ("We have a good marriage," "I am happy with my partner") and marital adjustment items referring to relationship processes (e.g., conflict, agreement, and decisions about household chores, among others). The inclusion of items from these two distinct domains creates a problem for attempts to validate correlates of satisfaction. As a result separate measures of quality and adjustment have been developed.

The Promise of Objectivity

The introduction of marital adjustment offers the promise of objectivity because adjustment redirects the focus of satisfaction onto events that can be observed. No longer does the satisfaction construct rest upon statements made about some inner state; the focus shifts to accomplishments. In an earlier behavioral model (Weiss, 1978) the quality of a marriage was said to depend upon transactions between the spouses, which were assessed not only by self-report, but also by controlled observation. Accordingly, this behaviorally based model of marriage posited four areas, or task categories, of accomplishment that couples must master. The categories required skills in *communication, supportiveness, problem solving,* and *behavior change.* These categories of accomplishment were cross-tabulated with specific interaction occasions, grouped according to their functionality, for example, appetitive transactions (socioemotional), instrumental transactions, and "by-products." (Appetitive transactions are those that spouses seek for enjoyment and fulfillment; instrumental transactions refer to the work-related functions of daily relationship life; by-products are defined as the forces that annoy or potentially pull partners apart.) The resulting matrix (4 accomplishments by 3 interaction categories) provided a template with which to assess how well a couple was functioning in each of the 12 cells; interventions were designed specifically to correct areas of deficit (Weiss, 1978). Although this model defined marital adjustment functionally in terms of what couples did, by focusing on their interaction, it also defined a priori what was necessary for a quality relationship. And therein lies the rub. Who among us is to define the criteria for an ideal relationship?

Prescriptive Satisfaction

There is a long tradition in the history of marital satisfaction to prescribe ideal marriages (e.g., Erbert & Duck, 1997). In Western cultures, where romantic love and voluntary mate selection are deemed essential to marital success, most people will agree on a list of elements believed to be important for satisfaction. For example, Feeney, Noller, and Ward (1997) found that spouses could rate given aspects of their marriage as important regardless of whether these were actually reported as present in their own relationship (p. 178). As expected, they found that discrepancies between persons' ratings of their ideal and actual marriages were related to their ratings of disappointment and dissatisfaction with their own marriages (p. 179). Both popular culture and pronouncements from nonsecular quarters not only define but also reinforce expectancies of the ideal relationship.

The early behavioral model (Weiss, 1978), described above, sought a priori to define satisfaction as the synthesis of specific relationship transactions thought to be essential if the participants were to experience satisfaction; even as a skills-based template it was nonetheless prescriptive. Thus, the answer to the question, "Who defines the criteria for an ideal relationship?" seems to be everybody. It depends on what we ask from couples and ourselves: (a) spouses and researchers may be asking about ideal types (stereotypes) of relationships, (b) spouses are asked to evaluate relationship quality, and (c) both spouses and researchers are asking about adjustment transactions. The result is a mix of subjective and objective sources of data that all seem obviously real.

Satisfaction in the Mind of the Beholder

Among the intraindividual correlates of marital satisfaction described in the literature (cf. Karney & Bradbury, 1995), certain cognitive process variables stand out as particularly relevant to the present discussion. At base is an epistemological challenge for both spouses and researchers alike: how do they or we "know" satisfaction (Weiss, 1978)? In this section I address some of the issues relevant to spouses' knowing about their satisfaction, a matter of cognitions.

The Ambience-Salience Dialectic. Self-reported satisfaction likely confuses ambient or background (distal) conditions with more salient (proximal) events of daily relationship life. Describing oneself as "happy," because one is generally optimistic, open to experience, and has self-efficacy about many aspects of daily life, reflects ambient, trait, or dispositional happiness. However, "happy" may be conditional on specific events (i.e., limited to time and situation). Self-reported relationship satisfaction can reflect either (a) a global or ambient "experience" (the evaluative component discussed above) or (b) the experience of salient (day-to-day) events (the actual transactions of the day). Do primacy and recency availability heuristics interfere when couples report on how happy they are in general with their relationship ("All things considered, how satisfied are you with your marriage?")? Likewise, it may not always be clear whether the target of the report is the self, the spouse, or the relationship.

Upon what do spouses base their judgments? For example, satisfaction as cognition or an attitude may be detachable from events, as with the evaluative component of marital satisfaction (Fincham & Bradbury, 1987; Norton, 1983) discussed above. Evaluative judgments of one's relationship are but one ambient factor that floats, as it were, more or less independently of the input of day-to-day relationship accomplishments. The sentiment override hypothesis (Weiss, 1980) pertains to the disconnect between cognition (judgment) and the goods and services (events) spouses actually exchange on a day-to-day basis. (For an excellent summary of how various behavioral exchange-based models address marital satisfaction, see Berscheid & Lopes, 1997, pp. 130–135). A cognition (belief, evaluative attitude) held about a partner may override that person's actual behavior toward the spouse; a prevailing uncharitable view will greatly lessen the impact of positive partner behaviors (Kluwer, 2000, discusses other examples from the social cognition literature, pp. 69, 70). Hawkins, Carrere, and Gottman (2002), using an oral history interview method, determined that compared to wives in unhappy marriages, those in happier marriages viewed their husband's anger as neutral; the unhappy wives viewed it as negative. The experience of positivity depends ultimately on the beholder, again invoking the issue of subjective interpretation.

From a social cognition perspective Fincham, Garnier, Gano-Phillips, and Osborne (1995) elaborated further on the sentiment override hypothesis by introducing *attitude availability* as a moderator in establishing correlates of marital satisfaction: "Satisfaction can vary not only in degree but also in the strength of the association between the evaluation (i.e., self-reported satisfaction) and the object of the evaluation (i.e., the partner)" (cited in Bradbury et al., 2000, p. 974). (Attitude availability was measured independently of self-reported satisfaction, thus making it possible to study correlates of satisfaction as a function of attitude availability.) For spouses showing high accessibly sentiment override would be most noticeable since satisfaction for them operates in a top-down rather than a bottom-up manner (i.e., rather than being dependent on the actual behavioral events in the relationship).

Whereas Fincham's approach to sentiment override has stressed underlying cognitive processes, it has also figured prominently in Gottman's investigations of basic processes derived from observational studies (Gottman, Murray, Swanson, Tyson, & Swanson, 2002) and in his empirically based model of marital therapy (Gottman, 1999).

Is Satisfaction Unidimensional?   Still another facet of cognitive processes underlying "how do they know" is whether reported satisfaction is unidimensional. Is dissatisfaction just the other end of the satisfaction continuum? A therapeutic truth in working with distressed couples is that the circumstances, the events, and the nature of day-to-day exchanges differentially impact marital satisfaction. The three general categories of interaction described earlier (appetitive, instrumental, and by-products) impact "satisfaction" quite differently, ranging from dissatisfaction, through neutrality, to satisfaction (Weiss, 1978). The key lies in the fact that the presence of some events *increments satisfaction,* whereas the presence of other events *increments dissatisfaction.* For example, the absence of appetitive events (e.g., affection, sex) decrements satisfaction (perhaps experienced as a vague sense of something missing), but the absence of other annoying or effortful events (by-products and some instrumental activities) only moves one to a neutral state, not to a state of satisfaction. The absence of adversity (in all its forms) is not satisfaction, and the removal of annoyances in a relationship is not sufficient to produce satisfaction. Couples experiencing relationship distress fail to recognize the dual nature of satisfaction; initially they request therapists to reduce the adversity. However, we do not hit our head against the wall just because it feels so good when we stop.

More recently in their decade review discussion of developments in conceptualizing marital satisfaction, Bradbury et al. (2000) state, "Factors that lead to marital distress may not be the simple inverse of the factors that lead to a satisfying relationship" (p. 973). References to nondistressed couples actually fail to appreciate this understanding. (Their review includes other relevant sources that define healthy marriages, attributes of long-term relationships, and the role of social support as expressions of a contemporary interest in conceptualizing the unique dimensions of satisfying and dissatisfying relationships.)

Fincham and colleagues (Fincham, Beach, & Kemp-Fincham, 1997; Fincham & Linfield, 1997) have devised a self-report measure of quality that separately assesses positive and negative dimensions (Positive and Negative Quality in Marriage Scale: PANQIMS). Accordingly, individuals can score either high or low on each of the dimensions. The four quadrants defined by the resulting 2×2 matrix indicate very different forms of satisfaction. For example, wives who had identical marital adjustment scores (MAT: Locke & Wallace, 1959), but who differed in their placement in the PANQIMS quadrants (e.g., high in both positivity *and* negativity vs. low in both positivity *and* negativity), differed reliably in their attributions about their husbands and in their scores based on behavioral observations. Unique variance accounted for by the separation of positive and negative items might well encourage researchers to look further into how couples know their satisfaction.

Beliefs and Values in Satisfaction.   To conclude this section on factors related to satisfaction in the mind of the beholder, consider next examples of constructs derived from folk experience that reflect beliefs and values. Constructs appropriated from the popular domain often create the illusion of explanation when in fact they are only descriptive or, at worst, tautological. The question should be, "Does holding a belief or value enhance marital satisfaction and/or predict something relevant to the functioning of a relationship?" Do beliefs and values serve as mediators of statements or actions, or as moderators, such that when present certain other relations are more or less likely? For example, research on attributions in marriage has shown that couples who report low marital quality also tend to make negative attributions about their partner's behaviors (Fincham, 1994). Are attributions motivational in that they somehow instigate action? Not surprisingly, unhappy spouses report their unhappiness in more than one way. Fincham and colleagues have been able to show that attributions are related to behaviors observed in marital interactions. In this sense the attributions serve motivational ends.

Two folk constructs, commitment and sacrifice, have found their way into the satisfaction literature. Like satisfaction, commitment and sacrifice are usually assessed by self-report (Stanley & Markman, 1992; Whitton, Stanley, & Markman, 2002). Descriptively these may be sources of important data; what a person says about the likelihood of remaining in a relationship, and whether one takes a long-term view, is worth knowing. The larger issue is whether and under what conditions beliefs predict behavior. Rusbult and colleagues (cf. Rusbult & Martz, 1995; Rusbult, Martz, & Agnew, 1998) have studied various conditions that affect the "validity" of predictions made from measured commitment. For married couples, statements about commitment reflect intentions to remain and to the extent that they prove to be accurate, the commitment construct is motivational. Both commitment and sacrifice reflect an ideal, that is, a strong belief in the viability of the relationship. Undoubtedly beliefs can and do determine actions (e.g., belief in the sanctity of marriage would most likely be related to efforts exerted to maintain it). Do we know that people are committed to relationships by virtue of their remaining in them, or do they remain because they are committed? Many constructs of this genre reflect beliefs that come into play because someone now asks about them (i.e., via self-report devices). Caution is needed lest we ascribe explanatory power to constructs that are descriptive.

■ Marital Satisfaction: An Integrated Model

To a large extent most past research on marital satisfaction has been successful in establishing correlates of reported relationship quality, but there has been relatively little written about the underlying mechanisms of such associations. Various theories about close relationships have been either appropriated or de novo proposed to understand marital satisfaction and stability (cf. Berscheid & Lopes, 1997; Kluwer, 2000, pp. 64–67). Karney and Bradbury (1995) offered an integration of intra-individual, interactional, and contextual variables—all of which were described piecemeal in the literature—as a model of marital satisfaction and stability. (Their model was based largely on a review of 115 longitudinal studies, comprising some 200 variables that predicted marital outcome over time.) Two features of their approach are noteworthy for the present discussion: (a) an emphasis on developmental changes in relationships and (b) the bidirectional role marital quality (the evaluative component) and adaptive processes play in marital stability. Their insistence that relationships must be understood from a developmental perspective is consistent with the view offered here, namely, that satisfaction be seen as a moving target. In the Karney and Bradbury model, adaptive processes equate to the adjustment component of the satisfaction construct. Spouses' actual adaptive capabilities and their perceptions of them, taken together, are said to predict stability. Adaptive processes in turn are separately affected by enduring vulnerabilities and stressful events. In part, as a reflection of the research available when the model was being developed, the "vulnerabilities" component was by definition heavily weighted toward individual and resource deficiencies. Research on so-called supportive capabilities might also figure in this model, as suggested by Roberts and Greenberg's (2002) description of an intimacy process model of marital distress. The salient role that negativity has played in assessing marital quality is based in large part on the tasks used to elicit interaction behaviors, namely, conflict-eliciting tasks. Roberts and Greenberg (citing work by Roberts, using partner reports of behavioral responses) "demonstrated that partner withdrawal in response to confiding behavior ('intimacy avoidance') is related to marital dissatisfaction *independently* of withdrawal responses in the context of conflict" (2002, italics added, p. 122). To further emphasize the point: work by Huston (cited in Roberts & Greenberg) indicated that marital outcome was predicted not by negative affect but rather by decreases in affectional expression and partner responsiveness (p. 121). (See above the discussion of satisfaction not being unidimensional.)

Karney and Bradbury (1995) and Roberts and Greenberg (2002), among others, lament the lack of interest in possible mediation and moderation effects between and among the simple correlations that are reported in the satisfaction literature. I would add that any developmental model of marriage must address which couples are successful in recovering from the natural storms of married life, i.e., not just the familiar stresses, but serious breaches that threaten the continuation of the marriage. Analyses of developmental trajectories might well include the dynamic interplay between these times of success and (if they occur) crises. Relying on zero order correlations merely encourages the belief that satisfaction is static.

■ Does Marital Distress Inform Satisfaction?

Might the enterprises of marital assessment and therapy provide a wealth of data about how well, or not, couples mange their relationship distress? What better place to look for the topography and the effectiveness of how couples manage accommodation? In this section I address the question "Does marital distress inform satisfaction?" by considering what can be gleaned, on the one hand, from activities in assessment and diagnosis and, on the other hand, activities described in marital therapies. The extensive literature in both domains necessitates being selective in the choice of examples for addressing marital satisfaction.

Assessment and Diagnosis

Research and clinical work would be facilitated if there were an agreed upon standard for describing distress status. Efforts to standardize diagnoses in psychopathology suggest an interesting parallel for understanding marital (dis)satisfaction. (The stated aim of diagnosis is to facilitate communication about disorders, explain etiology, and indicate effective treatments.) The *Diagnostic and Statistical Manual of Mental Disorders,* rev. fourth edition (*DSM-IV*), is an atheoretical compendium of more or less specific conditions, their frequency, and the time courses that define various diagnoses. The idea of specifying fairly objective criteria to be met in order to make a diagnosis has both advantages and disadvantages. Diagnoses are now based on information about the frequency and duration of specific behaviors, obtained through standardized interviews (First, Gibbon, Spitzer, & Williams, 1997). The disadvantage of this approach is that it freezes diagnosable conditions by overlooking significant yet relevant deviations from the specified criteria. (Some of the categories themselves are questionable, reflecting committee judgments more than actual conditions of concern.) In spite of many limitations and dissatisfaction expressed among professional groups, the widespread use of the *DSM* approach continues.

Is a *DSM* approach to marital satisfaction possible? Can relationships be diagnosed? Whether relationship "diagnosis" will ever make sense, the use of objective assessment technology remains an option. A study by Heyman, Feldbau-Kohn, Ehrensaft, Langhinrichsen-Rohling, and O'Leary (2001) tested how well the Dyadic Adjustment Scale (DAS) and a newer similar self-report measure can diagnose relationship distress using a modified structured diagnostic interview as the criterion. (For example, relationship quality items in the interview included "happiness," "thoughts of termination," "negative attributions.") The authors conclude that the widespread use of the DAS to diagnose marital distress is inadvisable; both questionnaires tended to overdiagnose couples as distressed. Although face valid, the interview protocol was based on important criteria for defining distress based on the literature describing correlates of satisfaction and the findings from the observational coding literature.

Assessment, unlike diagnosis, is less concerned with establishing symptoms and underlying conditions, but is more generally descriptive and functional. Even assessment used as a basis for developing typologies of marital interaction is much more descriptive of functions than a mere recitation of impairments. Among the many approaches used to describe marriages—for purposes of classification, developing correlates of satisfaction, or determining distress status—the impact of behavioral observation coding technology stands out in the satisfaction literature (e.g., Weiss & Heyman, 1990, 1997). More recently Weiss and Heyman (2004) have critically reviewed how authors of both microanalytic and global coding systems introduce constructs through their codes that seem to take on a life of their own (i.e., lack external validity). There is ample evidence to show that couples who self-report marital dissatisfaction also display classes of negative interaction behaviors. The concern is not whether a complex observational system to determine marital distress when asking the couple is sufficient. At issue is the relevance of the constructs defined by the code categories (and those based on statistical or graphical analytic techniques) for theory development.

How constructs based largely on graphical methodology come into being is best illustrated in a longitudinal study of newly married couples reported by Johnson and Bradbury (1999). They developed an analysis of the topography of Time 1 interaction patterns that predicted distinct levels of satisfaction assessed at 6 and 12 months. Based on microanalytic coding of problem-solving interactions, individual point graphs (Gottman, 1979) displayed the cumulative net positive-negative trend within each couple's interaction. The behavior coded at each successive unit of the interaction (turn at speech) was assigned a point score reflecting the degree of positive or negative valence of the codes. By accumulating the scores at each speech turn and displaying them as a function of time (the successive units), the graph displays the affective trend of the interaction for each spouse's behavior. Two features of the graphs are noteworthy: symmetry and slope. Spouses' trajectories are symmetrical if they both follow the same slope. The acceleration of the slopes of the lines, whether positive (upward) or negative (downward), indicates the affective changes over the time course of the interaction. Those couples that started out in synchrony, but whose graphs became asymmetrical (e.g., one spouse's graph became increasingly positive while the other's turned increasingly negative) reported lower marital satisfaction at 6 and 12 months. By describing interactions in this manner (along with further refinements as to when the asymmetry occurred) provides tantalizing leads that may eventually fit into a broader theory of marriage quality. Specifying patterns of affective change observed during an interaction at the beginning of a marriage that predict changes in satisfaction is a noteworthy effort. Yet as with so many behavioral observational studies focusing on marital satisfaction issues, descriptive rather than explanatory power rules the day.

By adopting a behavioral analytic approach (cf. Weiss & Heyman, 2004) the issue of who selects the diagnostic criteria for use in identifying marital distress might be circumvented. In brief, this approach follows a series of steps that assure the content validity of items by having samples of couples enumerate significant instances of conflict and mastery that occurred in their relationships. Other samples of couples would categorize the adequacy (in their judgments) of the method used to adapt to each situation. The result would be a means for presenting couples with situations and potential modes of adaptation prescaled for effectiveness. How well a given couple's assessment agreed with the standards set by the functional behavioral analytic methodology would be used to determine their status. Whether (a) it would it be possible to obtain a broad enough picture of the ecology of marriages by meaningfully describing situations and adaptive modes and whether (b) whether "knowledge" translates into actual relationship behaviors can only be decided empirically. But the prospect offers an interesting challenge.

Marital Therapy and Distress

To what extent does marital therapy inform marital distress or marital satisfaction? Marital satisfaction is the accepted product of marital therapy for both consumer and researcher, perhaps even the gold standard outcome variable, at least in the short run. Couples seen in marital therapy are typically in major distress and realistically or not they seek change in their plight. Therapists are highly motivated to reduce levels of distress. All therapies must operate from a theory of relationships, which defines criteria for desirable outcomes. (The theory of practice directs how these goals are to be met.) Couples presenting for marital therapy are not truly representative of marital distress; theirs is a picture of intimacy gone awry and of those who, for whatever reasons, turn to professional outsiders. Not all such couples seek help. Are techniques effective in reducing distress also the elixir for maintaining marital quality?

The rapid growth of and enthusiasm for skills-based treatment approaches made it seem that "one size fits all" was sufficient. Teaching distressed couples specific skills based on sound pedagogy reduced their distress. In practice this often meant teaching spouses to become more behavioral (e.g., learning how situations and consequences control the quality of their interactions). Enhancing positive exchanges, learning communication skills, and improving time management were among the salient techniques (cf. Weiss & Perry, 2001).

Both Gottman (Gottman, Coan, Carrere, & Swanson, 1998) and Halford (2001, 2002) have questioned the routine application of skills-based intervention on two grounds: the techniques were not always predictive of outcome (stability) and the absence of these skills among nondistressed couples did not matter. (Although aspirin helps reduce headaches, the absence of aspirin does not cause headaches.) Many of the skills-training modules were developed to overcome deficits seen in distressed couples, especially in the case of communication skills training. Halford (2002) argues, based on a review of past intervention research, that since finding particular behaviors that will enhance relationships for all couples is unlikely, "then the prediction and promotion of relationship satisfaction and stability need to be focused on a broader concept of what is adaptive to promote satisfying and stable relationships. We suggest that a useful focus to consider is how effectively people *work at* their relationship, rather than whether they use specific behaviors" (Halford, 2002, p. 498, italics added).

Halford has developed specific intervention modalities that focus on process and only secondarily on content (Halford, 2001, 2002). In this approach the adaptation component of the Karney and Bradbury model is given center stage. Halford proposes that self-regulation of couple relationships consists of four key meta-competencies: *self-appraisal, self-directed goal setting, self-implementation of change, and self-evaluation of change efforts.* The potential for describing self-initiated work as a core ingredient of satisfaction customizes the construct. By placing emphasis on individuals attaining their defined relationship goals, rather than on the more familiar static end state, satisfaction embodies processes that maintain the relationship. Relationship success might be measured quite simply by the extent to which the spouses attained their goals rather than by the usual self-reported satisfaction measures. As a first approximation, Halford has shown that employing the self-regulation metaskills improves reported satisfaction as well as longer term intervention (Halford, 2002). However, as we have seen throughout this discussion, researchers rely on the usual self-report measures of satisfaction when more process-oriented approaches seem possible. Halford's metacompetencies go beyond what is offered in the many skills-training approaches.

Another current approach to couple therapy, described as acceptance and change (Christensen & Jacobson, 2000), is similar to Halford's notion of meta-competencies. In this therapy the goal is to enable spouses to recast their struggles to change one another into a more benign acceptance of contradictions. The notion here is not so much removing the annoyances of a relationship as it is separating oneself from having to do something about them (i.e., changing the other). In both approaches skills are still taught, but the focus is on enabling each individual to achieve self-regulatory abilities. By helping couples get untangled from their costly efforts at making things better by changing each other, it is assumed that they will accommodate more satisfactorily.

In the final section I consider approaches to satisfaction that embody process considerations even more broadly than those alluded to thus far.

■ Satisfaction in Flux

My critique of current approaches to satisfaction has emphasized the implicit acceptance of marital satisfaction as a static phenomenon. Although longitudinal studies assess satisfaction at multiple time periods they do so with the same (usually single) satisfaction measure. As relationships change over time so do spouses' definitions of satisfaction. The average reported satisfaction scores decline linearly over years married, quite in contrast to the view that satisfaction follows an inverted U curve (Bradbury et al., 2000, p. 965). Does the ecological validity of measures change as couples are assessed at later life stages? Many self-report measures heavily weight agreement in determining satisfaction scores (e.g., DAS; Spanier, 1976). However, agreement may be a much less salient factor for couples in longer term relationships. Current usage merely provides snapshots of satisfaction (i.e., satisfaction frozen in some time frame). This encourages spouses (and researchers) to experience satisfaction as an end state. Erbert and Duck's (1997) dialectical theory of satisfaction describes a dynamic tension occasioned by contradictions. Steady-state notions of satisfaction imply an ideal to be achieved, thereby priming spouses to believe a *state* of satisfaction is attainable. An alternative view would suggest that remaining in the game *is* winning at the game; "satisfaction" is less important than the dynamics of "accommodation." (Accommodation is also misleading if it is defined as a linear process of increasingly discernible steps of fulfillment.) From a dialectic perspective conflict or other forms of misalignment are very much part and parcel of marital satisfaction, although this may be a hard sell for spouses whose relationship is characterized more by struggle than happiness.

Focus on Process

In their temporal model of relationship satisfaction and stability Berscheid and Lopes (1997) refer to interaction as the The Relationship Organism. "A relationship between two people resides in neither of the partners, but rather in the interaction that takes place between them. That interaction can be viewed as constituting the living organism, or dynamic system, we call an interpersonal 'relationship' " (p. 136).

How to move from metaphor to testable models and theory building? Two avenues of very different complexity are described in the literature. As already discussed above (e.g., Halford's self-regulation approach), the satisfaction construct can be expanded more broadly to include adaptive processes. The quality of the experience can be determined by focusing on relationship accomplishments in how well couples manage challenges *and* joyfulness. In an ambitious study, Gottman and Ryan (ch. 3 in this volume) further exemplified this approach by tailoring self-report outcome measures to tap the four specific facets of Gottman's theory of intervention, the Sound Marital House (Gottman, 1999), namely, *marital friendship, creating positive sentiment override, regulating conflict,* and *creating shared symbolic meaning.* Although the aim of their study was to assess the outcomes of various conditions of their theory-based intervention, the relevance for the satisfaction construct is quite direct. Gottman and Ryan stress a point alluded to above, namely, that Locke-Wallace (and the DAS) scores, as quintessential measures of outcome satisfaction, are based on the extent of spousal agreements. However, if conflict-based interventions enable couples to disagree in nondestructive ways, their scores will reflect less satisfaction than those of conflict avoidant couples, clearly an un-intended consequence that is inherent in instruments focusing on agreement. Agreement is not the most content valid way of expressing marital experience.

The second option for getting beyond the appeal of metaphor in describing satisfaction in dynamic terms is more complicated and entails implementing concepts from theories of complex dynamical systems (e.g., Eidelson, 1997; Lewis & Granic, 2000; Nowak & Vallacher, 1998); applications will be slower to emerge. To date Gottman and colleagues (2002) have done the most systematic marital work with marriages. In what follows I attempt to identify some key concepts from complex dynamical systems theory germane for understanding satisfaction. I briefly describe how Gottman has used marital interaction data to implement these ideas.

Marital Quality and Complex Systems

Complex dynamical systems (and complex adaptive systems: Eidelson, 1997; Lewis & Granic, 2000; Nowak & Vallacher, 1998) deal with complexities of nonlinear change in processes among interdependent elements (i.e., dynamic systems). Rather than accepting homeostasis as a basic system principle, change within complex dynamic systems produces ever more expansive organizations. Random elements, guided by the simplest rules, self-organize into patterns of often greater complexity. A useful portrayal of a dynamic system compares the roles of error terms in linear and nonlinear equations. Linear prediction equations assume error terms that are based on random sampling fluctuations and are therefore readily ignored. However, in a nonlinear equation the error term cannot be ignored because its very existence feeds back into the system, potentially causing major (sudden or catastrophic) qualitative changes. If a spouse acts in a certain unpremeditated manner (essentially a random act that should have no consequence for their interaction) the act itself can cause a cascade of events that could not be predicted just from the known values of variables describing the interaction. A complex dynamic system is one in which "change" jumps nonlinearly, thereby affecting the next values of the elements of the system. The trajectories of the interdependencies are not linear and predictions cannot be made using linear analytic methods.

The tendency for spouses to become stuck in their interaction patterns was noted in the discussion above. In complex dynamic systems, when elements are perturbed they return to, or are drawn to, attractors depicted in phase space. (Phase space is a graphical representation of either (a) the values of one variable plotted against its successive changes or (b) the values of two elements plotted on separate axes (as coordinates) as they move in time; time is represented by the succession of the points). When perturbed from a starting position the elements are drawn back to that point in phase space. Plotting husband and wife scores on separate axes describes the trajectory of how they (the unit) move together toward the attractors that operate in that system.

In order to develop a theory of marital interaction Gottman's group has undertaken the task of mathematically modeling changes in couples' interactions that predict either their satisfaction or stability. For such an undertaking to have any chance of succeeding a (small) number of parameters, empirically related to criterion variables, have to be identified and entered into complex mathematical equations. Based on data from behavioral coding of couples' affect during interactions (see the discussion of Johnson & Bradbury, 1999, above) Gottman has successfully modeled relationship dynamics that instruct therapeutic interventions as well as likely stability outcomes. Among the constructs of interest to the present discussion are parameters of uninfluenced (baseline) and influenced (in response to partner behavior) points, negativity and positivity thresholds, and attractors. It is possible to see that how an interaction begins constrains where it will end. As noted, Gottman's research has shown the importance of the balance between positivity and negativity for satisfaction and stability. (Typically, spouses who start out with high uninfluenced negative states do less well in maintaining their relationships.) Among the more interesting findings is that wives who had very low negativity thresholds (early in marriage) were more likely to be among the stably married; if it took less negativity from the husband to have a negative impact on the wife, the couple showed higher marital satisfaction. When the wife's affect moved the couple into a positive attractor area of the phase space a *repair function* was said to have occurred. Failure to move toward the positive attractor (i.e., being attracted to the negative area) reflected the *stuckedness* mentioned above. Determining whether a couple will be able to break out of negative affect reciprocity is the challenge of successful intervention. Also identifying the transaction events that produce catastrophic change (the "straw that broke the camel's back") for a given relationship will further develop our understanding of satisfaction.

To suggest that *interaction* is the relationship organism (Berscheid & Lopes, 1997) appropriately focuses our attention on process. As seen with the various approaches considered here, processes do predict outcomes, either satisfaction or stability. The argument advanced here is that process is the royal road to defining marital quality. This is all the more likely given that relationships survive under a broad spectrum of living conditions, suggesting that static variables may ultimately be less important in understanding quality. Perhaps the next steps should be more descriptive of quality rather than satisfaction.

From the perspective of complex dynamic systems, marital quality would be addressed by describing patterns of change and the control variables that presage major change. What are the conditions (magnitude of control variables) the presence of which are associated with nonlinear system changes? What are the attractors for a given marital system—the temporal stabilities that the couple returns to after some perturbation? *Marital quality is a temporal map, phase space, not a state, describing how the system moves through various phases.*

Implementing such a suggestion is the challenge. Realistically it will be some time before discrete variables can be defined for use in the mathematical equations necessary to model such events. However, short of this ultimate goal it is possible to have couples produce data on interaction events that are both highly pleasurable (appetitive) and that demand high degrees of coping. Among the latter are relationship relevant upheavals, economic or health-related challenges, and instances of betrayal, among many others. Such an approach would require teaching couples how to track their experiences in more detail than is customary. It would require descriptions of how they coped with events and, more importantly, where they ended up after such perturbations. This way of approaching marital quality does not produce single satisfaction scores, but it does have the potential to aid in understanding quality on a content appropriate scale.

■ Conclusions

The verbal reports people make about the state of their marital bliss have considerable utility for learning about their health and their cognitive and behavioral processes. Those wishing to remedy marital distress obviously need outcome measures. Marital satisfaction seems to be the all-purpose proxy, albeit a very static one. It promotes the view of an end state or an ideal that one must obtain, experiences notwithstanding. Even ambitious longitudinal studies have settled for single satisfaction measures that emphasize spousal agreement. Although appealing as an outcome variable, marital stability by itself hides important information about process. Both satisfaction and stability are moving targets. Many marriage-related constructs exist with relatively little theory development. My recommendation is to promote efforts to understand as many aspects of process as we can. Interest in adaptive processes has to go beyond cataloging individual resources and vulnerabilities. Process is a difficult beast to tame. Complex dynamical systems provide a paradigm for describing and understanding functionality. Hopefully we will see more applications of this approach that will enhance theory development.

■ References

Berscheid, E., & Lopes, J. (1997). A temporal model of relationship satisfaction and stability. In R. J. Sternberg & M. Hojjat (Eds.), *Satisfaction in close relationships* (pp. 129–159). New York: Guilford Press.

Bradbury, T. N., Fincham, F. D., & Beach, S. R. H. (2000). Research on the nature and determinants of marital satisfaction: A decade review. *Journal of Marriage and the Family, 62,* 964–980.

Christensen, A., & Jacobson, N. S. (2000). *Reconcilable differences.* New York: Guilford Press.

Coyne, J. C., Rohraugh, M. J., Shoham, V., Sonnega, J. S., Nicklas, J. M., & Cranford, J. A. (2001). Prognostic importance of marital quality for survival of congestive heart failure. *American Journal of Cardiology, 88,* 526–552.

Davila, J., & Bradbury, T. N. (2001). Attachment insecurity and the distinction between unhappy spouses who do and do not divorce. *Journal of Family Psychology, 15,* 371–393.

Eidelson, R. J. (1997). Complex adaptive systems in the behavioral and social sciences. *Review of General Psychology, 1,* 42–71.

Erbert, L. A., & Duck, S. W. (1997). Rethinking satisfaction in personal relationships from a dialectical perspective. In R. J. Sternberg & M. Hojjat (Eds.), *Satisfaction in close relationships* (pp. 190–216). New York: Guilford Press.

Feeney, J. A., Noller, P., and Ward, C. (1997). Marital satisfaction and spousal interaction. In R. J. Sternberg and M. Hojjat (Eds.), *Satisfaction in close relationships* (pp. 160–189). New York: Guilford Press.

Fincham, F., Beach, S. R. H., & Kemp-Fincham, S. I. (1997). Marital quality: A new theoretical perspective. In R. J. Sternberg & M. Hojjat (Eds.), *Satisfaction in close relationships* (pp. 275–304). New York: Guilford Press.

Fincham, F. D. (1994). Cognition in marriage: Current status and future challenges. *Applied and Preventive Psychology, 3,* 185–198.

Fincham, F. D., & Bradbury, T. N. (1987). The assessment of marital quality: A reevaluation. *Journal of Marriage and the Family, 49,* 797–809.

Fincham, F. D., Garnier, P. C., Gano-Phillips, S. D., & Osborne, L. N. (1995). Pre-interaction expectations, marital satisfaction and accessibility: A new look at sentiment override. *Journal of Family Psychology, 9,* 3–14.

Fincham, F. D., & Linfield, K. (1997). A new look at marital quality: Can spouses be positive and negative about their marriage? *Journal of Family Psychology, 11,* 489–502.

First, M. B., Gibbon, M., Spitzer, R. L., & Williams, I. B. W. (1997). *Structured clinical interview for DSM-IV axis I disorders—clinician version.* Washington, DC: American Psychiatric Press.

Fitzpatrick, M. A. (1988). *Between husbands and wives: Communication in marriage.* Beverly Hills, CA: Sage.

Gottman, J. (1982). Temporal form: Toward a new language for describing relationships, *Journal of Marriage and the Family, 44,* 943–962.

Gottman, J., Coan, J., Carrere, S., & Swanson, C. (1998). Predicting marital happiness and stability from newlywed interactions. *Journal of Marriage and the Family, 60*(1), 5–22.

Gottman, J. M. (1979). *Marital interaction: Experimental investigations.* New York: Academic Press.

Gottman, J. M. (1993). A theory of marital dissolution and stability. *Journal of Family Psychology, 7,* 57–75.

Gottman, J. M. (1999). *The marriage clinic.* New York: Norton.

Gottman, J. M., Murray, J. D., Swanson, C. C., Tyson, R., & Swanson, K. R. (2002). *The mathematics of marriage: Dynamic non-linear models.* Cambridge, MA: MIT Press.

Halford, W. K. (2001). *Brief couple therapy: Helping partners help themselves.* New York: Guilford Press.

Halford, W. K. (2002). Does working at a relationship work? Relationship self-regulation and relationship outcomes. In P. Noller & J. A. Feeney (Eds.), *Understanding marriage: Developments in the study of couple interaction* (pp. 493–517).Cambridge: Cambridge University Press.

Hawkins, M. W., Carrere, S., & Gottman, J. M. (2002). Marital sentiment override: Does it influence couples' perceptions? *Journal of Marriage and the Family, 64,* 193–201.

Heyman, R. E., Feldbau-Kohn, S. R., Ehrensaft, M. K., Langhinrichsen-Rohling, J., & O'Leary, K. D. (2001). Can questionnaire reports correctly classify relationship distress and partner physical abuse? *Journal of Family Psychology, 15,* 334–346.

Johnson, M. D., & Bradbury, T. N. (1999). Marital assessment and topographical assessment of marital interaction: A longitudinal analysis of newlywed couples. *Personal Relationships, 6,* 19–40.

Karney, B. R., & Bradbury, T. N. (1995). The longitudinal course of marital quality and stability: a review of theory, method, and research. *Psychological Bulletin, 118,* 3–34.

Kluwer, E. (2000). Marital quality. In R. M. Milardo & S. W. Duck (Eds.), *Families as relationships* (pp. 59–78). London: Wiley.

Lewis, M. D., & Granic, I. (Eds.). (2000). *Emotion, development and self-organization: Dynamic systems approaches to emotional development.* New York: Cambridge University Press.

Locke, H. J., & Wallace, K. M. (1959). Short marital adjustment and prediction tests: Their reliability and validity. *Journal of Marriage and the Family, 21,* 251–255.

Norton, R. (1983). Measuring marital quality: A critical look at the dependent variable. *Journal of Marriage and the Family, 45,* 141–151.

Nowak, A., & Vallacher, R. R. (1998). *Dynamical social psychology.* New York: Guilford Press.

Roberts, L., & Greenberg, D. R. (2002). Observational "windows" to intimacy: processes in marriage. In P. Noller & J. A. Feeney (Eds.), *Understanding marriage: Developments in the study of couple interaction* (pp. 118–149). Cambridge: Cambridge University Press.

Rogge, R. D., & Bradbury, T. N. (1999). Till violence does us part: The differing role of communication and aggression in predicting adverse marital outcomes. *Journal of Consulting and Clinical Psychology, 67,* 340–351.

Rusbult, C. E., & Martz, J. M. (1995). Remaining in an abusive relationship: An investment model analysis of non-voluntary dependence. *Journal of Social and Personal Relationships, 10,* 175–293.

Rusbult, C. E., Martz, J. M, & Agnew, C. R. (1998). The investment model scale: Measuring commitment level, satisfaction level, quality of alternative, and investment size. *Personal Relationship, 5*, 357–392.

Sabatelli, R. M. (1988). Measurement issues in marital research: A review and critique of contemporary survey instruments. *Journal of Marriage and the Family, 50*, 891–915.

Spanier, G. B. (1976). Measuring dyadic adjustment: New scales for assessing the quality of marriage and similar dyads. *Journal of Marriage and the Family, 37*, 63–275.

Stanley, S. M., & Markman, H. J. (1992). Assessing commitment in personal relationships. *Journal of Marriage and the Family, 54*, 595–608.

Weiss, R. L. (1978). The conceptualization of marriage from a behavioral perspective. In T. J. Paolino & B. S. McCrady (Eds.), *Marriage and marital therapy: Psychoanalytic, behavioral and systems theory perspectives* (pp. 165–239). New York: Brunner/Mazel.

Weiss, R. L. (1980). Strategic behavioral marital therapy: Toward a model for assessment and intervention. In J. P. Vincent (Ed.), *Advances in family intervention, assessment and theory* (Vol. 1, pp. 229–271). Greenwich, CT: JAI Press.

Weiss, R. L., & Heyman, R. E. (1990). Observation of marital interaction. In F. Fincham & T. Bradbury (Eds.), *The psychology of marriage: Basic issues and applications* (pp. 87–117). New York: Guilford Press.

Weiss, R. L., & Heyman, R. E. (1997). Marital interaction. In W. K. Halford & H. Markman (Eds.), *Clinical handbook of marriage and marital interaction* (pp. 13–35). New York: Wiley.

Weiss, R. L., & Heyman, R. E. (2004). Couples observational research: An impertinent, critical overview. In P. K. Kerig & D. H. Baucom (Eds.), *Couple observational coding systems* (pp. 11–25). Mahwah, NJ: Erlbaum.

Weiss, R. L., & Perry, B. A. (2001). Behavioral couples therapy: Prospect and retrospect. In T. Patterson (Ed.), *Comprehensive handbook of psychotherapy, Vol. Two: Cognitive/ behavioral/functional approaches* (pp. 295–419). New York: Wiley.

Whisman, M. (1997). Satisfaction in close relationships: Challenges for the 21st century. In R. J. Sternberg & M. Hojjat (Eds.), *Satisfaction in close relationships* (pp. 385–410). New York: Guilford Press.

Whitton, S. W., Stanley, S. M., & Markman, H. J. (2002). Sacrifice in romantic relationships: An exploration of relevant research and theory. In H. T. Reiss, M. A. Fitzpatrick, & A. L. Vangelisti (Eds.), *Stability and change in relationship behavior across the lifespan* (pp. 156–181). Cambridge: Cambridge University Press.

2

A Science of Couple Therapy: For What Should We Seek Empirical Support?

Andrew Christensen, Brian D. Doss, and David C. Atkins

As scientist-practitioners, we want our clinical efforts to be supported by scientific evidence. Indeed, science can provide the most compelling evidence that our treatments are beneficial to our clients rather than ineffective or harmful for them. Not only does scientific evidence meet our own values and standards for the credibility of psychotherapeutic treatment, it provides accountability to our clients and to third-party payers, who increasingly want evidence that what they pay for is effective. Thus, the demand for scientific evidence is high, and many treatments and providers seek the mantle of scientific respectability.

However, the process of determining what constitutes scientific or empirical support can be difficult. Data are always subject to interpretation and thus to controversy, and science is home to regular debates about whether some hypothesis has been properly supported by the data. However, in the realm of psychotherapeutic intervention, there is also controversy surrounding what specifically we should seek empirical support for. One notion is that, analogous to seeking data about the efficacy of drug and surgical interventions, we should seek empirical support for the efficacy of particular psychological treatments. In contrast to this notion, others have suggested that the interpersonal relationship is most crucial to psychotherapeutic success and that we should seek empirical support for particular kinds of therapeutic relationships. More recently, others have suggested that we seek empirical support for principles of change. Since the goal of intervention is change, proponents of this position emphasize that we should garner scientific data on what brings about change.

In this chapter we review each of these three approaches for garnering scientific evidence in support of psychotherapeutic treatment, using couple therapy as an example. We describe some of the advantages and disadvantages of each approach: empirically supported treatments (ESTs), empirically supported relationships (ESRs), and empirically supported principles of change (ESPs). We focus specifically on the latter and describe how our science might investigate the effectiveness of fundamental principles of change in couple therapy.

■ Empirically Supported Treatments

In 1995, the Task Force on Promotion and Dissemination of Psychological Procedures (Task Force), organized by Division 12 of the American Psychological Association and chaired by Dianne Chambless, issued its first report on criteria for empirically validated treatments and a list of treatments that met those criteria (Task Force, 1995). Subsequent task forces have modified those criteria and expanded the list of treatments that meet the criteria (Chambless et al., 1996, 1998). In the 1998 report, two levels of empirical support were specified: "well-established treatments" and "probably efficacious treatments." The first and highest level of support required (a) at least two methodologically rigorous between-group designs or a large series of single case designs showing the superiority of the treatment to a placebo or alternative treatment or equivalence to an already established treatment, (b) use of treatment manuals, (c) clear definitions of the client sample, and (d) effects demonstrated by at least two different investigators or investigating teams. For probably efficacious treatments there could be a variety of positive evidence that did not meet the standards for well-established treatments. Over time, the term *empirically validated treatments* has been replaced by the term *empirically supported treatments* or *evidence-based treatments*. Currently, the Web site for Division 12 Empirically Supported Treatments (http://www.apa.org/divisions/div12/rev_est/index.shtml) lists marital distress as one problem for which there are ESTs. The marital distress site (http://www.apa.org/divisions/div12/rev_est/marital.shtml) lists behavioral marital therapy as a well-established treatment but also lists emotionally focused couple therapy and insight-oriented marital therapy as having some evidence for them (presumably probably efficacious treatments). However, the most recent update of manuals (http://pantheon.yale.edu/%7Etat22/est_docs/manual498.pdf) by Woody and Sanderson (1998) only lists treatment manuals by Jacobson and Margolin (1979) and Baucom and Epstein (1990); the first is a manual for behavioral marital therapy and the second for cognitive-behavioral marital therapy.

This effort to identify and promote ESTs was motivated by a desire to place psychological treatments, similar to drug treatments, on a firm empirical base. Perhaps its most important accomplishment was to specify criteria for empirical support and to draw attention to treatments that had received empirical support. However, this laudatory effort was met with a variety of criticisms. Practitioners were concerned that ESTs might inhibit clinical creativity, force them to operate in the straightjackets of treatment manuals, prevent them from using effective treatments that had not been subjected to empirical scrutiny, and be misused by managed care companies (Chambless & Ollendick, 2001). For our purposes here, we focus on two assumptions and one consequence of the EST approach.

The search for ESTs assumes first of all that bona fide treatments differ in their effectiveness and that we should therefore seek the most efficacious of them. As reasonable as this assumption seems, there is considerable evidence questioning it. Ever since Luborsky and his colleagues first proposed the "Dodo Bird Verdict" that all have won and all must have prizes (Luborsky, Singer, & Luborsky, 1975), this verdict has pestered psychotherapy researchers. Luborsky and his colleagues (2002) summarized recent evidence for the Dodo Bird conclusion.

In the area of couple therapy, we certainly have examples where two different treatments do not appear to have differential outcomes. When compared with behavioral marital therapy, cognitive-behavioral marital therapy produces similar positive effects (Baucom, Sayers, & Sher, 1990). However, there are cases in which one couple treatment has performed better than another. Goldman and Greenberg (1992) found that integrated systemic therapy and emotionally focused therapy were superior to a control group and equally effective at the termination of treatment but that integrated systemic therapy showed greater maintenance of gains from termination to 4-month follow-up. Also, Snyder and his colleagues (Snyder & Wills, 1989; Snyder, Wills, & Grady-Fletcher, 1991a, 1991b) have shown that behavioral marital therapy and insight-oriented marital therapy were better than a control condition and equally effective at termination and 6-month follow-up, but that insight-oriented marital therapy was superior at a 4-year follow-up. However, despite these studies, there is not sufficient data to conclude that any existing couple treatment is clearly superior to the others (Christensen & Heavey, 1999).

The failure to find robust differences in outcome from interventions that are manifestly different in theory and execution could reflect the operation of common factors, as some of the proponents of the Dodo Bird hypothesis suggest (Messer & Wampold, 2002). However, rather than being a substantive finding, the failure to find robust differences may reflect methodological problems with the comparisons themselves. For example, differences between treatments may be more likely to show up in long-term than in short-term outcomes, such as was found in the Snyder et al. (1991a) study above. Yet few studies in the therapy literature in general, or the couple therapy literature in particular, conduct follow-ups beyond the first year posttreatment (Westen & Morrison, 2001). Many treatment studies may not be sufficiently powered to detect other than large differences in effect size (Rossi, 1990). In addition, treatment studies may not employ sensitive measures of outcome. Most studies use only intake to termination measures of change during treatment when repeated measures over treatment might show different trajectories of change during treatment. For example, Christensen and colleagues (2004) demonstrated different trajectories of change during treatment between two couple therapies when a simple pre–post analysis would have rendered them "not significantly different." Finally, Christensen et al. (2004) suggest that differential outcome may be most apparent when severe clinical problems characterize the treatment sample. Most treatments may achieve success with uncomplicated cases.

If the first assumption behind the EST movement is correct—that there are genuine differences in outcome between bona fide treatments—then a second assumption follows: that these differences can be objectively detected. Some investigators have suggested that the *allegiance effect,* an investigator's bias toward a favorite treatment, casts doubt on data showing differences between treatments

(Luborsky et al., 1999). Indeed, the data indicate that when treatments differ, the treatment favored by the investigator is much more likely than the alternative treatment to come out on top. Luborsky et al.'s recent review (1999) suggested that 69% of the variance in outcome could be explained by the allegiance effect!

In the marital area, the above mentioned study by Snyder et al. (1991a) was the subject of controversy related to the allegiance effect. Jacobson (1991) suggested that behavioral marital therapy had not been given a fair test in this study, arguing that the behavioral treatment was not "up-to-date" and excluded important, nonspecific therapist skills. Snyder et al. (1991b) responded to these allegations by citing, in part, their adherence data on the two treatments they examined. It is not our concern to evaluate these criticisms, but merely to show that issues of investigator allegiance have been raised against couple therapy studies, in fact against what is surely one of the best outcome studies to date of couple therapy.

The issue of allegiance is not limited to psychotherapy studies and has recently been raised with medical studies. In a recently published analysis, Bekelman, Li, and Gross (2003) found that industry-sponsored medical research is 3.6 times more likely to find results favorable, rather than unfavorable, to the company that paid for it. The solution to this serious problem is of course to institute more rigorous controls over outcome research (Moher, Schulz, & Altman, 2001). Psychotherapy studies should use therapists and supervisors who are expert in each of the treatments being compared, not just the treatment favored by the principal investigator (Hollon, 1999).

Even when we can meet these two essential assumptions of the EST approach—that psychotherapeutic treatments differ and that these differences can be detected objectively—we are not in an altogether comfortable situation. We may know that treatment A is better than treatment B for condition X, but we don't know why. ESTs are defined by treatment manuals, which are usually book-length descriptions of treatments to be read by and implemented by therapists. For example, the treatment manual for behavior marital therapy, which is currently listed as a well-established treatment for marital discord, is a 200+ page book by Jacobson and Margolin (1979). Although we have evidence that the use of the treatment specified in this book leads to positive outcomes, we don't know why. It is extremely unlikely that each procedure in the package of treatments described in the book is equally relevant to success or is even necessary for success. The book may include "little bits of superstitious behavior here and there" (Kazdin, 2001, p. 147).

There is a children's story about how humans first learned to eat meat. In a village by the ocean, where people lived in huts on stilts above the ground, a fire started in a village hut and a pig trapped underneath was burned to death. The villagers came by afterward to look at the poor pig, who had been a favorite pet. One villager bravely put his finger on the pig to see if the animal was indeed dead, his finger got burned, he instinctively put it in his mouth, and he discovered the new and wonderful taste of cooked meat. This lucky fellow with the burnt finger and happy taste buds encouraged others to stick their fingers into the pig and soon the whole village was having a feast. Sometime later the village wanted to enjoy such a meal again, so they naturally tied another pig underneath a hut and burned the hut down!

When we don't know why a treatment works, we may engage in much unnecessary behavior. Perhaps more importantly, we don't know what active ingredient we need to potentiate in order to make the treatment more effective. Similarly, we don't know what active ingredient to preserve or what modifications to make when we adapt a treatment to a different population, such as a different ethnic group or age cohort than the group on which the treatment was developed.

Of course, we can conduct studies to investigate the active ingredients in a treatment package. So far, these investigations have not been very encouraging in pointing to specific mechanisms of change. For example, an increase in communication skills is an hypothesized mechanism of change in behavioral marital therapy. However, studies investigating the relationship between change in communication skills and change in satisfaction have found no relationship, a positive relationship, as well as a negative relationship (Schilling, Baucom, Burnett, Allen, & Ragland, 2003; Whisman & Snyder, 1997).

These investigations of change mechanisms are few and far between (see Doss, Thum, Sevier, Atkins, & Christensen, in press, for a recent example). Certainly we can and should do more, an issue to which we return later in this chapter. However, the emphasis in the EST approach is finding a treatment package that is successful in treating a disorder, not so much on finding the specific ingredients that account for that success.

■ Empirically Supported Relationships

Many researchers (Ackerman et al., 2001) argue that the field knows what the active ingredients in successful therapy are and these ingredients are not treatment techniques but therapeutic relationships. Based on data showing the importance of the therapeutic relationship to outcome and data revealing small effect sizes associated with treatment approaches (Lambert & Barley, 2001), they argue that we should pay greater attention to the empirical data on relationship factors in treatment outcome.

In a reaction to the movement on ESTs, Division 29 of the American Psychological Association (APA), the Division of Psychotherapy, created a task force to "identify, operationalize, and disseminate information on empirically supported therapy relationships. We aimed to identify empirically supported (therapy) relationships rather than empirically supported treatments—or ESRs rather than ESTs" (Ackerman et al., 2001, pp. 347, 348). Their report (Ackerman et al., 2001) summarizes the evidence on relationship factors in psychotherapy outcome and uses categories of empirical support like those for ESTs. For example, they conclude that "empathy" and "goal consensus and collaboration" are general elements of the therapeutic relationship that are "demonstrably effective" and that "feedback," "positive regard," "management of transference," and "self-disclosure" are elements that are "promising and probably effective." In addition, they discuss levels of empirical support for strategies for "customizing the therapy relationship to individual patients."

The data in support of ESRs and the recommendations made about ESRs refer primarily to individual therapy, the usual constellation of one client and one therapist. Evidence clearly shows that a good therapeutic relationship with a client is associated with better outcome for that client. However, it is not clear if and how that positive outcome would spread to the client's relationships with others. For example, if a wife sees an individual therapist and has a good relationship with that individual therapist, will the simple fact of her having a good relationship with her therapist lead to benefit in her relationship with her husband?

Couple therapy is usually done conjointly. Certainly the client-therapist relationship is also important in conjoint therapy, but it is likely to be less important and less intense than in individual therapy, where the therapist-client relationship is the only relationship in the room. When a therapist works conjointly with a couple, there are three dyadic relationships in the room: the therapist and wife, the therapist and husband, and the wife and husband. More significantly, the most important and intense relationship—the presenting problem for treatment—is the relationship between the couple (see Pinsof, 1994, and Rait, 2000, for a detailed analysis of the therapeutic alliance in couple and family therapy).

Although such features as empathy and goal consensus are likely to be important features of the therapeutic relationship with a couple as well as with an individual (Bourgeois, Sabourin, & Wright, 1990), there are additional features of the therapeutic relationship that are important in conjoint therapy that are not relevant to individual therapy. Neutrality and balance are especially important. A couple therapist should usually maintain a position of neutrality for the partners' opposing positions on conflict and should balance his or her attention and support for each partner.

Beutler (2002) has argued that, while the relationship attributes identified by the ESR movement are important to individual therapy, they account "for no more of the treatment outcomes than that attributed to various specific treatments—about 10%" (p. 3). Unfortunately, there are few data on therapist qualities and the outcome of couple therapy. However, given its more limited role in conjoint couple therapy, the therapist relationship may well account for even less than 10% of the outcome—not a firm foundation on which to build empirical support.

■ Empirically Supported Principles of Change

Perhaps the earliest and latest candidates for empirical support are principles of therapeutic change. Rosen and Davison (2003) note that the earliest writings on behavior therapy called for the application of experimentally derived principles of behavior change to the amelioration of clinical problems. Over 20 years ago, Goldfried (1982) proposed that psychotherapeutic treatment should be based on empirically defined principles of change rather than on specific techniques or broad theories. More recently, Beutler and his colleagues (Beutler, 2000; Beutler, Clarkin, & Bongar, 2000) have developed the notion of empirically supported principles of therapeutic change both conceptually and empirically and have generated a series of empirically based principles for the treatment of depression (Beutler et al., 2000).

Beutler (2002) describes principles of therapeutic change as follows: "Principles are not theories—they are descriptions of observed relationships. They are more general than techniques and they are more specific than theories. They are the "if . . . then" relationships that tell us when to do and what to do, and who to do it to" (p. 3).

Beutler's (2000) model proposes four levels for which principles of therapeutic change can be developed. Level 1 refers to "patient predisposing variables," such as severity, resistance, social support, and coping styles. An example principle is "The likelihood of improvement (prognosis) is a positive function of social support level and a negative function of functional impairment." Level 2 refers to the "context of treatment," such as treatment intensity, individual versus group, and medical versus psychosocial. An example of a relevant principle from the treatment of depression would be "Psychoactive medication exerts its best effects among those patients with high functional impairment and high complexity/chronicity." Level 3 refers to therapist variables such as therapist skill and therapist alliance as well as therapist interventions. An example of the former would be that "Therapeutic change is greatest when the therapist is skillful and provides trust, acceptance, acknowledgment, collaboration, and respect for the patient within an environment that both supports risk and provides maximal safety." An example of the latter would be that "Therapeutic change is most likely when the patient is exposed to objects or targets of behavioral and emotional avoidance." Finally, Level 4 refers to the match between patient characteristics and type of treatment. An example is the principle that "Therapeutic change is greatest when the relative balance of interventions either favors the use of skill building and symptom removal procedures among patients who externalize or favors the use of insight and relationship-focused procedures among patients who internalize."

As President of Division 12 of APA, Beutler, in collaboration with Louis G. Castonguay, formed a Task Force in 2002 on "Defining the Principles of Effective Therapeutic Change." The Task Force met in 2003 to prepare a series of integrative chapters and presented its findings at the August 2003 APA; a book (Castonguay & Beutler, 2005) describes this work. The focus is on depressive disorders, anxiety disorders, personality disorders, and substance use disorders (L. E. Beutler & L. G. Castonguay, personal communications).

There are several advantages to the ESP approach. It avoids the raw, blind empiricism of both ESTs and ESRs. Rather than the static assertion that "interpersonal psychotherapy works for depression" or "Empathy improves outcome," the ESP approach asserts specific "if-then" connections that summarize empirically discovered relationships. The ESP approach can also incorporate some of the findings from EST and ESR research without the name brand adherence of ESTs and the ironically context-free approach of ESRs. Empirically supported principles refer to links between therapist and client behavior, whether that therapist behavior is more akin to relationship factors or specific techniques. Finally, ESPs can point toward possible mechanisms of action. Whereas ESTs and ESRs can successfully avoid any explanation of why treatments or relationships are beneficial, ESPs specify "if-then" relationships that move the field toward greater understanding of the mechanisms of human change. As we noted above, with knowledge of mechanisms, we are in a better position to improve the efficacy of our treatments and adapt them to different client circumstances.

If the field adopts the ESP approach, there will be less focus on competing *models* or *schools* of therapy. Instead, the focus will be on particular principles that can achieve particular goals at different time points and choice points in therapy. This focus on a smaller unit of analysis—a principle of change rather than an entire treatment package or a characteristic of the therapeutic relationship—won't necessarily make the empirical work any easier. Just as a psychological treatment comes in the context of a relationship and just as a therapeutic relationship exists in the context of some treatment activity, so a principle of change can only occur in the context of a broader treatment and a therapeutic relationship. The challenge is to conceptualize particular principles of change and to gather evidence for these principles within this broader context of treatment.

None of the work done to date on ESPs has focused on couple or family relationships. Nor will the work planned by the Task Force focus on these relationships. Therefore, in the remainder of this paper, we focus on how ESPs might be conceptualized from within couple therapy and how we might gather evidence to support or disconfirm them.

■ ESPs for Couple Therapy

Doss (2004) has recently presented a model for studying change in psychotherapy. We will borrow from this model in explicating ESPs for couples. His model distinguishes four sequential variables: Therapist change processes (the therapist's actions and re-actions during the therapy session that are often coded as adherence to treatment protocol or competence in delivering the treatment protocol), client change processes (client reactions and actions during the therapy session), client change mechanisms (client behavior outside of the therapy session), and client outcomes (the final changes we seek in clients as a result of therapy). As a simple example, the therapist teaches assertiveness in the therapy session (therapist change processes), the client practices those skills with the therapist in the session (client change processes), then the client practices those skills in real life, which helps him or her achieve goals and avoid resentment, which in turn increases a sense of self-efficacy (client change mechanisms), all of which then relieves the client's depression (client outcome). In our view, an ideal principle of change in couple therapy would specify each of these aspects of change, which could then be subject to empirical investigation.

In couple therapy, and perhaps in individual therapy as well, we can distinguish between two types of intervention, based on the model of therapeutic change for in-session and out-of-session behavior. In prescriptive interventions, the therapist instructs or trains the couple in how to behave in the outside world and these behaviors in the outside world then improve outcome. In evocative interventions, the therapist tries to create, elicit, or evoke new experiences in the therapy session that, even if they are not repeated outside of the therapy session, will have an impact on the couple's affective-cognitive-behavioral reactions outside the session and thus affect outcome. Traditionally, outcome in couple therapy has referred to changes in reports of relationship satisfaction and, less frequently, to relationship status (e.g., still married, separated, divorced). Weiss (ch. 1 in this volume) provides an interesting analysis of some of the problems with the construct of relationship satisfaction. Although we will often use relationship satisfaction as an example of outcome, the logic of the Doss (2004) model and our discussion below are not limited to any particular outcome measure.

Prescriptive Interventions

Prescriptive interventions can involve simple instruction or extensive training by the therapist. If both members of the couple have the necessary behaviors in their repertoire, then the therapist can simply instruct the couple in what to do. A common example would be "time-outs" as a way of dealing with heated arguments. A therapist describes when to take the time-outs, what to say (e.g., "I am getting too upset to have a constructive discussion and am going to take a time-out"), what not to say (e.g., "You are getting hysterical so I am going to take a time-out"), how long the time-out should last, and perhaps even the appropriate attitude toward the time-outs (e.g., as a way to avoid negative escalation, not as a punishment for the other). The therapist and couple may discuss different "what ifs" that may cause difficulty. The therapist may engage the couple in a negotiation of some features of the time-out (e.g., how long it should last, when they should return to the topic of discussion), and the therapist may adapt his or her suggestions to the client's style. If, for example, a husband would not think of himself as getting too upset to have a constructive discussion, the therapist might work out another message to signal time-outs (e.g., "I think this conversation is getting out of control and am going to take a time-out"). Nevertheless, despite these variations and complications, the therapist is essentially instructing and encouraging the couple to engage in a set of behaviors outside of the session.

If the couple does not have the necessary behaviors within their repertoire, a prescriptive intervention may involve training by the therapist. A common example would be "communication skills." A therapist might have the couple read about communication skills, such as the use of "I" statements and "paraphrasing," may instruct the couple in what to do, may model the requisite behaviors for the couple, may have them practice the behaviors in the session, and may provide corrective feedback.

Whether the prescriptive intervention involves simple instruction or more elaborate teaching and training, the therapist uses the session to encourage the couple to engage in the prescribed behaviors outside of the session, debriefs the efforts by the couple to use these behaviors, and provides instructive and rein-forcing feedback.

The primary interventions of traditional behavioral marital therapy (Jacobson & Margolin, 1979), such as behavior exchange, communication training, and pro-blem-solving training, are all essentially prescriptive interventions. The interven-tions of cognitive-behavioral couple therapy (Baucom & Epstein, 1990; Epstein & Baucom, 2002) are also usually prescriptive. For example, the therapist might teach the couple about cognitive errors such as "all or nothing" thinking, ask them in the session to generate exceptions to particular "all or nothing" statements, and en-courage them to challenge their thinking similarly outside of the session.

In prescriptive interventions, the mechanism of change is at least partly spec-ified. The first links in the causal chain—that the instructions and teaching in the sessions lead directly to changes in the relevant behaviors both in and outside the session—is clearly assumed if not stated. For example, the therapist not only teaches communication skills such as the use of "I" statements and paraphrasing, but has the couple practice the skills in the session and gives them homework assignments to practice these skills outside the session.

The next link in the mechanism of change, how the increased use of the be-haviors taught in session leads to changes in outcome, is often not specified but assumed. For example, use of the communication skills taught in the session might lead to reduced conflict outside the session, to greater achievement of goals, or to an increased sense of self-efficacy, but the therapist assumes that through one or more of these ways, the communication skills will lead to greater satisfaction and stability in the relationship, the primary outcome measures.

Given the clarity of proposed mechanisms in most prescriptive interventions, it is relatively easy to conduct empirical tests of those mechanisms. For example, if teaching and instruction do not lead to the expected changes in behavior outside the session, then the prescriptive intervention has clearly failed. If a couple does not use time-outs to control escalating arguments outside of the session, then the time-out intervention was not successful. Jacobson, Schmaling, and Holtzworth-Munroe (1987) presented data that 2 years after treatment, less than half of treated couples were using communication skills appropriately, as they were trained in therapy to do. Jacobson et al. then suggested that the lack of skill use may have accounted for the poor outcome at 2 years follow-up.

The failure to use behaviors taught in the therapy session could have more than just the neutral outcome of "no improvement"; the failure might lead to a wors-ening of outcome. Both members could get discouraged that they were unable to use the medicine the doctor recommended. If one member of a couple used the skills and the other did not, the user of the skills could blame the other for "not going along with the program" and another conflict could be created by the very inter-vention designed to reduce conflicts. Even if the couple were able to implement the recommended behaviors and experience some improvement as a result, they might not be able to maintain those behaviors over the long term, and then they would experience the ultimate discouragement of a pyrrhic success.

However, a failure to consistently implement the instruction or training obtained in therapy would not necessarily lead to a negative or neutral outcome. It is possible that the work in therapy, even if never implemented, could have salutary effects. For example, the discussion of communication skills could make each realize their own difficulties with communication and make them less blaming toward the other. Also, couples might learn from even sporadic efforts to implement training and instruction that therapy provided. For example, they might become more attuned to their communication and better able to recover from communication difficulties. Thus, a failure to implement prescriptive interventions outside of therapy only means, by itself, that the putative mechanism of action did not occur. If we discover that there was no improvement in outcome as well, we don't know whether the failure to implement the prescriptions doomed the outcome or whether the intervention itself would have been a failure, even if implemented.

If the prescriptive intervention does result in a consistent increase in the recommended behavior outside of the therapy session, then at least one link in the mechanism of change has been validated. However, then we need to determine that the increase in behavior outside of therapy results in a change in outcome, either directly or through some mediator. Even if a couple uses the prescribed behaviors, those behaviors may not have the expected impact. Consider a recent study by Schilling et al. (2003) that examined the impact of training in communication skills on engaged couples' risk of becoming maritally distressed. Although the data on men fit with predictions, in that increases in male positive communication and decreases in male negative communication decreased the risk of future marital distress, increases in female positive communication *increased the risk* of future marital distress. Thus, a therapeutically desired, and presumably induced, change led to poorer outcome! In an attempt to understand this finding, the authors examined results from other studies and examined some of their own self-report data, which suggested that increases in female positive communication and decreases in female negative communication were associated with greater avoidance of problem discussion by the couple. They suggest that "... it is possible that the emphasis on approaching conflict positively may send some premarital women an unintended message to be avoidant. They might then refrain from participating with their husbands in the *constructive engagement* of addressing relationship problems" (pp. 49, 50).

Earlier we illustrated that just because couples do not do what we prescribe for them does not mean that we have no impact upon them. Despite our failure to alter certain target behaviors, we could have either a positive or a negative impact on outcome. Similarly, the study above indicates that just because we have been successful in altering therapeutically targeted behaviors, we may not have improved outcome and, in some cases, may have jeopardized it. To provide convincing evidence for the putative mechanism of change in prescriptive interventions, we must show that therapists instruct and train the desired behaviors in session, that clients can perform these behaviors or understand these instructions in session, that couples do the prescribed behaviors outside of therapy, and that those behaviors have the intended effects.

Evocative Interventions

Rather than prescribing useful behavior, couple therapists often try to evoke an emotional response, elicit a new conceptualization or attitude, or provoke different in-session behavior in one or both partners. The therapeutic goal is not for the couple to "now go out and do this on your own" because the experience may require the active intervention of the therapist. However, the therapist assumes that the experience is powerful enough that it can, particularly if repeated in therapy, have an impact on the couple outside of therapy and result in an improvement in outcome. The idea is that evocative interventions lead to corrective experiences for the couple.

Experiential approaches are perhaps the clearest examples of evocative approaches. "Experiential approaches attempt to foster new corrective experiences for clients that emerge as part of personal encounters in the here-and-now of the therapy session" (Johnson & Denton, 2002, pp. 222, 223). The therapist tries to elicit emotional reactions in the session that are more direct, less defensive, more honest, or more complete than the reactions the partners usually have toward each other. From these emotional reactions, partners create new interactions with each other and come to new understandings of each other. For example, in emotionally focused couple therapy, the therapist tries to elicit a "softening" in one partner and "accessibility" in the other that can lead to a "bonding event" between them. "A softening involves a vulnerable request by a usually hostile partner for reassurance, comfort or some other attachment need to be met. When the other, now accessible partner is able to respond to this request, then both partners are mutually responsive and bonding interactions can occur" (Johnson & Denton, 2002, p. 237).

As a result of this "bonding event," partners are able to interact with each other more constructively and feel better about themselves. "A bonding event occurs in the session. This bond then allows for open communication, flexible problem solving, and resilient coping with everyday issues. . . . There are shifts in both partners' sense of self" (Johnson & Denton, 2002, p. 238).

Although the elicitation of emotional events in the session is perhaps the best illustration of evocative interventions, therapists often want to elicit new understandings or new perspectives in therapy. Consider, for example, "unified detachment" in integrative behavioral couple therapy (Christensen, Jacobson, & Babcock, 1995; Jacobson & Christensen, 1998). The therapist tries to foster a view of the problem as an "it" that both partners experience rather than a "you" that one does to the other. To elicit this third-party view of the problem, the therapist may describe a problematic sequence of interaction that the two experience, may discuss this sequence as a dance the two of them go through, may sympathize with each partner's sense that they feel compelled to their respective actions, may engage the couple in a name for their problem, and may use humor to highlight the ironies or contradictions in their actions. As a result of a number of these interventions in the session, integrative behavioral couple therapy suggests that partners will become more "emotionally accepting" and less judgmental about their own and their partner's roles in these interactions. Therefore, even though the pattern may still appear in their lives, it may generate less emotional heat for them and they may recover from the interaction more quickly. Thus, the problematic pattern may undergo some important but subtle changes as a result of the intervention.

To specify an evocative intervention as a principle of change and to empirically test this intervention, one would first have to specify the desired behaviors of the therapist and the desired behaviors of the client in session. For example, in emotionally focused couple therapy (Johnson & Denton, 2002), the therapist explores and reformulates emotions, which leads to "softening" by the clients and bonding events between them. The therapist's exploration and reformulation includes, among other actions, reflection and validation of emotional experience, "empathic conjecture or interpretation" (p. 235) of emotions, and requests for client enactments to heighten emotional responding. During softening, clients have "an expansion of experience, especially an accessing of attachment fears and of the longing for contact and comfort" (pp. 237, 238). From this expansion of experience, they may voice more vulnerable statements or requests; bonding occurs when a partner is open to these statements or requests and responds sensitively to them.

As can be seen in this example, it may be difficult to specify the therapist's behavior, because a variety of different actions can be used to elicit particular client responding. Also, it may be difficult to specify the client's response, particularly when that response is an internal experience, such as an expansion of emotional experience or achievement of a new perspective. The latter may need to be measured with self-reports after the session rather than simple observation of the behaviors in the session.

As with prescriptive interventions, it is not sufficient simply to establish that particular therapist behavior leads to particular client behavior in the session. The goal of couple therapy is to create changes outside of the session that lead to greater relationship satisfaction and stability. To fully specify a principle of change and to empirically test that principle, one must specify how the evocative experience creates changes outside of the session and how these changes ultimately improve outcome. In emotionally focused therapy, it seems that the goal of therapy is to create a more secure attachment bond between partners, a bond that persists outside of therapy. In turn, this bond enables them to communicate and cope more effectively and to achieve the ultimate outcome of happiness and stability. Thus, to validate a principle of EFT, one would need to show that therapy produces more secure attachments between partners, which then lead to improvements in communication and satisfaction outcomes.

■ Advantages and Disadvantages of Prescriptive Interventions

A major advantage of prescriptive interventions is their portability. Because these interventions are essentially educational, they are not confined to professional treatment but can be prescribed in educational contexts by nonprofessional therapists. For example, Fals-Stewart and Birchler (2002) recently demonstrated that bachelor's-level therapists can effectively deliver behavioral marital therapy to highly distressed couples in which one partner is abusing alcohol. Prescriptive interventions may also be adapted for courses, self-help books, magazine articles, computer software, and internet sites and on audio and video tapes. Because of popular interest in relationships, prescriptive advice on "how to improve your relationship" is offered regularly in these formats.

A major difficulty with prescriptive interventions is compliance. Even when people believe the advice they are given, they have difficulty implementing it on a consistent basis. Consider, for example, medical prescriptions. The "dirty little secret in health care" (Ornstein, 2002) is that patients often do not take the medicine that the doctor prescribes. Studies using electronic monitoring methods have shown that patients take their medication less often than they should and less often than they report, even when the consequences could be serious. For example, a study on glaucoma patients found a 97% compliance rate based on patient report but only a 76% compliance rate based on an eyedrop monitoring device, even though the consequences of not taking the medication can be blindness (study cited in Ornstein, 2002). The reasons for not taking medications include simple forgetting, feeling fine without the medication, the cost of the medications, and side effects.

Consider another example of medical advice where compliance is not affected by cost or side effects: the advice to maintain a healthy body weight and to engage in regular physical exercise. Although countless articles and programs have given advice to loose weight and exercise, about 60% of American adults are now overweight or obese (Stewart, 2003). It is estimated that Americans consumed 340 more calories a day in the late 1990s than they did in the mid-1980s and at least 500 more calories a day than in the 1950s (Wellness Facts, 2002). It is estimated that more than 60% of Americans are not physically active on a regular basis (Fulmer & Allen, 2002). Clearly the majority of Americans are not following valuable and regularly prescribed medical advice that could increase their health and longevity.

Therefore, we should hardly be surprised if our clients don't follow our prescriptions, even when we have taken pains to ensure that they understand what to do and have learned how to do it. It requires considerable effort to make consistent changes in our behavior. Such changes are especially difficult when we face circumstances, such as delicious food or interesting TV programs, which elicit behavior contrary to what we are advised to do. Consider the example of time-out. If spouses and parents would take a time-out before they got emotionally out of control, the rates of physical and psychological abuse would plummet. Relationships would be safer and healthier. Yet when emotions are strong and press for action, it can be extremely difficult to turn away and leave the situation. It is likely that people who get most emotionally aroused in relationships, and thus who would benefit most from time-out, are least likely to be able to implement it. This is not to say that we should abandon good prescriptions, such as the advice to exercise or take time-outs, but we need to focus on ways to get people to implement this advice.

Some couple therapies that focus on prescriptive interventions engage in evocative interventions in order to increase the chances that couples will follow through with the recommended prescriptions. For example, in solution-focused couple therapy (Hoyt, 2002), the therapist asks "Agency (Efficacy) Questions" that are "intended to call attention to clients' self-efficacy—that is, their abilities to make a difference in the desired direction" (p. 344). With a greater awareness of their self-efficacy, clients presumably are more willing and able to engage in prescribed tasks or homework. In brief strategic couple therapy (Shoham & Rohrbaugh, 2002), the goal is to break problematic interaction patterns in which couples are caught, but therapists from this approach are well aware that direct prescriptions to break the pattern can often backfire. Therefore, they often employ indirect and paradoxical methods. For example, Shoham and Rohrbaugh (2002) write that one way to break a pattern is "to redefine what one partner is doing in a way that stops short of prescribing change, yet makes it difficult for them to continue." They illustrate this approach with a demand-withdraw pattern in which a wife repeatedly reminds a withdrawn husband of what he should do. They might comment to the wife that "I've noticed that your reminding him and telling him what you think seems to give him an excuse to keep doing what he's doing without feeling guilty—he can justify it to himself simply by blaming you" (p. 13).

Although compliance is probably the major problem with prescribed interventions, there are other difficulties, such as authenticity and iatrogenic processes. Whereas some desired changes can be satisfied by simple behavior change and are well suited for prescribed interventions such as problem solving and negation, other changes require appropriate accompanying motivations and emotions so that they are genuine and ring true. Desires for the spouse to "take out the garbage" or "do the dishes" regularly can be fulfilled with simple behavioral compliance, no matter what the motivation or emotion. However, desires that the partner show more interest, express more appreciation, display more physical affection, or generate greater desire for sexual contact may not be satisfied with simple behavioral compliance, unless it appears genuine. An obligatory compliment or sexual servicing may not lead to satisfaction in either partner.

Prescribed interventions may lead to anticipations that interfere with their execution. For example, spouses often have a sense of urgency about their problems and can implement methods designed to solve the problem in such a way that the problem becomes worse. A partner might do a positive act, expect the other to respond with great appreciation, be dismayed at the lack of positive response, and then criticize the partner for this lack of response. Indeed, behavioral couple therapy has been shown to increase the likelihood that a spouse responds to their partner's negative statement with a negative statement of their own (Hahlweg, Revenstorf, & Schindler, 1984; Sayers, Baucom, Sher, Weiss, & Heyman, 1991). In brief strategic couple therapy, the therapist often urges clients to "go slow" and cautions them about the dangers of too rapid progress as a means to reduce urgency and anxiety. The rationale is that "go slow" messages can "make clients more likely to cooperate with therapeutic suggestions, and they relax the sense of urgency that often fuels clients' problem-maintaining efforts at solution" (p. 13).

In couple therapy, interventions are often prescribed for both partners, so that one does not seem to be the identified patient and the target of treatment. However, partners are often not equally able or willing to comply with the interventions. One partner may then criticize the other for lack of compliance, seek special therapeutic approval for compliance, or define the lack of compliance as a final straw: "you can't even do therapy right!" In these cases, as well as in the case above with anticipations about treatment, the prescribed interventions backfire and create additional problems for the couple and the therapist.

■ Advantages and Disadvantages of Evocative Interventions

In doing evocative interventions, the therapist tries to shift the context between partners and elicit a different emotional, cognitive, and/or behavioral reaction in each. Couples typically come to therapy in what Wile (2002) describes as an adversarial position, in which one or both react to the other as an enemy through criticism and defense, or in a withdrawn position, in which one or both react to the other as a stranger, by not revealing their concerns and feelings. A goal in most therapies is to shift couples out of these positions into a more collaborative position. No matter how powerful the therapy, couples often shift in and out of these various positions as they discuss their difficulties.

A major advantage of evocative interventions compared with prescriptive interventions is that the therapist has greater control over what happens in the session than on what happens outside the session. Couples typically tell the therapist important information about their feelings and thoughts that they may not share with their closest friends. Therefore, the therapist often has unique and substantial power to influence the couple as they share what are usually vulnerable experiences for them. The therapist can often elicit important shifts in feeling and thinking and can interrupt any iatrogenic processes or comment on any shifts that don't seem authentic.

However, evocative interventions are not as straightforward as prescriptive interventions. Often there are many possible interventions that need to be adapted to the particular couple. For example, in integrative behavioral couple therapy, therapists can use a variety of interventions to evoke a sense of "unified detachment" in couples. They may provide a nonblaming conceptualization of the couple's problem, they may engage the couple in a description of the couple's typical pattern of interaction, they may engage the couple in a comparison of their patterns of interaction under different circumstances, they may generate metaphors for the couple's pattern of interaction, and they may use humor to describe the ironies and contradictions in their pattern of interaction. Whether to use a particular tactic depends on the how the couple responds. A serious couple that views their conflicts as moral battles might not be a good candidate for humorous interventions.

Also, evocative interventions usually do not specify the changes that will take place outside of therapy as a result of the evoked states. Emotionally focused therapy suggests that "bonding events" in therapy will lead to more secure attachments between partners, but it is not clear how these secure attachments specifically reveal themselves in daily partner behavior and affect satisfaction and stability. Similarly integrative behavioral couple therapy indicates that "unified detachment" will lead to greater emotional acceptance, which then leads to greater satisfaction and stability, but the specifics of these relationships are missing. The notion that greater emotional acceptance is manifested by the enactments of previous patterns of conflict but with less emotional intensity and with quicker recovery does provide the kind of detail that is helpful in providing empirical support for the principle.

The major disadvantage of evocative interventions is that they require professional expertise. Presumably, a trained person must interact with the couple in order to elicit and evoke these cognitive, affective, and/or behavioral states that are central to change in the relationship; evocative interventions are thus less portable. They cannot be as easily adapted for self-help books, articles, and computer programs. Thus, they are more expensive interventions and are less likely to reach a large number of people.

Both prescriptive and evocative interventions are needed in work with couples. Certain combinations may be particularly useful, as when an evocative intervention makes the couple more likely to follow through with a prescriptive intervention. Also, these interventions may need to be tailed to particular couples. Consider the analogy of diet and exercise. People who are able, on their own, to eat a reasonable diet and exercise regularly do not need a medical consultation with a physician, a nutritionist, or a personal trainer. However, those who do not eat a reasonable diet or exercise regularly may need such additional professional help. Interventions for couples may need to be tailored so that eventually the least expensive but effective intervention can be provided where needed. For example, research on prevention of future relationship problems often takes a prescriptive approach and emphasizes skill building (Halford & Moore, 2002).

■ Conclusions

We all want our psychological treatments, such as couple therapy, to be based on empirical evidence. But for what should we seek empirical support? In this chapter we have reviewed the ideas of empirical support for particular treatments (ESTs) for certain kinds of therapy relationships (ESRs), and for principles of change (ESPs). We believe that treatments, which are packages of interventions defined by lengthy manuals, are too large a unit of analysis. When we find empirical support for a particular treatment, we advance very little in our knowledge of change in human behavior. We have little basis for adapting treatments to different populations or to particular clients. Also, attachments to and competition between brand name treatments may complicate efforts at objective empirical evaluation. Similarly, we believe that therapy relationships are also too large a unit of analysis. To know that empathy in relationships leads to better outcome does not provide information about what to do in particular situations with clients. Also, the heavy emphasis on the quality of the client-therapist relationship may not be as applicable to conjoint therapy as to individual therapy.

Thus, we believe that a focus on principles of change, and efforts to find empirical support for particular principles of change, is the best course for our science to take. Principles of change should specify particular therapist actions that lead to particular client responses, which then affect client behaviors outside the session, which then affect desired outcomes (Doss, 2004). These kinds of principles can concern treatment techniques as well as particular aspects of the therapist-client relationship. These principles can provide needed guidance to practitioners in the field who want to know which actions they take will lead to which responses in their clients.

In this chapter we have outlined two major classes of interventions for which we can seek empirical support, prescriptive interventions and evocative interventions. We have shown how principles of change can be developed for each and how empirical efforts can test each kind of principle. Effective intervention will likely depend on both types of intervention and combinations of the two may need to be adapted for particular types of clients. Research in the last 25 years has shown that a science of intervention generally, as well as a science of couple therapy in particular, is possible. Now we need to develop the kind of science that most rapidly advances our field and maximizes the information applicable to practitioners.

■ References

Ackerman, S. J., Benjamin, L. S., Beutler, L. E., Gelso, C. J., Goldfried, M. R., Hill, C., et al. (2001). Empirically supported therapy relationships: Conclusions and recommendations of the Division 29 Task Force. *Psychotherapy, 38*(4), 495–497.

Baucom, D. H., & Epstein, N. (1990). *Cognitive behavioral marital therapy.* New York: Brunner/Mazel.

Baucom, D. H., Sayers, S. L., & Sher, T. G. (1990). Supplementing behavioral marital therapy with cognitive restructuring and emotional expressiveness training: An outcome investigation. *Journal of Consulting and Clinical Psychology, 58,* 636–645.

Bekelman, J. E., Li, Y., & Gross, C. P. (2003). Scope and impact of financial conflicts of interest in biomedical research: A systematic review. *Journal of the American Medical Association, 289,* 454–465.

Beutler, L. E. (2000). Empirically based decision making in clinical practice. *Prevention & Treatment, 3,* Article 27. Retrieved September 1, 2000, from http://journals.apa.org/prevention/volume3/pre0030027a.html

Beutler, L. E. (2002). Can principles of therapeutic change replace the need for manuals? *The Clinical Psychologist, 55*(1), 3–4.

Beutler, L. E., Clarkin, J. F., & Bongar, B. (2000). *Guidelines for the systematic treatment of the depressed patient.* New York: Oxford University Press.

Bourgeois, L., Sabourin, S., & Wright, J. (1990). Predictive validity of therapeutic alliance in group marital therapy. *Journal of Consulting and Clinical Psychology, 58*(5), 608–613.

Castonguay, L. G., and Beutler, L. E. (2005). *Principles of therapeutic change that work.* New York: Oxford University Press.

Chambless, D. L., Baker, M., Baucom, D. H., Beutler, L. E., Calhoun, K. S., Crits-Christoph, P., et al. (1998). Update on empirically validated therapies, II. *Clinical Psychologist, 51*(1), 3–16.

Chambless, D. L., & Ollendick, T. H. (2001). Empirically supported psychological interventions: Controversies and evidence. *Annual Reviews, 52,* 685–716.

Chambless, D. L., Sanderson, W. C., Shoham, V., Bennett Johnson, S., Pope, K. S., Crits-Christoph, P., et al. (1996). An update on empirically validated therapies. *Clinical Psychologist, 49*(2), 5–18.

Christensen, A., Atkins, D. C., Berns, S., Wheeler, J., Baucom, D. H., & Simpson, L. E. (2004). Traditional versus integrative behavioral couple therapy for significantly and chronically distressed married couples. *Journal of Consulting and Clinical Psychology, 72*(2), 176–191.

Christensen, A., & Heavey, C. L. (1999). Interventions for couples. In J. T. Spence, J. M. Darley, & D. J. Foss (Eds.), *Annual review of psychology* (pp. 165–190). Palo Alto, CA: Annual Reviews.

Christensen, A., Jacobson, N. S., & Babcock, J. C. (1995). Integrative behavioral couple therapy. In N. S. Jacobson & A. S. Gurman (Eds.), *Clinical handbook of marital therapy* (2nd ed., pp. 31–64). New York: Guilford Press.

Doss, B. D. (2004). Changing the way we study change in psychotherapy. *Clinical Psychology: Science and Practice, 4,* 368–386.

Doss, B. D., Thum, V. M., Sevier, M., Atkins, D. C., & Christensen, A. (in press). Improving relationships: Mechanisms of change in couple therapy. *Journal of Consulting and Clinical Psychology.*

Epstein, N. B., & Baucom, D. H. (2002). *Enhanced cognitive-behavioral therapy for couples: A contextual approach.* Washington, DC: American Psychological Association.

Fals-Stewart, W., & Birchler, G. R. (2002). Behavioral couples therapy with alcoholic men and their intimate partners: The comparative effectiveness of bachelor's- and master's-level counselors. *Behavior Therapy, 33,* 123–147.

Fulmer, M., & Allen, J. (2002, September 6). Panel urges doubling exercise, eating "healthy fats." *Los Angeles Times,* p. A17.

Goldfried, M. R. (l982). Trends in psychodynamic, humanistic, and behavioral practice. In M. R. Goldfried (Ed.), *Converging themes in psychotherapy* (pp. 3–49). New York: Springer Publishing.

Goldman, A., & Greenberg, L. (1992). Comparison of integrated systemic and emotionally focused approaches to couples therapy. *Journal of Consulting and Clinical Psychology, 60,* 962–969.

Hahlweg, K., Revenstorf, D., & Schindler, L. (1984). Effects of behavioral marital therapy on couples' communication and problem-solving skills. *Journal of Consulting and Clinical Psychology, 52,* 553–566.

Halford, W. K., & Moore, E. N. (2002). Relationship education and the prevention of couple relationship problems. In A. S. Gurman & N. S. Jacobson (Eds.), *Clinical handbook of couple therapy* (pp. 400–419). New York: Guilford Press.

Hollon, S. D. (1999). Allegiance effects in treatment research: A commentary. *Clinical Psychology: Science and Practice, 6*(1), 107–112.

Hoyt, M. F. (2002). Solution-focused couple therapy. In A. S. Gurman & N. S. Jacobson (Eds.), *Clinical handbook of couple therapy* (pp. 335–369). New York: Guilford Press.

Jacobson, N. S. (1991). Behavioral versus insight-oriented marital therapy: Labels can be misleading. *Journal of Consulting and Clinical Psychology, 59,* 142–145

Jacobson, N. S., & Christensen, A. (1998). *Acceptance and change in couple therapy: A therapist's guide to transforming relationships.* New York: Norton.

Jacobson, N. S., & Margolin, G. (1979). *Marital therapy: Strategies based on social learning and behavior exchange principles.* New York: Brunner/Mazel.

Jacobson, N. S., Schmaling, K. B., & Holtzworth-Munroe, A. (1987). Component analysis of behavioral marital therapy: 2-year follow-up and prediction of relapse. *Journal of Marital and Family Therapy, 13,* 187–195.

Johnson, S. M., & Denton, W. (2002). Emotionally focused couple therapy: Creating secure connections. In A. S. Gurman & N. S. Jacobson (Eds.), *Clinical handbook of couple therapy* (pp. 221–250). New York: Guilford Press.

Kazdin, A. E. (2001). Progression of therapy research and clinical application of treatment require better understanding of the change process. *Clinical Psychology: Science and Practice, 8,* 143–151.

Lambert, M. J., & Barley, D. E. (2001). Research summary on the therapeutic relationship and psychotherapy outcome. *Psychotherapy, 38,* 357–361.

Luborsky, L., Diguer, L., Seligman, D. A., Rosenthal, R., Kruase, E. D., Johnson, S., et al. (1999). The researcher's own therapy allegiances: A "wild card" in comparisons of treatment efficacy. *Clinical Psychology: Science and Practice, 6*(1), 95–106.

Luborsky, L., Rosenthal, R., Diguer, L., Andrusyna, T. P., Berman, J. S., Levitt, J. T., et al. (2002). The dodo bird verdict is alive and well—mostly. *Clinical Psychology: Science and Practice, 9*(1), 2–12.

Luborsky, L., Singer, B., & Luborsky, L. (1975). Comparative studies of psychotherapies: Is it true that "everybody has won and all must have prizes"? *Archives of General Psychiatry, 32,* 995–1008.

Messer, S. B., & Wampold, B. E. (2002). Let's face facts: Common factors are more potent than specific therapy ingredients. *Clinical Psychology: Science and Practice, 9*(1), 21–26.

Moher, D., Schulz, K. F., & Altman, D. G. (2001). The CONSORT statement: Revised recommendations for improving the quality of reports of parallel-group randomized trials. *Annals of Internal Medicine, 134,* 657–662.

Ornstein, C. (2002, February 18). A tough pill to swallow. *The Los Angeles Times,* pp. A1, A12.

Pinsof, W. M. (1994). An integrative systems perspective on the therapeutic alliance: Theoretical, clinical and research implications. In A. Horvath & L. Greenberg (Eds.), *The working alliance: Theory, research, and practice* (pp. 173–195). New York: Wiley.

Rait, D. S. (2000). The therapeutic alliance in couples and family therapy. *Journal of Clinical Psychology, 56,* 211–224.

Rosen, G. M., & Davison, G. C. (2003). Psychology should list empirically supported principles of change (ESPs) and not credential trademarked therapies or other treatment packages. *Behavior Modification, 27*(3), 300–312.

Rossi, J. (1990). Statistical power of psychological research: What have we gained in 20 years? *Journal of Consulting and Clinical Psychology, 58,* 646–656.

Sayers, S. L., Baucom, D. H., Sher, T. G., Weiss, R. L., & Heyman, R. E. (1991). Constructive engagement, behavioral marital therapy, and changes in marital satisfaction. *Behavioral Assessment, 13,* 25–49.

Schilling, E. A., Baucom, D. H., Burnett, C. K., Allen, E. S., & Ragland, L. (2003). Altering the course of marriage: The effect of PREP communication skills acquisition on couples' risk of becoming maritally distressed. *Journal of Consulting and Clinical Psychology, 17,* 41–53.

Shoham, V., & Rohrbaugh, M. J. (2002). Brief strategic couple therapy. In A. S. Gurman & N. S. Jacobson (Eds.), *Clinical handbook of couple therapy* (pp. 5–25). New York: Guilford Press.

Snyder, D. K., & Wills, R. M. (1989). Behavioral versus insight-oriented marital therapy: Effects on individual and interspousal functioning. *Journal of Consulting and Clinical Psychology, 57,* 39–46.

Snyder, D. K., Wills, R. M., & Grady-Fletcher, A. (1991a). Long-term effectiveness of behavioral versus insight-oriented marital therapy: A 4-year follow-up study. *Journal of Consulting and Clinical Psychology, 59,* 138–141.

Snyder, D. K., Wills, R. M., & Grady-Fletcher, A. (1991b). Risks and challenges of long-term psychotherapy outcome research: Reply to Jacobson. *Journal of Consulting and Clinical Psychology, 59,* 146–149

Stewart, K. J. (2003, February). Working in an effective workout. *Health after 50: The Johns Hopkins Medical Letter, 14,* 6.

Task Force For the Promotion and Dissemination of Psychological Procedures. (1995). Training in and dissemination of empirically-validated psychological treatments: Report and recommendations. *Clinical Psychologist, 48*(1), 3–23.

Wellness Facts. (2002, January). *University of California Berkeley Wellness Letter, 18,* 1.

Westen, D., & Morrison, K. (2001). A multidimensional meta-analysis of treatments for depression, panic, and generalized anxiety disorder: An empirical examination of empirically supported therapies. *Journal of Consulting and Clinical Psychology, 69,* 875–899.

Whisman, M. A., & Snyder, D. K. (1997). Evaluating and improving the efficacy of conjoint couple therapy. In W. K. Halford & H. J. Markman (Eds.), *Clinical handbook of marriage and couples intervention* (pp. 679–693). New York: Wiley.

Wile, D. B. (2002). Collaborative couple therapy. In A. S. Gurman & N. S. Jacobson (Eds.), *Clinical handbook of couple therapy* (pp. 281–307). New York: Guilford Press.

Woody, S. R., & Sanderson, W. C. (1998). Manuals for empirically supported treatments: 1998 update. *Clinical Psychologist, 51*(1), 17–21.

3

The Mismeasure of Therapy: Treatment Outcomes in Marital Therapy Research

John Gottman and Kimberly Ryan

The purpose of this chapter is to review outcome measures in marital therapy research, to suggest that these measures are fatally flawed, to propose an alternative measurement package, and to demonstrate that differential treatment and relapse effects are a function of the outcome measurement package.

■ History and Choice of Outcome Assessment
   in Marital Therapy Research

The major construct for assessing the effect of couples' intervention has been *relationship quality*, usually assessed by some form of the Locke-Wallace Marital Adjustment Test (MAT; Locke & Wallace, 1959), or the very closely related Spanier Dyadic Adjustment Scale (DAS; Spanier, 1976).[1] Effect sizes in meta-analyses of couple and marital therapy studies have been estimated almost entirely based upon these two scales (Shadish, Montgomery, Wilson, Bright, & Okuwambua, 1993; Shadish, Ragsdale, Glaser-Renita, & Montgomery, 1995; see Hahlweg & Markman, 1988, and Bray & Jouriles, 1995, for a summary of these meta-analyses).

Fincham and Bradbury (1987) rightly criticicized these scales as adequate measures of marital quality, because they tend to include heterogeneous item types, including statements of happiness or unhappiness, statements of agreement or disagreement on a variety of topics (recreation, affection, sex, in-laws, and so on), confiding in partner, frequency of quarreling, the way disagreements are resolved (give and take, one partner giving in, and so on), discussing sex, and so on. Their major point was that self-report research on the *correlates* of marital quality is conceptually confounded by item overlap in criterion and predictive measures.

[1]The Dyadic Adjustment Scale was actually derived directly from the Locke-Wallace items; Spanier added some items and reworded the items he kept.

They therefore recommended that measures of marital quality be confined to measuring happiness or misery in the relationship, rather than tapping allied processes.

The original researchers on marriage agreed with Fincham and Bradbury's analysis. Historically, the measurement of marital satisfaction evolved from the general assessment of the concept of marital "success," spearheaded by Louis Terman (Terman, Buttenweiser, Ferguson, Johnson, & Wilson, 1938). Terman, one of the designers of the IQ test, who believed in a general factor of intelligence, also believed that there was a general factor of marital relationship competence, or what might currently be called "emotional intelligence" (Goleman, 1996). He developed various scales for measuring marital happiness. The first problem they tackled was how many points the scale of happiness should have. Terman employed a 7-point scale: "extraordinarily happy," "decidedly more happy than average," "somewhat more happy than average," "about average," "somewhat less happy than average," "decidedly less happy than average," "extremely unhappy." Locke suggested an alternative approach to the tendency of subjects to rate their marriages as very happy, happy, or average using 10 possible spaces on a line ranging from "very happy" to "very unhappy." This issue of scale design is a nontrivail problem even today. It is still an important source of unreliability in surveys that use single-item measures of marital quality. For example, the author recently participated in a random survey of marriages designed by a survey company for *Reader's Digest*. In this survey participants were asked whether their marriages was "extremely happy," "very happy," "very unhappy," or "extremely unhappy." With these choices 90% of American people classified their marriage as either very or extremely happy, which was clearly a spurious result. The same issue of unreliability in measuring marital quality has contributed to Waite and Doherty's recent questionable conclusion from the National Survey of Households that 86% of unhappy couples become happy after 5 years with no intrervention, a result that contravenes every controlled clinical trial of marital therapy, in which unhappily married people deteriorate significantly with no treatment.

Returning to the history of measurement of marital "success," there were many years of self-report measurement of a wide variety of constructs, such as the number of problems the couple had, the judged permananence of the relationship, happiness, satisfaction, whether they would remarry the same person again, sexual satisfaction, self-disclosure or areas of reserve, the integration of their separate personalities, companionship, consensus, affectional intimacy, wife accommodation, euphopria, differences between partners (correlations between partners tended to be in the .50s) (Burgess & Cottrell, 1939; Burgess & Wallin, 1953; Hamilton, 1929; Locke & Williamson, 1958). The overwhelming majority of these studies relied on pencil-and-paper measures, not worrying about cross-method validity. Terman et al.'s (1938) study was unusual in that it also asked the couple's friends to rate the couple's relationship; they obtained moderately high correlations between insider and outsider reports.

In the 1950s researchers decided that most of the various measures they had designed to assess couple relationships were actually quite highly correlated, and they concluded that they were probably measuring one construct after all (Burgess, Locke, & Thomes, 1970). Subsequent research on attributional processes confirmed, or perhaps rediscovered is a better word, a robust halo effect, which is that unhappily married people tend to endorse almost all negative items about their partner, whereas happily married people tend to endorse almost all positive items about their partner. This halo effect makes it very difficult to create true profiles of couple relationships, because most self-report scales do not give nonredundant information. In fact, in our experience designing and validating scales, it is only since designing an empirically based theory of couple relationships called the "Sound Marital House" (now known as the "Sound Relationship House") theory that a set of scales has emerged that provide some promise that we will one day be able to develop a useful profile of couple functioning that deals effectively with the halo effect.

■ Problems With the Measurement of Treatment Outcome in Marital Therapy Research

The most frequently used scales for assessing marital satisfaction are flawed measures for assessing outcome in most marital interventions for another reason, one that Fincham and Bradbury (1987) neglected to discuss. This flaw is that there are two ways of getting a high score on these scales. One way to get a high score is to rate one's relationship as closer to Perfectly Happy (the scale ranges from Very Unhappy to Happy to Perfectly Happy), a heavily weighted single item, along with several other items that assess overall happiness. Presumably these items tap the pure marital quality dimension that Fincham and Bradbury recommended. However, a second way of obtaining a high score is *to not disagree* very much, rating the following items closer to Agree (on a scale that ranges from Always Disagree to Always Agree): Handling Family Finances, Matters of Recreation, Demonstrations of Affection, Friends, Sex Relations, Conventionality (right, good, or proper conduct), Philosophy of Life, and Ways of Dealing With In-Laws. In the Locke-Wallace scale, taken together, the disagreement items account for much of the range in the combined marital satisfaction scale, from 0 to 53, which is a sizable part of the total score.

Hence, one way couples can score high on the Locke-Wallace scale is to be conflict avoiders. Conflict avoiding couples do indeed exist (see Gottman, 1993, 1994; Raush, Barry, Hertl, & Swain, 1974). Yet all of the couples intervention programs that have been researched have focused on changing the nature of the couple's conflict, and they have all included the admonition for couples to disagree, and they have included training for couples to do so in what they believe is a more constructive fashion. Hence, if these programs were totally successful, couples would find themselves facing their conflicts more directly and hence, at least initially, disagreeing more, and therefore these programs would be penalizing themselves by using the Locke-Wallace scale as a means for evaluating effectiveness. It would thus be more likely that control group couples would avoid conflict than intervention group couples.

Indeed, a clinical aside is relevant here. In our practice we see many conflict-avoiding couples who have relatively high Locke-Wallace scores but who also report on our other questionnaires that they have horrible fights that escalate out of control. We have found that these couples have no blueprint for dealing with disagreements when they do arise. Yet they often have reasonably high Locke-Wallace scores.

■ Snyder's Profile Approach to Marital Quality Measurement

Snyder's (Berg & Snyder, 1981; Scheer & Snyder, 1984) 280-item Marital Satisfaction Inventory (MSI) consists of a global marital quality scale and nine additional scales focusing on specific areas of reported marital interaction. These areas include the affective triad communication scales, disaffection and disharmony (Snyder & Regts, 1982), sexual satisfaction, problem-solving communication, sex-role orientation, and conflict over child rearing. Snyder's nontheoretical checklist approach to a more detailed profile of marital functioning is a commendable effort to expand a description of marital functioning beyond a single global marital satisfaction dimension. Snyder's MSI has demonstrated its usefulness in cluster analyses and across measurement domains (Snyder & Smith, 1986). We propose an alternative in this chapter, one based on a simple theory of marital functioning called the Sound Marital House (SMH) theory (Gottman, 1999).

■ Alternative Approach: Assessment of Progress Toward Specific Treatment Goals

Self-report measures that describe people's perceptions of their couple relationship are needed if they are to be widely used by clinicians for assessment, treatment planning, and evaluation of treatment effectiveness. While a multimethod approach is desirable in treatment outcome studies, it is rarely employed. Therefore, the field would be greatly enhanced if there were a self-report measurement package that provided a theoretically useful profile of a couple's relationship. We report our initial and highly tentative research designed to develop such a self-report package.

This chapter proposes that instead of relying on global measures of marital satisfaction, we design measures of an intervention program's effectiveness that *derive from the specifically stated objectives of the intervention.* We propose and employ such a measurement package, with specific objectives. We then present an evaluation of five different and theoretically specific interventions designed to accomplish these objectives and compare the effectiveness of the interventions. Thus, we suggest a change in measurement frameworks.

We believe that a change in measurement frameworks may eventually change some of the conclusions that meta-analyses have drawn from marital therapy outcome studies. It is possible that because in the field marital therapy researchers have relied on marital satisfaction as the sole outcome measure, we may have come to misleading conclusions about the effectiveness of our interventions. Specifically, it is possible that the use of the Locke-Wallace and DAS as primary outcome measures across studies in the marital area may have led to the erroneous conclusion that all of our interventions are equally effective. This view has dominated much of the review of the marital therapy outcome literature (e.g., Pinsof & Wynne, 1995), but we suspect that the conclusion may be an artifact of the poor choice of outcome measures.

■ If Not Marital Quality, What Should Be Measured in Marital Therapy Research?

Theory, the Interventions, and a Measurement Package

The objectives of an intervention program will depend on one's theory of marital function and dysfunction, and they will depend on one's analysis of what distressed couples need. We summarize one such formulation here, Gottman's (1999) empirically based seven-process theory of marital relationships, called SMH, which he developed to summarize the results of his longitudinal studies with well-functioning, stable couples versus distressed and stable or divorcing married couples. Self-report questionnaires were designed by Gottman for each component of this theory. The components can be grouped into outcomes and processes.

Sound Marital House Theory Outcomes

It is clear that one can view the processes in the SMH theory as processes or as outcomes. Here we treat them as outcomes because we view them as needed for a thorough description of the functioning of a marital relationship. However, in other studies, for example, on domestic abuse, they could just as easily be considered processes. One outcome variable in the SMH theory describes the quality of the *couple's friendship*. It has three elements: (a) Love Maps, which refers to interest in and knowledge of one's partner's inner psychological world (the fundamental process that determines making Love Maps is asking open-ended questions); (b) the Fondness and Admiration system (F&A), which assesses affection and respect (the fundamental process that determines the existence of F&A is small but frequent communications of affection and respect); and (c) Turning Toward Versus Turning Away, which assesses the quality of everyday emotional connection, using the "bid" for emotional connection by one partner and the "turning toward, away, or against" response by the other partner (the fundamental process of Turning Toward is mindfulness of one's partner's bids and a willingness to meet one's partner's immediate needs for emotional connection). Bids are arranged in a hierarchy from requesting one's partner's attention, interest, conversation, affection, humor, playfulness, emotional support, and sexual touch to existential conversations we call "dreaming" together. Another outcome is the quality of the couple's *sexual satisfaction, romance, and passion.* The SMH theory proposed that the three elements of friendship will determine, in part, the quality of a couple's sexual satisfaction, romance, and passion. This outcome is also determined, in part, by the natural way the couple deal with their conflicts.

The outcome of the amount of *constructive versus destructive marital conflict* was described by Gottman (1999) as follows. Destructive conflict has the following elements: (a) Gridlocked Conflict referred to repeating cycles of negative affect or emotional disengagement on recurring, unsolvable (or Perpetual) marital issues (see also Wile, 1988); (b) marital behaviors called the Four Horsemen of the Apocalypse: Criticism, Defensiveness, Contempt, and Stonewalling; (c) not accepting influence from the partner; (d) not compromising; and (e) harsh startup of the conflict.[2] Constructive conflict has the following elements: softened startup, accepting influence from one's partner, and compromise. Strongly related to the effective management of conflict is the final outcome of SMH, the development of a *shared meaning system*; the shared meaning system is based on shared rituals of connection (Doherty, 1997), shared central role definitions (husband, wife, mother, father, son, daughter, friend, work roles), shared values and life goals, and the shared definition of central symbols (e.g., a home, love). These are the four outcomes of the SMH theory.

Sound Marital House Theory Processes

In addition to these four outcomes there are three processes. Once again, these processes could be viewed as outcomes in other studies. The first process is called *sentiment override.* The sentiment override concept adds great precision to the idea of the halo effect we mentioned earlier. The concept of sentiment override comes from a paper by Weiss (1980). Weiss proposed that a spouse is in a state of either *negative sentiment override* or *positive sentiment override.* In negative sentiment override (NSO) the spouse's general negative evaluation of the partner and their relationship overrides momentary positivity, whereas in positive sentiment override the spouse's general positive evaluation of the partner and their relationship overrides momentary negativity. In research this concept is often operationalized as a discrepancy between insider and outsider perspectives on the interaction (recall Terman et al., 1938; for a modern definition see Vanzetti, Notarius, & NeeSmith, 1992). The concept of negative sentiment override can be thought of as a predisposition to respond negatively to even neutral partner events, or as having a "chip on one's shoulder" that makes one hypervigilant for slights and other negativity.

The SMH theory proposes that sentiment override is determined by the three elements of a couple's friendship. If these three elements are functioning well, the couple will be in positive sentiment override. If any of the three are not functioning well, the couple will be in negative sentiment override.

---

[2]In the measurement package the first two scales are negatively keyed, while the last two scales are positively keyed; *destructive conflict* is Gridlock, plus the Four Horsemen, minus Accepting Influence, minus Compromising. Negative numbers are a good sign here.

The second process is the effectiveness of *repair attempts*. Repair attempts are behavioral events couples use to repair negative interaction as it occurs, which are either successful in reducing negativity or not. Gottman (1999) proposed that sentiment override mediates the success of repair attempts during or after a conflict marital interaction. The theory is that positive sentiment override will make it more likely that repair attempts during conflict will be effective, while negative sentiment override will make it less likely that repair attempts during conflict will be effective.

The third process, posited to be related to negative sentiment override, is *flooding*. The concept of flooding, derived, in part, from Ekman (1984), is that some marital partners become overwhelmed and disorganized by the way their partner raises issues and therefore wish to flee or escalate the fight to silence the partner. Flooding has been identified as part of a "distance and isolation cascade" that is predictive of divorce (Gottman, 1994; Gottman & Levenson, 1992). It is closely related to the concept of *diffuse physiological arousal* (DPA), which refers to the diffuse activation of both the hypothalamic-pituitary-adrenocortical axis (which secretes cortisol) and the sympathetic-adrenomedullary axis (which secretes adrenaline). In DPA the processing of information is severely compromised and people tend to rely on overlearned behavior patterns. According to the Henry-Stephens model of stress (Henry & Stephens, 1977), DPA is generated by a blend of hostility and helplessness.

■ The Measurement Package Assesses
  Progress Toward Specific Goals

Given that relapse is one of the major problems facing the marital intervention field (Jacobson & Addis, 1993), it is essential to track changes in these objectives for several years. In this chapter we report the effectiveness of five interventions with respect to the goals we just proposed. We are tracking these changes over a 5-year period. In this chapter we report follow-up assessments at 1 year after the interventions ended to test the long-term effectiveness of these interventions. Here we describe the findings at 1 year from our marital outcome study of five theoretically different and distinct interventions. These interventions were designed as components of a total intervention to test what specific intervention processes might be related to progress toward the specific objectives specified by the SMH assessment instruments.

■ Correlation of the Sound Marital House Scales
  With Locke-Wallace Total Score and Psychopathology
  Using the Derogatis SCL-90 Scale

The participants in this study were 51 couples who took a 2-day workshop in marital communication. They filled out the SMH questionnaires, the Locke-Wallace questionnaire, the Symptom Checklist SCL-90 (Derogatis, Lipman, & Covi, 1973), and the Weiss-Cerreto Marital Status Inventory, which measures persistent thoughts and actions about divorce (Weiss & Cerreto, 1980). They received no subject fees.

TABLE 3.1   *Validity Check on the Seven SMH Variables*

	Weiss-Cerreto	SCL-90
Wife flooding	.33*	−.31*
Wife repair	−.43**	.35**
Wife NSO	.25*	−.37**
Wife sex/passion/romance	−.42**	.44**
Wife shared meaning	−.42**	.38**
Wife friendship	−.41**	.48***
Wife destructive conflict	.40**	−.48***
Husband flooding	.27*	−.36**
Husband repair	−.41**	.31*
Husband NSO	.19	−.24
Husband sex/passion/romance	−.40**	.33*
Husband shared meaning	−.37**	.41**
Husband friendship	−.43**	.45***
Husband destructive conflict	.33*	−.38**

Note. $*p < .05$. $**p < .01$. $***p < .001$. NSO = negative sentiment override.

Husbands were an average of 45.3 years old ($SD = 8.8$), had an education of college plus 0.1 years of graduate work, and earned an average of $80,000, and wives were an average of 43.7 years old ($SD = 8.5$), had an education of 3.7 years of college, and earned an average of $67,200. The mean Locke-Wallace scores were husband, 66.69 ($SD = 15.71$), and wife, 72.16 ($SD = 16.36$). The SMH scales had high reliability for both husbands and wives—Cronbach alphas were, for husband and wife, respectively, as follows: *friendship*, .95 and .94; *sex, romance, and passion*, .90 and .89; *negative sentiment override*, .92 and .92; *destructive or constructive marital conflict* (abbreviated as *destructive conflict*), .94 and .94; *repair effectiveness*, .87, and .87; *flooding*, .89 and .88; and *shared meaning total score*, .93 and .90.

The correlations of the SMH variables with SCL-90 total score and the Weiss-Cerreto inventory are summarized in table 3.1. As can be seen from the table, as expected, the SMH variables all correlate with these two established scales. While these results are encouraging, they are highly limited. This was not a clinical sample, it was a small sample, the validity measures are not multimethod, and the correlations obtained, while statistically significant, are moderate in size. To deal with some of these limitations, two studies are under way to create multimethod databases with couples at two points in the life course, couples with elementary school children and couples going through the transition to parenthood.

■ The Seattle Marital Therapy Outcome Study

Participants

Beginning with a volunteer sample of 400 couples from the greater Seattle metropolitan area recruited with radio and television interviews, newspaper advertisements, and flyers, 100 couples were selected for participation in the folowing way. Demographic information and telephone Locke-Wallace marital satisfaction scores were first obtained from all 400 couples. They answered a set of telephone survey questions that assessed their availability to attend the intervention, demographic characteristics, marital status, years married, marital satisfaction, and health. To be eligible for the study, couples were required to be living together, to be legally married, and to be able to attend the scheduled marital intervention and at least one spouse had to have a marital satisfaction score below 93 on the Locke-Wallace Marital Adjustment Test (0.5 SD) below the mean on this measure; Locke & Wallace, 1959). If the couples met the initial selection criteria, they were mailed a pretreatment packet of questionnaires to complete individually, a questionnaire consent form, a cover letter with directions, and a prepaid return envelope. Following the application of the screening criteria (described below), 100 distressed couples were then selected to match the racial demographics of the greater Seattle metropolitan area (based on the current City of Seattle's Planning Commission Report), and these demographics were balanced across the five groups of the study.

Procedure

Outcome and Process Assessment.   The following self-report scales were administered to these couples. In the area of *friendship:* Love Maps (20 items, sample item: I know my partner's current worries), Fondness and Admiration (20 items, sample item: I am really proud of my partner), Turning Toward (sample item: My partner is usually interested in hearing my views on things), and Emotional Disengagement (20 items, sample item: Sometimes our marriage feels empty to me). In the area of *sex, romance, and passion* (two 6-item scales from the 17-areas scale, the romance and passion scale, and the sex problems scale; sample romance item: The fire has gone out of this marriage; sample sex item: One problem is the amount of love in our love making). In the area of *conflict:* Harsh Startup (sample item: I hate the way my partner raises an issue), Accepting Influence (20 items, sample item: I believe in lots of give and take in our discussions), Compromise (20 items, sample item: In discussing issues we can usually find our common ground of agreement), The Four Horsemen (33 items, sample item: I can get mean and insulting in our disputes), and Gridlock on Perpetual Issues (20 items, sample item: The same problems keep coming up again and again in our marriage). In the area of *shared meaning:* shared goals (10 items, sample item: We share many of the same goals in our life together), shared roles (7 items, sample item: My partner and I have compatible views about the role of work in one's life), shared rituals (20 items, sample item: During weekends we do a lot of things together that we enjoy and value), and shared symbols (20 items, sample item: We see eye to eye about what a "home" means). There were seperate scales for *negative sentiment override* (20 items, sample item: In the recent past in my marriage, I felt innocent of blame for this problem), *flooding* (15 items, sample item: I have a hard time calming down), and *repair* (20 items, sample item: I can say that I am wrong). For data reduction purposes, these scales were combined to form the seven constructs previously described. The *friendship score* was the sum of the following scales: Love Maps, Fondness and Admiration, Turning Toward, minus Emotional Distance. *Sex, romance,* and *passion* was a combination of two 6-item scales. The scale for sex, romance, and passion is a checklist of problems, so a lower score is indicative of higher quality on this outcome variable. There were 12 items, and each item is scored 1 if it is not a problem and 2 if it is a problem, so the scale varies from 12 to 24. *Destructive-to-constructive conflict* was the sum of the following scales: Harsh Startup, plus the Four Horsemen and Gridlock, minus Accepting Influence, and minus Compromise; lower or more negative scores on this composite indicate constructive rather than destructive conflict. The *shared meaning* total score was the sum of the four shared meaning scales, rituals, roles, goals, and symbols. The final Cronbach alphas were, for husband and wife, respectively, as follows: *friendship,* .95 and .94; *sex, romance, and passion,* .90 and .89; *negative sentiment override,* .92 and .92; and *destructive or constructive marital conflict* (abbreviated as *destructive conflict*), .94 and .94. The three process measures were *repair effectiveness,* .87 and .87; *flooding,* .89 and .88; and *shared meaning total score,* .93 and .90. These self-report scales also had demonstrated acceptable levels of reliability and validity in a previous study with a separate sample (Ryan, 2001; Ryan & Gottman, unpublished manual).

Experimental Design.   Using a stratified random sampling method to insure that all intervention groups were balanced by race and ethnicity, all couples passing through the screening process were randomly assigned to one of five treatment conditions. The treatments logically followed a 2×2 factorial design, with one added comparison group designed to minimize relapse at 1-year follow-up by supplementing the core treatment with nine sessions of marital therapy (a treatment manual is available from the second author). The couples were then scheduled for preworkshop and postworkshop laboratory sessions. Couples were assessed at three points in time using the SMH self-report measures.

Pretreatment.   The pretreatment packet of questionnaires was completed during the recruitment and screening phase of the study. At the conclusion of the pretreatment laboratory session, the procedures for the intervention, postassessment questionnaire packet, posttreatment laboratory session, and follow-up questionnaires were explained to the participants.

Intervention.   The treatment outcome study employed brief interventions administered in a psychoeducational workshop format, with lectures, demonstrations, and exercises completed by husband and wife. These workshops were conducted by Drs. John and Julie Gottman at the University of Washington. The 2-day intervention has been used in workshops with 4,000 couples (8,000 people) to date by the Gottman Institute. There is other evidence to suggest that a purely psychoeducational format can be effective in treating marital problems (Kaiser, Hahlweg, Fehm-Wolfsdorf, & Groth, 1998). One of our goals in this study was to assess whether very specific interventions would produce very specific changes in realizing some outcome goals and yet leave other goals unrealized. The interventions (1) either included or did not include a component with lectures and exercises designed to enhance a couple's friendship (building love maps, building fondness and admiration, and emotional connection through turning toward one another in everyday interaction); this intervention also contained an abbreviated section on repair by processing fights by having a recovery conversation after the fight, using our Aftermath of a Fight procedure, and (2) either included or did not include a component with lectures and exercises designed to teach a couple to regulate conflict through (a) the management of gridlocked perpetual conflict (moving from gridlock to dialogue), with our dreams-within-conflict exercises, and (b) the management of solvable conflicts through softened startup, accepting influence, effective repair, physiological self and partner soothing, taking effective breaks, and compromise. There were three manuals distributed to couples and followed in the workshops. Thus, some couples received the full 2-day workshop (improving friendship and regulating destructive marital conflict) and others one of the more limited 1-day workshops, focused either on improving the couples' friendship or in regulating destructive marital conflict. The manual for the 1-day friendship enhancement workshop was not quite a carbon copy of that for the first day of the 2-day workshop. For the sake of providing a reasonably complete theory of how marriages function, exercises were added that discussed the repair of negative interaction and processing a fight, and lectures were added that claimed that the enhancement of friendship was all that was necessary for repair to be effective. The manual for the 1-day conflict regulation workshop was a carbon copy of that for Day 2 of the 2-day workshop. Each day of the workshop lasted 8 h. The exercises and the lectures for these workshops have been published (Gottman, 1999).

While these very specific and brief psychoeducational interventions cannot be considered marital therapy, they may produce some useful changes that could be an important prelude to marital therapy. Furthermore, they are far less expensive than marital therapy, and for some couples they may be adequate as an intervention or as a preventive intervention. Since marital therapy research has consistently shown that couples in either a waiting-list or no-treatment control group either do not improve or deteriorate in marital quality, and have high divorce rates, it was considered unethical to employ such a control group in this study. Instead of a no-treatment control, the control group in this 2 × 2 design (see table 3.2) was a minimal treatment Bibliotherapy control group. Every couple in the Bibliotherapy group

TABLE 3.2 *Diagram of the 2 ×2 Design*

	Teach Regulation of Conflict	Don't Teach the Regulation of Conflict
Build friendship and shared meaning	Two-day workshop	One-day friendship workshop
Don't build friendship and shared meaning	One-day conflict workshop	Bibliotherapy group

received Gottman and Silver's (1999) trade book *The Seven Principles for Making Marriage Work* and up to 3 h of telephone consultation with a doctoral student in clinical psychology.

In one additional treatment, called the 2-day-workshop-plus-relapse-prevention condition, couples also participated in a 2-day marital workshop. This design is economical, but it is also somewhat flawed. Ideally we would have run two studies, the 2 × 2 factorial study and then a second study in which we randomly assigned couples to the 2-day workshop and a 2-day-workshop-plus-relapse-prevention condition. Couples in this latter group couples would also receive nine sessions of manualized marital therapy. In the current study they received these therapy sessions from a graduate student in clinical psychology (therapists followed the Ryan and Gottman *Marital Relapse Prevention Manual* [unpublished], which was based, in part, on the SMH theory [Gottman, 1999] and in part on current thinking about preventing relapse). In future studies we would prefer the therapy to be administered by our experienced clinic therapists. Couples within the workshop-plus-relapse-prevention group were randomly assigned to one of five graduate student therapists who had been trained in the manualized treatment. The sessions with couples were conducted under the supervision of the author, as well as Dr. John Slattery, a clinical psychologist, and Kim Ryan. The relapse prevention program consisted of nine 50-min sessions, carried out over the course of 1 year. The general plan of the intervention follows the SMH theory, individualized for each couple (Gottman, 1999). This latter group was the basis of Ryan's (2001) dissertation. Given the work suggesting that treatment conditions should be perceived as equally credible by participants (Jacobson & Baucom, 1977), the procedures for assignment described each condition as a similarly effective treatment for marital distress. This brief marital therapy condition is not quite up to a full marital therapy, but it does serve as a brief therapy analogue.

Post- and Follow-Up Assessment.   Approximately 1 week and 1 year after the end of the workshop, a packet of posttreatment questionnaires was mailed out.

■ Analysis Plan for Assessing the Effectiveness of the Interventions and Differential Treatment Effects

Experimental Design

For each of the four outcome measures, a 2 × 3 × 2 × 2 repeated measures factorial analysis of variance was conducted, with the within-subject variables being spouse (two repeated measures levels: Husband and Wife) and time of measurement (three repeated measures levels: Pre, Post, and 1-year follow-up) and the between-subjects factorial variables being Increasing Friendship (yes or no) and Regulating Destructive Conflict (yes or no). This was followed by a specific comparison of the 2-day workshop with the 2-day workshop plus nine sessions of marital therapy in a $2 \times 3 \times 2$ repeated measures analysis of variance, with within-subject variables being spouse (two repeated measures levels: Husband and Wife) and time of measurement (three repeated measures levels: Pre, Post, and 1-year follow up) and the between subject variable being the two interventions. For tests subsequent to the analyses of variance, the mean square error term was used to construct the appropriate t ratio. To test the relationship between change in the three process variables and change in the four outcome variables a set of multiple regressions were conducted.

■ Results Assessing Effectiveness With Total Locke-Wallace Score and With the Full Four Objectives of the SMH Theory

Preliminary Analyses

Demographics. Chi-square analyses and t tests revealed no significant differences between any of the groups on any of the demographic variables (ethnicity, years married, age, income). As such, the demographics of the groups are reported together. Consistent with the city of Seattle's demographics, the sample was predominately White or European American, with 68% of both the husbands and wives identifying as such. The remainder of the sample was split fairly evenly among African American, Asian American, and Hispanic participants. Multiple ethnic/racial identities were permitted in our demographics. For husbands and wives, respectively, the breakdown was Hispanic American, 6.5 and 8.7%; African American 9.7 and 10.9%; Asian American, 4.3 and 8.8%; Pacific Islander or Hawaiian, 3.2 and 2.1%; and Native American, 3.2 and 1.1%. The mean number of years the participants had been married to their current partners was 13.0. Wives in the study had a mean age of 41.99 ($SD = 11.41$) years, while husbands had a mean age of 44.64 ($SD = 12.19$) years. The average income for wives was $20,800 and for husbands $48,900. The screening mean marital satisfaction scores were, for husbands, 80.77 ($SD = 23.49$), and for wives 74.85 ($SD = 22.45$). This sample was more distressed than the typical marital therapy study (for example, Greenberg & Johnson, 1988, reported two studies; in the first study the premarital satisfaction levels for the experimental group were 92.8, and they were 86.3 in the second study). Couples were effectively randomized within strata across groups so that each treatment group was equivalent by race/ethnicity and income.

Attrition. Across experimental groups, attrition from the preworkshop assessment to the 1-year follow-up was low. All couples completed the preworkshop and postworkshop assessments. Furthermore, analyses also showed that the couples who failed to complete the entire assessment did not differ significantly from the remaining sample in their marital satisfaction scores during the previous two assessments, nor did they differ on relevant demographic variables from the overall sample.

Assessing Effectiveness Using Locke-Wallace Marital Quality Total Score

With the husband and wife marital quality scores used as dependent variables, there were only three statistically significant effects, the time-linear effect, $F(1, 60) = 5.38$, $p < .024$, the time-quadratic effect, $F(1, 60) = 13.04$, $p < .001$, and the spouse effect, $F(1, 60) = 4.77$, $p = .033$. There was a systematic increase in marital satisfaction over time, from couples' mean of 80.67 at Time-1, to 88.64 at Time-2, to 86.34 at 1 year. The significant quadratic effect was not evidence of relapse in marital quality from postassessment to 1 year, but evidence of the convex shape of the growth curve, $t(60) = 0.55$, n.s., and, thus, the 2.3-point drop in marital quality from the post-assessment to the 1-year follow-up assessment was not statistically significant. Males had significantly higher marital quality than females (overall means were 89.10 compared to 81.33, respectively). Thus, the Locke-Wallace total score data suggested that there were no differences between the various treatments or interactions of any of the factors of the 2 × 2 design with the two treatment factors, conflict regulation and friendship enhancement. Comparing the 2-day workshop with the 2-day workshop plus marital therapy, there were no significant time by treatment inter-actions (the linear, $F(1, 29) = 1.81$, n.s., and the quadratic, $F(1, 29) = 2.80$, n.s.), nor was there a significant interaction of treatment by spouse, $F(1, 29) = 0.01$, n.s., and there was not a significant treatment main effect, $F(1, 29) = 0.42$, n.s. Hence, using the Locke-Wallace score as the marital quality outcome measure, one would con-clude that all treatments were effective in increasing marital quality over time, with no evidence of relapse at 1 year, but that no one treatment was better than another.

Assessing Effectiveness Using the Sound Marital House Scales

With the four SMH outcome variables univariate repeated measures analyses of variance were conducted. We summarize the results of these analyses for each of the four objectives of our interventions. We do not discuss the results for the process variables in this chapter, because the major point we wish to make is about outcome assessment.

Objective 1: Increasing the Quality of the Couple's Friendship

Differential Treatment Effects. With respect to the increasing friendship goal, we predicted that there would be *a conflict regulation component effect on friendship.* Consistent with this prediction, there was a marginally significant linear inter-action of time by spouse with the conflict regulation factor, $F(1, 59) = 2.82$, $p = .098$. Subsequent post hoc tests showed that when there was *no* conflict regulation component, men, but not women, increased significantly in friendship from Pre to Post (for women, $t(59) = 2.23$, n.s., but for men $t(59) = 4.13$, $p < .01$). With no conflict regulation component, the relapse at 1 year was not significant for men or for women (from Post to 1-year, for women, $t(59) = -1.07$, n.s.; for men, $t(59) = -1.74$, n.s.). When there *was* a conflict regulation component, both men and women again increased significantly in friendship from Pre to Post (for women,

$t(59) = 2.69$, $p < .01$; for men, $t(59) = 3.35$, $p < .01$). Neither men nor women relapsed from Post to 1-year in friendship when there was a conflict regulation component (for men, $t(59) = 0.04$, n.s.; for women, $t(59) = -2.08$, n.s.). We note that, unlike with the Locke-Wallace results, there were significant differences between treatments with the friendship outcome variable.

Time and Spouse Effects.   There was a significant linear and quadratic trend, with linear $F(1, 59) = 10.60$, $p = .002$, and quadratic $F(1, 59) = 24.37$, $p < .001$. These overall means were Pre, 39.61, Post, 45.75, and 1-year, 43.36. There is thus evidence of significant linear increase. There was a significant spouse effect, $F(1, 59) = 7.11$, $p = .010$. Husbands averaged 44.84, and wives averaged 40.97, with husbands describing their friendship with their wives more positively than wives described their friendship with their husbands. There was a significant quadratic interaction of time by spouse, $F(1, 59) = 5.11$, $p = .028$. Across all interventions husbands went from Pre, 41.93, to Post, 46.80, to 1-year, 45.79; wives went from Pre, 37.29, to Post, 44.71, to 1-year, 40.92. Testing for relapse, using our post hoc experiment-wise protection alpha of .01, across treatments, wives initially improved more (from Pre to Post: husbands, $t(59) = 2.45$, n.s.; wives, $t(59) = 3.75$, $p < .001$), but there was no significant difference in relapse across spouses (from Post to 1-year: husbands, $t(59) = -0.51$, n.s.; wives, $t(59) = -1.91$, n.s.).

Avoiding Relapse.   Comparing the 2-day workshop with the 2-day workshop plus marital therapy, there was a significant effect for time, linear, $F(1, 31) = 13.10$, $p < .001$, and a quadratic trend, $F(1, 31) = 13.09$, $p < .001$. As we predicted, in the planned comparison examining for relapse using the error term from the time by treatment interaction, relapse for both husbands and wives combined was statistically significant for the 2-day workshop, $t(31) = -1.70$, $p < .05$, whereas for the 2-day workshop plus marital therapy, there was no significant relapse, $t(31) = -0.40$, n.s. The relapse results, collapsed across spouses, are presented as figure 3.1 *To summarize,* there were significant differences between treatments with the friendship outcome variable and no relapse for both men and women only with the 2-day workshop plus nine sessions of marital therapy. Thus, as predicted, the addition of nine sessions of marital therapy did enhance the 2-day workshop for the outcome of minimizing relapse on the enhancing friendship outcome variable.

Objective 2: Decreasing Destructive and Increasing Constructive Marital Conflict

Differential Treatment Effects.   In complimentary fashion, as predicted, there was a significant main effect for the *friendship-enhancing component effect on conflict,* $F(1, 58) = 4.62$, $p = .036$. As predicted based on SMH theory, when the friendship-enhancing component was omitted, the destructive conflict mean was 10.30 (mostly destructive), whereas when the friendship-enhancing component was included the destructive conflict mean was -0.71 (mostly constructive). No other effects were significant. The overall means are plotted in figures 3.2a and 3.2b to summarize

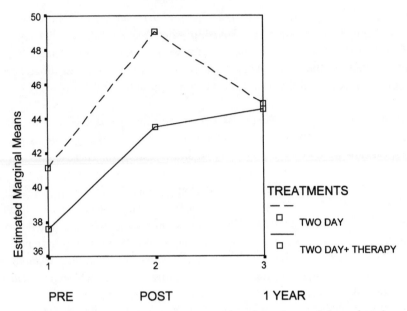

FIGURE 3.1 Two-day workshop compared to the 2-day workshop plus nine sessions of marital therapy for the increasing friendship quality outcome, averaged across spouses (Objective 1).

the four groups' means over time. The 2-day workshop intervention was the best intervention for reducing destructive marital conflict. Once again, there were significant differential treatment effects.

Time and Spouse Effects. There was a significant linear and significant quadratic effect for time (linear, $F(1, 58) = 17.06$, $p < .001$; quadratic, $F(1, 58) = 8.12$, $p = .006$). The means were Pre, 12.31, Post, 1.33, and 1-year, 0.77. The quadratic component in this case shows no evidence of relapse, but merely the convex character of the plot.

Avoiding Relapse. Comparing the 2-day workshop with the 2-day workshop plus marital therapy, there was a significant linear effect for time, $F(1, 31) = 20.03$, $p < .001$, and a significant quadratic effect for time, $F(1, 31) = 6.19$, $p = .018$. The time means were Pre, 10.12, Post, −1.43, and 1-year, −3.32. The quadratic effect again was not evidence of relapse but of the shape of the curve. There were no significant treatment effects or significant interaction effects of time or spouse with treatment. Thus, the addition of nine sessions of marital therapy *did not enhance* the 2-day workshop for the outcome of reducing destructive marital conflict.

Objective 3: Increasing the Quality of Sex,
Romance, and Passion in the Marriage

Differential Treatment Effects. There was a statistically significant interaction of spouse by the conflict regulation factor, $F(1, 50) = 6.81$, $p = .012$. Adding the

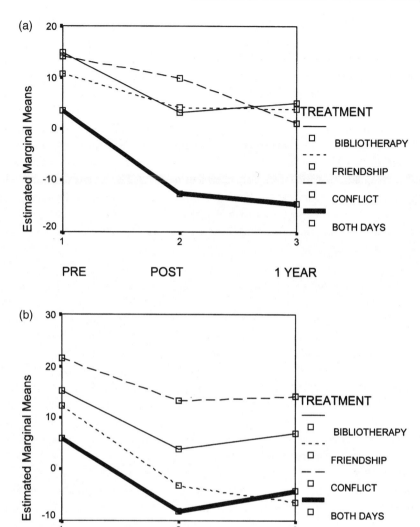

FIGURE 3.2   (a) Two-day workshop compared to the 2-day workshop plus nine sessions of marital therapy for decreasing destructive and increasing constructive marital conflict, husband (Objective 2). (b) Two-day workshop compared to the 2-day workshop plus nine sessions of marital therapy for decreasing destructive and increasing constructive marital conflict, wife (Objective 2).

conflict-reducing component produced a significant improvement in sex, romance, and passion for husbands, but not for wives.

Time and Spouse Effects.   There was a marginally significant quadratic effect for time, $F(1, 50) = 3.28$, $p = .076$. The means were Pre, 19.25, Post, 18.38, and 1-year, 18.77. There is no relapse here, but a convex shape effect; the t ratio from Post to 1-year was $t(50) = 0.42$, n.s. There was a significant spouse main effect,

$F(1, 50) = 14.42$, $p < .001$, with means for wives 19.58 and means for husbands 18.02, so husbands perceive more problems in this area than wives.

Avoiding Relapse.   Comparing the 2-day workshop with the 2-day workshop plus marital therapy, there was a significant quadratic effect for time, $F(1, 50) = 9.35$, $p = .005$. The means were Pre, 19.56, Post, 17.62, and 1-year, 18.95. There was no significant drop from Post to 1-year, $t(31) = 0.87$, n.s. Thus, there is *no evidence of relapse* for either of these two interventions. Also, the added nine sessions of marital therapy provided no increased benefit on this outcome. There was a significant spouse by quadratic time effect, $F(1, 31) = 5.31$, $p = .028$. The means were, for wives: Pre, 19.52, Post, 16.72, and 1-year, 18.91; and for husbands: Pre, 19.61, Post, 18.52, and 1-year, 18.98. The relapse for husbands from Post to 1-year was not significant, $t(31) = 1.21$, n.s., and the relapse for wives from Post to 1-year was also not significant, $t(31) = 0.26$, n.s.

Objective 4: Increasing the Quality of the Shared Meaning System

Differential Treatment Effects.   There was a marginally significant conflict by friendship interaction, $F(1, 57) = 3.92$, $p = .053$. The means were Bibliotherapy, 36.14, Friendship, 32.52, Conflict, 34.23, and Two-day, 38.67. The comparison between Bibliotherapy and Friendship was not significant, $t(57) = 2.36$, n.s.; couples did not do better in the Friendship enhancement workshop than in the Bibliotherapy group. The post hoc comparison between friendship enhancement and the 2-day workshop was significant, $t(57) = 4.02$, $p < .01$; couples did better in the 2-day workshop than in the friendship enhancement workshop on this objective. Once again, there were significant differential treatment effects.

Time and Spouse Effects.   The linear time effect was marginally significant, $F(1, 57) = 3.50$, $p = .067$, while the quadratic time effect was statistically significant, $F(1, 57) = 20.45$, $p < .001$. The means were Pre, 33.00, Post, 37.91, and 1-year, 35.03. The drop from Post to 1-year was not significant, $t(57) = 1.23$, n.s. There was a significant spouse effect, $F(1, 57) = 4.69$, $p = .034$. The means were Husbands, 37.11, Wives, 33.52; husbands see more shared meaning in the marriage than wives do. There was a significant quadratic interaction of spouse by time, $F(1, 57) = 4.31$, $p = .042$.

Avoiding Relapse.   Neither wives nor husbands relapsed from Post to 1-year ($t(57) = -2.28$, n.s., for wives; $t(57) = -0.83$, n.s., for husbands). There was a significant spouse by linear time by conflict factor interaction, $F(1, 57) = 5.95$, $p = .018$. In our post hoc comparisons, regardless of whether the conflict regulation component was present or not, wives relapsed in the shared meaning system from Post to 1-year assessments: for conflict regulation the relapse was significant, $t(57) = -3.73$, $p < .01$; but for no conflict regulation, the relapse was not significant, $t(57) = -1.77$, n.s. Husbands did not relapse significantly in either case from Post to 1-year assessments: for conflict regulation the relapse was not significant, $t(57) = -1.51$, n.s.; for no conflict regulation, the relapse was also not significant, $t(57) = -0.51$, n.s.

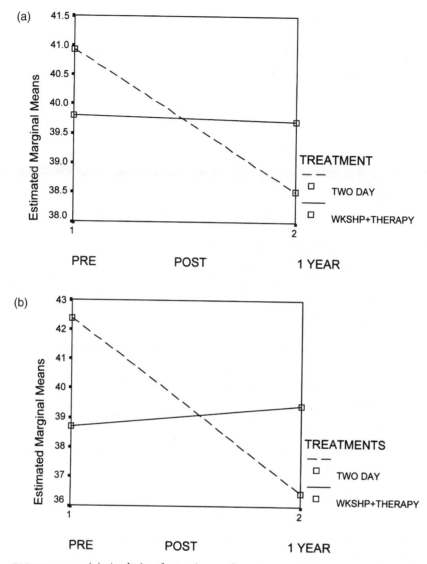

FIGURE 3.3   (a) Analysis of covariance: the 2-day workshop compared to the 2-day workshop plus nine sessions of marital therapy for increasing the quality of the shared meaning system, husband (Objective 4). (b) Analysis of covariance: the 2-day workshop compared to the 2-day workshop plus nine sessions of marital therapy for increasing the quality of the shared meaning system, wife (Objective 4).

Comparing the 2-day workshop with the 2-day workshop plus marital therapy, there was a significant linear and quadratic effect for time (linear, $F(1, 27) = 12.95$, $p = .001$; quadratic, $F(1, 27) = 15.04$, $p = .001$). The means were Pre, 34.61, Post, 40.44, and 1-year, 38.51. There is thus evidence of improvement as well as some evidence of relapse in the quality of the shared meaning system. No other factor was significant. To investigate the relapse more closely, since the Pre scores on shared meaning were somewhat different between the 2-day workshop and the

2-day workshop plus marital therapy (35.14 vs. 34.08, respectively), we conducted an analysis of covariance, with the husband and wife Pre scores as covariates. With this analysis, the time by treatment effect was marginally significant, $F(1, 27) = 3.88$, $p = .059$. The means from the analysis of covariance are plotted in figures 3.3a and 3.3b. We are particularly interested in the fact that in the covariance analysis, with the 2-day workshop plus marital therapy there was no relapse for either husbands or wives. In the subsequent tests, for wives, with only the 2-day workshop the drop from Post to 1-year was significant, $t(27) = -3.02$, $p < .01$, whereas for the 2-day workshop plus marital therapy there was an increase, which was not significant, $t(27) = 0.36$, n.s. Hence, the addition of the therapy sessions was sufficient for preventing relapse in shared meaning for wives.

■ Discussion and Conclusions

The concept proposed in this chapter is that the measurement network for evaluating marital interventions for distressed couples should emerge from the objectives of the intervention rather than relying on standard marital satisfaction scores (which do not control for conflict avoidance) or relying a global measure of marital quality. We suggested that the standard measures of marital quality were not entirely appropriate for measuring marital intervention outcomes because they do not control for conflict avoidance. We designed a study with five theoretically different interventions and demonstrated that there was no treatment effect for total score marital satisfaction, but there was a differential treatment effect for the marital happiness item.

However, our major point was to evaluate an alternative self-report measurement package of four outcome variables for each spouse (and three process variables), which we employed in a study evaluating our interventions. Unlike the Locke-Wallace total score of marital satisfaction, we found differential treatment outcomes with this new measurement package for each of the four objectives. The differential treatment effects did not mirror those obtained with the marital happiness score, but instead followed the predictions of the SMH theory.

Rather than a horse race between competing interventions, the psychoeducational interventions themselves were designed to test some *theoretical* hypotheses. The first two of these hypotheses were that the major effect of the conflict reduction intervention (by itself) would be on the friendship outcome, whereas, the major effect of the friendship-enhancing intervention (by itself) would be on the conflict outcome. Both components are presumed necessary to accomplish both goals. These hypotheses were supported by the results. We can therefore tentatively suggest that there may be a circular relationship between these two domains. If this conclusion is supported by subsequent studies it would suggest that a single global marital quality measure of outcome, which was recommended by Fincham and Bradbury (1987), may not be appropriate for measuring the outcomes of marital interventions.

The Objective of Enhancing Friendship

For the objective of enhancing the couple's friendship quality, the conflict re-duction psychoeducational intervention was not complete by itself. With only the psychoeducational conflict regulation intervention, there was significant relapse in the friendship quality outcome for wives from Post to 1-year. However, with the nine marital therapy sessions added to the full 2-day workshop there was no relapse from Post to 1-year. If the measurement package we are proposing proves valid in subsequent research, it would suggest the hypothesis that the psycho-educational component may need to be supplemented by marital therapy to pro-duce lasting change in the enhancing friendship objective. These findings are preliminary and need to be validated with a multimethod study and replicated before we can have confidence in the conclusion that we need to utilize more than a single global marital quality measure of outcome.

The Objective of Decreasing Destructive and Increasing
Constructive Marital Conflict

There was no relapse in destructive versus constructive marital conflict with the psychoeducational workshops, and the effect was not enhanced by the added nine sessions of marital therapy. The 2-day workshop that focused on both reducing destructive marital conflict and increasing the quality of the couple's friendship demonstrated the most effectiveness and absence of relapse for reducing destruc-tive marital conflict. Thus, the psychoeducational component does not need to be supplemented by marital therapy to produce lasting change in the conflict ob-jective. This is also important information that could not have been obtained by a single global marital quality measure of outcome.

The Objective of Increasing the Quality of Sex-Romance-Passion

Similar to the constructive versus destructive conflict objective, for the goal of improving the quality of sex, romance, and passion, every intervention was effec-tive, and there was no relapse. There was also a treatment by spouse interaction. As predicted, husbands improved on this outcome if the conflict-reducing compo-nent was present, but this was not the case for wives. Adding the nine sessions of marital therapy to the 2-day workshop did not affect relapse on this variable at all. Husbands saw more problems in this area than wives, so on this dimension men more than women are the barometers of the relationship's quality. Thus, the psychoeducational component does not need to be supplemented by marital ther-apy to produce lasting change in the quality of the sex-romance-passion objective. However, our hypothesis that the friendship component alone will improve this outcome for wives was not supported. Again, this was also important information that could not have been obtained by a single global marital quality measure of outcome.

The Objective of Increasing the Quality of the Shared Meaning System

For this goal there was no relapse effect for husbands but there was a relapse effect for wives. There was an interaction of spouse with the conflict reduction component, which showed that wives relapsed significantly from Post to 1-year but husbands did not relapse when there was a conflict reduction component in the intervention. There was also an interaction of spouse and time with the friendship-enhancing component. The Bibliotherapy group did no better than the friendship-enhancing component, but the 2-day workshop did better than the friendship-enhancing component. With the addition of the nine sessions of marital therapy, fortunately there was no longer any relapse effect for wives. Thus, the psychoeducational component does need to be supplemented by marital therapy to produce lasting change in the quality of shared meanings objective.

It was quite clear from these data that while psychoeducational interventions definitely have their place for two of the four objectives (conflict and sex), we need to supplement our workshops with marital therapy for the objectives of enhancing friendships and improving the shared meaning system.

Among the limitations of the present investigations is the problem of the common method variance of the outcome measures. Because of budgetary considerations, we were unable to evaluate a multimethod assessment package in this study. More recently, we have been able to begin collecting interview and observational data in conjunction with the SMH self-report measures in two groups of couples, one group experiencing the transition to parenthood and another group with preadolescent children. The early results are encouraging about the cross-method validity of the SMH measures.

Some scores dropped from posttest to follow-up at 1 year. In general we think that a 1-year follow up is inadequate for properly assessing an intervention with couples. For many couples the intervention gets them to face their unresolved issues, and that may lead to increased conflict and lower scores on self-report inventories of any kind. This is true despite the fact that the intervention program taught more constructive conflict management or conflict resolution skills. It still takes time to work these problems out and time for the skills to become integrated into the couple's repertoire so that they are constructive instead of destroying the peace produced by conflict avoidance. Hopefully, longer follow-up will bear out the long-term usefulness of the interventions. Our plan is to follow these couples for 5 years.

One important limitation of the present report is that we only reported 1-year follow-up data. This means that the workshop-plus-therapy group was just completing the therapy. Even though there were only nine sessions of therapy, and these were massed at the start of therapy and tapered out across a year of therapy, there was still a therapy session close to the final assessment for this group only. Hence, more follow-up is necessary before we can confidently conclude that the relapse prevention was effective. Indeed, we plan to follow these couples in the years to come to address that limitation of the present report.

We note, in passing, that, in general, men changed more on our measures than women. We consider this encouraging, because in our longitudinal research men's variables tended more than women's variables to be the lead indicators of longitudinal outcomes. For example, in the dimension of accepting influence, it was men's rejecting influence from women and not the converse that predicted divorce in a 6-year longitudinal study of newlyweds (Gottman, Coan, Carrere, & Swanson, 1998). Another example is provided by the behavior-physiology link. We reported (Gottman, Murray, Swanson, Tyson, & Swanson, 2002) that when women's affective behavior drove men's heart rates (and not the converse) divorce was the likely outcome. Based on these and other outcome data, it is clear that changing men ought to be a major goal in marital interventions. We need to examine how to obtain larger changes in women.

Subsequent research and clinical practice might attempt to fit the intervention to the specific areas of marital functioning that need most improvement. Because the SMH questionnaires reveal information in a differentiated and complex manner that can provide a profile of specific areas to focus on in intervention with a couple, these measures have promise for recommending specific components of treatment for specific marital concerns. They thus have clinical utility in addition to research utility.

■ References

Berg, P., & Snyder, D. K. (1981). Differential diagnosis of marital and sexual distress: A multidimensional approach. *Journal of Sex and Marital Therapy, 7*, 290–295.

Bray, J. H. & Jouriles, E. N. (1995). Treatment of marital conflict and prevention of divorce. *Journal of Marital and Family Therapy, 21*(4), 461–473.

Burgess, E. W., & Cottrell, L. S. (1939). *Predicting success or failure in marriage.* New York: Prentice Hall.

Burgess, E. W., Locke, H. J., & Thomes, M. M. (1970). *The family.* New York: Van Nostrand–Reinhold.

Burgess, E. W., & Wallin, P. (1953). *Engagement and marriage.* Philadelphia: Lippincott.

Derogatis, L. R., Lipman, R. S., & Covi, L. (1973). The SCL-90: An outpatient psychiatric rating scale—preliminary report. *Psychopharmacology Bulletin, 9*, 13–25.

Doherty, W. J. (1997). *The intentional family.* Reading, MA: Addison-Wesley.

Ekman, P. (1984). Expression and the nature of emotion. In K. R. Scherer & P. Ekman (Eds.), *Approacheds to emotion* (pp. 319–344). Hillsdale, NJ: Erlbaum.

Fincham, F. D., & Bradbury, T. N. (1987). The assessment of marital quality: A reevaluation. *Journal of Marriage and the Family, 49,* 797–809.

Goleman, D. (1996). *Emotional intelligence.* New York: Bantam Books.

Gottman, J. (1999). *The marriage clinic.* New York: Norton.

Gottman, J. M. (1993). The roles of conflict engagement, escalation, or avoidance in marital interaction: A longitudinal view of five types of couples. *Journal of Consulting and Clinical Psychology, 61*, 6–15.

Gottman, J. M. (1994). *What predicts divorce: The relationship between marital processes and marital outcomes.* Hillsdale, NJ: Erlbaum.

Gottman, J. M., Coan, J., Carrere, S., & Swanson, C. (1998). Predicting marital happiness and stability from newlywed interactions. *Journal of Marriage and the Family, 60*, 5–22.

Gottman, J. M., & Levenson, R.W. (1992). Marital processes predictive of later dissolution: Behavior, physiology, and health. *Journal of Personality and Social Psychology, 63*, 221–233.

Gottman, J. M., Murray, J., Swanson, C., Tyson, R., & Swanson, K. (2002). *The mathematics of marriage.* Cambridge, MA: MIT Press.

Gottman, J. M., & Silver, N. (1999). *The seven principles for making marriage work.* New York: Crown.

Greenberg, L. S., & Johnson, S. M. (1988). *Emotionally focused therapy for couples.* New York: Guilford Press.

Hahlweg, K., & Markman, H. J. (1988). Effectiveness of behavioral marital therapy: Empirical status of behavioral techniques in preventing and alleviating marital distress. *Journal of Consulting and Clinical Psychology, 56*(3), 440–447.

Hamilton, G. V. (1929). *A research in marriage.* New York: Albert and Charles Boni.

Henry, J. P., & Stephens, P. M. (1977). *Stress, health, and the social environment.* New York: Springer-Verlag.

Jacobson, N. S., & Addis, M. E. (1993). Research on couples and couple therapy: What do we know? Where are we going? *Journal of Consulting and Clinical Psychology, 61*(1), 85–93.

Jacobson, N. S., & Baucom, D. H. (1977). Design and assessment of nonspecific control groups in behavior modification research. *Behavior Therapy, 8*(4), 709–719.

Kaiser, A., Hahlweg, K., Fehm-Wolfsdorf, G., & Groth, T. (1998). The efficacy of a compact psychoeducational group training program for married couples. *Journal of Consulting and Clinical Psychology, 66*(5), 753–760.

Locke, H. J., & Wallace, K. M. (1959). Short marital-adjustment and prediction tests: Their reliability and validity. *Marriage and Family Living, 21*, 251–255.

Locke, H. J., & Williamson, R. C. (1958). Marital adjustment: A factor analysis study. *American Sociological Review, 23*, 562–569.

Pinsof, W. M., & Wynne, L. C. (1995). The effectiveness of marital and family therapy: An empirical overview, conclusions and recommendations. *Journal of Marital and Family Therapy, 21*, 341–343.

Raush, H. L., Barry, W. A., Hertl, R. K., & Swain, M. A. (1974). *Communication, conflict, and marriage.* San Francisco: Jossey-Bass.

Ryan, K. (2001). *A relapse prevention program for distressed couples following a workshop-based marital intervention.* Unpublished doctoral dissertation, University of Washington, Seattle.

Scheer, N. S., & Snyder, D. K. (1984). Empirical validation of the Marital Satisfaction Inventory in a nonclinical sample. *Journal of Consulting and Clinical Psychology, 52*, 88–96.

Shadish, W. R., Montgomery, L. M., Wilson, P., Bright, M. R., & Okuwambua. (1993). Effects of family and marital psychotherapies: A meta-analysis. *Journal of Consulting and Clinical Psychology, 61*(6), 992–1002.

Shadish, W. R., Ragsdale, K., Glaser-Renita, R., & Montgomery, L. M. (1995). The efficacy and effectiveness of marital and family therapy: A perspective from meta-analysis. *Journal of Marital and Family Therapy, 21*(4), 345–360.

Snyder, D. K., & Regts, J. M. (1982). Factor scales for assessing marital disharmony and disaffection. *Journal of Consulting and Clinical Psychology, 50*, 736–743.

Snyder, D. K., & Smith, G. T. (1986). Classification of marital relationships: An empirical approach. *Journal of Marriage and the Family, 48*, 137–146.

Spanier, G. B. (1976). Measuring dyadic adjustment: New scales for assessing the quality of marriage and similar dyads. *Journal of Marriage and the Family, 38*, 15–25.

Terman, L. M., Buttenweiser, P., Ferguson, L. W., Johnson, W. B., & Wilson, D. P. (1938). *Psychological factors in marital happiness.* New York: McGraw-Hill.

Vanzetti, N. A., Notarius, C. I., & NeeSmith, D. (1992). Specific and generalized expectancies in marital interaction. *Journal of Family Psychology, 6,* 171–183.

Weiss, R. L. (1980). Strategic behavioral marital therapy: Toward a model for assessment and intervention. In J. P. Vincent (Ed.), *Advances in family intervention, assessment and theory* (Vol. 1, pp. 229–271). Greenwich, CT: JAI.

Weiss, R. L., & Cerreto, M. (1980). Marital status inventory: Development of a measure of dissolution potential. *The American Journal of Family Therapy, 8,* 80–86.

Wile, D. (1988). *After the honeymoon.* New York: Wiley.

4

Emotion and the Repair
of Close Relationships

Susan M. Johnson

Couple therapy is a journey. It is a journey from the territory called marital distress, where depression, anxiety, and the disruption of families and children's development are part of the landscape, to a place called a good relationship that sustains people in their lives and promotes mental and physical health. This territory was for many years a dark and mysterious place. The vagaries of adult love and intimacy were not even considered to be an area of legitimate study for social scientists. This has now changed. We now have a rapidly expanding science of close relationships that offers the couple therapist a map to the territory of adult love and to the process of relationship repair. Specifically, the new science of close relationships can help the therapist to construct pivotal change events in couple therapy sessions and also to deal with impasses in such change events. A major part of this new science is a new understanding of the key role of emotion in the definition and redefinition of close relationships.

This focus on emotion highlights a central paradox in the field of couple and family therapy. The general public and popular culture take it for granted that emotion, whether negative and relationship threatening or positive and relationship building, is a major part of adult love relationships. Many individual therapists (e.g., Greenberg, Rice, & Elliott, 1993; Yalom, 1980) have also stressed the role of emotional experience and expression in the process of individual change. Even seminal figures who helped to build the discipline of couple therapy agreed that affect had to change if a relationship was to be repaired (Jacobson & Margolin, 1979). However, emotion has been generally marginalized in the field of couple and family therapy. The field has focused on cognition and behavior and on techniques such as skill building and the creation of cognitive insight. In fact, if emotion is considered at all, it is, even now, often seen as the enemy of relationship repair or at best as irrelevant to this repair (Miller & de Shazer, 2000). This chapter addresses the role of emotion in love relationships and their repair and suggests that new theoretical, research, and clinical developments are putting the "heart"—a focus on emotion—back into couple therapy in a way that informs clinicians how to actively use emotion to create lasting change in couple relationships.

■ Why Has the Field of Couple and Family Therapy Marginalized Emotion?

There seem to be many reasons emotion has been marginalized, but three reasons stand out. First, the cultural and professional context in which couple and family therapy developed has been highly ambivalent about emotion. As feminist writers point out, patriarchal models of health and well-being emphasize rationality and self-control over emotion and emotional expression, which has been associated with the feminine. Passion has been seen as dangerous and associated with dysfunction, while reason has been idealized. Strong emotions have been viewed as signs of immaturity and invitations to chaos (Kennedy-Moore & Watson, 1998). However, new conceptualizations of emotion actually integrate emotion and "intelligence" (Goleman, 1995). More specifically, the professional cultural context, as reflected in both behaviorism (which viewed emotion as an "internal" variable that was simply an epiphenomenon accompanying behavior) and systems theory, marginalized emotion. In fact, there is nothing inherently "unsystemic" about emotion. Indeed emotion and emotional communication can be viewed as an organizing or "leading element" in social systems (Johnson, 1998).

In recent years, emotion has perhaps begun to appear as less inherently dangerous as it has become more of a known quantity, and distinctions between problematic experiences, such as negative affect flooding, and emotion as a source of functional behavior have been made. Research has emerged that allows us to begin to differentiate when and how emotion is a source of functional adaptation, indeed an essential ingredient in that adaptation, and when it is part of problematic responses. Salovey, Rothman, Detweiler, and Stewart (2000) found that being aware of emotions is not distressing or problematic but chronically trying to figure them out is. Pennebaker (1993; Pennebaker & Traue, 1993) found that the ability to express emotions after trauma led to better functioning and less depression, distress, and somatizing, although here it is a little unclear whether it was the confiding itself that was of benefit or the realization that someone cared enough to listen. Moderate levels of emotional arousal after depressing life events also seemed to potentiate cognitive restructuring (Hunt, 1998); attempting to use cognitive restructuring while suppressing negative emotion led to worsening moods.

Second, emotion may have been marginalized because the nature of emotion was not clearly articulated. This not only was a problem in itself but then resulted in emotion being considered in rather superficial and polarized ways as an agent of therapeutic change. In the past, the humanistic psychology movement, for example, advocated catharsis and ventilation as a therapeutic tool, whereas behaviorists eschewed the use of emotion altogether. If clinicians are not clear about the nature of emotion and do not have guidelines for how to deal with and use emotion to create positive change, then it is not surprising if they tend to avoid it. This is especially true in couple and family therapy, where emotional interactions can be so powerful. Past formulations of emotion have named as many as 39 emotions (Solomon, 1976). This number of emotions is difficult to conceptualize and even more difficult to use systematically as a therapeutic tool. Other writings on affect have named 6 to 8 core affects (Ekman & Friesen, 1975; Izard, 1979) and offered clearer conceptualizations. As a result the ways in which core emotions can be used to create positive movement in therapy and foster adaptive behavior have recently been differentiated and refined (Greenberg, Korman, & Paivio, 2002; Johnson, 2004).

Third, emotion may have been marginalized because it is only recently that research has substantially validated the primacy of emotion in the arena of intimate relationships and the definition of adult partnerships, and it is only recently that a model of couple and family therapy that espouses the primacy of emotion and its use as a change agent has been shown to be effective (Johnson, Hunsley, Greenberg, & Schindler, 1999). A new science of the nature of relationship distress, the nature and function of emotion in relationships, and the nature of adult love is developing that offers a powerful resource to the therapist interested in helping clients transform their closest and most emotionally significant relationships. For example, in terms of understanding the exact nature of marital distress, Gottman, Coan, Carrere, and Swanson (1998) found that positive affect was the best predictor of relationship satisfaction and stability for newlywed couples over a 6-year period. Conversely, affective disengagement seems to be particularly associated with dissatisfaction in relationships (Smith, Vivian, & O'Leary, 1990). Facial expressions of emotion, specifically fear on the face of the husband and angry contempt on the face of the wife, have been found to be powerful predictors of the future trajectory of marital partnerships (Gottman, 1994). For the first time, couple therapists have available a coherent body of research on the nature of marital distress and on the nature of adult love (Johnson, 2003a) and the beginnings of a body of research on change in empirically validated models of couple therapy (Johnson et al., 1999), all of which stress the central role of emotion and offer a coherent perspective that holds great promise for the future practice of couple and family therapy.

■ What Is Emotion?

If one of the real barriers to recognizing and using emotion in therapy has been a lack of clear definition, do we now have a clear perspective on this phenomenon? Perhaps one of the most elegant ways, which is also compatible with other recent and more complex conceptualizations, is that of Arnold (1960). Emotion is a high-level information processing system rather than simply a sensation or a "feeling." It is composed of the following elements:

1. Rapid appraisal of environment cues as they relate to key survival needs and imperatives.
2. *Body sensations.* The word emotion comes from the Latin word to move. Emotion "moves" us physically and mentally.

3. *Reappraisal.* The meaning of cues and sensations is here considered and evaluated and this meaning linked and integrated into cognitive frameworks.
4. *Action priming.* Emotion primes us to act in a compelling manner. Anger, for example, often primes assertion of needs and fear often primes flight or freeze responses.

In general, in the therapy literature, emotions are viewed as action tendencies that arise from automatic appraisals of the relevance of situations to a person's basic concerns and needs (Frijda, 1986; Johnson & Greenberg, 1994; Lazarus, 1991). It is anything but a primitive, irrational response. It is a high-level information processing system that integrates innate biological and emotional needs with past experience, present perceptions of the environment, and anticipated interpersonal consequences (Frijda, 1988).

Although the exact number of emotions that can be recognized across cultures by distinct facial configurations varies somewhat, there seems to be general agreement that the core emotions are the following: anger, sadness, fear, joy, disgust, and surprise and excitement (Ekman & Friesen, 1975; Izard, 1979). These emotions appear to be universal and to be associated with specific neuroendocrine patterns and brain sites (Panksepp, 1998). Emotions often have "control precedence" (Tronick, 1989) and can easily override other cues and behaviors, especially in important interactions in relationships with those we depend on the most. As Bowlby states (1980, p. 40), "The most intense emotions arise during the formation, the maintenance, the disruption and renewal of attachment relationships. The formation of a bond is described as falling in love, maintaining a bond as loving someone, and losing a partner as grieving over someone. Similarly, threat of loss arouses anxiety and actual loss gives rise to sorrow, while each of these situations is likely to arouse anger. The unchallenged maintenance of a bond is experienced as a source of security and the renewal of a bond as a source of joy. Because such emotions are usually a reflection of the state of a person's affectional bonds, the psychology and the psychopathology of emotion is found to be in large part the psychology and psychopathology of affectional bonds."

The functions of emotion have also been outlined. In summary this literature gives a picture of emotion as a powerful organizer of inner realities and key interpersonal interactions. These functions as outlined by various authors (Frijda, 1988; Greenberg & Johnson, 1986; Safran & Greenberg, 1991) are the following:

1. Emotion orients us and directs us to focus on what is important in our environment. Damascio (1994) points to research where people who cannot access emotion due to brain injuries cannot make rational decisions and choices. They become caught in pondering all possible possibilities. They have no internal compass to tell them what they want and need—to give a felt sense of what matters to them.
2. Emotion is a vital part of meaning creation. It primes key cognitions and guides the creation of meaning (Frijda, 1986; Leventhal, 1984). Emotion colors the perception of self and other and is a powerful factor in the ongoing construction of personal identity (Bowlby, 1988; Guidano, 1987).

3. Emotion motivates and primes for action in a rapid compelling manner (Tomkins, 1984).

4. Emotion communicates to others concerning our intentions and inner states and also pulls for specific responses from others. So seeing another's grief and fear pulls for empathic caring and a movement toward that other. Affective expression organizes the "interpersonal reflex" (Leary, 1959) of the other. As a primary signaling system the expression of emotion organizes interactions; it can be viewed as the music of the dance between intimates (Johnson, 2004) and this music has the ability to dramatically alter social interactions (Keltner & Kring, 1998).

Emotion has also been differentiated into three levels, primary or core, secondary reactive, and instrumental (Greenberg & Johnson, 1988; Greenberg & Safran, 1987). It can also be described as hard (such as anger and disgust) or soft (such as sadness and vulnerability) (Jacobson & Christensen, 1996). Both of the most recent models of couple therapy, emotionally focused (EFT) and integrative behavioral (IBMT), assume that hard emotions have underlying soft emotions associated with them. EFT actively advocates evoking the softer emotions to shift the interactional stances partners take with their spouse and to pull for new, more positive responses to that spouse (Johnson & Greenberg, 1988).

Given the advances in understanding summarized above, what other specific advances have been made in our understanding of the role of emotion in close relationships from descriptive studies and new explanatory theoretical perspectives and research?

■ New Insights Into Emotion and the Definition of Close Relationships

Generally, the research by Gottman and colleagues (Gottman, 1994, 1999; Gottman et al., 1998) and by other investigators, such as Pasch and Bradbury (1998), tells us that the presence of negative affect and conflict is far from the whole story in distressed relationships. Happy couples become upset, fight, and often do not resolve issues. The essential difference between distressed and nondistressed couples resides more in whether partners can sustain emotional engagement and move to repair and renew this engagement after a fight or a rift. In more specific terms, recent research has found that wives in more satisfied relationships tend to use "softer" forms of emotional expression when bringing up an issue. Her spouse is then able to stay engaged and listen to her complaint and negative emotion, rather than react by withdrawing or defending (Gottman, 1999; Stanley, Bradbury, & Markman, 2000). Soothing responses—the offering of support, contact comfort, and reassurance—appear to be crucial to the maintenance of close relationships. There are then specific kinds of emotional engagement that seem to be critical for the maintenance of positive partnerships. When these partnerships are defined negatively there are also specific patterns of emotional expression that emerge. Specific emotions appear to be linked to the demand/criticize-withdraw/defend interactional patterns that characterize distress and predict divorce. Both contempt on the face of female partners, who are usually in the demanding role, and fear on the face of withdrawing male partners are associated with divorce. In the most general terms, this research directs the therapist's attention to compelling states of negative emotion, such as contemptuous anger and fear, and rigid patterns of interaction that prevent safe emotional engagement. There is also evidence that these strong negative emotions are most often accompanied by more negative, characterological rather than more benevolent, situational attributions for a partner's behavior.

The image of a satisfying relationship that emerges from this research is one of emotional safety and engagement together with an ability to regulate negative emotion and so exit from the negative patterns that hold distressed relationships hostage, such as criticize/withdraw. The ability to respond to the partner's need for soothing and to stay engaged when partners bring up relationship issues also seems crucial. This research is pivotal in that it suggests that a focus on emotion, emotion regulation, and patterns of emotional expression are key in the ongoing definition and redefinition of a close relationship.

However, the therapist also needs more than this descriptive research. Such research is often very general, correlational, and not context specific. For example, it may be true that positive relationships demonstrate five times the amount of positive to negative affect (Gottman, 1994). However, the therapist must ask what affect, in what form, and at what specific moments defines a relationship as satisfying or distressed and either hinders or promotes recovery from distress? What are the specific times when emotional engagement is particularly necessary? Research on change events in EFT (Johnson & Greenberg, 1988), which shift interactions in the direction of positive bonding interactions, suggests that a deepening of emotional experience is a key ingredient in such pivotal change events. Observation without a theoretical framework does not tell us how best to label and understand key emotional processes. Even if descriptive research is not to be used as a direct guide to intervention, it is still necessary to label and interpret the results of research observations. For example, partners who respond to another's "softened start-up" can be viewed as "accepting influence," or they can be viewed as being able to tolerate negative emotions and so maintain engagement (Stanley et al., 2000). If this research is to be used as a basis for fostering change, these labels become extremely important, for they have different implications for intervention. Theory is the explanation of pattern and placing these observational results in the context of a theory of adult love may not only elucidate their meaning but also help to translate them into a specific guiding framework for relationship change which includes a focus on emotion as a positive force in such change (Johnson & Whiffen, 2003).

■ A Theory of Adult Love and the Role of Emotion

The general findings of the above research would seem to fit very well with the huge and ever expanding literature on adult attachment (Bartholomew & Perlman, 1994;

Cassidy & Shaver, 1999; Johnson & Whiffen, 1999; Simpson & Rholes, 1998). The application of Bowlby's attachment theory (1969, 1973, 1980, 1988) to adult relationships only occurred in the late 1980s (Hazan & Shaver, 1987; Johnson, 1986), although Bowlby might be considered to have written the very first book on family therapy, entitled *Forty-Four Juvenile Thieves* (1946). The central tenets of attachment theory are as follows.

Seeking and maintaining contact with significant others is an innate, primary motivating principle in human beings across the life span. Dependency, which has been pathologized in our culture (Bowlby, 1988), is an innate part of being human rather than a childhood trait that we outgrow. Secure dependence is complementary to rather than dichotomous with autonomy. According to attachment theory, there is no such thing as complete independence from others or true overdependency (Bretherton & Munholland, 1999). There is only effective or ineffective dependency. Secure dependence fosters autonomy and self-confidence. The more securely connected we are, the more separate and different we can be. This secure connection is a felt sense, an emotional attunement.

Attachment offers a *safe haven.* As the Irish proverb goes, "We live in the shelter of each other." Maintaining proximity to an attachment figure is an innate survival mechanism and a primary method of regulating emotions, particularly fear. The presence of an attachment figure, which usually means parents, children, spouses, and lovers, provides comfort and security, while the perceived inaccessibility of such a figure creates emotional distress. A felt sense of secure attachment also offers a *secure base* from which individuals can explore their universe and most adaptively respond to their environment. The presence of such a base encourages exploration and a cognitive openness to new information. It promotes the confidence necessary to risk, learn, and continually update cognitive models of self and the world.

The basic building blocks of secure bonds are emotional accessibility and responsiveness. As found in recent research on marital satisfaction (Gottman, 1994), it is emotional engagement that is crucial. In attachment terms, any response (even anger) is better than none. If there is no engagement, no emotional responsiveness, the message from the attachment figure reads as "Your signals do not matter, and there is no connection between us." When an individual is threatened, by traumatic events, by the negative aspects of everyday life such as illness, or by any assault on the security of the attachment bond itself, powerful affect arises. As Bowlby points out this affect communicates to the self and to others the needs of the individual, especially needs for comfort, contact, and caring. These needs for comfort and connection then become particularly salient and compelling, and attachment behaviors, such as proximity seeking, are activated. Proximity to a loved one is an inbuilt emotional regulation device.

If attachment behaviors fail to evoke comforting responsiveness and contact from attachment figures, a prototypical process of angry protest, clinging, depression, and despair occurs, culminating eventually in detachment. Depression is a natural response to loss of connection. Bowlby distinguished between the anger of hope and the anger of despair. The latter tends to become desperate and coercive and can then make engagement with significant others more difficult. Attachment theory gives the clinician an explanatory framework for and a map to the emotional terrain of significant relationships. For example, in a model such as emotionally focused couple therapy, the critical demanding behaviors that are so typical of distressed couples (Gottman, 1994) are understood in terms of loss of connection, attachment protest, and insecurity. This theory would predict that, as found in the research described above, wives whose spouses were able to tolerate this protest and stay emotionally engaged would have happier partnerships.

Attachment theory predicts that the dance of distress in a close relationship will manifest in three basic patterns. There are only so many ways of coping with a negative response to the question "Can I depend on you when I need you?" These patterns correspond with the basic ways of expressing emotion (Ekman & Friesen, 1975): exaggerating, minimizing, and substituting one emotion for another. Attachment emotions and expressive behaviors become heightened as anxious clinging, pursuit, and even aggressive attempts to obtain a response from the loved one escalate. The second strategy for dealing with the lack of safe emotional engagement is to attempt to suppress attachment needs and emotions, focus on tasks, and limit or avoid distressing attempts at emotional engagement with attachment figures. These two ways of regulating emotion, anxious hyperactivation and numbing avoidance, can develop into habitual styles of engagement with intimate others. When fear of contact and fear of isolation are both high, a third strategy, which combines clinging in the face of distance and fearful avoidance in the face of contact, occurs. This is associated with being violated and traumatized by past attachment figures (Alexander, 1993). These strategies are "self-maintaining patterns of social interaction and emotion regulation" (Shaver & Clark, 1994, p. 119). While these habitual forms of engagement can be modified by new relationships, they can also mold current relationships and so become self-perpetuating. They involve specific behavioral responses to regulate emotions and protect the self from rejection and abandonment.

Strong emotion in attachment relationships also cues associated cognitive representations or working models of self and other. Strong affect accesses key cognitive schemas concerning identity and the nature of relationships (Greenberg & Safran, 1987). Secure attachment is characterized by a working model of self that is worthy of love and care and is confident and competent. And indeed research has found secure attachment to be associated with self-efficacy and a more coherent and articulated sense of self (Mikulincer, 1995). Securely attached people, who believe others will be responsive when needed, tend to have working models of others as dependable and worthy of trust. These working models are formed, elaborated, maintained, and, most important for the couple therapist, changed through emotional communication (Davila, Karney, & Bradbury, 1999). In fact, to be optimally useful they must be constantly revised and kept up to date as changes occur in interpersonal contexts.

Finally, attachment theory offers a map to key pivotal emotionally "hot" events that, out of all proportion to their frequency, tend to define the quality of an attachment relationship. Events where partners experience abandonment at times of intense need (Johnson, Makinen, & Millikin, 2001), for example, seem to create impasses to the creation of secure connection and must be repaired if a couple are to recover from distress. This theory also helps a couple therapist to structure key events of mutual accessibility and responsiveness that have the ability to transform a distressed relationship and create new positive emotions (Johnson & Greenberg, 1988).

Research has found that secure attachment is linked to more positive and intense positive emotion and less frequent and intense negative emotion. Insecure attachment is also associated with more inhibited displays of emotion in marriages (Feeney, 1999). Attachment affect regulation strategies predict key relationship behaviors, such as responses to conflict and responses to seeking and giving support. Those with a secure style are generally happier and more able to reach out for and provide support (Simpson, Rholes, & Nelligan, 1992; Simpson, Rholes, & Phillips, 1996). Those with secure styles have closer, more stable, and more trusting, satisfying relationships (Collins & Read, 1994; Simpson, 1990). They can better acknowledge and communicate their needs and are less likely to be verbally aggressive or withdraw during problem solving (Senchak & Leonard, 1992). Research suggests that partnerships containing at least one secure partner are more harmonious and have fewer conflictual interactions (Cohn, Silver, Cowan, Cowan, & Pearson, 1992).

This perspective on relationships privileges emotion and emotional communication and is consonant with the research on marital distress. Both bodies of research stress the importance of variables, such as sustainable emotional engagement and soothing supportive interactions, that foster the regulation of negative emotions. Attachment theorists would predict that the defensive stonewalling associated with escalating marital distress (Gottman, 1994) would naturally elicit a strong emotional distress response and exacerbate marital problems. These theorists would also predict that the avoid and defend strategy is most often employed in the hope of preserving connection by minimizing conflict and demands on the other spouse. Attachment theory helps us understand the plot behind the drama of intense emotional distress and how fears of loss, abandonment, and isolation fuel the intense emotions that are the music of the attachment dance (Johnson, 2003a).

New conceptualizations of emotion, descriptive research on distress in key relationships, and explanatory frameworks, such as attachment, are changing the way clinicians view emotion. It is being viewed as a crucial agent of positive change (Fosha, 2000), especially in therapies that focus on changing relational realities. Outcome research suggests that both individual therapy (Paivio & Nieuwenhuis, 2001) and couple and family therapy that evoke and use emotion to create new experiences of emotional connection and new interactions are effective (Johnson et al., 1999; Johnson, Maddeaux, & Blouin, 1998). Research also suggests that in couple therapy a model that focuses on emotion may be more adept at fostering lasting change and minimizing relapse than other approaches that do not address affect in the same way (Clothier, Manion, Gordon Walker, & Johnson, 2002).

■   The Use of Emotion in Change Events in Emotionally
    Focused Couple Therapy

One way to explore how emotion can be used to create in-session change is to consider key change events in EFT. As discussed above recent descriptive and explanatory frameworks offer guidance to clinicians as to the nature and process of transformational tasks and events in relationship rift and repair and the part emotion plays in such events (Johnson, 2002).

The goals of EFT are to help partners restructure the key attachment emotions that organize partners' interactions and so shift responses in the direction of secure attachment. The relationship repair process moves from the de-escalation of negative interactional cycles, to the creation of interactions characterized by emotional accessibility and responsiveness, and finally to the consolidation and integration of positive changes (Johnson & Denton, 2002). EFT is a humanistic constructivist approach (Neimeyer, 1993) that uses emotion in the way Bowlby (1991) suggested it be used, that is, as a primary source of information to the self and to others about needs and motives and as a primary route to connecting with attachment figures. In general, the EFT therapist tracks, accesses, and evokes emotion as a source of information about people's needs and fears and how these "move" partners and so structure the relational dance. The therapist also helps clients to shift their habitual ways of processing and regulating their emotions in interactions with their spouses, for example, expressing anger indirectly through criticism and hiding softer emotions such as fear. The therapist also helps clients unfold and restructure key emotional experiences that may be marginalized in their awareness, such as the experience of loss and abandonment that fuels expressions of apathy or numbness. The therapist also uses primary "soft" attachment emotions to shape new responses—responses that are crucial to secure attachment, such as the ability to assert needs or ask for comfort and caring. The EFT therapist assumes that it is not simply reframing negative emotions or naming emotions that is crucial for change, but a new experience of emotion that then organizes new interactional responses.

Two key change events are associated with success in the second stage of EFT, withdrawer reengagement and blamer softening. In the first event the more withdrawn spouse is able to express the emotional realities and imperatives underlying his or her withdrawn, self-protective stance and coherently assert his or her needs to be met in a way that invites more positive emotional engagement from the other partner. Process research has linked the successful completion of the second task, blamer softening, which allows for mutual engagement and responsiveness between partners, to successful outcome in EFT. In this event a previously hostile spouse is able to access and express vulnerability and ask for comfort and reassurance in a manner that maximizes the other's ability to respond with empathy and engagement (Johnson & Greenberg, 1988).

Process research that focuses on the client behaviors leading to important moments of change in therapy sessions is a priority for clinicians (Beutler, Williams, & Wakefield, 1993). One well-articulated approach to such research is the task analytic model (Greenberg, 1984, 1986). In this model, change episodes are explored and competent performance that leads to positive outcomes delineated. Specific steps in the change process can then be articulated, as well as the therapist interventions that best foster the change process as outlined. A key task is first identified from clinical experience and theoretical understanding, and a rational model of possible performance steps in this task is identified. The features that mark the beginning of an event are specified, and the steps toward change are then coded on process measures in a small number of individual cases. The coded steps are then compared to the steps set out in the rational model. The emerging pattern is then used to refine this model of task completion. This model is then examined in a number of cases where successful performance is contrasted with unsuccessful performance. If the components of the model discriminate between these performances, then the validated model is linked to in-session and/or end of treatment outcome (e.g., Greenberg & Foerster, 1996).

A task analytic study of key softening events in "best sessions" (as identified by clients) of stage two of EFT found that in couples who successfully completed these events, and went on to achieve positive treatment outcomes, blaming partners were more affiliative when coded on the Structural Analysis of Social Behavior Scale (SASB; Benjamin, 1986) and were rated as showing deeper levels of emotional experiencing (on the Experiencing Scale: Klein, Mathieu, Gendlin, & Miesler, 1969) in the session. Couples who did not benefit from therapy were also observed as not being able to complete these events. In addition, a sequence of steps in the successful performance of this task could be identified. This task ends in mutual comforting interactions and appears to redefine the relationship as a more secure bond where partners emotionally engage and directly ask for their attachment needs to be met. The couple can then move into the final consolidation phase of EFT.

So what does the plot line—the prototypical sequence of interactions—look like in this change event that appears to be pivotal in the change process in EFT? This event would typically evolve in the following manner.

Encouraged by the therapist, the blaming spouse (say, the wife) begins to connect with and touch softer emotions, such as pain and hurt in the relationship. For example, the therapist asks Rita if she sees that Ted is much more open and present in the relationship. She agrees he is. The therapist asks if she believes that now he understands her hurt in the relationship. She replies that she does not believe he really understands. The therapist asks her to help him and she replies that she cannot and she weeps. She says that she knows he will not be able to hear and respond to it. The therapist helps Ted to offer clear, congruent reassurance and further, to request that Rita open up and risk with him. She becomes very tearful and refuses to speak. Then, with much support, she, step by step, gives shape and form to her fears/insecurities and voices her vulnerability. She shares hopelessness. He will not be able to tolerate or respond to her hurt, and she gives instances when he did not. Her catastrophic fear is that if she expresses her hurts and fears, she will also be branded as demanding/difficult/impossible to love and so be left feeling even more alone.

Grief and different forms of fear—fear of risking, fear of being hurt again, fear of abandonment and helplessness, as well as shame at needing caring—are the universal emotional themes that arise here. Rita then shares all of this directly with

her partner in an enactment. Her partner explicitly reassures, validates, and comforts his wife. He continues to request that she reach for him and risk letting him in. The therapist heightens her need and her longing and helps Rita to structure specific requests for these needs to be met. Ted is able to respond and the couple engage in a bonding event where both are vulnerable, open, and asking for attachment needs to be met. Both are intensely engaged, self-disclosing as to their emotions, and empathically responsive to each other.

These events are powerful. What we also see is that as partners speak their most heartfelt fears and needs and find the other responsive many changes occur on many different levels. Attachment theory helps us understand these observed changes. We see that partners see each other in a more compassionate light. New emotions evoke new cognitions and meanings. They make different attributions about each other's behavior. If the negative cycle recurs, they can exit from it much faster and it does not define the relationship. In fact, after these events partners demonstrate the key responses associated in research studies with more secure attachment. Secure attachment is associated, for example, with less reactivity and better affect regulation, more cognitive openness and toleration of uncertainty and ambiguity, more ability to be empathic and assert needs, and a sense of self that is more elaborated, positive, and coherent (Johnson & Whiffen, 1999). In these powerful emotional events, new feedback is given about the nature of self, as when a previously blaming spouse says, "You do like this softer side of me? When I talk like this you feel closer to me—even if I am weak and needy?" And the partner concurs. New, more generous attributions are also made about the other and his or her ability to be responsive and dependable. There are some preliminary data to suggest that a partner's model of self can change after successful relationship repair in EFT (Sims, 1999). These change events are characterized by shifts in emotional content, the previously angry critical spouse allows him- or herself to access and express fear and despair, and shifts in how emotion is processed. Softer emotions are held and processed at a "working distance" (Gendlin, 1981); they are allowed and explored but are not experienced as overwhelming and so are not denied or replaced by secondary emotions, such as anger.

If we know what steps the couple takes to transform their relationship in EFT, how does the therapist promote these events in the moment? The theoretical writing on EFT would suggest that the therapist uses evocative responding (such as, "what happens to you as you say that?" or "what is it like for you to see your partner cry and ask for your help?") to help partners connect with attachment-oriented emotions. The therapist heightens these emotions, adding color, shape, and form, by the use of images and repetition in a way that leads into specific enactments that form bonding interactions. Bradley and Furrow (2004) studied tapes of successful softenings in couples and coded therapist interventions and found that indeed in successful softenings therapists used these interventions. However, they also made a discovery that has now been used to refine EFT interventions. They found that when the therapist offered an image—a model of how attachment needs might be expressed in more secure relationships—together with a validation of how anxiety inducing this would be to do in a particular couple's relationship, this seemed to foster successful task completion. So the therapist might say, "So you could never turn to him and say, 'I need you—come and be with me because I need you . . .'; that would be too scary?" This intervention seems to focus the blaming partner on the fears and vulnerabilities that block emotional disclosure and engagement and so foster the resolution of these difficulties.

This kind of research can bridge the gaps between theory, research, and practice. The conceptualizations of emotion that stress the primacy of anger, fear, sadness, and shame fit with the patterns of emotional expression observed in these events. Attachment theory and the map it offers of the emotional terrain of close relationships helps the EFT therapist understand the intrapsychic and interpersonal drama of such events and how they impact the definition of a relationship. These events and their impact on relationship repair also recursively lend validation to the attachment perspective on adult attachment. We can observe that these change events characterized by emotional accessibility and responsiveness and the expression of attachment needs create level two change as defined by Watzlawick, Weakland, and Fisch (1974); that is, they reorganize the couple's relational system and directly foster recovery from distress. On a more specific level, the pattern of responses in these events fits with descriptions of distressed couples' behaviors and with the postulates of attachment theory. For example, in attachment theory, defensive withdrawal or an avoidant style is viewed as a fragile strategy that masks but does not eliminate anxiety. Gottman also suggests (1994) that defensive withdrawn partners are, in fact, highly aroused and flooded with anxiety. In change events of withdrawer reengagement, these spouses do indeed routinely articulate the desperation and sense of helplessness and failure that cues their withdrawal from their partner. They describe this withdrawal as a desperate coping strategy to avoid being overwhelmed by a sense of loss and inadequacy, but they note that it does not eliminate their insecurities and anxieties. This kind of research can also give the therapist a guide to how and when to focus on emotion and how to use emotion to shape transforming events in therapy.

There are times, however, when negative emotion arises and blocks positive change. In fact, this is one of the reasons clinicians have been reluctant to focus on emotion in therapy sessions. This occurs in EFT when, in a change event as described above, a partner suddenly becomes flooded with hurt and anger from a past hurt and cannot risk or trust the other.

■ Impasses in EFT: Reversing Pivotal Moments
    of Negative Relationship Definition

Just as certain specific kinds of events can begin to define a relationship as a secure bond, so certain kinds of negative events can undermine trust and define a relationship as distressed and not to be depended on. Attachment theorists point out that when a partner responds (as in a softening) or fails to respond at a time of urgent need these incidents will influence the quality of an attachment relationship disproportionately (Simpson & Rholes, 1994). We have conceptualized events where a partner fails to respond at such times, and so wounds the other partner, as attachment injuries (Johnson et al., 2001). Such events, usually experienced as betrayals or abandonments, would logically become extremely relevant when, during the process of relationship repair, partners are asked to take risks and confront difficulties with trust and emotional engagement. In general, the couple therapy literature has recently turned its attention to incidents of betrayal or trauma that call for forgiveness and how these events can, if this forgiveness is not forthcoming, block relationship repair. However, views of forgiveness have not been integrated into marriage (Coop Gordon, Baucom, & Snyder, 2000), and there is little consensus as to the critical elements of forgiveness and how or why particular kinds of events impact relationships in particular ways. Couple therapists are, in fact, concerned with more than forgiveness per se; most often they are concerned with facilitating the renewal of trust and active reconciliation between intimates.

This concept arose from an integration of the observation of negative emotional shifts in key therapy sessions, especially sessions where therapists were structuring change events, both withdrawer reengagement and blamer softening. We saw that some of the partners were not able to complete the steps in these key change events. In fact, as the therapist encouraged partners to risk and reach for the other and voice their attachment needs, many of these spouses would actively block and vividly recount a past incident in which their trust was destroyed. This past incident was described in an emotionally alive and vibrant manner and culminated with a refusal to be open and allow the possibility of being hurt again. If the therapist helped the couple work through this incident, the couple often were able to complete the change process and reach recovery; however, this did not always happen. We began then to study case examples of these impasses and how, if the therapist did focus on them, partners were able to successfully work through their hurt and mistrust and move into softening events and more secure bonding interactions. As we did this our understanding of these impasses expanded and we termed them attachment injuries. An attachment injury occurs when, at a time of extreme need and vulnerability, such as a miscarriage, a medical crisis, or the death of a parent, attachment needs for emotional accessibility and responsiveness become particularly salient and compelling. When partners are unresponsive at such times, they shatter implicit assumptions that they will be responsive when urgently needed and so injure their spouses, who experience being abandoned to cope with their vulnerability alone. This isolation then exacerbates a partner's anxiety and sense of traumatic helplessness. When these events are evoked in couple therapy, they resemble traumatic flashbacks in their vivid intensity and they severely limit the trust and sense of security the injured partner experiences in the relationship. Injured partners describe becoming hypervigilant to any possible hurts or reminders of these injuries and also as numbing themselves in the manner described in classic examples of posttraumatic stress disorders. These events are best viewed as relationship traumas and illustrate the "indelible imprint" (Herman, 1992, p. 35) of traumatic experience. The other spouse often also helps to maintain this injury by refusing to discuss the incident or remaining unresponsive to the wounded partner's protests and desire to explore the event.

In general, healing from trauma involves the ability to construct an integrated narrative of the traumatic event together with its meaning and its consequences, to process and integrate the emotion associated with the event, and to risk emotional engagement with others that offer corrective experiences of efficacy and belonging (Harvey, 1996). More specifically, from the observations of cases and the construction of a rational outline of the conjectured steps in the change process, the process of resolution of attachment injuries appears to be as follows (this is now being tested in a current research project):

1. As the EFT therapist begins to encourage a spouse to risk connecting with the partner, this spouse then becomes flooded by emotion from an incident in which he or she felt abandoned and helpless, experiencing a violation of trust that damaged belief in the relationship as a secure bond. This spouse relates this incident in an alive, highly emotional manner rather than as a calm recollection. The partner either discounts, denies, or minimizes the incident and the injured partner's pain and moves to a defensive stance.

2. With the therapist's help, the injured spouse stays in touch with the injury and begins to articulate its emotional impact and its attachment significance. New emotions frequently emerge at this point. Anger evolves into clear expressions of helplessness, fear, and shame. The connection of the emotional impact of the injury to present negative cycles in the relationship becomes clear. For example, a spouse says, "I promised myself never again to give him the chance to hurt me like that. I watch for it now. I guard myself. It's like he has become the enemy. I keep testing him, but. . . ." The therapist attempts to attune to the injured partner's emotion and to act as a surrogate processor, helping this partner articulate and organize this overwhelming negative emotion and the meaning it has for the person and his or her stance in the relationship.

3. The other partner, supported by the therapist, begins to hear and understand the significance of the injurious event and to understand it, as the therapist frames it, in attachment terms, that is, as a reflection of how crucial his or her comfort and reassurance is to the injured spouse. This partner then is able to explicitly acknowledge and emotionally connect with the injured partner's pain and suffering. He or she elaborates on how the event evolved in a manner that makes his or her response more predictable and understandable to the injured partner.

4. The injured partner then tentatively moves toward a more integrated and complete articulation of the injury and expresses grief at the loss involved in it and fear concerning the specific loss of the attachment bond. This partner allows the other to witness his or her vulnerability. The therapist supports the injured partner to "make sense of" his or her experience and validates that experience.

5. The other spouse then becomes more emotionally engaged and is able to acknowledge explicit responsibility for his or her part in the attachment injury and express empathy, regret, and/or remorse in a congruent and emotionally

compelling manner that the injured spouse finds comforting and reassuring. Injured spouses make comments such as, "I do matter to him—he does care."

6. The injured spouse then risks asking for the comfort and caring from the partner which were unavailable at the time of the injurious event. This is done, as in softening events, in a way that pulls the partner toward him or her.

7. The other spouse is now able to respond in a caring manner that appears to act as an antidote to the traumatic experience of the attachment injury. The partners are then calm and able to reflect on the event and to construct together a new narrative of this event.

Once the attachment injury is resolved, the therapist can more effectively "foster the growth of trust and the beginning of general positive cycles of bonding and connection. The couple can then complete change events, such as a softening, where the more blaming spouse can confide his or her attachment needs and the other can respond (Johnson, 2004). Let us look at a case example of how attachment injuries are resolved in the practice of EFT.

■ An Antidote Change Event: Steps in Healing
   an Attachment Injury in EFT

Never mind—be quiet and just get on with it.

Trevor and Yolanda had been married since they were 18, that is, for 30 years. They had quite recently decided to emigrate to Canada and this transition had been very stressful for both of them, although they had both continued to successfully pursue careers in finance and administration. However, very soon after they arrived in Canada, their children left home and Trevor lost his job and become depressed and very withdrawn from his wife. She tried to support him but then had also begun to withdraw out of frustration. Trevor then became intensely romantically involved with a colleague who supported him in a newfound job. Yolanda discovered his affair and promptly left him. However, after a few weeks she returned, and the couple agreed that Trevor would end his affair and they would attempt to mend their marriage. Nine months later, Trevor called to see a couple therapist, stating that he and his wife just could not seem to resolve this rift between them.

Trevor began talking about the affair as a result of Yolanda's turning away from him and how he had come to believe that their marriage was ending and had then turned to another for consolation. Yolanda then exploded and told him that the real story was that he had shut her out and then betrayed her. She had not come to therapy to listen to excuses. The couple agreed that the Yolanda pursue/Trevor withdraw cycle that they had always struggled with in their marriage had been intensely exacerbated by the stress of immigration and by Trevor's depression. Yolanda had also moved into a new stance when, instead of pursuing, she had decided to turn away and let Trevor come to her. She bitterly remarked, "But of course, he didn't reach for me. After I had reached for him for 20 years or so, I only had to turn away for a few weeks and he found someone else. He threw our relationship away and now he just wants me to forget it and go on like nothing happened." Trevor sighed dejectedly and commented that he felt "battered" and "defeated" by her comments and that his motto in life had indeed been to ignore feelings and to "just get on with it"; but he agreed that this time simply trying to go back to the routines of married life wasn't working. In this couple the attachment injury did not emerge out of the shadows at a crucial moment in couple therapy, it was front and center from the beginning. The therapist helped the couple move through the usual process of stage one in EFT—de-escalation of the negative cycle and the emotion associated with it. Here they put the affair in the context of their interactional cycle and accessed underlying emotions in that cycle. Yolanda was able to talk about how she would feel "desperate and shut out" and create fights to try to reach him, while he commented that he did not know how to "do closeness, or talk about feelings" and would then feel "useless" and "shut down to avoid a bigger fight." He felt "guilty" about the affair and "accepted" Yolanda's rage, but he did not know what to do to change it. He stressed that he loved her very much and was totally committed to the marriage and that it hurt him to see her pain over his "big mistake." She replied she wasn't sure she could trust him ever again and that she could not "just get on with" being married to him. Both partners formed an excellent alliance with the therapist and as the relationship became less volatile, we began to work on the injury of the affair more directly. If we could take snapshots of the steps in resolution they would appear as follows:

1. As the couple talked about their relationship, Trevor admitted his sorrow and guilt, as well as his tendency to withdraw and so leave his wife feeling isolated. He asked her to try to learn to trust him again so they could really renew their marriage. Yolanda then became angry and dissolved in tears, at which point Trevor, although generally more engaged and responsive, then stated that there was obviously nothing he could do and stare at the floor. Yolanda then wept and rocked herself and said that she could not talk about this. She had spent the weeks after she had left him weeping like this or just "numbed out," and although they had reunited and improved their relationship, this had not changed. When she and Trevor tried to talk about this at home she experienced him as just "shutting down" and repeating to her that he had, after all, come back to her and they should stop trying to deal with this and "just get on with life—just do the job."

2. In order to articulate the injury and its attachment significance the therapist began by reflection, evocative questions, and heightening to help Yolanda articulate and organize her emotional responses. She began to articulate the core aspects of her pain. As she saw it, "As soon as I stopped building the bridge—reaching and pursuing him—after all those years, as soon as I stopped, he went off. It was like I didn't matter, and it was me that pulled him back here—this relationship is shifting sand. I was just the easiest option—so I won't put my heart on the line again." She was able to articulate and express

to him her grief, her helplessness, and her dismay at his "abandonment" of her, as well as her rage and sense of not being valued and her fear of being hurt again. The validation of the therapist and the therapist's help in processing Yolanda's emotion allowed her to stay engaged but not be overwhelmed by it.

3. Trevor began to hear and acknowledge his injured wife's pain and elaborate on the event. With the therapist's support, he was able to stay engaged and respond to his wife's hurt. He spoke of his "guilt" and how he had decided that he was "totally emotionally incompetent" as a spouse and had decided that he would never be able to please Yolanda and so would still numb out under the "pressure to perform." When he lost his job he told himself that he had even failed as a provider. He also believed that she was about to leave him in the weeks before he initiated his other relationship. He acknowledged how emotionally overwhelmed he used to be when his wife expressed concern about their relationship and how "terrified" he was of the fights in which he heard her disappointment with him. He was now also able to articulate how moved he was that she had come back and "fought" for him and still loved him. He explicitly told her that he saw her pain and her fear of risking with him and it moved him, especially when he understood the cycles they had been caught in and how she had been "knocking on the door" all these years and trying to get him to open up to her.

4. At this point in the process the injured partner then moves to a more integrated expression of the injury: Yolanda was now able to allow herself to touch and express the helplessness and terror she had experienced when she discovered Trevor's affair and how this sense of "abandonment and being alone" seemed to "take the breath right out" of her. The fear that, if she risked opening up to him, it would all happen again was now very tangible for her.

5. Trevor was now able to stay engaged and responsive and validate her emotions, while expressing deep regret and remorse. The couple also talked about how he was much more emotionally accessible and open at home and how he could now tell her when he was "overwhelmed" and couldn't "formulate sentences," rather than just withdrawing. He expressed puzzlement over this, since to express difficulty and not be able to "solve the problem" was failure in his terms. His wife assured him that his emotional presence was what she needed.

6. At this point the injured spouse can explicitly move to asking for caring and comfort: Yolanda stated that she still did not feel "chosen and valued" and needed reassurance from Trevor. He began to explicitly frame his withdrawal when she spoke of the affair as a response to his own "excruciating terror" that he had totally failed as a spouse and would then lose her, and he told her how much he wanted to be there for her. He told her, "I want to be with you; I chose you. You are the center of my life." She asked to be taken care of when she felt "assailed" by all these emotions, for example, on significant anniversaries or when other reminders of negative events occurred, and he

responded by telling her that he would like to do that and was learning how to do that better. He then offered to hold her and she accepted.

This process seemed to facilitate the growth of trust and secure bonding for this couple. Yolanda and Trevor were now able, in the session and outside, to reach for each other, to confide needs and fears, to comfort each other and use each other as a safe haven in which to deal with difficult emotions. They experienced their relationship as a more secure bond and were able to formulate a coherent narrative of how their relationship went to "the brink" and how they were able to repair it. The ability to regulate difficult emotions and to create coherent narratives of close relationships and difficult events in those relationships is associated with secure attachment (Main, Kaplan, & Cassidy, 1985). Trevor ended the sessions (10 in all) by telling his wife, "I love you; I am committed to you and I am finding I like learning to be close. Maybe that is more fun than just putting your head down and getting on with life like it's a job."

The steps in the resolution of attachment injuries are still being refined in process studies. However, it is already apparent that the process above appears to validate the power of emotion and specific emotional cues and experiences to define attachment relationships for good or ill. This process also validates the nature of the specific interactional responses that are needed to repair trust and create the safe emotional engagement that typifies a secure bond.

■ Conclusions

The field of couple therapy is coming of age (Johnson, 2003a; Johnson & Lebow, 2000). There is a growing coherence in our understanding of the nature of emotion, descriptive maps of emotional distress and satisfaction arising from research, the emerging attachment theory of adult love and the maps to emotional experience it has generated, and research that helps us understand specific events in the change process in couple therapy. This chapter has argued that we are clearer about the nature of emotion, the role it plays in organizing interactions, and how to use it in the change process. It may be time then to consider that for some kinds of change, such as rekindling love and compassion, working actively with emotion is not only the fastest route to change, it can be the primary route to change. At times in the therapeutic endeavor, Yalom may be right; as he remarks (1980), "It is only when therapy enlists deep emotions that it becomes a powerful force for change."

■ References

Alexander, P. C. (1993). Application of attachment theory to the study of sexual abuse. *Journal of Consulting and Clinical Psychology, 60*, 185–195.

Arnold, M. B. (1960). *Emotion and personality.* New York: Columbia University Press.

Bartholomew, K., & Perlman, D. (1994). *Attachment processes in adulthood.* London, PA: Jessica Kingsley.

Benjamin, L. (1986). Adding social and intra-psychic descriptors to axis 1 of DSM-III. In T. Millon & G. Kerman (Eds.), *Contemporary directions in psychopathology* (pp. 215–232). New York: Guilford Press.

Beutler, L., Williams, R., & Wakefield, P. (1993). Obstacles to disseminating applied psychological science. *Applied and Preventative Psychology, 2,* 53–58.

Bowlby, J. (1946). *Forty-four juvenile thieves: Their characters and home life.* London: Bailliere, Tindall, & Cox.

Bowlby, J. (1969). *Attachment and loss: Vol. 1. Attachment.* New York: Basic Books.

Bowlby, J. (1973). *Attachment: Vol. 2. Separation.* New York: Basic Books.

Bowlby, J. (1980). *Attachment: Vol. 3. Loss.* New York: Basic Books.

Bowlby, J. (1988). *A secure base.* London: Routledge.

Bowlby, J. (1991). Postscript. In C. Murry Parkes, J. Stevenson-Hinde, & P. Marris (Eds.), *Attachment across the life cycle.* New York: Routledge.

Bradley, B., & Furrow, J. (2004). Toward a mini-theory of blamer softening event. *Journal of Marital and Family Therapy, 30,* 233–246.

Bretherton, I., & Munholland, K. A. (1999). Internal working models in attachment relationships: A construct revisited. In J. Cassidy & P. Shaver (Eds.), *Handbook of attachment: Theory, research and clinical implications* (pp. 89–114). New York: Guilford Press.

Cassidy, J., & Shaver, P. (1999). *Clinical handbook of attachment: Theory, research and clinical applications.* New York: Guilford Press.

Clothier, P. F., Manion, I., Gordon Walker, J., & Johnson, S. M. (2002). Emotionally focused interventions for couples with chronically ill children: A 2 year follow-up. *Journal of Marital and Family Therapy, 28,* 391–398.

Cohn, D., Silver, D., Cowan, C., Cowan, P., & Pearson, J. (1992). Working models of childhood attachment and couple relationships. *Journal of Family Issues, 13,* 432–449.

Collins, N., & Read, S. (1994). Cognitive representations of attachment: The structure and function of working models. In K. Bartholomew & D. Perlman (Eds.), *Attachment processes in adulthood* (pp. 53–92). London, PA: Jessica Kingsley.

Coop Gordon, K., Baucom, D. S., & Snyder, D. K. (2000). The use of forgiveness in marital therapy. In M. McCullough, K. I. Pargament, & C. E. Thoresen (Eds.), *Forgiveness: Theory, research and practice* (pp. 203–227). New York: Guilford Press.

Damascio, A. R. (1994). *Descartes' error: Emotion, reason and the human brain.* New York: Putnam.

Davila, J., Karney, B., & Bradbury, T. N. (1999). Attachment change processes in the early years of marriage. *Journal of Personality and Social Psychology, 76,* 783–802.

Ekman, P., & Friesen, W. V. (1975). *Unmasking the face.* Englewood Cliffs, NJ: Prentice Hall.

Feeney, J. A. (1999). Adult attachment, emotional control and marital satisfaction. *Personal Relationships, 6,* 169–185.

Fosha, D. (2000). *The transforming power of affect.* New York: Basic Books.

Frijda, N. H. (1986). *The emotions.* Cambridge: Cambridge University Press.

Frijda, N. H. (1988). The laws of emotion. *American Psychologist, 43,* 349–358.

Gendlin, E. T. (1981). *Focusing* (2nd ed.). New York: Bantam Books.

Goleman, D. (1995). *Emotional intelligence.* New York: Bantam Books.

Gottman, J., Coan, J., Carrere, S., & Swanson, C. (1998). Predicting marital happiness and stability from newlywed interactions. *Journal of Marriage and the Family, 60,* 5–22.

Gottman, J. M. (1994). *What predicts divorce?* Hillsdale, NJ: Erlbaum.

Gottman, J. M. (1999). *The marriage clinic: A scientifically based marital therapy.* New York: Norton.

Greenberg, L. S. (1984). Task analysis: The general approach. In L. N. Rice & L. S. Greenberg (Eds.), *Patterns of change: Intensive analysis of psychotherapy process* (pp. 124–148). New York: Guilford Press.

Greenberg, L. S. (1986). Change process research. *Journal of Consulting and Clinical Psychology, 54,* 4–9.

Greenberg, L. S., & Foerster, F. S. (1996). Task analysis exemplified: The process of resolving unfinished business. *Journal of Consulting and Clinical Psychology, 64,* 439–446.

Greenberg, L. S., & Johnson, S. M. (1986). Affect in marital therapy. *Journal of Marital and Family Therapy, 12,* 1–10.

Greenberg, L. S., & Johnson, S. M. (1988). *Emotionally focused therapy for couples.* New York: Guilford Press.

Greenberg, L. S., Korman, L. M., & Paivio, S. C. (2002). Emotion in humanistic psychotherapy. In D. J. Cain & J. Seeman (Eds.), *Humanistic psychotherapies: Handbook of research and practice* (pp. 499–530). Washington, DC: APA Press.

Greenberg, L. S., Rice, L., & Elliott, R. (1993). *Facilitating emotional change.* New York: Guilford Press.

Greenberg, L. S., & Safran, J. (Eds.). (1987). *Emotion, psychotherapy and change.* New York: Guilford Press.

Guidano, V. F. (1987). *Complexity of the self: A developmental approach to psychopathology and therapy.* New York: Guilford Press.

Harvey, M. (1996). An ecological view of trauma and trauma recovery. *Journal of Traumatic Stress, 9,* 3–23.

Hazan, C., & Shaver, P. (1987). Conceptualizing romantic love as an attachment process. *Journal of Personality and Social Psychology, 52,* 511–524.

Herman, J. L. (1992). *Trauma and recovery.* New York: Basic Books.

Hunt, M. G. (1998). The only way out is through: Emotional processing and recovery after a depressing life event. *Behavior Research and Therapy, 36,* 361–384.

Izard, C. E. (1979). *Emotion in personality and psychotherapy.* New York: Plenum.

Jacobson, N. S., & Christensen, A. (1996). *Integrative couples therapy: Promoting acceptance and change.* New York: Norton.

Jacobson, N. S., & Margolin, G. (1979). *Marital therapy: Strategies based on social learning and behavioral exchange principles.* New York: Brunner/Mazel.

Johnson, S. M. (1986). Bonds or bargains: Relationship paradigms and their significance for marital therapy. *Journal of Marital and Family Therapy, 12,* 259–267.

Johnson, S. M. (1998). Listening to the music: Emotion as a natural part of systems theory. *Journal of Systemic Therapies: Special Edition on the Use of Emotions in Couple and Family Therapy, 17,* 1–17.

Johnson, S. M. (2002). *Emotionally focused couple therapy with trauma survivors: Strengthening attachment bonds.* New York: Guilford Press.

Johnson, S. M. (2003a). Attachment theory—a guide for couple relationships: The EFT model. In S. M. Johnson & V. Whiffen (Eds.), *Attachment: A perspective for couple and family therapy* (pp. 103–123). New York: Guilford Press.

Johnson, S. M. (2003b). The revolution in CT: A practitioner–scientist perspective. *Journal of Marital and Family Therapy, 29,* 365–384.

Johnson, S. M. (2004). *The practice of emotionally focused couple therapy: Creating connection* (2nd ed.). New York: Brunner/Routledge.

Johnson, S. M., & Denton, W. (2002). Emotionally focused couples therapy: Creating secure connections. In A. S. Gurman (Ed.), *The clinical handbook of couple therapy* (3rd ed., pp. 221–250). New York: Guilford Press.

Johnson, S. M., & Greenberg, L. S. (1988). Relating process to outcome in marital therapy. *Journal of Marital and Family Therapy, 14*, 175–183.

Johnson, S. M. & Greenberg, L. S. (1994). Emotion in intimate relationships: Theory and implications for therapy. In S. Johnson & L. Greenberg (Eds.), *The heart of the matter: Perspectives on emotion in marital therapy* (pp. 3–22). New York: Brunner/Mazel.

Johnson, S. M., Hunsley, J., Greenberg, L., & Schindler, D. (1999). Emotionally focused couples therapy: Status and challenges. *Clinical Psychology: Science and Practice, 6*, 67–79.

Johnson, S. M., & Lebow, J. (2000). The coming of age of couple therapy: A decade review. *Journal of Marital and Family Therapy, 26*, 9–24.

Johnson, S. M., Maddeaux, C., & Blouin, J. (1998). Emotionally focused family therapy for bulimia: Changing attachment patterns. *Psychotherapy, 35*, 238–247.

Johnson, S. M., Makinen, J., & Millikin, J. (2001). Attachment injuries in couple relationships: A new perspective on impasses in couples therapy. *Journal of Marital and Family Therapy, 27*, 145–155.

Johnson, S. M., & Whiffen, V. (1999). Made to measure: Attachment styles in couples therapy. *Clinical Psychology: Science and Practice, Special Edition on Individual Differences and Couples Therapy, 6*, 366–381.

Johnson, S. M., & Whiffen, V. (Eds.). (2003). *Attachment theory: A perspective for couple ad family therapy.* New York: Guilford Press.

Keltner, D., & Kring, A. M. (1998). Emotion, social function and psychopathology. *Review of General Psychology, 2*, 320–342.

Kennedy-Moore, E., & Watson, J. C. (1998). *Expressing emotion.* New York: Guilford Press.

Klein, M. H., Mathieu, P. L., Gendlin, E. T., & Miesler, D. J. (1969). *The experiencing scale.* Madison: Bureau of AV Instruction, University of Wisconsin.

Lazarus, R. S. (1991). Cognition and motivation in emotion. *American Psychologist, 46*, 352–367.

Leary, T. (1959). *The interpersonal diagnosis of personality.* New York: Ronald.

Leventhal, H. (1984). A perceptual motor theory of emotion. In L. Berkowitz (Ed.), *Advances in experimental social psychology.* New York: Academic Press.

Main, M., Kaplan, N., & Cassidy, J. (1985). Security in infancy, childhood and adulthood: A move to the level of representation. In I. Bretherton & E. Waters (Eds.), Growing points of attachment theory and research. *Monographs of the Society for Research in Child Development, 50*, 66–106.

Mikulincer, M. (1995). Attachment style and the mental representation of the self. *Journal of Personality and Social Psychology, 69*, 1203–1215.

Miller, G., & de Shazer, S. (2000). Emotions in solution focused therapy: A re-examination. *Family Process, 39*, 5–24.

Neimeyer, R. A. (1993). An appraisal of constructivist psychotherapies. *Journal of Consulting and Clinical Psychology, 61*, 221–234.

Paivio, S., & Nieuwenhuis, J. A. (2001). Efficacy of emotion focused therapy for adult survivors of child abuse: A preliminary study. *Journal of Traumatic Stress, 14*, 115–133.

Panksepp, J. (1998). *Affective neuroscience: The foundation of human and animal emotions.* New York: Oxford University Press.

Pasch, L. A., & Bradbury, T. N. (1998). Social support, conflict and the development of marital dysfunction. *Journal of Consulting and Clinical Psychology, 66,* 219–230.

Pennebaker, J. W. (1993). Putting stress into words: Health, linguistic and therapeutic implications. *Behavior Research and Therapy, 31,* 539–548.

Pennebaker, J. W., & Traue, H. C. (1993). Inhibition and psychosomatic processes. In H. C. Traue & J. W. Pennebaker (Eds.), *Emotion, inhibition and health* (pp. 146–163). Seattle, WA: Hogrefe & Huber.

Safran, J. D., & Greenberg, L. S. (Eds.). (1991). *Emotion, psychotherapy and change.* New York: Guilford Press.

Salovey, P., Rothman, A., Detweiler, J., & Stewart, W. T. (2000). Emotional states and physical health. *American Psychologist, 55,* 110–121.

Senchak, M., & Leonard, K. (1992). Attachment styles and marital adjustment among newly wed couples. *Journal of Social and Personal Relationships, 9,* 51–64.

Shaver, P. R., & Clark, C. L. (1994). The psychodynamics of adult romantic attachment. In J. Masling & R. Bornstein (Eds.), *Empirical perspectives on object relations theory* (pp. 105–156). Washington, DC: APA Press.

Simpson, J., & Rholes, W. (1994). Stress and secure base relationships in adulthood. In K. Bartholomew & D. Perlman (Eds.), *Attachment processes in adulthood* (pp. 181–204). London, PA: Jessica Kingsley.

Simpson, J. A. (1990). The influence of attachment styles on romantic relationships. *Journal of Personality and Social Psychology, 59,* 971–980.

Simpson, J. A., & Rholes, W. S. (1998). *Attachment theory and close relationships.* New York: Guilford Press.

Simpson, J. A., Rholes, W. S., & Nelligan, J. S. (1992). Support seeking and support giving within couples in an anxiety provoking situation: The role of attachment styles. *Journal of Personality and Social Psychology, 62,* 434–446.

Simpson, J. A., Rholes, W. S., & Phillips, D. (1996). Conflict in close relationships: An attachment perspective. *Journal of Personality and Social Psychology, 71,* 899–914.

Sims, A. E. B. (1999). *Working models of attachment: The impact of emotionally focused marital therapy.* Unpublished doctoral thesis, University of Ottawa, Ottawa, Ontario, Canada.

Smith, D. A., Vivian, D., & O'Leary, K. D. (1990). Longitudinal prediction of marital discord from premarital expressions of affect. *Journal of Consulting and Clinical Psychology, 58,* 790–798.

Solomon, R. (1976). *The passions.* New York: Doubleday/Anchor.

Stanley, S. M., Bradbury, T. N., & Markman, H. J. (2000). Structural flaws in the bridge from basic research on marriage to interventions for couples. *Journal of Marriage and the Family, 62,* 256–264.

Tomkins, S. S. (1984). Affect theory. In K. Scherer & P. Ekman (Eds.), *Approaches to emotion* (pp. 163–196). Hillsdale, NJ: Erlbaum.

Tronick, E. Z. (1989). Emotions and emotional communication in infants. *American Psychologist, 44,* 112–119.

Watzlawick, P., Weakland, J. H., & Fisch, R. (1974). *Change: Principles of problem formation and problem resolution.* New York: Norton.

Yalom, I. (1980). *Existential psychotherapy.* New York: Basic Books.

5

A Sampling of Theoretical, Methodological, and Policy Issues in Marriage Education: Implications for Family Psychology

Howard J. Markman, Galena H. Kline, Jacqueline G. Rea, Samantha Simms Piper, and Scott M. Stanley

Come learn about relationships.
　　　　　—*"A Marriage Cure,"* The New Yorker, *August 2003*

The above quote is from a recent article about the possibilities that relationship and marriage education classes offered in Oklahoma can foster economic stability by helping people have healthier relationships and marriages. There is growing national consensus from both liberals and conservatives that children who grow up in stable and healthy families do better in terms of economic and social well-being and that relationship and marriage education programs are one way to help people have healthier relationships and marriages. Yet discussions of education approaches to helping couples are relatively new to the field of family psychology. Thus, our goal in this chapter is to review some of the major theoretical and methodological issues in the areas of preventing poor marital/relational outcomes and promoting healthy relationships and marriages through education programs.

The content of journals and at conferences even into the early part of the new millennium indicates that mainstream family psychology has been primarily focused on efforts to understand and treat marital and family distress rather than prevent it. Back when the senior author (senior by age, at any rate) entered the field of prevention back in the mid 1970s, he was virtually alone in focusing on the prevention of marital distress and divorce in the field of clinical psychology and there was no such area as family psychology. Rather than starting to do prevention based on non-empirically based assumptions, Howard and his colleagues (e.g., Frank Floyd, Scott Stanley) decided to conduct longitudinal research to provide empirical foundations for future prevention efforts (for a review of some of the history of this aspect of the field, see Notarius & Markman, 1993). More recently, interest in the prevention of poor marital outcomes and the promotion of marital success is dramatically increasing. For example, there is now an annual conference (Smart Marriages/Happy Families) that focuses on prevention and educational approaches to helping couples have healthy marriages (see www.smartmarriages. com). Funds for marriage education programs at the federal and state levels are increasingly available, including a proposed 200 million federal dollars a year (of the $16 billion a year for the welfare-related budget) for marriage promotion (with a strong emphasis on marriage education) as part of the reauthorization of the Welfare Reform Act of 1996 (Temporary Assistance for Needy Families; TANF; Toner & Pear, 2002). Already, states have been using a wide range of approaches to providing relationship or marriage education (for a review, see Parke & Ooms, 2002), often in nontraditional settings such as TANF classes, high schools, and prisons. Moreover, as illustrated by the American Psychological Association Division 43 (Family Psychology) conference that spawned this book, some researchers and therapists are developing and evaluating relationship and marriage education programs using a prevention science model in which interventions are based on longitudinal research that identifies risk and protective factors for future marital and family outcomes (Coie et al., 1993).

■ What's in a Name: Prevention or Education?

The field of prevention with couples has grown so large that there are now reviews of reviews (e.g., Markman, Stanley, & Kline, 2003). There have been various names for the key focus of the field, such as divorce prevention, relationship enhancement, and marriage education. Most prevention efforts are educational, in that couples are taught skills and principles linked to healthy marriages/relationships, even before the onset of distress, in order to prevent distress and sustain satisfying and stable relationships over time. We use the terms relationship or marriage education because they are broad enough to cover the content of most current research and intervention programs and specific enough to highlight that education is at the core of efforts to prevent relationship distress and promote healthy partnerships. The goal of marriage education from a prevention perspective is to reach couples when they are still happy to keep them happy.

■ Overview of the Chapter

In the next section of this chapter we provide a review of relationship and marriage education as it applies to family psychology. Specifically we (a) briefly define relationship education, (b) discuss why relationship education is important, (c) present our model of a healthy relationship, (d) describe the best practices in relationship and marriage education, and (e) briefly review the effectiveness of marriage education programs. Next we consider two issues facing the field of marital education: (a) using divorce as an outcome and (b) working with lower income and culturally diverse couples.

At the outset, we want to acknowledge that we are only at the tip of the iceberg in having the knowledge we need about healthy marriages and families, particularly when it comes to diverse populations. One goal of this chapter is to stimulate research, both basic and applied, to add to the knowledge base in this area. However, as we have noted elsewhere (e.g., Markman et al., 2003; Stanley, 2001) practitioners and policy makers are acting now, and we want to make sure that couples and families in the community are receiving the best possible, scientifically informed knowledge to guide such efforts.

A basic premise of our chapter is that research clearly indicates that people from all walks of life desire to be in happy, long-lasting, healthy marriages and that healthy marriages benefit children, adults, and our society at large (see Markman, Stanley, Blumberg, Jenkins, & Whiteley, 2004). Because it is beyond the scope of this chapter, we will not examine the interesting question posed by Pinsof (2002) concerning the extent to which the focus in the family psychology field should be on marriage versus other forms of family relationships. For now, we note that, even if marriage were not the main family form in our culture (just over 50% of U.S. households are two married adults [Fields & Casper, 2001]), most people would like to be married (Halford, Markman, Kline, & Stanley, 2003). As noted by Stanley (2003), this is true even for people receiving government assistance and who often cannot see a clear path from where they are to marriage. For example, research from the Fragile Families Project (e.g., Carlson, McLanahan, & England, 2003) suggests that marriage is viewed as the "crowning achievement" for many of the low-income people in their studies. Further, there is increasing evidence that children benefit when they grow up in stable and happy homes (Doherty et al., 2002; McLanahan & Sandefur, 1996). Throughout the rest of the chapter we use illustrations from our own work with PREP (the Prevention and Relationship Enhancement Program) and other research-based approaches to marriage education as examples of the choices researchers and providers in the field have made to address some of the issues raised here.

■ Overview of Marriage Education

Below, we provide an overview of the state of the art and science in relationship and marriage education.

What Is Marriage Education? A Working Definition for Family Psychology

Marriage education refers to curricula that include a set of evidence-based tools and principles that can be used to prevent marital distress and divorce and strengthen relationships and marriages. In addition, the field is using this term to include programs or curricula that target individuals, married or not, with the goal of educating people about the benefits of marriage as well as preparing people for having healthy relationships and marriages in the future by helping them develop reasonable expectations, teaching them better communication and conflict management, promoting ways of thinking that foster healthy relationships, and, where possible, helping people make healthy choices about potential partners in life. Often these programs are offered to people as part of other community-based activities, including premarital counseling in religious organizations, high school classes on relationships, college courses on marriage, prison rehabilitation, workforce development programs for women receiving TANF funds, couples entering the U.S. Army, and couples planning a first child. Typically programs are conceived of as classes and offered to groups of couples or individuals. In our own with work with PREP and its applications, we use groups because it enables us to reach larger numbers of people. We use the term *class* since we offer education, and, in our experience, the idea of going to a class is more appealing to many potential consumers than terms such as therapy. The notion of attending a class versus attending therapy may be especially appealing to young men who may be at higher risk for a variety of problems than young women and who are likely more reluctant to come to couple interventions than young women.

Why Is Marriage Education Important?

Given the high social and emotional costs of family disruption on children and adults (e.g., negative effects of divorce, nonmarital relationship breakup, out of wedlock births, relationship aggression) there is a strong and increasingly recognized need for programs to increase healthy marriage and family relationships. Yet, as a field, family psychology (and our sister fields such as marriage and family therapy) is faced with challenges in reaching people who need our services. Consider the following example from the marital therapy field. Many reviews are available that document how much high-quality, research-based couple therapy can help distressed couples (Jacobson & Christensen, 1998; Sprenkle, 2002). However, we know that in the United States the majority of couples who have divorced (about 80%) have not consulted a mental health professional (C. A. Johnson et al., 2002). In general, people with marital problems are more likely to see a member of clergy for help than a mental health professional (C. A. Johnson et al., 2002). In other words, mental health and marital therapy practitioners generally have poor penetration in their efforts to help couples who are on a trajectory toward divorce and other negative outcomes. Thus, an important way that traditional mental health fields can broaden their reach to couples is by collaborating with clergy in offering marriage education (for more background on the role of religious organizations in marriage education see Stanley, Markman, St. Peters, & Leber, 1995). Such efforts can help those with a strong preventive mind-set and access to couples to engage couples with best practices strategies to prevent marital declines (discussed below).

To summarize, the rationale for marriage education includes three key points. First, key findings converge across studies to point to risk and protective factors that can be targeted. For example, many studies have suggested that it is not the differences between couples that matter in predicting distress and divorce as much as how differences are handled (e.g., Markman & Hahlweg, 1993). In fact, the National Institute of Mental Health considers destructive parental and couples conflict management a generic risk factor for a variety of adult and child mental health problems (Coie et al., 1993). Second, there is growing evidence that couples can be taught to lower specific risks; for example, how to handle differences and to talk without fighting about important issues. Third, outcome results are promising, suggesting that couples can protect positives, decrease negatives, and increase chances for marital happiness over time (e.g., Carroll & Doherty, 2003; Hahlweg, Markman, Thurmaier, Engl, & Eckert, 1998; Markman, Renick, Floyd, & Stanley, 1993). Taken together, these findings have helped us develop a model of healthy relationship functioning.

A Model of a Healthy Marriage

As part of the conference that led to this book, some of the presenters were asked to articulate the model of healthy relationship functioning that framed their research. As we expand in the next section upon best practices in marriage education, we have been working on a model of a healthy marriage using a model that we call *safety theory* (Stanley, Markman, & Whitton, 2002). Research and theory strongly suggest that there are two types of safety: (a) safety in interaction (i.e., being able to talk openly and well [enough] about key issues) and (b) safety in commitment. (e.g., having the security of support and a sense of a clear future). Safety theory dovetails with family psychology's major theories of healthy family functioning, including attachment theory (Furman & Flanagan, 1997), Jacobson and Christensen's (1998) work on acceptance, and emotional expression theory (S. M. Johnson, 1996). Safety theory has guided our intervention work both in PREP and in our clinical practices. For example, If we had one session with a couple or one opportunity to educate a group of couples, based on research and clinical experience, we would help partners to take personal action to do two things: (a) help them stop (or avoid the tendency toward) fighting destructively and talk without fighting about important issues and (b) help them protect and preserve a lasting love though nurturing positive connections and being committed to one another. This will help couples be "safe at home"!

Our experience training a diverse range of couples and professionals suggests that the concept of being safe at home has wide appeal, acceptance, and educational value. For the talk at the conference that spawned this book, we expanded the safety theory to reflect what we now call the baseball model of a healthy marriage.

Safety Theory in Action: A Baseball Model of a Healthy Marriage

Picture a baseball diamond in your mind and then imagine each of the bases. Each base represents one of the three pillars of a happy, healthy marriage. At first base is handling negative emotions or being able to talk without fighting about important issues. In our research we have identified four key destructive ways of handling negative emotions that characterize couples heading for problems. In PREP we call these patterns *danger signs* and they include escalation, invalidation, negative interpretations, and withdrawal. Because the danger signs predict distress, couples need a way to avoid or counteract these behaviors in order to handle their (inevitable) differences constructively.

At second base is developing and protecting the positive connections in the relationship. Fun, friendship, romance, going on dates, talking as friends, and even philosophizing together during quiet times—all these activities help solidify the bond between partners. At third base is commitment and the need to sacrifice for one's relationship. In baseball, sometimes the players have to sacrifice their at-bat to move the runners forward. Similarly, one way to keep a relationship moving forward is to be willing to sacrifice one's own inclinations and time so that the partner, and ultimately the relationship, may benefit. Maintaining a firm commitment to the relationship and not threatening its existence permits stability and happiness to grow. At the pitchers mound is to "do your own part" in the relationship to make it as healthy and happy as possible. Partners in relationships on the road to distress often blame each other for problems, instead of focusing on what they can do to be the best possible partner they can be. Finally, when all of the above is working, people feel safe at home—which in our model is, of course, home plate.

Marriage education programs, like PREP, teach couples skills to handle negative emotions and preserve the positive connections, as well as teach critical principles of healthy relationship functioning, such as commitment (e.g., not threatening the stability of the relationship when angry), making one's marriage a major priority, and having a long-term view for one's marriage and family. These are crucial aspects of maintaining both kinds of elemental safety.

Marriage education also includes information that differences are to be expected, so that when they occur, partners will know that they are a natural part of the marital terrain, rather than a fault line that dooms them and indicates they made the wrong choice in a marital partner. Finally, when men and woman are asked about their major relationship complaints/goals, women generally describe a desire to talk more and to have more closeness, while the major desire of men is to fight less (Markman & Kraft, 1989; Markman, Stanley, et al., 2004). Therefore, one of the objectives of best practices marriage education is to help couples talk, in a safe way, without fighting. At the same time, especially working with younger and happier couples, we try to help couples protect and preserve the great things in their relationship—the reasons people want to be married in the first place (e.g., friendship, fun, sexuality, spiritual connection).

Negatives Versus Positives (First Versus Second Base)

Early interactional research clearly suggested that negative interaction predicted outcomes significantly better than positive interaction. Based on this research, Notarius and Markman (1993) suggested that one "zinger" erased 5–20 positive actions of kindness. However, more recent research is finding support for positive factors being just as, if not more, important (Karney & Bradbury, 1995). We suggest that negative interaction is more predictive of divorce as an outcome, but when predicting overall satisfaction, positives and negatives should (and in some cases do) predict equally well.

There is some evidence that, when it comes to divorce proneness (i.e., thoughts and actions that lead to divorce), males are more sensitive to the presence of negatives and females are more sensitive to the absence of positives (Stanley, Markman, & Whitton, 2002). Thus, an important issue for future research is to assess how well positives and negatives predict as a function of gender and the outcome measure used. However, there is likely to be more heterogeneity on the positive side of things. For example, Notarius and Markman (1993) note that the famous Russian writer Tolstoy wrote in the introduction of his novel Anna Karenina (and we are paraphrasing here), "All happy families are alike and each unhappy family is different, each in its own fashion." Notarius and Markman (1993) note that marital research shows that "Tolstoy was wrong!" Instead, research suggests that marital unhappiness comes in only a few forms (e.g., interactional danger signs), while marital happiness is "a many-splendored thing" (i.e., there are a variety of ways to have a great marriage).

Best Practices in Marital/Relationship Education

In this section we list and briefly review five major aspects of the best practices in marriage education as they relate to family psychology. For a more detailed discussion see a recent paper by Halford et al. (2003).

1. *Risk and protective factors for marital happiness and divorce.* Best practices in marriage education are based on a model of prevention that focuses on empirically confirmed risk and protective factors (Coie et al., 1993). In other words, evidence-based marriage education programs are based on a model of a healthy marriage. Table 5.1 displays many of these factors and is organized by the extent to which these factors are static or dynamic. Static factors are not likely to change as a function of intervention, whereas dynamic factors are more modifiable (Stanley, 2001). More focus should be directed toward the dynamic factors because they are easier to change in interventions than are static factors. For example, destructive interaction patterns are dynamic risk factors that erode the positive elements of

TABLE 5.1   *Examples of Empirically Informed Risk Factors for Marital Distress and Divorce*

Static Factors	Dynamic Factors
Some personality factors	Interaction danger signs
Parental divorce	Communication and conflict management ability
Cohabitation history	Physical aggression (some types)
Previous divorce	Unrealistic expectations
Religious dissimilarity	Commitment and motivation
Young age at marriage	
Economic status	
Psychopathology	
Racism	

Note. Reprinted with permission from PREP, Inc.

marital relationships and thus should be the focus of couples intervention, both preventative and therapeutic. Similarly, because fun and friendship are dynamic protective factors they also should be intervention targets (Markman et al., in press). It is beyond the scope of this chapter to provide a more comprehensive review of the research on risk and protective factors, but good reviews can be found elsewhere (e.g., Halford et al., 2003; Karney & Bradbury, 1995; Stanley, 2001).

2. *Best practices programs are dynamic and evolving.* Best practice programs are dynamic in that they are regularly updated based on ongoing research (Stanley, Markman, & Jenkins, 2002). For example, we regularly modify the content of the PREP program based on our own basic and evaluation research as well as based on other advancements in the field. Thus, best practices marriage education programs are not only a research-based and evaluated curriculum, but also are a vehicle (and metaphor) for the process of building and delivering empirically based concepts to couples (Markman, Whitton, et al., 2004).

3. *Best practices programs are flexible.* Best practices programs are also highly modular and flexible so that they can be tailored to specific audiences (Stanley, Markman, & Jenkins, 2002). For example, we do not think that *all* the existing content is appropriate for all the variations of people who can benefit from marriage education (e.g., low-income women without partners, high school students); thus, adapting programs to various consumers is recommended. Such adaptations are more viable in a program with a modular and flexible structure. Best practice programs can also be used by a variety of providers. We believe that research-based programs can reach those couples who need them the most by using a dissemination approach that targets naturally occurring community organizations and training service providers in these settings to effectively use the program (Markman, Whitton, et al., 2004). This model encourages collaboration with experts who work with diverse community populations and encourages practitioners who are "experts" with these couples and families to apply the curriculum to specific contexts. For example, the Oklahoma Marriage Initiative offers guidelines for providers who complete the regular PREP training to apply the curriculum in high schools.

One of the benefits of this dissemination model is that people tend to relate better and have a more positive alliance when the service provider is close to the audience on dimensions relevant to them in terms of ethnicity, culture, and communication styles. In general, research suggests that research-based interventions tend to be the most effective when people in their community have been trained specifically to work with a particular program (Laurenceau, Stanley, Olmos-Gallo, Baucom, & Markman, in press; Markman, Whitton, et al., 2004; Stanley et al., 2001).

4. *Best practices programs are short term.* Best practices marriage education programs are generally short term for several reasons. First, time is a major issue for everyone and couples are reluctant to make commitments for long-term interventions. Second, in prevention, the motivation associated with marital distress is often not present. While people cite strong interest in taking programs to achieve the goals of learning skills and principles to prevent problems from developing (C. A. Johnson et al., 2002), our experience indicates that when it comes time to sign

up and attend, translating interest to attendance is a major problem. In our experience couples will be more likely to make a commitment to attend a short-term class than a longer program. Third, there is growing evidence that short-term prevention approaches are reasonably effective (Carroll & Doherty, 2003). It has been suggested that a weakness of a short-term interventions (8–12 sessions) is how difficult it is to try to impact emotionally laden (even unconscious) processes and distal outcomes (Pinsof, 2002). Yet, as we review below, there are some empirical data to suggest that couples can learn the skills associated with having a healthy marriage in short-term interventions, that when using these skills to talk safely, couples can access emotionally laden material with each other, and that these couples may have reduced risk for future relationship distress (Halford et al., 2003).

5. *Best practices programs help couples get more intervention when needed.* In marriage education classes, where we see a large number of couples, we recognize that many people in the room are dealing with many other issues and problems. Perhaps one of the most useful outcomes for some people who come to marriage education classes is learning about and being more motivated to utilize resources in their community for current or future problems.

We strongly recommend that all leaders of marriage education classes have available a referral document that lists the common issues people in the room may be experiencing and provides local resources for dealing with these problems. We have developed such an instrument and it is included as an appendix to this chapter. In addition, we are currently investigating the hypothesis that when someone with serious problems has a good experience in a relationship education class, they are more likely to seek help for problems, now and in the future. There is some evidence that this is so (Schumm, Silliman, & Bell, 2000). In addition, qualitative evaluations of our work with women who are in unhealthy relationships suggest that one outcome of participating in marriage education is that they now know enough about what makes a great marriage to know what to avoid in the future, and they may decide to break up with a current partner.

■ Is Marriage Education Effective?

It is beyond the scope of the present chapter to provide a detailed review of the state of the art in evaluating prevention and education programs for couples. Readers are referred to one of the excellent reviews that are available (e.g., Carroll & Doherty, 2003; Fagan, Patterson, & Rector, 2002; Halford et al., 2003; Silliman, Stanley, Coffin, Markman, & Jordan, 2002). In brief, just about every research-based program that has been evaluated preintervention to postintervention (e.g., PREP, Couples Communication, Relationship Enhancement) shows that couples can learn skills which link to marital success (e.g., Giblin, Sprenkle, & Sheehan, 1985; Guerney & Maxson, 1990; Silliman et al., 2002).

PREP is the only program that has been evaluated in terms of long-term effects. As noted by Halford et al. (2003) in a review of the best practices in marriage education: "Only five published studies have follow-ups of more than 12 months, and all of these studies have focused on PREP or a variant of PREP. Markman and colleagues found in two studies that skills-based relationship education was associated with enhanced relationship satisfaction or functioning 2 and 5 years after marriage (Hahlweg et al., 1998; Markman et al., 1993). The Markman et al. study also found that across the 3-, 4-, and 5-year follow-ups, the intervention couples reported significantly fewer instances of spousal physical violence than control couples (p. 17)." Most important, there is evidence in a number of studies that couples can learn to reduce patterns of negative interaction and that such changes can hold up over years (Hahlweg et al., 1998; Markman et al., 1993). There is also, in some studies, evidence of an effect for lowering the risks of divorce (Halford et al., 2003).

While results are promising, it is important to note that the longitudinal follow-up studies of PREP do not show consistent long-term effects (e.g., Van Widenfelt, Hosman, Schaap, & van der Staak, 1996). Further, in other fields, long-term outcome studies conducted by investigators other than the primary program developers have not been as positive as earlier studies. On the other hand, there are very encouraging findings on programs such as variations on PREP from a range of researchers on numerous continents (Hahlweg et al., 1998; Halford, Sanders, & Behrens, 2001; Markman et al., 1993; Stanley et al., 2001)

Mechanisms of Change

While evaluations of research-based prevention programs like PREP have yielded promising results, relatively little is known about the mechanisms that link processes to outcomes. Recent efforts by several research teams are starting to make some headway in this important area (Schilling, Baucom, Burnett, Allen, & Ragland, 2003; Stanley, Kline, Olmos-Gallo, & Markman, 2005). One key theory underlying most best practices marriage education programs is that an increased ability to manage negative emotions well will be associated with positive relationship outcomes. As noted by Coie et al. (1993), prevention trials, especially those with random assignment that modify key causal variables, are the best way to test predictions concerning casual mechanisms. Thus, one important future direction for research is to conduct studies that use the results of prevention trails to examine questions concerning mechanisms of change.

■ Two of the Issues Facing the Field

For the purposes of this chapter we have decided to focus on two of the major issues facing the field of marriage education: divorce as an outcome and marriage education programs for welfare and lower income families. Our goal here is to briefly explore the theoretical, methodological, and/or application aspects of these issues rather than provide definitive solutions. Further, we note that there are many other important issues facing this field that we are not covering here.

Divorce as an Outcome

In past intervention outcome research with couples, relationship dissolution has typically been viewed as a negative outcome. As such, one aim of prevention efforts has often been to reduce the probability of divorce or breakup. From this perspective, prevention programs are considered to be *successful* if completion of the program leads to a greater likelihood that the couple stays together compared to control groups or alternative interventions.

It is not surprising that divorce has traditionally been viewed as a negative outcome or that the reduction of breakup has been considered a positive outcome. From a research perspective, the process of divorce is typically viewed as a stressful life transition that increases the likelihood of negative emotional, behavioral, and heath outcomes for adults and children (see Amato, 2000, 2001a). However, some scholars suggest that divorce, in and of itself, is not inherently bad or good (Hetherington & Kelly, 2002; Pinsof, 2002). Researchers have often failed to consider the full range of factors that affect adjustment pre- and postseparation, such as the presence of interspousal aggression (Jaffe, Poisson, & Cunningham, 2001). In general, research suggests that the relationship between divorce and negative outcomes for children is not driven by divorce per se, but by the amount and severity of interspousal conflict and aggression witnessed by the child before, during, and after the divorce (Amato, 2001a; Johnston, 1994). There is some evidence that children from high-conflict homes may actually be better off if their parents divorce, especially if the conflict subsides following the divorce (Amato, 2001b). Many divorces may actually occur in the context of low-conflict, devitalized marriages, rather than high-conflict marriages. From a marriage education perspective, these are the divorces that may be the most preventable, and they are also the ones that, if prevented, may have the clearest, unequivocally good implications for child outcomes.

Further, some researchers have found that factors such as interparental conflict and violence account for more variance in adjustment difficulties than does divorce (Gano-Phillips & Fincham, 1995). When exposed to interparental aggression and violence, children tend to have more internalizing (e.g., anxiety, depression) and externalizing (aggression, disobedience) problems than do nonexposed children, and they tend to show poorer school and social competence (Graham-Bermann, 1998; Graham-Bermann & Levedosky, 1998; Grych & Fincham, 1990; Rossman, Hughes, & Rosenberg, 2000; Wolfe, Jaffe, Wilson, & Zak, 1985). On the other hand, there is accumulating evidence that there are negative outcomes for children resulting from divorce independently of the effects of conflict (e.g., Cherlin, Chase-Lansdale, & McRae, 1998), and there is growing evidence that family structure matters for child outcomes (McLanahan & Sandefur, 1996).

In light of such findings, it is possible that divorce or breakup, compared to continued exposure to high levels of interpersonal conflict, may represent a more beneficial outcome for some couples and children. We suggest that prevention and intervention researchers carefully consider the assumptions underlying their reasons for using divorce as an outcome measure, particularly as a measure of *negative* outcome. Yet not even the coauthors of this chapter would agree, in general terms, about the conditions under which divorce is desirable or not. While it is easy to agree on the extremes (for example, no one we know seriously advocates that dangerously conflicted couples remain together for the sake of the children), there is a vast gray area here where the shades of gray look quite different depending on one's background and perspectives. What is not hard to determine is the fact that marital therapists, in general, are a good deal more liberal in their attitudes about most everything, including divorce, than the average person who might desire (or need) their services. So, it is not merely researchers who should evaluate their assumptions in various ways, but it is important for practitioners to do so as well.

In general, both couples and those who work closely with them in marriage education programs (e.g., clergy, marriage educators) are likely to view divorce as a negative outcome, yet marital therapists are sometimes neutral about how to view divorce as outcome (Stanley, Markman, & Lobitz, 1988). Future research should carefully examine the hypothesis that many partners, especially men, may avoid mental health counselors and seek out clergy instead when maritally distressed because of perceptions that therapists are neutral about divorce (Waite et al., 2002). This hypothesis is supported by research data that shows that most couples who divorce do not seek out marital therapy and when they do it is more often from clergy than by mental health or marital counselors (C. A. Johnson et al., 2002). In general, more research is needed on how divorce is viewed by adults, children, and mental health professionals.

A challenge for future researchers is to continue to elucidate the circumstances in which relationship dissolution may be considered a positive outcome. Further, it would be helpful for researchers and clinicians to work together and establish research-based methods to determine when the benefits of a couple's breaking up outweigh the risks they may incur if they stay together.

Yet another issue for future research and theory is that the goals of marital education (or marital therapy) may be different in terms the goals of adults and the needs of children. For example, from a child welfare perspective having a marriage that is stable and devoid of major destructive conflict may be a good enough marriage (Amato, 2001b), but may be very unsatisfying for most adults.

In sum, if a couple is in a high-conflict and aggressive relationship, breaking up *before* marriage or having kids might actually be considered a positive outcome. We suggest that researchers recognize that these are complicated issues that deserve thoughtful consideration in the development, evaluation, and dissemination of prevention and education programs in family psychology. For example, the physical and mental health of couples and their children should be assessed prior to breakup, immediately after breakup, and several years post breakup. In addition, the potential mediating and moderating variables, such as the level of interparental conflict, socioeconomic status, and availability of social support or other community resources, should be evaluated.

Last, there is one circumstance in which it is no controversy at all whether dissolution is a good thing: among couples who have been contemplating a future, but who have not yet married or had children and where there are reasons to believe that their relationship will be high risk with little hope for mitigation. If relationship education were generally able to help more people make wiser choices earlier on, and if such educational efforts were disseminated to people who were at earlier stages, this would be a useful, noncontroversial benefit to countless couples who likely need help breaking up before they are constrained into unhealthy or unwise relationships.

Intervening With Welfare or Low-Income Families

As noted earlier, there is growing evidence of the positive effects of marriage education programs (with premarital and marital couples) with primarily middle-class couples. Recently, Stanley (2003) summarized situations in which research is lacking, yet there is great interest in moving forward with marriage education interventions. These include couples with (a) very low income and high economic stress, (b) lower education levels, (c) ambiguous commitment between partners, including about a future and exclusivity, (d) a child out of wedlock, and (e) a male partner with serious problems, such as substance abuse, domestic violence, poor job history/opportunities, or a criminal history.

A key question is To what extent do best practices marriage education programs transport to populations that have not (to date) been the major focus of marriage education research (Stanley, 2003)? For example, how generalizable are these programs to couples who have a child and might not be together if not for the child? These are empirical questions that are starting to be addressed, and it is hoped that new research funds will encourage more dissemination efforts, clinical trials, and basic research studies.

Situations Where We Have Somewhat More Confidence.   There are three types of lower income couples about whom recent research gives us somewhat more confidence in applying current marriage education programs (Stanley, 2003). These include (a) younger couples with clear commitment, (b) working class (lower income but not in poverty) couples, and (c) interracial and interethnic couples. For example, we conducted a recent program evaluation of a version of PREP being used in the U.S. Army with young soldiers and their spouses (Stanley et al., 2003). Over 50% of the sample consisted of couples in which one or both were ethnic minorities, and most were married and low income (though at least one partner had a job). The effect sizes of the positive impact of this intervention (from pre to post to a 1-month follow-up) were among the strongest in the marriage education and marriage intervention fields on measures of satisfaction, negative communication, and confidence in handling conflict. Further, these effects were as strong for minority couples as for other couples. We do need to note that this was a pilot study that lacked random assignment and a control group and had a relatively short follow-up. We have planned a more in-depth research study with random assignment and richer assessment.

There are numerous complexities when it comes to transporting marriage education programs to those lower income couples with whom many in the family psychology field have little clinical or research experience (and even those with whom we have somewhat more confidence in working). For now, we highlight two general themes for readers to consider.

Low-Income and Welfare Families and Marriage

First, as noted earlier, a basic desire of most adults, regardless of age, income, or ethnicity, is to have a long-term, loving, happy relationship. Further, most people clearly want to achieve this relationship within the context of marriage. Much research now demonstrates why so many couples have this goal: stable and happy marriages benefit children, adults, and society. Recent federally funded, multisite research on fragile families (e.g., families who are low income, highly disadvantaged, and have a child out of wedlock) has demonstrated that this goal is also held by many whom policy experts had presumed were not interested in marriage because of the lower frequency of marriage (McLanahan, Garfinkel, & Mincy, 2001). In fact, both liberals and conservatives tend to agree that research indicates there are benefits of marriage to most low-income people, although the benefits for African Americans may be less clear (Blankenhorn, 2003).

Although low-income and ethnic minority individuals report that they value marriage as much other ethnic and income groups, there are considerable barriers to successful and lasting marriages for these groups. These couples face additional stressors that may put them at higher risk for marital dissatisfaction, discord, violence, and relationship dissolution (Seefeldt & Smock, 2004). These stressors include financial hardship, employment difficulties, dangerous living conditions, poor access to resources, lack of community support, and discrimination.

Practical survival matters may often take precedence over relationship difficulties, which make it difficult to access and engage these couples. Disagreements or marital dissatisfaction often must take a backseat to finding work or paying bills. In addition, such couples face great challenges in staying together because of the external forces straining their individual resources and a sense of fatalism if the relationship is failing. The developmental course of relationships is also different for low-income and some ethnic minority couples, in that these couples tend to have unplanned children before marriage, which creates further stressors on relationship development (Ooms, 2002). For example, according to recent census data, 70–75% of African American women are expected to marry compared to 91% of White women (Fields & Casper, 2001), and African American women are twice as likely to divorce as White or Latino women (Tucker & Mitchell-Kernan, 1995).

Based on all of the above, some critics of promoting marriage education for welfare families suggest that marriage education classes may push people who do not want to be married, or should not be married, into unhealthy marriages. In fact, best practices programs that are designed to help couples have healthy marriages are focused on communication skills, marriage preparation, helping individuals clarify whether they are indeed suited for marriage, or whether marriage (or a future) would be wise with a specific partner. Most of the themes in best practices marriage education programs are universal in terms of communication skills and principles of handling negative emotions and thus can be used with a variety of people, both individuals and couples. For example, a woman who has a child and is not interested in marrying the father but is interested in marriage at some point can benefit from learning about risk factors for divorce, how to handle conflict in any relationship, knowing what to expect in relationships, and mate selection issues. Therefore, there is reason to believe that some of the preventive benefits of marriage education might be universal, regardless of whether this is or should be a trajectory toward marriage.

Nevertheless, for historical reasons, there is a mistrust of professionals in health care, social services, and psychology for both lower income and ethnic minority populations, which provides an additional barrier to prevention and intervention with these couples. Because of this mistrust, religious or community organizations may present a better base for outreach to low-income minority couples (Stanley et al., 1995). Furthermore, there are significant differences among African American, Native American, Latino, and Asian low-income couples, as well as differences between the urban and rural poor. This means that service providers who are familiar with these populations need to adapt best practices programs to the population they are working with and that the field needs to explore empirically the results of these efforts. On a more optimistic note, recent surveys have indicated a strong interest among both lower income men and women in participating in marriage education programs. For example, over 70% of survey participants in a recent random survey in Oklahoma said they would like to participate in a relationship education program (C. A. Johnson et al., 2002). Of particular note is that interest in relationship education was higher among lower income and higher risk people. In addition, the Oklahoma survey also indicated that most citizens (85%) supported a statewide initiative to curb divorce rates and strengthen families. This support was particularly high among minority and low-income respondents (C. A. Johnson et al., 2002).

Making empirically supported programs available to interested couples and individuals who have traditionally not received services from the mainstream mental health community can be seen as an equal access to resources issue (Markman, 2000; Ooms, 2002). While more research is needed on low-income groups, using a dissemination model in which program deliverers are known by the couples (discussed below) is one way to tailor relationship intervention programs for each group (Markman, Whitton, et al., 2004).

Dissemination of Research-Based Programs

As noted earlier, one key to transporting marriage education to welfare and low-income families is to train program leaders who are experts with their audiences—those who can reach out to underserved groups and use illustrations and examples relevant to their audiences. Modifications made to the intervention model are typically in a number of key categories: literacy, learning style, the use of culturally appropriate metaphors, the nature of the relationship (committed or not), and stories and terminology (Markman, Stanley, et al., 2004; Stanley & Markman, 1997).

Further, experts who work with minority and low-income couples are often very vocal about not changing the empirically based content even if research has not yet shown effectiveness with the populations they serve. As George Young suggests, they feel that it is *their* job to translate the empirically supported principles to populations they serve (Stanley & Young, 2003). We believe that, with appropriate modifications and service providers, adhering to empirically based content even if not tested with the target populations is better than offering no services or services that are not research based. Of course, conducting both basic research and evaluations of marriage education services with lower income couples and individuals is a high priority.

■ Conclusions and Future Directions

In conclusion, prevention work, whether it is offered through private organizations, religious organizations, private practitioners, or federally funded programs, should be based on research. Several research-based relationship education programs are available (see Halford et al., 2003; Silliman et al., 2002); however, future research is needed to assure the generalizability of these programs to diverse populations and circumstances. As noted above, little research has focused on the effectiveness of marriage education programs with minority couples. Moreover, certain circumstances may call for additional or modified educational materials, such as with domestic violence, mental illness, drug abuse, unmarried partners with children, or serious economic strain. In addition, there are virtually no research-based programs available that target the specific issues associated with remarriage and with cohabitation. The need for attention to these areas stems from the facts that being remarried and cohabiting before marriage are both risk factors for future divorce and that both situations are increasing at fairly dramatic rates.

Furthermore, since society tends to benefit from healthy marriages, it has made sense to policy makers to invest in the marital well-being of couples. As noted in the introduction, various branches of federal and local government are increasingly involved in supporting happy, healthy, long-term marriages by funding opportunities for marriage education (and marital therapy) for those couples who desire it (e.g., Horn, 2003). Substantial new funds are also available for research evaluating the effects of marriage education programs, especially those delivered in community settings to low-income couples with children. Many innovative efforts are already under way, for example, some states are providing free handbooks or videos on keys to strong marriages, effects of divorce, and community resources to couples applying for marriage licenses. In some areas, public service announcements describe the benefits of being married. Oklahoma has taken the lead in providing free relationship education to a wide array of married or soon-to-be married couples in high schools and even in the juvenile justice and prison systems. Though not without some controversy, these federal and state initiatives will spark new large-scale and large sample research, new interventions, and theory that will shape the field for years to come.

Finally, it is clear that much more basic, applied, and intervention research needs to be done in the marriage and family fields in general and with lower income and welfare families in particular. Nevertheless, we believe that we know enough to move forward now with thoughtful, carefully designed applications of research-based marriage education programs. As Stanley has said, "We know enough to act, and we should take action to know more" (Stanley, 2001, p. 278). The next decade will be a fertile time for both basic and applied research in the marriage education and family psychology fields. We hope this chapter has provided some directions to guide these fields as we head into these exciting times.

■ Appendix: Getting More Help When There Are Serious Problems

The workshop you are taking is an educational program that teaches you skills and principles that can help you build strong and healthy marriages and couple or family relationships. However, it is not designed to address serious relationship and individual problems.

Since you are taking this time to think more about your life and relationships, it may also be a good time to think about other services that you or others you care about may need. We provide this sheet of information to ALL couples and individuals in these workshops so that you will be aware of other available services.

Even if your main goal right now is to improve your marriage or relationship, difficulties in other areas could make it that much harder to make your relationship work. Likewise, if you are having really severe problems in your relationship, it can make dealing with any of these other problems that much harder.

The good news is that participating in this workshop can be a gateway to getting other services. It can provide you with awareness, motivation, and tools to help you take other steps to improve your life. Here are some areas where seeking additional help could be really important for you and your family.

Financial Problems

- Serious money problems make everything else harder.
- Unemployment/job loss can be one of the key sources of conflict and stress for couples.
- While this workshop can help you as a couple to work more as a team, you may need more help to learn to manage your finances or find a job.

Serious Marital or Other Family Problems or Stresses

- If you have serious marital or adult relationship problems where more help is needed than can be provided in this educational workshop, you can seek counseling from someone who specializes in helping couples.
- Coping with a serious, life threatening, or chronic illness or disability in a child or adult can place a lot of stress on caregivers and their family relationships. Community resources often exist to help families with these kinds of issues.

Substance Abuse, Addictions, and Other Compulsive Behaviors

- No matter what else you have to deal with in life, it will be harder if you or your partner, or another close family member, has a substance abuse problem.

- Drug or alcohol abuse and addiction robs a person of the ability to handle life well, have close relationships, and be a good parent.
- Alcohol abuse can also make it harder to control anger and violence.
- Other problems families sometimes face include eating disorders, sexual addictions, and gambling.

You need to decide to get help with these problems to make your life better and the life of those you love. It will make it easier if your partner or spouse supports this decision.

Mental Health Problems

- Mental health problems come in many forms, from anxiety to depression to schizophrenia, and place a great deal of stress on couple and family relationships.
- Depression is particularly common when there are serious relationship problems.
- Having thoughts of suicide is often a sign of depression. Seek help if you struggle with such thoughts.

The good news is that there are now many effective treatments for mental health problems with services available in all counties, including options for those with less means to pay.

Domestic Aggression and Violence

- While domestic violence can take many forms, *the key is doing whatever is needed to make sure you and your children are safe.*
- While domestic aggression and violence of any sort is wrong and dangerous, experts now recognize different types, for example:
  — Some couples have arguments that get out of control, with frustration spilling over into pushing, shoving, or slapping. This can be dangerous, especially if you don't take strong measures to stop the patterns from continuing.
  — The type of domestic violence that is usually the most dangerous of all and least likely to change is when a male uses aggression and force to scare and control a woman. Verbal abuse, threats of harm, and/or forced sexual activity can be part of this pattern.
- This workshop/program is not a treatment program for physical aggression. If you are dealing with aggression and violence in your relationship, you need more help than what can be offered in this program. That might mean seeking marital or relationship counseling or seeking the advice of domestic violence experts.
- If you have any questions about the safety of your relationship, you should contact a domestic violence program or hotline, especially if you feel like you are in danger of being harmed.

The bottom line is doing what you need to do to assure that you and your children are safe. If you ever feel you are in immediate danger from your partner or others, call 911 for help or contact your domestic violence hotline.

Where Can We Get More Help?

If you, your partner, or your relationship experiences any of these special problems, we strongly recommend that you get more help.

Your workshop leaders may have attached additional contact information for some resources in your area. You can also ask your leaders directly (in person or by phone) if you would like any other suggestions.

National Resources

- A national domestic violence hotline: SAFELINE, 1-800-522-7233
- A national Web site with links for help with substance abuse and mental health issues:
  — www.samhsa.gov/public/look_frame.html
  — A national hotline for referrals to substance abuse treatment: 1-800-662-HELP
  — A national hotline for suicide prevention: National Hopeline Network, 1-800-SUICIDE (784-2433)

Local resources to consider: There are community mental health centers in all areas of the U. S. Other counseling centers and mental health professionals are often available as well (both nonreligious and religious). Also, both clergy and family physicians are usually well aware of resources for various needs in their communities, so consider asking them for suggestions.

■ Acknowledgments

Support for this research and for preparation of the manuscript was provided in part by Grant 5-RO1-MH35525-12, "The Long-Term Effects of Premarital Intervention" (awarded to Howard Markman, Scott Stanley, and Lydia Prado), from the National Institute of Mental Health, Division of Services and Intervention Research, Adult and Geriatric Treatment and Prevention Branch. The handout reproduced in the appendix was produced and is distributed by PREP, Inc. It was reprinted here with permission from PREP, Inc. Input was provided by the Oklahoma Marriage Initiative along with Scott Stanley, Howard Markman, Theodora Ooms, Natalie Jenkins, and Bruce Carruth. Special thanks to both Marcia Smith, the executive director of the Oklahoma Coalition Against Domestic Violence and Sexual Assault, for her feedback and recommendations and Larry Didier, Prevention Programs Coordinator for the Oklahoma Department of Mental Health and Substance Abuse Services.

■ References

Amato, P. R. (2000). The consequences of divorce for adults and children. *Journal of Marriage and the Family, 62*(4), 1269–1287.

Amato, P. R. (2001a). Children of divorce in the 1990s: An update of the Amato and Keith (1991) meta-analysis. *Journal of Family Psychology, 15*(3), 355–370.

Amato, P. R. (2001b). Good enough marriages: Parental discord, divorce, and children's well-being. *The Virginia Journal of Social Policy and the Law, 9*, 71–94.

Blankenhorn, D. (2003). The marriage problem. *American Experiment Quarterly, 6*, 61–71.

Carlson, M., McLanahan, S., & England, P. (2003). *Union formation in fragile families* (Working Paper No. 01-06-FF). Princeton, NJ: Center for Research on Child Wellbeing.

Carroll, J. S., & Doherty, W. J. (2003). Evaluating the effectiveness of premarital prevention programs: A meta-analytic review of outcome research. *Family Relations: Interdisciplinary Journal of Applied Family Studies, 52*(2), 105–118.

Cherlin, A. J., Chase-Lansdale, P. L., & McRae, C. (1998). Effects of parental divorce on mental health through the life course. *American Sociological Review, 63*, 239–249.

Coie, J. D., Watt, N. F., West, S. G., Hawkins, J. D., Asarnow, J. R., Markman, H. J., et al. (1993). The science of prevention: A conceptual framework and some directions for a national research program. *American Psychologist, 48*(10), 1013–1022.

Doherty, W. J., Galston, W., Glenn, N. D., Gottman, J. M., Markey, B., Markman, H. J., et al. (2002). *Why marriage matters: Twenty-one conclusions from the social sciences.* New York: Institute for American Values.

Fagan, P. F., Patterson, R. W., & Rector, R. E. (2002). *Marriage and welfare reform: The overwhelming evidence that marriage education works.* Washington, DC: The Heritage Foundation.

Fields, J., & Casper, L. (2001). *America's families and living arrangements: March 2000.* (Current Population Report, P20-537). Washington DC: U.S. Census Bureau.

Furman, W., & Flanagan, A. S. (1997). The influence of earlier relationships on marriage: An attachment perspective. In W. K. Halford & H. J. Markman (Eds.), *Clinical handbook of marriage and couples interventions* (pp. 179–202). New York: Wiley and Sons.

Gano-Phillips, S., & Fincham, F. D. (1995). Family conflict, divorce, and children's adjustment. In M. A. Fitzpatrick & A. L. Vangelisti (Eds.), *Explaining family interactions* (pp. 206–231). Thousand Oaks, CA: Sage.

Giblin, P., Sprenkle, D. H., & Sheehan, R. (1985). Enrichment outcome research: A meta-analysis of premarital, marital, and family interventions. *Journal of Marital and Family Therapy, 11*(3), 257–271.

Graham-Bermann, S. A. (1998). The impact of woman abuse on children's social development: Research and theoretical perspectives. In G. W. Holden & R. Geffner (Eds.), *Children exposed to marital violence: Theory, research, and applied issues* (pp. 21–54). Washington, DC: American Psychological Association.

Graham-Bermann, S. A., & Levedosky, A. A. (1998). The social functioning of pre-school age children whose mothers are emotionally and physically abusive. *Journal of Emotional Abuse, 1*(1), 59–84.

Grych, J. H., & Fincham, F. D. (1990). Marital conflict and children's adjustment: A cognitive-contextual framework. *Psychological Bulletin, 108*(2), 267–290.

Guerney, B. G., & Maxson, P. (1990). Marital and family enrichment research: A decade review and a look ahead. *Journal of Marriage and the Family, 52,* 1127–1135.

Hahlweg, K., Markman, H. J., Thurmaier, F., Engl, J., & Eckert, V. (1998). Prevention of marital distress: Results of a German prospective longitudinal study. *Journal of Family Psychology, 12*(4), 543–556.

Halford, W. K., Markman, H. J., Kline, G. H., & Stanley, S. M. (2003). Best practice in couple relationship education. *Journal of Marital and Family Therapy, 29*(3), 385–406.

Halford, W. K., Sanders, M. R., & Behrens, B. C. (2001). Can skills training prevent relationship problems in at-risk couples? Four-year effects of a behavioral relationship education program. *Journal of Family Psychology, 15,* 750–768.

Hetherington, E. M., & Kelly, J. (2002). *For better or worse: Divorce reconsidered.* New York: Norton.

Horn, W. (2003, June). *Going to the chapel: The president's healthy marriage initiative.* Paper presented at the Smart Marriages Conference, Reno, NV.

Jacobson, N. S., & Christensen, A. (1998). *Acceptance and change in couple therapy: A therapist's guide to transforming relationships.* New York: Norton.

Jaffe, P. G., Poisson, S. E., & Cunningham, A. (2001). Domestic violence and high-conflict divorce: Developing a new generation of research for children. In S. A. Graham-Bermann & J. L. Edleson (Eds.), *Domestic violence in the lives of children: The future of research, intervention, and social policy* (pp. 189–202). Washington, DC: American Psychological Association.

Johnson, C. A., Stanley, S. M., Glenn, N. D., Amato, P. A., Nock, S. L., Markman, H. J., et al. (2002). *Marriage in Oklahoma: 2001 baseline statewide survey on marriage and divorce* (S02096 OKDHS). Oklahoma City: Oklahoma Department of Human Services.

Johnson, S. M. (1996). *The practice of emotionally focused marital therapy: Creating connection.* New York: Taylor & Francis.

Johnston, J. R. (1994). High conflict divorce. *The Future of Children, 4*(1), 165–182.

Karney, B. R., & Bradbury, T. N. (1995). The longitudinal course of marital quality and stability: A review of theory, method, and research. *Psychological Bulletin, 118,* 3–34.

Laurenceau, J.-P., Stanley, S. M., Olmos-Gallo, P. A., Baucom, B., & Markman, H. J. (in press). Community-based prevention of marital dysfunction: Multilevel modeling of a randomized effectiveness study. *Journal of Consulting and Clinical Psychology.*

Markman, H. J. (2000, December). *Adaptation of evidence-based divorce prevention programs in religious organizations: Strange bedfellows or healthy marriages?* Paper presented at the World Congress on the Prevention of Mental Health Problems conference, Carter Center, Atlanta, GA.

Markman, H. J., & Hahlweg, K. (1993). The prediction and prevention of marital distress: An international perspective. *Clinical Psychology Review, 13*(1), 29–43.

Markman, H. J., & Kraft, S. A. (1989). Men and women in marriage: Dealing with gender differences in marital therapy. *The Behavior Therapist, 12,* 51–56.

Markman, H. J., Renick, M. J., Floyd, F. J., & Stanley, S. M. (1993). Preventing marital distress through communication and conflict management training: A 4- and 5-year follow-up. *Journal of Consulting and Clinical Psychology, 61*(1), 70–77.

Markman, H. J., Stanley, S. M., Blumberg, S. L., Jenkins, N., & Whiteley, C. (2004). *Twelve hours to a great marriage.* San Francisco: Jossey-Bass.

Markman, H. J., Stanley, S. M., & Kline, G. H. (2003). Why marriage education can work and how government can be involved: Illustrations from the PREP approach. In W. D. Allen & L. L. Eiklenborg (Eds.), *Vision 2003: Contemporary family issues* (pp. 16–26). Minneapolis, MN: National Council on Family Relations.

Markman, H. J., Whitton, S. W., Kline, G. H., Thompson, H., St. Peters, M., Stanley, S. M., et al. (2004). Use of an empirically-based marriage education program by religious organizations: Results of a dissemination trial. *Family Relations, 53,* 504–512.

McLanahan, S., Garfinkel, I., & Mincy, R. B. (2001). *Fragile families, welfare reform, and marriage* (No. 10). Washington, DC: Brookings Institute.

McLanahan, S., & Sandefur, G. (1996). *Growing up with a single parent: What hurts, what helps.* Cambridge, MA: Harvard University Press.

Notarius, C., & Markman, H. J. (1993). *We can work it out: Making sense of marital conflict.* New York: Putnam.

Ooms, T. (2002). *Marriage and government: Strange bedfellows?* Washington, DC: Center for Law and Social Policy.

Parke, M., & Ooms, T. (2002). *More than a dating service? State activities designed to strengthen and promote marriage.* Washington, DC: Center for Law and Social Policy.

Pinsof, W. M. (2002). The death of "till death us do part": The transformation of pair-bonding in the 20th century. *Family Process, 41*(2), 135–157.

Rossman, B. B. R., Hughes, H. M., & Rosenberg, M. S. (2000). *Children in violent families: The impact of exposure.* Washington, DC: Taylor & Francis.

Schilling, E. A., Baucom, D. H., Burnett, C. K., Allen, E. S., & Ragland, L. (2003). Altering the course of marriage: The effect of premarital communication skills acquisition on couples' risk of becoming maritally distressed. *Journal of Family Psychology, 17*(1), 41–53.

Schumm, W. R., Silliman, B., & Bell, D. B. (2000). Perceived premarital counseling outcomes among recently married army personnel. *Journal of Sex and Marital Therapy, 26*(2), 177–186.

Seefeldt, K. S., & Smock, P. J. (2004). *Marriage on the public policy agenda: What do policy makers need to know from research?* PSC Research Report No. 04-554. Ann Arbor, MI: Population Studies Center.

Silliman, B., Stanley, S. M., Coffin, W., Markman, H. J., & Jordan, P. L. (2002). Preventive interventions for couples. In H. A. Liddle & D. A. Santisteban (Eds.), *Family psychology: Science-based interventions* (pp. 123–146). Washington, DC: American Psychological Association.

Sprenkle, D. H. (Ed.). (2002). *Effectiveness research in marriage and family therapy.* Alexandria, VA: American Association for Marriage and Family Therapy.

Stanley, S. M. (2001). Making the case for premarital education. *Family Relations, 50,* 272–280.

Stanley, S. M. (2003, May). *Marriage and premarriage education research in welfare populations.* Paper presented at the Welfare Reform Evaluation Conference, Washington, DC.

Stanley, S. M., Kline, G. H., Olmos-Gallo, P. A., & Markman, H. J. (2005). *Predicting marital distress from changes in communication following PREP: Findings and methodological concerns.* Manuscript submitted for publication.

Stanley, S. M., & Markman, H. J. (1997, June). *Acting on what we know: The hope of prevention.* Paper presented at the Family Impact Seminar, Washington, DC.

Stanley, S. M., Markman, H. J., & Jenkins, N. (2002). *Marriage educations and government policy: Helping couples who choose marriage achieve success.* Denver, CO: PREP.

Stanley, S. M., Markman, H. J., & Lobitz, W. C. (1988, May). Marital therapy in Colorado. *Colorado Psychological Association Bulletin.*

Stanley, S. M., Markman, H. J., Prado, L. M., Olmos-Gallo, P. A., Tonelli, L., St. Peters, M., et al. (2001). Community-based premarital prevention: Clergy and lay leaders on the front lines. *Family Relations, 50*(1), 67–76.

Stanley, S. M., Markman, H. J., St. Peters, M., & Leber, B. D. (1995). Strengthening marriages and preventing divorce: New directions in prevention research. *Family Relations: Journal of Applied Family and Child Studies, 44*(4), 392–401.

Stanley, S. M., Markman, H. J., Saiz, C. C., Schumm, W. R., Bloomstrom, G., & Bailey, A. E. (2003). *Building strong and ready families: Interim report.* Washington, DC: SAIC.

Stanley, S. M., Markman, H. J., & Whitton, S. W. (2002). Communication, conflict and commitment: Insights on the foundations of relationship success from a national survey. *Family Process, 41*(4), 659–675.

Stanley, S. M., & Young, G. (2003, June). *Realities, possibilities & myths of the marriage movement.* Paper presented at the Smart Marriages Conference, Reno, NV.

Toner, R., & Pear, R. (2002, February 27). Bush urges work and marriage programs in welfare plan. *New York Times.*

Tucker, M. B., & Mitchell-Kernan, C. (1995). Social structural and psychological correlates of interethnic dating. *Journal of Social and Personal Relationships, 12*(3), 341–361.

Van Widenfelt, B., Hosman, C., Schaap, C., & van der Staak, C. (1996). The prevention of relationship distress for couples at risk: A controlled evaluation with nine-month and two-year follow-ups. *Family Relations, 45,* 156–165.

Waite, L. J., Browning, D., Doherty, W. J., Gallagher, M., Lou, Y., & Stanley, S. M. (2002). *Does divorce make people happy? Findings from a study of unhappy marriages.* New York: Institute for American Values.

Wolfe, D. A., Jaffe, P., Wilson, S. K., & Zak, L. (1985). Children of battered women: The relation of child behavior to family violence and maternal stress. *Journal of Consulting and Clinical Psychology, 53*(5), 657–665.

PART II

PARTNER VIOLENCE: PARTICIPANT PERSPECTIVES AND TREATMENT

Partner violence has become an increasingly prominent problem within the United States and the rest of Western civilization within the last quarter of the 20th century. Most researchers doubt that this is a new phenomenon in the life of the human species. The emergence of this problem in large part derives from changing cultural norms and values that have allowed social scientists, and in particular family psychologists, to "see" the problem that was once taken for granted or hidden. What we are seeing is indeed frightening. As the chapters in this part of our book attest, partner violence is very dangerous, and not infrequently, it is even fatal.

Furthermore, the study and treatment of partner violence have become highly politicized endeavors, with different public constituencies arguing for different perspectives and policies. Particular attention and controversy have surrounded the issues of what constitutes partner violence, who is responsible, and who should be involved in what way in its prevention and treatment.

The chapters here truly represent a mini-manual for the study and treatment of partner violence. Deborah M. Capaldi, Joann Wu Shortt, and Hyoun K. Kim elaborate a comprehensive, life span perspective on partner violence that provides an emerging "map" of the terrain that needs to be studied in research and traversed in intervention. Amy Holtzworth-Munroe and Jeffrey C. Meehan examine the contribution of males to partner violence, exploring critical issues pertaining to the typing or categorizing of relationally violent men, their potentially distinct developmental trajectories, and possible alternative treatment strategies. Mary Ann Dutton and her colleagues explore the role of women in partner violence, exploring who gets involved and why, with a much needed emphasis on historically neglected variables, such as culture. Additionally, their chapter includes an excellent examination of treatment and prevention options and issues for women in violent relationships. Ernest N. Jouriles, Renee McDonald, and Nancy A. Skopp provide an invaluable examination of theory and research pertaining to the impact of partner violence on children. Their work pushes the envelope of understanding and ameliorating the impact of witnessing parental violence, ranging all the way from the biological to the social and intellectual. K. Daniel O'Leary and Edward M. Vega argue for a more differentiated perspective on partner violence, in which different intervention and prevention strategies can be tailored to different types and levels of partner violence. They also bravely address the controversial role of individual versus conjoint intervention and acknowledge the enormity and complexity of the task of reducing and preventing partner violence.

These chapters cover the gender and developmental spectrum in regard to partner violence. They also collectively argue for a more sophisticated and differentiated understanding of the phenomenon of partner violence and its treatment. In mapping the terrain of this problem and its treatment, as a group they provide a comprehensive overview of the research challenges and opportunities in this vitally important area.

6

A Life Span Developmental Systems Perspective on Aggression Toward a Partner

Deborah M. Capaldi, Joann Wu Shortt, and Hyoun K. Kim

The use of physically aggressive tactics during disagreements between partners has gained national attention as domestic violence. Former Surgeon General Novello announced in 1992 that domestic violence is the leading cause of injuries to women aged 15–44 years and that addressing the issue of violence against women has become a national priority (Biden, 1993). For perhaps as many as 25 to 30% of those who report first instances of physical aggression in early dating relationships, such aggression becomes more serious across time (O'Leary et al., 1989; Roscoe & Benaske, 1985). Understanding the causes and course of physical aggression directed at women by male partners is a critical issue. Aggression in couples, however, is a larger issue than this alone. First, men also are injured by their partners (Archer, 2000). Furthermore, physical aggression that does not result in injuries severe enough to require medical attention can have other impacts that are destructive to the relationship and to the well-being of the partners (Bradbury & Lawrence, 1999; Gelles & Harrop, 1989). Possible impacts include decline in relationship satisfaction, relationship breakdowns, and divorce, with accompanying negative effects such as loss of income and housing; personal distress including fear, depressive symptoms, and posttraumatic stress disorder (PTSD); and consequences such as substance use. Finally, such aggression between parents has been related to negative outcomes for the children (Jouriles, Norwood, McDonald, & Peters, 2001; Simons, Johnson, Beaman, & Conger, 1993). In this chapter, we discuss the prevalence of physical aggression in romantic relationships, current theoretical perspectives on couples' aggression, and the need for a developmental systems perspective to move the field forward in its endeavors to explain the etiology of and processes involved in aggression toward a partner.

■   The Prevalence of Physical Aggression in Couples

In recent decades, the issue of physical aggression in married, cohabiting, and dating couples has received increasing attention. In a nationally representative sample of married and cohabiting couples, namely, the National Family Violence Survey (NFVS; Straus & Gelles, 1986), 16% of the couples reported physical aggression by either partner. Aggressive acts ranged from more minor, such as pushing and shoving, to more severe. About 6% of the sample reported that severe assaults, including kicking, punching, biting, choking, and use of a weapon had occurred in the relationship. Studies based on community samples found even higher rates of physical aggression between partners. O'Leary et al. (1989) found that physical aggression occurred in 57% of couples 1 month before marriage. Similarly, McLaughlin, Leonard, and Senchak (1992) found that 36% of couples reported at least one instance of husband-to-wife aggression in the past year.

Prevalence of Physical Aggression in Young Couples

Carlson (1987) reviewed rates of physical aggression among dating couples for high school and college students, generally as self-reported on the Conflict Tactics Scale (CTS; Straus, 1990a). Rates for less serious physical acts (e.g., slapping) were variable and ranged between 13 and 61%. The most serious types of physical aggression, such as threatening with or using a weapon, were much less common, with prevalence rates ranging from 1 to 4%. Moffitt and Caspi (1999) compared the findings of three studies with large samples for rates of physical aggression in late adolescence and young adulthood (under age 25 years): Two U.S. studies with data collection in the mid 1980s, namely, the NFVS (Fagan & Browne, 1994) and the National Youth Survey (NYS; Elliott, Huizinga, & Morse, 1985), and 1993–1994 findings from their study with a New Zealand sample. Across these studies, perpetration rates ranged from about 36 to 51% for women and 22 to 43% for men, somewhat higher than those in college samples. Findings across these reviews indicate surprisingly high prevalence rates of physical aggression, particularly among young couples.

Prevalence of Physical Aggression Across Age

Rates of physical aggression toward a partner have been found to be highest at young ages and to decrease with time (Gelles & Straus, 1988). O'Leary (1999) estimated the prevalence of physical aggression by men toward their women partners from cross-sectional data. The estimates indicated a sharp rise from ages 15–25 years, a peak prevalence at around age 25 years, and a sharp decline to about age 35 years. It is not clear if the hypothesized rise to age 25 years reflects the fact that many more individuals are engaged in romantic relationships at age 25 years than age 15 years. It may be that for individuals engaged in a relationship, the peak engagement in aggression toward a partner is at the younger ages (controlling for length of relationship) and that there is a gradual decline after about ages 18–21 years.

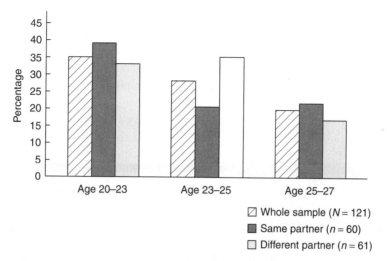

FIGURE 6.1   Prevalence of any physical aggression toward a partner by young men.

Longitudinal evidence from our study (Capaldi & Kim, 2002) as well as from a study by Lorber and O'Leary (2002) also indicates that physical aggression declines over time in young couples. Capaldi and Kim (2002) examined the frequency of aggression at three time points in young adulthood for men; ages 20–23, 23–25, and 25–27 years, respectively. Self- and partner reports on the CTS (Straus, 1990a) were used to create a dichotomous score indicating whether the men used any physical aggression toward their partner. Shown in figure 6.1 are prevalence rates for men in the whole sample who participated at the three time points and also for those who participated with the same or a different partner at the prior time point. The prevalence of physical aggression decreased across this developmental age span, with a decrease between ages 20–23 and 23–25 years for men with the same partner and between ages 23–25 and 25–27 years for men with different partners between these two time points.

■ Physical Aggression and Gender

Many survey data of both marital and dating couples indicate highly similar or slightly higher rates of physical aggression against men by women than vice versa for both married (e.g., Straus & Gelles, 1986) and dating couples (Laner & Thompson, 1982; Sugarman & Hotaling, 1989). In a meta-analysis of sex differences in aggression, Archer (2000) found a higher prevalence of female than male physical aggression for the younger age group (aged 14–22 years) and that injury rates were almost equal at these ages.

Recent studies also have indicated that aggression between adolescent partners is often bidirectional or mutual. Of adolescent dating couples showing any physical aggression toward a partner, reported rates of bidirectional aggression are as high as

59 to 71% (Capaldi & Crosby, 1997; Gray & Foshee, 1997; Henton, Cate, Koval, Lloyd, & Christopher, 1983). Most often the partners in mutually aggressive couples report about equal frequency and severity of physical aggression perpetrated and sustained (Gray & Foshee, 1997; Henton et al., 1983) and that both partners were equally responsible for initiating the behavior (Henton et al., 1983). These couples also report sustaining and initiating greater amounts of physical aggression, more types of physical aggression, and more injuries than those who report unidirectional physical aggression in their relationship. Individuals participating in bidirectional aggression are also more likely to be involved in physical aggression across relationships.

In sum, these findings suggest that efforts to address the issues of partner aggression should include women's aggression as well as men's and should also incorporate the role of both partners within a dyad. This requires a conceptual perspective that views partner aggression within the context of the relationship, thus differing from some dominant theories of partner aggression and from predominant treatment approaches. To date, little attention has been paid to developmental dyadic processes, or how both partners contribute to aggression and how the pattern may change over time. Before we describe such a perspective, predominant theoretical approaches to partner aggression and limitations of those conceptualizations are discussed.

■ Predominant Theories of Couple Violence

Feminist Theory

The two dominant theoretical approaches to examining partner violence are feminist-based perspectives (e.g., Walker, 1984) and family conflict perspectives (e.g., Straus, 1990b). The feminist theoretical approach posits that physical aggression in couples is due to patriarchy, and it is thus directed from men toward women in order to maintain the predominant position of men in Western society through the process of controlling and subjugating women (Dobash & Dobash, 1979; Kurz, 1993; Martin, 1976; Walker, 1984). Most treatment programs are based on this perspective and address men's battering of women (Hamby, 1998). Studies based on feminist approaches generally employ three types of samples: women recruited from women's shelters or agencies, couples recruited from professional referrals by therapists or lawyers, and couples recruited from newspaper ads and flyers. Couples are then usually screened for participation on the basis of the presence of men's aggression toward the women. If women's aggression is acknowledged as occurring, this aggression is generally posited to be much less frequent and serious and as occurring in self-defense.

Research based on the feminist approach does not include the etiology of physical aggression within couples, and women's behavior is considered not to play a role in the origin or occurrence of such aggression. Furthermore, it is generally considered that men who are aggressive toward their partner will not desist from this behavior, but will get worse over time (Walker, 1984).

Family Conflict Theory

The family conflict perspective posits that conflicts occur in family relationships due to factors such as differing goals, personalities, and behavioral styles of family members. If these family conflicts involve aggression, socialization to aggression occurs. Once socialized to aggression, participants then resort to using aggressive tactics to resolve conflicts in their romantic relationships. Physical aggression is viewed mainly as a system product rather than the result of individual pathology (Straus, 1973). Processes within families can maintain, escalate, or reduce levels of physical aggression.

Much work based on this perspective has involved phone surveys that, in particular, seek to establish the topography of couple aggression (e.g., prevalence, types, and association with individual characteristics including gender and other demographic characteristics). Findings from these studies indicate that women engage in physical aggression toward a partner at rates similar to men's (Archer, 2000). Work from this perspective has increased our understanding of the ubiquitous nature of aggression within couples and some associated risk factors that are common to both men and women. A significant contribution of this perspective is that it led to recognition of the possibility that partner aggression might involve a complex process in which both men and women partners may play roles. However, most studies based on this approach have been descriptive and have not adequately addressed the influence of both partners and interactions between partners on partner aggression and how the pattern and degree of aggression change over time.

Typological Approaches to Aggression

Much recent research effort in the area of aggression toward a partner has focused on defining typologies of aggression (M. P. Johnson, 1995, 1999; M. P. Johnson & Leone, 2000) and of batterers (Gottman et al., 1995; Holtzworth-Munroe & Stuart, 1994).

Patriarchal Terrorism Versus Common Couple Violence.   M. P. Johnson (1995) attempted to explain the discrepant findings from feminist and family violence research by positing two theoretically different kinds of violence in couples, namely, common couple violence and patriarchal terrorism. He posits that common couple violence is due to conflicts between partners that are poorly managed and occasionally escalate to minor violence, but rarely to serious violence. He speculates that such violence is likely to be mutual, low frequency, and less likely to persist. On the other hand, patriarchal terrorism is patterned male violence against women with the purpose of maintaining male domination, and such violence is likely to be frequent, persistent, and almost exclusively done by men.

Although the Johnson dichotomy has intuitive appeal and validates different theoretical approaches and bodies of findings, there is little compelling empirical evidence to support a clear-cut distinction between patriarchal terrorism and mutual couple violence. Johnson and Ferraro (2000) cite three studies as providing supportive evidence, but each has sampling or assessment design features likely to have influenced the identification of two groups (M. P. Johnson, 1999; M. P. Johnson & Leone, 2000; Leone, Johnson, Cohan, & Lloyd, 2001). Currently, it has not been demonstrated that these two groups of men show different motivations for physical aggression or that the more parsimonious hypothesis of a continuous distribution of aggression and controlling behavior in men from almost absent to very severe is less valid than the proposed typology. Furthermore, the sampling techniques and study designs, so far, have not been adequate to demonstrate that women (although likely in lower numbers) are not present among those showing higher frequencies of physical aggression and controlling behaviors.

Batterer Typologies.　The work to define batterer typologies appears to be driven largely by the goal of improving the outcomes of treatment programs for men by defining subtypes who may respond to different forms of treatment and intervention, rather than by understanding the etiology and cause of physical aggression toward women. Holtzworth-Munroe and Stuart (1994) identified three subtypes of batterers, namely, generally violent/antisocial, dysphoric/borderline, and family only. Recent research indicates that there may be an additional subtype (Holtzworth-Munroe, Meehan, Herron, Rehman, & Stuart, 2000) and overlap between subtypes (Holtzworth-Munroe, Meehan, Herron, Rehman, & Stuart, 2003). Gottman et al. (1995) identified two subtypes based on physiological responses during marital conflict. Type 1 men were violent toward others (e.g., coworkers) and exhibited high levels of antisocial behavior and sadistic aggression. Type 2 men were dependent on their partners. Apart from the family-only group, these typologies seem to converge in identifying a group of men who are high in general antisocial behavior and a group who may still be elevated in antisocial behavior to some degree, but also show depressive and anxious characteristics.

The batterer typology approach is based on the explicit assumption that physical aggression toward a partner by men, as well as other controlling behaviors, is inherently based in male individual differences. In other words, if one considers social behaviors as caused by an individual–environmental interaction, batterer typology theorists focus only on the *individual* part of the equation, whereas environment, particularly in the form of the partner and her behavior, are not examined nor considered to be important influences. The majority of batterer treatments are based solely on changing men's behaviors. As acknowledged, whether tailoring treatment to the subtype of batterer improves the outcome of treatment programs has not yet been tested (Holtzworth-Munroe et al., 2000).

Theories that assume that individual differences are the sole cause of an outcome, perhaps with other contextual factors (e.g., stress and job loss considered as possible contextual effects), are based also on the usually implicit assumption that men's aggressive behavior toward a partner is relatively stable across time and across partners. In other words, if the partner's behavior is not a factor in the men's aggression, then changes in partner behavior and changes in actual partners should not be associated with changes in men's aggression. Thus far, no robust evidence on high levels of stability in men's aggression toward a partner has been found (Holtzworth-Munroe et al., 2003) and none of this work includes men in representative community samples. Whether and to what degree stability can be demonstrated over time and across partners in men's aggression toward women and the relative balance of influence of individual differences versus partner behavioral (environmental) characteristics across early adulthood are critically important issues in advancing our understanding of aggression and of the utility and applications of typologies of aggressive men. If the typologies are not stable over time or replicable across samples with differing characteristics (Babcock, Green, Webb, & Graham, 2004; Gottman, 2001; Meehan & Holtzworth-Munroe, 2001; Meehan, Holtzworth-Munroe, & Herron, 2001), then using them to differentiate men for treatment purposes may not be effective.

Preliminary work on a typology of women who have been violent toward their male partners indicates that women can also be subtyped by their use of aggression (Babcock, Miller, & Siard, 2003). In comparison to women who used violence only toward their partners, women who used violence toward their partners and others reported witnessing their mothers being violent toward their fathers in childhood, supporting the thinking that using aggressive strategies to resolve conflict has roots in family interaction patterns (e.g., Patterson, 1982). Typologies of women, however, will have the same limitations as the typologies of men.

■ Definitional and Methodological Issues

As discussed by Capaldi and Gorman-Smith (2003), researchers studying aggression in couples face a number of definitional and methodological challenges. As recently as 1997, Gortner, Gollan, and Jacobson concluded that very little was known about the causes of domestic violence, partly due to methodological limitations of studies of this topic, such as sample selection issues (e.g., battered women's shelter samples and samples of convenience) and limited study designs (cross-sectional or retrospective in nature). Some of the issues in the area are partly due to the heavy focus on men's aggression toward women partners and to individual differences rather than to process oriented mechanisms. Below, we describe four critical issues in the area that must be addressed in order to further advance our understanding of aggression toward a partner or domestic violence, namely, definitional, design, assessment, and sampling issues.

Definitional Issues

Clearer conceptualization and definition of types of aggression, particularly physical and psychological aggression, as well as further consideration of the consequences of aggression, would advance understanding in this field. Archer (1994, 2000) and Heyman, Slep, Capaldi, Eddy, and Stoolmiller (1999) recommend that the *impacts* or consequences of aggression be considered separately from the *acts,* avoiding the assumption that all physical aggression has the same degree of damaging consequences for all individuals. The impacts of aggression include such psychological consequences as fear and depression, as well as physical injury (Capaldi & Owen, 2001; Dutton & Painter, 1993; Gelles & Harrop, 1989).

Aggression toward a partner that is not physical has been considered in many studies, including verbal abuse and psychological aggression. Stets (1991) stated that "Psychological aggression refers to acting in a verbally offending or degrading manner toward another. The mistreatment may take the form of insults or behavior that results in making another feel guilty, upset, or worthless" (p. 101). Follingstad, Rutledge, Berg, Hause, and Polek (1990) identified six types of psychological aggression: Threats of abuse, ridicule, jealousy, threats to change relationship, restriction, and damage to property.

Recently, relational aggression, a construct originally theorized to characterize peer aggression in girls, has been applied to aggression in couples (Linder, Crick, & Collins, 2002). According to this theory, girls are less likely to be directly aggressive and, therefore, use indirect aggressive tactics against other girls, specifically targeting relationships. It is theorized that as girls place a high value on relationships, they are vulnerable to aggression in this area. Linder et al. define such aggression as ". . . any behavior that causes harm by damaging relationships or feelings of acceptance and love. Examples of relational aggression in romantic relationships include flirting with others to make a romantic partner jealous, threatening to break up with a partner if the partner will not comply, or giving a partner the silent treatment when angry" (Linder et al., 2002, p. 70). Linder et al. (2002) state that psychological aggression is a broader construct than relational aggression. Whereas psychological aggression may target perceptions, thoughts, feelings, or behaviors, the target of relational aggression is always relationships, whether the specific behaviors are verbal, nonverbal, direct, or indirect.

It is not clear how controlling or manipulating a relationship (relational aggression) is different from controlling a partner within the relationship (i.e., that it is possible to separate the effects of relational aggression from broader psychological aggression). The construct of relational aggression seems to confound the behavior with its impact. For example, is an individual jealous and interpreting a partner's behavior as provoking jealousy on purpose because the partner is actually intentionally provoking jealousy or because the individual easily experiences the emotion of jealousy and has a higher level of hostile attribution bias? Thus, the items used to assess relational victimization in the Linder et al. (2002) study include *both* the behavior and the victim's interpretation of the actor's intention. Further work on describing, defining, and examining dimensions of nonphysical aggression toward a partner is needed.

Cross-Sectional Versus Longitudinal Designs

As discussed by Bradbury (2002), relationships naturally unfold over time and are unlikely to be well understood unless time is incorporated into the research design. Despite the obvious validity of this assertion, studies of couples' aggression have been predominantly cross-sectional or of very limited longitudinal design, rarely involving more than two points in time. In order to advance our understanding of aggression, study designs must accommodate the dynamic nature of relationships and aggression. To examine growth in aggression using growth curve analyses (Muthén & Muthén, 2000) or heterogeneity in trajectories of aggression over time (Muthén & Muthén, 2000; Nagin, 1999), at least three time points are required, involving multiple assessments within a relationship and possibly across relationships.

Assessment

A third area of weakness, as well as controversy, is assessment. The most widely used instrument for assessing physical aggression in couples is the CTS (Straus, 1990a), on which respondents are asked to report the extent to which they have used various types of aggression during an argument or disagreement with their partner. Reliance on the CTS as the sole measure of physical aggression has been criticized, particularly for the lack of attention to the context and consequences of the physical aggression (Dobash, Dobash, Wilson, & Daly, 1992; White, Smith, Koss, & Figueredo, 2000). For example, there is no way to determine whether or how much the behavior was in self-defense. Critics argue that most of women's reported aggression toward a partner is likely to be in self-defense, rather than initiated by the woman. Similarly, it has been argued that the consequences of aggression toward women are much more severe; women suffer more serious injuries as a result of the men's aggression (Cantos, Neidig, & O'Leary, 1994). Prior versions of the CTS did not allow for any measurement of injuries sustained. Additional issues included the lack of a comprehensive list of the types of aggression that could be perpetrated and the scaling of the CTS. The scaling of the CTS involves aggregating across all of the items and does not weight items based on severity. Thus, critics argued that even if women report greater use of aggression on the CTS, it is likely that women use less severe forms of aggression. Despite these criticisms, the CTS is the most widely used instrument to measure aggression toward a partner. Recent revisions have improved the CTS. The CTS2 includes sexual coercion and physical injury scales and improved distinction between minor and severe aggression (Straus, Hamby, Boney-McCoy, & Sugarman, 1996).

Issues of bias in self-report data have been recognized for some time (e.g., Patterson, 1982), and it may be particularly problematic in examining the processes involved in marital conflict (Markman, Notarius, Stephen, & Smith, 1981). Many studies of aggression toward a partner only involve questionnaires and the report of one partner. Schafer, Caetano, and Clark (2002) found relatively low concordance between self- and partner reports of the presence of any violence. Szinovacz and Egley (1995) found some divergence between predictor models based on one-partner and couple scores of violence.

In assessing the constructs related to process in couples relationships, observational data can help identify the behavioral processes that distinguish unhappy and violent couples and that are associated with relationship deterioration (Gottman, Coan, Carrere, & Swanson, 1998). The behavior of violent couples during problem solving has been examined in several studies (Burman, John, & Margolin, 1992; Cordova, Jacobson, Gottman, Rushe, & Cox, 1993; Jacobson et al., 1994; Margolin, John, & Gleberman, 1988). Findings indicate significant observable differences in the behavior of the violent couples. Distressed violent couples generally show more aversive and less facilitative behavior than either distressed nonviolent or happily married couples. Violent couples have been found to be more likely to engage in negative reciprocal exchanges than comparison couples (Cordova et al., 1993; Gottman, 1980; Gottman & Levenson, 1984). However, any single assessment method is subject to measurement error, and multiple method and agent approaches increase the validity of measurement (Patterson, Reid, & Dishion, 1992). Similarly, in a review of observational studies of couples, Heyman (2001) argued that observational data alone were not adequate and recommended a move toward the use of multimethod constructs and more concern for establishing construct validity.

Sampling

A further limitation of studies of aggression in couples is related to sampling. Apart from the NFVS, the majority of studies have been conducted using convenience samples (e.g., in response to advertising), rather than samples recruited as representative of a targeted community population. Such approaches to studying relationships have been criticized repeatedly as inadequate (e.g., Bradbury, 2002; de Jong Gierveld, 1995). It is difficult to assess the nature and extent of bias caused by such sampling of volunteers or the generalizability of the findings. Volunteers have been shown to have differing characteristics from nonvolunteers, including higher levels of education, social class, intelligence, approval motivation, sociability, altruism, and self-disclosure, as well as being less authoritarian (Rosenthal & Rosnow, 1975). Potential biases are more complex in couples research than in research with individuals. It is predominantly women who respond to advertising for such studies. Their motivation for doing so may well relate to characteristics of the couple (e.g., that the woman is dissatisfied with her partner).

Issues that may arise from differing sampling techniques are highlighted by M. P. Johnson (1995), who argues that studies of agency samples and family violence studies have utilized samples showing almost no overlap in levels of physical aggression. Two studies that used the CTS (Straus, 1979) with shelter samples found that women reported an average of 69 (Giles-Sims, 1983) and 65 (Okun, 1986) acts of physical aggression against them by partners in the past year. In contrast, only a tiny proportion of couples in the larger survey studies conducted by Straus and colleagues showed frequencies of physical aggression as high as the mean levels that have been found for shelter samples (less than one tenth of 1%, $n = 4$, in the 1985 NFVS; Straus, 1990b). We have argued that sampling bias for both the agency and family violence survey studies contributes to this discrepancy (Capaldi & Owen, 2001). Straus (1990b) has speculated that couples in which the man is frequently physically aggressive may be less likely to respond to telephone surveys. Further, women entering a shelter may be more likely to do so during the breakdown of the relationship, when levels of stress and conflict are particularly high.

■ Current Challenges in Understanding Couples' Aggression

The urgency of the need for a fresh conceptual focus and assessment approach is highlighted by the findings of a rapidly growing body of prospective developmental studies examining childhood and adolescent predictors of later aggression toward a partner. These findings indicate that antisocial behavior that develops by adolescence predicts later aggressive behavior toward a romantic partner, not only for young men (e.g., Capaldi & Clark, 1998; Magdol, Moffitt, Caspi, & Silva, 1998; Simons & Johnson, 1998) but also for young women (Andrews, Foster, Capaldi, & Hops, 2000; Ehrensaft, Cohen, Brown, Smailes, & Johnson, 2003; Giordano, Millhollin, Cernkovich, Pugh, & Rudolph, 1999; Magdol et al., 1998; Woodward, Fergusson, & Horwood, 2002). This suggests the importance of individual psychopathology as a predictor of aggression for both men and women and some similarity in developmental pathways of aggression toward a partner for men and women, indicating that they both play some active role in physical aggression in couples.

The need for a new conceptual approach is also found in work regarding the mutuality and stability of partner aggression. O'Leary et al. (1989) and others (Capaldi & Crosby, 1997; Gray & Foshee, 1997) found that when physical aggression occurred within dyads, it tended to be bidirectional or mutual, suggesting that both partners are responsible for aggression in the relationship. Another important finding in this area is that the presence and degree of physical aggression toward a partner tend to fluctuate over time. For instance, O'Leary and colleagues (1989) found that only 51% of the men and 41% of the women who were aggressive 1 month before marriage remained aggressive 18 months later. On the other hand, for those who were not initially aggressive, 15% became aggressive after 18 months. These findings indicate that, despite prediction from psychopathology, aggression toward a partner changes over time, indicating the likely influence of contextual factors.

The current challenge for researchers in the area of couples' aggression is to develop a theoretical approach that can explain more fully the phenomenon of partner violence. In order to progress, we need to address fundamental questions regarding physical aggression in couples that have not been answered adequately. A strong theoretical framework would be one that suggests fruitful hypotheses for addressing the following questions:

1. What is physical aggression in couples—what forms does it take? Is it a heterogeneous or homogeneous phenomenon?
2. What are the functions of physical aggression in couples' relationships?
3. Why and how does physical aggression develop?
4. What is the course of aggression over time? Does physical aggression toward a partner change over time with the developmental age of the partners and the developmental age of the relationship itself? Is the occurrence of physical aggression relatively stable over time, both within and across relationships?
5. What is the role and involvement of each partner in aggression—or of men and women in heterosexual relationships?
6. What are the impacts of aggression?

7. Who is at risk for physical aggression and for the differing impacts of physical aggression?

Whereas we cannot address all these questions in this chapter, we describe a theoretical approach below, along with some recent findings based on such a perspective that illustrate how we may move forward in addressing them.

■ A Developmental Systems Perspective

The predominant theories of partner aggression provide limited frameworks to address issues regarding the developmental risk factors for aggression and the bidirectional nature and course of physical aggression through adulthood. These issues require a new approach that involves multilevel factors and assumes dynamic interactions and changes among the factors over time. We need to explain how each partner's developmental history, and behaviors, and interactions within the dyad and interactions of the dyad and individual partners with other contextual factors and social systems are related to partner aggression. We have argued that aggression toward a partner is best understood within a life span developmental-contextual or developmental-interactional framework (Capaldi & Gorman-Smith, 2003; Capaldi, Shortt, & Crosby, 2003). This approach is perhaps best characterized as a developmental systems perspective. The developmental systems perspective emphasizes the interplay between biology (e.g., genetic influences), individual characteristics (e.g., temperament), contextual factors (e.g., parental divorce), and socialization experiences, especially within the family of origin and peer group (e.g., Dishion, French, & Patterson, 1995) in explaining behaviors (e.g., Baltes, 1983; Cairns & Cairns, 1995; Capaldi, Dishion, Stoolmiller, & Yoerger, 2001; Caspi & Elder, 1988; Dishion et al., 1995; Dishion & Patterson, 1997; Elder, 1985; Hetherington & Baltes, 1988; Magnusson & Toerestad, 1993; Rutter, 1989).

In a similar theoretical approach applied to the etiology of conduct problems, Bronfenbrenner (1979, 1986) has posited an ecological model conceptualized as a hierarchy of four nested systems involving intrapersonal factors, microsystems of face-to-face interactions, behavioral settings, and finally macrocontextual factors involving cultural and community practices. Developmental change occurs at multiple levels, including the biological level, the individual or psychological level, the social relational level (e.g., family of origin, peer groups, work groups, intimate partner), and the sociocultural level. As these levels are structurally and functionally integrated, a systems view is needed to understand human development and changing behavior over time (Lerner, 2002; Sameroff, 1983). In a recent discussion of developmental systems models, Lerner and Castellino (2002) stressed that plasticity exists across the life span, although the magnitude of this plasticity varies across developmental periods. Thus, levels and types of aggressive behavior vary across development.

The developmental systems approach emphasizes the importance of considering first the characteristics of both partners as they enter and then move through the relationship, including personality, psychopathology, ongoing social influences (e.g., peer associations), and individual developmental stage. The second emphasis is on the nature of the relationship itself, primarily the interaction patterns within the dyad as they are initially established and as they change over time, as well as factors affecting the context of the relationship. Shown in figure 6.2 is a summary of the developmental systems model of partner aggression from childhood through adulthood, depicted in characteristic developmental time.

As depicted, parental genetic and behavioral risk factors and unskilled parenting tend to co-occur within families that also experience higher levels of contextual risk factors, such as low socioeconomic status, employment problems, and parental transitions or divorce. These factors are associated with the emergence of depressive symptoms and particularly of conduct problems in childhood and adolescence. In fact, conduct problems and depressive symptoms tend to co-occur in childhood and adolescence (Capaldi, 1991, 1992). Conduct problems, in turn, are associated with rejection by prosocial peers and association with deviant peers or other antisocial adolescents. As the adolescents begin dating, they tend to meet partners in their peer group and date partners who have similar tastes. Assortative partnering (i.e., the tendency for individuals to engage in romantic relationships with partners with background characteristics similar to their own) can result in couples who both have higher levels of risk factors for aggression toward a partner. These couples then are at risk for unskilled relationship process, aggression toward a partner, ongoing negative context, such as arrests and unemployment, and eventually for more persistent and severe aggression and for the impacts of aggression, such as injury. These developmental processes are described in more detail below.

The Development of Conduct Problems

The characteristics of partners as they enter a relationship are products of their entire developmental history, including both genetic and socialization histories.

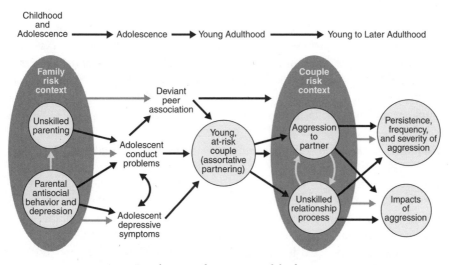

FIGURE 6.2   Developmental systems model of partner aggression.

When history and prior experience are considered in relation to intimate relationship behavior, it is often the case that only matching experience is considered. In the partner violence area, this has particularly pertained to examining whether violence between the parents predicts the offspring's later violence toward a partner in adulthood (Rosenbaum & O'Leary, 1981; Stets, 1991). Capaldi and Clark (1998) found that, for boys, how they were treated by their parents (particularly discipline and monitoring practices) was more predictive of later aggression toward a partner than was aggression between the parents and that the association was mediated by the development of conduct problems.

The model depicts similar developmental factors for risk for boys' conduct problems, as detailed in Capaldi and Clark (1998) and Capaldi, Pears, Patterson, and Owen (2003), namely, antisocial behavior and depression in the parents (i.e., genetic and contextual risk), associated unskilled parenting (especially poor discipline and monitoring), and contextual risk factors (e.g., poor neighborhood, parental marital transitions). Similar etiological factors are posited for the development of girls' conduct problems. Although we know considerably less about the development of conduct problems in girls than in boys, the weight of evidence suggests risk factors that are similar to those of boys (Keenan, Loeber, & Green, 1999).

Peer Socialization Toward Aggression

As depicted in figure 6.2, association with other aggressive peers is highly related to conduct problems during childhood and adolescence. Such associations have also been found to predict later aggression toward a partner (Capaldi et al., 2001). Capaldi et al. (2001) also found that male dyads with higher levels of conduct problems are more likely to be observed to use hostile and aggressive terminology during discussions of girls and women and that such mutual hostile talk predicts their later aggression toward a partner, even controlling for conduct problems. Thus, the reinforcement of conduct problems, which has been found among adolescent male dyads (Dishion, Eddy, Haas, Li, & Spracklen, 1997), may be part of a specific socialization process related to aggressive behavior toward women partners. Association with deviant peers is also posited to be involved in the process of assortative partnering (Kim & Capaldi, 2004), and continued association with deviant peers may also be an aspect of an ongoing risk context for the young couple, related to such factors as problematic substance use.

Assortative Partnering by Conduct Problems and Depressive Symptoms

Assortative partnering by conduct problems or antisocial behavior and/or by depressive symptoms is posited to result in young couples who are at considerable risk for aggression in their relationships, including physical violence. Couples in which both the young man and woman show higher levels of antisocial behavior occur more often than predicted by chance due to assortative partnering by antisocial behavior. Significant associations between partners' levels of antisocial behavior have been found in late adolescence for the Oregon Youth Study (OYS) sample (Capaldi & Crosby, 1997), as well as in other studies (Krueger, Moffitt, Caspi, Bleske, & Silva, 1998; Merikangas, 1982). Assortative partnering tends to occur because of at least two individual-environment interaction effects. The first effect is by active selection of environments (e.g., a young woman who likes to "party" and use substances is likely to meet young men with the same preferences at these social occasions). Second, engagement in conduct problems and related adjustment failures (Capaldi & Shortt, 2003) leads to unintended restriction of environmental options (e.g., an adolescent who drops out of high school may not attend a 4-year college and is less likely to date a young woman attending such a college).

Interactions between the partners can provoke or reinforce aggressive behaviors within dyads (Buss, 1987; Scarr & McCartney, 1983). Aggressive characteristics of the partner may tend to support or to evoke aggressive characteristics of the individual. If the partner accepts aggressive behavior by a mate, this may be supportive of the continuance of the behavior. Aggressive responses may be evoked by verbal aggression (e.g., threats and jealous accusations may be responded to with similarly aggressive responses) or by physical aggression (e.g., if one partner hits, the other may hit back). Such aggressive exchanges may be more likely when both partners are higher in levels of antisocial behavior and may be more likely to escalate. Coercive exchanges may occur in which one partner tries to get his or her own way and to get the partner to back down by making verbally aggressive attacks (e.g. threats; Patterson et al., 1992). When both individuals are higher in antisocial behavior, such exchanges may be more prolonged and become more heated and aggressive before one of the partners is prepared to back down.

Evidence has also indicated assortative partnering by affective disorders, such as anxiety or depression (Merikangas, 1982). Researchers have consistently found significant associations for affective disorders between partners within dyads and concluded that such concordance was mainly due to assortative partnering, rather than to interactions subsequent to partnering (e.g., Maes et al., 1998; McLeod, 1995; Merikangas & Spiker, 1982). This argument was supported by high prevalence rates of affective disorders among the affected partner's first-degree relatives (Merikangas & Spiker, 1982). In addition, they found that the level of concordance did not increase as partners spend more time together, and thus they rejected the alternative hypothesis that partners became similar through mutual interactions and modeling. However, most of the previous studies involved samples from clinical settings (e.g., psychiatric patients); therefore, there is little knowledge available regarding assortative partnering by depressive symptoms and how it is associated with aggression within dyads among couples from the general population.

Depressive Symptoms and Aggression Toward a Partner

The association of aggression toward a partner and depressive symptoms is most commonly thought of as explained by the aggression causing depression. However, there is evidence that depressive symptoms may play a causal role in aggression toward a partner. Couples with a depressed spouse have been found to have interactional difficulties, including elevated levels of hostility, sad affects, lack of affection, and negative communication styles (see Gotlib & Hooley, 1988, for a review). Depressed couples, particularly depressed wives, tend to show increased verbal negativity during marital interactions. In addition, depressed individuals perceive that their partners are more dominant, hostile, and less friendly than do nondepressed individuals (McCabe & Gotlib, 1993). There is some evidence that depressed wives showed increasing negative behaviors over the course of their interactions with their partners (McCabe & Gotlib, 1993). Studies on marital interaction and depression further indicate that behaviors by the depressed spouse and the partner's reaction to the depressed partner differ by gender. S. L. Johnson and Jacob (1997) found that depressed wives showed more negative and less positive communication than did depressed husbands, suggesting that depression among wives was associated with more disturbed marital interaction than depression among husbands. Capaldi and Crosby (1997) also found that depressive symptoms and low self-esteem in young women were concurrently associated with both physical and psychological aggression toward a partner in late adolescence (an average age of 18 years) for young women, but not for young men.

The combination of previously developed aggressive and coercive behaviors and risk associated with depressive symptoms (e.g., negative affect and irritability) is hypothesized to lead directly to aggressive behaviors in interaction with the partner and also to unskilled relationship behavior and process (e.g., poor problem solving, unfaithfulness), as well as to the continuance of risk context from the family of origin and adolescence (e.g., low education, poor neighborhood) and associated stress events (e.g., being fired from work, unemployment, low income). These factors, in turn, are expected to predict both the frequency and severity of future aggression and the impacts of aggression (e.g., injury, increase in depressive symptoms, family disruption).

Assortative Partnering and Its Association With Partner Violence

In an effort to test effects of both partners' characteristics on aggression within dyads, Kim and Capaldi (2004) examined whether high levels of antisocial behavior and depressive symptoms on the part of the young women predict aggression in their relationship over and above prediction from the young men's antisocial behavior and depressive symptoms (i.e., whether assortative partnering by antisocial behavior and depressive symptoms was associated with increased risk for aggression in the relationship). Evidence of assortative partnering by antisocial behavior and depressive symptoms was found, in that levels of antisocial behavior of both partners were significantly associated, as were depressive symptoms. In addition, for both men and women, antisocial behavior and depressive symptoms predicted their own physical or psychological aggression toward a partner.

Predicting from the developmental systems model, it was expected that partners' psychopathology would account for additional variance in aggression concurrently over and above prediction from the individual's own levels of psychopathology. In predicting physical aggression, hierarchical regression analyses indicated that women's depressive symptoms predicted men's physical aggression. In predicting psychological aggression, women's antisocial behavior and depressive symptoms predicted men's psychological aggression. In analyses over time, predicting from each partner's psychopathology and controlling for the individual's prior level of aggression, women's depressive symptoms also predicted her male partner's future psychological aggression. These findings indicate that antisocial behavior and depressive symptoms in both men and women are risk factors for aggression in their romantic relationships and that depressive symptoms in women may be a particularly strong risk factor for psychological aggression.

■ Time Dynamics and Developmental Systems

Some concepts of dynamic systems theory are helpful in considering the interplay between developmental systems levels over time. Granic, Dishion, and Hollenstein (2003) discussed the concept of the interplay between interdependent time scales, for example, between real time and developmental time. As there is evidence that the level of aggression in couples is related to the age of the partners (O'Leary, 1999), as well as to the length of the relationship (Capaldi & Crosby, 1997), it is important to consider the potential effects of multiple levels of time on the couples' behaviors, including each partner's developmental time, length of the relationship or couple time, and chronological time.

Developmental time may have various components (e.g., social maturity, career stage) and may differ for partners even when they are the same chronological age. Developmental time includes some periods of rapid change and others of greater stability. However, despite individual variations, developmental age shows strong associations with chronological age—consider the likely differences between a group 18 years of age and a group 40 years of age in social behaviors. The developmental stage of the couple's relationship itself—again related to, but not identical with, the chronological length of the relationship—may strongly affect the couple's interactions. For example, early stages may be more marked by insecurity and vulnerability to jealousy and later stages by more concerns around division of labor and lower levels of satisfaction. The couple's experience of their relationship and sequencing of events, among other factors, will be experienced in real or chronological time. One of the challenges for those studying couples is the timing of study assessments in relation to these levels of time that affect the couple.

The associations of levels of time with relationship process would be considerably more complex for individuals passing through multiple relationships with partners in different developmental life stages. Furthermore, the courses of developmental and relationship time are unlikely to be linear, but rather show times of rapid change and others of consolidation or relatively little change.

Whereas the developmental constructs shown in figure 6.2 tend to push for, or predict, stability or increasing severity of aggression, the age trend runs counter to a model of increasing severity. As noted previously, the evidence from cross-sectional (O'Leary, 1999) and recent longitudinal (Capaldi & Kim, 2002; Lorber & O'Leary, 2002) studies is that the prevalence of physical aggression declines across adulthood.

Therefore, it may be the case that the posited factors predict initiation of aggression in young couples and less tendency to desistance with age (i.e., a failure to make normative developmental progress). Antisocial behaviors generally show some improvement with age. For example, the prevalence and frequency of criminal acts peaks in late adolescence (Blumstein, Cohen, Roth, & Visher, 1986) and declines quite rapidly thereafter. Aggression toward a partner may therefore show some similar developmental trends to antisocial behavior in general.

Stability and Change in Aggression Toward a Partner Over Time

From a developmental systems perspective, young men's aggression toward a partner is predicted to show some stability across partners, but also to show some changes with new partners. If aggression is *entirely* associated with something within the man (e.g., patriarchal dominance or antisocial behavior), aggression toward a partner should be as stable over time for men with new partners as for men with the same partner. If aggression toward a partner is more stable over time for men with the same partner than with a different partner, this suggests that characteristics of the partner or the dyadic context and interaction are involved in the occurrence of such aggression.

Stability in physical and psychological aggression toward a partner from late adolescence to young adulthood was examined using both reports by partners and observational data. For the OYS couples' sample, there was significant stability in physical and psychological aggression toward a partner by *both* the young man and woman if the couple remained intact over that period (Capaldi, Shortt, & Crosby, 2003). However, if the young man was with a new partner, there was no significant association in reported aggression across this period. There was some evidence of significant stability in aggression by men toward their partners across relationships from the observational data, although lower than that for men with the same partner.

Additional evidence that change in aggression over time is a dyadic process came from examining the association of the levels of change for both young men and their partners. For both physical and psychological aggression, significant associations were found between the partners for change over time within couples who stayed together (same-partner couples) and couples who had repartnered (different-partner couples). Thus, the same-partner couples tended to move in the same direction in their level of aggression. The association for the different-partner group likely indicated that if the new woman partner had a greater or lesser level of aggression than the previous partner, the man would also move in that direction. Aggression thus appears to be predominantly bidirectional, and the direction of change over time tends to be synchronous between partners for both physical and psychological aggression toward a partner.

Women's Perpetration and Their Own Risk for Injury

The importance of a developmental systems approach to understanding the risk of impacts of aggression is seen in the work on women's perpetration of aggression and their own risk for injury. Capaldi and Owen (2001) found that when a young woman was frequently aggressive toward her partner, she herself had a three-times-greater likelihood of injury, and she also had a higher probability of more frequent and severe injuries. These findings are in keeping with the contention of Straus and colleagues that one reason physical aggression toward a partner by women is an important problem is that it may put them in danger of retaliation by their partners that may result in injury (Feld & Straus, 1989; Straus, 1999).

Dissatisfaction and Relationship Instability

Further impacts of aggression for couples may include declining satisfaction with the relationship and a greater likelihood of separation or divorce. It may be that consequences for hostility (associated with psychological aggression) and for physical aggression are rather different. In an analysis of the UCLA newlywed sample at 4-year follow-up, Rogge and Bradbury (1999) found that dyadic hostile negative affect (husband and wife anger and contempt), humor (husband and wife humor, negatively correlated with hostile negative affect), and self-reports of husbands' propensity toward anger discriminated between happy and unhappy intact marriages, whereas reported dyadic physical aggression discriminated between couples who were together and couples who were separated/divorced. This study is the only one that we know of that includes both couples' aggression and affective processes in prediction and is rare for its incorporation of multiple approaches and outcomes of both marital satisfaction and separation/divorce.

■ Conclusions

Recent studies on aggression in couples indicate that this is a complex behavior, and advancement of our understanding of this behavior is most likely with a developmental systems approach that takes into account the multiple levels of factors involved in initial emergence, as well as the course of this behavior. Fundamental questions still need to be answered regarding the nature of aggression in couples in order for us to understand this behavior and to improve prevention and treatment programs. At this stage of our knowledge, findings certainly indicate that psychopathology and social interactions are implicated in the prediction of aggression for men and women. In addition, study of the couple as a developing dyad is critical to understanding aggressive behavior. For prevention and intervention programs to be most effective, it seems that individual psychopathology, socialization, dyadic aspects of aggression in relationships, and the roles of both men and women in the etiology and process of aggression must be addressed in order to reach the goal of decreasing aggression in romantic relationships and the damaging impacts of such aggression.

■ Acknowledgments

The authors would like to thank Jane Wilson, Rhody Hinks, and the data collection team staff for their commitment to high quality and complete data and Sally Schwader for editorial assistance. Support for this work was provided by Grant RO1 MH 50259 from the Prevention, Early Intervention, and Epidemiology Branch, National Institute of Mental Health (NIMH), U.S. PHS. Additional support was provided by Grant R37 MH 37940 from the Prevention, Early Intervention, and Epidemiology Branch, NIMH, U.S. PHS; Grant R01 HD 34511 from the Center for Research for Mothers and Children, National Institute of Child Health and Human Development, U.S. PHS; and Grant MH P30 46690 Prevention, Early Intervention, and Epidemiology Branch, NIMH, and ORMH Office of Research on Minority Health, U.S. PHS.

■ References

Andrews, J. A., Foster, S. L., Capaldi, D., & Hops, H. (2000). Adolescent and family predictors of physical aggression, communication, and satisfaction in young adult couples: A prospective analysis. *Journal of Consulting and Clinical Psychology, 68,* 195–208.

Archer, J. (1994). Introduction. In J. Archer (Ed.), *Male violence* (pp. 1–20). London and New York: Routledge.

Archer, J. (2000). Sex differences in aggression between heterosexual partners: A meta-analytic review. *Psychological Bulletin, 126,* 651–680.

Babcock, J. C., Green, C. E., Webb, S. A., & Graham, K. H. (2004). A second failure to replicate the Gottman et al. (1995) typology of men who abuse intimate partners . . . and possible reasons why. *Journal of Family Psychology, 18,* 396–400.

Babcock, J. C., Miller, S. A., & Siard, C. (2003). Toward a typology of abusive women: Differences between partner-only and generally violent women in the use of violence. *Psychology of Women Quarterly, 27,* 153–161.

Baltes, P. B. (1983). Life-span developmental psychology: Observations on history and theory revisited. In R. M. Lerner (Ed.), *Developmental psychology: Historical and philosophical perspectives* (pp. 79–11). Hillsdale, NJ: Erlbaum.

Biden, J. R., Jr. (1993). Violence against women: The congressional response. *American Psychologist, 48,* 1059–1061.

Blumstein, A., Cohen, J., Roth, J. A., & Visher, C. A. (Eds.). (1986). *Criminal careers and career criminals* (Vol. 1). Washington, DC: National Academy Press.

Bradbury, T. N. (2002). Invited program overview: Research on relationships as a prelude to action. *Journal of Social and Personal Relationships, 19,* 571–599.

Bradbury, T. N., & Lawrence, E. (1999). Physical aggression and the longitudinal course of newlywed marriage. In X. B. Arriaga & S. Oskamp (Eds.), *Violence in intimate relationships* (pp. 181–202). Thousand Oaks, CA: Sage.

Bronfenbrenner, U. (1979). *The ecology of human development: Experiments by nature and by design.* Cambridge, MA: Harvard University Press.

Bronfenbrenner, U. (1986). Ecology of family as a context for human development: Research perspectives. *Developmental Psychology, 22,* 723–742.

Burman, B., John, R. S., & Margolin, G. (1992). Observed patterns of conflict in violent, nonviolent, and nondistressed couples. *Behavioral Assessment, 14,* 15–37.

Buss, D. M. (1987). Selection, evocation, and manipulation. *Journal of Personality and Social Psychology, 53,* 1214–1221.

Cairns, R. B., & Cairns, B. D. (1995). Social ecology over time and space. In P. Moen, J. G. H. Elder, & K. Luscher (Eds.), *Examining lives in context* (pp. 397–421). Washington, DC: American Psychological Association.

Cantos, A. L., Neidig, P. H., & O'Leary, K. D. (1994). Injuries of women and men in a treatment program for domestic violence. *Journal of Family Violence, 9,* 113–124.

Capaldi, D. M. (1991). The co-occurrence of conduct problems and depressive symptoms in early adolescent boys: I. Familial factors and general adjustment at Grade 6. *Development and Psychopathology, 3,* 277–300.

Capaldi, D. M. (1992). The co-occurrence of conduct problems and depressive symptoms in early adolescent boys: II. A 2-year follow-up at grade 8. *Development and Psychopathology, 4,* 125–144.

Capaldi, D. M., & Clark, S. (1998). Prospective family predictors of aggression toward female partners for at-risk young men. *Developmental Psychology, 34,* 1175–1188.

Capaldi, D. M., & Crosby, L. (1997). Observed and reported psychological and physical aggression in young, at-risk couples. *Social Development, 6,* 184–206.

Capaldi, D. M., Dishion, T. J., Stoolmiller, M., & Yoerger, K. (2001). Aggression toward female partners by at-risk young men: The contribution of male adolescent friendships. *Developmental Psychology, 37,* 61–73.

Capaldi, D. M., & Gorman-Smith, D. (2003). Physical and psychological aggression in male/female adolescent and young adult couples. In P. Florsheim (Ed.), *Adolescent romantic relationships and sexual behavior: Theory, research and practical implications* (pp. 244–278). Mahwah, NJ: Erlbaum.

Capaldi, D. M., & Kim, H. K. (2002, November). *Aggression toward a partner in young adulthood: Longitudinal pattern and predictors.* Paper presented at the annual meeting of the Association for Advancement of Behavior Therapy, Reno, NV.

Capaldi, D. M., & Owen, L. D. (2001). Physical aggression in a community sample of at-risk young couples: Gender comparisons for high frequency, injury, and fear. *Journal of Family Psychology, 15,* 425–440.

Capaldi, D. M., Pears, K. C., Patterson, G. R., & Owen, L. D. (2003). Continuity of parenting practices across generations in an at-risk sample: A prospective comparison of direct and mediated associations. *Journal of Abnormal Child Psychology, 31,* 127–142.

Capaldi, D. M., & Shortt, J. W. (2003). Understanding conduct problems in adolescence from a lifespan perspective. In G. R. Adams & M. D. Berzonsky (Eds.), *Blackwell handbook of adolescence* (pp. 470–493). Oxford, UK: Blackwell.

Capaldi, D. M., Shortt, J. W., & Crosby, L. (2003). Physical and psychological aggression in at-risk young couples: Stability and change in young adulthood. *Merrill-Palmer Quarterly, 49,* 1–27.

Carlson, B. E. (1987). Dating violence: A research review and comparison with spouse abuse. *Social Casework: The Journal of Contemporary Social Work, 68,* 16–23.

Caspi, A., & Elder, G. H. (1988). Childhood precursors of the life course: Early personality and life disorganization. In E. M. Hetherington, R. M. Lerner, & M. Perlmutter (Eds.), *Child development in life-span perspective* (pp. 115–142). Hillsdale, NJ: Erlbaum.

Cordova, J. V., Jacobson, N. S., Gottman, J. M., Rushe, R. H., & Cox, G. (1993). Negative reciprocity and communication in couples with a violent husband. *Journal of Abnormal Psychology, 104,* 559–564.

De Jong Gierveld, J. (1995). Research into relationship research designs: Personal relationships under the microscope. *Journal of Social and Personal Relationships, 12,* 583–588.

Dishion, T. J., Eddy, J. M., Haas, E., Li, F., & Spracklen, K. (1997). Friendships and violent behavior during adolescence. *Social Development, 6*, 207–225.

Dishion, T. J., French, D. C., & Patterson, G. R. (1995). The development and ecology of antisocial behavior. In D. Cicchetti & D. J. Cohen (Eds.), *Developmental psychopathology: Risk, disorder, and adaptation* (Vol. 2, pp. 421–471). New York: Wiley.

Dishion, T. J., & Patterson, G. R. (1997). The timing and severity of antisocial behavior: Three hypotheses within an ecological framework. In D. M. Stoff, J. Breiling, & J. D. Maser (Eds.), *Handbook of antisocial behavior* (pp. 205–217). New York: Wiley.

Dobash, R. E., & Dobash, R. (1979). *Violence against wives: A case against the patriarchy.* New York: Free Press.

Dobash, R. P., Dobash, R. E., Wilson, M., & Daly, M. (1992). The myth of sexual symmetry in marital violence. *Social Problems, 39*, 71–91.

Dutton, D. G., & Painter, S. L. (1993). Emotional attachments in abusive relationships: A test of traumatic bonding theory. *Violence and Victims, 8*, 105–120.

Ehrensaft, M. K., Cohen, P., Brown, J., Smailes, E., & Johnson, J. (2003). Intergenerational transmission of partner violence: A 20-year prospective study. *Journal of Consulting and Clinical Psychology, 71*, 741–753.

Elder, G. H., Jr. (1985). Perspectives on the life course. In J. G. H. Elder (Ed.), *Life course dynamics: Trajectories and transitions* (pp. 23–49). Ithaca, NY: Cornell University Press.

Elliott, D. S., Huizinga, D., & Morse, B. J. (1985). *The dynamics of delinquent behavior: A National Survey Progress Report.* Boulder: University of Colorado, Institute of Behavioral Sciences.

Fagan, J., & Browne, A. (1994). Violence between spouses and intimates: Physical aggression between women and men in intimate relationships. In A. J. Reiss & J. A. Roth (Eds.), *Understanding and preventing violence: Social influences* (Vol. 3, pp. 115–292). Washington, DC: National Academy Press.

Feld, S. L., & Straus, M. A. (1989). Escalation and desistance of wife assault in marriage. *Criminology, 27*, 141–161.

Follingstad, D. R., Rutledge, L. L., Berg, B. J., Hause, E. S., & Polek, D. S. (1990). The role of emotional abuse in physically abusive relationships. *Journal of Family Violence, 5*, 107–120.

Gelles, R. J., & Harrop, J. W. (1989). Violence, battering, and psychological distress among women. *Journal of Interpersonal Violence, 4*, 400–420.

Gelles, R. J., & Straus, M. A. (1988). *Intimate violence: The causes and consequences of abuse in the American family.* New York: Simon & Schuster.

Giles-Sims, J. (1983). *Wife battering: A systems theory approach.* New York: Guilford Press.

Giordano, P. C., Millhollin, T. J., Cernkovich, S. A., Pugh, M. D., & Rudolph, J. L. (1999). Delinquency, identity, and women's involvement in relationship violence. *Criminology, 27*, 17–40.

Gortner, E. T., Gollan, J. K., & Jacobson, N. S. (1997). Psychological aspects of perpetrators of domestic violence and their relationships with the victims. *The Psychiatric Clinics of North America, 20*, 337–352.

Gotlib, I. H., & Hooley, J. M. (1988). Depression and marital distress: Current status and future directions. In S. Duck & D. F. Hay (Eds.), *Handbook of personal relationships: Theory, research and interventions* (pp. 543–570). New York: Wiley.

Gottman, J. M. (1980). Consistency of nonverbal affect and affect reciprocity in marital interaction. *Journal of Consulting and Clinical Psychology, 48*, 711–717.

Gottman, J. M. (2001). Crime, hostility, wife battering, and the heart: On the Meehan et al. (2001) failure to replicate the Gottman et al. (1995) typology. *Journal of Family Psychology, 15,* 409–414.

Gottman, J. M., Coan, J., Carrere, S., & Swanson, C. (1998). Predicting marital happiness and stability from newlywed interactions. *Journal of Marriage and the Family, 60,* 5–22.

Gottman, J. M., Jacobson, N. S., Rushe, R. H., Shortt, J. W., Babcock, J., La Taillade, J. J., et al. (1995). The relationship between heart rate reactivity, emotionally aggressive behavior, and general violence in batterers. *Journal of Family Psychology, 9,* 227–248.

Gottman, J. M., & Levenson, R. W. (1984). *Why marriages fail: Affective and physiological patterns in marital interaction.* San Diego, CA: Academic Press.

Granic, I., Dishion, T. J., & Hollenstein, T. (2003). The family ecology of adolescence: A dynamic systems perspective on normative development. In G. R. Adams & M. D. Berzonsky (Eds.), *Blackwell handbook of adolescence* (pp. 60–91). Oxford, UK: Blackwell.

Gray, H. M., & Foshee, V. A. (1997). Adolescent dating violence: Differences between one-sided and mutually violent profiles. *Journal of Interpersonal Violence, 12,* 126–141.

Hamby, S. L. (1998). Partner violence: Prevention and intervention. In J. L. Jasinski, L. M. Williams, & D. Finkelhor (Eds.), *Partner violence: A comprehensive review of 20 years of research* (pp. 210–258). Thousand Oaks, CA: Sage.

Henton, J. M., Cate, R. M., Koval, J., Lloyd, S., & Christopher, F. S. (1983). Romance and violence in dating relationships. *Journal of Family Issues, 4,* 467–482.

Hetherington, E. M., & Baltes, P. B. (1988). Child psychology and life-span development. In E. M. Hetherington & R. M. Lerner (Eds.), *Child development in life-span perspective* (pp. 1–19). Hillsdale, NJ: Erlbaum.

Heyman, R. E. (2001). Observation of couple conflicts: Clinical assessment applications, stubborn truths, and shaky foundations. *Psychological Assessment, 13,* 5–35.

Heyman, R. E., Slep, A. M. S., Capaldi, D. M., Eddy, J. M., & Stoolmiller, M. (1999, April). *Physical aggression in couples' relationships: Toward understanding violent acts and their impacts.* Paper presented at the SUMMARY of the Raymond and Rosalie Weiss Foundation Think Tank on Aggression in Couples, Oregon Social Learning Center, Eugene, OR.

Holtzworth-Munroe, A., Meehan, J. C., Herron, K., Rehman, U., & Stuart, G. L. (2000). Testing the Holtzworth-Munroe & Stuart (1994) batterer typology. *Journal of Consulting and Clinical Psychology, 68,* 1000–1019.

Holtzworth-Munroe, A., Meehan, J. C., Herron, K., Rehman, U., & Stuart, G. L. (2003). Do subtypes of maritally violent men continue to differ over time? *Journal of Consulting and Clinical Psychology, 71,* 728–740.

Holtzworth-Munroe, A., & Stuart, G. L. (1994). Typologies of male batterers: Three subtypes and the differences among them. *Psychological Bulletin, 116,* 476–597.

Jacobson, N. S., Gottman, J. M., Waltz, J., Rushe, R., Babcock, J., & Holtzworth-Munroe, A. (1994). Affect, verbal content, and psychophysiology in the arguments of couples with a violent husband. *Journal of Consulting and Clinical Psychology, 62,* 982–988.

Johnson, M. P. (1995). Patriarchal terrorism and common couple violence: Two forms of violence against women. *Journal of Marriage and the Family, 57,* 283–294.

Johnson, M. P. (1999, November). *Two types of violence against women in the American family: Identifying patriarchal terrorism and common couple violence.* Paper presented at the National Council on Family Relations, Irvine, CA.

Johnson, M. P., & Ferraro, K. J. (2000). Research on domestic violence in the 1990s: The discovery of differences. *Journal of Marriage and the Family, 62,* 948–963.

Johnson, M. P., & Leone, J. M. (2000, July). *The differential effects of patriarchal terrorism and common couple violence: Findings from the National Violence Against Women Survey.* Paper presented at the Tenth International Conference on Personal Relationships, Brisbane, Australia.

Johnson, S. L., & Jacob, T. (1997). Marital interactions of depressed men and women. *Journal of Consulting and Clinical Psychology, 1,* 15–23.

Jouriles, E. N., Norwood, W. D., McDonald, R., & Peters, B. (2001). Domestic violence and child adjustment. In J. H. Grych & F. D. Fincham (Eds.), *Interparental conflict and child development: Theory, research, and applications* (pp. 315–336). New York: Cambridge University Press.

Keenan, K., Loeber, R., & Green, S. (1999). Conduct disorder in girls: A review of the literature. *Clinical Child and Family Psychology Review, 2,* 3–19.

Kim, H. K., & Capaldi, D. M. (2004). The association of antisocial behavior and depressive symptoms between partners and risk for aggression in romantic relationships. *Journal of Family Psychology, 18,* 82–96.

Krueger, R. F., Moffitt, T. E., Caspi, A., Bleske, A., & Silva, P. A. (1998). Assortative mating for antisocial behavior: Developmental and methodological implications. *Behavior Genetics, 28,* 173–186.

Kurz, D. (1993). Physical assaults by husbands: A major social problem. In R. J. Gelles & D. R. Loseke (Eds.), *Current controversies on family violence* (pp. 88–103). Newbury Park, CA: Sage.

Laner, M. R., & Thompson, J. (1982). Abuse and aggression in courting couples. *Deviant Behavior, 3,* 229–244.

Leone, J. M., Johnson, M. P., Cohan, C. L., & Lloyd, S. (2001, June). *Consequences of different types of domestic violence for low-income, ethnic women: A control-based typology of male-partner violence.* Paper presented at the International Network on Personal Relationships, Prescott, AZ.

Lerner, R. M. (2002). *Concepts and theories of human development* (3rd ed.). Hillsdale, NJ: Erlbaum.

Lerner, R. M., & Castellino, D. R. (2002). Contemporary developmental theory and adolescence: Developmental systems and applied developmental science. *Journal of Adolescent Health, 22,* 122–135.

Linder, J. R., Crick, N. R., & Collins, W. A. (2002). Relational aggression and victimization in young adults' romantic relationships: Associations with perceptions of parent, peer, and romantic relationship quality. *Social Development, 11,* 69–86.

Lorber, M. F., & O'Leary, K. D. (2002, November). *Psychological aggression at engagement predicts increases in male physical aggression in early marriage.* Paper presented at the annual meeting of the Association for Advancement of Behavior Therapy, Reno, NV.

Maes, H. H. M., Neale, M. C., Kendler, K. S., Hewitt, J. K., Silberg, J. L., Foley, D. L., et al. (1998). Assortative mating for major psychiatric diagnoses in two population-based samples. *Psychological Medicine, 28,* 1389–1401.

Magdol, L., Moffitt, T. E., Caspi, A., & Silva, P. A. (1998). Hitting without a license: Testing explanations for differences in partner abuse between young adult daters and cohabitors. *Journal of Marriage and the Family, 60,* 41–55.

Magnusson, D., & Toerestad, B. (1993). A holistic view of personality: A model revisited. *Annual Review of Psychology, 44,* 427–452.

Margolin, G., John, R. S., & Gleberman, L. (1988). Affective responses to conflictual discussions in violent and nonviolent couples. *Journal of Consulting and Clinical Psychology, 56,* 24–33.

Markman, H. J., Notarius, C. I., Stephen, T., & Smith, T. (1981). Behavioral observation systems for couples: The current status. In E. E. Filsinger & R. A. Lewis (Eds.), *Assessing marriage: New behavioral approaches* (pp. 234–262). Beverly Hills, CA: Sage.

Martin, D. (1976). *Battered wives.* San Francisco: Glide.

McCabe, S. B., & Gotlib, I. H. (1993). Interactions of couples with and without a depressed spouse: Self-report and observations of problem-solving situations. *Journal of Social and Personal Relationships, 10,* 589–599.

McLaughlin, I. G., Leonard, K. E., & Senchak, M. (1992). Prevalence and distribution of premarital aggression among couples applying for a marriage license. *Journal of Family Violence, 7,* 309–319.

McLeod, J. D. (1995). Social and psychological bases of homogamy for common psychiatric disorders. *Journal of Marriage and the Family, 57,* 201–214.

Meehan, J. C., & Holtzworth-Munroe, A. (2001). Heart rate reactivity in male batterers: Reply to Gottman (2001) and a second look at the evidence. *Journal of Family Psychology, 15,* 415–424.

Meehan, J. C., Holtzworth-Munroe, A., & Herron, K. (2001). Maritally violent men's heart rate reactivity to marital interactions: A failure to replicate the Gottman et al. (1995) typology. *Journal of Family Psychology, 15,* 394–408.

Merikangas, K. R. (1982). Assortative mating for psychiatric disorders and psychological traits. *Archives of General Psychiatry, 39,* 1173–1180.

Merikangas, K. R., & Spiker, D. G. (1982). Assortative mating among in-patients with primary affective disorder. *Psychological Medicine, 12,* 753–764.

Moffitt, T. E., & Caspi, A. (1999). *Findings about partner violence from the Dunedin Multidisciplinary Health and Development Study* (NCJ 170018). Washington, DC: U.S. Department of Justice, Office of Justice Programs, National Institute of Justice.

Muthén, B. O., & Muthén, L. K. (2000). Integrating person-centered and variable-centered analyses: Growth mixture modeling with latent trajectory classes. *Alcoholism: Clinical and Experimental Research, 24,* 882–891.

Nagin, D. S. (1999). Analyzing developmental trajectories: A semiparametric, group-based approach. *Psychological Methods, 4,* 139–157.

Okun, L. (1986). *Woman abuse: Facts replacing myths.* Albany: State University of New York Press.

O'Leary, K. D. (1999). Developmental and affective issues in assessing and treating partner aggression. *Clinical Psychology: Science and Practice, 6,* 400–414.

O'Leary, K. D., Barling, J., Arias, I., Rosenbaum, A., Malone, J., & Tyree, A. (1989). Prevalence and stability of physical aggression between spouses: A longitudinal analysis. *Journal of Consulting and Clinical Psychology, 57,* 263–268.

Patterson, G. R. (1982). *Coercive family process.* Eugene, OR: Castalia.

Patterson, G. R., Reid, J. B., & Dishion, T. J. (1992). *A social learning approach: Antisocial boys* (Vol. 4). Eugene, OR: Castalia.

Rogge, R. D., & Bradbury, T. N. (1999). Till violence does us part: The differing roles of communication and aggression in predicting adverse marital outcomes. *Journal of Consulting and Clinical Psychology, 67,* 340–351.

Roscoe, B., & Benaske, N. (1985). Courtship violence experienced by abused wives: Similarities in patterns of abuse. *Family Relations: Journal of Applied Family and Child Studies, 34,* 419–424.

Rosenbaum, A., & O'Leary, K. D. (1981). Marital violence: Characteristics of abusive couples. *Journal of Consulting and Clinical Psychology, 49,* 63–71.

Rosenthal, R., & Rosnow, R. L. (1975). Characteristics of the volunteer subject. In R. Rosenthal & R. L. Rosnow (Eds.), *The volunteer subject* (pp. 84–90). New York: Wiley.

Rutter, M. (1989). Pathways from childhood to adult life. *Journal of Child Psychology and Psychiatry and Allied Disciplines, 30,* 23–51.

Sameroff, A. J. (1983). Developmental systems: Contexts and evolution. In W. Kessen (Ed.), *Handbook of child psychology: History, theory and methods* (Vol. 1, pp. 237–294). New York: Wiley.

Scarr, S., & McCartney, K. (1983). How people make their own environments: A theory of genotype leading to environment effects. *Child Development, 54,* 424–435.

Schafer, J., Caetano, R., & Clark, C. L. (2002). Agreement about violence in U. S. couples. *Journal of Interpersonal Violence, 17,* 457–470.

Simons, R. L., & Johnson, C. (1998). An examination of competing explanations for the intergenerational transmission of domestic violence. In Y. Danieli (Ed.), *International handbook of the Plenum series on stress and coping* (pp. 553–570). New York: Plenum.

Simons, R. L., Johnson, C., Beaman, J., & Conger, R. D. (1993). Explaining women's double jeopardy: Factors that mediate the association between harsh treatment as a child and violence by a husband. *Journal of Marriage and the Family, 55,* 713–723.

Stets, J. E. (1991). Psychological aggression in dating relationships: The role of interpersonal control. *Journal of Family Violence, 6,* 97–114.

Straus, M. A. (1973). A general systems theory approach to a theory of violence between family members. *Social Science Information, 12,* 105–125.

Straus, M. A. (1979). Measuring intrafamily conflict and violence: The Conflict Tactics (CT) Scale. *Journal of Marriage and the Family, 41,* 75–88.

Straus, M. A. (1990a). The Conflict Tactics Scales and its critics: An evaluation and new data on validity and reliability. In M. A. Straus & R. G. Gelles (Eds.), *Physical violence in American families: Risk factors and adaptations to violence in 8,145 families* (pp. 49–73). New Brunswick, NJ: Transaction.

Straus, M. A. (1990b). Injury and frequency of assault and the "representative sample fallacy" in measuring wife beating and child abuse. In M. A. Straus & R. G. Gelles (Eds.), *Physical violence in American families: Risk factors and adaptations to violence in 8,145 families* (pp. 75–91). New Brunswick, NJ: Transaction.

Straus, M. A. (1999). The controversy over domestic violence by women: A methodological, theoretical, and sociology of science analysis. In X. B. Arriaga & S. Oskamp (Eds.), *Violence in intimate relationships* (pp. 17–44). Thousand Oaks, CA: Sage.

Straus, M. A., & Gelles, R. J. (1986). Societal change and change in family violence from 1975 to 1985 as revealed by two national surveys. *Journal of Marriage and the Family, 48,* 465–478.

Straus, M. A., Hamby, S. L., Boney-McCoy, S., & Sugarman, D. B. (1996). The revised conflict tactics scales (CTS2): Development and preliminary psychometric data. *Journal of Family Issues, 17,* 283–316.

Sugarman, D. B., & Hotaling, G. I. (1989). Dating violence: Prevalence, context, and risk markers. In M. A. Pirog-Good & J. E. Stets (Eds.), *Violence in dating relationships: Emerging social issues* (pp. 3–32). New York: Praeger.

Szinovacz, M. E., & Egley, L. C. (1995). Comparing one-partner and couple data on sensitive marital behaviors: The case of marital violence. *Journal of Marriage and the Family, 57,* 995–1010.

Walker, L. E. (1984). *The battered women syndrome.* New York: Springer.

White, J. W., Smith, P. H., Koss, M. P., & Figueredo, A. J. (2000). Intimate partner aggression—What have we learned? Comment on Archer (2000). *Psychological Bulletin, 126,* 690–696.

Woodward, L. J., Fergusson, D. M., & Horwood, L. J. (2002). Romantic relationships of young people with childhood and adolescent onset antisocial behavior problems. *Journal of Abnormal Child Psychology, 30,* 231–243.

7

Partner Violence and Men: A Focus on the Male Perpetrator

Amy Holtzworth-Munroe and Jeffrey C. Meehan

T he present chapter addresses male violence against an intimate female partner. The chapter consists of three main sections. First, we consider a series of questions that we are often asked about this research area, including such issues as why we study male rather than female violence, why we often focus on the individual rather than the dyad, and what the relationship between psychological abuse, physical violence, and marital distress may be. Growing out of our consideration of these issues, we next focus much of the chapter on the consideration of batterer typologies, presenting our own typology theory and study findings, discussing the clinical implications of our data, and considering some limitations of our approach. Finally, we end with a discussion of issues for future researchers to consider.

■ Why Focus on Male-Perpetrated Physical Aggression?

As discussed in the previous chapter, in the United States, physical aggression against an intimate partner is a serious problem with many negative consequences. The present chapter focuses on male aggression toward an intimate female partner. When the first author (A.H.M) began conducting research on marital violence, in the early 1980s, it was politically incorrect to even consider studying female aggression. Battered women's advocates had been working long and hard to draw attention to the problem of male violence and to establish safe shelters for battered women. Feminist theories of relationship violence were prevalent, focusing on male aggression as a socially sanctioned means for men to control and dominate women in our patriarchal country (e.g., Dobash & Dobash, 1979). Rumor had it that supporters of battered women had once protested any discussion of female aggression at a scientific conference so loudly that the presenters gave up and left the podium. Federal funding agencies were reluctant to fund research on female aggression (e.g., reviews of one of our early grant submissions instructed us that female aggression was not a problem and to focus on male aggression).

Thus, when the first author entered this research environment, as a graduate student, it was clear that the focus of her research should be on male aggression! Interestingly though, she never felt at odds with this focus, as her clinical experience working with violent couples was consistent with the field's greater concern regarding male violence than female violence. Specifically, her clinical work with couples in conjoint therapy, men in batterers' treatment programs, and women in battered women's support groups suggested that women were more likely to be injured and upset by male violence than vice versa.

This issue represents a case where, in our opinion, research eventually "caught up" with the rest of the field, providing empirical data to support what began as a political stance—the importance of focusing on male violence. To be clear, research does demonstrate that both men and women engage in physical aggression in their intimate relationships; indeed, in young samples, the prevalence of female aggression often exceeds the prevalence of male aggression (Archer, 2000). Yet the vast majority of available studies demonstrate that male aggression has more negative consequences than female aggression. While there are a very few exceptions to this finding (i.e., Capaldi & Owen, 2001, did not find higher rates of injury and fear among women than among men), most researchers have consistently documented gender differences in the consequences of relationship violence. For example, Holtzworth-Munroe, Smutzler, and Bates (1997) reviewed nine studies that were not focused on batterers or severe levels of violence (i.e., three studies of nationally representative samples, four of couples seeking marital therapy, and two of couples with a partner in the military). Such studies consistently demonstrated that, even among couples in which both partners used physical aggression, women were more likely than men to be physically injured and, when such factors were examined, women were more likely than men to suffer psychological consequences of partner aggression (e.g., depression, marital dissatisfaction). Similarly, Archer (2000), in a review of 20 studies, found that women were more likely to be injured by male violence than men were to be injured by female violence. Studies of severe levels of domestic violence (e.g., battered women's shelter or domestic violence treatment samples) find even more striking differences between the consequences of male and female violence.

Given such data, while we have never suggested that female aggression is not important, we have argued that it is particularly important to focus on male aggression. As a result, our research program has focused on trying to understand husband, not wife, violence.

■ Why Focus on One Individual (the Husband) Versus the Dyad or Family System?

As the first author's graduate training involved working with Neil Jacobson, a prominent marital therapy researcher, it may seem odd that her work (and that of many other marital violence researchers) focuses so heavily on the individual characteristics of maritally violent men, rather than on dyadic processes that may underlie marital violence. At least two explanations of this focus are presented here.

Research Comparing Violent and Nonviolent Men
and Battered and Nonbattered Women

There are dozens of studies showing that maritally violent men differ from non-violent men on a wide variety of factors, including psychopathology, personality disorders, substance abuse, criminality, beliefs and attitudes, attachment patterns, social skills and communication behaviors, and exposure to violence in their family of origin (see one review of this research in Holtzworth-Munroe, Bates, Smutzler, & Sandin, 1997). As the first author jokingly tells colleagues, the husband violence research area was a great research field to enter, at the time when she did so, because almost every study she has ever conducted, comparing violent and nonviolent husbands on almost any variable, has resulted in significant group differences and thus been publishable! Such findings clearly suggest that violent men differ in many ways from nonviolent men and thus hint that the causes of marital violence may lie within individual characteristics of the man.

In contrast to the burgeoning research findings on the characteristics of violent men, the role of women in relationship violence has not been well studied, perhaps due to concerns about blaming the victim (i.e., examining a battered woman's role in relationship violence). Such biases likely have affected the types of research conducted and variables examined. The field's biases have led most researchers to interpret studies in a manner that suggests that male problems are determinants of male's perpetration of violence, while female problems are more likely a consequence of being a victim of violence. For example, while researchers examine whether women's psychological symptoms decrease following their leaving an abusive relationship, to our knowledge, researchers have not studied whether men's psychological symptoms lessen the longer they are out of a relationship in which they perpetrated violence. Such issues may be examined in future research.

In the meantime, despite such biases, research comparing battered and non-battered women does not consistently show the same strong group differences as research comparing violent and nonviolent men (see review in Holtzworth-Munroe, Smutzler, & Sandin, 1997). There certainly are some group differences. For example, women with violent husbands engage in more negative communication behaviors during marital interactions than wives in nonviolent relationships; however, there are not consistent differences between these groups on other variables, such as sex-role attitudes or exposure to violence in the family of origin. In addition, some of the research on battered women does suggest that their psychopathology may be a consequence, not a cause, of experiencing relationship violence. For example, longitudinal studies suggest that the occurrence of husband violence temporally precedes women's depression and marital dissatisfaction and that women's psychological distress symptoms lessen the longer the time elapsed following exit from a violent relationship (see review in Holtzworth-Munroe, Smutzler, & Sandin, 1997).

In summary, the existing data suggest that there are more consistent group differences between maritally violent and nonviolent men than between battered and nonbattered women. Such findings may support the notion that the causes of violence may lie within the individual man, rather than within the relationship.

Differing Causes (Individual Versus Dyadic)
for Differing Types of Male Violence

Related to this issue, researchers in this area seem to be reaching a consensus about two related issues: (a) there are differing types of male violence, with at least two differing levels of marital violence, and (b) the causes of these differing levels of violence may be different, with one reflecting more dyadic processes and the other seeming to lie within the individual man.

Regarding the first point, researchers in this field are beginning to reach some tentative agreement that differing levels and types of husband aggression exist and that differing terms might be used for these levels of violence (e.g., Holtzworth-Munroe & Stuart, 1994; Lawrence, 2002). In general, the term batterer is used for more severe husband violence. However, to our knowledge, there is no agreement regarding exactly what defines a batterer. Some researchers discuss the severity/frequency of violence alone, while others insist that some degree of wife injury, fear of the partner, psychological abuse, or control/domination is also necessary.

In addition, to our knowledge, there is no agreed upon term for lower levels of violence (e.g., minor violence, O'Leary, 1993; common couple violence, Johnson, 1995; family-only men, Holtzworth-Munroe & Stuart, 1994), suggesting that one can debate whether the term *batterer* is the best label for less violent men. Indeed, many in the field are not comfortable using differing labels to refer to differing levels of husband violence. For example, some battered women advocates believe that any physical aggression on the part of the husband makes him a batterer. Similarly, legally, if a husband is arrested for even one shove or slap, he is a "batterer," charged with "battery."

More important than semantics, there is a growing movement in the field to view lower levels of marital violence as due to dyadic, relationship factors (e.g., Johnson's 1995 term, common couple violence), while more severe husband violence is often seen as being primarily due to the man's characteristics (e.g., Johnson's patriarchal terrorism). For example, this idea is discussed in a recent review article by Lawrence (2002): "Researchers have begun to view domestic violence as encompassing two types of phenomena. The first type is alternatively referred to as situational violence ... or family-only violence, and the second type as battering ... antisocial/general violence, or terrorism. Stable aggression [the second type] suggests importance of biological and intrapersonal factors whereas unstable aggression [the first type] reflects environmental or interactional factors" (pp. 3, 4).

In our own typology work, we have made similar hypotheses. As discussed in Holtzworth-Munroe, Meehan, Herron, Rehman, and Stuart (2003), the question of whether batterer subtypes' behavior and characteristics are stable over time has been the subject of theoretical debate. Some have suggested that the subtypes of maritally violent men, identified cross-sectionally, may represent different phases of marital violence, with violent husbands progressing from one, less violent subtype to another, more severely violent subtype, as their violence escalates over time (Gondolf, 1988; Saunders, 1992). Such predictions are consistent with the assumption that husband violence, once begun, inevitably escalates in frequency and severity (e.g., Pagelow, 1981; Walker, 1979). In contrast to this suggestion, the few longitudinal studies of husband violence conducted to date suggest that the initial severity level of violence is the best predictor of violence continuation, such that men engaging in low levels of violence do not necessarily escalate their violence level over time (e.g., Aldarondo, 1996; Feld & Straus, 1989; Jacobson, Gottman, Gartner, Berns, & Shortt, 1996; Lawrence & Bradbury, 2001; O'Leary et al., 1989; Quigley & Leonard, 1996). Thus, we did not predict that subtypes would represent phases in the escalation of relationship violence. Instead, we hypothesized that the violence levels of the subtypes of maritally violent men would continue to differ significantly over time. More severely violent men would continue to engage in more marital violence and related relationship abuse (e.g., sexual and psychological aggression), while less severely violent men would maintain lower levels of abuse or even desist from relationship violence over time. As discussed below, our study findings supported this notion.

In addition, to our knowledge, few researchers have yet examined the stability of batterer characteristics that are theoretically linked to a man's use of violence. In doing so in our typology study, we predicted that, over time, the subtypes would continue to differ in the same manner in which they differed initially. Our prediction of subgroup stability on individual differences assumed to be related to violence perpetration is based on our implicit hypothesis that the relationship violence of severely violent men is related to stable individual characteristics of these men. Indirectly, our model proposes that the individual characteristics of some men put them at high risk for perpetrating severe relationship violence; in these relationships, the man is the cause of the relationship violence and is likely to carry his violence forward, across time and across relationships. Thus, the individual characteristics of these men that are theoretically linked to their use of violence (e.g., antisociality, insecure attachment, impulsivity) should remain relatively constant across time. In contrast, the low levels of violence perpetrated by our least violent subgroup, while reflecting some individual characteristics of the man, may also be more strongly related to dyadic factors (e.g., marital conflict), life stressors (e.g., job loss), and the cultural acceptability of low levels of relationship aggression (e.g., media portrayals of couples using aggression to resolve conflicts). If this is correct, then the men in our least violent subgroup are not men in the early phases of developing a life-long pattern of escalating relationship aggression, but rather, over time, should use violence inconsistently and should continue to evidence low levels of risk factors for relationship violence (e.g., relative to the other subtypes, these men should report less psychopathology, less positive attitudes toward violence, less impulsivity). Thus, our prediction was that the subtypes of maritally violent men would not change over time. As reviewed below, our study data generally supported this hypothesis.

In summary, to date, the research field has focused more attention on individual characteristics of men as causes for violence than on female or dyad characteristics, and research has demonstrated a wide variety of group differences between maritally violent and nonviolent men. Yet there also is a growing consensus, and some supporting evidence, for the notion that differing types or levels of male violence may have differing causes, with severe violence being more directly related to individual characteristics of men and lower levels of violence perhaps involving dyadic factors.

■ How Does Psychological Abuse Fit Into the Picture?

Increasingly, researchers also are examining husband-to-wife psychological aggression as an important correlate and predictor of physical abuse (e.g., see the special issue of *Violence and Victims*, 1999, on the topic). Interestingly, behaviors that are labeled psychological aggression (e.g., swearing, name-calling, yelling) are found to be prevalent among all couples, including engaged couples and nonviolent couples seeking marital therapy, not just among physically violent couples. The widespread nature of these behaviors raises the question of when such actions can be labeled abusive. Perhaps such behaviors only become abusive when they reach a certain level of severity and frequency (e.g., when a husband calls his wife names on a daily basis, not just during heated conflicts) or when they begin to differ, qualitatively, from what is statistically normal relationship conflict behavior (e.g., a husband who called his wife a whore and spit at her vs. less extreme name-calling). Similarly, it may be easier to identify certain subcategories of behavior as abusive (e.g., controlling jealous behaviors, such as tapping the phone or checking the mileage on a wife's car to make sure she only went where she said she was going) than others (e.g., swearing). Alternatively, it is possible that such behaviors primarily become abusive in the context of a physically violent relationship, as it is assumed that such actions carry an additional threat when they have previously preceded violence.

While such definitional issues have yet to be resolved, we do know that psychological aggression is a correlate of physical aggression and has damaging consequences for battered women. Indeed, many battered women report that emotional abuse has a more negative impact on them than physical violence (e.g., Follingstad, Rutledge, Berg, Hause, & Polek, 1990). In addition, available data suggest that psychological aggression may predict physical aggression. For example, Murphy and O'Leary (1989) found that husbands' use of psychological aggression at 18 months after marriage significantly predicted physical aggression 30 months after marriage. Given a growing interest in this important problem, it is hoped that future research will lead to a better understanding of psychological abuse, as we have yet to fully understand the relationship between emotional abuse, marital distress and conflict, and physical violence in relationships.

■ Do We Need a Unique Focus on Marital Violence, as Opposed to Marital Distress?

Early studies in this research area compared couples experiencing relationship violence to nonviolent couples. Such work methodologically confounded marital distress and marital violence, as these two problems are correlated with one another. In such studies, the nonviolent couples were more likely to have been more happily married than the violent couples. Thus, as research in this area has become more methodologically sophisticated, researchers have split their nonviolent comparison sample into a happily married group and other comparison groups, such as nonviolent but maritally distressed couples or verbally (but not physically) aggressive couples.

Such comparison groups are necessary to help us understand how some couples are able to experience marital conflict and distress but not engage in physical aggression, while others couples "cross the line" to use violence. The results of such studies are mixed. Some research has demonstrated group differences between violent and nonviolent/distressed couples. For example, relative to happy/nonviolent couples, while nonviolent/distressed couples show elevated levels of wife demand/husband withdraw communication, violent couples show elevated levels of both wife demand/husband withdraw and husband demand/wife withdraw. On the other hand, some research has not been able to differentiate between nonviolent/unhappy couples and violent couples. For example, as reviewed below, our own typology study failed to reveal any consistent differences between our nonviolent/distressed comparison sample and the least violent subtype of maritally violent man; our study thus failed to provide any information regarding why some men who are unhappily married sometimes engage in physical aggression and others do not.

It is important to note that we do not fully understand the relationship between marital distress and violence. For example, studies of community samples make it increasingly clear that there are couples who report marital satisfaction even though they have experienced physical aggression in their relationship. As would make sense, however, such marital satisfaction is usually absent in the presence of severe husband violence and may disappear over time even with exposure to only lower levels of violence. Indeed, studies of newlywed couples suggest that wives, in particular, begin to experience marital distress as a violent relationship progresses (e.g., Heyman, O'Leary, & Jouriles, 1995; Quigley & Leonard, 1996) and that violent newlywed marriages are more likely to be dissolved over time than nonviolent marriages (Rogge & Bradbury, 1999). In other words, physical aggression may precede, and lead to, marital distress.

Another issue we do not yet understand is whether marital distress and violence differ only quantitatively (i.e., violent is a more extreme version of marital distress) or also qualitatively (i.e., something about relationship violence is inherently different than marital distress). The discussion above, regarding differing types of male aggression, may be relevant to this issue. For example, one could argue that low levels of marital violence (e.g., common couple violence) is one version of marital dissatisfaction in a society that normalizes and accepts low levels of relationship violence as an expression of frustration and anger. As noted above, such a hypothesis would be consistent with our inability to differentiate less severely violent husbands from nonviolent/distressed men. In contrast, one could hypothesize that more severe marital violence may be qualitatively different than marital distress, being more related to individual psychopathology (e.g., anti-sociality) and having a differing impact on the relationships (e.g., physical injury, fear of the partner). Given the possible importance of considering varying types of male violence, we focus the rest of this chapter on batterer typologies.

■ Batterer Typologies

As discussed above, recent research has made it clear that samples of maritally violent men are heterogeneous, varying along theoretically important dimensions. Along with others, we have suggested that our understanding of husband violence will be advanced by drawing attention to these differences. Comparing subtypes of violent men to each other, and understanding how each type differs from non-violent men, may help us to identify different underlying processes resulting in violence. Attention to batterer typologies also might lead to improved outcome in batterers' treatment, by allowing us to better understand which subtypes of men benefit from treatment and to design treatments addressing the clinical issues of each subgroup.

The Holtzworth-Munroe and Stuart Typology

Holtzworth-Munroe and Stuart (1994) conducted a comprehensive review of the 15 published batterer typologies available at that time. Across these studies, we observed that batterer subtypes could be classified along three descriptive dimensions: (a) severity/frequency of the husband's marital violence, (b) generality of the man's violence (i.e., marital only or extrafamilial), and (c) the batterer's psychopathology or personality disorders. We proposed that, using these dimensions, three subtypes of batterers would be identified. *Family-only* (FO) batterers were predicted to engage in the least marital violence, the lowest levels of psychological and sexual abuse, and the least violence outside the home. Men in this group were predicted to evidence little or no psychopathology. *Dysphoric/borderline* (DB) batterers were predicted to engage in moderate to severe wife abuse. Their violence would be primarily confined to the wife, although some extrafamilial violence might be evident. This group would be the most psychologically distressed and the most likely to evidence borderline personality characteristics (e.g., extreme emotional lability; intense, unstable interpersonal relationships; fear of rejection). *Generally violent/antisocial* (GVA) batterers were predicted to be the most violent subtype, engaging in high levels of marital violence and the highest levels of extrafamilial violence. They would be the most likely to evidence characteristics of antisocial personality disorder (e.g., criminal behavior, arrests, substance abuse).

Holtzworth-Munroe and Stuart (1994) then integrated several intrapersonal theories of aggression into a developmental model of these differing types of husband violence. The model highlighted the importance of correlates of male violence, including both distal/historical correlates (e.g., violence in the family of origin, association with delinquent peers) and proximal correlates (e.g., attachment/

dependency; impulsivity; social skills in marital and nonmarital relationships; and attitudes, both hostile attitudes toward women and attitudes supportive of violence) as risk factors for differing batterer subtypes.

Based on this model, we predicted that among maritally violent men, family-only men would evidence the lowest levels of risk factors. The violence of family-only men was proposed to result from a combination of stress (personal and/or marital) and low-level risk factors (e.g., childhood exposure to marital violence, lack of relationship skills), such that, on some occasions, during escalating marital conflicts, these men would engage in physical aggression. Following such incidents, however, their low levels of psychopathology and related problems (e.g., low impulsivity, low attachment dysfunction), combined with their lack of hostility toward women and lack of positive attitudes toward violence, would lead to remorse and prevent their aggression from escalating. As noted above, our newer conceptualization of this subtype suggests that dyadic factors may be important to understanding the violence of FO men.

In contrast, dysphoric/borderline batterers were hypothesized to come from a background involving parental abuse and rejection. As a result, these men would have difficulty forming a stable, trusting attachment with an intimate partner. Instead, they would be very jealous and highly dependent upon, yet fearful of losing, their wives. They would tend to be impulsive, lack marital skills, and have attitudes that were hostile toward women and supportive of violence. This group resembles batterers studied by Dutton (1995), who suggests that their early traumatic experiences lead to borderline personality organization, anger, and insecure attachment which, when frustrated, result in violence against the adult attachment figure (i.e., the wife).

Finally, generally violent/antisocial batterers were predicted to resemble other antisocial, aggressive groups. Relative to the other subtypes, they were expected to have experienced high levels of family of origin violence and association with deviant peers. They would be impulsive, lack skills (marital and nonmarital), have hostile attitudes toward women, and view violence as acceptable. Their marital violence was conceptualized as a part of their general use of aggression and engagement in antisocial behavior.

Tests of Our Typology

We conducted a study testing our batterer typology (Holtzworth-Munroe, Meehan, Herron, Rehman, & Stuart, 2000). From the community, we recruited 102 men who had been physically aggressive toward their wives in the past year; their wives also participated in the study, providing information about the men. We included men who had engaged in a wide range of violence, in contrast to previous batterer typologies that have been based on either clinical samples (i.e., men in treatment for domestic violence) or severely violent community samples.

We conducted a series of cluster analyses using measures of the three descriptive dimensions (i.e., marital violence, general violence, personality disorder). The three predicted subgroups of violent men (i.e., FO, BD, and GVA) emerged, along with one additional subgroup, labeled *low-level antisocial* (LLA). Among the 102 maritally violent men in the study, 37 were classified as FO, 34 as LLA, 15 as BD, and 16 as GVA. The three predicted subgroups generally differed as hypothesized on both the descriptive dimensions and the model correlates of violence (i.e., childhood home environment, association with deviant peers, impulsivity, attachment, skills, and attitudes).

The fourth, unpredicted, cluster, the LLA group, had moderate scores on measures of antisociality, marital violence, and general violence. On many measures, this group fell intermediate to the FO and GVA groups (i.e., FO men scored lower; GVA men scored higher). This new group is probably akin our originally proposed FO group; their levels of violence and antisociality are similar to those predicted for the FO group, as derived from previous typologies of severely violent men. In contrast, as our study sample was recruited from the community and included less violent men, we believe that the FO group emerging in our study has not been included in previous batterer typologies, but rather resembles the less severely violent men often found in studies with community, newlywed, and/or marital therapy samples. If this is correct, then our four cluster typology helps to bridge a recognized gap in this research area—between research examining generally low levels of violence among community samples and research examining severe violence among clinical samples (e.g., common couple violence vs. patriarchal terrorism, Johnson, 1995).

In addition to our own study, batterer typologies published since the Holtzworth-Munroe and Stuart (1994) review have often been consistent with our proposed typology. While some research groups have identified only two subgroups, these subgroups have resembled two of our proposed subtypes (Chase, O'Leary, & Heyman, 2001; Gottman et al., 1995; Tweed & Dutton, 1998). Other researchers have identified three subgroups resembling our proposed subtypes (Langhinrichsen-Rohling, Huss, & Ramsey, 2000; Waltz, Babcock, Jacobson, & Gottman, 2000). Such work includes two studies with large samples (i.e., each with over 800 men starting domestic violence treatment; Hamberger, Lohr, Bonge, & Tolin, 1996; White & Gondolf, 2000).

Do the Subgroups Continue to Differ Over Time?

While at least 23 published batterer typology studies have identified batterer subtypes cross-sectionally, only one previous typology study included any longitudinal data, and that study included only longitudinal data on subtype differences in relationship stability (Gottman et al., 1995). We believed that it was important to examine a wider variety of possible longitudinal changes in the characteristics, behaviors, and relationships of the differing batterer subgroups.

Thus, in our typology study, we reassessed men at 18- and 36-month follow-ups. We were able to obtain information on 95 of the original sample of 102 maritally violent men at both time points. We compared the four subgroups of violent men, identified at Time 1, over time. As noted above, we had predicted that the subgroups would continue to differ, both in level of marital violence and on individual characteristics theoretically related to their violence. These findings have been presented by Holtzworth-Munroe et al. (2003).

As predicted, the aggression of men who initially engaged in lower levels of violence was less stable over time than that of more severely violent men. Among men still having at least monthly contact with their partner (i.e., the opportunity for continued violence), 40% of FO men and 23% of LLA men desisted from violence over a 3-year period; in contrast, only 7% of GVA men and 14% of BD men desisted from violence. In the absence of longitudinal studies of subtypes of maritally violent men, some theorists had hypothesized that the FO subgroup represented men in the early stages of relationship violence, such that these men would progress to more severe violence over time (e.g., Gondolf, 1988; Saunders, 1992). In contrast, our data suggest that the FO group may be a stable one.

Of course, this does not mean that all men who are cross-sectionally identified as engaging in low levels of physical aggression will not escalate to more severe violence. Instead, our data suggest that among men engaging in low levels of violence, those who resemble FO men, in terms of evidencing low levels of other risk factors (e.g., little concurrent psychopathology or generally violent behavior, low risk from other factors such as impulsivity and negative attitudes), may continue to have a low risk of marital violence over time. In contrast, for example, one would predict that a man who has, to date, only engaged in low levels of marital violence, but resembles the GVA subgroup on risk factors (e.g., criminal behavior, delinquent friends, substance abuse, impulsivity, attitudes), is at high risk to escalate his marital aggression over time. Such predictions, if confirmed in future research, have important implications for prevention (e.g., targeting men who are at high risk for escalating relationship violence before they have engaged in severe violence).

The men's initial subgroup placements also predicted relationship variables. For example, we examined how many couples had remained stably living together versus how many had experienced separations or were separated or divorced at the follow-up assessments. While one quarter to one third of FO and LLA had experienced relationship instability, this figure was over 75% in the BD and GVA subgroups. In addition, high proportions of LLA, BD, and GVA men and their wives had Time 2 marital satisfaction questionnaire scores suggestive of marital distress.

Some of the relationships of couples in our study simply defied the traditional categorizations of couples as together versus separated/divorced. For example, we had couples who told us, during the follow-up phone interviews, that they had separated during the follow-up period, but were currently living together and wanted to come to the lab together, only to have one spouse arrive at the lab alone, saying that they had filed for divorce and separated again. These changing relationships create methodological difficulties when collecting longitudinal data from severely violent men and their partners (e.g., Gondolf, 2001). On a positive note, however, this finding of relationship instability among the most severely violent men (BD and GVA men) may reflect the fact that some of the wives are in the process of leaving their relationships and attempting to end the violence in their lives. As research has shown, this process may consist of multiple attempts to separate before a final separation or end to violence is achieved (see review in Holtzworth-Munroe, Smutzler, & Sandin, 1997).

Many of our longitudinal study findings supported our hypotheses that the subtypes would continue to differ in men's individual characteristics assumed to be related to their use of violence. While GVA and BD men did not always differ significantly from one another in post hoc tests, across time, one or both of these more severely violent groups was "worse" than the less violent men (FO and/or LLA), in the manner predicted, on a variety of measures, including: levels of wife injury (both GVA and BD), borderline personality organization (BD), problems resulting from substance use (GVA), psychological (BD) and criminal (GVA) interventions received, fearful/preoccupied attachment (BD), jealousy and spouse-specific dependency (BD), impulsivity (both), positive attitudes toward violence (both), and hostile attitudes toward women (both).

Related to this, an issue emerging from the recent research on batterer typologies is the question of whether the GVA and BD subgroups are distinct groups. For example, in their batterer subtype study, Waltz et al. (2000) identified a pathological subtype that scored highest on questionnaire scales of both antisocial and borderline personality disorders. Similarly, in our study, the GVA and BD groups did not always differ significantly. Of course, given our small sample sizes at some of the follow-ups (e.g., 8 BD men in some analyses), a lack of statistical power might be blamed for the lack of differentiation of these two subtypes on some measures. However, part of the problem in differentiating GVA and BD men stems from the fact that these groups are predicted to be similar in their levels of marital aggression and on several of the model correlates of violence, including impulsivity, positive attitudes toward violence, and negative attitudes toward women (Holtzworth-Munroe & Stuart, 1994). Yet it is important to note that, as predicted, over time the GVA and BD groups did differ on some variables. For example, the GVA men were the most likely to spend time in jail over the study follow-up period, and the BD men scored highest on a composite measure of jealousy and spouse-specific dependency and were the most likely to have been treated for depressive symptoms over the follow-up period. Our study findings do not conclusively resolve the debate regarding how different the BD and GVA subtypes are from one another; future researchers will need to address the issue of overlapping psychopathology across these groups.

Our findings do suggest, however, the potential importance of two types of personality-related characteristics (i.e., antisociality and borderline) when studying husband violence. Highlighting the potentially important role of antisocial behavior in understanding husband violence, it is possible to conceptualize three of our violent subtypes (i.e., FO, LLA, and GVA) as falling along a continuum of antisociality (e.g., FO batterers have the lowest levels of violence, antisocial behavior, and risk factors; GVA men have the highest; and the LLA group has intermediate levels). The BD group, however, cannot be easily placed along this continuum, as these men had the highest scores on variables that cluster in a theoretically coherent manner (i.e., fear of abandonment, preoccupied/fearful attachment, dependency). This raises the possibility that two dimensions (i.e., antisociality and borderline personality characteristics) are needed to describe all of the subgroups.

■ A Dimensional Versus a Clustering Approach

Related to this point, until now we have argued that identifying subtypes of maritally violent men is a useful method to account for the heterogeneity among maritally violent men on theoretically important variables. Yet is it time to reify these subtypes? Do we believe that these subgroups are true diagnostic categories that identify underlying taxonomical differences across subtypes of men? We have not yet conducted the taxonomical research necessary to definitively answer that question. In the meantime, we are hesitant to reify any typology.

Unfortunately, we have been told of misuses of our typology, including a battered woman who was assured by a clinician that it was safe for her to return to her abusive husband because he was "an FO man" and a judge who was reportedly classifying batterers into subtypes to determine their sentences! Data are not yet available to support such uses of the typology.

Until proven otherwise, it is quite possible to argue that while some men are prototypes of the different subtypes, the majority of men fall along dimensions of theoretical importance rather than forming distinctly identifiable groups. Given our model and study findings, we currently propose that the dimensions of antisociality and borderline personality characteristics might be as useful a manner of conceptualizing the data as is our typology. Theoretically, we see advantages to a dimensional approach. Most important, our typology requires that one consider current level of husband violence when categorizing men, which makes it less useful for predicting the onset of violence among young samples who are not yet in relationships. In contrast, a dimensional approach focusing on the dimensions of antisociality and borderline characteristics would allow one to predict future violence levels without knowledge of current violence levels. Thus, for example, one could conduct a study of adolescents who have not yet begun dating to predict the onset of male intimate violence. Most of the existing research using a dimensional approach to predict the onset of violence (e.g., Andrews, Foster, Capaldi, & Hops, 2000; Capaldi & Clark, 1998) has focused only on the dimension of antisociality. Thus, attention to our typology adds to this work by suggesting the need to also consider the dimension of borderline personality characteristics.

■ Can We Provide Cutoff Points to Identify the Subtypes?

Some clinicians and researchers have requested that we provide cutoff scores on the measures we used to identify subgroups of maritally violent men, so that these subgroups can be identified in other settings. We are concerned, however, that cutoff points may not be generalizable from one sample to another.

Our concern stems from research we have been conducting with Frank Dunford to identify subtypes of maritally violent men among men in the Navy who have engaged in substantiated cases of spouse abuse. Dunford has been administering abbreviated versions of the clustering measures used by Holtzworth-Munroe et al. (2000) to these men. In general, the Navy sample has lower levels of antisociality than the Holtzworth-Munroe et al. (2000) sample; for example, men with a criminal record are not recruited into the Navy and men who are found to use drugs are discharged.

In preliminary cluster analyses of Dunford's data, we derived a four-subgroup solution. These four groups differed from one another in the same manner as did the four groups in Holtzworth-Munroe et al. (2000), and we gave these four groups the same names (i.e., FO, LLA, BD, and GVA). For example, the subgroup we labeled the FO group in Dunford's sample has the lowest scores on all of the descriptive dimension measures used in the cluster analyses; the GVA group has high levels of marital violence and the highest levels of general violence; the BD group has high levels of marital violence and the highest scores on the fear of abandonment measure; and the LLA group falls intermediate to the FO and GVA groups. These data suggest that, when similar measures of the descriptive dimensions are used in other settings, the structure of our typology is replicable. Interestingly, however, the subgroup means on the clustering variables in the Dunford subgroups are substantially lower than the comparable subgroup means in the Holtzworth-Munroe et al. (2000) sample. For example, the levels of marital and general violence among the Dunford GVA men are much lower than the violence reported among the Holtzworth-Munroe et al. GVA men. These data suggest that while the same subgroups may emerge in different samples, the scores used to identify these subgroups may differ across samples.

Thus, at this time, we believe that absolute cutoff scores cannot be provided to identify subtypes. Rather, until further research can be conducted to address this issue, we suggest that, within each sample, cutoff scores for that sample need to be established. For this reason, it is premature for clinicians and others (e.g., judges, researchers) to use the subgroup means presented in Holtzworth-Munroe et al. (2000) to type the batterers in their samples.

■ Clinical Implications of the Typology

While the issue is still being debated, many in the field have concluded that the overall effectiveness of batterers' treatment is not impressive (e.g., Green & Babcock, 2000; Rosenfeld, 1992). One hope is that a valid typology of batterers might allow us to distinguish subtypes likely to benefit from treatment from those unlikely to improve following clinical interventions. Indeed, some recent data suggest that consideration of a batterer typology may help us to better understand the generally disappointing outcomes from batterer treatment.

Predicting Differences in Outcome in Standard Batterers' Treatment

Some recent study findings provide hints that standard batterer treatment may be ineffective for certain subtypes of maritally violent men. Using scores on a measure of personality dimensions, Dutton, Bornarchuk, Kropp, Hart, and Ogloff (1997) reported that batterers with high scores on measures of borderline, avoidant, and antisocial personality had the poorest outcomes among men completing domestic violence treatment. Identifying the Holtzworth-Munroe and Stuart (1994) batterer subgroups based on measures of general violence and psychopathology, Langhinrichsen-Rohling et al. (2000) found that GVA batterers were the least likely to complete treatment and were rated, by their therapists, as being significantly less likely than the other groups to remain violence free posttreatment.

In contrast, examining personality profiles of batterers in a large study of the effectiveness of batterer treatment, Gondolf and his colleagues concluded that batterer personality characteristics do not predict recidivism following participation in standard treatment. Snow Jones and Gondolf (2001) reported that batterer personality profiles did not predict reassault following treatment. However, they did find that severe psychopathology at intake, history of arrest, and drunkenness during the follow-up period, all factors that are theoretically related to differentiating batterer subtypes, were predictive of reassault following treatment. Among the same sample, Gondolf and White (2001) reported that a wide variety of personality profiles were found among the repeat reassaulters and noted that the majority of repeat reassaulters had subclinical or low levels of personality dysfunction. They argue that group differences in personality were small enough to render them clinically meaningless; however, they found statistically significant group differences in the percentages of men showing psychopathic tendencies (i.e., 54% in the repeat reassaulter group, 35% among men with only one reassault, 39% in the no reassault group) and on other variables related to our typology (i.e., repeat reassaulters were more likely to have been severely violent toward their partner, violent outside the home, and previously arrested and to have substance use problems). It is important to note that the publications from the Gondolf study did not use two of our three proposed descriptive dimensions to identify subtypes of men (i.e., severity of marital violence, generality of violence); they used only one measure of personality disorder and psychopathology. Despite these limitations, their findings suggest that variables related to the typology (e.g., psychopathy, violence, substance abuse) may be statistically significant predictors of treatment outcome.

Indeed, Gondolf has graciously agreed to collaborate with us to attempt to identify our subtypes in his sample and to examine treatment outcome data across the subtypes (initial findings are reported in Clements, Holtzworth-Munroe, Gondolf, & Meehan [2002]). To do so, we created decision rules to place the men in Gondolf's sample into one of our four subtypes, using men's and women's reports of the level of male marital violence and men's self-reports on our MCMI-derived measures of fear of abandonment and antisociality (note: no measure of generality of violence was available). We were able to form the four subtypes in our typology and they differed, in the predicted manner, on available measures of related variables (e.g., BD men had received more psychological interventions; GVA men had the most substance abuse problems). Most importantly, we were able to compare treatment outcome across the subtypes. Our initial findings have revealed significant group differences. For example, as would be predicted, men in the GVA and BD subgroups were more likely than LLA and FO men to be re-arrested for domestic violence (at 15-month follow-up: 15% of GVA men, 22% of BD, 5.5% of LLA, 5.5% of FO), while GVA men were the most likely to be arrested for any violence (domestic violence or violence toward another individual; at 15 months: 47% of GVA, to 27% of LLA, 22% of BD, 16% of FO) or for any crime (at 15 months: 62% of GVA, 41% of BD, 47% of LLA, 39% of FO). Examining female partners' reports of further male violence, similar results were obtained; for example, a significant group difference emerges at the 15-month follow-up, with

21% of FO, 28% of LLA, 42% of GVA, and 44% of BD men reported to have engaged in further abuse. Taken together, the existing data suggest that identification of subtypes of maritally violent men may be predictive of treatment outcome in standard batterers' treatment programs.

Treatment-Patient Matching

A clinical implication of the findings just reviewed is that treatment outcome might be improved by matching interventions to batterer subtypes. To our knowledge, only one study has addressed this issue and has done so only indirectly. In a post hoc analysis of data from a study comparing cognitive-behavioral-feminist treatment to a new process, psychodynamic treatment, Saunders (1996) found that batterers scoring high on an antisocial measure did better in the structured cognitive-behavioral intervention, while batterers scoring high on a measure of dependency did better in the new intervention.

It is premature to recommend particular interventions for various subtypes of batterers. It may be time, however, to generate hypotheses for future testing. In particular, given the potential importance of the antisocial and borderline dimensions in understanding male intimate violence, we would suggest consideration of existing treatments for these personality disorders.

When considering the BD subtype, perhaps Saunders's (1996) process–psychodynamic batterers intervention would be useful, as his post hoc analyses suggest. In addition, Linehan (1993) has developed, and is empirically testing, a cognitive-behavioral treatment for borderline personality disorder; however, how her program, developed for female patients, would have to be modified for male batterers is unclear at this time. Stosny (1995) has developed a compassion workshop to treat *attachment abuse* that theoretically would be relevant for this subgroup. In addition, given the high levels of psychological distress found among our sample of BD men, combined with our study's longitudinal evidence that many of these men sought help for depression during the study follow-up period, it may prove useful to provide BD men entering batterers' programs with adjunct medication (e.g., antidepressants) and/or individual therapy for their immediate psychological distress. Doing so might allow them to resolve current psychological crises and thus more fully participate in batterers' treatment groups.

When considering the GVA batterer, reviews of the available research on treatment for violent offenders and individuals with antisocial personality disorder (e.g., Bonta & Cormier, 1999; Losel, 1998; Rice & Harris, 1997) suggest that while we know little about what is effective with antisocial personality disorder, some treatments (e.g., insight oriented) have been proven ineffective, while others (i.e., behavioral-cognitive approaches) may help reduce recidivism. Similarly, Saunders's (1996) findings suggest that structured cognitive-behavioral approaches may be the best available option for this group. In addition, however, it may be important to consider new interventions developed in other fields, such as criminal justice. For example, the potential usefulness of intensive rehabilitation supervision (e.g., close monitoring of offenders in the community, along with rehabilitation focused on criminogenic needs) is receiving attention in work with antisocial criminal groups (e.g., Gendreau, Cullen, & Bonta, 1994).

Finally, given their lower levels of behavioral, personality, and criminal problems, we would hypothesize that FO, and perhaps LLA, men are the most likely to benefit from existing batterer treatment programs (e.g., cognitive-behavioral approaches including anger management and feminist approaches encouraging these men to examine gender roles). We have also suggested that couples with an FO husband may be the only maritally violent couples appropriate for conjoint couple therapy, as the risk factors that characterize them (e.g., skills deficits) may be amenable to conjoint therapy. Indeed, as noted above, FO men do not differ in many ways from nonviolent but maritally distressed men who are the usual targets of marital therapy.

It is important to note that even if batterer typologies should not prove predictive of batterers' treatment outcomes, it does not mean that typologies are not a useful conceptual framework for understanding differing types of husband violence and for predicting the course of relationship violence without intervention. When we originally urged researchers in the husband violence area to adopt a typological approach to the study of battering, we made two main arguments regarding the potential usefulness of such an approach, suggesting that a valid typology could (a) "increase [our] understanding of marital violence and help in identifying different underlying processes resulting in violence . . . allow a systematic examination of how and why different men use violence against their wives" and (b) "lead to increases in therapy effectiveness, eventually resulting in patient-treatment matching" (Holtzworth-Munroe & Stuart, 1994, p. 476). We believe that batterer typologies are already proving useful with regard to the first goal. At this time, we believe that the second goal has not been thoroughly addressed and awaits further empirical investigation.

■ Future Research Issues

In this section, we briefly raise a few other issues for consideration by future researchers. One such issue is that of the meaning and impact of low-level husband violence. Low levels of physical aggression (e.g., FO men) are so prevalent as to be almost statistically normative in our culture; one third of engaged and newly married men engage in low-level physical aggression (e.g., O'Leary et al., 1989). As discussed above, we do not understand how these less violent men differ from men who are experiencing marital conflict but who do not engage in physical aggression. It is thus tempting to assume that low levels of aggression do not lead to pernicious outcomes above and beyond effects attributable to marital distress. This may not be the case, however, as a recent longitudinal study of newlyweds demonstrated that relatively low levels of physical aggression predicted marital separation/divorce better than did marital distress or negative marital communication (Rogge & Bradbury, 1999). Thus, while previous batterer typologies have focused on severely violent samples, we believe that lower levels of male physical aggression, resembling common couple violence (Johnson, 1995), also deserve attention.

Also, it is now time to examine the potentially differing impacts on women of being in a relationship with differing subtypes of batterers. For example, we found that while the percentage of wives experiencing marital distress in each subgroup differed at Time 1, these differences became even more pronounced at Time 2, with wives of more severely violent men reporting relationship distress. In addition, while not meaning to imply that women play any causal role in violence, researchers should consider how the characteristics and reactions of female partners of each subtype of man affect the probability of his violence. For example, we tentatively propose that challenging a GVA man's authority would be particularly dangerous, while jealousy issues would be more immediate precursors to violence among BD men. It would also be useful to consider how varying reactions on the part of the man's partner (e.g., appeasement vs. fighting back) affect the future risk of violence within each subtype. As another example of issues involving female partners, given assortative mating and very limited partner choice in some communities, we would hypothesize that a larger proportion of GVA men than the other subgroups have female partners who engage in antisocial behavior, including physical aggression, themselves. How the relationship dynamics between two antisocial individuals affects the male's use of violence is the type of question that should be addressed in future research.

We recommend that prospective, longitudinal studies be conducted to identify the developmental pathways resulting in different subtypes of violent husbands. In such studies, researchers could examine constructs assumed to predict the use of violence among samples of adolescents or children and then observe the relationship between these variables and the emergence of relationship violence as study participants enter intimate relationships. As discussed in our original presentation of our typology, it also is possible that there is a genetic contribution to batterer subtype differences (e.g., in predisposition to aggression, antisociality, impulsivity, or emotional dysregulation; Holtzworth-Munroe & Stuart, 1994). Studies of such issues will require different research designs (e.g., twin studies) than those commonly used in this field.

Similarly, we recommend that future researchers more systematically study the process of desisting from violence. In our typology study, almost half of FO men engaged in no further physical violence over a 3-year period. Other longitudinal studies have similarly shown that some men, particularly men who engage in "minor" violence, desist from violence. This issue deserves more attention, perhaps borrowing methods from related research areas. For example, in interviews with violent youth (Wilkinson, 2002) and violent criminal offenders (Horney, 2002), researchers have begun to compare the situational determinants of the perpetration of violence versus *avoided* violence (i.e., refraining from violence). Such work might have clinical implications, suggesting techniques and decisions that men have found useful in desisting from violence.

To our knowledge, batterer typologies have not been developed or tested in countries other than the United States and Canada. Whether such typologies will be replicated in other cultures is a question requiring empirical investigation. It is possible, given the role of societal factors (e.g., patriarchy, acceptance of interpersonal violence, availability of guns) in shaping the expression of husband violence, that existing typologies will require modification in other cultures. For example, in more patriarchal societies, in which husband violence is widely viewed as acceptable, there may be a weaker link between husband violence and psychopathology; instead, a larger proportion of FO men may be identified.

Individual Characteristics, Situational Factors, and Dyadic Processes

An important criticism of existing batterer typologies, including our own, is that they focus almost exclusively on relatively distal correlates and predictors of violence, with a heavy emphasis on personality disorders and characteristics. Even variables that are theoretically more immediately related to the onset of violence (e.g., fear of abandonment) are usually assessed at a more general, stable (rather than situational) level. Our typology emphasizes characteristics of the individual; it is an intrapersonal model focusing on individual differences. Yet husband violence occurs in the context of interpersonal relationships, communities and subcultures, and society.

As reviewed above, across studies, there is a clear convergence of data regarding the subtypes likely to emerge in most samples of violent husbands, the dimensions used to identify them, and the variables on which the identified subtypes will differ. We suggest that it is now time to begin examining more immediate variables that may explain why, in a particular situation, each subtype of man engages in violence. As one example, some researchers have begun to consider different motivations for relationship violence across subtypes of men (e.g., studies of instrumental/proactive vs. impulsive/reactive aggression; Chase et al., 2001; Tweed & Dutton, 1998). Such research, however, has generally still focused on characterizing stable traits (e.g., classifying men as reactively or proactively aggressive). We recommend going further, to study how stable characteristics (e.g., personality variables, motivations) are expressed in a given situation. As one example, consider the BD subgroup. How are an insecure attachment style and fear of abandonment, as relatively stable personality features, activated in a particular situation? And how do these activated fears translate into violence—Does the man act in rage, experiencing emotional dysregulation, or in a calculated manner to prevent his partner from leaving him? This expanded viewpoint should include a focus on situational variables and dyadic processes that immediately precede engagement in violent behaviors. In other words, it is now important to understand why, for each subtype of man, violence emerges within an ongoing dyadic relationship and within particular situations (e.g., Cavanaugh, 2001). The answers to such questions await future research.

■ Acknowledgments

This project was supported by NIH Grant PHS R01-MH51935 to A. Holtzworth-Munroe. We would like to thank the numerous research assistants and graduate and undergraduate students involved in conducting our study, particularly Gregory Stuart, Katherine

Herron, Uzma Rehman, and Amy Marshall. We also particularly thank Lori Buser for her excellent job in maintaining contact with study participants over the follow-up period.

■ References

Aldarondo, E. (1996). Cessation and persistence of wife assault: A longitudinal analysis. *American Journal of Orthopsychiatry, 66,* 141–151.

Andrews, J. A., Foster, S. L., Capaldi, D., & Hops, H. (2000). Adolescent and family predictors of physical aggression, communication, and satisfaction in young adult couples: A prospective analysis. *Journal of Consulting and Clinical Psychology, 68,* 195–208.

Archer, J. (2000). Sex differences in aggression between heterosexual partners: A meta-analytic review. *Psychological Bulletin, 126,* 651–680.

Bonta, J., & Cormier, R. B. (1999, April). Corrections research in Canada: Impressive progress and promising prospects. *Canadian Journal of Criminology,* 235–247.

Capaldi, D. M., & Clark, S. (1998). Prospective family predictors of aggression toward female partners for a-risk young men. *Developmental Psychology, 34,* 1175–1188.

Capaldi, D. M., & Owen, L. D. (2001). Physical aggression in a community sample of at-risk young couples: Gender comparisons for high frequency, injury, and fear. *Journal of Family Psychology, 15,* 425–440.

Cavanaugh, M. M. (2001, July). *Re-examining typology research on male domestic violence offenders from an escalation perspective.* Paper presented at the 7th International Family Violence Research Conference, Portsmouth, NH.

Chase, K. A., O'Leary, K. D., & Heyman, R. E. (2001). Categorizing partner-violent men within the reactive-proactive typology model. *Journal of Consulting and Clinical Psychology, 69,* 567–572.

Clements, K., Holtzworth-Munroe, A., Gondolf, E., & Meehan, J. (2002, November). *Testing the Holtzworth-Munroe et al. (2000) batterer typology among court-referred maritally violent men.* Poster presented at the annual meeting of the Association for the Advancement of Behavior Therapy, Reno, NV.

Dobash, R. E., & Dobash, R. P. (1979). *Violence against wives.* New York: Free Press.

Dutton, D. G. (1995). Intimate abusiveness. *Clinical Psychology: Science and Practice, 2,* 207–224.

Dutton, D. G., Bodnarchuk, M., Kropp, R., Hart, S. D., & Ogloff, J. P. (1997). Client personality disorders affecting wife assault post-treatment recidivism. *Violence and Victims, 12,* 37–50.

Feld, S. L., & Straus, M. A. (1989). Escalation and desistance of wife assault in marriage. *Criminology, 27,* 141–161.

Follingstad, D. R., Rutledge, L. L., Berg, B. J., Hause, E. S., & Polek, D. S. (1990). The role of emotional abuse in physically abusive relationships. *Journal of Family Violence, 5,* 107–120.

Gendreau, P., Cullen, F. T., & Bonta, J. (1994). Intensive rehabilitation supervision: The next generation in community corrections? *Federal Probation, 58,* 72–78.

Gondolf, E. (2001, July). *Fifteen-month outcome from four batterer treatment programs.* Presented at the International Conference on Family Violence, Portsmouth, NH.

Gondolf, E. W. (1988). Who are these guys?: Toward a behavioral typology of batterers. *Violence and Victims, 3,* 187–203.

Gondolf, E. W., & White, R. J. (2001). Batterer program participants who repeatedly reassault: Psychopathic tendencies and other disorders. *Journal of Interpersonal Violence, 16,* 361–380.

Gottman, J. M., Jacobson, N. S., Rushe, R. H., Short, J. Wu, Babcock, J., La Taillade, J. J., et al. (1995). The relationship between heart rate reactivity, emotionally aggressive behavior and general violence in batterers. *Journal of Family Psychology, 9,* 227–248.

Green, C., & Babcock, J. (2000, July). *A meta-analysis of the effectiveness of batterer treatment.* Paper presented at the 7th International Family Violence Research Conference, Portsmouth, NH.

Hamberger, L. K., Lohr, J. M., Bonge, D., & Tolin, D. F. (1996). A large sample empirical typology of male spouse abusers and its relationship to dimensions of abuse. *Violence and Victims, 11,* 277–292.

Heyman, R. E., O'Leary, K. D., & Jouriles, E. N. (1995). Alcohol and aggressive personality styles: Potentiators of serious physical aggression against wives? *Journal of Family Psychology, 9,* 44–57.

Holtzworth-Munroe, A., Bates, L., Smutzler, N., & Sandin, E. (1997). A brief review of the research on husband violence. Part I: Maritally violent versus nonviolent men. *Aggression and Violent Behavior, 2,* 65–99.

Holtzworth-Munroe, A., Meehan, J. C., Herron, K., Rehman, U., & Stuart, G. L. (2000). Testing the Holtzworth-Munroe and Stuart (1994) batterer typology. *Journal of Consulting and Clinical Psychology, 68,* 1000–1019.

Holtzworth-Munroe, A., Meehan, J. C., Herron, K., Rehman, U., & Stuart, G. L. (2003). Do subtypes of maritally violent men continue to differ over time? *Journal of Consulting and Clinical Psychology, 71,* 728–740.

Holtzworth-Munroe, A., Smutzler, N., & Bates, L. (1997). A brief review of the research on husband violence. Part III: Sociodemographic factors, relationship factors, and differing consequences of husband and wife violence. *Aggression and Violent Behavior, 2,* 285–307.

Holtzworth-Munroe, A., Smutzler, N., & Sandin, E. (1997). A brief review of the research on husband violence. Part II: The psychological effects of husband violence on battered women and their children. *Aggression and Violent Behavior, 2,* 179–213.

Holtzworth-Munroe, A., & Stuart, G. L. (1994). Typologies of male batterers: Three subtypes and the differences among them. *Psychological Bulletin, 116,* 476–497.

Horney, J. (2002, January). Commentary at workshop of the National Research Council on Setting the Future Research Agenda for Violence Against Women, Washington, DC.

Jacobson, N. S., Gottman, J. M., Gartner, E., Berns, S., & Shortt, J. W. (1996). Psychological factors in the longitudinal course of battering: When do couples split up? When does the abuse decrease? *Violence and Victims, 11,* 371–392.

Johnson, M. P. (1995). Patriarchal terrorism and common couple violence: Two forms of violence against women. *Journal of Marriage and the Family, 57,* 283–294.

Langhinrichsen-Rohling, J., Huss, M. T., & Ramsey, S. (2000). The clinical utility of batterer typologies. *Journal of Family Violence, 15,* 37–53.

Lawrence, E. (2002, Spring/Summer). Emerging perspectives in the study of physical aggression in intimate relationships. *Newsletter of the AABT Couples Research and Therapy Special Interest Group.*

Lawrence, E., & Bradbury, T. N. (2001). Physical aggression and marital dysfunction: A longitudinal analysis. *Journal of Family Psychology, 15,* 135–154.

Linehan, M. M. (1993). *Cognitive-behavioral treatment of borderline personality disorder.* New York: Guilford Press.

Losel, F. (1998). Treatment and management of psychopaths. In D. J. Cooke, A. E. Forth, & R. D. Hare (Eds.), *Psychopathy: Theory, research, and implications for society* (pp. 303–354). Dordrecht, The Netherlands: Kluwer Academic.

Murphy, C. M., & O'Leary, K. D. (1989). Psychological aggression predicts physical aggression in early marriage. *Journal of Consulting and Clinical Psychology, 57,* 579–582.

O'Leary, K. D. (1993). Through a psychological lens: Personality traits, personality disorders, and levels of violence. In R. J. Gelles & D. R. Ioseke (Eds.), *Current controversies in family violence* (pp. 7–29). Newbury Park, CA: Sage.

O'Leary, K. D., Barling, J., Arias, I., Rosenbaum, A., Malone, J., & Tyree, A. (1989). Prevalence and stability of physical aggression between spouses. *Journal of Consulting and Clinical Psychology, 57,* 263–268.

Pagelow, M. D. (1981). *Woman-battering: Victims and their experiences.* Newbury Park, CA: Sage.

Quigley, B. M., & Leonard, K. E. (1996). Desistance of husband aggression in the early years of marriage. *Violence and Victims, 11,* 355–370.

Rice, M. E., & Harris, G. T. (1997). The treatment of adult offenders. In D. M. Stoff, J. Breiling, & J. D. Maser (Eds.), *Handbook of antisocial behavior* (pp. 425–434). New York: Wiley.

Rogge, R. D., & Bradbury, T. N. (1999). Till violence does us part: The differing roles of communication and aggression in predicting adverse marital outcomes. *Journal of Consulting and Clinical Psychology, 67,* 340–351.

Rosenfeld, B. D. (1992). Court-ordered treatment of spouse abuse. *Clinical Psychology Review, 12,* 205–226.

Saunders, D. G. (1992). A typology of men who batter women: Three types derived from cluster analysis. *American Orthopsychiatry, 62,* 264–275.

Saunders, D. G. (1996). Feminist-cognitive-behavioral and process-psychodynamic treatments for men who batter. *Violence and Victims, 4,* 393–414.

Snow Jones, A., & Gondolf, E. W. (2001). Time-varying risk factors for reassault among batterer program participants. *Journal of Family Violence, 16,* 345–359.

Stosny, S. (1995). *Treating attachment abuse: A compassionate approach.* New York: Springer.

Tweed, R., & Dutton, D. G. (1998). A comparison of impulsive and instrumental subgroups of batterers. *Violence and Victims, 13,* 217–230.

Walker, L. E. (1979). *The battered woman.* New York: Harper & Row.

Waltz, J., Babcock, J. C., Jacobson, N. S., & Gottman, J. M. (2000). Testing a typology of batterers. *Journal of Consulting and Clinical Psychology, 68,* 658–669.

White, R. J., & Gondolf, E. W. (2000). Implications of personality profiles for batterer treatment. *Journal of Interpersonal Violence, 15,* 467–488.

Wilkinson, D. (2002, January). *Situational determinants of intimate violence.* Presentation at the workshop of the National Research Council on Setting the Future Research Agenda for Violence Against Women, Washington, DC.

8

Women in Intimate Partner Violence: Major Advances and New Directions

Mary Ann Dutton, Mai El-Khoury, Megan Murphy, Rachel Somberg, and Margret E. Bell

Understanding women in intimate partner violence (IPV) is necessary for developing ecologically valid and effective interventions to prevent further harm and to reduce the harm already incurred. Most of this chapter focuses on women's response to IPV, although we also include a section addressing women's own use of violence. Recognizing women as both victims of IPV and agents in the use of violence against their partners is complex, both politically and scientifically. Consideration of violent acts alone fails to do justice to the complex terrain of intimate partners' interactions, since most forms of violence can have quite different meanings depending on the social context. For example, when one partner initiates physical assault or a verbal threat and the other responds in kind, the two acts may differ in terms of the level of motivation to control or dominate the partner, injury, and fear or other psychological reactions by the partner. Assessing violent acts in ways that distinguish very different contexts is a noteworthy scientific challenge.

The goal of this chapter is to examine major advances and emerging issues pertaining to women in IPV. The first section includes a discussion of major advances in the field pertaining to women's response to IPV. The first type of response addressed is traumatic reactions that result from exposure to IPV (Saltzman, Fanslow, McMahon, & Shelley, 1999, 2002), such as posttraumatic symptoms, depression, and somatic problems. Strategic responses (Dutton, 1992), including help-seeking and other behaviors for coping with IPV and its aftermath, comprise the second type of response discussed. The distinction between women's traumatic and strategic responses to IPV recognizes both the psychological impact of traumatic exposure and the multiple strategies women employ in dealing with violence and abuse in their lives. In the second section, we discuss three emerging issues necessary to fill important gaps in our understanding of women in IPV. These include cultural and other social context factors, women's assessment of IPV risks, and women's use of violence.

■ Major Advances Concerning Women in Intimate Partner Violence

Intimate partner violence is actual or threatened physical or sexual violence or psychological and emotional abuse directed toward a spouse, ex-spouse, current or former boyfriend or girlfriend, or current or former dating partner. Intimate partners may be heterosexual or of the same sex. Some of the common terms used to describe IPV are domestic abuse, spouse abuse, domestic violence, courtship violence, battering, marital rape, and date rape (Saltzman et al., 1999, 2002). Researchers have made major strides in understanding the psychological impact of IPV in women's lives and, to a lesser extent, the strategies women employ to deal with violence and abuse or the effects of it. The next section includes a brief description of the major findings in these areas, including remaining gaps in our knowledge.

Women's Traumatic Response to Intimate Partner Violence

When individuals are exposed to traumatic events such as rape, disaster, or acts of violence, they often experience a variety of negative psychological effects (Kessler, 2000). More specifically, when women have experienced IPV, they too can experience similar traumatic outcomes. This section reviews literature concerning three leading traumatic stress reactions associated with IPV: posttraumatic stress disorder (PTSD), depression, and somatic concerns.

Posttraumatic Stress Disorder.   A well recognized aftermath of exposure to traumatic events is PTSD (Kessler, Sonnega, Bromet, Hughes, & Nelson, 1995). Serious IPV clearly fits the definition of a traumatic stress as defined by the *Diagnostic and Statistical Manual of Mental Disorders,* rev. fourth edition (*DSM-IV*):

- The person experienced, witnessed, or was confronted with an event or events that involved actual or threatened death or serious injury, or a threat to the physical integrity of self or others and
- The person's response involved intense fear, helplessness, or horror (American Psychiatric Association, 2000)

A recent meta-analysis of mental health effects of IPV have identified that the prevalence rates of PTSD among battered women range from 31 to 84.4% (Golding, 1999; Jones, Hughes, & Unterstaller, 2001). Not all women exposed to IPV develop PTSD. Three broadly defined factors have been identified which influence when exposure to traumatic events leads to PTSD, including characteristics of the event, individual characteristics, and characteristics of the recovery environment (Green, Lindy, & Grace, 1985). Numerous studies have examined the role of specific factors in predicting posttraumatic symptoms among battered women. Within these, one group of studies has focused on the nature of the IPV exposure. Greater severity and frequency of physical violence—especially that which includes life threat—has been shown to relate to the development of PTSD (Astin, Lawrence, & Foy, 1993; Houskamp & Foy, 1991; Kemp, Rawlings, & Green, 1991; Woods, 2000). Whether a weapon was used or whether IPV involved sexual abuse also has been shown to predict greater PTSD symptom severity and frequency (Dutton, 2003a, 2003b, 2003c; Hattendorf, Ottens, & Lomax, 1999). Others have placed less emphasis on the nature of the violent acts and focused more on women's perceptions of the abuse and their level of subjective distress in determining posttraumatic symptoms (Kemp et al., 1991). Greater psychological abuse has been shown to increase posttraumatic symptomatology as well. For example, researchers (Dutton, Goodman, & Bennett, 2001; Street & Arias, 2001) have found that psychological abuse is a stronger predictor of IPV than physical abuse among women. These results demonstrate that it is important to examine ways in which different forms of IPV—not merely the severity and frequency—contribute to women's traumatic responses.

Another collection of research has focused on individual characteristics, including historical factors and characteristics of the recovery environment. Particular attention has been given to history of abuse, specifically child sexual abuse, as a risk factor for PTSD. PTSD is reported to a greater extent among women with multiple experiences of victimization throughout both adulthood and childhood and especially among women experiencing current IPV with histories of childhood sexual abuse (Astin, Ogland-Hand, Coleman, & Foy, 1995; Messman-Moore, Long, & Siegfried, 2000; Schaaf & McCanne, 1998). Put simply, it is important to realize that IPV is often not an isolated experience. Many women have been exposed to violence—and other traumatic experiences—throughout their lifetimes. These additional traumatic experiences can lead to increased risk for PTSD, especially when coping strategies are ineffective and resources are not available. Another study found that time out of a relationship, coping disengagement, negative life events, perceived support, and a history of child abuse contributed to PTSD symptomatology in battered women (Kemp, Green, Hovanitz, & Rawlings, 1995).

While a number of factors predict greater likelihood of PTSD following exposure to IPV, other factors seem to buffer or protect against its development (social support and positive life events) (Astin et al., 1993). Yet we know little about these and other protective factors that might mitigate the risk of negative emotional consequences of IPV. Importantly, why some women who experience severe forms of violence escape posttraumatic symptoms is not well understood. This and other questions pertaining to women's resilience and recovery in the face of IPV require further research.

Depression. Depression has been identified as another common psychological reaction to traumatic exposure, including IPV (Cascardi, O'Leary, & Schlee, 1999; Watson et al., 1997; West, Fernandez, Hillard, Schoof, et al., 1990). In women who have been diagnosed with major depression, approximately 60% report histories of intimate partner abuse, a rate that is 2 times greater than that in the general population (Dienemann et al., 2000). A meta-analysis of studies examining mental disorders in women exposed to IPV (Golding, 1999) found a weighted average prevalence of 47.6% for depression. Some studies have found even greater lifetime prevalence rates of major depression, relative to PTSD, in samples of battered women (Gleason, 1993; Stein & Kennedy, 2001). Further, women experiencing IPV frequently develop comorbid depression and PTSD. Among women who develop PTSD following IPV, major depression is the most commonly cited comorbid disorder and occurs in greater than 50% of women (Cascardi et al., 1999; Stein & Kennedy, 2001). Yet we understand little about what predicts PTSD/depression comorbidity versus PTSD or depression, alone, among battered women.

As with PTSD, predictive factors for depression are both situational and individual. For example, levels of prior and current violence are related to depression. As the number of traumatic experiences increases, so does the number of trauma symptoms, including depression (Follette, Polusny, Bechtle, & Naugle, 1996). Cascardi and O'Leary (1992) found that as the severity of current physical violence increased so did levels of depression. Greater levels of both emotional abuse and prior physical abuse (Campbell, Kub, Belknap, & Templin, 1997) are related to greater depression. Dutton and colleagues found that higher severity and the inclusion of sexual violence in the pattern of IPV (Dutton, 2003a, 2003b), as well as continuing IPV over the course of a year (Dutton, 2003b), were associated with higher levels of depression. Campbell and colleagues also found that even low-intensity stressors, such as daily hassles, were positively correlated with levels of depression in women exposed to IPV, although women with certain individual characteristics, such as self-care agency, were less likely to develop depression. These results illustrate the individual and situational factors that contribute to depression in women exposed to IPV. As with PTSD, understanding the protective factors that contribute to battered women's resilience with respect to depression are less well developed and need further study.

Health Problems.   Exposure to IPV leads not only to psychological distress, but to physical symptoms as well. Women who have experienced partner violence are more likely to both experience higher rates of health problems and perceive their overall health as poor (Campbell & Soeken, 1999; Green, Flowe-Valencia, Rosenblum, & Tait, 1999; Lown & Vega, 2001; Resnick, Acierno, & Kilpatrick, 1997). The most common somatic complaints include headaches, insomnia, chocking sensations, hyperventilation, gastrointestinal symptoms, and chest, back, and pelvic pain (American College of Obstetricians and Gynecologists [ACOG], 1995; Dutton, Haywood, & El-Bayoumi, 1997). The relationship between negative health consequences and battering has been shown to be the strongest among low-income women (Sutherland, Sullivan, & Bybee, 2001).

Injury is an obvious and well-recognized health concern among battered women. Although any type of injury may be sustained from IPV, contusions, abrasions, minor lacerations, fractures or sprains; injuries to the head, neck, chest, breast, and abdomen; injuries during pregnancy; and repeated or chronic injuries are most common characteristics of domestic violence assaults (American Medical Association [AMA], 1992). Head injury is an often unrecognized form of injury to women who are exposed to IPV (Jackson, Philp, Nuttall, & Diller, 2002). Chronic pain syndromes are found more commonly in women with domestic violence and child abuse than in controls (Kendall-Tackett, Marshall, & Ness, 2003). Violence and abuse during pregnancy may also result in detrimental health outcomes to a mother and child, including low birth weight, fetal death by placenta abruption, antepartum hemorrhage; fetal fractures; rupture of the uterus, liver, or spleen; and premature labor (Bullock, 1989; Huth-Bocks, Levendosky, & Bogat, 2002; McFarlane, Campbell, Sharps, & Watson, 2002; McFarlane, Parker, & Soeken, 1995; Saltzman, 1990; Torres et al., 2000). IPV also places women at higher risk for other physical health concerns, including HIV and STDs, alcohol and drug abuse, and attempted suicides (AMA, 1992; Zierler, Witbeck, & Mayer, 1996).

Recognizing the need to differentiate the health outcomes for women with varied violent and abuse experiences, more recent studies have sought to investigate how different types of IPV can influence women's perceived health outcomes. For example, psychological abuse has been found to uniquely contribute to pain and poorer physical health outcomes beyond the influence of physical violence (Murphy, Dutton, & Somberg, 2002). Sexual abuse histories have been specifically linked to increased gynecological symptoms and to pelvic, abdominal, and stomach pain symptoms (Campbell & Soeken, 1999; Green et al., 1999; Lown & Vega, 2001), although it is difficult to assess the influence of sexual violence alone on health outcomes in women, because sexual abuse among this population seldom occurs without any physical violence (Coker, Smith, McKeown, & King, 2000). Nevertheless, sexual and physical violence has been found to be more detrimental to physical and emotional health than experiencing physical violence alone.

In spite of the body of research linking IPV to physical health outcomes, research is needed to examine further how different types of violence and abuse contribute to specific health outcomes and to explore pathways from IPV to these health impairments. For example, PSTD has been found to lead to negative health behaviors (Brunello et al., 2001; Cohen, Alfonso, Hoffman, Milau, & Carrera, 2001; Hutton et al., 2001). Given that many battered women experience posttraumatic stress symptoms, future studies might investigate the unique consequences of these symptoms on physical health outcomes through the potential pathways of medical adherence and compliance, as well as coping strategies for dealing with PTSD. These issues might be particularly relevant to chronic illnesses such as diabetes, cancer, HIV/AIDS, heart disease, and sickle cell anemia. Understanding the pathways between IPV and health status could lead to more effective means of treating illness among women who have experienced partner violence (Kendall-Tackett, 2003).

■ Women's Strategic Responses to Intimate Partner Violence

Women's strategic response to IPV is the second major area in which IPV researchers have made important advances. This research has focused almost exclusively on women's problem-focused strategies (Folkman & Lazarus, 1990) for dealing with the violence and abuse, rather than on their emotion-focused strategies (Folkman & Lazarus, 1990) for dealing with the aftermath of violent experiences.

Women deal with IPV using a variety of problem-focused strategies, including seeking help from others and from community agencies. This section examines women's use of domestic violence advocacy, civil protection orders, the criminal justice system, physical and behavioral health care, and personal strategic responses to IPV.

Domestic Violence Advocacy

The most scientifically rigorous test of the effectiveness of *community-based advocacy* to date (Sullivan & Bybee, 1999) compared the effects of a 10-week intensive, individualized, and community-based advocacy intervention to no advocacy following shelter residency. The advocacy condition involved face-to-face contact twice a week for an average of 6.4 hr per week for 10 weeks. Advocates assisted women in trying to obtain education (84%), legal assistance (72%), employment (72%), services for their children (68% of mothers), housing (67%), child care (63% of mothers), transportation (62%), financial assistance (61%), health care (60%), and social support (47%).

Analyses of the effectiveness of this community-based advocacy intervention examined five different outcomes: (a) involvement with the assailant across time, (b) involvement in new relationships over time, (c) effectiveness and difficulty in obtaining resources, (d) short-term outcomes, and (d) long-term outcomes, including physical assault, psychological abuse, depression, quality of life, and social support. At the first interview, immediately after leaving a shelter for battered women, 75% reported wanting to end the relationships with the men who had abused them. Women who worked with advocates were more effective in ending the relationship when they wanted to than were women in the control condition (96% vs. 87% at 24-month follow-up). Of the women who reported that they intended to remain in the relationship, 55% had ended the relationship by the 24-month follow-up and there was no difference between advocacy and control conditions. There was also no difference between women in the advocacy versus control conditions in terms of women's involvement in new relationships. During the 24-month follow-up period, 73% of the women reported having been in a new relationship at some point during that time.

Women in the advocacy condition reported that they both were more effective and experienced fewer difficulties in obtaining needed resources than controls. Further, the difficulty in obtaining resources decreased more quickly for women in the advocacy condition. Preintervention-postintervention (10 weeks) changes revealed significantly lower levels of physical violence, psychological abuse, and depression and higher levels of social support and quality of life compared to the control condition. At 24-month follow-up, the advocacy condition was associated with significantly lower levels of physical violence and significantly higher levels of quality of life, compared to the control condition. Survival analysis indicated that for women in the advocacy condition, the hazard for reoccurrence of violence leveled off at about 15 months, whereas for those in the control condition, the hazard continued to escalate through to the end of the 24-month follow-up period. Median time to reabuse was 3 months for the control condition, compared to 9 months for the advocacy condition. By the end of the 24 months, only 11% of the control condition women had not experienced further violence from a current or ex-partner, compared to 24% of women in the advocacy condition, suggesting that multiple types of interventions may be necessary to protect most women even more effectively from IPV.

These results demonstrate the effectiveness of domestic violence advocacy for assisting abused women to obtain needed resources more easily, to escape physical violence and psychological abuse more effectively, and to experience greater quality of life. Results showed that working with a domestic violence advocate increased safety even for those women who remained in the abusive relationship. These findings have yet to be replicated with abused women who have not first received shelter services.

Further analysis of the community-based advocacy study (Bybee & Sullivan, 2002) found that quality of life entirely mediated the effect of the advocacy intervention on later reabuse. That is, it was the effect of the advocacy intervention on increasing social support and increasing resources at postintervention (10 weeks), which in turn enhanced victims' quality of life (at 10 weeks and 12 months), that decreased victims' reabuse and increased access to resources (at 24 months). The authors explain that quality of life can affect the likelihood of reabuse through multiple pathways. First, it may simply reflect the increase in women's support and resources relevant to their needs. Second, increased quality of life may predict women's ability to generate resources and mobilize supports in the future. Third, subjective well-being or quality of life may expand or contract their sense of what it is possible to achieve (self-efficacy). Finally, enhanced quality of life may be associated with positive emotions and may increase women's thought-action repertoires, resulting in greater ability to mobilize resources and supports (Bybee & Sullivan, 2002). In sum, these findings suggest that advocacy interventions that increase victims' quality of life through increased access to resources and increased social support are necessary for preventing reabuse among women.

In one of the only studies of its kind, Bell and Goodman (2001) examined the effectiveness of a *legal advocacy* intervention program involving IPV victims. Compared to women who received standard civil protection order court services, 21 women working with law student advocates reported significantly less physical and psychological reabuse and marginally better emotional support after 6 weeks. This study highlights the important role of advocacy in the context of legal intervention for IPV as a way of enhancing the safety of IPV victims. Determining why advocacy is associated with greater effectiveness is not addressed by this study. While cases are not randomly connected to a legal advocate, the bias should operate in the opposite direction. That is, IPV victims with more serious cases are often those whose case is referred for assistance from legal advocates, while less serious cases often precede pro se.

Safety planning is an intervention common to advocates across varied settings. The literature describes safety planning with (a) women in an internal domestic violence program in a public child welfare office (Whitney & Davis, 1999), (b) abused women with developmental disabilities (Carlson, 1997), (c) heterosexual women arrested for domestic violence (Hamberger & Potente, 1994), (d) women whose partners are involved in a batterer treatment program (Campbell, 2002), and (e) women involved in the health care system (McFarlane, Greenberg, Weltge, & Watson, 1995). Davies and her colleagues (Davies, Lyon, & Monti-Catania, 1998) delineate the complexity of batterer-generated risks that confront women, as well as the life-generated risks (e.g., poverty) not specific to domestic violence, yet are the fault lines along which domestic violence takes its toll. Not only are battered victims at ongoing physical risk, they face risks of psychological harm, loss of children, loss of relationship with their abusive intimate partner, financial loss, destruction of property, and loss of connection with family and friends.

Safety planning for IPV is a dynamic process (Campbell, 2002; Davies et al., 1998; Dutton, Mitchell, & Haywood, 1996), not merely a one-time plan, in which victims assess risks and plan strategies for avoiding or reducing domestic violence risks. The level of risk and surrounding circumstances can change dramatically and quickly, necessitating a shift in plans. Safety planning may occur in advance of the next immediate threat and involve actions that require a great deal of time and effort (e.g., civil protection orders) or it may occur only moments before a victim acts on those plans (i.e., running out of the house or calling police to avoid a violent attack). Advocates and other professionals working with victims of IPV provide assistance with safety planning in domestic violence programs, health care settings, mental health services, law enforcement crime scenes, courts, social services offices, and almost anywhere that victims are identified.

Although a victim can engage in safety planning on her own, when it involves a service provider, safety panning involves discussion of the risks faced by the battered woman and the generation of potential strategies for avoiding or reducing both ongoing and imminent risks. Safety plans should not be generic, since victims' risks differ, as do their circumstances and resources for dealing with them. A woman who has separated from her abusive husband, has filed for divorce, and is living with the children in the couples' home faces different risks than a woman who remains in the home, is unemployed, and has no money or transportation. Although the IPV risks may be high in both cases, strategies for addressing them may vary considerably.

A recent randomized clinical trial examined the increase in safety behaviors of abused women (McFarlane, Malecha, et al., 2002) among 150 women qualifying for a civil protection order within a family violence unit of a district attorney's office. An advocacy intervention involved six phone calls (one within 48–72 hr of initial visit to the district attorney's office and one each 1, 2, 3, 5, and 8 weeks later), averaging 9 min each (range, 3–25 min). A review of risk behaviors and safety behaviors was conducted with 75 women in the intervention condition, while the other 75 received the "usual" services of the district attorney's office. Follow-up interviews were conducted at 3 and 6 months to determine change in the use of safety behaviors. The intervention group engaged in a significantly greater number of safety behaviors at both 3-month (12.5 vs. 9.9 safety behaviors, $F = 29.55$, $df = 1$, 147, $p \leq .001$) and 6-month (11.9 vs. 10.4, $F = 16.27$, $df = 1$, 147, $p \leq .001$) follow-up periods. Determining the clinical significance of these differences is an important next step.

Most research has examined the impact of advocacy for women who use it. However, a recent study of the female partners of men involved in battered treatment (Gondolf, 2002) found that only about a third of the women in the study had contact with an advocate other than in the courtroom. Over half of the women reported they felt no need for such services. Thus, while it is important to examine the effectiveness of advocacy services for women who utilize them, an equally important question is how to make such services more accessible—or more relevant— to greater numbers of women who are striving to keep themselves and their children safe from violence and abuse.

With the exception of these few studies, there is little research concerning women's use or the effectiveness of advocacy on IPV victims—especially across varied settings, such as domestic violence courts, prosecutor's offices, law enforcement, social service agencies, or other settings. Further, we need studies that examine women's use of and response to advocacy based on characteristics of the IPV, their abusive partners, the women themselves, and an array of other contextual determinants. There are many gaps in our knowledge of safety planning, and the most central is an understanding of its effectiveness in reducing future harm to adult victims and to their children. With the exception of research by McFarlane, Malecha, et al. (2002), described above, safety planning has not been empirically tested, in either quasi-experimental or more rigorous controlled studies. Such an undertaking would require well-developed definitions of safety planning, clear specification of the target population for whom such an intervention was deemed appropriate, and well-considered outcomes variables. Further, the effectiveness of safety planning cannot be considered in isolation, but would require examination in the context of the abuser's behavior as well as other relevant moderating and mediating variables (e.g., access to resources).

Civil Protection Orders

Civil protection orders provide a legal avenue for battered women's efforts to increase their protection from IPV and for remedies that address related needs, such as stay-away orders, support for herself and her children, exclusive use of the home, access to transportation, removal of weapons, and temporary custody of children. However, many IPV victims do not use protection orders, even among those with police involvement. Only about 20% of women who have experienced IPV obtain a civil protection order (Holt, Kernic, Lumley, Wolf, & Rivara, 2002).

A recent study (Holt et al., 2002) examined 2691 episodes of IPV involving a female victim and a male offender which were reported to police in Seattle during a 17-month period where no permanent civil protection order had been in effect during the previous 12 months. In only 12% of these police-reported IPV incidents did the woman file for a protection order. Only 57% of those who obtained a temporary order went on to get a permanent order. IPV females who obtained permanent (vs. temporary) orders did not differ in terms of age, pregnancy status, or IPV history from those who did not. However, alcohol and drug use of both IPV victims and their abusers was significantly less for those who obtained a protection order than for those who did not. Additionally, those who obtained a protection order were more likely ever to have been married to their abusers and less likely to have been living with them at the time of the incident.

Another study (Wolf, Holt, Kernic, & Rivara, 2000) compared characteristics of a protection-order group, with and without a previous police-reported domestic violence incident, to a non-protection-order group who had police contact for a domestic violence incident in the previous year. Multivariate analyses found that women who obtained protection orders, compared to those who did not, were more likely to (a) be employed, (b) be married to the abuser, but no longer living with him, (c) be older, (d) be pregnant, (e) have family members or friends threatened or abused, (f) report severe depression (CES-D > 27), and (g) have been recently sexually abused. Generally, women with more severe partner violence—or more severe effects—were more likely to seek protection orders. However, women who obtained a protection order were less likely to have been living or involved with the abuser or assaulted or injured (but more likely to report threats, stalking, and assault to other family members or friends) during the *index* incident. Data from these two studies suggest that female IPV victims more often use protection orders at a later stage in the course of their violence history when they have been, but are not currently, seriously involved in the relationship.

A recent study by Gondolf and colleagues (Gondolf, 2001) found that a relatively small percentage of total cases involving a petition for a civil protection order court also involved a criminal domestic violence charge. That is, 13% of civil court cases and 19% of criminal cases were overlap cases involving both a petition for a civil protection order and criminal domestic violence prosecution. Comparing overlap cases to civil-only or criminal-only cases found that the overlap cases were generally more serious. Women in overlap cases, compared to civil-only cases, were more likely to have filed prior petitions (20% vs. 7%) and to have filed a greater number of prior petitions. The overlap cases were also more likely to have had accompanying divorce petitions (16% vs. 7%). Overlap cases, compared to criminal court only cases, were more likely to involve charges of harassment or threats (36% vs. 26%) and to have a greater number of total charges. Together, these findings suggest that cases involving both a petition for a civil protection order and criminal domestic violence charges may indicate greater intent of women to leave more abusive partners.

There remain a number of questions about women's use of civil protection orders in response to IPV. We need a better understanding of why IPV victims choose not to seek protection orders in the first place and why, once they are initiated, they often do not pursue protection orders. Studies of this type require interview data from victims to identify their motivations for seeking protection orders, perceptions of their effectiveness, and obstacles to obtaining them. Also, there has been relatively little research examining women's efforts to seek protection orders or their perceptions of specific remedies. Further, the "cost" to women of pursuing a protection order has not been examined. Even when the fee for the court proceeding is waived, the cost to women in terms of lost income or child care when they wait for hours or must return repeatedly when their case is postponed, repeatedly, is often unrecognized. Emotional costs have been almost entirely neglected in this research.

Criminal Justice System

The criminal justice system offers another avenue of intervention for battered women. Most women become involved with the criminal justice system at some point during their abusive relationships (Tjaden & Thoennes, 2000; Gondolf, 1998). This involvement can range from a single encounter with the police to many months in criminal prosecution. Although the nature and the extent of victims' contact with the system is often not under their control (Hanna, 1996), there is evidence that women, nonetheless, find ways to shape the system's response to make it more useful to their particular situation. One way is by attempting to drop charges, recanting, or refusing to participate in a criminal prosecution, particularly if it is a *no-drop prosecution* brought against her wishes (Rebovich, 1996; Smith, 2000). Thus, even those women who attempt to drop the charges against their partner may be using the system in a strategic fashion. For example, using qualitative data from 25 women seeking to file misdemeanor charges against their partners, Ford (1991) documented the ways in which prosecution can serve as a *power resource* for battered women. That is, rather than reflecting ambivalence or passivity, filing and then dropping charges may provide victims with the leverage they need to effect change in the power inequalities of their relationships. There are many important reasons victims might choose to do so, including fear of batterer retaliation, conflict over the possibility of his incarceration, emotional and/or economic dependence her partner, lack of social support, or confusion and frustration with the court process (e.g., Bennett, Goodman, & Dutton, 1999; Erez & Belknap, 1998; Goodman, Bennett, & Dutton, 1999; for a review, see Epstein, Bell, & Goodman, in press).

However, only a few empirical studies have examined factors that might affect battered women's cooperation with prosecution. Of these, Goodman et al. (1999) found that women experiencing more severe violence and those with lower levels of substance abuse, higher levels of tangible support, and children in common with the abuser were more likely to be rated by the prosecutor involved in the case as *cooperative* with the process. Weisz (2002) reported that women separated from the abuser, those whose abusers used alcohol or drugs during violent incidents, and those who did not feel pressured to pursue or drop charges were more likely to favor prosecution. Similarly (Bell, Goodman, & Dutton, 2003), interviews with low-income African American women found that economic independence from the abuser, plans not to continue the relationship, and perceptions of greater future violent risk were most predictive of desire for a criminal prosecution.

Overall, however, there has been very little work on how victims use the court system and what they find helpful about their involvement with it (Fleury, 2002). Information such as this is particularly important given that the needs and wishes of the victim for protection, prevention of future violence, rehabilitation, justice, and especially reconciliation with the batterer frequently do not correspond to the punishment- and deterrence-oriented outcomes pursued by prosecutors (Lewis, Dobash, Dobash, & Cavanagh, 2000). Particularly given the nationwide shift toward mandatory arrest and prosecution (Hanna, 1996), it is unclear how this tension affects victim safety, well-being, and willingness to turn to the justice system for help. Initial evidence from Ford and Regoli (1992) on this topic suggests that victims who are given the option to drop charges, but do not do so, may be less likely to experience subsequent violence. While there is clearly a great deal of work left to be done in the area, these results support the idea that allowing and supporting victims' strategic and flexible use of the system may ultimately be the most important intervention the court can provide (Epstein et al., in press; Ford, 1991).

Physical and Behavioral Health Care.   A small body of research has developed concerning the evaluation of health care interventions for IPV victims (Krasnoff & Moscati, 2002; McFarlane, Greenberg, et al., 1995; McFarlane & Parker, 1994; McFarlane, Soeken, & Wiist, 2000; Parker, McFarlane, Soeken, Silva, & Reel, 1999) and for assessing the quality of hospital-based domestic violence programs (Coben, 2002). Health care-based programs typically include screening for partner violence, which involves a brief series of questions intended to identify those individuals for whom a more in-depth assessment of partner violence victimization—and intervention—is recommended. However, the results of a recent review of 22 studies, using the evidence-based methods of the Canadian Task Force on Preventive Health Care (Wathen & MacMillan, 2003), indicated that no study has examined, in a comparative design, the effectiveness of screening when the end point is improved outcomes for women, versus merely identification of prior abuse. One study (Koziol-McLain, Coates, & Lowenstein, 2001) found that a three-item domestic violence screen was useful for predicting reabuse 3 to 6 months later. Specifically, the relative risk for severe physical violence for women who screened positive was 46.6 times greater than that for those who did not. For women, having a positive screen and being separated were independent predictors of subsequent partner violence. Screening alone has been shown to be inadequate as a gateway for providing services to all the women who may require it, since screening protocols may identify severely abused women, but not those exposed to moderate or low levels of abuse (McNutt, Carlson, Rose, & Robinson, 2002).

Current literature suggests a positive correlation between IPV experiences and health care utilization. Although less than half of women in the United States who have been injured by IPV seek health care for related injuries (Bachman & Coker, 1995), battered women were found to be 3 times more likely to seek care from emergency departments and other medical professionals than were nonbattered women (Ratner, 1993). Studies also report that battered women generate between $1,775 and $2,790 more health care costs annually (Wisner, Gilmer, Saltzman, & Zink, 1999; Ulrich et al., 2003). Although evidence suggests that battered women make more medical visits, often in emergency rooms when they lack insurance (McNutt, van Ryn, Clark, & Fraiser, 2000; Dearwater et al., 1998), significant barriers to health care still exist for battered women (Bauer, Rodriguez, Quiroga, & Flores-Ortiz, 2000; Murphy, Dutton, & Kaltman, 2002).

Overall, studies suggest that women who have experienced partner violence feel dissatisfied with health care providers and report low levels of disclosure regarding

IPV, perhaps due to certain barriers to health care that make it more difficult to disclose IPV, which in turn robs them of the opportunity for the most appropriate medical care. These barriers, and perhaps women's experience of medical encounters, may be related to the psychological consequences of IPV. For example, Dutton and colleagues found a positive association between PTSD and women's perceived barriers to disclose IPV to a health care provider (Murphy, Dutton, & Kaltman, 2002).

A report of the U.S. Department of Health and Human Services (USDHHS; 2001) indicated that minority women are less likely to utilize traditional health services for personal problems. This suggests unique implications for the health care of battered women, since they find it more difficult than other women to discuss "what's on their mind" and other "private thoughts," making it more difficult to disclose abuse to a health care provider (McNutt et al., 2000).

Greater effort is needed focusing on training sensitive and effective health care providers to respond to IPV. For example, despite battered women's poorer health and increased health care utilization, domestic violence screening remains low (Hamberger et al., 2004; McNutt et al., 2000). A recent investigation of physician beliefs about IPV among four specialties (emergency medicine, family practice, obstetrics-gynecology, and psychiatry) indicated that one third of physicians held victim-blaming attitudes and 70% did not believe they had resources available to assist battered women.

While battered women use health care services at higher rates, they do not commonly utilize mental health or counseling services (Coker, Derrick, Lumpkin, Aldrich, & Oldendick, 2000; Gondolf, 1998). Further, there is a relatively little research that focuses on the development and systematic evaluation of mental health interventions for women who have experienced partner violence (Abel, 2000; Levendosky & Graham-Bermann, 2000; Lundy & Grossman, 2001). Depression is the leading cause of nonfatal burden and, correspondingly, the fourth leading cause of disease burden (Murray & Lopez, 1996), making attention to these and related conditions resulting from IPV a major priority.

A 2-year follow-up study of an advocacy, not a mental health, intervention showed sustained and significantly greater improvement in depression for battered women in a 10-week, 6- to 8-hr per week advocacy condition following shelter stay compared to controls (Sullivan & Bybee, 1999; Sullivan, Bybee, & Allen, 2002). Another study described a cognitive trauma therapy for battered women (Kubany, Hill, & Owens, 2003; Kubany & Watson, 2002) which was administered to 37 ethnically diverse women. In a delayed treatment, comparison group design, posttraumatic stress symptoms remitted in 30 of the 32 women who completed treatment and gains were maintained at 3-month follow-up. Finally, a study of group intervention with 60 battered women in Korea (Kim & Kim, 2001) found a reduction at postintervention in trait (but not state) anxiety, self-esteem, and depression, in the experimental, compared to the control, group. Dropout rates were comparable for both groups. Although gains have been made in terms of health and mental health care of women exposed to IPV, much remains to be done.

Personal Strategies for Responding to IPV.   Research is needed to understand more about women's personal efforts to increase their safety and to cope with the emotional and economic aftermath of IPV. Importantly, many strategies for attempting to avoid further violence and to protect their children often go unrecognized. The bulk of these studies on women's personal response to partner violence continue to concentrate on women's decisions to end their relationships, investigating such topics as the process women go through in deciding to do so (Lempert, 1996; Merritt-Gray & Wuest, 1995), predictors of their following through with the decision (Ulrich, 1998), and their ability to maintain the separation over time (Baker, 1997; Griffing et al., 2002; Wuest & Merritt-Gray, 1999).

Thus, ending the relationship often has been used as the central measure of whether women are "doing something" in response to IPV. It is clear that even when a woman decides to leave, it occurs in the context of a whole host of other responses. This emphasis on leaving the relationship persists even though the field has greatly progressed beyond earlier assumptions of battered women's learned helplessness (Walker, 1979). For example (Gondolf & Fisher, 1988), interviews with 6,612 women in Texas shelters documented victims' wide range of help-seeking efforts, efforts that increased as the level of violence escalated. Other studies have found similar results (Bowker, 1986; Follingstad, Hause, Rutledge, & Polek, 1992). Extending and expanding upon this body of knowledge, a number of qualitative works have examined the process that victims go through in moving from more private attempts to stop the abuse (such as hiding or not putting up a fight) to more public help-seeking efforts (such as seeking help from community agencies, family, or friends) (Brown, 1997; Lempert, 1996). A recent qualitative study (Patzel, 2001) explored the personal strengths and inner resources that contributed to women's decisions to terminate the abusive relationship and their ability to successfully follow through with their decisions. Themes of turning point, realization, reframing, agency, and self-efficacy emerged from the study.

Although the decision to leave an abusive relationship is an important area of study, leaving is not always the "right" choice by every woman. Some women may need to establish their ability to remain out of the relationship permanently before leaving in order to avoid severe retaliation, including death. In order to avoid having to return once temporary shelter or others' support is no longer available, some women wait until children have finished school or they have stable employment. Other women wait for an opportunity to leave that will minimize the likelihood of being intercepted or stalked by their abuser. Still others decide that leaving is not a viable option and attempt to avoid or minimize the violence while remaining in the relationship.

The focus on leaving a violent relationship has resulted in a marked lack of information about the strategies victims use on a day-to-day basis while still in an abusive relationship, the factors that influence their choices among different strategies, and the effectiveness of those strategies in reducing the violence and improving their quality of life. A recent longitudinal study of battered woman conducted by Dutton and her colleagues (Goodman, Dutton, Weinfurt, & Cook, 2003) reported on the development of a new measure of IPV-related strategies. In addition to two types of help-seeking strategies (legal strategies, formal networks), the IPV Strategies Index identified four categories of personal strategies (safety planning, resistance, use of informal networks, and placating). In a sample of 406 battered women recruited from civil and criminal courts and shelters, safety planning, use of informal networks, and legal strategies were rated as most helpful, although placating and resistance strategies were most commonly used. Interestingly, greater severity of violence was associated with increased strategy use in every category, even those that appear to be contradictory. For example, women both resisted and placated their abusive partner more as the severity of violence increased. There is need to further examine battered women's private and personal strategies.

■ Emerging Issues Concerning Women in Intimate Partner Violence

Notwithstanding the burgeoning field of IPV, there remain many unanswered questions pertaining to the understanding of women in IPV. Many variations in the ecology of women's lives have yet to be adequately addressed in explaining women's response to IPV. Further, describing and predicting patterns over time is needed. Below we examine three key emerging issues: (a) the influence of cultural and other contextual factors, (b) women's own assessment of their risks and the dangers that confront them, and (c) women's use of violence.

Influence of Culture and Social Context

Understanding social context women in IPV is important for virtually every form of intervention. Although we know relatively little about the influence of culture and other social contexts, as they interact with IPV, this research is beginning to emerge. Culture is a complex construct which includes various ethnic, social, and economic realities, all of which interplay in the shaping of women's responses to IPV (Bogard, 1999). Research suggests that African Americans, compared to Caucasians, underutilize traditional health and mental health services (Neighbors, 1985, 1988; Snowden, 1999; USDHHS, 2001). Gondolf and colleagues (Gondolf, Fisher, & McFerron, 1988) found that African American battered women were more likely than their Caucasian counterparts to contact ministers and the police. This difference in police use may be a result of African American women's perception that they have few resources outside of the police, a perception exacerbated by economic and historical challenges faced by the African American community (Asbury, 1987). On the other hand, African American women may be reluctant to use the police and other public resources in an effort to protect their male partners (and themselves and their communities) from a system that has traditionally been experienced as racist (Kanuha, 1996). Culture is a key factor in understanding women's readiness to use certain help-seeking strategies in response to partner violence. Further, culture can help inform women's perceptions regarding the efficacy of these strategies.

Minority women experiencing IPV may be placed in the position of addressing conflicting agendas, particularly when their needs as women are in conflict with their cultural needs (Crenshaw, 1994). For example, there may be "political costs of exposing gender violence" (Crenshaw, 1994), which serve to undermine the community's fight against racism and related negative stereotypes (Ayyub, 2000). A study examining domestic violence in Vietnamese American families (Bui & Morash, 1999) describes how "women whose husbands had been suffering for many years in the communist reeducation camps before moving to the United States probably would not want to be blamed by the community for causing their husbands to be arrested again in their new country" (1999, p. 790). Internalized cultural values, such as the virtue of sacrifice, playing nonassertive female roles, and family cohesiveness at all costs, can conflict with the desire to leave an abusive relationship (Ayyub, 2000; Yoshihama, 2000). Battered women who are recent immigrants to the United States are particularly vulnerable and may not seek help from authorities because of language barriers, an unfamiliarity with their rights, and, for some women, the risks that accrue from tenuous legal status (Crenshaw, 1994; Sharma, 2001).

After seeking help, minority women may not receive help which addresses their needs in a culturally relevant manner. Diala and colleagues (2000) found that, although there were no ethnic differences in terms of preutilization attitudes, African American women, compared to Caucasian women, reported more negative attitudes after using mental health services and less likelihood of using these services again. Using information gathered from 911 narratives of immigrant women of Japanese descent, Yoshihama (2000) identified several themes that should be considered when addressing domestic violence concerns among this minority group. These themes include the possibilities that Japanese women have a higher tolerance for hierarchies, are taught to avoid conflict, are concerned with the value of collective family welfare, and often feel obligated to keep family matters private (Yoshihama, 2000). Further, the importance of religion on women's responses to personal problems, including domestic violence, has been highlighted in interventions with African Americans (Queener & Martin, 2001) and South Asian Muslim women (Ayyub, 2000).

Research suggests that women frequently use religious resources, such as clergy, when coping with IPV (Alsdurf, 1985; Bowker & Maurer, 1987; Weaver, Koenig, & Ochberg, 1996). Alsdurf (1985) sent surveys to 5,700 clergy in the United States and Canada and found that 84% of the participating clergy reported having counseled at least one female who had experienced physical abuse from her husband. In a survey of 1,000 battered wives seeking medical assistance, Bowker and Maurer (1987) found that approximately one in every three women reported having sought help from clergy. Battered women may seek help from clergy for many reasons, including preexisting long-term relationships with clergy, the physical and financial accessibility of clergy, and the perception that clergy are sensitive to relevant cultural and environmental factors (Queener & Martin, 2001; Weaver et al., 1996).

Another appeal of clergy as counselors lies in their ability to address spirituality (Weaver et al., 1996), a construct that is not well integrated into mainstream mental health interventions. Among African Americans, religiosity and spirituality have been cited as primary coping strategies used in dealing with a variety of personal problems (Bell & Mattis, 2000; Bourjolly, Kerson, Schwaber, & Nuamah, 1999; Constantine, Lewis, Conner, & Sanchez, 2000; Cook & Wiley, 2000; El-Khoury et al., 2004; Neighbors, Musick, & Williams, 1998; Smith, 1981; Tully, 1999; Van, 2001). In a sample of battered women, El-Khoury and colleagues (2004) found that African Americans were significantly more likely than Caucasians to endorse prayer as a strategy to deal with their partner's abuse. Further, African Americans' ratings of the helpfulness of prayer were significantly higher when compared to Caucasian ratings of this strategy. Trauma, in general, poses a spiritual challenge (Garbarino, 1994). In the case of battered women, especially those from fundamentalist traditions, this challenge may be represented in conflicting ideologies revolving around one's self-concept and community and familial loyalties (Whipple, 1987).

Although clergy can be in a particularly advantageous position to counsel battered women, they may not be adequately trained and prepared to respond effectively to their mental health needs (Dixon, 1995; Fortune, 1993; Horton & Williamson, 1988; Weaver et al., 1996; Whipple, 1987). For example, clergy may engage in conservative religious interpretations of family integrity, sex roles, and marriage, which could hinder their ability to provide advice which both is supportive and does not place women in more physical and emotional danger (Alsdurf, 1985; Cooper-White, 1996; Whipple, 1987). There is much to be learned about minority women's perceptions of resource availability and efficacy. More research is needed to examine differences in cultural and other social context variables as they relate to all aspects of women in IPV.

Intimate Partner Violence Threat Appraisal

The potential ongoing threat characteristic of IPV defines it as a stressor different from other types of traumatic events for which there is a reasonably clear end point (e.g., assault by a stranger, combat exposure), even when the traumatic experience involves more than a single event. Yet we know relatively little about the role of threat appraisal for understanding the traumatic or strategic response to IPV. Threat appraisal has been shown to be influenced independently by both the severity and type of IPV (Mechanic, Weaver, & Resick, 2000), as well as by other contextual factors, such as the abuser's use of substances (Gondolf & Heckert, 2003), relationship status (Gondolf & Heckert, 2003), and family structure (Belamaric, 2003; Belamaric et al., 2002). In a recent study, Dutton and colleagues (Dutton, 2003c) found that both characteristics of IPV and other aspects of the social context (social support, PTSD, children in common with the abuser, employment) predicted battered women's level of threat appraisal, but differently for violent versus non-violent threat. Although the investigation of threat appraisal in IPV is relatively new, these data suggest the importance of examining the contribution of the context in which IPV occurs, in addition to characteristics of the IPV per se.

The investigation of threat appraisal in IPV requires attention to the risks of physical harm from the abuser, as well as to other potential risks (Davies et al.,

1998). These include risks of psychological harm (e.g., depression or other forms of emotional distress, suicide), loss of children (e.g., kidnapping, custody), loss of family and friends (e.g., isolation), financial harm (e.g., loss of income, costs of litigation against an abusive partner), legal problems (e.g., abuser reporting actual or falsified allegations to authorities), and loss of property (e.g., destruction of property, loss of use of home or car).

Disentangling the relationship between cognitive threat appraisal (how likely violence is thought to be) and fear (affective response to perceived danger) warrants examination. Understanding the influence of social context (social support, resources) of threat appraisal would potentially inform practitioners when intervening with persons with a history of IPV.

Women's Use of Violence

Recent increases in the number of women being arrested for IPV in the United States (Goldberg, 1999; Hamberger, 1997; Hamberger & Potente, 1994) have, in part, generated a renewed interest in addressing women's use of IPV. In a comprehensive meta-analysis (most of which used community and college samples) focusing on gender differences in IPV, Archer (2000) summarizes that, in general, women are using violence against men at equal, if not higher, rates than men use violence against women. However, regardless of whether IPV rates differ by gender, research suggests that women, compared to men, are significantly and systematically more likely to report experiencing severe, frequent levels and negative consequences of IPV (Archer, 2000; Berk, Berk, Loseke, & Rauma, 1983; Campbell, 1993; Dobash, Dobash, Wilson, & Daly, 1992; Follingstad, Wright, Lloyd, & Sebastian, 1991; Holtzworth-Monroe, Smutzler, & Bates, 1997; Molidor & Tolman, 1998; O'Leary, 2000; Zlotnick, Kohn, Peterson, & Pearlstein, 1998). In sum, women appear to be "more often than men the victims of severe partner assault and injury, not necessarily because men strike more often, but because men strike harder" (Morse, 1995).

Further, social context-based research emphasizes the importance of examining women's use of IPV within the context of male violence and abuse, particularly with regard to motivations for using IPV (Nazaroo, 1995; Swan & Snow, 2002). Women report using violence for a variety of reasons, including as a way to express their feelings (Hamberger, 1997), because of jealousy (Stets & Pirog-good, 1987), to control their partners and to seek retribution (Swan & Snow, 2003), and because they want something (Walker, 1984). However, the most frequently cited motivations for women's use of IPV are self-defense, as an effort to protect against an abusive partner (Barnett, Lee, & Thelen, 1997; Saunders, 1986; Swan & Snow, 2002), or as a reaction to male aggression against her and her children (Dobash et al., 1992). In a review of 75 IPV-related arrest reports involving female perpetrators in Duluth, Minnesota, McMahon and Pence (2003) found that at least one third of the arrested females were later found to have a legitimate claim for self-defense. Further, 41 of 75 women reported that, although they did not feel in danger when they used violence, they were using violence as part of a response to chronic abuse or to a recent (but not immediate) abusive incident (McMahon & Pence, 2003).

Various typologies have been proposed in trying to understand dimensions of couple violence (Johnson, 1995; Johnson & Ferraro, 2000) and, in particular, women's use of IPV (Swan & Snow, 2002, 2003). Johnson and colleagues (Johnson, 1995; Johnson & Ferraro, 2000) identify four relatively distinct types of couple violence: common couple violence (CCV), intimate terrorism (IT), violent resistance (VR), and mutual violent control (MVC). Johnson suggests that CCV, when compared to IT, is less frequent, less severe, less likely to escalate with time, less reflective of a motivation to control one's partner, and more likely to involve mutual violence. Studies which identify domestic violence among community and college dating samples may more likely be tapping into CCV, while couple violence that is more likely to be perpetrated by men and reflected in the experiences of female participants represented in shelter and criminal survey samples may more often reflect IT (Johnson, 1995; Johnson & Ferraro, 2000). The types VR and MVC are less understood dimensions of couple violence and reflect situations in which females perpetrate violence either to resist violence directed toward them or as an equally violent, controlling partner, respectively.

In one of the key studies addressing women's use of violence, Swan and Snow (2002) identified four patterns of female-perpetrated IPV in a sample of 108 heterosexual, low-income, predominately African American women recruited from a health clinic (73%), a family violence program (16%), family court (10%), and a domestic violence shelter (1 participant). These researchers identified four types of female perpetrators of IPV: victim (34%), aggressor (12%), mixed female coercive (17%), and mixed male coercive (33%) types. Although all of the women reported having used IPV at least once in the last 6 months against their male partners, women's use of violence was diverse in terms of severity. Women classified as *victims* and *aggressors* used less or more, respectively, severe forms of violence and coercion against their partners, whereas women in the mixed female coercive/mixed male coercive groups were in relationships characterized by mutual levels of violence, where either the male or female was more coercive. Regardless of type, approximately 94% of the women in the sample reported having experienced physical aggression by their partners. Perhaps this finding emphasizes the importance of examining women's use of violence within the context of their partners' abuse more than any other reason (Swan and Snow, 2002).

In a later study using data collected from the same sample, Swan and Snow (2003) found differences in motivation, behavior, and health among women in each of the four categories of female violence. In general, the mixed coercive groups included the most functional and healthy participants, in that they reported lower levels of violence use, anger, depression, and anxiety (Swan & Snow, 2003). The experiences of women of the victim and aggressor types were characterized by comparable high levels of avoidance coping, suppressed anger, poor anger control, psychological distress (elevated PTSD and depression), and physical injury (Swan & Snow, 2003). Women in the victim group differed from the rest of the sample in that they were most likely to have endorsed self-defense as a primary motivation for violence and to have engaged in higher levels of alcohol use (Swan & Snow, 2003). Women in the aggressor group differed from the rest of the women in that they reported the highest levels of childhood trauma and were the most likely to have endorsed control and retribution as motivations for using violence

(Swan & Snow, 2003). Thus, even though the latter group were more violent than those in the victim group and were the most likely (of all women) to have initiated the IPV aggression, the strategy was not any more effective (than the less frequent and more reactionary violence used by women in the victim group) in dealing with either their aggressors or their own internal feelings of distress (Swan & Snow, 2003). Further, these results point to the importance of understanding the role of lifetime history of violence victimization in women's (and men's) use of IPV.

In spite of this research, women's use of violence is not yet very well understood or documented. Prevalence rates remain largely undetermined, due, in part, to measurement limitations that fail to place women's (and men's) violence in the context of the partner's behavior. Further, battered women who use IPV may be placing themselves at a higher risk for more severe victimization, psychological distress, and legal sanctions. Research addressing gender differences in IPV would yield insight into the possible motivations and predictors of female perpetrated IPV. However, with the exception of a few empirical research studies (i.e., Swan & Snow, 2002, 2003), most of the literature addressing female IPV is theoretical and includes limited samples of heterosexual, college, dating, and/or community populations. Future studies should include women who differ in terms of recruitment sites, violence exposure, sexual orientation, relationship status, ethnicity, and socioeconomic status. Further, studies are needed to examine battered women's use of violence across time in order to capture time-variant patterns. Another important area for future inquiry is the correlates and consequences of battered women's use of IPV, particularly those related to traumatic stress reactions. Such research can inform the development of interventions which address battered women's needs in a fuller manner.

■ Conclusions: Conceptual Framework for Future Research

The review of major advances and emerging issues concerning women in IPV provides a foundation from which to consider an overall framework to guide future research (figure 8.1). In order to understand fully the traumatic and strategic responses to IPV, it is necessary to examine the influence of social, cultural, and historical factors as the context for both of these. That is, how does the context, such as race, ethnicity, social class, gender, immigration status, sexual preference, geographic (urban, rural, suburban), regional locality, social and political contexts, and history of prior violence victimization and/or perpetration, influence how women are affected by and how they respond to IPV? Future research should be explicit in defining the context of the IPV being examined and note the limitations defined by context.

A model of women in IPV must include an understanding of the nature and extent of that abusive experience. For example, more recent research has begun to examine the impact of psychological abuse, separately from physical violence (Arias & Pape, 1999; Dutton, Goodman, & Bennett, 1999; Sackett & Saunders, 1999; Street & Arias, 2001). The notion of violence typologies (Johnson & Ferraro, 2000; Swan & Snow, 2003) is another promising direction for understanding the sequence of events that define IPV for both men and women.

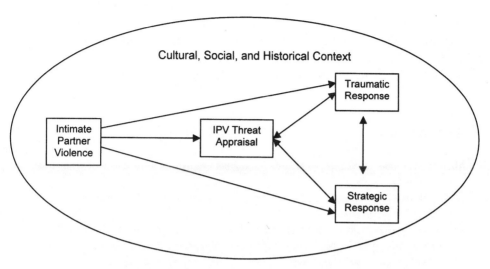

FIGURE 8.1 Conceptual model for guiding research concerning women's response to intimate partner violence.

Intimate partner violence threat appraisal occupies an important position in the proposed conceptual framework for understanding women in IPV. Research is needed to understand how not only the violence, but the social context in which it occurs determines the extent to which women perceive themselves to be in on-going danger. This understudied area of research could highlight the extent to which the impact of IPV on both traumatic and strategic responses is direct—or is mediated through the individual's appraisal of threat. The stress appraisal literature (Lazarus, 2000; Lazarus & Folkman, 1984) may guide IPV researchers in understanding women's response to IPV beyond an objective characterization of violence alone.

While research on women's traumatic response to IPV is perhaps among the most mature in any area, researchers would do well to examine the traumatic response to violence on four separate levels: (a) normal human emotions (e.g., anger, fear, hope), (b) symptomatology (e.g., depression, posttraumatic symptoms) that results from exposure to IPV, (c) cognitive schemas (e.g., trust, intimacy, power) and other consequences of chronic exposure to IPV, and (d) functioning (e.g., work, interpersonal, health, family roles). An understanding of these responses over time, as well as the interactions between them, is important to help define needs for interventions.

Research focusing on strategic responses to IPV is challenged by the wide range of possible types of coping responses (e.g., short vs. long term, private vs. public, ongoing vs. discrete responses, legal vs. illegal, delayed vs. immediate, resistant vs. compliant, behavioral vs. cognitive) that women use. Each domain of response is a context for understanding the others. For example, a study of the use of protection orders would do well to include information about what other strategies battered women had previously tried—and how helpful they were. Nevertheless, a framework for research concerning women in IPV would benefit from the inclusion of behavioral and cognitive coping strategies used for responding to IPV. Another potentially important area of inquiry is the extent to which traumatic and strategic responses to IPV influence each other. In all, the next generation of research on IPV needs would benefit from a contextually rich conceptual framework to guide the development of research questions and to formulate plausible hypotheses.

■ References

Abel, E. M. (2000). Psychosocial treatments for battered women: A review of empirical research. *Research on Social Work Practice, 10*(1), 55–77.

Alsdurf, J. (1985). Wife abuse and the church: The response of pastors. *Response to the Victimization of Women and Children, 8,* 9–11.

American College of Obstetricians and Gynecologists. (1995). *The abused women* (ACOG Patient Education Pamphlet No. APO83). Washington, DC: Author.

American Medical Association. (1992). *Diagnostic and treatment guidelines on domestic violence* [AA 22:92-406 20M]. Chicago: American Medical Association.

American Psychiatric Association. (2000). *Diagnostic and statistical manual of mental disorders* (4th ed., rev.). Washington, DC: Author.

Archer, J. (2000). Sex differences in physical aggression to partners: A reply to Frieze (2000), O'Leary (2000), and White, Smith, Koss, and Figueredo (2000). *Psychological Bulletin, 126*(5), 697–702.

Arias, I., & Pape, K. T. (1999). Psychological abuse: Implications for adjustment and commitment to leave violent partners. *Violence and Victims, 14,* 55–67.

Asbury, J. (1987). African American women in violent relationships: An exploration of cultural differences. In R. L. Hampton (Ed.), *Violence in the black family* (pp. 89–105). Lexington: D. C. Heath.

Astin, M. C., Lawrence, K. J., & Foy, D. W. (1993). Posttraumatic stress disorder among battered women: Risk and resiliency factors. *Violence and Victims, 8*(1), 17–28.

Astin, M. C., Ogland-Hand, S. M., Coleman, E. M., & Foy, D. W. (1995). Posttraumatic stress disorder and childhood abuse in battered women: Comparisons with maritally distressed women. *Journal of Consulting and Clinical Psychology, 63*(2), 308–312.

Ayyub, R. (2000). Domestic violence in the South Asian Muslim immigrant population in the United States. *Journal of Social Distress and the Homeless, 9*(3), 237–248.

Bachman, R., & Coker, A. L. (1995). Police involvement in domestic violence: The interactive effects of victim injury, offender's history of violence, and race. *Violence & Victims, 10*(2), 91–106.

Baker, P. L. (1997). And I went back: Battered women's negotiation of choice. *Journal of Contemporary Ethnography, 26*(1), 55–74.

Barnett, O., Lee, C., & Thelen, R. (1997). Gender differences in attributions of self-defense and control in interpersonal aggression. *Violence Against Women, 3*(5), 462–481.

Bauer, H. M., Rodriguez, M. A., Quiroga, S. S., & Flores-Ortiz, Y. G. (2000). Barriers to health care for abused Latina and Asian immigrant women. *Journal of Health Care for the Poor & Underserved, 11*(1), 33–44.

Belamaric, R. J. (2003). *The role of family structure in battered women's threat appraisals: Direct and moderator effects.* Washington, DC: George Washington University.

Belamaric, R. J., Dutton, M. A., Goodman, L. B., El-Khoury, M. Y., Engel, L., & Murphy, M. (2002). The role of family structure in battered women's threat appraisal and reabuse. *Family Violence and Sexual Assault Bulletin, 18*(3), 15–20.

Bell, C., & Mattis, J. (2000). The importance of cultural competence in ministering to African American victims of domestic violence. *Violence Against Women, 6*, 515–532.

Bell, M. E., & Goodman, L. A. (2001). Supporting battered women involved with the court system: An evaluation of a law-based advocacy intervention. *Violence Against Women, 7*(12), 1377–1404.

Bell, M. E., Goodman, L. A., & Dutton, M. A. (2003). Understanding domestic violence victims' decision-making in the justice system: Predicting desire for a criminal prosecution. *Family Violence and Sexual Assault Bulletin, 19*(2), 6–15.

Bennett, L., Goodman, L. A., & Dutton, M. A. (1999). Systemic obstacles to the criminal prosecution of a battering partner: A victim perspective. *Journal of Interpersonal Violence, 14*(7), 761–772.

Berk, R., Berk, S., Loseke, D., & Rauma, D. (1983). Mutual combat and other family victim myths. In D. Finkelhor, D. Gelles, G. Hotaling, & M. Straus (Eds.), *The dark side of families* (pp. 197–212). Beverly Hills, CA: Sage.

Bogard, M. (1999). Strengthening domestic violence theories: Intersections of race, class, sexual orientation and gender. *Journal of Marital and Family Therapy, 25*(3), 275–289.

Bourjolly, J., Kerson, T., Schwaber, T., & Nuamah, I. (1999). Differences in religious issues among Black and White women with breast cancer. *Social Work in Health Care, 28*, 21–39.

Bowker, L., & Maurer, L. (1987). The medical treatment of battered wives. *Women and Health, 12*(1), 25–45.

Bowker, L. H. (1986). *Ending the violence.* Holmes Beach, FL: Learning Publications.

Brown, J. (1997). Working toward freedom from violence. *Violence Against Women, 3*(1), 5–26.

Brunello, N., Davidson, J. R. T., Deahl, M., Kessler, R. C., Mendlewicz, J., Racagni, G., et al. (2001). Posttraumatic stress disorder: Diagnosis and epidemiology, comorbidity and social consequences, biology and treatment. *Neuropsychobiology, 43*(3), 150–162.

Bui, H., & Morash, M. (1999). Domestic violence in the Vietnamese immigrant community. *Violence Against Women, 5*(7), 769–795.

Bullock, L. (1989). Characteristics of battered women in primary care settings. *Nurse Practitioner, 14*, 47–55.

Bybee, D. I., & Sullivan, C. M. (2002). The process through which an advocacy intervention resulted in positive change for battered women over time. *American Journal of Community Psychology, 30*(1), 103–132.

Campbell, J. (1993). *Men, women and aggression.* New York: Basic Books.

Campbell, J. C. (2002). Safety planning based on lethality assessment for partners of batterers in intervention programs. *Journal of Aggression, Maltreatment and Trauma, 5*(2), 129–143.

Campbell, J. C., Kub, J., Belknap, R. A., & Templin, T. N. (1997). Predictors of depression in battered women. *Violence Against Women, 3*(3), 271–293.

Campbell, J. C., & Soeken, K. L. (1999). Forced sex and intimate partner violence: Effects on women's risk and women's health. *Violence Against Women, 5*(9), 1017–1035.

Carlson, B. E. (1997). Mental retardation and domestic violence: An ecological approach to intervention. *Social Work, 42*(1), 79–89.

Cascardi, M., & O'Leary, K. D. (1992). Depressive symptomatology, self-esteem, and self-blame in battered women. *Journal of Family Violence, 7*(4), 249–259.

Cascardi, M., O'Leary, K. D., & Schlee, K. A. (1999). Co-occurrence and correlates of posttraumatic stress disorder and major depression in physically abused women. *Journal of Family Violence, 14*(3), 227–249.

Coben, J. H. (2002). Measuring the quality of hospital-based domestic violence programs. *Academic Emergency Medicine, 9*(11), 1176–1183.

Cohen, M. A., Alfonso, C. A., Hoffman, R. G., Milau, V., & Carrera, G. (2001). The impact of PTSD on treatment adherence in persons with HIV infection. *General Hospital Psychiatry, 23*(5), 294–296.

Coker, A. L., Derrick, C., Lumpkin, J. L., Aldrich, T. E., & Oldendick, R. (2000). Help-seeking for intimate partner violence and forced sex in South Carolina. *American Journal of Preventive Medicine, 19*(4), 316–320.

Coker, A. L., Smith, P. H., McKeown, R. E., & King, M. J. (2000). Frequency and correlates of intimate partner violence by type: Physical, sexual, and psychological battering. *American Journal of Public Health, 90*(4), 553–559.

Constantine, M., Lewis, E., Conner, L., & Sanchez, D. (2000). Addressing spiritual and religious issues in counseling African Americans: Implications for counselor training and practice. *Counseling and Values, 45*, 28–38.

Cook, D., & Wiley, C. (2000). Psychotherapy with members of African American churches and spiritual traditions. In P. Richards & A. Bergin (Eds.), *Handbook of psychotherapy and religious diversity* (pp. 369–396). Washington DC: APA.

Cooper-White, P. (1996). An emperor without clothes: The church's views about treatment of domestic violence. *Pastoral Psychology, 45*(1), 3–20.

Crenshaw, K. (1994). Mapping the margins: Intersectionality, identity politics, and violence against women of color. In M. Fineman & Mykitiuk (Eds.), *The public nature of private violence* (pp. 93–120). New York: Routledge.

Davies, J. M., Lyon, E., & Monti-Catania, D. (1998). *Safety planning with battered women: Complex lives/difficult choices.* Thousand Oaks, CA: Sage.

Dearwater, S. R., Coben, J. H., Campbell, J. C., Nah, G., Glass, N., McLoughlin, E., & Bekemeier, B. (1998). Prevalence of intimate partner abuse in women treated at community hospital emergency departments. *JAMA: Journal of the American Medical Association, 280*, 433–438.

Diala, C., Muntaner, C., Walrath, C., Nickerson, K., LaVeist, T., & Leaf, P. (2000). Racial differences in attitudes toward professional mental health care and in the use of services. *American Journal of Orthopsychiatry, 70*, 455–464.

Dienemann, J., Boyle, E., Baker, D., Resnick, W., Wiederhorn, N., & Campbell, J. (2000). Intimate partner abuse among women diagnosed with depression. *Issues in Mental Health Nursing, 21*(5), 499–513.

Dixon, C. (1995). Violence in families: The development of a program to enable clergy to provide support. *Journal of Family Studies, 1*(1), 14–23.

Dobash, R., Dobash, R., Wilson, M., & Daly, M. (1992). The myth of sexual symmetry in marital violence. *Social Problems, 39*, 71–91.

Dutton, M. A. (1992). Understanding women's responses to domestic violence: A redefinition of battered woman syndrome. *Hofstra Law Review, 23*.

Dutton, M. A. (2003a, July). *Configurations of intimate partner violence.* Paper presented at the 8th International Family Violence Research Conference, Portsmouth, NH.

Dutton, M. A. (2003b, July). *Longitudinal patterns of intimate partner violence.* Paper presented at the 8th International Family Violence Research Conference, Portsmouth, NH.

Dutton, M. A. (2003c, October). *Determinants and social context of battered women's threat appraisal.* Paper presented at the International Society for Traumatic Stress Studies, Chicago.

Dutton, M. A., Goodman, L. A., & Bennett, L. (1999). Court-involved battered women's responses to violence: The role of psychological, physical, and sexual abuse. *Violence and Victims, 14*(1), 89–104.

Dutton, M. A., Haywood, Y., & El-Bayoumi, G. (1997). Impact of violence on women's health., *Health care for women: Psychological, social, and behavioral influences* (pp. 41–56). Washington, DC: American Psychological Association.

Dutton, M. A., Mitchell, B., & Haywood, Y. (1996). The emergency department as a violence prevention center. *Journal of the American Medical Women's Association, 51*(3), 92–95, 117.

El-Khoury, M. Y., Dutton, M. A., Goodman, L. A., Engel, L., Belamaric, R. J., & Murphy, M. (2004). Ethnic differences in battered women's formal help-seeking strategies: A focus on health, mental health and spirituality. *Cultural Diversity and Ethnic Minority Psychology, 10*, 383–393.

Epstein, D., Bell, M. E., & Goodman, L. A. (in press). Transforming aggressive prosecution policies: Prioritizing victims' long-term safety in the prosecution of domestic violence cases. *Journal of Gender, Social Policies, & the Law.*

Erez, E., & Belknap, J. (1998). In their own words: Battered women's assessment of the criminal processing system's responses. *Violence and Victims, 13*(3), 251–268.

Fleury, R. E. (2002). Missing voices: Patterns of battered women's satisfaction with the criminal legal system. *Violence Against Women, 8*(2), 181–205.

Folkman, S., & Lazarus, R. S. (1990). Coping and emotion. In N. L. Strein, B. Leventhal, & T. Trabasso (Eds.), *Psychological and biological approaches to emotion* (pp. 313–332). Hillsdale, NJ: Erlbaum.

Follette, V. M., Polusny, M. A., Bechtle, A. E., & Naugle, A. E. (1996). Cumulative trauma: The impact of child sexual abuse, adult sexual assault, and spouse abuse. *Journal of Traumatic Stress, 9*(1), 25–35.

Follingstad, D., Wright, S., Lloyd, S., & Sebastian, J. (1991). Sex differences in motivations and effects in dating violence. *Family Relations, 40*, 51–57.

Follingstad, D. R., Hause, E. S., Rutledge, L. L., & Polek, D. S. (1992). Effects of battered women's early responses on later abuse patterns. *Violence and Victims, 7*, 109–128.

Ford, D. A. (1991). Prosecution as a victim power resource: A note on empowering women in violent conjugal relationships. *Law & Society Review, 25*(2), 313–334.

Ford, D. A., & Regoli, M. J. (1992). The preventive impacts of policies for prosecuting wife batterers. E. S. Buzzawa & C. G. Buzzawa (Eds.), *Domestic violence: The changing criminal justice response* (pp. 181–207). Westport, CT: Auburn House.

Fortune, M. (1993). The nature of abuse. *Pastoral Psychology, 41*, 275–288.

Garbarino, J. (1994). The spiritual challenge of violent trauma. *American Journal of Orthopsychiatry, 66*(1), 162–163.

Gleason, W. J. (1993). Mental disorders in battered women: An empirical study. *Violence and Victims, 8*(1), 53–68.

Goldberg, C. (1999, November 23). Spouse abuse crackdown surprisingly nets many women. *The New York Times*, p. A16.

Golding, J. M. (1999). Intimate partner violence as a risk factor for mental disorders: A meta-analysis. *Journal of Family Violence, 14*, 99–132.

Gondolf, E., Fisher, E., & McFerron, R. (1988). Racial differences among shelter residents: A comparison of Anglo, Black and Hispanic battered. *Journal of Family Violence, 3*, 39–51.

Gondolf, E. W. (1998). The victims of court-ordered batterers: Their victimization, helpseeking, and perceptions. *Violence Against Women, 4*(6), 659–676.

Gondolf, E. W. (2001). *Civil protection orders and criminal court actions: The extent and impact of "overlap" cases.* Harrisburg: Pennsylvania Commission on Crime and Delinquency.

Gondolf, E. W. (2002). Service barriers for battered women with male partners in batterer programs. *Journal of Interpersonal Violence, 17*(2), 217–227.

Gondolf, E. W., & Fisher, E. R. (1988). *Battered women as survivors: An alternative to treating learned helplessness.* Lexington, MA: Lexington Books.

Gondolf, E. W., & Heckert, D. A. (2003). Determinants of women's perception of risk in battering relationships. *Violence and Victims, 18*, 371–386.

Goodman, L., Bennett, L., & Dutton, M. A. (1999). Obstacles to domestic violence victims' cooperation with the criminal prosecution of their abusers: The role of social support. *Violence & Victims, 14*, 427–444.

Goodman, L. A., Dutton, M. A., Weinfurt, K., & Cook, S. (2003). The Intimate Partner Violence Strategies Index: Development and application. *Violence and Victims, 9*(2), 163–186.

Green, B. L., Lindy, J. D., & Grace, M. C. (1985). Posttraumatic stress disorder: Toward DSM-IV. *Journal of Nervous and Mental Disease, 173*(7), 406–411.

Green, C. R., Flowe-Valencia, H., Rosenblum, L., & Tait, A. R. (1999). Do physical and sexual abuse differentially affect chronic pain states in women? *Journal of Pain and Symptom Management, 18*(6), 420–426.

Griffing, S., Ragin, D. F., Sage, R. E., Madry, L., Bingham, L. E., & Primm, B. J. (2002). Domestic violence survivors' self-identified reasons for returning to abusive relationships. *Journal of Interpersonal Violence, 17*(3), 306–319.

Hamberger, K. (1997). Female offenders in domestic violence: A look at actions in context. *Journal of Aggression, Maltreatment and Trauma, 1*(1), 117–129.

Hamberger, L., & Potente, R. (1994). Counseling heterosexual women arrested for domestic violence: Implications for theory and practice. *Violence and Victims, 9*(2), 125–137.

Hamberger, L. K., Guse, C., Boerger, J., Minsky, D., Pape, D., & Folsom, C. (2004). Evaluation of a health care provider training program to identify and help partner violence victims, *Journal of Family Violence, 19*, 1–11.

Hanna, C. (1996). No right to choose: Mandated victim participation in domestic violence prosecutions. *Harvard Law Review, 109*(8), 1850–1910.

Hattendorf, J., Ottens, A. J., & Lomax, R. G. (1999). Type and severity of abuse and posttraumatic stress disorder symptoms reported by women who killed abusive partners. *Violence Against Women, 5*(3), 292–312.

Holt, V. L., Kernic, M. A., Lumley, T., Wolf, M. E., & Rivara, F. P. (2002). Civil protection orders and risk of subsequent police-reported violence. *Journal of the American Medical Association, 288*(5), 589–594.

Holtzworth-Monroe, A., Smutzler, N., & Bates, L. (1997). A brief review of the research on husband violence. *Aggression and Violent Behavior, 2*(3), 285–307.

Horton, A. L., & Williamson, J. A. (Eds.). (1988). Abuse and religion: When praying isn't enough. Lexington, MA: Lexington Books/D. C. Heath and Company.

Houskamp, B. M., & Foy, D. W. (1991). The assessment of posttraumatic stress disorder in battered women. *Journal of Interpersonal Violence, 6*(3), 367–375.

Huth-Bocks, A. C., Levendosky, A. A., & Bogat, G. A. (2002). The effects of domestic violence during pregnancy on maternal and infant health. *Violence and Victims, 17*(2), 169–185.

Hutton, H. E., Treisman, G. J., Hunt, W. R., Fishman, M., Kendig, N., Swetz, A., et al. (2001). HIV risk behaviors and their relationship to posttraumatic stress disorder among women prisoners. *Psychiatric Services, 52*(4), 508–513.

Jackson, H., Philp, E., Nuttall, R. L., & Diller, L. (2002). Traumatic brain injury: A hidden consequence for battered women. *Professional Psychology: Research and Practice, 33*(1), 39–45.

Johnson, M. (1995). Patriarchal terrorism and common couple violence: Two forms of violence against women. *Journal of Marriage and the Family, 57,* 283–294.

Johnson, M., & Ferraro, K. (2000). Research on domestic violence in the 1990s: Making distinctions. *Journal of Marriage and the Family, 62*(4), 948–963.

Jones, L., Hughes, M., & Unterstaller, U. (2001). Post-traumatic stress disorder (PTSD) in victims of domestic violence: A review of the research. *Trauma Violence and Abuse, 2*(2), 99–119.

Kanuha, V. (1996). Domestic violence, racism and the battered women's movement in the United States. In J. Edleson & Z. Eisikovits (Eds.), *Future interventions with battered women and their families* (pp. 34–50). Thousand Oaks, CA: Sage.

Kemp, A., Green, B. L., Hovanitz, C., & Rawlings, E. I. (1995). Incidence and correlates of posttraumatic stress disorder in battered women: Shelter and community samples. *Journal of Interpersonal Violence, 10*(1), 43–55.

Kemp, A., Rawlings, E. I., & Green, B. L. (1991). Post-traumatic stress disorder (PTSD) in battered women: A shelter sample. *Journal of Traumatic Stress, 4*(1), 137–148.

Kendall-Tackett, K. (2003). *Health consequences of abuse in the family : A clinical guide for evidence-based practice.* Washington, DC: American Psychological Association.

Kendall-Tackett, K., Marshall, R., & Ness, K. (2003). Chronic pain syndromes and violence against women. *Women and Therapy, 26*(1, 2), 45–56.

Kessler, R. C. (2000). Posttraumatic stress disorder: the burden to the individual and to society. *Journal of Clinical Psychiatry, 61*(Suppl. 5), 4–12; discussion 13, 14.

Kessler, R. C., Sonnega, A., Bromet, E., Hughes, M., & Nelson, C. B. (1995). Posttraumatic stress disorder in the National Comorbidity Study. *Archives of General Psychiatry, 52,* 1048–1060.

Kim, S., & Kim, J. (2001). The effects of group intervention for battered women in Korea. *Archives of Psychiatric Nursing, 15*(6), 257–264.

Koziol-McLain, J., Coates, C. J., & Lowenstein, S. R. (2001). Predictive validity of a screen for partner violence against women. *American Journal of Preventive Medicine, 21*(2), 93–100.

Krasnoff, M., & Moscati, R. (2002). Domestic violence screening and referral can be effective. *Annals of Emergency Medicine, 40*(5), 485–492.

Kubany, E. S., Hill, E. E., & Owens, J. A. (2003). Cognitive trauma therapy for battered women with PTSD: Preliminary findings. *Journal of Traumatic Stress, 16*(1), 81–91.

Kubany, E. S., & Watson, S. B. (2002). Cognitive trauma therapy for formerly battered women with PTSD: Conceptual bases and treatment outlines. *Cognitive and Behavioral Practice, 9*(2), 111–127.

Lazarus, R. S. (2000). Toward better research on stress and coping. *American Psychologist, 55*(6), 665–673.

Lazarus, R. S., & Folkman, S. (1984). *Stress, appraisal, and coping.* New York: Springer.

Lempert, L. B. (1996). Women's strategies for survival: Developing agency in abusive relationships. *Journal of Family Violence, 11*(3), 269–289.

Levendosky, A. A., & Graham-Bermann, S. A. (2000). Trauma and parenting in battered women: An addition to an ecological model of parenting. *Journal of Aggression, Maltreatment & Trauma, 3*(1), 25–35.

Lewis, R., Dobash, R. P., Dobash, R. E., & Cavanagh, K. (2000). Protection, prevention, rehabilitation or justice? Women's use of the law to challenge domestic violence. *Domestic Violence: Global Responses, 7*(1–3), 179–205.

Lown, E. A., & Vega, W. A. (2001). Intimate partner violence and health: Self-assessed health, chronic health, and somatic symptoms among Mexican American women. *Psychosomatic Medicine, 63*(3), 352–360.

Lundy, M., & Grossman, S. (2001). Clinical research and practice with battered women: What we know, what we need to know. *Trauma Violence and Abuse, 2*(2), 120–141.

McFarlane, J., Campbell, J. C., Sharps, P., & Watson, K. (2002). Abuse during pregnancy and femicide: Urgent implications for women's health. *Obstetrics & Gynecology, 100*(1), 27–36.

McFarlane, J., Greenberg, L., Weltge, A., & Watson, M. (1995). Identification of abuse in emergency departments: Effectiveness of a two-question screening tool. *Journal of Emergency Nursing, 21*(5), 391–394.

McFarlane, J., Malecha, A., Gist, J., Watson, K., Batten, E., Hall, I., et al. (2002). An intervention to increase safety behaviors of abused women: Results of a randomized clinical trial. *Nursing Research, 51*(6), 347–354.

McFarlane, J., & Parker, B. (1994). Preventing abuse during pregnancy: An assessment and intervention protocol. *American Journal of Maternal and Child Nursing, 19*(6), 321–324.

McFarlane, J., Parker, B., & Soeken, K. (1995). Abuse during pregnancy: Frequency, severity, perpetrator, and risk factors of homicide. *Public Health Nursing, 12*(5), 284–289.

McFarlane, J., Soeken, K., & Wiist, W. (2000). An evaluation of interventions to decrease intimate partner violence to pregnant women. *Public Health Nursing, 17*(6), 443–451.

McMahon, M., & Pence, E. (2003). Making social change: Reflections on individual and institutional advocacy with women arrested for domestic violence. *Violence Against Women, 9*(1), 47–74.

McNutt, L.-A., Carlson, B. E., Rose, I. M., & Robinson, D. A. (2002). Partner violence intervention in the busy primary care environment. *American Journal of Preventive Medicine, 22*(2), 84–91.

McNutt, L.-A., van Ryn, M., Clark, C., & Fraiser, I. (2000). Partner violence and medical encounters: African-American women's perspectives. *Am J Prev Med, 19*(4), 264–269.

Mechanic, M. B., Weaver, T. L., & Resick, P. A. (2000). Intimate partner violence and stalking behavior: Exploration of patterns and correlates in a sample of acutely battered women. In *Violence and victims* (Vol. 15, pp. 55–72). New York: Springer. http://www.springerpub.com

Merritt-Gray, M., & Wuest, J. (1995). Counteracting abuse and breaking free: The process of leaving revealed through women's voices. *Health Care for Women International, 16*, 413–424.

Messman-Moore, T. L., Long, P. J., & Siegfried, N. J. (2000). The revictimization of child sexual abuse survivors: An examination of the adjustment of college women with child sexual abuse, adult sexual assault, and adult physical abuse. *Child Maltreatment: Journal of the American Professional Society on the Abuse of Children,* 5(1), 18–27.

Molidor, C., & Tolman, R. (1998). Gender and contextual factors in adolescent dating violence. *Violence Against Women,* 4(2), 180–194.

Morse, B. (1995). Beyond the conflict tactic scale: Assessing gender differences in partner violence. *Violence and Victims,* 10, 251–272.

Murphy, M., Dutton, M. A., & Kaltman, S. (2002). *PTSD and obstacles to battered women's disclosure to health care providers.* Paper presented at the annual meeting of the International Society for Traumatic Stress Studies, Baltimore, MD.

Murphy, M. M., Dutton, M. A., & Somberg, R. (2002). *Intimate partner violence: Health outcomes and healthcare.* Paper presented at the Family Violence Prevention Fund, Atlanta, GA.

Murray, C. J. L., & Lopez, A. D. (1996). *Global burden of disease and injury series: Vol. 1. The global burden of disease: A comprehensive assessment of mortality and disability from diseases, injuries and risk factors in 1990 and projected to 2020.* Cambridge, MA: Harvard University Press.

Nazaroo, J. (1995). Uncovering gender differences in the use of marital violence: The effect of methodology. *Sociology,* 29(3), 475–494.

Neighbors, H. (1985). Seeking professional help for personal problems: Black Americans' use of health and mental health services. *Community Mental Health Journal,* 21, 156–166.

Neighbors, H. (1988). Help-seeking behavior of Black Americans: A summary of findings from the National Survey of Black Americans. *Journal of the National Medical Association,* 80, 1009–1012.

Neighbors, H., Musick, M., & Williams, D. (1998). The African American minister as source of help for serious personal crises: Bridge or barrier to mental health care. *Health Education and Behavior,* 25, 759–777.

O'Leary, D. (2000). Are women really more aggressive than men in intimate relationships: Comment on Archer. *Psychological Bulletin,* 126, 685–689.

Parker, B., McFarlane, J., Soeken, K., Silva, C., & Reel, S. (1999). Testing an intervention to prevent further abuse to pregnant women. *Research in Nursing and Health,* 22(1), 59–66.

Patzel, B. (2001). Women's use of resources in leaving abusive relationships: A naturalistic inquiry. *Issues in Mental Health Nursing,* 22(8), 729–747.

Queener, J., & Martin, J. (2001). Providing culturally relevant mental health services: Collaboration between psychology and the African American church. *Journal of Black Psychology,* 27(1), 112–122.

Ratner, P. A. (1993). The incidence of wife abuse and mental health status in abused wives in Edmonton, Alberta. *Canadian Journal of Public Health,* 84(4), 246–249.

Rebovich, D. J. (1996). Prosecution response to domestic violence: Results of a survey of large jurisdictions. In E. S. Buzawa & C. G. Buzawa (Eds.), *Do arrests and restraining orders work?* (pp. 176–191). Thousand Oaks, CA: Sage Publications.

Resnick, H. S., Acierno, R., & Kilpatrick, D. G. (1997). Health impact of interpersonal violence: II. Medical and mental health outcomes. *Behavioral Medicine,* 23(2), 65–78.

Sackett, L. A., & Saunders, D. G. (1999). The impact of different forms of psychological abuse on battered women. *Violence and Victims,* 14(1), 105–117.

Saltzman, L. (1990). Battering during pregnancy. *Atlanta Medicine,* 64, 45–48.

Saltzman, L. E., Fanslow, J. L., McMahon, P. M., & Shelley, G. A. (1999, 2002). *Intimate partner violence surveillance: Uniform definitions and recommended data elements, Version 1*. Atlanta, GA: Centers for Disease Control, National Center for Injury Prevention and Control, Division of Violence Prevention.

Saunders, D. (1986). When battered women use violence: Husband abuse or self-defense? *Victims and Violence, 1*, 4760.

Schaaf, K. K., & McCanne, T. R. (1998). Relationship of childhood sexual, physical, and combined sexual and physical abuse to adult victimization and posttraumatic stress disorder. *Child Abuse and Neglect, 22*(11), 1119–1133.

Sharma, A. (2001). Healing the wounds of domestic abuse. *Violence Against Women, 7*(12), 1405–1428.

Smith, A. (1981). Religion and mental health among Blacks. *Journal of Religion and Health, 20*, 264–287.

Smith, A. (2000). It's my decision, isn't it? A research not on battered women's perceptions of mandatory intervention laws. *Violence Against Women, 6*(12), 1384–1402.

Snowden, L. (1999). African American service use for mental health problems. *Journal of Community Psychology, 27*, 303–313.

Stein, M. B., & Kennedy, C. (2001). Major depressive and post-traumatic stress disorder comorbidity in female victims of intimate partner violence. *Journal of Affective Disorders, 66*(2–3), 133–138.

Stets, J., & Pirog-good, M. (1987). Violence in dating relationships. *Social Psychology Quarterly, 50*, 237–246.

Street, A. E., & Arias, I. (2001). Psychological abuse and posttraumatic stress disorder in battered women: Examining the roles of shame and guilt. *Violence and Victims, 16*(1), 65–78.

Sullivan, C. M., & Bybee, D. I. (1999). Reducing violence using community-based advocacy for women with abusive partners. *Journal of Consulting and Clinical Psychology, 67*(1), 43–53.

Sullivan, C. M., Bybee, D. I., & Allen, N. E. (2002). Findings from a community-based program for battered women and their children. *Journal of Interpersonal Violence, 17*(9), 915–936.

Sutherland, C. A., Sullivan, C. M., & Bybee, D. I. (2001). Effects of intimate partner violence versus poverty on women's health. *Violence Against Women, 7*(10), 1122–1143.

Swan, S., & Snow, D. (2002). A typology of women's use of violence in intimate relationships. *Violence Against Women, 8*(3), 286–319.

Swan, S., & Snow, D. (2003). Behavioral and psychological differences among abused women who use violence in intimate relationships. *Violence Against Women, 9*(1), 75–109.

Tjaden, P., & Thoennes, N. (2000). Extent, nature, and consequences of intimate partner violence: Findings from the National Violence Against Women Survey. A report from the National Institute of Justice and Centers for Disease Control and Prevention.

Torres, S., Campbell, J., Campbell, D. W., Ryan, J., King, C., Price, P., et al. (2000). Abuse during and before pregnancy: Prevalence and cultural correlates. *Violence and Victims, 15*(3), 303–321.

Tully, M. (1999). Lifting our voices: African American cultural responses to trauma and loss. In K. Nader, N. Dubrow, & H. Stamm (Eds.), *Honoring differences: Cultural issues in the treatment of trauma and loss*. Philadelphia: Brunner/Mazel.

Ulrich, Y. C. (1998). What helped most in leaving spouse abuse: Implications for interventions. In J. Campbell (Ed.), *Empowering survivors of abuse: Health care for battered women and their children* (pp. 70–78). Thousand Oaks, CA: Sage.

Ulrich, Y. C., Caln, K. C., Sugg, N. K., Rivara, F. P., Rubanowice, D. M., & Thompson, R. S. (2003). Medical care utilization patterns in women with diagnosed domestic violence. *America Journal of Preventive Medicine, 24,* 9–15.

U.S. Department of Health and Human Services. (2001). *Mental health, culture, race, and ethnicity—a supplement to mental health: A report of the surgeon general.* Washington, DC: U.S. Department of Health and Human Services, Substance Abuse and Mental Health Services Administration, Center for Mental Health Services.

Van, P. (2001). Breaking the silence of African American women: Healing after pregnancy loss. *Health Care for Women International, 22,* 229–243.

Walker, L. (1984). *The battered women syndrome.* New York: Springer.

Walker, L. E. (1979). *The battered woman.* New York: Harper and Row.

Wathen, C. N., & MacMillan, H. L. (2003). Interventions for violence against women: Scientific review. *Journal of the American Medical Association, 289*(5), 589–600.

Watson, C. G., Barnett, M., Nikunen, L., Schultz, C., Randolph-Elgin, T., & Mendez, C. M. (1997). Lifetime prevalences of nine common psychiatric/personality disorders in female domestic abuse survivors. *Journal of Nervous and Mental Disease, 185*(10), 645–647.

Weaver, A., Koenig, H., & Ochberg, F. (1996). Posttraumatic stress, mental health professional, and the clergy: A need for collaboration, training and research. *Journal of Traumatic Stress, 9,* 847–856.

Weisz, A. N. (2002). Prosecution of batterers: Views of African American battered women. *Violence & Victims, 17*(1), 19–34.

West, C. G., Fernandez, A., Hillard, J. R., Schoof, M., et al. (1990). Psychiatric disorders of abused women at a shelter. *Psychiatric Quarterly, 61*(4), 295–301.

Whipple, V. (1987). Counseling battered women from fundamentalist churches. *Journal of Marital and Family Therapy, 13*(3), 251–258.

Whitney, P., & Davis, L. (1999). Child abuse and domestic violence in Massachusetts: Can practice be integrated in a public child welfare setting? *Child Maltreatment: Journal of the American Professional Society on the Abuse of Children, 4*(2), 158–166.

Wisner, C. L., Gilmer, T. P., Saltzman, L. E., & Zink, T. M. (1999). Intimate partner violence against women: Do victims cost health plans more? *Journal of Family Practice, 48*(6), 439–443.

Wolf, M. E., Holt, V. L., Kernic, M. A., & Rivara, F. P. (2000). Who gets protection orders for intimate partner violence? *American Journal of Preventive Medicine, 19*(4), 286–291.

Woods, S. J. (2000). Prevalence and patterns of posttraumatic stress disorder in abused and postabused women. *Issues in Mental Health Nursing, 21*(3), 309–324.

Wuest, J., & Merritt-Gray, M. (1999). Not going back: Sustaining the separation in the process of leaving abusive relationships. *Violence Against Women, 5*(2), 110–133.

Yoshihama, M. (2000). Reinterpreting strength and safety in a socio-cultural context: Dynamics of domestic violence and experiences of women of Japanese descent. *Children and Youth Services Review, 22*(3/4), 207–229.

Zierler, S., Witbeck, B., & Mayer, K. (1996). Sexual violence against women living with or at risk for HIV infection. *American Journal of Preventive Medicine, 12*(5), 304–310.

Zlotnick, C., Kohn, R., Peterson, J., & Pearlstein, R. (1998). Partner physical victimization in a national sample of American families. *Journal of Interpersonal Violence, 13*(1), 156–166.

9
Partner Violence and Children

Ernest N. Jouriles, Renee McDonald, and Nancy A. Skopp

Physical violence between partners in the context of an intimate relationship (referred to in this chapter as partner violence) is a prevalent problem in the United States (Schafer, Caetano, & Clark, 1998; Straus & Gelles, 1990; Tjaden & Thoennes, 1998). Although women may be the most obvious victims of such violence, it has become increasingly clear that the impact of partner violence extends to children as well. In fact, children of battered women (women who have experienced frequent and severe partner violence) appear to be at considerable risk for a wide range of adjustment difficulties (Jouriles, Norwood, McDonald, & Peters, 2001; Margolin, 1998; Wolfe & Korsch, 1994). Given the large number of children in the United States projected to be exposed to partner violence, there is a growing concern about the effects of such violence on children (Holden, Geffner, & Jouriles, 1998). In this chapter, we discuss several key aspects of the empirical literature on partner violence and children. We first review some of the epidemiological findings on partner violence and children, including estimates of the number of children in the United States exposed to partner violence. We then review findings suggesting that children's exposure to partner violence is associated with short- and long-term adjustment difficulties. The focus of our chapter, however, is on gaps in our knowledge pertaining to children's exposure to partner violence. These include the disconnect between studies on the prevalence of partner violence and those on the link between partner violence and child problems, the lack of knowledge on processes linking partner violence with child problems, and the dearth of research on interventions for children in families characterized by partner violence.

We start by offering a brief observation and comment about terminology and measurement in the literature on partner violence and children. The term *partner violence* implies men's violence toward women *as well as* women's violence toward men. As noted in Capaldi, Shortt, and Kim (ch. 6 in this volume), survey data suggest that both men's and women's partner violence are prevalent and often co-occur, particularly among young couples in community samples. There are also important differences between men's and women's partner violence. For example, in community samples women's partner violence appears to be slightly more prevalent than men's, but men's violence is more likely to result in injury (Archer, 2000; Johnson, 1995). In help-seeking samples, men's partner violence tends to be more prevalent and severe than women's violence (Archer, 2000; Johnson, 1995). Most research on partner violence and children appears to have an explicit focus on men's violence toward women (as suggested by phrases such as *children of battered women*). In fact, some investigators do not even measure women's violence toward men in their studies. Other investigators have assessed partner violence generally, not attempting to distinguish between (measure separately) men's violence toward women and women's violence toward men. Others have measured men's and women's partner violence separately and have combined them into one *partner violence* measure. In short, although the term partner violence is used throughout this chapter, many studies in this literature conceptualize and measure partner violence in different ways.

■ Prevalence of Children's Exposure to Partner Violence

In an early review of the literature on children and partner violence, Carlson (1984) projected that at least 3.3 million children in the United States are exposed to partner violence each year. This estimate was extrapolated from the 1975 National Family Violence Survey (NFVS; Straus, Gelles, & Steinmetz, 1980) and U.S. Census data. Carlson's estimate is perhaps the most commonly cited 1-year prevalence estimate of the number of children exposed to partner violence in the United States. However, it is also among the lowest estimates found in the scientific literature. For example, Straus (1992) reports that more than 10 million American children witness an act of partner violence each year. We recently estimated that approximately 15.5 million American children are exposed to partner violence each year (McDonald, Jouriles, Ramisetty-Mikler, Caetano, & Green, in press). Although the estimates vary, the primary point here is that a very large number of American children are exposed to partner violence, irrespective of the specific survey results.

Other epidemiological findings pertaining to the prevalence of partner violence are also worth noting. Prevalence rates for partner violence are particularly high among families with young children (e.g., children under 6 years of age) and in families with multiple children (Fantuzzo, Boruch, Beriama, Atkins, & Marcus, 1997; Lown & Vega, 2001). Black couples are more likely than White couples to report physical aggression between partners (Cazenave & Straus, 1990; Sorenson, Upchurch, & Shen, 1996; Straus et al., 1980), and differences across ethnic groups on the prevalence of partner violence suggest corresponding differences in children's exposure to such violence. In addition, partner violence typically occurs in the context of other risk factors for child problems, including low socioeconomic status, marital discord, and child maltreatment (Straus & Gelles, 1990). We believe these epidemiological findings are important to consider in future research on the topic of partner violence and children, and we return to them later in this chapter.

■ Partner Violence and Child Problems

Many children in families characterized by partner violence are reported to experience significant mental health problems, as well as a range of other adjustment difficulties. Early studies on this topic provided descriptive information on the types of problems exhibited by children in families seeking services (often at shelters providing refuge to women and children because of partner violence). The types of mental health problems typically noted included symptoms of trauma, anxiety, and depression, as well as defiant, aggressive, and delinquent behavior (e.g., Hilberman & Munson, 1977–1978; Roy, 1977; Walker, 1979). However, the problems experienced by these children were not limited to the domain of mental health. School problems, such as distractibility in completing assignments, erratic attendance, and poor grades, were common. Similarly, somatic complaints, such as headaches, stomachaches, asthma, and elimination problems, were also noted. In sum, the lists of child problems in these early studies were often long and diverse and pointed to a broad range of adjustment difficulties experienced by the children in these families.

These early descriptive studies were followed by more carefully controlled studies, which compared children from families characterized by partner violence (again, most often recruited from shelters) to children living at home with nonviolent parents (e.g., Christopoulos et al., 1987; Holden & Ritchie, 1991; Jouriles, Murphy, & O'Leary, 1989). Although the specific findings vary from study to study, it is clear from this literature, as a whole, that children from families characterized by partner violence have higher rates/levels of problems than children from nonviolent families (Jouriles, Norwood, et al., 2001; Margolin, 1998; Wolfe & Korsch, 1994). This is the case across mental health problems broadly conceived (e.g., externalizing problems, internalizing problems) and specific types of mental health difficulties (e.g., aggressive behavior, depressive symptoms), as well as other domains of adjustment (e.g., cognitive functioning, social skills).

It is also noteworthy that a substantial proportion of the children in families characterized by partner violence are reported, on standard measures, to experience mental health problems at clinical levels. For example, in an early review of this literature, McDonald and Jouriles (1991) reported that 25 to 70% of children from families characterized by partner violence exhibited clinical levels of mental health problems, in comparison to 10 to 20% of children from nonviolent, community control families. In a recent descriptive study of a large sample of children brought to battered women's shelters, approximately 50% of the children exhibited problems at clinical levels (Grych, Jouriles, Swank, McDonald, & Norwood, 2000). Clinical levels of conduct problems appear to be especially prevalent, with approximately one third of the children at battered women's shelters exhibiting such problems (Ware et al., 2001).

Most of our knowledge about partner violence and child problems is based on cross-sectional research and incorporates samples of help-seeking families. To date, only a handful of investigators have attempted to follow the children in these families over time, and the results of this research have been equivocal. For example, in a short-term longitudinal study that focused on families in which the children were exhibiting clinical levels of externalizing problems at the time of shelter residence (Ware et al., 2001), mothers' reports of children's externalizing problems remained stable between shelter residence and 2 months after shelter departure, whereas mothers' reports of children's internalizing problems decreased over this time period. In a longer follow-up of a similar but smaller sample, mothers' reports of children's externalizing problems remained at clinical levels over the 16-month follow-up period, with children's internalizing problems again decreasing (Jouriles, McDonald, Spiller, et al., 2001). In a small longitudinal study that suffered from a fairly high attrition rate (18 of the 50 original participants dropped out), mothers' reports of children's externalizing and internalizing problems were higher during shelter residence than 3–6 months after shelter departure (Holden, Stein, Ritchie, Harris, & Jouriles, 1998). These data appear to suggest that children's internalizing problems diminish within several months of shelter departure. Externalizing problems, on the other hand, tend to remain stable, at least among children with clinical levels of such problems.

Other longitudinal data suggest that exposure to partner violence may have long-term detrimental effects for children. For example, Yates, Dodds, Sroufe, and Egeland (2003) followed a sample of young families living in poverty from the children's early preschool years into adolescence. These investigators found that partner violence contributed in the prediction of child problems after controlling for child physical abuse and neglect, child cognitive ability, socioeconomic status, and life stress. McCloskey and colleagues (e.g., Herrera & McCloskey, 2001) followed a sample of children exposed to partner violence, which combined families recruited from women's shelters with families recruited from the community, and a comparison sample of children from nonviolent families for 6–9 years. Children from partner violent homes were found to be at risk for a variety of adjustment difficulties. In other longitudinal research, McCord (1979) found boys' exposure to *parental aggression* (this construct was a combination of partner violence and fathers' punitiveness) to be associated with adult criminal activity. McNeal and Amato (1998) found a single-item measure of adolescents' exposure to parental partner violence to be associated with a variety of negative outcomes in adulthood. In sum, the gathering longitudinal research is beginning to document that partner violence contributes to adjustment problems over the life span.

■ Gaps in Our Knowledge on Partner Violence and Children

It is clear from this brief review that many children in the United States live in families marked by incidents of partner violence and many experience significant adjustment difficulties. Unfortunately, our understanding of the effects of partner violence on children is constrained by numerous gaps in this literature. One important gap is the inability to integrate data on the prevalence of children's exposure to partner violence with findings linking partner violence to child problems. A second important gap is the lack of research on the processes linking partner violence with child problems and, in particular, the absence of knowledge on domestically violent men's contributions to child problems (beyond the effects of their violence). A third important gap is the paucity of data on interventions for children living in families characterized by partner violence. These gaps are explicated below.

Disconnect Between Epidemiological Findings and Findings
Linking Partner Violence to Child Problems

As noted above, a large number of children in the United States are exposed to partner violence. It is important to recognize, however, that estimates of children's exposure to partner violence are based on surveys of national community samples. Many of these surveys also suggest that very few families marked by partner violence seek shelter or other types of services pertaining to the partner violence. For example, only 2% of the women who were victims of violence in the National Family Violence Resurvey sought the services of a shelter (Straus, 1990), suggesting that the children brought to women's shelters are but a small proportion of children who are exposed to partner violence.

At the present time, most of our knowledge on partner violence and child problems is based on children who have been brought to battered women's shelters. In fact, in over 75% of the published empirical articles on partner violence and child problems, investigators have recruited most, if not all, of the participants that compose the violent groups from battered women's shelters (Jouriles, McDonald, Norwood, & Ezell, 2001; Margolin, 1998). Children who are brought to battered women's shelters are an extremely important group and one that we need to better understand. Again, a sizable proportion of these children are identified as exhibiting significant mental health problems at the time of their shelter residence (McDonald & Jouriles, 1991), and the shelter setting readily affords opportunities for providing services (Jouriles, McDonald, Stephens, et al., 1998). Yet it is misleading to think that the children in these women's shelters are generally representative of the large number of children projected to be exposed to partner violence.

There are several reasons to believe that children who are brought to women's shelters may experience greater mental health problems than children who have been exposed to partner violence, but who have not been brought to women's shelters. One reason stems from the differences in the partner violence that characterizes shelter and nonshelter families. Specifically, the violence that occurs in women's shelter families differs significantly—in degree and kind—from the violence that occurs in violent families identified in national survey studies (Johnson, 1995; Straus, 1990). Children who are brought to women's shelters often come from homes characterized by over 60 acts of physical violence per year;

approximately 80% of the children are exposed to wife beatings and over one half are exposed to partner violence involving the threat or use of knives or guns (Jouriles, McDonald, Norwood, et al., 1998). The pattern of violence observed among shelter samples is thought to be chronic and pervasive and has been described as a "form of terroristic control of wives by their husbands that involves the systematic use of not only [physical] violence, but economic subordination, threats, isolation, and other control tactics" (Johnson, 1995, p. 284). Such extreme violence is rarely documented in community survey research on nationally representative samples. In fact, in these surveys, the violence is typically a push, grab, or shove that occurs, on average, six times a year or less (Straus, 1990) and dissipates over time (Johnson, 1995). In contrast to the "terroristic control" that characterizes women's shelter samples, the violence that occurs in community samples is thought to emerge when conflict sometimes gets out of hand (Johnson, 1995). Some have labeled this ordinary (Straus, 1990) or *common couple* violence (Johnson, 1995) and consider it a different phenomenon altogether from the frequent, severe, and persistent violence of shelter families.

There are likely to be additional differences between shelter-seeking and non-shelter-seeking partner violent families—differences that have implications for the adjustment of children. For example, psychological maltreatment (economic subordination, threats, isolation, and other control tactics) and sexual coercion of women are likely to be more common among shelter families than violent families in which the mothers have not sought shelter (Johnson, 1995). There is evidence that psychological maltreatment and sexual coercion of women contribute in the prediction of child problems after accounting for physical violence toward women (Jouriles, Norwood, McDonald, Vincent, & Mahoney, 1996; Spiller, Marsh, Peters, Miller, & Jouriles, 1999). The literature on different types of batterers (Appel & Holden, 1998; Holtzworth-Munroe & Stuart, 1994; Simons, Wu, Johnson, & Conger, 1995) suggests several additional correlates of child problems that may be more common among families characterized by frequent, severe, and persistent violence toward women (i.e., the type of violence frequently found in shelter samples). These include child maltreatment, parental victimization experiences, financial hardship, parental substance abuse, nonviolent marital conflict, and children's exposure to other forms of deviant parental behavior and violence (e.g., violence in the community). In addition, these children have experienced massive changes in the structure of their lives (changes in residence, parental figures, and friends). It could reasonably be argued that one or more of these other variables may account for observed relations between partner violence and child problems.

The lack of knowledge about children of partner violent parents who have not sought shelter or other services is widely recognized as an important gap in our knowledge of the effects of children's exposure to partner violence (Jouriles, McDonald, Norwood, & Ezell, 2001; Margolin, 1998; Sternberg, Lamb, & Dawud-Noursi, 1997). Only a handful of investigators have attempted to compare children at battered women's shelters with children of domestically violent parents recruited from the community and/or agencies, and the results of these investigations are mixed (Fantuzzo et al., 1991; McCloskey, Figueredo, & Koss, 1995; Rossman & Rosenberg, 1992). Similarly, there have been relatively few studies comparing children in violent and nonviolent families recruited from the community. If it is indeed the case that only 2% of women in domestically violent families seek shelter to escape the violence (Straus, 1990), it could be argued that we currently know very little about how partner violence, *as it most commonly occurs in our society*, relates to child problems.

Young Children's Exposure to Partner Violence.   Epidemiological findings indicate that very young children (under 6 years of age) are at higher risk for exposure to partner violence than older children (Fantuzzo et al., 1997). However, at the present time, most of our knowledge on partner violence and child problems is based on children older than 7 years of age. In fact, according to recent reviews of this literature (Jouriles, Norwood, et al., 2001; Margolin, 1998), fewer than 10% of the controlled studies (studies comparing children from partner violent families to children in nonviolent families) focused on children less than 6.5 years of age (see Fantuzzo et al., 1991; Graham-Bermann & Levendosky, 1998; Hinchey & Gavelek, 1982; Onyskiw & Hayduk, 2001, for exceptions). These studies as a group, however, suggest that very young children are affected by partner violence. Specifically, the available research suggests that infants and toddlers exposed to partner or community violence manifest excessive irritability, immature behavior, sleep disturbances, emotional distress, fears of being alone, and regression in toileting and language (see Osofsky, 1999, for a review). The exposure of young children to partner violence may also interfere with the developing child's ability to trust and may curtail subsequent exploratory behaviors that foster autonomy (Osofsky, 1999). Given that children's risk of exposure to partner violence is heightened during this critical developmental period, research on the effects of partner violence on children between the ages of 0 and 6 is long overdue.

Partner Violence and Sibling Relationships.   Epidemiological data suggest that children with siblings are at greater risk for exposure to partner violence than children without siblings (Lown & Vega, 2001). We also know from the empirical literature on siblings that their experiences of their home environments often are not highly correlated (Daniels, Dunn, Furstenberg, & Plomin, 1985; Dunn, 1983), and siblings' differential appraisals of the home environment relate to siblings' differential adjustment (Daniels et al., 1985). Unfortunately, there is a paucity of research in the area of partner violence and child functioning that explicitly considers such findings. For example, there is no research examining whether siblings in homes marked by partner violence perceive their home environments in a similar manner. We have little knowledge about how partner violence might affect sibling interactions. We do not know if partner violence is a topic of siblings' conversations or how a sibling might influence the effects of partner violence on his or her brother or sister. Along these lines, it is possible that partner violence affects child problems indirectly through cross-sibling effects. That is, children who see their brothers or sisters suffering because of the violence may identify with their siblings' plight and become distressed as a result. In addition, children who interpret their parents' violence as threatening or who attribute blame for the violence to themselves might engender distress in their siblings by simply communicating these appraisals to them.

The existing empirical literature on interparental conflict and sibling relationships suggests that interparental conflict is associated with hostile and antagonistic sibling relationships (Dunn & Davies, 2001; Stocker & Youngblade, 1999). For example, a recent longitudinal study involving 3,681 pairs of young siblings (Dunn, Deater-Deckard, Pickering, Golding, & the ALSPAC Study Team, 1999) indicated that mother and partner reports of the quality of the marital relationship related negatively to the hostility and positively to the friendliness exhibited in sibling relationships 4 years later. However, there is also some indication that exposure to partner violence may foster a closer relationship among siblings. For example, it appears that siblings develop closer bonds when parental care is lacking (Boer, Goedhart, & Treffers, 1992; Bryant, 1992). Given that parenting behaviors may be compromised as a result of partner violence (see review below), it is quite plausible that children might become more closely allied in the face of such violence. In short, much more research on the dynamics of sibling relationships among children exposed to partner violence is needed to improve our understanding of the extent to which such relationships might serve protective or deleterious functions.

Ethnicity, Partner Violence, and Child Problems.   Another gap in our knowledge about partner violence and children pertains to how ethnicity might influence relations between partner violence and child problems. Again, we know from national survey data that physical aggression between partners is more frequently reported among Black than White couples (Cazenave & Straus, 1990; Sorenson et al., 1996; Straus et al., 1980) suggesting that Black children may be at greater risk for exposure to partner violence than their White counterparts. It thus seems particularly important to understand how partner violence relates to child problems within Black families and whether relations differ across different ethnic groups. Unfortunately, virtually no research exists on this topic.

Theory on ethnicity, interparental conflict, and child problems suggests a number of ways in which ethnicity might mark differences in relations between partner violence and child problems (McLoyd, Harper, & Copeland, 2001). One hypothesis suggests that the association between parental conflict and child problems might be attenuated in ethnic minority families (Amato & Keith, 1991). It is reasoned that interparental conflict experienced by ethnic minority children frequently occurs against the backdrop of a number of ethnicity-related stressors (e.g., racial prejudice), mitigating the salience of the conflict for these children. It is also reasoned that ethnic minority families are more likely than White families to be embedded in extended family networks and receive support from multiple sources. A plausible argument also could be made for the notion that the association between partner violence and child problems is stronger in ethnic minority families. For example, research suggests that psychosocial risk factors operate in a cumulative, or even a multiplicative, fashion such that one adverse event adds to, or potentiates, the effects of another (Rutter, 1983). Thus, one could reasonably assert that when children's exposure to partner violence occurs in conjunction with ethnicity-related stressors, it greatly increases the potential for child problems. Alternatively, because White children, in comparison to ethnic minority children, are more likely to live in favorable environments where they potentially have greater access to growth-enhancing experiences, they may be less vulnerable to the effects of partner violence because they are buffered by their more advantaged social circumstances. In short, it is evident that much more research is needed to evaluate how ethnicity might serve to attenuate or intensify the effects of partner violence on child problems.

Other Risk Factors Associated With Both Partner Violence and Child Problems.   Epidemiological data suggest that partner violence often occurs in the context of other risk factors for child problems. These risk factors are numerous and include low socioeconomic status, nonviolent marital discord, and child maltreatment. However, there is very little research examining how these other risk factors might interact with partner violence in influencing child functioning. In fact, there is very little research even attempting to account for these other risk factors, leaving open the possibility that these other risk factors, and not partner violence per se, are responsible for the documented association between partner violence and child problems. Given the cumulative and interactive effects of multiple risk factors noted above (Rutter, 1983), it would appear essential to assess for potential risk factors beyond partner violence. In fact, the failure to consider these other variables that are correlates of both partner violence and child problems clouds the interpretation of past research and renders it impossible to determine the extent to which partner violence per se increases the risk for child problems.

■ Theory Linking Partner Violence With Child Problems

To further our understanding of relations between partner violence and child problems, it is important to consider the psychological and family processes responsible for the relations. Knowledge pertaining to these processes is also likely to be important in the development of effective interventions for children adversely affected by partner violence. Early research focused almost exclusively on documenting that there was indeed a relation between partner violence and child problems. Only recently have there been systematic attempts to test theory on the processes linking these two family problems. Much of this research has focused on social learning theory explanations of the development of child problems in the context of partner violence. Specifically, much of the research has focused on (a) children's observation and interpretation of partner violence and (b) how partner violence might disrupt parenting, which, in turn, influences child adjustment. In our minds, both of these explanations seem reasonable and likely account, in part, for the link between partner violence and child problems. Below, we briefly present ideas emerging from these theories and then offer several potentially promising avenues.

Children's Observation and Interpretation of Partner Violence

Repeated observation of aggressive models—in particular, salient models such as parents—facilitates the development of beliefs and scripts that support the use of aggressive behavior in particular contexts (Bandura, 1973; Huesmann, 1988). These include the notion that aggression is an acceptable method for resolving disagreements and that its use can produce positive outcomes or, alternatively, will not result in negative outcomes. There is a large body of research indicating that beliefs and scripts hypothesized to support the use of aggression are associated with aggressive behavior among school-aged children (Hall, Herzberger, & Skowronski, 1998; Huesmann & Guerra, 1997; Perry, Willard, & Perry, 1990). There is also evidence that these beliefs and scripts may originate with the parents (Bandura, 1983), but it is not clear exactly how parents facilitate their development. With respect to partner violence and child behavior, it certainly seems plausible that these observational learning processes might be operating. In fact, much of the research in the field has been guided by this notion, and the results of numerous studies linking partner violence with children's aggression have been interpreted to be consistent with these ideas. However, it might also be argued that important aspects of this theory (e.g., the development of beliefs and scripts that support the use of aggressive behavior) have not yet been tested directly in partner violent families. Similarly, one can propose many alternative explanations for the development of aggressive behavior in partner violent families.

Grych, Fincham, and colleagues emphasize the importance of children's cognitive appraisals of marital conflict and partner violence (Grych, 2000; Grych & Fincham, 1990; Grych, Fincham, Jouriles, & McDonald, 2000). In their model, children are not passively influenced by their parents' conflict and violence; they attend to it, interpret it, and respond according to their interpretations of its meaning. Children are hypothesized to appraise conflict and violence along several dimensions, including the extent to which it is viewed as threatening to the child and/or to the stability of the family (e.g., scared the conflict/violence will spill over to the child, fear the family will split up), and the extent to which the children blame themselves for its occurrence. Perceived threat and self-blame for the conflict and violence are hypothesized to lead to child internalizing problems, such as anxiety and depression (Grych, Fincham, et al., 2000). For example, children who perceive marital conflict as threatening may develop persistent worries about their parents, the future of the family, and their own well-being. Children who blame themselves for causing parental conflict are hypothesized to develop feelings of guilt and shame, which are symptoms of depression. A number of cross-sectional studies and a recent longitudinal investigation have yielded data consistent with these suppositions. Specifically, children's threat and self-blame appraisals of marital conflict have been found to be associated with internalizing problems in community samples (e.g., Cummings, Davies, & Simpson, 1994; Grych, Harold, & Miles, 2003; Grych, Seid,

& Fincham, 1992), as well as in samples characterized by partner violence (Grych, Fincham, et al., 2000; Jouriles, Spiller, Stephens, McDonald, & Swank, 2000).

Effects of Partner Violence on Parenting

Another social learning theory account of the development of aggression in young children emphasizes the role of parenting (e.g., Patterson, 1982; Patterson, Reid, & Dishion, 1992). By virtue of their interactions with their children, parents are hypothesized to teach (often inadvertently) children to behave in an aggressive manner. Parental aggression toward children is hypothesized to be important in this process. As suggested above, a parent's use of aggression (especially in disciplinary confrontations) might facilitate the development of beliefs and scripts that aggressive behavior is an acceptable method for resolving disagreements and that it can result in positive outcomes. Another dimension of parenting hypothesized to be important in this teaching process involves inconsistent discipline, in which parents sometimes fail to follow through with directives or discipline, particularly when parents withdraw directives or discipline in response to oppositional or aggressive child behavior (such inconsistencies are hypothesized to teach children that oppositional or aggressive behavior can pay off). A third dimension of parenting hypothesized to be important is parental supportiveness and, in particular, encouragement for prosocial behavior. These three dimensions of parenting (aggression, inconsistent discipline, supportiveness) have been associated with child aggression in many previous studies (Patterson, 1982; Patterson et al., 1992).

Research on partner violence and parenting is sparse and focuses primarily on physical aggression directed toward children. It is clear that partner violence is positively associated with both mothers' and fathers' physical aggression toward children (Appel & Holden, 1998). Partner violence has also been positively associated with inconsistencies in parental discipline (Holden & Ritchie, 1991) and negatively associated with maternal warmth and supportiveness toward children (Levendosky & Graham-Bermann, 2000; McCloskey et al., 1995). However, the latter finding has not been documented consistently (Holden & Ritchie, 1991; McCloskey et al., 1995), and some investigators have theorized that partner violence might actually increase maternal supportiveness (Sullivan, Nguyen, Allen, Bybee, & Juras, 2000).

Promising New Directions: Thinking a Little Outside the Box

Extending Existing Parenting Models to Domestically Violent Men.   The notion that domestically violent men might play a role in the development of child problems—beyond the effects of violence—is almost completely absent from the literature. In fact, research on men's influence on child development, in general, remains relatively rare (Lamb, 1997; Phares, 1997). In the literature on partner violence and child problems, only a handful of studies include data collected from men (e.g., Crockenberg & Langrock, 2001; Jouriles et al., 1989; McDonald, Jouriles, Norwood, Ware, & Ezell, 2000; Sternberg, Lamb, & Dawud-Noursi, 1997; Sternberg et al., 1993).

Consequently, most of our knowledge about men's behavior within partner violent families, in relation to child problems, is based on data provided by mothers. It is quite conceivable that such data are biased (e.g., a battered woman might be more likely to perceive and describe her partner in a negative light). However, with this shortcoming in mind, the available evidence suggests that the parenting behavior of domestically violent men is likely to contribute to child problems. For example, mothers often indicate that domestically violent men are physically aggressive toward their children (e.g., Holden & Ritchie, 1991; Jouriles & LeCompte, 1991) and that they rarely engage in positive, supportive interactions with their children (Holden & Ritchie, 1991).

The research literature on fathering suggests that men's involvement in the children's lives may also be important. Specifically, fathers' involvement in their children's lives is positively related to a number of positive outcomes for children (Cabrera, Tamis-LeMonda, Bradley, Hofferth, & Lamb, 2000; Lamb, 1997; Phares, 1997). Yet it is interesting to consider the possible effects of domestically violent men's involvement with children. That is, it is reasonable to think that the involvement of a violent man in a child's life might be linked to poorer child outcomes. Although little is known about how a child's involvement with a man engaging in deviant behavior (such as frequent and severe partner violence) is likely to influence child development, there is evidence from the substance abuse literature suggesting that high levels of involvement between a child and a "deviant" man fosters deviant child outcomes (Andrews, Hops, & Duncan, 1997).

Parental Discussions With Children About Violent Events.   Parental discussions with a child about violent events warrant special attention as a potentially important aspect of family interaction that influences child functioning. It has been hypothesized that children exposed to violence need to talk about their experience with others in a way that will help them cope with and make sense of the violence (Campos, 1987; Garbarino, Dubrow, Kostelny, & Pardo, 1992; Kliewer, Lepore, Oskin, & Johnson, 1998). In the absence of such discussions, children are often left to their own devices in dealing with stressors, which can result in a variety of internalizing and externalizing problems (Bandura, 1973; Dodge, Bates, & Pettit, 1990). In our own pilot work, we have observed a great deal of variability in how parents and children talk about the violence that occurs in their home. We expect that some parental explanations will help children make sense of partner violence in a manner that fosters adaptive appraisals of violent events (e.g., "my father's violence is not my fault"). Other explanations, on the other hand, may exacerbate the effects of violence exposure (e.g., by blaming children for incidents of partner violence; Holden et al., 1998).

Thinking a Little Further Outside the Box.   It seems plausible that children's exposure to partner violence, particularly frequent and severe violence, affects them in many ways that have not yet been explored. It is also plausible that these effects might play an extremely important role in the development of psychopathology or other adjustment difficulties. For example, partner violence might influence developing physiological, affective, and regulatory systems in a way that leads to impaired behavioral and emotional functioning. Numerous examples could be offered. For instance, recent data suggest that environmental factors at certain developmental points have context-specific effects on biological markers associated with affective and behavioral regulation (toddlers in child care demonstrate fluctuating patterns in HPA axis functioning and cortisol levels; Watamura, Donzella, Alwin, & Gunnar, 2003). A randomized intervention trial to help at-risk preschoolers at school entry has demonstrated context-specific effects on HPA axis functioning and cortisol levels, in addition to preventive intervention effects on parenting and child social competence (Brotman, Gouley, Klein, Castellanos, & Pine, 2003). Effects on regulatory systems could be linked to a number of problematic mental health outcomes, in addition to being problems in and of themselves.

■ Interventions

Over the past decade some strides have been made with respect to the implementation and evaluation of interventions for children exposed to partner violence (see Lehmann & Rabenstein, 2002; Graham-Bermann, 2001, for reviews); however, research on the efficacy of these interventions is in the very early stages. Existing programs that have been evaluated vary in scope and treatment goals (e.g., treatments targeted at changing particular family processes or child behavior versus diffuse treatments aimed at ameliorating the impact of the violence more generally), venue (shelter, community, and home-based programs), targeted age range (e.g., children versus adolescents), and composition (e.g., individual children, children's groups, sibling groups, mother-child dyads; Graham-Bermann, 2001). Unfortunately, most of the outcome data with respect to these interventions are based upon preliminary findings derived from very small samples often lacking comparison groups (Graham-Bermann, 2001). Of the handful of studies that included posttreatment follow-up, none followed children beyond 8 months posttreatment (Graham-Bermann, 2001); thus the durability of reported treatment gains is unclear (see Jouriles, McDonald, Spiller et al., 2001, for an exception). Furthermore, despite the diversity of interventions, most are not tailored to children's individual needs or do not target specific populations or provide screening protocols (Graham-Bermann, 2001). In short, the outcome data on interventions for children exposed to partner violence are sparse and suffer from a number of methodological shortcomings.

Impeding the occurrence of violence is likely to be the most effective route to alleviating emotional distress and behavioral problems among children exposed to partner violence. Yet even when partner violence ceases, some children may continue to experience residual issues or problems associated with the violence. Interventions designed to address ensuing child problems and provide instrumental and emotional support to women who have attempted to establish residence independent of their partners might be useful in this regard. The encouraging results of Project SUPPORT highlight the potential utility of an intervention program targeting specific family processes in an attempt to change child behavior (Jouriles,

McDonald, Spiller et al., 2001). Very briefly, Project SUPPORT is an intervention designed for families (mothers and children) departing from a women's shelter, in which at least one child exhibited clinical levels of conduct problems, and the mother was attempting to establish a residence independent of her violent partner. The intervention included two main components: (a) providing instrumental and emotional support to mothers during their transition from women's shelters to new homes independent of their abusive partners and (b) teaching mothers to implement a set of child management and nurturing skills that have been shown to be effective in the treatment of clinical levels of conduct problems. Project SUPPORT's services were initiated shortly after shelter departure and lasted up to 8 months following shelter departure. Compared to children in the existing services comparison condition, the conduct problems among children in the Project SUPPORT intervention condition decreased more rapidly and were more likely to fall from clinical to normative levels. This latter finding was documented 8 months following the termination of services (16 months following shelter departure). There were also differences in observed parenting, with the proper use of child management skills increasing more rapidly among mothers in the Project SUPPORT intervention condition than in mothers in the existing services comparison condition.

Graham-Bermann (2001) offers a number of suggestions for designing more effective interventions for children exposed to partner violence. First of all, there is an urgent need for research to extend beyond families residing at shelters to encompass community families, given that only a fraction of families affected by partner violence seek refuge in such shelters. In addition, more research is indicated to compare and contrast divergent interventions; rather than comparing similar treatments, it would be potentially useful to evaluate divergent treatments to identify the most fruitful treatment approaches. In a similar vein, outcome studies targeting a range of child problems would be useful in increasing our understanding of which children are most likely to benefit from particular treatments. Research designed to develop risk profiles for children exposed to partner violence might be instrumental in targeting groups of children with similar profiles, violence experiences, and exposures. Research is also needed to systematically examine contextual elements of these interventions (e.g., setting, therapist characteristics, treatment techniques).

To conclude this section, we want to emphasize that there is a high degree of variability in adjustment among children from partner violent households. The notion that all children who have been exposed to partner violence inevitably experience psychological impairments requiring therapeutic intervention is most likely inaccurate, as an appreciable proportion of children from such households do not appear to manifest significant child problems (Grych, Jouriles, et al., 2000; Hughes & Luke, 1998). Thus, it would be essential for clinicians to individually assess the need for psychotherapeutic intervention among children from partner violent homes and to tailor treatments to the specific needs of particular children when treatment is indicated. In sum, it is evident that much more research is required to determine the efficacy and appropriateness of various intervention programs for children exposed to partner violence and to develop more efficacious ones.

■ Summary and Conclusions

Clearly much work remains to be done to fill the gaps in our knowledge of the prevalence of children's exposure to partner violence (and epidemiological data on partner violence in general) and the link between partner violence and child problems. In this chapter, we have highlighted several key domains within this literature that are in need of development. Prominent among the issues raised is the overreliance on shelter samples and the paucity of research on young children and sibling relationships. We have also noted the lack of research examining how ethnicity might attenuate or amplify the effects of partner violence on child problems, as well as insufficient attention to the concomitants (e.g., economic hardship, interparental conflict) of partner violence, which are also likely to increase the risk of child problems. There is a clear need to test existing theory and to develop new theory on the psychological and family processes linking partner violence and child problems, as well as the treatment of such problems. In this vein, we have suggested that existing parenting models be extended to include domestically violent men and that future research examine the influence of partner violence on the developing child's physiological, affective, and regulatory system. We have also have reviewed suggestions for increasing the rigor of treatment outcome studies and outlined the potential function of parent-child discussions about partner violence in the development, maintenance, or hindrance of child problems. In conclusion, a much more comprehensive understanding of the relations between children's exposure to partner violence and child problems will emerge after sustained and focused efforts are made to resolve the issues raised above.

■ References

Amato, P. R., & Keith, B. (1991). Parental divorce and adult well-being: A meta-analysis. *Journal of Marriage and the Family, 53,* 43–58.

Andrews, J. A., Hops, H., & Duncan, S. C. (1997). Adolescent modeling of parent substance use: The moderating effect of the relationship with the parent. *Journal of Family Psychology, 11,* 259–270.

Appel, A. E., & Holden, G. W. (1998). The co-occurrence of spouse and physical child abuse: A review and appraisal. *Journal of Family Violence, 2,* 139–149.

Archer, J. (2000). Sex differences in aggression between heterosexual partners: A meta-analytic review. *Psychological Bulletin, 126,* 651–680.

Bandura, A. (1973). *Aggression: A social learning analysis.* Englewood Cliffs, NJ: Prentice Hall.

Bandura, A. (1983). Psychological mechanisms of aggression. In R. G. Geen & E. I. Donnerstein (Eds.), *Aggression: Theoretical and empirical reviews* (pp. 1–40). New York: Academic Press.

Boer, F., Goedhart, A. W., & Treffers, P. D. A. (1992). Siblings and their parents. In F. Boer & J. Dunn (Eds.), *Children's sibling relationships: Developmental and clinical issues* (pp. 41–54). Hillsdale, NJ: Erlbaum.

Brotman, L. M., Gouley, K. K., Klein, R. G., Castellanos, F. X., & Pine, D. S. (2003). Children, stress, and context: Integrating basic, clinical, and experimental prevention research. *Child Development, 74,* 1053–1057.

Bryant, B. K. (1992). Sibling caretaking: Providing emotional support during middle childhood. In F. Boer & J. Dunn (Eds.), *Children's sibling relationships: Developmental and clinical issues* (pp. 55–69). Hillsdale, NJ: Erlbaum.

Cabrera, N. J., Tamis-LeMonda, C. S., Bradley, R. H., Hofferth, S., & Lamb, M. E. (2000). Fatherhood in the twenty-first century. *Child Development, 71,* 127–136.

Campos, B. E. (1987). Coping with stress during childhood and adolescence. *Psychological Bulletin, 101,* 393–403.

Carlson, B. E. (1984). Children's observations of interpersonal violence. In A. Roberts (Ed.), *Battered women and their families* (pp. 147–167). New York: Springer.

Cazenave, N. A., & Straus, M. (1990). Race, class, network embeddedness, and family violence: A search for potent support systems. In M. A. Straus & R. J. Gelles (Eds.), *Physical violence in American families: Risk factors and adaptations to violence in 8,145 families.* (pp. 321–329). New Brunswick, NJ: Transaction.

Christopoulos, C., Cohn, D. A., Shaw, D. S., Joyce, S., Sullivan-Hanson, J., Kraft, S. P., et al. (1987). Children of abused women: Adjustment at time of shelter residence. *Journal of Marriage and the Family, 49,* 611–619.

Crockenberg, S., & Langrock, A. (2001). The role of specific emotions in children's responses to interparental conflict: Test of the model. *Journal of Family Psychology, 15,* 163–182.

Cummings, E. M., Davies, P. T., & Simpson, K. S. (1994). Marital conflict, gender, and children's appraisals and coping efficacy as mediators of child adjustment. *Journal of Family Psychology, 8,* 141–149.

Daniels, E., Dunn, J., Furstenberg, F. F., & Plomin, R. (1985). Environmental differences within the family and adjustment differences within pairs of adolescent siblings. *Child Development, 56,* 764–774.

Dodge, K. A., Bates, J. E., & Pettit, G. S. (1990). Mechanisms in the cycle of violence. *Science, 250,* 1678–1683.

Dunn, J. (1983). Sibling relationships in early childhood. *Child Development, 54,* 787–811.

Dunn, J., & Davies, L. (2001). Sibling relationships and interparental conflict. In J. H. Grych & F. D. Fincham (Eds.), *Interparental conflict and child development* (pp. 273–290). Cambridge: Cambridge University Press.

Dunn, J., Deater-Deckard, K., Pickering, K., Golding, J., & the ALSPAC Study Team. (1999). Siblings, parents and partners: Family relationships within a longitudinal community study. *Journal of Child Psychology and Psychiatry, 40,* 1025–1037.

Fantuzzo, J. W., Boruch, R., Beriama, A., Atkins, M., & Marcus, S. (1997). Domestic violence and children: Prevalence and risk in five major U.S. cities. *Journal of the American Academy of Child and Adolescent Psychiatry, 36,* 116–122.

Fantuzzo, J. W., DePaola, L. M., Lambert, L., Martino, T., Anderson, G., & Sutton, S. (1991). Effects of interparental violence on the psychological adjustment and competencies of young children. *Journal of Consulting and Clinical Psychology, 59,* 258–265.

Garbarino, J., Dubrow, N., Kostelny, K., & Pardo, C. (1992). *Children in danger. Coping with the consequences of community violence.* San Francisco: Jossey-Bass.

Graham-Bermann, S. A. (2001). Designing intervention evaluations for children exposed to domestic violence. In S. A. Graham-Bermann & J. L. Edleson (Eds.), *Domestic violence in the lives of children: The future of research, intervention, and social policy* (pp. 237–267). Washington, DC: American Psychological Association.

Graham-Bermann, S. A., & Levendosky, A. A. (1998). The social functioning of preschool-age children whose mothers are emotionally and physically abused. *Journal of Emotional Abuse, 1,* 59–84.

Grych, J. H. (2000). Children's perspectives of family violence: Implications for research and intervention. In J. P. Vincent & E. N. Jouriles (Eds.), *Domestic violence: Guidelines for research-informed practice* (pp. 102–125). London: Jessica Kingsley.

Grych, J. H., & Fincham, F. D. (1990). Marital conflict and children's adjustment: A cognitive-contextual framework. *Psychological Bulletin, 108*, 267–290.

Grych, J. H., Fincham, F. D., Jouriles, E. N., & McDonald, R. (2000). Interparental conflict and child adjustment: Testing the mediational role of appraisals in the cognitive-contextual framework. *Child Development, 71*, 1648–1661.

Grych, J. H., Harold, G. T., & Miles, C. J. (2003). A prospective investigation of appraisals as mediators of the link between interparental conflict and child adjustment. *Child Development, 74*, 1176–1193.

Grych, J. H., Jouriles, E. N., Swank, R. McDonald, R., & Norwood, W. D. (2000). Patterns of adjustment among children of battered women. *Journal of Consulting and Clinical Psychology, 68*, 84–94.

Grych, J. H., Seid, M., & Fincham, F. D. (1992). Assessing marital conflict from the child's perspective: The children's Perception of Interparental Conflict Scale. *Child Development, 63*, 558–572.

Hall, J. A., Herzberger, S. D., & Skowronski, K. J. (1998). Outcome expectancies and outcome values as predictors of children's aggression. *Aggressive Behavior, 24*, 439–454.

Herrera, V. M., & McCloskey, L. A. (2001). Gender differences in the risk for delinquency among youth exposed to family violence. *Child Abuse and Neglect, 25*, 1037–1051.

Hilberman, E., & Munson, K. (1977–1978). Sixty battered women. *Victimology, 2*(3, Suppl., 4), 460–470.

Hinchey, F. S., & Gavelek, J. R. (1982). Empathic responding in children of battered mothers. *Child Abuse and Neglect, 6*, 395–401.

Holden, G. W., Geffner, R. E., & Jouriles, E. N. (Eds.). (1998). *Children exposed to marital violence: Theory, research, and applied issues.* Washington, DC: American Psychological Association.

Holden, G. W., & Ritchie, K. L. (1991). Linking extreme marital discord, child rearing, and child behavior problems: Evidence from battered women. *Child Development, 62*, 311–327.

Holden, G. W., Stein, J. D., Ritchie, K. L., Harris, S. D., & Jouriles, E. N. (1998). Parenting behaviors and beliefs of battered women. In G. W. Holden, R. Geffner, & E. N. Jouriles (Eds.), *Children exposed to marital violence: Theory, research, and applied issues* (pp. 289–334). Washington, DC: American Psychological Association.

Holtzworth-Munroe, A., & Stuart, G. L. (1994). Typologies of male batterers: Three subtypes and the differences among them. *Psychological Bulletin, 116*, 476–497.

Huesmann, L. R. (1988). An information processing model for the development of aggression. *Aggressive Behavior, 14*, 13–24.

Huesmann, L. R., & Guerra, N. G. (1997). Children's normative beliefs about aggression and aggressive behavior. *Journal of Personality and Social Psychology, 72*, 408–419.

Hughes, H. M., & Luke, D. A. (1998). Heterogeneity in adjustment among children of battered women. In G. W. Holden, R. Geffner, & E. N. Jouriles (Eds.), *Children exposed to marital violence: Theory, research, and applied issues* (pp. 185–221). Washington, DC: American Psychological Association.

Johnson, M. P. (1995). Patriarchal terrorism and common couple violence: Two forms of violence against women. *Journal of Marriage and the Family, 57,* 283–294.

Jouriles, E. N., & LeCompte, S. H. (1991). Husbands' aggression toward wives and mothers' and fathers' aggression toward children: Moderating effects of child gender. *Journal of Consulting and Clinical Psychology, 59,* 190–192.

Jouriles, E. N., McDonald, R., Norwood, W. D., & Ezell, E. (2001). Issues and controversies in documenting the prevalence of children's exposure to domestic violence. In S. A. Graham-Bermann & J. L. Edleson (Eds.), *Domestic violence in the lives of children: The future of research, intervention, and social policy* (pp. 13–34). Washington, DC: American Psychological Association.

Jouriles, E. N., McDonald, R., Norwood, W. D., Ware, H. S., Spiller, L. C., & Swank, P. R. (1998). Knives, guns, and interparent violence: Relations with child behavior problems. *Journal of Family Psychology, 12,* 178–194.

Jouriles, E. N., McDonald, R., Spiller, L., Norwood, W. D., Swank, P. R., Stephens, N., et al. (2001). Reducing conduct problems among children of battered women. *Journal of Consulting and Clinical Psychology, 69,* 774–785.

Jouriles, E. N., McDonald, R., Stephens, N., Norwood, W., Spiller, L. C., & Ware, H. (1998). Breaking the cycle of violence: Helping families departing from battered women's shelters. In G. W. Holden, R. Geffner, & E. N. Jouriles (Eds.), *Children exposed to marital violence: Theory, research, and applied issues* (pp. 337–369). Washington, DC: American Psychological Association.

Jouriles, E. N., Murphy, C. M., & O'Leary, K. D. (1989). Interspousal aggression, marital discord, and child problems. *Journal of Consulting and Clinical Psychology, 57,* 453–455.

Jouriles, E. N., Norwood, W. D., McDonald, R., & Peters, B. (2001). Domestic violence and child adjustment. In J. H. Grych & F. D. Fincham (Eds.), *Interparental conflict and child development: Theory, research, and application* (pp. 315–336). Cambridge: Cambridge University Press.

Jouriles, E. N., Norwood, W. D., McDonald, R., Vincent, J. P., & Mahoney, A. (1996). Physical violence and other forms of marital aggression: Links with children's behavior problems. *Journal of Family Psychology, 10,* 223–234.

Jouriles, E. N., Spiller, L. C., Stephens, N., McDonald, R., & Swank, P. (2000). Variability in adjustment of children of battered women: The role of child appraisals of interparent conflict. *Cognitive Therapy and Research, 24,* 233–249.

Kliewer, W., Lepore, S. J., Oskin, D., & Johnson, P. D. (1998). The role of social and cognitive processes in children's adjustment to community violence. *Journal of Consulting and Clinical Psychology, 66,* 199–209.

Lamb, M. (Ed.). (1997). *The role of the father in child development* (3rd ed.). New York: Wiley.

Lehmann, P., & Rabenstein, S. (2002). Children exposed to domestic violence: The role of impact, assessment, and treatment. In A. R. Roberts (Ed.), *Handbook of domestic violence intervention strategies: Policies, programs, and legal remedies* (pp. 343–364). New York: Oxford University Press.

Levendosky, A. A., & Graham-Bermann, S. A. (2000). Behavioral observations of parenting in battered women. *Journal of Family Psychology, 14,* 1–15.

Lown, E. A., & Vega, W. A. (2001). Prevalence and predictors of physical partner abuse among Mexican American women. *American Journal of Public Health, 91,* 441–445.

Margolin, G. (1998). Effects of domestic violence on children. In P. K. Trickett & C. J. Schellenbach (Eds.), *Violence against children in the family and the community* (pp. 57–101). Washington, DC: American Psychological Association.

McCloskey, L. A., Figueredo, A. J., & Koss, M. P. (1995). The effects of systemic family violence on children's mental health. *Child Development, 66*, 1239–1261.

McCord, J. (1979). Some child rearing antecedents to criminal behavior in adult men. *Journal of Personality and Social Psychology, 37*, 1477–1486.

McDonald, R., & Jouriles, E. N. (1991). Marital aggression and child behavior problems: Research findings, mechanisms, and intervention strategies. *The Behavior Therapist, 14*, 189–192.

McDonald, R., Jouriles, E. N., Norwood, W. D., Ware, H., & Ezell, E. (2000). Husbands' marital violence and the adjustment problems of clinic-referred children. *Behavior Therapy, 31*, 649–665.

McDonald, R., Jouriles, E. N., Ramisetty-Mikler, S., Caetano, R., & Green, C. (in press). Estimating the number of American children living in partner-violent families. *Journal of Family Psychology.*

McLoyd, V. C., Harper, D. I., & Copeland, N. L. (2001). Ethnic minority status, interparental conflict, and child adjustment. In J. H. Grych & F. D. Fincham (Eds.), *Interparental conflict and child development: Theory, research, and applications* (pp. 98–125). New York: Cambridge University Press.

McNeal, C., & Amato, P. R. (1998). Parents' marital violence: Long-term consequences for children. *Journal of Family Issues, 19*, 123–139.

Onyskiw, J. E., & Hayduk, L. A. (2001). Processes underlying children's adjustment in families characterized by physical aggression. *Family Relations, 50*, 376–385.

Osofsky, J. D. (1999). The impact of violence on children. *The Future of Children. Domestic Violence and Children, 9*, 33–49.

Patterson, G. R. (1982). *Coercive family process.* Eugene, OR: Castalia.

Patterson, G. R., Reid, J. B., & Dishion, T. J. (1992). *Antisocial boys.* Eugene, OR: Castalia.

Perry, D.G., Willard, J. C., & Perry, L. C. (1990). Peers' perceptions of the consequences that victimized children provide aggressors. *Child Development, 61*, 1310–1325.

Phares, V. (1997). *Fathers and developmental psychopathology.* New York: Wiley.

Rossman, B. B. R., & Rosenberg, M. (1992). Family stress and functioning in children: Moderating effects of children's beliefs about their control over parental conflict. *Journal of Child Psychology and Psychiatry, 33*, 699–715.

Roy, M. (Ed.). (1977). *Battered women: a psychosociological study of domestic violence.* New York: Van Nostrand-Reinhold.

Rutter, M. (1983). Stress, coping, and development: Some issues and some questions. In N. Garmezy & M. Rutter (Eds.), *Stress, coping, and development in children* (pp. 1–41). New York: McGraw-Hill.

Schafer, J., Caetano, R., & Clark, C. (1998). Rates of intimate partner violence in the United States. *American Journal of Public Health, 88*, 1701–1704.

Simons, R. L., Wu, C., Johnson, C., & Conger, R. D. (1995). A test of various perspectives on the intergenerational transmission of domestic violence. *Criminology, 33*, 141–171.

Sorenson, S. B., Upchurch, D. M., & Shen, H. (1996). Violence and injury in marital arguments: Risk patterns and gender differences. *American Journal of Public Health, 86*, 35–40.

Spiller, L. C., Marsh, W., Peters, B., Miller, P., & Jouriles, E. N. (1999). *Multiple types of wife abuse and child behavior problems.* Paper presented to the Society for Research on Child Development, Albuquerque, NM.

Sternberg, K. J., Lamb, M. E., & Dawud-Noursi, S. (1997). Using multiple informants and cross-cultural research to study the effects of domestic violence on developmental psychopathology: Illustrations from research in Israel. In S. S. Luthar, J. A. Burack, D. Cicchetti, & J. R. Weisz (Eds.), *Developmental psychopathology: Perspectives on adjustment, risk, and disorder* (pp. 417–436). Cambridge: Cambridge University Press.

Sternberg, K. J., Lamb, M. E., Greenbaum, C., Cicchetti, D., Dawud, S., Coretes, R. M., et al. (1993). Effects of domestic violence on children's behavior problems and depression. *Developmental Psychology, 29,* 44–52.

Stocker, C. M., & Youngblade, L. (1999). Marital conflict and parental hostility: Links with children's sibling and peer relationships. *Journal of Family Psychology, 13,* 598–609.

Straus, M. A. (1990). Injury and frequency of assault and the "representative sample fallacy" in measuring wife beating and child abuse. In M. A. Straus & R. J. Gelles (Eds.), *Physical violence in American families: Risk factors and adaptations to violence in 8,145 families* (pp. 75–91). New Brunswick, NJ: Transaction.

Straus, M. A. (1992). Children as witness to marital violence: A risk factor for lifelong problems among a nationally representative sample of American men and women. In D. F. Schwarz (Ed.), *Children and violence, report of the twenty-third Ross Roundtable on Critical Approaches to Common Pediatric Problems* (pp. 98–104). Columbus, OH: Ross Laboratories.

Straus, M. A., & Gelles, R. J. (1990). *Physical violence in American families: Risk factors and adaptations to violence in 8,145 families.* New Brunswick, NJ: Transaction.

Straus, M. A., Gelles, R. J., & Steinmetz, S. K. (1980). *Behind closed doors: Violence in the American family.* Garden City, NY: Doubleday.

Sullivan, C. M., Nguyen, H., Allen, N., Bybee, D., & Juras, J. (2000). Beyond searching for deficits: Evidence that physically and emotionally abused women are nurturing parents. *Journal of Emotional Abuse, 2,* 53–73.

Tjaden, P., & Thoennes, N. (1998). *Prevalence, incidence, and consequences of violence against women: Findings from the national violence against women survey.* Washington, DC: National Institute of Justice.

Walker, L. E. (1979). *The battered woman.* New York: Harper Perennial.

Ware, H. S., Jouriles, E. N., Spiller, L. C., McDonald, R., Swank, P. R., & Norwood, W. D. (2001). Conduct problems among children at battered women's shelters: Prevalence and stability of maternal reports. *Journal of Family Violence, 16,* 291–307.

Watamura, S. E., Donzella, B., Alwin, J., & Gunnar, M. R. (2003). Morning-to-afternoon increases in cortisol concentrations for infants and toddlers at child care: Age differences and behavioral correlates. *Child Development, 74,* 1006–1020.

Wolfe, D. A., & Korsch, B. (1994). Witnessing domestic violence during childhood and adolescence. *Pediatrics, 94,* 594–599.

Yates, T. M., Dodds, M. F., Sroufe, A., & Egeland, B. (2003). Exposure to partner violence and child behavior problems: A prospective study controlling for child physical abuse and neglect, child cognitive ability, socioeconomic status, and life stress. *Development and Psychopathology, 15,* 199–218.

10

Can Partner Aggression Be Stopped With Psychosocial Interventions?

K. Daniel O'Leary and Edward M. Vega

The problem of partner aggression or partner abuse has been gaining attention for the past 25 years, and research on the topic has burgeoned in the past decade. Research on correlates and predictors of physical aggression against partners has documented numerous factors associated with and/or predictive of partner aggression (Gelles & Loseke, 1993; O'Leary, 1993; Schumacher, Feldbau-Kohn, Slep, & Heyman, 2001). In addition, there have been significant advances in the formulation of arrest policies and community responses to violence (Aldarondo & Mederos, 2002). However, it has been difficult to implement and evaluate intervention research with men who abuse their partners and with the victims of such abuse. This difficulty is best evidenced in the reviews of the literature which suggest that interventions for physically abusive men may be effective, but also indicate that the evidence is not yet convincing (Edleson & Tolman, 1992; Rosenfeld, 1992). While a meta-analysis documents a very small but significant effect of interventions for partner aggression, the comparison group was men who dropped out of treatment (Babcock, Green, & Robie, 2004). Thus, as will later be discussed, despite the fact that there are numerous studies that show that about 66% of men do not engage in physical aggression following an intervention, there is no unequivocal evidence supporting the interventions themselves. In this chapter, we attempt to address some difficult problems that we believe have impeded progress in the area of treatment for partner abuse. Specifically, we address (a) the lack of conceptual diversity in the area, (b) the high dropout rate in programs for batterers, and (c) the lack of interventions or treatments that meet the American Psychological Association (APA) criteria for empirically supported treatments. We also address the types of research questions that need to be addressed in future research.

The continuum of partner aggressive behaviors ranges from psychological aggression, to mild physical aggression, to severe physical aggression. In consideration of the continuum of partner aggression, we feel that it is very important to understand that there are different correlates and causes of the different aggressive behaviors (O'Leary, 1993). Further, as importantly noted by Holtzworth-Munroe (2001), certain types of men (generally violent/antisocial) are less likely to benefit from most interventions. In turn, it seems important to consider that there likely should be different interventions designed to address the continuum of aggression.

■ Lack of Conceptual Diversity

One may first ask why different theoretical frameworks are useful and/or needed? When there is only one theoretical framework for viewing a problem, intellectual stagnation can occur. There have been changes in the views of science and its progression from paradigm shifts (Kuhn, 1962) to pluralistic and social constructivism conceptualizations (Cole, 2001). However, irrespective of the specific way in which progress in science is viewed, singular conceptualizations are generally seen as impeding progress. Intellectual stagnation can also occur in the context of having treatment standards to which all must adhere (Geffner & Rosenbaum, 2002; Gelles, 2001), and standards often help maintain a rigid orientation to a problem. While some standards for providers of service may be necessary and even desirable, standards regarding program format (group or individual), length of intervention, and licensing of providers seem quite premature (Murphy, 2001).

There have been two primary conceptual frameworks that have views of, and treatments for, physical aggression in intimate relationships. Those views are feminist (e.g., Adams, 1989; Yllo, 1993) and cognitive-behavioral (e.g., Hamberger & Lohr, 1989). These two views are not necessarily contradictory and, in fact, are often complementary; variants of the two are utilized in integrative approaches (Rosenbaum & Maiuro, 1989). Power and control are dominant concepts in most of the above models, especially the feminist models, which describe the manners in which an aggressor uses coercive acts to intimidate and undermine the victim. Men's aggressive behavior is not simply physical in nature; it is psychological as well. Psychological aggression serves to undermine the self-esteem of the generally female victim (Schechter, 1982). Moreover, psychological abuse is often more predictive of a battered women's traumatic responses than is physical violence (Dutton, Goodman, & Bennett, 2001).

The cognitive-behavioral model, building upon feminist concepts, introduced an emphasis on goal-directed, self-produced patterns of behavior that are "under the control of the batterer" (p. 66). This model emphasized the control of aggression through changes in physiological, cognitive, and behavioral processes and the need to address issues such as anger, anxiety, and stress (Hamberger & Lohr, 1989). Further, voices from the Battered Women's Movement led most states to provide laws designed to protect and provide services for battered women. It is important to acknowledge that the progress in the delivery of services and in the legal arena that has been made in the field of partner abuse has come largely from advocates and individuals holding views like those above. Moreover, we accept many of the above views, though for only a certain segment of the abusing population. Additionally, we have evaluated factors such as power and control in relationships and have compared gender-specific treatments for wife abuse to other therapy approaches (O'Leary, Heyman, & Neidig, 1999).

Other theoretical frameworks have been espoused, such as psychodynamic approaches (Saunders, 1996) and variants of the psychodynamic view, such as the attachment model (Stosny, 1995). However, there is little research on the application and/or outcome of such programs, except that of Saunders, who compared feminist cognitive-behavioral and process-psychodynamic treatments. Couples approaches have been presented to break destructive patterns of partner abuse (Geller, 1992) and have been compared with gender-specific approaches by Brannen and Rubin (1996) and O'Leary et al. (1999). An excellent summary of couples approaches has been given by Stith, Rosen, and McCollum (2002). Basically, there does not appear to be any difference in the effectiveness of the two intervention approaches. In addition, manuals are available for both the programs evaluated by Stosny (1995) and O'Leary et al. (1999). Despite these developments, the use of these alternatives in the treatment of aggression in intimate relationships appears to be relatively meager, except perhaps by family therapists and psychodynamically oriented therapists who may focus on working with the individual.

What is the problem with the dominant theoretical conceptualization? Variants of the feminist views have dominated programs for batterers and they have had a trickle-down effect of leading people who work in this field to believe that this is the only acceptable intervention, despite the lack of clear evidence that this program has unequivocal effects and/or effects that are superior to those of other programs. Consequently, there is lack of flexibility in the types of interventions offered. Moreover, there is little consideration of the lengths of treatment needed, depending upon the severity of the problem and or the typology of the aggressive man or woman.

The inadequacy of a "one size fits all" model of treatment for intimate partner violence has been discussed in many different forums, including in the Center for Disease Control and Prevention Expert Panel Meeting in March 2002. The increasing attention to categorizing men highlights the need to understand differing levels of partner aggression. Several approaches to categorizing physically aggressive men have been proffered, and the different categories are usually hypothesized to have different correlates/causes. Hamberger and Hastings (1985) classified men into three subgroups: Overcontrolled-Dependent, Impulsive-Borderline, and Instrumental-Antisocial. Similarly, Holtzworth-Munroe and Stuart (1994) classified men into three categories: Family-Only Violence, Dysphoric/Borderline, and Antisocial. In 1993, O'Leary presented a model with four levels of aggression placed on a continuum: Verbal Aggression, Physical Aggression, Severe Physical Aggression, and Murder. Chase, O'Leary, and Heyman (2001) classified men into two categories, Reactive and Proactive, following a similar distinction that has been used with aggressive children (Dodge & Coie, 1987). Tweed and Dutton (1998) classified types of aggression based on motivations for violence: Impulsive or Instrumental. Classifications based on severity, personality characteristics, or motivations for aggression all suggest different etiologies and associated treatments. Despite all the research on types of men who are physically aggressive with their partners, intervention efforts have typically focused only on the more severe group of partner aggressive men typically described as batterers. Further, there is almost no published research that attempts to link specific treatment to the particular type, frequency, or severity of violence.

The increasing need to prevent partner abuse may force some change in the conceptualization of the problem. The struggle to understand, define, and categorize intimate partner violence has already been intensified by recent evidence that challenges our traditional views that all partner violence is the same. For example, recent work has found that physical aggression against partners is very common among teens and young adults. Additionally, physical aggression is often reciprocal in young couples and physical aggression by females predicts later aggression against them (O'Leary & Smith Slep, 2003). Even young females report that they engage in physical aggression more often than they report that they are aggressed against (Archer, 2000). Regardless of the final outcome of the debates about aggression by males and females, it has become clear that both men and women aggress and that they start doing so in their teens and continue to escalate into their mid twenties (O'Leary, 1999). These facts make clear to these authors that any unilateral approach focusing only on the males to prevent and or treat partner aggression may be inadequate to address the problem, and it is likely to fail. A similar view was expressed by Capaldi, Shortt, and Kim (ch. 6 in this volume), who stated that the study of the couple as a developing dyad is crucial to the understanding of aggressive behavior toward a partner. They also argued that one needs to assess individual psychopathology, socialization, dyadic aspects of aggression, and the roles of both men and women to understand partner aggression. The relatively new emphasis on prevention, prompted in part by the Centers for Disease Control and Prevention, will also prompt more intensive discussions on the extent to which partner aggression can be stopped at various levels (mild, moderate, or severe) and stages (early, middle, or late). Thus, the answer to the question posed in the title of this chapter will not be a simple "yes" or "no." Rather, most likely, it may depend upon the level, stage, or type of problem. Given the history of almost all treatment of problems in the psychological and psychiatric fields, it will also depend upon the extent of comorbid conditions (such as substance abuse, personality disorders, and quite likely history of personal victimization).

■ High Dropout Rates

Another dramatic problem that is seen in evaluations of treatment programs for intimate partner violence is that a significant proportion of aggressive men refuse the treatment provided in mandated batterer programs. As noted by Gondolf (1997), "as few as 10% of the men referred to a program may actually complete it, as at least one published tabulation of program records indicates" (p. 89). Some of the men referred to batterer interventions are not severely aggressive and do not cause injury to the partner. Others beat their partners repeatedly and cause great physical injury. This heterogeneity of individuals can lead to a mismatch between the clients' perceptions of their treatment needs and the goals of the program. In turn, clients frequently drop out of gender-specific treatments for men. Previous research has demonstrated this unwillingness of many individuals to participate in gender-specific treatments (O'Leary et al., 1999); the dropout rate among men who initially volunteer for treatment is even higher than the 50% rate among men court-mandated to treatment (Edleson & Tolman, 1992; Rosenbaum, Gearan, & Ondovic, 1997). Dropout from some interventions has also been found to be linked to some treatment-related issues, such as the difficulty of addressing specific issues important to clients while working in a group format (Brown, O'Leary, & Feldbau, 1997). Additionally, dropout may be increased by the confrontational style that is common to, and in fact an integral part of, many interventions for partner aggressive men (Murphy & Baxter, 1997).

■ The Problem of Empirically Supporting Interventions

As briefly noted earlier, there is mixed evidence regarding the efficacy of current batterer intervention programs. There is some evidence, however, that men who complete batterer intervention programs are less likely to reassault than men who drop out (Gondolf, 2002). In an evaluation of four different sites using variations of the Duluth model (Pence & Paymar, 1993), Gondolf showed that at 30 months there was a reassault rate of 36% for attenders and 55% for dropouts. However, at 30 months, 49% of female partners of the completers reported that their partners continued to use threats against them and 76% of the female partners reported that their partners were verbally abusive. In short, physical abuse appeared to decrease but rates of verbal abuse and threats remained quite high. It is worth noting that in this research the use of dropouts as a comparison group is problematic because a dropout was defined as an individual who left treatment for any reason (including termination from the program) prior to completing 2 months. In the opinion of the second author, who has conducted group interventions with over 350 men mandated to treatment for physical aggression, men who are terminated from a program are often the most aggressive, resistant, and/or psychopathic. Hence, the definition of a treatment dropout may significantly skew outcome data. Nonetheless, this is the best large-scale, carefully conducted, naturalistic study to date. The burden of proof, however, is usually on the scientist to show that the dropouts did not differ from the completers. Gondolf (2002) does an excellent job of addressing this issue, and he showed that if he statistically controlled for a number of demographic factors, drunkenness, arrests, and severe assaults, and severe mental disorder there still appeared to be an effect of attenders versus dropouts. Nonetheless, Gondolf (2002) recognized that comparisons of attenders and dropouts often are statistically problematic (p. 142), because it is difficult, if not impossible, to be assured that the attenders did not differ from the dropouts on some significant variables. Further, the possibility remains that some variables, measured or unmeasured, associated with reduction in the assault rate could also have been associated with the men's attendance or dropout.

Babcock et al. (2004) conducted a meta-analytic review of interventions for men who were mandated to interventions for partner aggression, and the review provides a good synthesis of the effects of existing treatments. Using either a Duluth-type feminist model or a cognitive-behavioral therapy that is informed by a feminist orientation, the authors found that the overall treatment effects were .09 and .12 using victim and police reports, respectively, showing that there was a statistically significant improvement of the individuals mandated to the psychoeducational intervention (compared to a control group of treatment dropouts). The treatment dropout group may be problematic because in court-mandated interventions the men often are still subject to court monitoring or monitoring by probation officers. Thus, rather than a no-treatment control group, the psychosocial intervention is often compared with a legal intervention; in these cases the psychosocial intervention may have performed more favorably if compared to a condition in which there had not been court monitoring.

■ Empirically Supported Interventions?

There are a number of different criteria by which one can judge the effectiveness of an intervention or therapy, and these criteria have been reviewed in detail by Chambless and Ollendick (2001). While there are variations in the criteria, all of the systems are designed to help professionals and policy makers decide whether an intervention or therapy has sufficient scientific evidence to support its use. We have chosen the system adopted by Division 12 of the APA. According to the APA (Chambless & Ollendick, 2001), in order to have an empirically supported intervention (therapy) one must meet one of the following two criteria:

1. The intervention must prove superior to the effects of a "pill or psychotherapy placebo or to other treatment"
2. The intervention must be equivalent to an already established treatment with adequate sample sizes

Or one may have a large series of single case design experiments that demonstrate efficacy with

1. Use of good experimental design and
2. Comparison with (and superiority to) another treatment
3. Manuals to allow for replication across sites
4. Diagnostic criteria for selection of the participants that are enumerated
5. Effects that are demonstrated by at least two different investigative teams or investigators

For ethical reasons, interventions for men who physically abuse their wives usually do not have control groups which do not receive an active intervention or which are thought to be inert for the condition being treated (a placebo). The control groups usually involve some form of court-mandated intervention, such as monitoring by probation or some arm of the court. Thus, the psychosocial interventions that have been developed are being compared to legal interventions. As discussed in more detail later, it is in fact possible that that there is little effect of the psychoeducational or therapeutic intervention over and above the legal or community interventions, such as probation, court monitoring, or community service (Davis, Taylor, & Maxwell, 2000; Dunford, 2000; Feder & Forde, 2000).

To have an intervention that is *probably efficacious,* one must have (a) two experiments showing that the intervention is superior to the wait-list control group or (b) one or more experiments that meet established criteria of good experimental design, with random assignment to the interventions, comparison and superiority of the intervention to another treatment, evidence of treatment manuals, and well-specified samples.

There are three published studies that have involved random assignment of partner abusive men to intervention and control groups; given the above criteria, we discuss each of them briefly here. In 1992, Palmer, Brown, and Barrera randomly assigned 59 men who had been placed on probation and who had been court-mandated to participate in the evaluation. This study is important because of its experimental design and its attention to problems of data collection. The intervention was a 10-session psychoeducational group, involving a combination of modeling, information giving, teaching values for dealing with anger, reinforcing self-esteem, and improving relationships with women. Data were obtained 16–18 months after the treatment ended; 50% of the men in treatment and 50% of the controls completed the evaluation procedure. Due to the difficulty in obtaining reports from partners, the researchers relied on police report data. Recidivism was higher for the controls (31%) than the men in treatment (10%); the difference was statistically significant. For the men in the treatment program, there was no association between the treatment dose (i.e., the number of sessions attended) and recidivism. At the long-term follow-up both groups had equal numbers of police reports, though the reports were not simply about partner abuse. Reports were also made for assaulting men and driving while under the influence of alcohol or other drugs. There were police reports regarding three of the men in the treatment group for partner abuse, whereas eight of the men in the control group had such reports. Interestingly, according to the authors, the involvement with the police was usually alcohol related. As the authors themselves stated, this study provides modest support for the use of a psychosocial intervention. However, it is apparent that alternate sources of information about men's aggression are critical (e.g., information from the partner about abuse), since a great deal of abuse never gets reported to the police.

In 2000, Dunford reported on a research evaluation conducted in the Navy, involving random assignment of 861 men to one of four groups: a male-only intervention group, a conjoint treatment group, a rigorously monitored (nontreatment) group, and a control group. Cognitive-behavioral interventions were implemented for the male-only and the conjoint treatment groups. Fortunately, data were obtained from both the male abuser and his partner. Men in the rigorously monitored group were seen monthly for individual counseling, every 6 weeks a record search was conducted to see if there had been any arrests, and wives were called monthly to ask about abuse. Commanding officers were informed of any new instances of abuse. The female partner of the men in the control group received only safety planning information. There were no differences between the groups on any of the comparisons for the females' reports of abuse by their partners. According to the wives reports, approximately 30% of the men had pushed or hit their partner following the different interventions (treatment or controls). The decrease in the percentage of men in the control group (receiving only safety planning) who were reported as being physically aggressive presents a challenge to any easy interpretation of these results.

Davis et al. (2000) also conducted an experimental evaluation in which 376 men were randomly assigned to an intervention (a Duluth model, profeminist approach) or a control group (community service unrelated to issues of aggression). The intervention was a 39-hr psychosocial intervention involving groups for men who batter; in half of the cases the intervention was delivered in 8 weeks, and in the other half it was delivered in 26 weeks. Only defendants assigned to the 26-week-long intervention showed less recidivism than the control men. However, 77% of the men completed the 8-week-long intervention, whereas only 27% of the men completed the 26-week-long program. Using victim reports, there was a lower rate of abuse at follow-up (albeit not significantly lower) for the intervention versus the control groups (15% vs. 22%). However, according to police record data there was a significant difference favoring the intervention group (18% vs. 28%). Unfortunately, there was no evidence of change in attitudes as a result of treatment.

Thus, two of three published experimental design studies show some, but only moderate, support for the psychosocial interventions. Using victim reports, only one of the three experimental studies show support for the programs. Thus, the interventions evaluated so far do not meet the APA standards of a probably efficacious treatment. At present, our state of knowledge reflects that available intervention programs are *experimental* treatments.

Probably the most important impediment to establishing an intervention that meets standards such as those discussed by Chambless and Ollendick (2001) is the lack of control groups that do not involve an intervention that has a significant effect, as court monitoring appears to have (Dunford, 2000; Gondolf, 2002). Given this very significant research problem, we later discuss ways in which the problem of control groups can be addressed and still meet ethical standards. When an intervention is associated with a reduction in physical aggression for approximately 66% of men in programs for batterers, as many reviews have shown, many believe that the programs are effective (Gondolf, 2002). However, due to lack of the proper types of control groups, the interventions do not meet the standards for most psychosocial interventions. Gondolf (2002) provides a good discussion of the research designs that have been used to evaluate programs for men who batter, and he acknowledges that the problem of "with whom are the subjects to be compared is the most difficult and yet the most crucial" (p. 39). He also notes that the reality of being arrested, or maturing during the course of a year, could have a comparable outcome to the psychosocial intervention itself. Thus, the question remains as to what is an effective control group.

What Is a Reasonable Control Group?

The true experimental design is the gold standard for evaluating most treatments, such as medications for a disease or a condition like depression. In evaluating a treatment for depression, depressed patients are randomly assigned to an active medication group or a placebo group. This design has worked well in the medical and psychiatric fields, but the use of placebos is fraught with problems that have been discussed for decades (O'Leary & Borkovec, 1978). Another alternative in the use of the experimental design is the use of wait-list control groups, that is, groups who are not given any medication or therapy for a specified period. To address ethical problems with this design, an alternative is the wait list with a treatment on demand, in which depressed patients may be randomly assigned to the control group and told that they can call for a treatment if their situation becomes urgent and/or if they become suicidal (O'Leary & Beach, 1990). This design could be used for men (and women) who have low levels of physical aggression and who have not caused injury to, or fear in, their partner.

If the court system is monitoring an individual through probation or some other means, one has to be able to show that the psychosocial intervention or treatment does better than court monitoring and/or arrest. Often, the treatments themselves may not differ on all of the outcome variables. This problem is one that is quite complicated, but with rigorous designs and a theoretical framework for evaluating the treatment(s), it can be surmounted. There are ways in which a research design can be developed that allows one to evaluate mechanisms of change and how certain dependent measures will change with one treatment but not the other. Specifically, experiments must be designed with treatments that focus on *particular* outcomes that are theoretically tied to the individual intervention. Additionally, outcome should be measured broadly enough that the differences in treatment can be measured in terms of *differential* results after the treatment in performed. For example, although psychosocial interventions may not differ from court monitoring in terms of immediate reduction in aggression, there may be other differences in treatment effect, such as differences in long-term follow-up over many years, attitudinal differences, or differences in relationship satisfaction for those still with a partner.

What Treatment Questions Should We Address With Research?

Given that there is no unequivocal evidence demonstrating a consistent intervention effect of programs for court-mandated batterers, there are a number of important unanswered questions: (a) what alternative interventions work, (b) are there intervention techniques that have demonstrable effects, (c) how can client dropout be reduced, and (d) on what basis should clients be matched with interventions?

■ What Alternative Interventions Work?

As noted earlier, there are very few alternatives to the standard model that have received empirical evaluation. However, there are a variety of programs with a psychoeducational basis, and there are some variants thereof, as well as some programs developed by clinicians, and some cultural integration models. However, a perusal of a recent compendium of Programs for men who batter shows that there is "striking similarity" among the approaches (Aldarando & Mederos, 2002). The interventions are typically delivered in a group format, a psychoeducational approach is used, the programs are nonclinical in orientation, and the facilitators include professionals, paraprofessionals, and advocates. As noted by Mederos (2002), relatively few group facilitators are licensed mental health professionals. Part of the similarity comes from the Battered Women's Movement of the 1970s (Schecter, 1982), and part comes from the observation that men who abuse their partners do abuse their power to exert control over their partners. One unfortunate consequence of the similarity among programs is the lack of theoretical differences across interventions, across formats of intervention, and across the severity of the problem that is targeted.

To illustrate a few examples of interventions that differ considerably from the *power and control* orientation assumed by Duluth model type interventions (Pence & Paymar, 1993), we briefly discuss three approaches: the treatment of clients with both substance abuse and aggression issues (Fals-Stewart, 2003), the couples approach (to be used particularly with low levels of aggression), and the compassion approach (Stosny, 1995). These approaches have been chosen in part because there is some empirical evaluation of each of the interventions, especially the first two.

Treatment of substance abuse has been a controversial way to deal with partner violence because those who deal with men who engage in such behavior do not want the substance abuse to be used as an excuse for the violence. However, because there is so much overlap between alcohol abuse and partner violence in populations mandated for an intervention for one or the other problem, it has been fruitful for some to assess the changes in violence that are associated with interventions for alcohol abuse. The findings are quite positive. Specifically, when men complete programs for alcohol abuse, their physical aggression also decreases (Fals-Stewart, 2003; O'Farrell & Murphy, 1995). Further, the odds of men's using physical aggression against their partners following alcoholism treatment were 11 times higher on days when the men drank than when they did not (Fals-Stewart, 2003).

The failure to provide much of a context for the role of alcohol abuse in the etiology and treatment of partner abuse is illustrated by the compendium of programs for men who batter, which has only two entries on alcohol abuse and no index entries about how interventions should be structured given the presence of alcohol abuse. There is also a problem in the literature in that both researchers and clinicians fail to differentiate between clinical samples and representative samples. Further, it is sometimes argued that "frequency and drinking amount does not appear to significantly increase the risk of assault. The highest rates of abuse occur among binge drinkers" (Aldarondo & Mederos, 2002, pp. 2–8). However, based on two large representative samples we concluded that frequency of drinking has a small but significant association with partner aggression, though the greatest risk clearly comes from problem drinkers and binge drinkers (O'Leary & Schumacher, 2003). We also know from clinical samples of alcoholics and batterers that on the days in which they drink, the risk for partner abuse increases dramatically (Fals-Stewart, 2003).

Interventions for couples have been summarized by Brown and O'Leary (1997) and Stith et al. (2002). It is important to emphasize that the current authors do not recommend couples approaches for all men and/or women in physically aggressive relationships. Rather, a dyadic approach seems best suited for couples whose aggressive behavior is infrequent and mild; it is for couples in whom the female is not fearful of her partner (Cohen & O'Leary, 2002). There are two relatively large controlled studies of a couples intervention designed specifically to reduce physical aggression in couples. The first was that of Brannen and Rubin (1996), for 49 couples court-referred for treatment in Dallas, Texas. They assigned each couple to either gender-specific or couples intervention. The gender-specific program was based on a variation of the Duluth model; the couples intervention was based on a model developed by Neidig and Friedman (1984). Both treatments were associated with significant reductions in physical aggression, as assessed by the wife's report at both posttreatment and a 6-month follow-up. The second controlled study evaluated a couples intervention for 75 couples to reduce partner aggression (O'Leary et al., 1999). Like the Brannen and Rubin (1996) study, this study compared a gender-specific intervention for men and women to a couples intervention designed to reduce partner aggression. Unlike the Brannen study, however, this study involved all volunteer couples and included selection criteria to exclude couples in which husband-to-wife aggression lead to injury requiring medical attention. Additionally, wives were assessed (in individual interviews) for fear of their partner; in cases where a partner was fearful of participating, both partners were referred to local domestic violence centers for intervention. Both interventions resulted in significant reductions in psychological and physical aggression both posttreatment and at a 1-year follow-up.

Stosny (1995) developed the Compassion Workshop, which is designed for men "who are capable of forming emotional bonds." He excludes sociopaths and those with severe personality disorders, mental illness, and substance abuse. In addition, participants are expected to complete 63 pages of homework assignments. Stosny designed the program for child and partner abusers, and the goal of the program is to help the individual take the perspective of the other person and to value loved ones. The framework is attachment based, and the abusers are helped to recognize their emotional states. The format of the intervention is usually a group, but there is also a shortened version that can be used for individuals, groups, or families for prevention of family violence. The workshop intentionally includes each form of family abuse: child abusers, heterosexual partner abusers of both sexes, abusers of same-sex partners, and, when possible, adult abusers of parents. As many as 35 individuals can participate in a group, which is conducted largely in a didactic mode, since the bulk of the intervention work is accomplished through the completion of homework.

Three core concepts are central to the intervention: (a) the abuser is responsible for his emotions and behavior; (b) to the extent to which he blames another, he renders himself powerless; and (c) he must be able to take the emotional perspective of his loved ones. In a comparative outcome study, court-ordered partner abusers were randomly assigned to profeminist power and control programs offered by five agencies or to the Compassion Workshop. At the end of the interventions, 87% of the men in the Compassion Workshop were violence free, compared to 42% in the other intervention. The research herein has been presented in several books, but it has not appeared in refereed journal publications. Consequently, one must be cautious about interpreting the results. However, these data are presented because the approach differs significantly from many that have been tried.

■ Are There Intervention Techniques That Work?

Beyond the limited research available regarding the effectiveness of treatments for relationship aggression, there is, in fact, little outcome research to guide the search for empirically supported components or principles of change in the area of relationship aggression. Most intervention programs maintain a strong emphasis on the use of change strategies related to power and control, and some programs are selected for review and evaluation only if they have such an emphasis (Gondolf, 2002). However, there is no evidence of the utility of this particular orientation.

There remain the "tried and true" techniques often used in marital therapy, such as caring days and time-outs, as well as other techniques such as problem solving and reattribution of partner intent, yet there is little research to establish or support empirically these techniques for use in the realm of partner aggression. Thus, the field is still open to evaluation of many of the individual intervention strategies or techniques used in programs for men and women in physically aggressive relationships.

There is, of course, reason to believe that some basic therapeutic strategies may be useful in all interventions for partner aggressive men and women. For example, in the marital therapy arena, Johnson and Talitman (1997) found that the strength of the therapeutic alliance was a positive predictor of posttreatment marital satisfaction, accounting for 22% of the variance. In couple therapy, it has been argued that treatment works optimally when there is a positive alliance between each spouse and the therapist (Pinsof & Catherall, 1986). The formation of positive alliances has proven of value in predicting decreases in husband-to-wife psychological aggression, as well as mild and severe physical aggression (Brown & O'Leary, 2000).

Thus, we see that the building of a strong therapeutic alliance appears critical for the treatment of relationship aggression, as it is for other forms of therapy.

Thus, while the search goes on for demonstrations of effective intervention programs, it may also be useful to devote more effort to determining what components of treatments are effective in addressing relationship aggression, in the manner described by Rosen and Davison (2003). Research could be performed investigating whether the implementation of particular techniques by therapists, and in turn by couples, results in a decrease in aggressive behavior. For example, some treatment programs encourage the partners in a dyad to become aware of their own cognitive, emotional, and physical indicators of anger and to take time-outs when they are nearing a point at which they are likely to become aggressive; the question remains whether compliance with the program in terms of utilizing the time-out techniques results in a better treatment outcome (i.e., less aggression). A similar approach could be used with numerous techniques, e.g., other perspective taking, reattribution of intent, and relaxation techniques.

■ How to Reduce Dropout

A focus on the issue of treatment dropout in the area of prevention of partner aggression points out a major flaw in the current treatments. Even if there existed a treatment technique with perfect treatment efficacy, it would ultimately be of little utility if it were nested in a treatment program out of which most people typically drop. Indeed, evidence suggests that dropout is the *typical* outcome in programs for batterers; a dramatically high proportion of the population of aggressive men refuse the treatment provided in mandated batterer programs, as well as programs for men who volunteer for treatment. As noted earlier, treatment dropout may be as high as 50–90% in batterer intervention programs (Edleson & Tolman, 1992; Gondolf, 1997; Rosenbaum et al., 1997).

Dropout from some interventions has also been found to be linked to some treatment-related issues, such as the difficulty of addressing specific issues important to clients while working in a group format (Brown et al., 1997). This dramatically high dropout rate may also be due in part to a general failure to build a strong therapeutic alliance because of a lack of agreement between therapist and clients on treatment goals and treatment method. This failure may in turn stem from attempts to apply treatments without carefully considering the needs and preferences of the client. Given a highly heterogeneous population of people for whom relationship aggression is a problem, various treatments are also required. Gender-specific programs for men (designed primarily for batterers) have become the only programs offered in many facilities. Often, if a man is in a relationship characterized by low levels of bilateral grabbing, pushing, or slapping which does not escalate and does not result in injury to, or fear in, either partner, he will not see himself as a batterer. Moreover, according to the terminology of Jacobson and Gottman (1998), such a man is not a batterer. However, batterer intervention programs may often be the only type of treatment available to him. This apparent mismatch that sometimes occurs between the type of client and the treatment offered may play a part in the fact that many men with lower levels of physical aggression drop out of such programs. Similarly, even though approximately 53% of women seeking help for marital problems report that there has been some level of physical aggression in their relationship (O'Leary, Vivian, & Malone, 1992), the actual reason they seek help frequently is not for the aggression per se. Often, the primary problem they see in their relationship may be in the area of communication, sexuality, or personality styles. In cases such as these, the aggression is still a critical problem that must be addressed; however, it may prove problematic in terms of the therapeutic alliance (and, consequently, the high probability of client dropout) to focus on physical aggression as the only problem, or even the primary problem, in the relationship.

Elaborating on Bordin's (1979) earlier work, Pinsof (1994) describes three components critical in describing the content of the therapeutic alliance: Tasks (the actual activities in which the therapist and client engage, as well as the comfort/anxiety associated therewith), Goals (agreement on, and commitment to, the goals of therapy), and Bond (the affective component of therapy, in terms of the level of trust, respect, and caring between therapist and client). A weakness in any of these three components is problematic in the course of therapy, especially if the other components are not strong enough to compensate. A common problem is a mismatch between the clients' perceptions of their treatment needs and the goals of the program, resulting in a weakening of the therapeutic alliance and increased treatment dropout. When offering programs to the public for men and women in relationships characterized by physical aggression, it was found at our clinic that programs for couples were preferred over individual-focused gender-specific programs (O'Leary et al., 1999). Again, the research indicates that even among couples whose relationship involves low levels of physical aggression, the primary problems perceived by the couple are typically those of psychological aggression (heated arguing, yelling or shouting, cursing, and insults) and poor communication, rather than the physical aggression itself (O'Leary et al., 1992). In these cases, if the therapist focuses only on the physical aggression instead of also addressing the elements of psychological aggression that the clients perceive as more problematic, many clients will simply terminate therapy because of the disagreement with the therapist as to what the focus of therapy should be.

Just as agreement on treatment goals is critical to building a strong alliance with both individual clients and couples, the other elements of the therapeutic alliance must also be considered if one wishes to manage the difficult balancing of two competing demands (building a strong bond and ending aggressive behaviors). Addressing difficult problems, such as aggression in a relationship, can be understood as requiring a bond (value placed on the therapy relationship, based on trust, respect, and caring) that is strong enough to assist the client in being able to tolerate task-related anxiety (addressing problematic aggressive behaviors). Thus, when working with partner aggressive individuals, as with any client, it may be necessary to begin therapy by addressing the goals that the client(s) can easily recognize/acknowledge. As therapy progresses, the bond may become stronger, that is, the therapy and therapist mean more to the client, and trust increases. As a result, the therapist may be able to utilize stronger and bolder interventions, and goals that would have been too anxiety provoking earlier in therapy can be addressed, without threatening the therapeutic alliance in a way that would increase the likelihood of treatment dropout (Pinsof, 1994). Even in gender-specific treatments the use of an approach that is harshly confrontational is likely to increase, rather than overcome, defensiveness; conversely, a compassionate (but not colluding) approach may be more effective overall (Murphy & Baxter, 1997).

■ The Need to Match Clients With Appropriate Interventions

Researchers and clinicians specializing in the treatment of intimate partner aggression struggle with the task of incorporating ideological, theoretical, and practical considerations into the design of treatment programs. Engaging in controlling behaviors against a partner is a core descriptor as well as an explanation of partner abuse in feminist accounts of abusive behavior. As Yllo (1993) stated, "domestic violence is about gender and power"; this description may in some ways summarize the complex body of feminist theory and research. These ideas are critical to the field of treatment of intimate partner violence. Indeed, concerns about the protection and safety of victims of abuse are paramount; in cases of severe abuse, especially if abuse has resulted in injury or fear to either or both partners, it is critical for the therapist to consider the need for safety planning with the victim of abuse. Clearly, conjoint therapy is inappropriate in such cases.

   Given this critical focus on safety and justice for victims of violence, it is not surprising that gender-specific programs for men (designed primarily for batterers) have become the only programs offered in many facilities. However, even within the realm of aggressive relationships, there is much variation. At lower levels of physical aggression in relationships, both males and females may engage in controlling behaviors. We have seen, for example, that in high school dating samples, males and females sometimes engage in controlling behaviors at approximately equal rates (O'Leary & Smith Slep, 2003). Thus, while gender-specific treatments, such as batterer intervention programs, are appropriate for many men, in the case of a relationship characterized by a low level of bilateral aggression which does not escalate and does not result in injury or fear to either partner, neither partner may consider the situation to be a battering relationship. Often, the primary problem such a couple reports in their relationship is in the area of communication, sexuality, or personality styles. Clearly, the therapist must address physical aggression as a real and serious issue in the relationship. However, in cases where the members of the dyad conceptualize their problems as relationship issues, failure to acknowledge the dyadic elements of the problem (in addition to addressing the problem of the individual choice to use aggression) can result in dramatically increased treatment dropout or refusal to start treatment (O'Leary et al., 1999).

   The existing treatments for intimate partner aggression differ primarily in terms of form (i.e., with whom the treatment occurs—one partner or the other, or both individually, or both conjointly, or the entire family) and focus (e.g., family process, communication, physical aggression, etc.). As discussed above, there are no consistent differences in outcome based on the treatment modality. Additionally, the available treatments have not been established as being more effective than court monitoring. However, it remains true that there are other differences in the desirability of various treatments, especially in terms of safety considerations, as well as possible differences in terms of treatment dropout.

Even when dealing with low levels of aggression, individual treatment may be indicated in lieu of, or in addition to, conjoint treatment. In cases where individual problems, such as severe psychopathology or substance abuse, might interfere with couples treatment, individual treatment might precede couples work, or one or both partners might engage in individual therapy as well as couple therapy. Additionally, even in the case of couples with whom no physical aggression has occurred, if levels of anger/hostility are very high, it may be necessary to conduct several individual sessions with each partner prior to meeting conjointly, to assist each partner in managing the expression of anger toward the partner. Similarly, if such issues arise during the course of conjoint treatment, individual sessions may be held until such time as conjoint sessions can effectively/safely resume.

Both partners are responsible for changing their relationship, but even in conjoint therapy for intimate partner aggression *there has to be special emphasis on each person changing his or her own behavior.* To the extent that a therapist can encourage self-change, it becomes less likely that there will be blaming of the partner for past and current problems. A relatively new form of marital therapy, a *self-directed change approach,* has been evaluated in Australia (Halford, 2000). This approach places the onus of change on each partner individually from the outset of therapy. In relationships characterized by verbal aggression, one can expect that both individuals contribute to the arguments in one fashion or another, and it seems quite reasonable that both can take individual steps to make the arguments less frequent and less intense. However, even in situations where both partners contribute to relationship problems, each partner must accept responsibility for his or her own abusive/hurtful behaviors. Thus, one can discuss shared responsibility for the marital discord while at the same time emphasizing individual responsibility for any physical aggression. Also, throughout treatment there may be an alternating focus on individual issues (especially insofar as they impact the other partner or the relationship itself) and couple issues.

■ Summary and Conclusions

There are no interventions that we can say unequivocally reduce physical aggression against a partner. Part of the problem in reaching such a conclusion is that research designs that have been used thus far do not meet the criteria for empirically supported treatments as described by Chambless and Ollendick (2001) and the Clinical Division of the APA. Nonetheless, several reviews and summaries of interventions for batterers show that about 66% of the men reduce and/or cease their physical aggression against their partners. What is not clear is how many of the men would have reduced their physical aggression by the same amount if they had not been subject to court monitoring, a legal intervention that appears to have a significant effect in itself. Given the stability of partner aggression (Lorber & O'Leary, in press; O'Leary, 1993) and that as many as 75–80% of such men continue to engage in aggression if they do not receive any legal or psychosocial intervention, it may be the case that our community responses to partner abuse actually are working to reduce partner aggression but that the research designs to date have not allowed us to make firm conclusions regarding their effectiveness. If more studies on the stability of partner aggression in the absence of any intervention show a high stability of partner aggression, the fact that 66% of men in various programs desist in their aggression suggests that the interventions work

Dropout from interventions for batterers is often 50% or greater. This high dropout rate should alert both researchers and clinicians that there might be a problem with the programs themselves. Not all programs have such high dropout rates; it is worthwhile to investigate what is facilitating retention among programs in which the dropout rate is low. It is our belief that the failure to consider the levels and types of physically aggressive men (and women) when providing service is a key reason for much of the dropout.

The field is ripe for innovation and creativity since the dominant conceptualization centered on the abuse of power and control has been in existence for almost 20 years. It seems especially prudent to conceptualize partner abuse as a continuum of aggression ranging from psychological aggression, to mild physical aggression, to severe physical aggression. In turn, the factors that are correlated with these varied types of aggression vary. Of course the various forms and levels of aggression are likely to be etiologically different. Similarly, not all interventions are equally appropriate for all types of physical aggression. The forms of aggression that have been addressed in the court systems and in many batterer programs represent only the tip of the iceberg that is intimate partner aggression. The largest amount of physical aggression occurs among young couples; it is critical that we learn how to prevent aggression in its nascent form from escalating into more stable and intense forms. In addition, many couples seeking marital and family therapy engage in at least low levels of physical aggression against each other, though such aggression often is undetected or assessed.

■ References

Adams, D. (1989). Feminist-based interventions for battering men. In P. L. Caesar & L. K. Hamberger (Eds.), *Treating men who batter: Theory, practice and programs.* New York: Springer.

Aldarondo, E., & Mederos, F. (Eds.). (2002). *Programs for men who batter: Intervention and prevention strategies in a diverse society.* Kingston, NJ: Civic Research Institute.

Archer, J. (2000). Sex differences in aggression between heterosexual partners: A meta-analytic review. *Psychological Bulletin, 126,* 651–680.

Babcock, J. C., Green, C. E., & Robie, C. (2004). Does batterers' treatment work?: A meta-analytic review of domestic violence treatment. *Clinical Psychology Review, 23,* 1023–1053.

Bordin, E. S. (1979). The generalizeability of the psychoanalytic concept of the working alliance. *Psychotherapy: Theory, Research and Practice, 16,* 252–260.

Brannen, S. J., & Rubin, A. (1996). Comparing the effectiveness of gender-specific and couples groups in a court-mandated-spouse-abuse treatment program. *Research on Social Work Practice, 6,* 405–424.

Brown, P. D., & O'Leary, K. D (1997). Wife abuse in intact couples: A review of couples treatment programs. In G. K. Kantor & J. L. Jasinski (Eds.), *Out of the darkness* (pp. 194–207). Thousand Oaks, CA: Sage.

Brown, P. D., & O'Leary, K. D. (2000). Therapeutic alliance: Predicting continuance and success in group treatment for spouse abuse. *Journal of Consulting and Clinical Psychology, 68,* 340–345.

Brown, P. D., O'Leary, K. D., & Feldbau, S. R. (1997). Dropout in a treatment program for self-referring wife abusing men. *Journal of Family Violence, 12,* 365–387.

Chambless, D. L., & Ollendick, T. L. (2001). Empirically supported psychological interventions: Controversies and evidence. *Annual Review of Psychology, 52,* 685–716.

Chase, K. A., O'Leary, K. D., & Heyman, R. E. (2001). Categorizing partner violent men within the reactive-proactive typology model. *Journal of Consulting and Clinical Psychology, 69,* 567–572.

Cohen, S., & O'Leary, K. D. (2002). *Development and validation of the Fear of Partner scale.* Poster presented at the Annual convention of the Association for the Advancement of Behavior Therapy, Reno, NV.

Cole, S. (2001). *What's wrong with sociology?* New Brunswick, NJ: Transaction.

Davis, R., Taylor, B., & Maxwell, C. (2000). *Does batterer treatment reduce violence? A randomized experiment in Brooklyn.* Final report to the National Institute of Justice, Washington, DC.

Dodge, K. A., & Coie, J. D. (1987). Social information processing factors in reactive and proactive aggression in children's peer groups. *Journal of Personality and Social Psychology, 53,* 1146–1158.

Dunford, F. (2000). The San Diego navy experiment: An assessment of interventions for men who assault their wives. *Journal of Consulting and Clinical Psychology, 68,* 486–476.

Dutton, M. A., Goodman, L. A., & Bennett, L. (2001). Court-involved battered women's responses to violence: The role of psychological, physical, and sexual abuse. In K. D. O'Leary & R. D. Maiuro (Eds.), *Psychological abuse in violent domestic relations* (pp. 177–195). New York: Springer.

Edleson, J. L., & Tolman, R. M. (1992). *Intervention for men who batter: An ecological approach.* Newbury Park, CA: Sage.

Fals-Stewart, W. (2003). The occurrence of partner physical aggression on days of alcohol consumption: A longitudinal diary study. *Journal of Consulting and Clinical Psychology, 71,* 41–52.

Feder, L., & Forde, D. (2000). *A test of the efficacy of court-mandated counseling of domestic violent offenders: The Broward experiment.* Final Report to the National Institute of Justice, Washington, DC.

Geffner, R. A., & Rosenbaum A. (Eds.). (2002). *Domestic violence offenders: Current interventions, research and implications for policies and standards.* New York: Haworth.

Geller, J. A. (1992). *Breaking destructive patterns: Multiple strategies for treating partner abuse.* New York: Free Press.

Gelles, R. J. (2001). Standards for programs for men who batter? Not yet. In R. A. Geffner & A. Rosenbaum (Eds.), *Domestic violence offenders: Current interventions, research, and implications for policies and standards* (pp. 11–20). New York: Haworth.

Gelles, R. J., & Loseke, D. R. (1993). *Current controversies on family violence.* Newbury Park, CA: Sage.

Gondolf, E. W. (1997). Batterer programs: What we know and need to know. *Journal of Interpersonal Violence, 12,* 83–98.

Gondolf, E. W. (2002). *Batterer intervention systems: Issues, outcomes, and recommendations.* Thousand Oaks, CA: Sage.

Halford, K. (2000). *Brief couple therapy: Helping partners help themselves.* New York: Guilford Press.

Hamberger, L. K., & Hastings, J. E. (1985, March). *Personality correlates of men who abuse their partners: Some preliminary data.* Paper presented at the meeting of the Society of Personality Assessment, Berkeley, CA.

Hamberger, L. K., & Lohr, J. M. (1989). Proximal causes of spouse abuse: A theoretical analysis for cognitive-behavioral interventions. In P. L. Caesar & L. K. Hamberger (Eds.), *Treating men who batter: Theory, practice, and programs* (pp. 53–76). New York: Springer.

Holtzworth-Monroe, A. (2001). Standards for batterer treatment programs: How can research inform our decisions. In R. A. Geffner & A. Rosenbaum (Eds.), *Domestic violence offenders: Current interventions, research, and implications for policies and standards* (pp. 165–180). New York: Haworth.

Holtzworth-Monroe, A., & Stuart, G. L. (1994). Typologies of male partner violent men: Three subtypes and the differences among them. *Psychological Bulletin, 116,* 476–497.

Jacobson, N. S., & Gottman, J. (1998). *When men batter women: New insights into ending abusive relationships.* New York: Simon & Schuster.

Johnson, S. M., & Talitman, E. (1997). Predictors of success in emotionally focused marital therapy. *Journal of Marital and Family Therapy, 23,* 135–152.

Kuhn, T. (1962). *The structure of scientific revolutions.* Chicago: University of Chicago Press.

Lorber, M., & O'Leary, K. D. (in press). Predictors of persistent male aggression in early marriage: Continuities with antisociality? *Journal of Interpersonal Violence.*

Mederos, F. (2002). Changing our visions of intervention—the evolution of programs for physically abusive men. In E. Aldarondo & F. Mederos (Eds.), *Programs for men who batter: Intervention and prevention strategies in a diverse society.* Kingston, NJ: Civic Research Institute.

Murphy, C. M. (2001). Toward empirically-based standards for abuser intervention: The Maryland model. *Journal of Aggression, Maltreatment, and Trauma, 5,* 249–264.

Murphy, C. M., & Baxter, V. A. (1997). Motivating batterers to change in the treatment context. *Journal of Interpersonal Violence, 12,* 607–619.

Neidig, P. H., & Friedman, D. (1984). *Spouse abuse: A treatment program for couples.* Champaign, IL: Research Press.

O'Farrell, T. J., & Murphy, C. M. (1995). Marital violence before and after alcoholism treatment. *Journal of Consulting and Clinical Psychology, 63,* 256–262.

O'Leary, K. D. (1993). Through a psychological lens: Personality traits, personality disorders, and levels of violence. In R. J. Gelles & D. R. Loseke (Eds.), *Current controversies on family violence* (pp. 7–29). Newbury Park, CA: Sage.

O'Leary, K. D. (1999). Developmental and affective issues in assessing and treating partner aggression. *Clinical Psychology: Science and Practice, 6,* 400–414.

O'Leary, K. D., & Beach, S. R. H. (1990) Marital therapy: A viable treatment for depression and marital discord. *American Journal of Psychiatry, 147*, 183–186.

O'Leary, K.D., & Borkovec, T.D. (1978). Conceptual, methodological, and ethical problems of placebo groups in psychotherapy research. *The American Psychologist, 33*, 821–830.

O'Leary, K. D., Heyman, R. E., & Neidig, P. H. (1999). Treatment of wife abuse: A comparison of gender-specific and conjoint approaches. *Behavior Therapy, 30*, 475–505.

O'Leary, K. D., & Schumacher, J. A. (2003). The association between alcohol use and intimate partner violence: Linear effect, threshold effect, or both. *Addictive Behaviors, 28*, 1575–1585.

O'Leary, K. D., & Smith Slep, A. M. (2003). A dyadic longitudinal model of adolescent dating aggression. *Journal of Child and Adolescent Psychology, 32*(3), 314–327.

O'Leary, K. D., Vivian, D., & Malone, J. (1992). Assessment of physical aggression in marriage: The need for a multimodal method. *Behavioral Assessment, 14*, 5–14.

Palmer, S. E., Brown, R. A., & Barrera, M. E. (1992). Group treatment for the abusive husband: Long term evaluation. *American Journal of Orthopsychiatry, 62*, 276–283.

Pence, E., & Paymar, M. (1993). *Education groups for men who batter: The Duluth model.* New York: Springer.

Pinsof, W. M. (1994). An integrative systems perspective on the therapeutic alliance: Theoretical, clinical, and research implications. In A. O. Horvath & L. S. Greenberg (Eds.), *The working alliance: Theory, research, and practice* (pp. 173–195). New York: Wiley.

Pinsof, W. M., & Catherall, D. R. (1986). The integrative psychotherapy alliance: Family, couples, and individual therapy scales. *Journal of Marital and Family Therapy, 12,* 137–151.

Rosen, G. M., & Davison, G. C. (2003). Psychology should list empirically supported principles of change (ESPs) and not credential trademarked therapies or other treatment packages. *Behavior Modification, 27*(3), 300–312.

Rosenbaum, A., Gearan, P., & Ondovic, C. (1997, August). Completion and recidivism among court-referred and self-referred batterers in a psychoeducational group treatment program. In A. Rosenbaum (Chair), *Batterers treatment: Strategies, issues, and outcomes.* Symposium conducted at the annual meeting of the American Psychological Association, Chicago.

Rosenbaum, A., & Maiuro, R. D. (1989). Eclectic approaches in working with men who batter. In P. L. Caesar & K. L. Hamberger (Eds.), *Treating men who batter: Theory, practice, and programs* (pp. 165–195). New York: Springer.

Rosenfeld, B. D. (1992). Court ordered treatment of spouse abuse. *Clinical Psychology Review, 12*, 205–226.

Saunders, D. G. (1996). Feminist-cognitive-behavioral and process-psychodynamic treatments for men who batter: Interaction of abusers traits and treatment models. *Violence and Victims, 11*(4), 393–414.

Schechter, S. (1982). *Women and male violence: The visions and struggles of the battered women's movement.* Boston: South End.

Schumacher, J. A., Feldbau-Kohn, S., Slep, A., & Heyman, R. E. (2001). Risk factors for male-to-female partner physical abuse. *Aggression and Violent Behavior, 6*, 281–352.

Stith, S. M., Rosen, K. H., & McCollum, E. E. (2002). Developing a manualized couples treatment for domestic violence: Overcoming challenges. *Journal of Marital and Family Therapy, 28*, 21–25.

Stosny, S. (1995). *Treating attachment abuse.* New York: Springer.

Tweed, R. G., & Dutton, D. G. (1998). A comparison of impulsive and instrumental subgroups of batterers. *Violence and Victims, 13,* 217–230.

Yllo, K. A. (1993). Through a feminist lens: gender, power, and violence. In R. J. Gelles and D. R. Loseke (Eds.), *Current controversies on family violence* (pp. 47–62). Newbury Park, CA: Sage.

PART III

FAMILIES IN DIVORCE AND REMARRIAGE: FAMILY MEMBER PERSPECTIVES

As the divorce rate surged to 50% in the United States and close to that level in the rest of the Western world in the last quarter of the 20th century, divorce and remarriage virtually became "normal" (in the statistical sense) life crises in the lives of families, with important ramifications for all nuclear and extended family members. There are few areas of investigation in the social sciences in which the importance of solid methodological investigation has been as dramatically demonstrated. For instance, American society has yet to recover from the powerful reactions of families and social policy makers to the publication, in 2000, of Wallerstein's widely publicized, but small, uncontrolled and primarily qualitative study demonstrating the long-term, negative effects of divorce. Despite the needs of the public and policy makers for simple, "headline" information, the findings of better research present a more complex picture. It is only in the context of the best research that we can fully understand the effects of divorce and remarriage on specific groups of people and how to help families with the stresses that inevitably accompany these transitions.

This part of our book presents a wide range of methods of research for examining divorce and remarriage. James H. Bray and Irene Easling provide an overview of research on stepfamilies, highlighting key issues and summarizing salient findings from a major, quantitative study of stepfamilies. Sanford L. Braver and his colleagues examine the long-neglected domain of research about fathers in families after divorce, discussing programs, particularly their own, aimed at building better relationships between nonresident divorced fathers and their children. Addressing an even more neglected research domain, Melvin N. Wilson, Anthony L. Chambers, and LaKeesha N. Woods tackle the problems of fathers in African American families, focusing in particular on a large study (the Fragile Families Study) that examined the factors that facilitate and the consequences of different levels of paternal involvement in children's lives. Bernadette Marie Bullock and Marion S. Forgatch center their chapter on their work in the Oregon Divorce

Study, which accents how divorce affects mothers, their mothering, and, ultimately, their children. They also describe the impact of programs to help mothers and their children, emphasizing in particular their own preventive intervention program.

Each chapter examines postdivorce families through a lens (or lenses) accenting a different piece (or pieces) of the overall postdivorce family puzzle: fathers, mothers, children, remarriage, and culture. This part as a whole provides a relatively comprehensive picture of the entire family system and its parts, as well as the complex interactions between the members and the larger cultural context. This part, and its specific chapters, illustrate the complex research challenges and the strategies that are needed to further illuminate postdivorce families, as well as the kinds of programs and program evaluation research that are needed to ameliorate the negative effects of divorce and remarriage on families.

11

Remarriage and Stepfamilies

James H. Bray and Irene Easling

S tepfamilies are a fast-growing family structure in the United States due to the high divorce rate and numbers of children born outside of marriage (Bramlett & Mosher, 2001; U.S. Bureau of the Census, 1992). Many adults and children will experience multiple divorces and remarriages during their lifetime, as the divorce rate for second and subsequent marriages is even higher than that for first marriages. Before adulthood, about a third of U.S. children will live in a remarried or cohabiting stepfamily (Bumpass, Raley, & Sweet, 1995; Seltzer, 1994). It is likely that about 40% of adult women will live in a remarried or cohabiting stepfamily as a parent or stepparent at some time, and 40% of all families include step-grandparents (Szinovacz, 1998).

There are several demographic trends that contribute to the increased numbers of stepfamilies. These include the high divorce and remarriage rates and the increase in numbers of children born outside of marriage. It is not possible to get exact numbers and percentages concerning these demographic changes because the federal government and many states have stopped collecting information about marriage, divorce, and remarriage, as was the case with the 2000 U.S. Census.

This chapter reviews the literature on stepfamilies and remarriages and some of the findings from the Developmental Issues in Stepfamilies (DIS) Research Project, which investigated the longitudinal impact of divorce and remarriage on children's social, emotional, and cognitive development (Bray, 1988, 1999; Bray & Berger, 1993a, 1993b; Bray & Kelly, 1998). The DIS study was a multimethod, multiperspective study of parents, children, and extended family members that included extensive interviews, psychological assessments, family assessments, and videotapes of family interactions. The data provide a rich source of information about divorce and remarriage and their impact on children and adults.

■ Stepfamilies

A stepfamily is defined as a household in which there is an adult couple of whom one or both persons has a child from a previous relationship (Visher & Visher, 1988). The popular and research literatures include many names for stepfamilies: remarried families, reconstituted families, REM families, blended families, binuclear families, second families, and/or two-fams. In this chapter, we use the term stepfamily, which encompasses families that have custody of the children and those that do not, married and unmarried couples, opposite-gender and same-gender couples, families with one or two biological parents, and divorced, widowed, and previously unmarried families. Types of stepfamilies include stepfather families, stepmother families, and blended families, in which both parents have custody of children from a previous marriage. The vast majority of residential stepfamilies are stepfather families, because of the high percentage of children who reside with their mothers after birth or after a divorce. Stepfamilies differ from other family types with respect to patterns of functioning, organization, and relationships (Bray, 1999; Hetherington & Stanley-Hagan, 1999; Spruijt, 1997). Among stepfamilies, there is great diversity in structures, histories, and circumstances (Hetherington & Stanley-Hagan, 1999). This review focuses on stepfather families because they are the most common type. Important differences between stepfamily types are also discussed.

■ Theories and Models of Remarriage and Stepfamilies

Just as there is diversity in stepfamilies, there are multiple and varied theories to explain their development and functioning. Most researchers have based their studies on more than one theory and many theories are interrelated (Hetherington, Henderson, & Reiss, 1999). Table 11.1 provides a list of the major perspectives used to study stepfamilies. In some cases these viewpoints are general perspectives that can be applied to a broad range of families, and in other cases they are specific to stepfamilies.

Incomplete Institution Model

Historically, the incomplete institution model was one of the first explanations for differences in stepfamily functioning (Cherlin, 1978). The model posits that the absence of societal norms for stepfamily roles, the shortage of socially accepted methods for problem resolution, and the lack of institutionalized social support contribute to increased stress levels for remarried families (Cherlin, 1978). Although some researchers have criticized this hypothesis (Coleman, Ganong, & Cable, 1997; Jacobson, 1995), it is generally accepted that expectations for stepparents are not as clear as those for biological parents (Bray, Berger, & Boethel, 1994; Bulcroft, Carmody, & Bulcroft, 1998; Fine, Coleman, & Ganong, 1998). However, there is not strong empirical support for the model and few recent studies have used this as a basis for investigation.

TABLE 11.1   *Theories and Models of Remarriage and Stepfamilies*

Name	Focus	Authors
Incomplete institution	Lack of social norms for stepfamilies	Cherlin (1978)
Deficit family structure	Stepfamilies are considered deficient relative to first-marriage families	Ganong & Coleman (1994); Orleans, Palisi, & Caddell (1989)
Family systems	Interactional patterns and relationships	Bray, Berger, Silverblatt, & Hollier (1987); Bray & Berger (1993a); McGoldrick & Carter (1988); Hetherington & Clingempeel (1992); Hetherington, Henderson, & Reiss (1999)
Developmental	Issues and factors related to normative and nonnormative changes and life cycles	Bray, Berger, Silverblatt, & Hollier (1987); Bray & Berger (1993); McGoldrick & Carter (1988); Hetherington & Clingempeel, (1992); Hetherington, Henderson, & Reiss (1999)
Risk and resiliency	Positive and negative factors related to adjustment	Bray (1999); Hetherington, Henderson, & Reiss (1999)
Evolutionary	Biological factors	Daly & Wilson (1987); Hetherington, Henderson, & Reiss (1999)
Individual risk and vulnerability	Individual pathology that impacts outcomes	Capaldi & Patterson (1991); Hetherington, Bridges, & Insabella (1998)
Stress and marital transitions	Impact of stress and change	Brody, Neubaum, & Forehand (1988); Capaldi & Patterson (1991); Hetherington, Bridges, & Insabella (1998)

Deficit Family Structure

Much of the early research on stepfamilies was based on a deficit model that compared the relationships, circumstances, and outcomes of stepfamilies to those within first-marriage families (Ganong & Coleman, 1994; Orleans, Palisi, & Caddell, 1989). Differences between the family types were considered signs of poor functioning and adjustment in stepfamilies. Early studies often focused on the absence of the father as a cause for the dysfunction (Hetherington, Bridges, & Insabella, 1998). First-marriage families were considered normative and stepfamilies were considered deviant or dysfunctional. The focus of research was comparisons between family types, with little or no interest in within-family type functioning or predictors of successful adjustment in stepfamilies.

The deficit model has been largely replaced by family systems, developmental, and risk and resiliency models (Amato & Keith, 1991; Bray, 1999; Garmezy, 1993; Hetherington et al., 1992; Wolin & Wolin, 1993). The models' frameworks facilitate examination of individual, family, and external factors and processes that expose them to or protect them from negative outcomes during and after family transitions (Hetherington, 1993).

Family Systems Theories

Theories developed within systems perspectives provide rich and diverse perspectives on stepfamily functioning. While there are multiple family systems theories, in general they view family members as part of an interdependent emotional and relational system that mutually influences other aspects of the family system. Stepfamily systems include not only the residential family, but also nonresidential family members (Bray, 1999; Bray & Berger, 1993a; Bray, Berger, Silverblatt, & Hollier, 1987; McGoldrick & Carter, 1988). The lack of attention to these complex relationships in previous research limits our understanding of stepfamilies. This perspective, as it relates to stepfamilies, requires the definitions of external boundaries identifying who is a member of the stepfamily and internal boundaries that are made operational by rules, roles, alliances, and membership (Anderson, Greene, Hetherington, & Clingempeel, 1999; Bray & Berger, 1993a; Crosbie-Burnett, 1989; McGoldrick & Carter, 1988). Our work and the research of Hetherington and colleagues (Hetherington & Clingempeel, 1992; Hetherington et al., 1999) have drawn heavily on this perspective.

Family systems theories provide models for identifying family processes, such as conflict, problem solving, and parenting, that are related to family functioning and individual adjustment. Disruptions in family relationships and processes, for example, in diminished parenting, may mediate the effects of remarriage on children's adjustment (Forgatch, Patterson, & Ray, 1995; Hetherington, 1993; Simons & Beaman, 1996; Simons & Johnson, 1996).

Developmental and Life Cycle Perspectives

In addition to the interactional aspects of family relationships, developmental factors for both the family and individual members are considered important for understanding stepfamilies. Families undergo predictable and unpredictable life cycle changes that mutually influence individual family members' development (Carter & McGoldrick, 1988). However, the normative family life cycle progression is disrupted by divorce and remarriage, and these transitions interact with the developmental trajectories of children and adolescents. Therefore, factors such as length of time since the divorce, time since remarriage, and ages of adults and children are important factors to consider in delineating the family life cycle progression of remarried families.

Further, it is important to look at the multiple developmental trajectories of individuals and the family. For example, new stepfamilies with adolescents may experience more stress and conflict because the developmental need of the adolescent to separate from the family may be in conflict with the developmental process of the stepfamily to come together and be cohesive (Bray, 1995). Research using this perspective attempts to identify the developmental tasks and issues for stepfamilies and how they change over time. In addition, it considers the individual developmental issues of family members and how they interact with family process and change.

Risk and Resiliency

This perspective grows out of the general developmental literature that examines factors related to positive and negative outcomes for children (Garmezy, 1993). Risk factors are related to increases in negative outcomes, while protective factors help individuals cope with adversity and obtain positive outcomes. This perspective is useful as it provides a normative context for remarriage and links our understanding of stepfamilies to the broader context of coping and adaptation to changing life circumstances.

This theoretical perspective was used by Hetherington and her colleagues in their longitudinal study of adolescent siblings in stepfamilies (Hetherington et al., 1999). Responses to remarriage and to stepfamily life vary considerably and involve individual, family, and extrafamilial vulnerability and protective factors (Hetherington, 1989, 1991; Werner, 1993). Examples of the former are increased stress, problems in family relationships, and anger and acrimony (Bray & Berger, 1993a; Hetherington, 1989; Hetherington & Jodl, 1994) and the latter include the opportunity to develop satisfying relationships that are good for both children and adults (Bray & Kelly, 1998; Hetherington, Cox, & Cox, 1985). Most stepchildren show resiliency in the face of changes and problems associated with stepfamily formation and adjust to family life (Hetherington et al., 1999).

Evolutionary Theory

This perspective posits that humans use reproduction to increase the probability of their genes' survival into the next generation, so their priority is to nurture and protect their biological children (Daly & Wilson, 1987). From this viewpoint, stepparents limit their involvement in their stepchildren's lives because they are not genetically related to them (Daly & Wilson, 1996). The theory suggests that differences between stepfamilies and first-marriage families are primarily due to these biological underpinnings and the problems seen in stepfamilies are due to the conflict between biological and social needs and desires.

Stepparents who are also biological parents are expected to pay more attention to their biological children. Stepfathers' interactions with stepchildren are aimed at impressing their new partners to facilitate the mating relationship, rather than at encouraging their stepchildren's positive development. Some research supports this theory (Flinn, 1999; Mekos, Hetherington, & Reiss, 1996), while other studies do not (Bray, 1999; Bulcroft et al., 1998; Menaghan, Kowaleski-Jones, & Mott, 1997). The theory was also used frequently in studies of child abuse to explain why stepchildren are more likely to be abused (Coleman, Ganong, & Fine, 2000), although several other theories were proposed in this type of research (Giles-Sims, 1997).

Evolutionary theory, together with attachment theory, guided the conceptualization of the adolescent sibling study (Hetherington et al., 1999). Attachment theory, which has its basis in evolutionary theory, posits that when behaviors in parents and children, which have evolved to encourage bonding and survival of the latter, are not practiced in the first year of a relationship, secure attachments will be less likely to be forged (Bowlby, 1969). Both theories suggest that it is more difficult to develop strong, caring relationships between stepparents and stepchildren than between biological parents and children (Hetherington et al., 1999). However, the influence of biological relationships can be modified by later experiences and family relationships. For example, research has shown that some stepfathers invest more resources in their residential stepchildren than in their nonresidential biological offspring (Bray, 1999; Furstenberg & Cherlin, 1991).

Individual Risk and Vulnerability

The characteristics of some adults increase their risk for marital discord, multiple marital transitions, and other negative experiences (Brody, Neubaum, & Forehand, 1988; Capaldi & Patterson, 1991; Kitson & Morgan, 1990; Patterson & Dishion, 1988; Simons, Johnson, & Lorenz, 1996). The marital selectivity hypothesis posits that adults with psychological problems often select partners with such problems (Merikangas, Prusoff, & Weissman, 1988), thereby increasing their risk for marital discord and divorce. Further, divorced adults may have relationship skills deficits (i.e., poor communication skills) that make it difficult to sustain a marriage (Bray et al., 1987). Individual characteristics, such a depression, can also impact family relationships and parenting, which in turn may lead to more behavior and adjustment problems for children (Forgatch et al., 1995). Some children's characteristics also make them more likely to be either affected by or, conversely, protected from the stresses related to their parents' marital transitions (Amato & Booth, 1991; Bray, 1991; Emery & Forehand, 1994; Hetherington, 1991).

Stress and Marital Transitions

The stress perspective proposes that marital transitions have negative effects, such as social and economic changes and disruption, on parents and children (Hetherington et al., 1998). Custodial mothers and their children are likely to suffer economically as a result of divorce, while single mothers find that they often have higher incomes after remarriage (McLanahan & Sandefur, 1994). Both economic (the focus of much stress-related research) and other types of stress resulting from changes in family roles and relationships can affect both divorced and remarried families (Cherlin & Furstenberg, 1994; Hetherington & Stanley-Hagan, 1995; Simons et al., 1996).

Negative stress from divorce and remarriage may cause parental distress and can lead to psychological problems, such as depression, anxiety, irritability, and health problems, that interfere with the adaptive functioning of other family members (Capaldi & Patterson, 1991; Forgatch et al., 1995; Hetherington, 1989, 1991; Kiecolt-Glaser et al., 1987; Lorenz, Simons, & Chao, 1996; Simons & Johnson, 1996). In the DIS study, adults in stepfamilies reported 2 to 4 times as much stress as adults in first-marriage families (Bray, 1988; Bray & Berger, 1993a, 2004). Responses to life changes vary, with some parents coping well, while others develop problems. The cumulative effects hypothesis proposes that the more marital disruption and number of marital transitions a parent experiences, the more internalizing and externalizing problems the children have as a result of coping with marital changes (Brody et al., 1988; Capaldi & Patterson, 1991).

Research provides varying degrees of support for these various perspectives, even though they are often seen as incompatible (Hetherington et al., 1998), leading to the suggestion that they be viewed as complementary hypotheses (Amato & Keith, 1991; Simons, 1996). In some cases, variations in sample size, research methods, and statistical techniques produced conflicting results and misleading conclusions. In addition, linkages and interactions between the perspectives have been identified and the included variables sometimes serve as moderators or mediators to others, particularly in studies using causal modeling (Conger & Conger, 1996; Forgatch et al., 1995; Hetherington et al., 1999; Simons & Associates, 1996)

Often the scope of more general perspectives, such as family systems theories and evolutionary theory, has been narrowed and adapted to the study of stepfamilies. Concepts, such as that of risk and protective factors, appear in several models, illustrating that there are links between them. Researchers have frequently based their studies on more than one theory and have developed models based on a combination of concepts, such as our developmental family systems model (Bray, 1999; Bray et al., 1987) and the transactional model of risks developed by Hetherington and her colleagues (Hetherington et al., 1999). While there are unique characteristics and issues for stepfamilies, it is important that future research place these in a broader theoretical context that considers the biopsychosocial nature of individuals and families. In addition, future theories need to consider the cultural and ethnic diversity of stepfamilies by including more diverse samples from varying ethnicities and socioeconomic backgrounds.

■ Children's Adjustment in Stepfamilies

Many stepchildren are at risk for behavioral and emotional problems during the period after their parents' divorce and remarriage (Bray, 1999; Hetherington & Clingempeel, 1992; Hetherington & Jodl, 1994). In both cross-sectional and longitudinal research, children in stepfamilies have been found to be less well adjusted than those in first-marriage families. They have more behavioral, emotional, and health problems, lower academic achievement, and lower social competence and social responsibility than children in first-marriage families (Acock & Demo, 1994; Borgers, Dronkers, & van Praag, 1996; Furstenberg & Cherlin, 1991; Hetherington & Jodl, 1994; Zill, 1994). Although most stepchildren adapt over time, for some the problems are severe and long lasting (Amato & Keith, 1991).

There has been a considerable amount of disagreement concerning how widespread, serious, and persistent the adjustment problems of stepchildren are (Bray, 1999; Hetherington et al., 1999; Spruijt, 1997). In most studies the differences have been small, as illustrated by the effect sizes in the meta-analysis of Amato (1994), which ranged from −0.07 (academic achievement) to −0.37 for psychological adjustment; −0.32 was the effect size for problems in conduct and/or behavior. The small size of the differences is further demonstrated by the fact that on the Child Behavior Checklist (Achenbach & Edelbrock, 1983), a standardized measure of children's adjustment, 70–80% of children in stepfamilies function within a normal range, compared to 10–15% of children in first-marriage families (Bray, 1999, 2001; Hetherington & Stanley-Hagan, 1999). When socioeconomic factors, such as differences in education and early age at first marriage, are controlled for, the differences are marginal (Coleman, 1994). Thus, most children in stepfamilies do not experience adjustment problems, are able to adapt to their new family structure, and become competent individuals.

It should be noted that problem behaviors may be present even prior to the divorce and may result from experiences in a first marriage or conflict in a single-parent family (Amato & Booth, 1996; Block, Block, & Gjerde, 1986; Cherlin et al., 1991). Children's problems tend to worsen for a period of time after remarriage (Bray & Berger, 1993a; Hetherington & Clingempeel, 1992; Hetherington & Jodl, 1994), but often their behavior improves with time spent in a stepfamily.

Gender Differences

Initial studies of stepfamilies suggested that girls had more difficulty adjusting to stepfamily life than did boys (Hetherington, 1987). However, clear and consistent gender differences are not reported in the literature. Some studies have shown boys to have more problems than girls (Coley, 1998; Dunn, Deater-Deckard, Pickering, O'Connor, & Golding, 1998), while other studies have shown the opposite (Needle, Su, & Doherty, 1990). Lee, Burkam, Zimiles, and Ladewski (1994) found the latter to be true only for girls living with stepfathers and for girls living with stepmothers (Suh, Schutz, & Johanson, 1996). Consistent gender differences were not found in the DIS study (Bray, 1999) or by Hetherington and colleagues (1992, 1999).

Adolescents' Adjustment

Adolescence can be a difficult transition period and may be exacerbated by a parental remarriage. Research has shown that adolescent stepchildren are more likely to have externalizing behavioral problems than adolescents in first-marriage families (Bray, 1999; Hetherington & Clingempeel, 1992). These problems include the use of drugs and alcohol (Hoffman & Johnson, 1998, Needle et al., 1990), early sexual intercourse (Day, 1992), unmarried motherhood (Astone & Washington, 1994), being arrested (Coughlin & Vuchinich, 1996), and higher rates of suicide attempts (Garnefski & Diekstra, 1997). Other investigators found that such characteristics as dropping out of school, academic difficulties, unemployment, conduct disorders, teenage pregnancy, and overall behavior problems were about twice as common in stepfamilies as in first-marriage families (Hetherington, 1989, 1991; Hetherington & Jodl, 1994; McLanahan & Sandefur, 1994; Zill, Morrison, & Coiro, 1993).

The hypotheses about the emergence of behavior problems for adolescents in stepfamilies relate to the struggle to individuate and develop identity during this period (Bray, 1999). Part of the individuation process is to interact with parents as a means of determining self-identity and autonomy. However, in stepfamilies there is often an important person not present, the nonresidential parent, who is usually the father. Thus, the individuation process is transferred to the stepfather and may become problematic because adolescents need their other birth parent to complete this process. As part of this process, it is common for children in stepfamilies to develop an increased interest in their nonresidential parent and they may request to live with that parent.

Further, the stepparent may respond to the increased behavior problems by disengaging, which also contributes to externalizing behavior by adolescents. In the DIS study, stepfathers made statements such as, "I don't understand why he is sullen and rude with me. It seems like he is angry about something, but he won't talk with me about it." These findings and those by Hetherington et al. (1999) give new meaning to the common occurrence in stepfamilies in which a stepchild says to a stepparent, "I don't have to do what you say because you are not my *real* dad or mom!" The findings also indicate that stepparents may really be saying, "I don't have to deal with you because you are not my *real* child" (Bray, 1999). While the DIS study found that stepfather disengagement occurred in long-term stepfamilies, Hetherington and Clingempeel (1992) reported that it was more frequent and difficult for new stepfamilies with adolescents. Comparison of the two studies suggests that it is particularly difficult to form a new stepfamily with young adolescents.

Ethnicity

Most research on stepfamilies has used samples of White, middle-class families. The diversity of American families in terms of ethnicity has not been sufficiently studied. Given the different marriage, divorce, and remarriage rates among different ethnic groups, further research is needed to examine ethnic diversity in response to marital and nonmarital transitions.

Black adolescents may get more benefit from living in a stepfamily than their White counterparts, although there are gender differences in its impact on adjustment (Hetherington & Stanley-Hagan, 1999). The rates of teenage births in young Black women in stepfamilies are the same as for those in two-parent, first-marriage families and young Black men in stepfamilies are no more likely to drop out of high school than those in two-parent families (McLanahan & Sandefur, 1994); neither finding is true for White youths. A posited reason for the ethnic differences is that the income, supervision, and role model provided by a stepfather may have greater impact on Black children, who are more likely to live in poor neighborhoods with many risks and few resources and social controls. However, comparatively few Black children have stepfathers, because of Black families' low rates of remarriage (Amato, 1994; Clarke & Wilson, 1994; Dawson, 1991; Hetherington & Jodl, 1994).

It should be pointed out that family structure explains only a modest amount of the variance in emotional problems, indicating that other factors may be associated with such problems (Bray & Berger, 1993a; O'Connor, Dunn, Jenkins, Pickering, & Rasbash, 2001). O'Connor et al. (2001) found that 41% of child psychopathology could be explained by family factors, such as the compromised quality of the parent-child relationship, parental depression, and socioeconomic adversity (income, maternal education). Family and social factors are strong mediators of child adjustment in stepfamilies. The rest of this chapter focuses on family process factors that influence children's adjustment in stepfamilies.

■ Factors Influencing Children's Adjustment in Stepfamilies

There are a number of risk factors that impact children in stepfamilies, including marital problems, difficulties in the stepparent-child relationship, family conflict, and problems with the nonresidential parent. In addition, the presence of adolescents in stepfamilies increases the risk for family problems. Stepfamilies may thrive and be resilient because of previous experiences in which they learned to cope more effectively with stress, the social maturity and responsibility of parents, effective parenting practices, and marital and family support and satisfaction.

Remarriages

Strong, well-functioning marital relationships in stepfamilies differ from those in first-marriage families (Hetherington & Stanley-Hagan, 1999). Spouses in the former see their relationship as less romantic but more pragmatic, and they tend to share both household and childrearing responsibilities more than occurs in first-marriage families (Furstenberg, 1987).

It has been thought that the quality of a marital relationship between remarried adults is damaged by the presence of stepchildren (Brown & Booth, 1996), although the impact is not always big. After the marriage, newlywed couples normally spend time alone and create a marital bond; however, in stepfamilies, this is compromised by the demands of caring for children from the beginning of the relationship (Bray & Berger, 1993b; Bray et al., 1987; Hetherington, 1993; Hetherington & Clingempeel, 1992).

The quality of the marital relationship is poorer when both parents have children from previous relationships than when only one adult is a stepparent, probably because of increased complexity and more opportunities for conflict (Hobart, 1991). There are exceptions; for instance, Kurdek (1999) found that children of first marriages lowered the quality of marital relationships more than did stepchildren. There were few differences in marital adjustment and interactions between first-marriage and remarried couples in the DIS study for each period after remarriage

(Bray & Berger, 1993b; Bray et al., 1987). After 5 years of remarriage, stepfathers reported higher marital satisfaction than did first-marriage husbands; however, in behavioral observations first-marriage couples were rated as more positive in their interactions than remarried couples during this same period. There were also no differences between groups in marital satisfaction at the longitudinal follow-up. As Vemer, Coleman, Ganong, and Cooper (1989) reported in their review of the remarriage literature, marital relations and satisfaction with marriages in first and second marriages are usually quite similar. Overall, research finds that having children is associated with lower marital satisfaction. Thus, these findings are consistent with the view that residential children may impact marital satisfaction and may further explain the lack of a honeymoon effect for newly remarried couples.

However, in contrast to the self-report findings of marital satisfaction, observations of couples' interactions indicated that remarried couples were more negative and less positive toward each other than first-marriage couples (Bray, 1988; Bray & Berger, 1993a). In the follow-up interviews remarried couples were also more negative toward each other and stepfathers were less positive toward their wives than couples in first-marriage families.

The marital subsystem appears to impact other family subsystems differently in stepfamilies than in first-marriage families (Bray, 1988a; Bray & Berger, 1993a), yet marital conflict is a crucial factor in both family types (Bray & Jouriles, 1995). Sources of such conflict experienced by remarried couples include boundary ambiguity, conflicting loyalties, stepparent-stepchild relationships, and stepparents' disciplinary role (Burrell, 1995; Daly & Wilson, 1996; Kheshgi-Genovese & Genovese, 1997). There seem to be more disruption and conflict in parent-child relationships during the early stages of remarriage than in first-marriage families, and parents exercise less authority (Hetherington & Stanley-Hagan, 1999). Disagreements between couples usually focus on stepchildren issues, such as discipline, rules from children, and the distribution of resources to children (Hobart, 1991; Pasley, Koch, & Ihinger-Tallman, 1993).

During early remarriage, marital adjustment and satisfaction are not related to children's behavior problems (Bray, 1988a; Hetherington & Clingempeel, 1992). This is in contrast to first-marriage families, in which marital relationships are usually predictive of adjustment difficulties for children (Emery, 1988). After several years in a stepfamily, marital relationships have more impact on children's adjustment and parent-child interactions, similar to that in first-marriage families (Bray & Berger, 1993b; Hetherington & Clingempeel, 1992).

Areas for Future Research

The behavioral, emotional, and physiological patterns of marital relations related to subsequent divorce or happiness identified in Gottman's research (1994) need to be examined in remarried couples. Replication of his work with stepfamilies would provide useful information regarding interactional patterns that lead to happy remarriages. Some current data sets of stepfamilies might be reanalyzed to evaluate these patterns. However, the research would need to examine context (e.g., presence of children) and content (e.g., meaning of conflict) differences between first marriages and remarriages. Some new studies need to be conducted that will provide the physiological data on emotion and arousal that are not available in existing data sets.

In addition, bidirectional effects (how stepchildren are affected by their parents and vice versa), such as those in the study of Hetherington and her colleagues (Hetherington et al., 1999), should be examined. The dynamic nature of family relations needs further study to determine patterns of interactions and change over time. These types of studies will help us understand the unique developmental issues for stepfamilies. There is some evidence that stepchildren's responses to stepparents may be vital to the development of happy marital relationships, particularly for longer term stepfamilies. Longitudinal studies with multiple observations are needed to evaluate these types of relationships.

Since the divorce rate for remarriages is higher than that in first marriages, additional research is needed to examine the role of multiple marital transitions on children's adjustment. More research on the adverse effects of multiple marital transitions on parents and children would be valuable (Amato & Booth, 1991). These studies should examine the diverse adaptive trajectories associated with marital transitions, the timing and patterns of risks, and risk and protective factors contributing to adverse outcomes or resiliency resulting from marital transitions.

■ Relationships in Stepfamilies

Researchers generally agree that family process has greater impact on children's adjustment than does family structure (Bray & Berger, 1993a; Fine & Kurdek, 1995; Hetherington & Clingempeel, 1992; Visher & Visher, 1988). Family relationships in stepfamilies, and particularly the stepparent-child relationship, are more distant and have more conflict than those in first-marriage families (Bray, 1988b; Bray & Berger, 1993a; Hetherington & Clingempeel, 1992; Perkins & Kahan, 1979; Santrock, Warshak, Lindberg, & Meadows, 1982). In addition, the relationships have more coalitions and triangles than do first-marriage families (Anderson & White, 1986; Bray, 1992). Thus, parent-child relationship problems are a higher risk in stepfamilies, especially with adolescents, and individual behavioral and emotional problems are also more likely to appear in response to these difficulties (Bray & Harvey, 1995; Garbarino, Sebes, & Schellenbach, 1984).

However, similar family processes among stepfamilies and first-marriage families have been reported in some research (Bogenschneider, 1997; O'Connor, Hetherington, & Reiss, 1998; Waldren, Bell, Peek, & Sorell, 1990), and quite a large proportion of stable, long-term stepfamilies seem to function in a similar way to first-marriage families (O'Connor et al., 1998; Vuchinich, Hetherington, Vuchinich, & Clingempeel, 1991). It is possible that stepfamilies function similarly to first-marriage families over time (Coleman et al., 2000). Over a 2-year period, mother-stepfather-preadolescent stepson triads resembled first-marriage family triads in problem-solving effectiveness (Vuchinich, Vuchinich, & Wood, 1993). Agreement between parents (but not parental coalitions) made problem solving easier in both family types. In neither family type was marital conflict associated with successful problem solving.

There are more disruption and conflict in parent-child relationships during the early stages of remarriage than in first-marriage families (Hetherington & Stanley-Hagan, 1999). Over time, however, biological residential parents in stepfamilies tend to resemble their counterparts in first-marriage families with respect to parenting. Furthermore, stepchildren have more relationship problems with parents and siblings and with spouses in adulthood than do their counterparts in first-marriage families (Amato & Booth, 1991; Amato & Keith, 1991). The types of problems encountered, however, can vary according to the children's development status, gender, and ethnicity.

Boys appear to accept and adapt to a stepfather faster than girls (Brand, Clingempeel, & Bowen-Woodward, 1988). Preadolescent and early adolescent stepdaughters often have a more negative attitude and show resistance toward stepparents (Bray & Berger, 1993a; Clingempeel, Brand, & Ievoli, 1984). Thus, the development of a good relationship between stepparent and child is related not only to the stepparent's desire and attempts to form a close relationship, but also to the child's readiness and developmental status. When stepparents attempt to be involved with their stepchildren too quickly, even when they behave in positive and otherwise reasonable ways, the children may withdraw or be hostile toward the stepparent. This may result in the stepparent disengaging from the children (Bray & Berger, 1993a; Hetherington, 1987; Hetherington & Clingempeel, 1992). Over time, this disengagement is related to poorer behavioral adjustment of children. A close relationship with a stepfather is more likely to improve the well-being and achievement of stepsons than of stepdaughters (Amato & Keith, 1991; Hetherington, 1993; Hetherington & Clingempeel, 1992; Lindner-Gunnoe, 1993; Zill et al., 1993). The presence of a stepfather can exacerbate the problems of girls (Amato & Keith, 1991). Hetherington and Stanley-Hagan (1999) suggest that gender differences in adjustment to stepparents may be due more to children's reactions to stepparents than to stepparents' initial parenting efforts.

At the follow-up interviews in the DIS Project, stepfathers reported being more negative and less positive in their interactions with their stepchildren than were nuclear fathers. In addition, children in stepfamilies were less positive toward their stepfathers than were children in first-marriage families. Stepfathers were less positive toward their stepchildren over time than were nuclear fathers. Stepfathers and stepsons had the largest decreases in positive interactions over time. These findings are in essential agreement with Anderson and White's (1986) and Hetherington and Clingempeel's (1992) findings that stepfathers have more distant and less positive relationships with their stepchildren than do biological fathers and children.

However, it is important to note that while these relationships are more negative in stepfamilies than in first-marriage families, they are not necessarily pathological or problematic (Bray, 1999). Most of the measures used in these studies are based on nonclinical families and characteristics, such as warmth and parenting. This finding is applicable to both the self-report measures and the behavioral ratings. While there are differences between family structure groups on various measures and ratings of family relations, they are relatively small and represent differences in a "normal" range. While there are often more negative and conflictual relationships in stepfamilies, compared to non-stepfamilies, the mean ratings for *both* groups are in the positive range. Specifically, if you look at the behavioral ratings of the Hetherington and Bray studies, the scales are usually 1–5, with 5 being highly negative. Most of the means are in the 1 to 2 ranges for both types of families. Thus, it is not accurate to characterize stepfamilies as "negative, conflictual, and distant." If this is done, then both scholars and social policy analysts will misinterpret the data.

Areas for Future Research

Research identifying interactional patterns of successful and problematic stepfamily relationships, similar to Gottman's (1994) work in marital relations, would benefit prevention and intervention efforts. Again, some current data sets of stepfamilies might be reanalyzed with molecular coding systems and longitudinal designs to evaluate these patterns. In addition, it is important to examine interactional patterns that are related to negative behavioral outcomes, such as child abuse, early teen pregnancy, or deviant behavior, to determine if there are causal sequences that might be identified.

From a family systems perspective, it is important to identify bidirectional influences among parents, stepparents, and stepchildren. Dyadic and triadic patterns related to successful or problematic outcomes need to be studied further. Longitudinal studies with multiple observations are needed to evaluate these types of relationships.

■ Parenting and Stepparenting

Parenting and stepparenting are a major challenge for all stepfamilies, regardless of how long they have been in existence. The former appears to be the more difficult and stressful aspect of stepfamily life (Bray, 1988a; Bray & Kelly, 1998). Forgatch et al. (1995) found that parenting mediates the impact of divorce and other family changes on children's adjustment. The DIS study indicates that the role of parenting on children's adjustment varies depending on the developmental status of the stepfamily and child.

During the early months of remarriage, stepparents may have difficulty playing a parental role, even when they use authoritative parenting. Stepchildren have been shown to reject stepparents who exercise discipline and control early in the relationship (Ganong, Coleman, Fine, & Martin, 1999). In new stepfamilies, even when stepparents used effective parenting skills, they were often rebuffed and the children responded with more behavior problems (Bray, 1999). This was quite surprising, since the videotaped interactions demonstrated the stepparents using authoritative parenting skills that are usually associated with positive child outcomes in first-marriage families. Functioning as a friend or camp counselor rather than as a parent can facilitate the children's acceptance of the stepparent (Bray, 1988a; Visher & Visher, 1988). Children were more likely to accept stepparents when they first attempted to form a relationship with the children instead of actively trying to discipline or control them (Bray & Berger, 1993a). However, over time, after 2.5 years in a stepfamily, the stepparent played an important parental role and the use of authoritative parenting was related to positive outcomes for children.

Active monitoring of children's behavior and activities by the stepparent is a beneficial parental activity that facilitates children's adjustment during both the early and later stages of remarriage (Bray, 1988b; Hetherington, 1987; Hetherington & Clingempeel, 1992). After a relationship is formed—a process that may take several months to over a year—more active authoritative parenting by the stepparent can be beneficial to children. Boys seem to respond more quickly to this process than girls in stepfather families (Bray, 1988b; Hetherington & Clingempeel, 1992). This developmental flow is important for the near-term adjustment of children and is also predictive of better adjustment during later remarriage (Bray & Hetherington, 1993).

Older adolescents rely on peer relationships and extrafamilial sources of support as they become more independent of the family (Baumrind, 1991; Bray, Adams, Getz, & Baer, 2001). However, effective parenting and stepparenting are still important for adolescents, as seen from the DIS study's longitudinal findings. A consistent association between more paternal monitoring and better adjustment in stepchildren highlights the importance of this parenting practice for stepfathers over time (Bray, 1999; Hetherington, 1993). Mothers in both family types reported the development of warmer and more involved relationships with their children (Bray, Berger, Boethel, Maymi, & Touch, 1992). However, stepfathers' warmth decreased over time toward both stepsons and stepdaughters. Stepfathers' reduced warmth appears to be contraindicated, as less warmth and involvement are related to poorer adjustment for stepchildren.

Increases in authoritarian parenting by mothers and stepfathers were the most consistent correlates of behavior problems and lower social competency for adolescents in stepfamilies and girls in first-marriage families (Bray, 1994). Parenting in long-term stepfamilies and first-marriage families was quite similar. Authoritative parenting related to fewer behavior problems and higher social competency, while authoritarian parenting was associated with poorer adjustment. Disengaged parenting was also related to poorer adjustment for boys in stepfamilies and girls in first-marriage families.

Areas for Future Research

Research that identifies successful parenting practices for stepfamilies would benefit prevention and intervention efforts. However, this research would need to consider the developmental status of the children and the stepfamily. For example, in the DIS study early parenting styles were not strong longitudinal predictors of later adolescent adjustment, particularly for stepfathers (Bray, 1994). This finding is not surprising given the changes in parenting styles in stepfamilies and the rapid changes that frequently occur during the early years of remarriage. In contrast, there were many similarities between parenting in long-term stepfamilies and first-marriage families. This suggests that after 4 to 5 years these two family types converge in their parenting and opinions about what is best for adolescent's adjustment. In addition, it is important to examine parenting practices and styles that are related to negative behavioral outcomes, such as child abuse, substance abuse, or deviant behavior, to determine if there are causal sequences that might be identified.

There is little research on intra- and extrafamily influences on successful parenting in stepfamilies. Intrafamily influences include factors such as the role of marital relations on parenting practices. It is believed that a strong marital bond facilitates the formation of a strong parenting coalition, but this needs to be validated. Child characteristics, such as learning disabilities or psychopathology (attention deficit disorder, depression), have also not been studied extensively and how they impact parenting is of theoretical and practical significance. In addition, external factors, such as the role of the nonresidential parent or grandparents, on parenting need further investigation to better understand the stepfamily system.

■ Conflict in Stepfamilies

Previous research on divorced families indicated that family conflict mediates the relationship between family structure and children's behavior problems (Borrine, Handal, Brown, & Searight, 1991; Hetherington, Cox, & Cox, 1982; Kurdek & Sinclair, 1988). In addition, given the increased levels of stress and potential conflict between ex-spouses in stepfamilies, it was hypothesized that these processes may also be mediators. In the DIS Project, the parents' life stress and family conflict mediated family structure differences in children's stress and internalizing problems, but not those in children's externalizing problems and social competency. However, stress and conflict explained a significant amount of the variance in externalizing problems and children's adjustment in both family types (Bray & Berger, 2004). Thus other factors, in addition to conflict and stress, account for the higher level of behavior problems and lower social competency of children in stepfamilies.

Nuclear family conflict can include marital conflict, interparental conflict, parent-child conflict, sibling conflict, parent-grandparent conflict, and other general forms of family disharmony. Stepfamilies can also experience conflict like first-marriage families and there is also the possibility for stepparent-parent conflict, stepparent-child conflict, and conflict between former spouses. Family and interparental conflict involving the children are key predictors of children's adjustment, especially in divorced or remarried families (Borrine et al., 1991; Hetherington & Clingempeel, 1992; Johnston, Kline, & Tschann, 1989; Kline, Johnston, & Tschann, 1991; Kurdek & Sinclair, 1988).

In the DIS Project various types of family conflict significantly predicted children's adjustment. While there were similarities in types of conflict present in stepfamilies and first-marriage families, such as conflict between parents over childrearing issues and parenting and physical conflict, there were also notable differences. These differences are not identified in studies that fail to distinguish among various types of conflict within families (e.g., Borrine et al., 1991). In stepfamilies, stepfather-child conflict was an important predictor, while mother-child conflict was an important predictor in first-marriage families. Overall, conflict was more predictive of children's adjustment in stepfamilies than in first-marriage families. Further, conflict has a stronger contemporaneous and longitudinal effect on children's externalizing problems than other indices of adjustment.

Areas for Future Research

Gottman's (1994) work in marital relations indicated that marital conflict was not related to divorce or long-term negative outcomes. A central question is whether this finding applies to stepfamilies and whether family conflict, as opposed to just marital conflict, has a different relationship over the life cycle of stepfamilies. Again, some current data sets of stepfamilies might be re-analyzed with molecular coding systems and longitudinal designs to evaluate these patterns. In addition, the meanings attributed to conflict in stepfamilies need further study. They may explain why conflict has more impact on children in stepfamilies than children in first-marriage families. For children of divorce, family relationships are more tenuous, so that children are sensitized to the negative impact that conflict plays in marital transitions and family breakups. Thus, they respond to conflict by acting out and exhibiting other externalizing behaviors. Further, a high level of conflict in families can interfere with effective parenting, which is also directly related to child outcomes (Forgatch et al., 1995). Since Gottman (1994) found that certain types of marital conflict and disagreements may facilitate the resolution of problems over time in first-marriage couples, it is important to determine what, if any, types of family conflict have a positive effect in stepfamilies and how they can manage conflict effectively to prevent a detrimental impact on children.

From a family systems perspective, it is important to identify bidirectional influences of conflict among parents, stepparents, and stepchildren. Dyadic and triadic patterns related to successful or problematic outcomes need to be studied further through longitudinal observational studies, which are invaluable in helping to develop successful prevention and intervention strategies.

■ Nonresidential Parents in Stepfamilies

After a divorce or having a child outside of marriage, many nonresidential fathers withdraw and have limited or no contact with their children (Furstenberg, 1988; Hetherington & Jodl, 1994; Seltzer, 1991). Those who remain in contact often adopt the role of a companion rather than that of a disciplinarian or parent figure

(Furstenberg & Cherlin, 1991; Hetherington, 1993; Lindner-Gunnoe, 1993). This may account for the fact that the involvement of the nonresidential father does not obstruct the stepfather's efforts to exercise authority over the children; in fact, their contact with both fathers may benefit the children, particularly boys (Hetherington, 1993; Hetherington & Jodl, 1994; Lindner-Gunnoe, 1993).

Nonresidential mothers are more likely than nonresidential fathers to continue to be active parents and, not surprisingly, children feel closer to the former than to the latter (Lindner-Gunnoe, 1993). However, the mother's continued parenting involvement may result in conflict between mother and stepmother. Children in stepfamilies often feel trapped between the mothers and the perceived divided loyalties can make the stepmother-stepdaughter relationship difficult (Furstenberg, 1987; Lindner-Gunnoe, 1993; Salwen, 1990).

The relationship between children's adjustment and contact with their non-residential parents varies. While some studies find a direct correlation between more contact and a better relationship between nonresidential parents and children and better adjustment for children and adolescents, others find that this is mediated by such factors as interparental conflict and parenting (Emery, 1988; Hetherington, 1993; Hetherington et al., 1982; Johnston et al., 1989; Kline et al., 1991). Enduring anger and animosity from the divorce may reemerge after remarriage. However, even many years after the remarriage, some children still want their divorced parents to reunite (Bray & Berger, 1992). After the remarriage some children may begin to treat the stepparent with animosity and hostility, despite a good relationship before the remarriage. This seems to be a common pattern in stepfamilies.

Though the relationship with the nonresidential father is important to the concurrent behavioral adjustment of children in the early months after remarriage, this impact is less after several years in the stepfamily (Bray & Berger, 1990, 1993b). More contact and a better relationship between father and child were related to better behavioral adjustment for both boys and girls after 6 months in a stepfather family. For girls, a positive impact was also found after 2.5 years of remarriage. After 5 years of living in a stepfather family, however, there was no concurrent relationship between either the amount of contact or the quality of the nonresidential father-child relationship and children's behavioral adjustment (Bray & Berger, 1990, 1993b). Given the limited amount of time children spend with their fathers and their older ages in the longer remarried families, these results are not entirely surprising. During adolescence, children are often influenced more by their peer relationships than family relationships (Baumrind, 1991; Bray et al., 2001).

Areas for Future Research

While there is significant research on nonresidential parent-child relationships in stepfamilies, there is insufficient study of their long-term impact. For example, a better relationship seems to be related to better behavioral outcomes for children and adolescents, but it is not clear how this relationship impacts later adolescent and young adult adjustment and development. If there is a tenuous or no relationship between fathers and children, are the fathers more or less likely to help with college, purchasing cars, or finding employment? Does the lack of a relationship have a later impact on the offspring's intimate relationships and marriage? Future research is needed to answer these questions.

■ Recommendations for Future Research on Stepfamilies

It is hoped that the quality of studies on remarriage and stepfamilies will continue to improve. Below are listed some recommendations for future research, which build on what has already been accomplished and identify some new directions.

Research Designs

There is a need for more longitudinal research that assesses changes over time (long and short term) in stepfamily members' experiences, perceptions, interactions, and adjustment. These designs need to include multiple sources of data (self-reports, observations, external evaluations) and repeated observations to evaluate the developmental trajectories and impacts of stepfamily life on child and adult outcomes. Convergence and divergence among different methods of data are needed to examine the relationships between attitudes and perceptions and interactional patterns of behavior within stepfamilies.

Such research is also recommended to examine individual adjustment and family relationship dynamics in families with less typical structures, such as stepmother families, mixed stepfamilies, or families headed by single parents marrying for the first time or by cohabitating adults (Hetherington & Stanley-Hagan, 1999). Longitudinal studies would also be useful in charting the development of beliefs in myths about stepfamilies and linking changes in the myths to observations of interactions within the stepfamily system.

More within-group designs are needed. They would provide more knowledge of factors associated with healthy and adaptive functioning in stepfamilies. The use of a variety of quantitative and qualitative methods and the study of processes in stepfamilies (e.g., marital conflict) and their relationship to individuals' adjustment would help those who design interventions and educational programs (Coleman et al., 2000).

There should be more qualitative studies on the experiences, perceptions, and reflections of stepfamily members (Coleman et al., 2000). In-depth interviewing and grounded theory approaches to data analysis should be used. Both qualitative and quantitative methods are recommended for the study of stepfamily processes, as is the combination of biological, psychological, interpersonal, and cultural influences on individuals and families.

Measures

Fine and his colleagues (Fine, McKenry, Donnelly, & Voydanoff, 1992) point out that, with the exception of the CES Depression Scale (modified for use in the National Survey of Households and Families), the measures used in their adjustment study had no psychometric properties, except for adequate internal consistency. Standardized measures should be used in the future, particularly when it comes to assessing outcomes such as psychopathology. It is unfortunate that some researchers and social policy analysts misinterpret research findings and place too much emphasis on the negative effects of divorce and remarriage on adults and children. It is only with the use of normative measures that we can make these comparisons and interpretations.

General Research Topics

In each of the above areas, suggestions were made for future studies on stepfamilies. In addition to these areas, some broader contextual areas are needed. These broader areas might include the previously discussed aspects of stepfamily life.

Overall, there is a need for research on the diversity of stepfamilies, including cohabiting couples and gay or lesbian couples with children, which should provide new insights into stepfamily dynamics (Coleman et al., 2000). In addition, the ethnic diversity of stepfamilies has been sorely understudied. Differences in outcomes for minority stepfamilies need to be examined, the diversity and complexity of these families recognized, and family relations and dynamics investigated.

Future research should place more emphasis on the factors contributing to the success of stepfamilies and to the development of healthy and happy children. To date, there has been too much emphasis on problems and not enough on effective solutions in various types of stepfamilies.

Thus far, there has been little research on the relationship between children and grandparents (Lussier, Deater-Deckard, Dunn, & Davies, 2002) and it is recommended that the topic should be further examined. It would be worthwhile to use data from 3 generations (grandparents, adult children, grandchildren) to address issues of cultural diversity. Other suggested topics include the roles played by grandparents, such as caregiver, supportive friend, or playmate, and their relationship to family functioning and children's adjustment.

How stepfamilies interface with other social institutions should be further examined (Coleman et al., 2000); topic examples include social policies and cultural attitudes. Members of stepfamilies adopt roles from cultural norms, and their created roles influence cultural attitudes and, at a later date, social policy.

It is critical that research efforts should be used to develop prevention and intervention programs to help children and adults cope with and adjust to the stress and upheaval caused by marital transitions (Bray, 2001). The longitudinal research on divorce and remarriage strongly indicates that the programs need to focus on both the short- and long-term adjustment issues that stepfamilies face in order to prevent or minimize some of the problems and enhance the positive adjustment for family members.

■ Conclusions

Stepfamilies are here to stay in American culture and our research efforts need to focus more on the diversity of these families. The changing landscape of U.S.

families, particularly in terms of ethnic and racial diversity, demands that we expand and adapt our current efforts to modern U.S. stepfamilies. The remarriage process entails a number of risk factors for children in stepfamilies, such as increased stress, diminished parenting practices, disrupted family roles, and increased conflict. Warm supportive relationships between children and custodial parents and step-parents, co-operative, understanding relationships between custodial and noncus-todial parents, and authoritative parenting by custodial parents and stepparents are all important factors that contribute to children's adjustment in stepfamilies. There has been enough research focusing on the deficits and problems—we need a closer examination of the factors that contribute to the success of stepfamilies and how they can contribute to the development of healthy and happy children. Finally, research on stepfamilies points to the need to establish social policies that support both marriages and remarriages.

■ Acknowledgments

Work on this chapter was supported by NIH Grants RO1 HD 18025 and RO1 HD 22642 from the National Institute of Child Health and Human Development and Grant RO1 AA08864 from the National Institute of Alcoholism and Alcohol Abuse. I would like to thank my collaborator, Sandra Berger, and all of the staff and students who have worked on these projects.

■ References

Achenbach, T. M., & Edelbrock, C. S. (1983). *Manual for the Behavior Checklist and Revised Child Behavior Profile.* Burlington: University of Vermont, Child Psychiatry.

Acock, A. C., & Demo, D. H. (1994). *Family diversity and well being.* Thousand Oaks, CA: Sage.

Amato, P. R. (1994). The implications of research findings on children in stepfamilies. In A. Booth & J. Dunn (Eds.), *Stepfamilies: Who benefits? Who does not?* (pp. 81–87). Hillsdale, NJ: Erlbaum.

Amato, P. R., & Booth, A. (1991). Consequences of parental divorce and marital unhappiness for adult well-being. *Social Forces, 69,* 895–914.

Amato, P. R., & Booth, A. (1996). A prospective study of divorce and parent-child relationships. *Journal of Marriage and the Family, 58,* 356–365

Amato, P. R., & Keith, B. (1991). Parental divorce and the well-being of children: A meta-analysis. *Psychological Bulletin, 110,* 26–46.

Anderson, E. R., Greene, S. M., Hetherington, E. M., & Clingempeel, W. G. (1999). The dynamics of parental remarriage: adolescent parent and sibling influences. In E. M. Hetherington (Ed.), *Coping with divorce, single parenting, and remarriage.* Hillsdale, NJ: Erlbaum.

Anderson, J. Z., & White, G. D. (1986). An empirical investigation of interactional and relationship patterns in functional and dysfunctional nuclear and stepfamilies. *Family Process, 25,* 407–422.

Astone, N. M., & Washington, M. L. (1994). The association between grandparental coresidence and adolescent childbearing. *Journal of Family Issues, 15,* 574–589.

Baumrind, D. (1991). Effective parenting during the early adolescent transition. In P. A. Cowan & E. M. Hetherington (Eds.), *Family transitions* (pp. 111–164). Hillsdale, NJ: Erlbaum.

Block, J. H., Block, J., & Gjerde, P. F. (1986). The personality of children prior to divorce: A prospective study. *Child Development, 57,* 827–840.

Bogenschneider, K. (1997). Parental involvement in adolescent schooling: A proximal *process* with transcontextual validity. *Journal of Marriage and the Family, 59,* 718–733.

Borgers, N., Dronkers, J., & van Praag, B. (1996). Different forms of two- and lone-parent families and the well-being of their children in secondary education. *Society for Psychological Education, 1,* 147–169.

Borrine, M. L., Handal, P. J., Brown, N. Y., & Searight, H. R. (1991). Family conflict and adolescent adjustment in intact, divorced, and blended families. *Journal of Consulting and Clinical Psychology, 59,* 753–755.

Bowlby, J. (1969). *Attachment and loss: I. Attachment.* London: Hogarth.

Bramlett, M. D., & Mosher, W. D. (2001). *First marriage dissolution, divorce, and remarriage: United States* (Advance Data, No. 323). Washington, DC: National Center for Health Statistics, Centers for Disease Control and Prevention.

Brand, E., Clingempeel, W. G., & Bowen-Woodward, K. (1988). Family relationships and children's adjustment in stepmother and stepfather families. In E. M. Hetherington & J. D. Arasteh (Eds.), *The impact of divorce, single parenting, and stepparenting on children.* Hillsdale, NJ: Erlbaum.

Bray, J. H. (1988a). Children's development during early remarriage. In E. M. Hetherington & J. Arasteh (Eds.), *The impact of divorce, single-parenting and step-parenting on children* (pp. 279–298). Hillsdale, NJ: Erlbaum.

Bray, J. H. (1988b). *Developmental issues in stepfamilies research project: Final report (grant number R01 Hd18025).* Bethesda, MD: National Institute of Child Health and Human Development.

Bray, J. H. (1991). Psychosocial factors affecting custodial and visitation arrangements. *Behavioral Sciences and the Law, 9,* 419–437.

Bray, J. H. (1992). Family relationships and children's adjustment in clinical and nonclinical stepfather families. *Journal of Family Psychology, 6,* 60–68.

Bray, J. H. (1994, February). *Longitudinal impact of parenting on adolescent adjustment in stepfamilies.* Paper presented at the Society for Research on Adolescence, San Diego, CA.

Bray, J. H. (1995). Family oriented treatment of stepfamilies. In R. Mikesell, D. D. Lusterman, & S. McDaniel (Eds.), *Integrating family therapy: Handbook of family psychology and systems therapy* (pp. 125–140). Washington, DC: American Psychological Association.

Bray, J. H. (1999). From marriage to remarriage and beyond: Findings from the Developmental Issues in Stepfamilies Research Project. In E. M. Hetherington (Ed.), *Coping with divorce, single-parenting and remarriage: A risk and resiliency perspective* (pp. 253–271). Hillsdale, NJ: Erlbaum.

Bray, J. H. (2001). Therapy with stepfamilies: A developmental systems approach. In D. D. Lusterman, S. H. McDaniel, & C. Philpot (Eds.), *Integrating family therapy: A casebook* (pp. 127–140). Washington, DC: American Psychological Association.

Bray, J. H., Adams, G., Getz, J. G., & Baer, P. E. (2001). Developmental, family, and ethnic influences on adolescent alcohol usage: A growth curve approach. *Journal of Family Psychology, 15,* 301–314.

Bray, J. H., & Berger, S. H. (1990). Noncustodial parent and grandparent relationships in stepfamilies. *Family Relations, 39,* 414–419.

Bray, J. H., & Berger, S. H. (1992). Stepfamilies. In M. E. Procidano & C. B. Fisher (Eds.), *Contemporary families: A handbook for school professional* (pp. 57–79). New York: Teachers College Press.

Bray, J. H., & Berger, S. H. (1993a). Developmental issues in stepfamilies research project: Family relationships and parent-child interactions. *Journal of Family Psychology, 7,* 76–90.

Bray, J. H., & Berger, S. H. (1993b). Nonresidential family-child relationships following divorce and remarriage. In C. E. Depner & J. H. Bray (Eds.), *Noncustodial parents: New vista in family living* (pp. 156–181). Newbury Park, CA: Sage.

Bray, J. H., & Berger, S. H. (2004). *Length of remarriage, conflict, stress, and children's adjustment in stepfather families and nuclear families.* Manuscript submitted for publication.

Bray, J. H., Berger, S. H., & Boethel, C. (1994). Role integration and marital adjustment in stepfather families. In K. Pasley & M. Ihinger-Tallman (Eds.), *Stepfamilies: Issues in research, theory, and practice* (pp. 69–86). New York: Greenwood.

Bray, J. H., Berger, S. H., Boethel, C., Maymi, J. R., & Touch, G. (1992, August). *Longitudinal changes in stepfamilies: Impact on children's adjustment.* Paper presented at the American Psychological Association, Washington, DC.

Bray, J. H., Berger, S. H., Silverblatt, A., & Hollier, A. (1987). Family process and organization during early remarriage: A preliminary analysis. In J. P. Vincent (Ed.), *Advances in family intervention, assessment and theory* (Vol. 4, pp. 253–280). Greenwich, CT: JAI.

Bray, J. H., & Harvey, D. M. (1995). Adolescents in stepfamilies: Developmental and family interventions. *Psychotherapy, 32,* 122–130.

Bray, J. H., & Hetherington, E. M. (1993). Families in transition: Introduction and overview. *Journal of Family Psychology, 7,* 3–8.

Bray, J. H., & Jouriles, E. (1995). Treatment of marital conflict and prevention of divorce. *Journal of Marital and Family Therapy, 21,* 461–473.

Bray, J. H., & Kelly, J. (1998). *Stepfamilies: Love, marriage, and parenting in the first decade.* New York: Broadway Books.

Brody, G. H., Neubaum, E., & Forehand, R. (1988). Serial marriage: A heuristic analysis of an emerging family form. *Psychological Bulletin, 103,* 211–222.

Brown, S. L., & Booth, A. (1996). Cohabitation versus marriage: A comparison of relationship quality. *Journal of Marriage and the Family, 58,* 668–678.

Bulcroft, R., Carmody, D., & Bulcroft, K. (1998). Family structure and patterns of independence giving to adolescents. *Journal of Family Issues, 19,* 404–435.

Bumpass, L., Raley, R. K., & Sweet, J. A. (1995). The changing character of stepfamilies implications of cohabitation and nonmarital childbearing. *Demography, 32,* 425–436.

Burrell, N. A. (1995). Communication patterns in stepfamilies: Redefining family roles, themes, and conflict styles. In A. Fitzpatrick & A. L. Vangelisti (Eds.), *Explaining family interaction* (pp. 290–309). Newbury Park, CA: Sage.

Capaldi, D. M., & Patterson, G. R. (1991). Relation of parental transitions to boys' adjustment problems: I. A linear hypothesis. II. Mothers at risk for transitions and unskilled parenting. *Developmental Psychology, 27,* 489–504.

Carter, B., & McGoldrick, M. (1988). *The changing family life cycle: A framework for family therapy* (2nd ed.). New York: Gardner.

Cherlin, A. J. (1978). Remarriage as an incomplete institution. *American Journal of Sociology, 84,* 634–649.

Cherlin, A. J., & Furstenberg, F. F. (1994). Stepfamilies in the United States: A reconsideration. In J. Blake & J. Hagen (Eds.), *Annual review of sociology* (pp. 359–381). Palo Alto, CA: Annual Reviews.

Cherlin, A. J., Furstenberg, F. F., Chase-Lansdale, P. L., Kiernan, K. E., Robins, P. K., Morrison, D. R., et al. (1991). Longitudinal studies of effects of divorce in children in Great Britain and the United States. *Science, 252,* 1386–1389.

Clarke, S. C., & Wilson, B. F. (1994). The relative stability of remarriages: A cohort approach using vital statistics. *Family Relations, 43,* 305–310.

Clingempeel, W. G., Brand, E., & Ievoli, R. (1984). Stepparent-stepchild relationships in stepmother and stepfather families. *Child Development, 57,* 474–484

Coleman, M. (1994). Stepfamilies in the United States: challenging biased assumptions. In A. Booth & J. Dunn (Eds.), *Stepfamilies: Who benefits? Who does not?* (pp. 29–36). Hillsdale, NJ: Erlbaum.

Coleman, M., Ganong, L., & Cable, S. (1997). Perceptions of stepparents: An examination of the incomplete institutionalization and social stigma hypotheses. *Journal of Divorce and Remarriage, 26,* 25–48.

Coleman, M., Ganong, L., & Fine, M. (2000). Reinvestigating remarriage: Another decade of progress. *Journal of Marriage and the Family, 62,* 1288–1307.

Coley, R. L. (1998). Children's socialization experiences and functioning in single-mother households: The importance of fathers and other men. *Child Development, 69,* 219–230.

Conger, R. D., & Conger, K. J. (1996). Sibling relationships. In R. L. A. Simons (Ed.), *Understanding differences between divorced and intact families: Stress, interaction, and child outcome* (pp. 157–175). Thousand Oaks, CA: Sage.

Coughlin, C., & Vuchinich, S. (1996). Family experience in preadolescence and the development of male delinquency. *Journal of Marriage and the Family, 58,* 491–501.

Crosbie-Burnett, M. (1989). Impact of custody arrangement and family structure on remarriage. *Journal of Divorce, 13,* 1–16.

Daly, M., & Wilson, M. I. (1987). The Darwinian psychology of discriminative solicitude. *Nebraska Symposium on Motivation, 35,* 91–144.

Daly, M., & Wilson, M. I. (1996). Evolutionary psychology and marital conflict: The relevance of stepchildren. In D. M. Buss & N. M. Malamuth (Eds.), *Sex, power, conflict: Evolutionary and feminist perspectives* (pp. 9–28). New York: Oxford University Press.

Dawson, D. A. (1991). Family structure and children's health: United States, 1988. *Vital Health Statistics, 10,* 1–47.

Day, R. D. (1992). The transition to first intercourse among racially and culturally diverse youth. *Journal of Marriage and the Family, 54,* 749–762.

Dunn, J., Deater-Deckard, K., Pickering, K., O'Connor, T. G., & Golding, J. (1998). Children's adjustment and prosocial behavior in step-, single-parent, and non-stepfamily settings: Findings from a community study. ALSPAC Study Team. Avon Longitudinal Study of Pregnancy and Childhood. *Journal of Child Psychology and Psychiatry, 39,* 1083–1095.

Emery, R. E. (1988). *Marriage, divorce, and children's adjustment.* Newbury Park, CA: Sage.

Emery, R. E., & Forehand, R. (1994). Parental divorce and children's well-being: A focus on resilience. In R. J. Haggerty, L. R. Sherrod, N. Garmezy, & M. Rutter (Eds.), *Stress, risk, and resilience in children and adolescents* (pp. 64–99). Cambridge: Cambridge University Press.

Fine, M. A., Coleman, M., & Ganong, L. (1998). Consistency in perceptions of the stepparent role among stepparents, parents, and stepchildren. *Journal of Social and Personal Relationships, 15,* 810–828.

Fine, M. A., & Kurdek, L. A. (1995). Relation between marital quality and (step)parent-child relationship quality for parents and stepparents in stepfamilies. *Journal of Family Psychology, 9,* 216–223.

Fine, M. A., McKenry, P. C., Donnelly, B. W., & Voydanoff, P. (1992). Perceived adjustment of parents and children: Variations by family structure, race, and gender. *Journal of Marriage and the Family, 54,* 118–127.

Flinn, M. (1999). Growth and fluctuating asymmetry of stepchildren. *Evolution and Human Behavior, 20,* 465–479.

Forgatch, M. S., Patterson, G. R., & Ray, J. A. (1995). Divorce and boys' adjustment problems: Two paths with a single model. In E. M. Hetherington & E. A. Bleckman (Eds.), *Stress, coping, and resiliency in children and families* (pp. 67–105). Mahway, NJ: Erlbaum.

Furstenberg, F. F. (1987). The new extended family: The experience of parents and children after remarriage. In K. Pasley & M. Ihinger-Tallman (Eds.), *Remarriage and stepparenting: Current research and theory* (pp. 42–51). New York: Guilford Press.

Furstenberg, F. F. (1988). Child care after divorce and remarriage. In E. M. Hetherington & J. D. Arasteh (Eds.), *Impact of divorce, single parenting, and stepparenting on children* (pp. 245–261). Hillsdale, NJ: Erlbaum.

Furstenberg, F. F., & Cherlin, A. (1991). *Divided families: What happens to children when parents part.* Cambridge, MA: Harvard University Press.

Ganong, L., & Coleman, M. (1994). *Remarried family relationships.* Thousand Oaks, CA: Sage.

Ganong, L., Coleman, M., Fine, M., & Martin, P. (1999). Stepparents' affinity-seeking and affinity-maintaining strategies with stepchildren. *Journal of Family Issues, 2,* 299–327.

Garbarino, J., Sebes, J., & Schellenbach, C. (1984). Families at risk for destructive parent-child relations in adolescence. *Child Development, 55,* 174–183.

Garmezy, N. (1993). Stressors of childhood. In N. Garmezy & M. Rutter (Eds.), *Stress, coping, and development in children* (pp. 43–84). New York: McGraw-Hill.

Garnefski, N., & Diekstra, R. F. W. (1997). Adolescents from one parent, stepparent and intact families: Emotional problems and suicide attempts. *Journal of Adolescence, 20,* 201–208.

Giles-Sims, J. (1997). Current knowledge about child abuse in stepfamilies. In I. Levin & M. Sussman (Eds.), *Stepfamilies: History, research, and policy* (pp. 215–230). New York: Haworth.

Gottman, J. M. (1994). *What predicts divorce?* Hillsdale, NJ: Erlbaum.

Hetherington, E. M. (1987). Family relations six years after divorce. In K. Pasley & M. Ihinger-Tallman (Eds.), *Remarriage and stepparenting today: Current research and theory* (pp. 185–205). New York: Guilford Press.

Hetherington, E. M. (1989). Coping with family transitions: Winners, losers, and survivors. *Child Development, 60,* 1–14.

Hetherington, E. M. (1991). Families, lies, and videotapes. *Journal of Research on Adolescence, 1,* 323–348.

Hetherington, E. M. (1993). An overview of the Virginia longitudinal study of divorce and remarriage. *Journal of Family Psychology, 7,* 39–56.

Hetherington, E. M., Bridges, M., & Insabella, G. M. (1998). What matters? What does not? Five perspectives on the association between marital transitions and children's adjustment. *American Psychologist, 53*, 167–184.

Hetherington, E. M., & Clingempeel, W. G. (1992). Coping with marital transitions: A family systems perspective. *Monographs of the Society for Research in Child Development, 57*(2, 3), Serial No. 227.

Hetherington, E. M., Cox, M., & Cox, R. (1982). Effects of divorce on parents and children. In M. E. Lamb (Ed.), *Nontraditional families: Parenting and child development* (pp. 233–288). Hillsdale, NJ: Erlbaum.

Hetherington, E. M., Cox, M., & Cox, R. (1985). Long-term effects of divorce and remarriage on the adjustment of children. *Journal of the American Academy of Child Psychiatry, 24*, 518–530.

Hetherington, E. M., Henderson, S., & Reiss, D. (1999). *Adolescent siblings in stepfamilies: Family functioning and adolescent adjustment.* Malden, MA: Blackwell.

Hetherington, E. M., & Jodl, K. M. (1994). Stepfamilies as settings for child development. In A. Booth & J. Dunn (Eds.), *Stepfamilies: Who benefits? Who does not?* (pp. 55–79). Hillsdale, NJ: Erlbaum.

Hetherington, E. M., & Stanley-Hagan, M. (1995). Parenting in divorced and remarried families. In M. Bornstein (Ed.), *Handbook of parenting* (pp. 233–255). Hillsdale, NJ: Erlbaum.

Hetherington, E. M., & Stanley-Hagan, M. (1999). Stepfamilies. In M. E. Lamb (Ed.), *Parenting and child development in "nontraditional" families* (pp. 137–159). Mahwah, NJ: Erlbaum.

Hobart, C. (1991). Conflict in remarriages. *Journal of Divorce and Remarriage, 15*, 69–86.

Hoffman, J. P., & Johnson, R. A. (1998). A national portrait of family structure and adolescent drug use. *Journal of Marriage and the Family, 60*, 633–645.

Jacobson, D. S. (1995). Incomplete institution or culture shock: Institutional and processual models of stepfamily instability. *Journal of Divorce and Remarriage, 24*, 3–18.

Johnston, J. R., Kline, M., & Tschann, J. M. (1989). Ongoing postdivorce conflict: Effects on children of joint custody and frequent access. *American Journal of Orthopsychiatry, 59*, 1–17.

Kheshgi-Genovese, Z., & Genovese, T. A. (1997). Developing the spousal relationship within stepfamilies. *Families in Society, 78*, 255–264.

Kiecolt-Glaser, J. K., Fisher, L. D., Ogrocki, P., Stout, J. C., Speicher, C. E., & Glaser, R. (1987). Marital quality, marital disruption, and immune function. *Psychosomatic Medicine, 49*, 13–34.

Kitson, G. C., & Morgan, L. A. (1990). The multiple consequences of divorce. *Journal of Marriage and the Family, 52*, 913–924.

Kline, M., Johnston, J. R., & Tschann, J. M. (1991). The long shadow of marital conflict: A model of children's post-divorce adjustment. *Journal of Marriage and the Family, 53*, 297–309.

Kurdek, L. A. (1999). The nature and predictors of the trajectory of change in marital quality for husbands and wives over the first 10 years of marriage. *Developmental Psychology, 35*, 1283–1296.

Kurdek, L. A., & Sinclair, R. J. (1988). Adjustment of young adolescents in two-parent nuclear, stepfather, and mother-custody families. *Journal of Consulting and Clinical Psychology, 56*, 91–96.

Lee, V., Burkam, D., Zimiles, H., & Ladewski, B. (1994). Family structure and its effect on behavioral and emotional problems in young adolescents. *Journal of Research on Adolescence, 4*, 405–437.

Lindner-Gunnoe, M. L. (1993). *Noncustodial mothers' and fathers' contributions to the adjustment of adolescent stepchildren.* Unpublished dissertation, University of Virginia.

Lorenz, F. O., Simons, R. L., & Chao, W. (1996). Family structure and mother's depressions. In R. L. A. Simons (Ed.), *Understanding differences between divorced and intact families: Stress, interaction, and child outcome* (pp. 65–77). Thousand Oaks, CA: Sage.

Lussier, G., Deater-Deckard, K., Dunn, J., & Davies, L. (2002). Support across two generations: children's closeness to grandparents following parental divorce and remarriage. *Journal of Family Psychology, 16,* 363–376.

McGoldrick, M., & Carter, E. A. (1988). Forming a remarried family. In E. A. Carter & M. McGoldrick (Eds.), *The changing family life cycle* (pp. 399–429). New York: Gardner.

McLanahan, S., & Sandefur, G. (1994). *Growing up with a single parent. What hurts, what helps?* Cambridge, MA: Harvard University Press.

Mekos, D., Hetherington, E. M., & Reiss, D. (1996). Sibling differences in problem behavior and parental treatment in nondivorced and remarried families. *Child Development, 67,* 2148–2165.

Menaghan, E. G., Kowaleski-Jones, L., & Mott, F. L. (1997). The intergenerational costs of parental social stressors: academic and social difficulties in early adolescence for children of young mothers. *Journal of Health and Social Behavior, 38,* 72–86.

Merikangas, K. R., Prusoff, B. A., & Weissman, M. M. (1988). Parental concordance for affective disorders: psychopathology in offspring. *Journal of Affective Disorders, 15,* 279–290.

Needle, R., Su, S., & Doherty, W. (1990). Divorce, remarriage, and adolescent substance use: A prospective longitudinal study. *Journal of Marriage and the Family, 52,* 157–169.

O'Connor, T. G., Dunn, J., Jenkins, J. M., Pickering, K., & Rasbash, J. (2001). Family settings and children's adjustment: differential adjustment within and across families. *British Journal of Psychiatry, 179,* 110–115.

O'Connor, T. G., Hetherington, E. M., & Reiss, D. (1998). Family systems and adolescent development: Shared and nonshared risk and protective factors in nondivorced and remarried families. *Developmental Psychopathology, 10,* 353–375.

Orleans, M., Palisi, B. J., & Caddell, D. (1989). Marriage adjustment and satisfaction of stepfathers: Their feelings and perceptions of decision making and stepchildren relations. *Family Relations, 38,* 371–377.

Pasley, K., Koch, M., & Ihinger-Tallman, M. (1993). Problems in remarriage: An exploratory study of intact and terminated remarriages. *Journal of Divorce and Remarriage, 20,* 63–83.

Patterson, G., & Dishion, T. J. (1988). Multilevel family process levels: Traits, interactions, and relationships. In Hinde. R. & J. Stevenson-Hinde (Eds.), *Relationships within families: Mutual influences* (pp. 288–310). Oxford, UK: Clarendon.

Perkins, T. F., & Kahan, J. P. (1979). An empirical comparison of natural-father and step-father family systems. *Family Process, 18,* 175–183.

Salwen, L. V. (1990). The myth of the wicked stepmother. *Women and Therapy, 10,* 117–125.

Santrock, J. W., Warshak, R. A., Lindberg, C., & Meadows, L. (1982). Children's and parent's observed social behavior in stepfather families. *Child Development, 53,* 472–480.

Seltzer, J. A. (1991). Relationships between fathers and children who live apart: The father's role after separation. *Journal of Marriage and the Family, 53,* 79–101.

Seltzer, J. A. (1994). Intergenerational ties in adulthood and childhood experience. In A. Booth & J. Dunn (Eds.), *Stepfamilies: Who benefits? Who does not?* (pp. 153–163). Hillsdale, NJ: Erlbaum.

Simons, R. L. (1996). The effect of divorce on adult and child adjustment. In R. L. A. Simons (Ed.), *Understanding differences between divorced and intact families: Stress, interaction, and child outcome* (pp. 3–20). Thousand Oaks, CA: Sage.

Simons, R. L., & Associates. (1996). *Understanding differences between divorced and intact families: Stress, interaction, and child outcome.* Thousand Oaks, CA: Sage.

Simons, R. L., & Beaman, J. (1996). Father's parenting. In R. L.A. Simons (Ed.), *Understanding differences between divorced and intact families: Stress, interaction, and child outcome* (pp. 94–103). Thousand Oaks, CA: Sage.

Simons, R. L., & Johnson, C. (1996). Mother's parenting. In R. L. A. Simons (Ed.), *Understanding differences between divorced and intact families: Stress, interaction, and child outcome* (pp. 81–93). Thousand Oaks, CA: Sage

Simons, R. L., Johnson, C., & Lorenz, F. O. (1996). Family structure differences in stress and behavioral predispositions. In R. L. A. Simons (Ed.), *Understanding differences between divorced and intact families: Stress, interaction, and child outcome* (pp. 45–83). Thousand Oaks, CA: Sage.

Spruijt, E. (1997). Stepfamily lifestyles and adolescent well-being in the Netherlands. *Journal of Divorce and Remarriage, 26,* 137–153.

Suh, T., Schutz, C. G., & Johanson, C. E. (1996). Family structure and initiating non-medical drug use among adolescents. *Journal of Child and Adolescent Substance Abuse, 5,* 21–36.

Szinovacz, M. E. (1998). Grandparents today: A demographic profile. *Gerontologist, 38,* 37–52.

U.S. Bureau of the Census. (1992). *Marriage, divorce, and remarriage in the 1990s* (Current Population Reports). Washington, DC: U.S. Government Printing Office.

Vemer, E., Coleman, M., Ganong, L. H., & Cooper, H. (1989). Marital satisfaction in remarriage: A meta-analysis. *Journal of Marriage and the Family, 51,* 713–725.

Visher, E. B., & Visher, J. S. (1988). *Old loyalties, new ties: Therapeutic strategies with stepfamilies.* New York: Brunner/Mazel.

Vuchinich, S., Vuchinich, R., & Wood, B. (1993). The interparental relationship and family problem solving with preadolescent males. *Child Development, 64,* 1389–1400.

Vuchinich, S., Hetherington, E. M., Vuchinich, R. A., & Clingempeel, W. G. (1991). Parent and child interaction and gender differences in early adolescents' adaptation to stepfamilies. *Developmental Psychology, 27,* 618–626.

Waldren, T., Bell, N., Peek, C., & Sorell, G. (1990). Cohesion and adaptability in post-divorce remarried and first-married families: Relationships with family stress and coping styles. *Journal of Divorce and Remarriage, 14,* 13–28.

Werner, E. E. (1993). Risk, resilience, and recovery: Perspectives from the Kauai Longitudinal Study. *Development and Psychopathology, 54,* 503–515.

Wolin, S., & Wolin, S. (1993). *The resilient self: How survivors of troubled families rise above adversity.* New York: Villard.

Zill, N. (1994). Understanding why children in stepfamilies have more learning and behavior problems than children in nuclear families. In A. Booth & J. Dunn (Eds.), *Stepfamilies: Who benefits? Who does not?* (pp. 97–106). Hillsdale, NJ: Erlbaum.

Zill, N., Morrison, D. R., & Coiro, M. J. (1993). Long-term effects of parental divorce and parent-child relationships, adjustment, and achievement in young adulthood. *Journal of Family Psychology, 7,* 91–103.

12

Promoting Better Fathering Among Divorced Nonresident Fathers

Sanford L. Braver, William A. Griffin, Jeffrey T. Cookston,
Irwin N. Sandler, and Jason Williams

As Bray and Easling (ch. 11 in this volume) have documented, the divorce or marital separation of their parents is a very common condition faced by children in America today. Currently, over 40% of children are expected to live in a divorced home before the age of 16 (Cherlin, 1999), more than double the proportion 30 years ago (Shiono & Quinn, 1994). A substantial empirical literature has now arisen and been summarized most aptly by Amato (Amato, 2000, 2001, 2003; Amato & Keith, 1991a, 1991b) documenting the potentially adverse effect of divorce on children. This literature also suggests that divorced fathers have a substantial role to play in impacting their children's well-being. For example, Amato and Keith (1991a) showed that the following factors (listed roughly in order of effect size) negatively affect children's postdivorce outcomes: (a) high levels of postdivorce interparental conflict, (b) a disturbed relationship with an impaired custodial parent (typically the mother), (c) an absent or ineffective nonresident parent (typically the father), (d) increased economic hardship, (e) substantial levels of environmental changes (i.e., moves, other losses), etc., and (f) the child's poor or ineffective coping skills. While the factor above most obviously impacted by the nonresident father is (c), each of the others is plausibly also affected to some degree by fathers' actions and reactions. For example, fathers are one of the two parties involved in conflict (factor a, above); fathers may fail to adequately support the child economically after divorce (factor d); and fathers can assist their children in coping better with the divorce circumstances (factor f) either by modeling good coping techniques or by doing what is possible to minimize the adversities with which the child most cope. Even the child's relationship with the mother (b), which seemingly involves *only* the mother, and discussed in more detail by Bullock and Forgatch (ch. 14 in this volume), is nonetheless substantially impacted by fathers, since mothers report that one of the most stressful aspects of divorce that disturbs their parenting is their relationship with their ex-husbands (Ahrons, 1981; Brandwein, Brown, & Fox, 1974; Tschann, Johnston, Kline, & Wallerstein, 1989). Thus, there is plausibly considerable benefit to children that will accrue by enhancing the fathering of their nonresidential parent.

■ Deficit Model Versus Modifiable Potentiality

Much of the literature of the 1980s on divorced fathers adopted a deficit model, which emphasized the shortcomings and failures of divorced fathers. For example, the media are full of daily news stories about "deadbeat dads" (e.g., Davis, 2003; Weitzstein, 2003). Moreover, Furstenburg, Nord, Peterson, and Zill (1983) reported that 49% of the children in their sample had not seen their nonresidential parent in the past year and that only one child in six averaged one or more contacts per week. Furstenburg and Nord (1985) suggest that this infrequent contact occurs because most of the fathers are only weakly attached to their children. Popenoe (1996), too, echoes this conclusion, writing that "male biology pulls men away from long-term parental investment . . . men are only weakly attached to the father role" (pp. 173, 184). Furstenburg refers to these men as "bad dads" (1988) or "disappearing dads" (Furstenburg & Harris, 1992). A deficit perspective assumes that many or most divorced fathers are characterologically inept or uncaring fathers, who simply volitionally and irresponsibly abandon their emotional, financial, and physical involvement with their children without good—or any—cause.

In the present chapter, we refrain from adopting a deficit model. While its accuracy has certainly been called into question (Braver & O'Connell, 1998; Garfinkel, Miller, McLanahan, & Hanson, 1998; Hawkins & Dollahite, 1997; Parke & Brott, 1999; Pasley & Minton, 1997; Schwartz, 2001) and its prominence in the more recent literature on fathers is rapidly diminishing, the primary justification for abandoning it is that is simply not helpful or useful. Rather, the deficit approach leads to hand-wringing, wholesale condemnations, and occasionally draconian and coercive policies that have generally proven ineffective in promoting better fathering and thereby improving the lives of their children.

Since the goal of this chapter is to discuss how best to promote better fathering in divorced fathers, we instead review the literature on divorced fathers using the lens or filter of *modifiable potentiality*. By this term we mean we search for factors or attributes that are *modifiable* and have the *potential to optimize* divorced fathers' beneficial influence on their children's well-being. Focusing exclusively on the malleable and beneficial aspects of the father-child relationship allows for the development of parsimonious and streamlined programming. This is a constructive approach that builds strengths and is far more hopeful than the deficit perspective, which condemns weaknesses (Maton, Ledbetter, Schellenbach, & Solarz, 2004). Rather than pursue inherent limitations and/or failures and deficits, we address capabilities and potential but unrealized strengths. What does the literature tell us is necessary and plausible to alter fathers' impact on children for the better? How can these changes best be accomplished? What programs are needed? What additional research would be required? Using this perspective, we hope to conclude with reasonable interventions that are feasible and can improve the relationship between fathers and their children.

The organization of the remainder of this chapter is as follows. First, we discuss the functions and roles of divorced fathers in the postdivorce family by reviewing what fathers *do*—or fail to do—after divorce and the impact these behaviors have on their children, the child's environment, and their relationship with the ex-spouse. After synthesizing this evidence, we propose the essential dimensions of divorced nonresidential parenting. Second, we attempt to explain variation among fathers in their fulfillment of their fathering responsibilities. In order to understand how best to enhance divorced fathering, we need to recognize what the "levers" are, what factors contribute to or detract from adequate enactment of adaptive achievement of enhanced fathering. The search for what we term *modifiable potentiators* is aided by a theoretical perspective, so, in our third section, we discuss six theories that have been offered to predict father involvement and impact. Fourth, we draw this literature together into an integrated proposal for an intervention targeting the modifiable potentiators that has promise of promoting better fathering. Fifth, we discuss such a program we have designed, based on this review, called "Dads for Life." Sixth, we present details of an experimental trial we have conducted to evaluate the impact of Dads for Life. Seventh, we briefly discuss the program's encouraging preliminary results. Finally, we mention other promising programs to enhance divorced fathering, and we propose a research agenda on nonresidential fathering for the future.

■ The Dimensions of Divorced Nonresidential Fathering

Although things appear to be slowly changing (Cancian & Meyer, 1998; Meyer & Garasky, 1993), the vast majority of fathers become "nonresidential" parents after divorce, in the sense that their children will no longer reside with them for the majority of time. Current estimates are that, following divorce, 90% of children live primarily with their mothers, with the remainder roughly evenly divided between children who reside primarily with their fathers and those who are in "true" joint custody, spending virtually half of their time residing with each parent (Nord & Zill, 1996) As many writers have pointed out (Blankenhorn, 1995; Stewart, 1999; Wallerstein & Corbin, 1986), the nonresidential parent role is one with a number of constraints that greatly interfere with "normal" parent-child relationships. Most obviously, the time with the child is substantially restricted by the visitation arrangement the decree specifies. This interferes with continuity: considerable time may have elapsed between visits and many events of important meaning to either parent or child may have occurred without mutually taking note of them. Moreover, since disciplining often requires follow-through (e.g., "grounding"), the father's normal role in limit setting and regulation cannot be effectively implemented. Next, parenting occurs in a solo parenting environment. The two parents, who may have reinforced and relieved each other before divorce, uncommonly do so after divorce. Also, the postmarital relationship may be strained or hostile, especially around the issues of visitation (Arendell, 1995; Kruk, 1993; Wolchik, Fenaughty, & Braver, 1996) and childrearing (Braver & O'Connell, 1998; Fox,

1985; Fox & Blanton, 1995; Lund, 1987). Finally, unique to the postdivorce period, the father's relationship to his children, especially his financial support, is a matter for governmental and legal scrutiny and control.

There is substantial agreement in the literature that these issues, combined with the normal stresses of the end of the marital relationship, exact a heavy emotional toll on divorced fathers (Albrecht, 1980; Bloom, Asher, & White, 1978; Bloom & Caldwell, 1981; Chiraboga & Cutler, 1977; Price & McKenry, 1988; Riessman, 1990). In one early study, the suicide rate of recently divorced fathers was found to be greater than that of nondivorced fathers, as well as recently divorced mothers (Bloom et al., 1978). More recently, Umberson and Williams (1993) found that this psychological distress can be explained in large degree by the conflicts and role strains engendered by the confusion of the divorced fathering role. An additional, and well-verified, part of the distress is that it was generally the mother who wanted the marriage to end and initiated the divorce over the opposition of the father, oftentimes leaving the father confused by the divorce itself (Ahrons, 1994; Braver, Whitley, & Ng, 1993; Kitson & Holmes, 1992; Pettit & Bloom, 1984; Wallerstein & Blakeslee, 1989) Moreover, mothers' reported reasons for seeking the divorce were primarily because of inter-personal or emotional problems such as "differences in lifestyles or values" and "spouse not able or willing to meet my needs" rather than matters which involve more blameworthy behavior, such as domestic or substance abuse or adultery (Braver & O'Connell, 1998; Gigy & Kelly, 1992; Kitson, Babri, & Roach, 1985) and, in turn, they do so primarily because they are confident that they will win full custody of the children (Brinig & Allen, 2000).

As a result of these stresses, divorced fathers typically encounter great dis-locations and substantial difficulty in being effective parents. Research has focused on four dimensions of father parenting that impact the long-term well-being of their children: (a) frequency of father-child contact, (b) father-child relationship quality, (c) father's financial support, and (d) quality of postdivorce mother-father relations.

Frequency

The typical visitation clause of a divorce decree allows nonresidential fathers contact only on alternating weekends (Lamb, 1999), effectively setting a maximum legal limit on contact. As noted, however, older research (e.g., Amato, 1986; Fulton, 1979; Furstenburg & Nord, 1985; Hetherington, Cox, & Cox, 1982; Hetherington & Hagan, 1986) had shown discouragingly low levels of contact, well below that allowed by the decree, and far too many fathers disengaging completely. However, more current research (Braver, Wolchik, Sandler, Fogas, & Zvetina, 1991; Braver, Wolchik, Sandler, Sheets, et al., 1993; Bray & Berger, 1990; Maccoby, Depner, & Mnookin, 1988; Seltzer, 1991) has shown higher levels of contact, and Cooksey and Craig (1998) have shown this to be a cohort difference (i.e., current generations of divorced fathers visit more). Recent research (Fabricius & Hall, 2000) has also shown that both young adult children and their fathers reported that they had wished for more contact. More contact was precluded because the divorce decree conformed closely to the mothers' desires for more mother-child contact and, subsequently, less father-child contact.

Frequency of the father's contact alone has an inconsistent relationship to child well-being, with some studies showing positive outcomes for children (e.g., Guidubaldi et al., 1986; Hetherington, Cox, & Cox, 1978, 1982; Wallerstein & Kelly, 1980), but others showing no effect or even negative effects (Amato, 1993; Baydar & Brooks-Gunn, 1994; Furstenburg & Harris, 1993; Healy, Malley, & Stewart, 1990; King, 1994; Seltzer, 1994).

Quality

In contrast to the weak or inconsistent effects found for frequency of contact per se, quality of contact has more compelling effects on child well-being. In a meta-analysis of 63 published studies, Amato and Gilbreth (1999) found consistent positive effect sizes on children's well-being for fathers' authoritative parenting practices, such as limit setting, instrumental assistance, and talking about problems, and for fathers' emotional closeness to their children. For example, Simons, Whitbeck, and Beaman (1994) found that fathers who praised children's accomplishments and disciplined them for misbehavior had adolescents who were better adjusted. Similarly, Buchanan, Maccoby, and Dornbusch (1996) found that adolescents who had strong emotional ties with their nonresident fathers were better adjusted. Of course, strong emotional ties and effective authoritative parenting are precluded with insufficient contact; in effect, quantity provides opportunity for quality. But for many divorced fathers whose decrees permit ample contact, these visits are restricted to dinners in restaurants and recreational activities (Hetherington & Hagan, 1986; Stewart, 1999), which appear ineffective in benefiting their children.

Financial Support

In addition to emotional support, another obligation of postdivorce fathers is to provide financial support to the child. After divorce this support primarily takes the form of child support, a court-ordered arrangement mandating that a certain amount be paid by the noncustodial parent to the custodial parent in support of the child. However, evidence shows that many nonresidential fathers fail to financially support their children (Beller & Graham, 1993; Meyer, 1999; Pearson & Thoennes, 1986; Peterson & Nord, 1990; Sorensen, 1997; Teachman & Paasch, 1994). Several of the large national studies have also found that adequate payment of child support is related to better child outcomes, such as better grades and less school dropout (Argys, Peters, Brooks-Gunn, & Smith, 1998; Baydar & Brooks-Gunn, 1994; King, 1994; McLanahan & Sandefur, 1994; Seltzer, 1994). In a meta-analysis, Amato and Gilbreth (1999) showed that this relationship held up over all published studies. Some intriguing recent evidence found, however, that child support payment might be a proxy for fathers' demonstration of high concern about and regard for their children that is also transmitted in other ways. For example, child support that is voluntary or otherwise uncoerced is better for children because it conveys more concern and love than mandated or ordered child support (Argys et al., 1998; Hernandez, Beller, & Graham, 1995).

Interparental Conflict

While the previous three factors mentioned concerned the father's relationship and actions relevant to the child, the final dimension of father's impact is a bit less direct, but no less potent. It concerns the nonresidential father's relationship to the mother. Studies indicate that most divorcing couples with children tend to experience high levels of conflict immediately after the divorce (Fulton, 1979; Hetherington et al., 1982) and that high levels of conflict and hostility commonly persist for 3 years or more after the divorce is final (Ahrons & Wallisch, 1986; Masheter, 1991; Pearson & Thoennes, 1988). After that, the majority of couples appear to disengage from protracted conflict and instead go into a parallel parenting mode (Ahrons, 1994; King & Heard, 1999; Maccoby & Mnookin, 1992) or, more beneficially, become *coparental* (Ahrons, 1981; Arditti & Kelly, 1994; Whiteside, 1998). Perhaps 25%, however, persist in high conflict more or less indefinitely (Ahrons, 1994).

Data suggest that the effects of divorce on children are exacerbated by high levels of conflict between the parents of the divorced child (Amato & Rezac, 1994; Camara & Resnick, 1989; Emery, 1982) and meta-analyses have shown such conflict to be among the leading stressors for children of divorce and best predictors of child maladjustment (Amato & Keith, 1991a). Such findings are not surprising given the large and consistent body of research showing the association between conflict in married couples and the elevated risk for children (e.g., Cummings, 1998; Cummings, Ballard, & El-Sheikh, 1991; Cummings & Davies, 1994; Grych & Fincham, 1993). Particularly damaging to children is conflict between parents that the child witnesses. Conflict witnessed by children is associated with conduct problems, anxiety, and depression; between 9 and 25% of children's externalizing problems are accounted for by marital conflict (Cummings & Davies, 1994); this increased risk may result from decreased parenting efficacy (Krishnakumar & Buehler, 2000).

Interdependence of the Dimensions

Although the four foregoing dimensions of fathering have been discussed separately, they are empirically interdependent. For example, we have already noted that *frequency* of contact puts a ceiling on *quality* of contact. Fathers are unlikely to develop an authoritative relationship with their child, nor to maintain close emotional ties, if they visit too infrequently. Studies have also shown a strong correlation between visiting (both quality and frequency) and child support (Braver, Wolchik, Sandler, Sheets, et al., 1993; Furstenburg et al., 1983; Pearson & Thoennes, 1986; Peterson & Nord, 1990; Seltzer, 1991; Seltzer, Schaeffer, & Charng, 1989). Explanations of this latter finding have included the idea that paying is the causal factor (Weiss & Willis, 1985), since fathers who are forced to pay will want to look in on their investment; that visiting is the causal factor, because it induces an urge to shelter and financially enhance the child (Chambers, 1979; Tropf, 1984); and that some third variable accounts for the relationship between visiting and child support compliance. Seltzer et al. (1989) suggest the factor might be a sense of paternal responsibility, while Braver, Wolchik, Sandler, Sheets, et al. (1993) have presented evidence that it is a sense of perceived control over postdivorce issues that causes both visiting and paying.

Finally, there is an empirical link between each of the above dimensions and interparental conflict. For example, researchers have found correlations between post-divorce interparental conflict and the quality of children's relationships with nonresidential fathers. Conflict with the ex-spouse seems to account for significant variance in the amount (Ahrons, 1981; Hetherington, Cox, & Cox, 1976; Johnston, Kline, & Tschann, 1989; Koch & Lowery, 1984; Tschann et al., 1989) and quality of fathers' postseparation involvement with their children. One explanation for these findings is that postdivorce interparental conflict often involves child-rearing issues (Ahrons & Wallisch, 1986; Clingempeel, 1981), which may make children a direct target of parental anger or draw children into the conflict as intermediaries. Also, because interparental conflicts in the postdivorce period tend to focus on visitation arrangements and other child-related matters, these conflicts may be particularly threatening to child self-esteem and mental health (Kurdek, 1981; Wolchik, Braver, & Sandler, 1985).

The four dimensions may be linked in some as yet undiscovered causal sequence. For example, in the Tschann et al. (1989) study, the effect of conflict levels on child adjustment were mediated by the quality of parent-child relationships after the divorce. Each of the aforementioned dimensions has implications for child well-being, and fortunately their interconnectedness has encouraging implications for intervention. Plausibly, for example, an intervention attempting to enhance the postdivorce mother-father relationship might have salutary unintended benefits for the father-child relationship or for the payment of child support. While a more circumspect intervention strategy would be to try to impact each and every one of the dimensions independently, it is certainly plausible that an intervention targeting only one will have ramifying beneficial effects on the others. Also plausible is that a failed intervention effort to directly alter one dimension can nonetheless find success because another one of the correlated dimensions was successfully improved.

The voluntary component of child support compliance seems strongly related to the other three dimensions; however, it is also strongly related to fathers' income or employment (Peters, Argys, Maccoby, & Mnookin, 1993) and with new enforcement mechanisms, such as automatic wage withholding (Meyer, 1999), support is frequently paid nonvoluntarily. As a result, we focus instead on the two primary dimensions: the relationship with the child (which for future purposes subsumes both quantity and quality) and the relationship with the mother/ex-spouse.

■ Modifiable Potentiators of Nonresidential Fathering

The two primary dimensions of fathering outlined above, father-child relationships and father-mother relationships, are clearly the ones that can affect children's outcomes and should be investigated. Next, we need to understand what contributes to variation in those two dimensions. What is it about some fathers and families that leads fathering to be both frequent and effective and relationships with the mother to be coparental and cooperative, while other fathers have disengaged or have consistently hostile relationships with the mothers, to the child's detriment? Again, we have exclusive interest in the aspects of fathers' postdivorce relations, whether moderators or mediators, that are *modifiable* by interventions and beneficial to children.

There has now accumulated an appreciable empirical literature that investigates correlates of how well fathers visit and pay child support, how satisfied or outraged they are by the new postdivorce arrangements, and how much conflict versus cooperation characterizes their relationships with their ex-wives. Several authors (e.g., Arendell, 1995; Kruk, 1992) have conducted primarily qualitative or ethnographic investigations, while others (e.g., Braver, Wolchik, Sandler, Sheets, et al., 1993; Leite & McKenry, 2002; Rettig, Leichtentritt, & Stanton, 1999) have used quantitative methodologies with either regional or national data sets. Before attempting to summarize this literature to derive a set of modifiable potentiators, we describe the work that has attempted to synthesize these factors into *theories* of father-child relationships.

■ Theories of Postdivorce Fathering

Interactionist-Feminist Theory

Arendell (1992a, 1992b, 1994, 1995) adopts an interactionist-feminist vantage point in interpreting results from her qualitative study of 75 recently divorced nonresident fathers. The dominant theme she recorded was one of fathers' rage at the legal system and at their ex-wives. The large majority of her interviewees experienced "injustice, discrimination, resistance, and frustration and discontent." Most of these, "passionately committed to resisting perceived oppression . . . had very limited, if any, relationships with their children" (1995, pp. 16, 17). Generally unsympathetic to their plight, however, Arendell dismissed their complaints as "masculinist discourse" and just "rhetoric."

Family Systems Theory

Arditti and Kelly (1994) formulated a family systems perspective, which focused on fathers' interdependence in their relationship with their ex-wives. They found that fathers whose relationships with their ex-wives were closer and involved less conflict had better relationships with their children. An important factor, reminiscent of Arendell's findings, was satisfaction with custody and visitation arrangements. Those who felt these matters were unjust and unsatisfactory had poorer relationships both with their children and their ex-wives (cf. Madden-Derdich & Leonard, 2000, 2002).

Role-Identity Theory

Ihinger-Tallman, Pasley, and Buehler (1993) developed a "midrange" role-identity theory, in which the principle theoretical predictor of father involvement and child well-being was posited to be father's parenting role identity. However, the effect of this role identity was theorized to be moderated by a number of factors, including the coparental relationship, mother's views of his parenting, his emotional well-being, and the encouragement he received from others to engage in parenting. The theorists empirically tested the postulates of the theory, as did Minton and Pasley (1996) and Stone and McKenry (1998). All found support for the theory, but, like previous theorists, Stone and McKenry also found dissatisfaction with the legal system and the custody and visitation arrangements to detract from how well father role identity predicted involvement.

Role-Enactment Theory

Based on the preceding finding, Leite and McKenry (2002) reformulated the above theory into role-enactment theory, in which role satisfaction and "institutional role clarity" (involving clearly specified legal arrangements for custody and visitation) were added as predictors. They tested their model with the National Survey of Families and Households national data set (Sweet & Bumpass, 1996). Consistent with the theoretical assumptions, fathers' low involvement with their children was related to ongoing conflict with the mother, to greater geographic distance from children, and to a lack of clarity about how they should behave in their parenting role.

Resource Theory

Rettig et al. (1999) used Foa and Foa's (1980) resource theory as the basis of their model. According to this notion, people exchange resources through give and take between individuals. Behaviors and satisfaction, as a result, are a function of how these resource exchanges flow between partners. Involvement with children was thus theorized to be related to the father's own perceived economic and social psychological well-being, his communication with the mother during coparenting, and their degree of conflict. Results supported the theory.

Social Exchange Theory

Braver, Wolchik, Sandler, and Sheets (1993) formulated a theory closely related to resource theory, social exchange theory. The fundamental notion is that in deciding how much of an investment to make in a specific relationship, such as the father's relationship to the child, one implicitly calculates the rewards of that relationship in comparison to its costs. The more positive the reward-cost ratio, the more invested in the relationship the individual will be. Potential rewards to the father include the father's idea that his relationship is valuable to the child, his commitment to the fathering role, and supports he receives for the relationship from significant others. Costs include conflict with the ex-spouse, awkward or disturbing visits, dissatisfaction with the divorce arrangements, and his perceived lack of control over the postdivorce relationship with the child. The model was strongly supported in longitudinal analyses by Braver, Wolchik, Sandler, Sheets, et al. (1993).

■   Synthesizing the Findings to Spotlight Modifiable
     Potentiators of the Dimensions of Fathering

Tests of the above theories, as well as less theoretical, more exploratory empirical
investigations by Dudley (1991a, 1991b, 1991c, 1996), Kruk (1991a, 1991b, 1992, 1993),
Arditti (1990, 1991, 1992a, 1992b; Arditti & Allen, 1993; Arditti & Keith, 1993), Hoffman
(1995), McKenry (McKenry, McKelvey, Leigh, & Wark, 1996; McKenry, Price, Fine, &
Serovich, 1992), and others, have yielded information about a number of variables
significantly related to enhanced fathering (i.e., father-child and father-mother relationships) across several studies. Several of the factors that have predicted father
involvement and effectiveness are not ready candidate variables for interventions,
however. For example, having substantial economic or educational resources emerges
as a predictor of positive involvement in several studies (e.g., Rettig et al., 1999; Stone &
McKenry, 1998), but such factors are not readily modified or improved by any
plausible intervention. Other variables in this category include geographic barriers,
emotional health, and having obtained favorable custody and visitation arrangements,
or at least being satisfied with the arrangements one has. On the other hand, the
following factors that *are* plausibly modifiable by an intervention have been related to
better fathering and greater child well-being consistently across studies: a strong
fathering role identity or strong commitment to the fathering role; an authoritative
parenting orientation; an understanding of how to effectively parent in nonresidential
mode; cooperation versus conflict with the ex-spouse; support from the ex-spouse for
continued involvement with the child; and support for continued involvement with
the child from important others. We slightly recategorize these as follows.

Commitment to the Parental Role

Many studies have indicated that level of commitment to the role of parent is a strong
predictor of level of father involvement with his children after divorce (e.g., Ihinger-
Tallman et al., 1993; Minton & Pasley, 1996; Rosenthal & Keshet, 1981; Stone & McKenry,
1998; Tepp, 1983). For example, Tepp (1983) found that a sense of responsibility to the
children was significantly correlated with amount of visitation. Data also indicate that
fathers' withdrawal from their children tends to occur gradually, as they feel increasingly
unimportant or unrewarded for their efforts (Fulton, 1979; Furstenberg & Nord, 1985).
Most fathers initially feel a reasonably high level of interest in contact with their children
(Hetherington et al., 1978; Kruk, 1992), but this level sometimes decreases because of
inadequate coping with the difficulties of visitation, such as hampered or difficult
visitation arrangements, escalated child misbehavior, or conflict with the ex-spouse
(Braver et al., 1991; Wolchik et al., 1996). As a coping response, a father may decide to
sacrifice his relationship with the children, without fully considering the implications of
this choice. Thus, we hypothesize that any process of withdrawal from the commitment
to the parenting role may be interrupted by an intervention that presents factual
information on the importance of a positive father-child relationship to children's well-
being and an emotional appeal which vividly demonstrates children's emotional vulnerability and need for paternal support.

Skills for Nonresidential Parenting

Many divorced fathers complain about the difficulty of parenting as an infrequent and nonprimary parent. However, the literature is clear (Amato & Gilbreth, 1999) that positive child outcomes accrue with a warm and authoritative nonresidential parenting style. Two decades of research have also shown that both parental warmth and effectiveness in limit setting can be enhanced by parenting skills training interventions, which aim at emphasizing communication skills and the use of positive reinforcement and noncoercive limit setting (e.g., appropriate commands, logical consequences, and time out from reinforcement) (Baum & Forehand, 1981; Patterson, Chamberlin, & Reid, 1982; Spaccarelli, Cotler, & Penman, 1992). Also, because parenting skill and effectiveness are influenced by stressful events in parents' lives, many parent training programs have been specifically geared to parents who have recently experienced a stressor such as spouse death (Sandler et al., 1992). Wolchik et al. (1993, 2002) and Bullock and Forgatch (ch. 14 in this volume) taught parenting skills to recently divorced custodial mothers and find that these skills can be significantly improved through preventive intervention and that they are important mediators of adjustment for children of divorce, yielding remarkable improvements in child outcomes even 6 years later (Wolchik et al., 2002).

Unfortunately, most of the research on parenting programs has excluded fathers. Coplin and Houts (1991) reviewed 35 studies on behavioral parent training published between 1981 and 1988 and found that only 13 included any fathers as subjects. One notable exception is the work of Webster-Stratton and colleagues, in which parents with conduct-disordered children were trained in a variety of parenting skills through videotape modeling (Webster-Stratton, Kolpacoff, & Hollinsworth, 1988). These investigators have found that fathering skills (measured via home observational data) were significantly improved by the videotape modeling program in combination with therapist-led group discussion and also by a self-administered version of the videotape program (Webster-Stratton, Hollinsworth, & Kolpacoff, 1989; Webster-Stratton et al., 1988). Thus we hypothesize that an intervention that teaches parenting skills and tailors them to the demands and constraints of the nonresidential parent situation can successfully overcome the obstacles to nonresidential parenting and both keep fathers involved and increase the child's well-being.

Fathers' Motivation and Skills for Conflict Management With the Ex-Spouse

Perhaps the most consistent yet multifaceted factor found in the literature to be related to fathering after divorce is the relationship with the ex-spouse. A conflictual relationship is deleterious to all three parties, yet ramifies into myriad domains (Wolchik et al., 1996). For example, the conflict level is strongly related to whether the mother supports the father's continued involvement (Arditti, 1992b; Kruk, 1993; Seltzer, 1994). And, as Braver and O'Connell (1998) put it, "The most important pathway [to father involvement] is having an ex-wife who desires the father to be connected to the child, who supports and encourages his involvement, as compared to one who wants the father altogether out of the way" (p. 175). Thus an extremely important modifiable potentiator to target for an intervention is motivation and skill to reduce or manage conflict with the child's mother.

Despite its potential importance, there is little in the literature that offers encouragement that this can be successfully accomplished. Several projects proposed a more modest goal, teaching fathers to "keep the child out of the war zone," that is, not to argue with their ex-spouses when children are present (Kurkowski, Gordon, & Arbuthnot, 1993; Wolchik et al., 1993). This theoretically can be accomplished by providing vivid illustrations of the effect of conflict on children of divorce. However, there have been no successful attempts we are aware of in the literature to actually decrease overall levels of postdivorce conflict and promote better coparenting. A promising candidate approach is the stress inoculation training approach (Meichenbaum, 1975), which helps people accomplish goals even while experiencing stress, for example, when a father feels provoked by the ex-wife. This approach teaches parents to better understand and manage situations that prompt intense anger (Moon & Eisler, 1983; Novaco, 1977). Anger management skills training based on the stress inoculation model focuses the trainee on (a) increasing awareness of personal anger process (e.g., identification of specific situations, thoughts, and cues that initiate and maintain the response), (b) identifying, challenging, and modifying irrational thoughts (using thought stopping and self-talk) that lead to loss of control, and (c) learning alternative coping strategies, such as relaxation, assertiveness, and problem solving. It has been shown that this approach can even be effective with men at high risk for domestic violence (Deschner & McNeil, 1986).

Fathers' Perceived Control Over the Divorce Process

Finally, we believe an intervention to promote better nonresidential fathering should target countering their sense of helplessness and powerlessness noted by so many researchers (Arditti, 1992a, 1992b; Arditti & Allen, 1993; Arditti & Kelly, 1994; Arendell, 1995; Kruk, 1992; Umberson & Williams, 1993). Increasing perceptions of control, we hypothesize, will tend both to increase quality of involvement with the children and to decrease interparental conflict. Studies indicate that fathers' perceptions of control over family issues are affected by the divorce settlement and/ or its implementation (e.g., visitation arrangements, child-rearing decisions) and are strongly related to their level of postdivorce involvement with the children, by far the strongest predictor of the 27 Braver, Wolchik, Sandler, Sheets, et al. (1993) studied. Father's perceived control was also an important predictor of the level of postdivorce conflict between parents (Bay & Braver, 1990). This finding suggests that fathers who believe they have little control over postdivorce family life may also be angrier and have greater difficulty getting along with the ex-spouse. Furthermore, if these fathers believe that visitation will inevitably result in negative interactions with the ex-wife, one coping choice would be to skip visitation and thereby sacrifice their relationship with the children. These effects of perceived control theoretically provide an important focus for intervening with fathers to reduce interparental conflict. Instilling a sense of control in the father may also reduce general postmarital distress, resulting in less interparental conflict.

One way to attempt to counter the powerlessness often experienced by noncustodial parents is by focusing on those areas in which they do in fact exert substantial control. Specifically, we hypothesize that it is important to teach fathers that they have ample opportunity to impact the child's life while the child is in their care on visits. In addition, if the father masters an interpersonal encounter with his ex-wife by using conflict management skills in his repertoire instead of giving in to the impulse to show anger or escalate, he has demonstrated a great deal of control. One could also focus on perceptions of secondary, as well as primary, control (Rothbaum, Weisz, & Snyder, 1982). Primary control reflects action by an individual used to gain control over the environment in order to be consistent with wishes or desires, whereas secondary control reflects attempts by the individual to recognize and mentally adjust to environmental events or situations over which they have no or limited control. In effect, secondary control, while appearing passive, allows the individual to cope with an uncontrollable situation. Recent work has shown that individuals can be taught how to adjust to and recognize the difference between those events in which action can or should be taken and those events or situations that are undesirable and nonmalleable (e.g., decisions or prejudices of judges), yet can be understood and mastered via secondary control processes (Reich & Zautra, 1990).

■ Designing an Intervention to Impact These Modifiable Potentiators: Dads for Life

We developed an intervention program that targeted the above four modifiable potentiators. With the aid of a 5-year NIMH grant, we designed a program for nonresidential fathers with the goal of benefiting children's well-being by promoting better nonresidential father behaviors. Our program, Dads for Life (DFL), consisted of 10 sessions in all, 8 group sessions of 1 hr and 45 min, occurring weekly, in the evening, and 2 individual sessions of 45 min each. The material presented and the method of group leadership were heavily scripted and manualized for ease of export. The core of each group session was specially developed videotaped material of about 10 min each, using professional child and adult actors. The videotape, called *Eight Short Films About Divorced Fathers*, was emotionally and dramatically powerful, yet didactically sound. Literature has shown videotape to be an efficacious change modality (Golub, Espinosa, Damon, & Card, 1987; Mayadas & Duehn, 1977; O'Dell, Krug, Patterson, & Faustman, 1980; O'Dell et al., 1982; Webster-Stratton, 1984). In general, the videotapes were used by the group leader to either introduce a topic or reiterate it through a different medium. For most skills, two-person vignettes modeled one incorrect and one correct example of the skill being utilized in common postdivorce situations faced by nonresidential fathers. All the videotapes were constructed with special attention to the needs of ethnic minority families, both in terms of the ethnicity and race of the actors and also in terms of the cultural context of the issues. For example, in one video in which the Latino parents were fighting, the issues about which the fight occurred were appropriate for the Latin culture and the actors reverted to yelling in Spanish.

Table 12.1 contains a summary of session contents. The first session provides a program overview and reviews normal processes that are associated with divorce (normalizing). Considerable attention is given to motivating fathers to maintain regular attendance in the program. It also focuses on the two modifiable potentiators of increasing commitment to the parenting role and enhancing parenting skills (encouraging the fathers to introduce special family time and one-on-one time as strategies for building a relationship between fathers and their children). The videotape accomplishes the former goal by presenting information on fathers' impact on children both by summarizing research findings and expert opinions about the effects of father absence on children and by having children share feelings about visitation (e.g., fears of losing dad, sensitivity to missed visitations) which emphasize their emotional attachment to father. Sessions 2 and 3 are devoted to the modifiable potentiator of enhanced parenting skills. Session 2 works on listening and communication skills, such as being ready and open to the child's attempt to communicate, while session 3 works on discipline strategies. The

TABLE 12.1   *Dads for Life Program*

Meetings	Activities
1: Remodeling Your Life	Film: *Being There* ☐ Introduction ☐ Effects of divorce on children and fathers ☐ Special family time ☐ One-on-one time
2: Catching Your Kids' Messages	Film: *Field of Dreams* ☐ Listening
3: Checking Kids' Messages and Getting Clear on Yours	Film: *Careful, He Might Hear You* ☐ Listening ☐ Discipline—part I
4: Keeping Kids Out of the War Zone	Film: *Shot Through the Heart* ☐ Conflict—part I ☐ Self-control
5: Reducing Conflict	Film: *Blue in the Face* ☐ Conflict—part II ☐ Engagement and de-escalation
6: Following Through on Discipline	Film: *Five Easy Pieces* ☐ Discipline—part II
7: Magic and Romance	Film: *Fear of Flying* ☐ Problem solving ☐ Dating and relationships
8: Looking Back, Looking Ahead	Film: *In the Middle of the Night in a Dark House Somewhere in the World*

videotapes of session 2 model giving reassurance, using active listening, etc., while those of session 3 model clear communication of behavioral expectations. Sessions 4 and 5 deal with the two modifiable potentiators of building the motivation and skills for conflict management and enhancing perceived control. Session 4 focuses initially on the consequences of conflict on the child, and then the fathers are taught the importance of keeping the kids out of the war zone. The remainder of session 4 is devoted to emphasizing self-control and controlling high-risk topics and situations. Session 5 again focuses on self-control and then teaches very specific engagement skills for deescalating conflict with the ex-wife. Videotaped vignettes on control show how, by assuming control over the situation, both the father and the child will have better adjustment. Other material teaches the concept of secondary control, i.e., mentally adjusting to events over which they have limited control (Rothbaum et al., 1982). Videotape scenes on conflict management illustrate the specific skills for anger control (Anderson, Fodor, & Alpert, 1976). In short, sessions 4 and 5 consists of a series of exercises that teach each father to refrain from enacting behaviors that would otherwise escalate the conflict and to minimize the behaviors his ex-wife may be expecting that increase animosity. Specifically, we got fathers to show attending behaviors (e.g., looking), reduce contemptuous behaviors (e.g., eye roll), and in general, acknowledge the issue being discussed. Notice that we were not trying to get a father to change his ex-wife's behavior, nor did we ask him to do something radically different. Instead we requested a few simple attending behaviors, and we asked that he give her views a respectful hearing. Preliminary data from our pilot studies indicate that these were behaviors that, if not performed, seem to instigate animosity and negative behavior cycles during interactions (Braver & Griffin, 2000). Session 6 returns to the modifiable potentiator of parenting skills, primarily working with effective discipline techniques such as positive reinforcement. The videotaped segments teach limit setting, imposing consequences, etc. Session 7 returns to the modifiable potentiator of building commitment to the parenting role. Specifically addressed here are manifestations of that commitment, such as maintaining child support payments and maintaining a consistent visitation pattern. The videotaped segments describe the importance of the father's visits from the child's perspective. The final session addresses maintenance of acquired skills and problem solving. Also covered is where to acquire additional information about parenting, especially handling developmental changes. We provide fathers with extensive reference material covering the divorce process and material about local (Phoenix area) educational and recreational facilities for children.

Each session was accompanied by homework assignments and considerable practice at skill acquisition. Each group session consisted of didactic teaching, group discussions and role playing.

Individual Sessions

Two individual sessions were also scheduled, at weeks 3 and 6. One of these dealt with the relationship with the ex-wife and the other with the parent-child dyad. In the individual sessions, the fathers were helped to develop individualized strategies for ensuring that they would succeed in implementing program skills in their particular family situations (Lambermon & van Ijzendoorn, 1989). Leaders helped problem solve to remove obstacles to the appropriate use of program material.

Group Leaders

The group sessions were led by a team of one male and one female master's-level counselor. Leaders participated in ten 3-hr training sessions prior to beginning and had weekly supervision meetings led by an experienced doctoral-level clinician.

■ Evaluating Dads for Life

In order to evaluate the preventive effect of DFL on children of divorce, an experimental evaluation was conducted, with fathers being assigned at random either into DFL or a self-study control condition. Evaluation involved standardized assessments of children's behavior problems, using father, mother, child, and teacher reports at pretest and three follow-up waves: an immediate posttest, a 4 month follow-up (chosen based on our estimates about how long it would take any changes in a father's behavior to affect or be recognizable to a mother and child), and a 1-year follow-up. Primary participants were 214 recently divorced fathers, 127 in DFL, 87 in control. In addition, evaluation data were obtained from the ex-wives of these men, as well as from one child (the "target" child) and the child's teacher, when the child was of school age. Potential participants were identified through public court divorce records, including computerized child support files. Initial eligibility requirements included that the couple's legal divorce was between 4 and 10 months previously, that they had at least one child between the ages of 4 and 12, that the mother had primary physical custody, and that both parents continued to reside in the geographic area. Fathers we were successful in contacting by phone were informed of the potential benefits of participation, but were cautioned to decline participation unless they could commit to complete whichever of the two conditions randomness (an actual lottery) dictated. Forty-seven percent agreed to participate in either DFL or the home study control condition (see below) and to accept random assignment to either. Families were told in advance about the follow-up assessments and tentatively volunteered to participate in these as well. The assignment to condition was achieved at the orientation; the father himself drew the lot that assigned his condition, a procedure designed to improve commitment and decrease attrition (Wortman, Hendricks, & Hillis, 1976).

In addition to the self-report measures we also collected observational data that included a problem-solving task involving the ex-spouses and a father-child task. Of the 214 families, a subsample of couples agreed (27 DFL and 16 control) to be videotaped while having a 15-min problem-solving discussion about postdivorce child-rearing and scheduling problems. Dyadic interactions were assessed across the four waves of data collection. For each interaction we coded Verbal Negative, Problem Solution, Verbal Agree, Back Channel, Head Nod, Eye Gaze, and Eye Roll using a variant of the MICSEASE coding system (Griffin, Greene, & Decker-Haas, 2004). As part of the observation assessment, each member of the dyad provided a real-time rating of his or her affect during the interaction (see Griffin, 1993, for details). This allows us to combine the traditional observation codes with an internal affect reference in assessing the quality and structure of postdivorce dyadic interactions.

Self-Study Placebo Control Group

Fathers assigned at random to this condition, which we described for them as the "home version" of DFL, received by mail a copy of what we deemed the best self-help books available at the time,* *Divorced Fathers: Reconstructing a Quality Life* (Oakland, 1984) and *Divorced Dad Dilemma* (Mayer, 1994). These books offer practical advice to divorced fathers on four major areas, including (a) personal life adjustment, (b) improvement of existing relationships with children, (c) establishment of a separate home, and (d) constructive methods for handling legal matters connected with divorce.

■ Preliminary Results of the DFL Randomized Trial

We report here preliminary results on the child adjustment measures and some of the modifiable potentiators as assessed only on mothers and fathers (i.e., we do not report on teacher or child report outcomes). Since we wished in the analysis to look for patterns over the posttest waves, the analysis needed to allow examination of trends over these periods. Furthermore, since similar prevention programs (e.g., Wolchik et al., 2000, 2002) have disclosed that the impact of the treatment often depends on the level of difficulties the child displays at pretest, we needed to choose an analysis that had the capability to detect "baseline by treatment" interactions. That is, we wished to be able to recognize whether the differences between DFL and control effects were different depending on the levels of initial (pretest) problems. These data-analytic considerations led us to the random coefficient analysis or "mixed model" (programmed on SAS PROC MIXED).

We found such a significant baseline by treatment interaction for both mother's and father's report of child internalizing problems, as well as for mother's report of total problems on the Child Behavior Checklist (Achenbach, 1991). For each dependent variable, graphs disclosed that children in the DFL condition had fewer such problems than control children, but this occurred primarily for children who were initially more troubled. We also found that families in the DFL condition had less interparental conflict (according to father's report; again the impact of DFL was most pronounced for families who were initially highly conflicted) and were more

---

*Several books we regard as superior have subsequently been published (Bernstein, Worth, & Worth, 1997; Brott, 1999; Condrell & Small, 1998; Feuer, 1997; Klatte, 1999; Knox & Leggett, 1998; McClure & Saffer, 2000; Prengel & Yale, 1999; Wasson & Hefner, 2002).

coparental, according to mother's report (Braver, Griffin, Cookston, Sandler, & Williams, 2001).

A subset of the couples also interacted live for behavioral observation. Initial analyses of the affect rating data taken from this interaction task clearly show that dyads containing a father who had been assigned to the DFL group reported significantly higher (positive) affect than those couples containing a control group father. Using a PROC MIXED procedure, and using the Pre-test affect rating as a covariate, these significant group differences were sustained through Wave 4 (Griffin, Braver, & Cookston, 2003).

■ Conclusions and an Agenda for the Future

In sum, preliminary results with DFL are encouraging. We had hoped to secure better outcomes for children of divorce by advancing the parenting characteristics of their nonresidential father. Preliminary indications are that we were successful, primarily by impacting the relationship between father and mother.

Of course, we need to continue our analyses, adding reports by the children and teachers, and we need to probe and refine our understanding of which of the modifiable potentiators are responsible for our effects. But assuming that more conclusive analyses support our preliminary ones, how does DFL compare to other actual or potential programs for this population? While there is some anecdotal indication that other programs for nonresidential fathers exist, spurred by the support of The Fatherhood Initiative funding, only two others are in the published literature, and neither has impressive empirical support. Devlin, Brown, Beebe, and Parulis (1992) have developed an intervention which addresses unique parenting issues faced by divorced fathers. The only significant effect found for the Devlin et al. (1992) intervention was a tendency to increase fathers' sense of competence in the parenting role; however, methodological weaknesses make it difficult to draw conclusions as to the effectiveness of this program in changing fathers' behaviors. The study did not employ random assignment to conditions or use observational measures of fathering behavior, and it involved a small sample with substantial opportunity for self-selection biases. Similarly, Hall and Kelly (1996) discuss a "counseling group" for nonresidential fathers that has content and structure similar to those of DFL; no evaluation of the program is described.

What should be the future research agenda to promote better fathering among divorced nonresident fathers? What are the advances in knowledge concerning nonresidential divorced fathers we will need in the coming years to expand our understanding and to improve outcomes for children? We begin by specifying a potential agenda that we *do not* see as helpful.

Although coming from a variety of theoretical and ideological traditions, there is remarkable uniformity in the findings of most researchers. The same issues, variables, and predictors surface from study to study; thus there is considerable consensus about what the important variables are. The theories are similar and complementary enough that the results in support of one theory can also largely be regarded as simultaneously supporting the others. Accordingly, we do not see additional theoretical development or clarification as being a priority for subsequent research. Analogously, we do not see it as useful to attempt to empirically support one theory at the expense of another, to develop critical tests between them, nor even to attempt to make distinctions at a purely theoretical or conceptual level. Moreover, because of considerable replication of findings concerning predictors, we would not assign priority to additional psychosocial nonintervention research, the kind that would give program developers more ideas about what variables are the important ones to attempt to change to reap positive benefits for children and parents; we believe we already know what variables are critical.

Instead, we recommend the following areas as the focus for additional research. First, the *causal relationship* among these variables is still very open to question and is a priority for future research to untangle. An excellent example is the causal primacy of the conflictual relationship between the parents, identified as crucial by so many of the studies. Are parents in conflict because of residual anger concerning the marital break-up, because they disagree about parenting, because fathers visit too much or too little, because of child support, etc., or are the causal relationships the reverse? Since almost all the studies in the literature are cross-sectional correlational studies, all of these and more remain plausible interpretations of the results, whatever the theoretical preferences of the investigators or whether analytic techniques such as path analysis (which are sometimes wrongly concluded to imply causality) are used. More cross-sectional correlational studies, no matter how carefully designed and executed, cannot presume to clarify these matters and thus should be given lower priority. In contrast, both longitudinal studies and experimental designs can dissect the processes to illuminate the causal sequences and should be preferred. While a few longitudinal studies were among those reviewed above, and while they clearly offer more promise than cross-sectional correlational investigations in untangling causal linkages, they only do so conclusively if the timing of the study waves matches well with the "causal lags" (McCleary & Welsh, 1992). That is, only if the longitudinal researchers were perspicacious or fortunate enough to time a study wave shortly after the next causal microprocess has taken effect, and only if there were limited causal circularity, would one be able to properly infer the causal chain with analyses.

Here is where the enormous advantage of experimental investigations may be leveraged. An experimental study in which the investigator is successful at reducing (for example) interparental conflict on a randomly selected portion of the sample is able more adeptly and conclusively to trace the causal impact of that reduced conflict on the remaining variables. Thus, for this reason especially, as well as to improve the outcomes for divorced families, we call for more experimental studies of fathering in divorced families (cf. Sandler, Wolchik, Davis, Hainer, & Ayers, 2003).

Second, while it is quite clear *what variables* to attempt to change, it is far less clear how, exactly, to change them. Again, conflict between the parents is a clear example. Many specialists in parenting have observed that if we could only make (married or divorced) parents get along better, their children would do better (not to mention the parents themselves). However, it is far more difficult to find an effective intervention technique for ameliorating conflict than to recognize that we need one. This is even more obvious with divorced families, who have less motivation to stifle conflict than still-married ones and for whom their quite distinct and rival interests and their bout with the adversarial legal system, in addition to whatever relationship factors and events drove them to dissolve their marriage, contribute to conflict levels. Thus, finding an intervention that shows significant evidence of reducing interparental conflict is rare in the literature (Goodman, Bonds, Sandler, & Braver, 2004), though we were apparently quite successful in doing so with DFL. Research that searches for and finds more powerful and consistent change techniques for any of the modifiable potentiators should be high on the agenda.

Third, future research can address the wisdom of separately developing or needing or integrating programs for divorced *mothers,* for divorced *fathers,* and for their *children.* If we successfully intervene with one party, is there potential benefit in also intervening with either or both of the other two family members? If so, to what degree do the separate interventions need to be coordinated and/or integrated? There are hints in data analyzed by me and my colleagues that there will be incremental benefits to intervening with both mother and father, but not also with their children, and only *in some but not all cases.* This important but complicated question needs more research attention, as does the question of *how does one know* when each intervention component is needed or preferred.

Finally, a critical, formidable but familiar issue for family psychology more generally is how to incorporate DFL or similar research-based programs into regular practice (Rotheram-Borus & Duan, 2003). Transporting interventions that have been shown to be efficacious in rigorous studies into the community for widespread deployment is one of the most vexing and recurring yet unsolved and even unapproached problems in psychology. It is also one of the highest priorities of the NIMH research agenda (Lamb, Greenlick, & McCarty, 1998; National Advisory Mental Health Council, 1998, 2001). A promising avenue for interventions with divorced families is to partner with family courts for dissemination of their programs (Braver, Hipke, Ellman, & Sandler, 2004). Courts can readily identify all divorcing families and have very substantial authority over them, far more so than courts have over other law-abiding citizens. Family courts have also quite recently begun supplementing their traditional roles as adjudicators by greatly expanding their social service and education roles (Blaisure & Geasler, 1996; Geasler & Blaisure, 1999). Moreover, surveys have shown that family courts are interested in expanding their programming of the DFL type of program (Arbuthnot, 2002; Cookston, Braver, Sandler, & Genalo, 2002). Whether one can successfully embed DFL or similar programs within a court system, and if so, how to do so while preserving both the efficacy of the intervention and the family's legal rights are tricky but crucial dissemination problems that remain to be solved. In this context, it is obvious that special attention needs to be paid to the appropriateness of any intervention for the various cultural and ethnic groups that come under the court's authority. It would be wise for programs to face this contingency early, in the program development stage, as did DFL, and to continually evaluate whether modifications are needed to preserve the cultural competence.

◼ References

Achenbach, T. M. (1991). *Manual for the child behavior checklist/4-18 and 1991 profile.* Burlington: University of Vermont, Department of Psychiatry.

Ahrons, C. (1994). *The good divorce: Keeping your family together when your marriage comes apart.* New York: Harper Collins.

Ahrons, C. R. (1981). The continuing coparental relationship between divorced spouses. *American Journal of Orthopsychiatry, 51,* 415–428.

Ahrons, C. R., & Wallisch, L. (1986). The relationship between spouses. In S. Duck & D. Pearlman (Eds.), *Close relationships: Development, dynamics and deterioration.* Beverly Hills, CA: Sage.

Albrecht, S. L. (1980). Reactions and adjustment to divorce: Differences in the experiences of males and females. *Family Relations, 29,* 59–68.

Amato, P. R. (1986). Marital conflict, the parent-child relationship and child self-esteem. *Family Relations, 35,* 403–410.

Amato, P. R. (1993). Children's adjustment to divorce: Theories, hypotheses, and empirical support. *Journal of Marriage and Family, 55*(1), 23–39.

Amato, P. R. (2000). The consequences of divorce for adults and children. *Journal of Marriage and the Family, 62,* 1269–1287.

Amato, P. R. (2001). Children of divorce in the 1990s: an update of the Amato and Keith (1991) meta-analysis. *Journal of Family Psychology, 15,* 355–370.

Amato, P. R. (2003). Reconciling divergent perspectives: Judith Wallerstein, quantitative family research, and children of divorce. *Family Relations: Interdisciplinary Journal of Applied Family Studies, 52*(4), 332–339.

Amato, P. R., & Gilbreth, J. G. (1999). Nonresident fathers and children's well-being: A meta-analysis. *Journal of Marriage and the Family, 61*(3), 557–573.

Amato, P. R., & Keith, B. (1991a). Consequences of parental divorce for the well-being of children: A meta-analysis. *Psychological Bulletin, 110,* 26–46.

Amato, P. R., & Keith, B. (1991b). Parental divorce and adult well-being: A meta-analysis. *Journal of Marriage and the Family, 53,* 43–58.

Amato, P. R., & Rezac, S. J. (1994). Contact with nonresidential parents, interparental conflict, and children's behavior. *Journal of Family Issues, 15*(2), 191–207.

Anderson, L., Fodor, I., & Alpert, M. (1976). A comparison of methods for training self-control. *Behavior Therapy, 7,* 649–658.

Arbuthnot, J. (2002). A call unheeded: Courts' perceived obstacles to establishing divorce education programs. *Family Court Review, 40,* 371–382.

Arditti, J. A. (1990). Noncustodial fathers: An overview of policy and resources. *Family Relations, 39*(4), 460–468.

Arditti, J. A. (1991). Child support non compliance and divorced fathers: Rethinking the role of paternal involvement. *Journal of Divorce and Remarriage, 14,* 107–119.

Arditti, J. A. (1992a). Differences between fathers with joint custody and noncustodial fathers. *American Journal of Orthopsychiatry, 62*(2), 186–195.

Arditti, J. A. (1992b). Factors related to custody, visitation, and child support for divorced fathers: An exploratory analysis. *Journal of Divorce and Remarriage, 17,* 23–42.

Arditti, J. A., & Allen, K. R. (1993). Understanding distressed fathers' perceptions of legal and relational inequities post divorce. *Family and Conciliation Court Review, 31*(4), 461–476.

Arditti, J. A., & Keith, T. Z. (1993). Visitation frequency, child support payment, and the father-child relationship postdivorce. *Journal of Marriage and the Family, 55*(3), 699–712.

Arditti, J. A., & Kelly, M. (1994). Fathers' perspectives of their co-parental relationships postdivorce: Implications for family practice and legal reform. *Family Relations, 43*, 61–67.

Arendell, T. (1992a). Father absence: Investigations into divorce. *Gender and Society, 6*, 562–586.

Arendell, T. (1992b). Social self as gendered: A masculinist discourse of divorce. *Symbolic Interaction, 5*(2), 151–181.

Arendell, T. (1994). Divorce: It's a gender issue. *Family Advocate, 17*(1), 30–34.

Arendell, T. (1995). *Fathers and divorce.* Thousand Oaks, CA: Sage.

Argys, L. M., Peters, H. E., Brooks-Gunn, J., & Smith, J. R. (1998). The impact of child support on cognitive outcomes of young children. *Demography, 35*, 159–172.

Baum, C. G., & Forehand, R. (1981). Long-term follow-up assessment of parent training by use of multiple outcome measures. *Behavior Therapy, 12*, 643–655.

Bay, R. C., & Braver, S. L. (1990). Perceived control of the divorce settlement process and interparental conflict. *Family Relations, 40*, 180–185.

Baydar, N., & Brooks-Gunn, J. (1994). The dynamics of child support and its consequences for children. In I. M. Garfinkel, S. S. McLanahan, & P. K. Robins (Eds.), *Child support and child well being* (pp. 257–279). Washington, DC: Urban Institute.

Beller, A.H., & Graham, J.W. (1993). *Small change: the economics of child support.* New Haven, CT: Yale University Press.

Bernstein, R., Worth, R., & Worth, D. (1997). *Divorced dad's handbook: 100 questions and answers.* Tempe, AZ: Blue Bird.

Blaisure, K. R., & Geasler, M. J. (1996). Results of a survey of court-connected parent education programs in U.S. counties. *Family and Conciliation Courts Review, 34*, 23–40.

Blankenhorn, D. (1995). *Fatherless America: Confronting our most urgent social problem.* New York: Basic Books.

Bloom, B. L., Asher, S. J., & White, S. W. (1978). Marital disruption as a stressor: A review and analysis. *Psychological Bulletin, 85*(4), 867–894.

Bloom, B. L., & Caldwell, R. A. (1981). Sex differences in adjustment during the process of marital separation. *Journal of Marriage and the Family, 43*(3), 693–701.

Brandwein, R. B., Brown, C. A., & Fox, E. M. (1974). Women and children last: The social situation of divorced mothers and their families. *Journal of Marriage and the Family, 36*, 498–514.

Braver, S. L., & Griffin, W. A. (2000). Engaging fathers in the post-divorce family. *Marriage and Family Review, 29*(4), 247–267.

Braver, S. L., Griffin, W. A., Cookston, J. T., Sandler, I. N., & Williams, J. (2001, May). *An evidenced-based program for divorced noncustodial fathers: Dads for Life.* Paper presented at the Association of Family and Conciliation Courts, Chicago.

Braver, S. L., Hipke, K. N., Ellman, I. M., & Sandler, I. N. (2004). Strengths-building public policy for children of divorce. In K. Maton, C. Schellenbach, B. Ledbetter, & A. Solarz (Eds.), *Investing in children, youth, families, and communities: Strengths based public policies* (pp. 53–72). New York: American Psychological Association.

Braver, S. L., & O'Connell, D. (1998). *Divorced dads: Shattering the myths.* New York: Tarcher/Putnam.

Braver, S. L., Whitley, M., & Ng, C. (1993). Who divorced whom? Methodological and theoretical Issues. *Journal of Divorce & Remarriage, 20,* 1–19.

Braver, S. L., Wolchik, S. A., Sandler, I. N., Fogas, B. S., & Zvetina, D. (1991). Frequency of visitation by divorced fathers: Differences in reports by fathers and mothers. *American Journal of Orthopsychiatry, 61,* 448–454.

Braver, S. L., Wolchik, S. A., Sandler, I. N., & Sheets, V. L. (1993). A social exchange model of nonresidential parent involvement. In C. Depner & J. H. Bray (Eds.), *Nonresidential parenting: New vistas in family living.* Newbury Park, CA: Sage.

Braver, S. L., Wolchik, S. A., Sandler, I. N., Sheets, V. L., Fogas, B. S., & Bay, R. C. (1993). A longitudinal study of noncustodial parents: Parents without children. *Journal of Family Psychology, 7,* 9–23.

Bray, J. H., & Berger, S. H. (1990). Noncustodial father and paternal grandparent relationships in stepfamilies. *Family-Relations: Journal of Applied Family and Child Studies, 39*(4), 414–419

Brinig, M. F., & Allen, D. W. (2000). "These boots are made for walking": Why women file for divorce? *American Law and Economics Review, 2,* 141–167.

Brott, A. (1999). *The single father: A dad's guide to parenting without a partner.* New York: Abbeville.

Buchanan, C. M., Maccoby, E. E., & Dornbusch, S. M. (1996). *Adolescents after divorce.* Cambridge, MA: Harvard University Press.

Camara, K. A., & Resnick, G. (1989). Styles of conflict resolution and cooperation between divorced parents: Effects on child behavior and adjustment. *American Journal of Orthopsychiatry, 59*(4), 560–575.

Cancian, M., & Meyer, D. R. (1998). Who gets custody? *Demography, 35,* 147–157.

Chambers, D. (1979). *Making fathers pay.* Chicago: University of Chicago Press.

Cherlin, A. J. (1999). Going to extremes: Family structure, children's well being, and social science, *Demography, 36,* 421–428

Chiraboga, D. A., & Cutler, A. (1977). Stress responses among divorcing men and women. *Journal of Divorce, 1,* 95–106.

Clingempeel, W. G. (1981). Quasi-kin relationships and marital quality in stepfather families. *Journal of Personality and Social Psychology, 5,* 890–901.

Condrell, K. N., & Small, L. L. (1998). *Be a great divorced dad.* New York: St. Martin's.

Cooksey, E. C., & Craig, P. H. (1998). Parenting from a distance: The effects of paternal characteristics on contact between nonresidential fathers and their children. *Demography, 35,* 187–200.

Cookston, J. T., Braver, S. L., Sandler, I. N., & Genalo, M. T. (2002). Prospects for expanded parent education services for divorcing families with children. *Family Court Review, 40,* 190–203.

Coplin, J. W., & Houts, A. C. (1991). Father involvement in parent training for oppositional child behavior: Progress or stagnation? *Child and Family Behavior Therapy, 13*(2), 29–51.

Cummings, E. M. (1998). Children exposed to marital conflict and violence: Conceptual and theoretical directions. In G. W. Holden, R. Geffner, & E. N. Jouriles (Eds.), *Children exposed to marital violence: Theory, research, and applied issues.* Washington, DC: American Psychological Association.

Cummings, E. M., Ballard, M., & El-Sheikh, M. (1991). Responses of children and adolescents to interadult anger as a function of gender, age, and mode of expression. *Merrill-Palmer Quarterly, 37,* 543–560.

Cummings, E. M., & Davies, P. (1994). *Children and marital conflict: The impact of family dispute and resolution*. New York: Guilford Press.

Davis, D. (2003, March 2). State names top 25 deadbeat dads. *Santa Fe New Mexican*.

Deschner, J. P., & McNeil, J. S. (1986). Results of anger control training for battering couples. *Journal of Family Violence, 1*, 111–120.

Devlin, A. S., Brown, E. H., Beebe, J., & Parulis, E. (1992). Parent education for divorced fathers. *Family Relations, 41*, 290–296.

Dudley, J. R. (1991a). The consequences of divorce proceedings for divorced fathers. *Journal of Divorce and Remarriage, 16*(3, 4), 171–193.

Dudley, J. R. (1991b). Exploring ways to get divorced fathers to comply willingly with child support arrangements. *Journal of Divorce and Remarriage, 16*, 121–135.

Dudley, J. R. (1991c). Increasing our understanding of divorced fathers who have infrequent contact with their children. *Family Relations: Interdisciplinary Journal of Applied Family Studies, 40*(3), 279–285.

Dudley, J. R. (1996). Noncustodial fathers speak about their parental role. *Family and Conciliation Courts Review, 34*(3), 410–426.

Emery, R. E. (1982). Interparental conflict and the children of discord and divorce. *Psychological Bulletin, 92*, 310–330.

Fabricius, W. V., & Hall, J. (2000). Young adults' perspectives on divorce: Living arrangements. *Family and Conciliation Courts Review, 38*, 446–461

Feuer, J. (1997). *Good men: A practical handbook for divorced dads*. New York: Avon Books.

Foa, E. B., & Foa, U. G. (1980). Resource theory: Interpersonal behavior as exchange. In K. J. Gergen, M. S. Greenberg, & R. H. Willis (Eds.), *Social exchange and advances in theory and research* (pp. 77–94). New York: Plenum.

Fox, G. L. (1985). Noncustodial fathers. In S. M. H. Hanson & F. W. Bozett (Eds.), *Dimensions of fatherhood* (pp. 393–415). Beverly Hills, CA: Sage.

Fox, G. L., & Blanton, P. W. (1995). Noncustodial fathers following divorce. *Marriage and Family Review, 20*(1, 2), 257–282.

Fulton, J. A. (1979). Parental reports of children's post-divorce adjustment. *Journal of Social Issues, 35*, 126–139.

Furstenberg, F. F., Jr. (1988). Good dads—bad dads: Two faces of fatherhood. In A. J. Cherlin (Ed.), *The changing American family and public policy. The changing domestic priorities series* (pp. 193–218). Washington, DC: Urban Institute.

Furstenberg, F. F., & Harris, K. M. (1992). The disappearing American father? Divorce and the waning significance of biological parenthood. In S. J. South & S. E. Tolnay (Eds.), *The changing American family: Sociological and demographic perspectives* (pp. 197–223). Boulder, CO: Westview.

Furstenberg, F. F., & Harris, K. M. (1993). When and why fathers matter: Impacts of father involvement on the children of adolescent mother. In R. I. Lerman & T. J. Ooms (Eds.), *Young unwed fathers: Changing roles and emerging policies* (pp. 117–138). Philadelphia, PA: Temple University Press.

Furstenberg, F. F., & Nord, C. (1985). Parenting apart: Patterns of childrearing after marital disruption. *Journal of Marriage and the Family, 47*, 893–904.

Furstenberg, F. F., Nord, C. W., Peterson, J. L., & Zill, N. (1983). The life course of children of divorce: Marital disruption and parental contact. *American Sociological Review, 8*, 656–668.

Garfinkel, I., Miller, C., McLanahan, S. S, & Hanson, T. L. (1998) Deadbeat dads or inept states? A comparison of child support enforcement systems. *Evaluation Review, 22*(6), 717–750.

Geasler, M. J., & Blaisure, K. R. (1999). 1998 nationwide survey of court-connected divorce education programs. *Family and Conciliation Court Review, 37,* 240–256.

Gigy, L., & Kelly, J. B. (1992). Reasons for divorce: Perspectives of divorcing men and women. *Journal of Divorce and Remarriage, 18*(1, 2), 169–187.

Golub, J. S., Espinosa, M., Damon, L., & Card, J. (1987). A videotape parent education program for abusive parents. *Child Abuse and Neglect, 11,* 255–265.

Goodman, M., Bonds, D., Sandler, I. N., & Braver, S. L. (2004). Teaching conflict resolution skills in parent education courses. *Family Court Review, 42*(2), 263–279.

Griffin, W. A. (1993). Event history analysis of marital and family interaction: A practical introduction. *Journal of Family Psychology, 6,* 211–229.

Griffin, W. A., Braver, S. L., & Cookston, J. T. (2003, October). *Behavioral observations of interaction between divorced parents: Evaluating a conflict-reducing intervention program.* Paper presented at American Association of Marriage and Family Therapists, Long Beach, CA.

Griffin, W. A., Greene, S. M., & Decker-Haas, A. (2004). The MICSEASE: An observational coding system for capturing social processes. In P. K. Kerig & D. Baucom (Eds.), *Couple observational coding systems.* Mahwah, NJ: Lawrence Erlbaum.

Grych, J. H., & Fincham, F. D. (1993). Children's appraisals of marital conflict: Initial investigations of the cognitive-contextual framework. *Child Development, 64,* 215–230.

Guidubaldi, J., et al. (1986). The role of selected family environment factors in children's post-divorce adjustment. *Family Relations: Interdisciplinary Journal of Applied Family Studies, 35,* 141–151.

Hall, A. S., & Kelly, K. R. (1996). Noncustodial fathers in groups: Maintaining the parenting bond. In M. Andronico (Ed.), *Men in groups: Insights, interventions, and psychoeducational work* (pp. 243–256). Washington, DC: American Psychological Association.

Hawkins, A. J., & Dollahite, D. C. (Eds.). (1997). *Generative fathering: Beyond deficit perspectives.* Thousand Oaks, CA: Sage.

Healy, J., Malley, J., & Stewart, A. (1990). Children and their fathers after parental separation. *American Journal of Orthopsychiatry, 60,* 531–543.

Hernandez, P. M., Beller, A. H., & Graham, J. W. (1995). Changes in relationships between child support payments and educational attainment of offspring, 1979–1988. *Demography, 32,* 249–260.

Hetherington, E. M., Cox, M., & Cox, R. (1976). Divorced fathers. *The Family Coordinator, 25,* 417–428.

Hetherington, E. M., Cox, M., & Cox, R. (1978). The aftermath of divorce. In J. H. Stevens & M. Mathews (Eds.), *Mother/child, father/child relationships* (pp. 110–155). Washington, DC: National Association for the Education of Young Children.

Hetherington, E. M., Cox, M., & Cox, R. (1982). Effects of divorce on parents and children. In M. E. Lamb (Ed.), *Nontraditional families* (pp. 237–288). Hillsdale, NJ: Erlbaum.

Hetherington, E. M., & Hagan, M. S. (1986). Divorced fathers: Stress, coping and adjustment. In M. E. Lamb (Ed.), *The father's role: Applied perspectives* (pp. 103–134). New York: Wiley.

Hoffman, C. D. (1995). Pre- and post-divorce father–child relationships and child adjustment: Noncustodial fathers' perspectives. *Journal of Divorce and Remarriage, 23*(1, 2), 3–20.

Ihinger-Tallman, M., Pasley, K., & Buehler, C. (1993). Developing a middle-range theory of father involvement postdivorce. *Journal of Family Issues, 14*(4), 550–571.

Johnston, J., Kline, M., & Tschann, J. (1989). Ongoing postdivorce conflict: Effects on children of joint custody and frequent access. *American Journal of Orthopsychiatry, 59,* 576–592.

King, V. (1994). Variation in the consequences of nonresident father involvement for children's well-being. *Journal of Marriage and the Family, 56*(4), 963–972

King, V., & Heard, H. E. (1999). Non-resident father visitation, parental conflict, and mother's satisfaction: what's best for child well-being. *Journal of Marriage and the Family, 61,* 385–396.

Kitson, G. C., Babri, K. B., & Roach, M. J. (1985). Who divorces and why: A review. *Journal of Family Issues, 6,* 255–293.

Kitson, G. C., & Holmes, W. M. (1992). *Portrait of divorce: Adjustment to marital breakdown.* New York: Guilford Press.

Klatte, W. C. (1999). *Live-away dads: Staying a part of your children's lives when they aren't a part of your home.* New York: Penguin.

Knox, D., & Leggett, K. (1998). *The divorced dad's survival book: How to stay connected with your kids.* Cambridge, MA: Perseus.

Koch, M. A., & Lowery, C. R. (1984). Visitation and the noncustodial father. *Journal of Divorce, 8,* 47–65.

Krishnakumar, A., & Buehler, C. (2000). Interparental conflict and parenting behaviors: A meta-analytic review. *Family Relations, 49*(1), 25–45.

Kruk, E. (1991a). Discontinuity between pre- and post-divorce father-child relationships: New evidence regarding paternal disengagement. *Journal of Divorce and Remarriage, 16*(3, 4), 195–227.

Kruk, E. (1991b). The grief reaction of noncustodial fathers subsequent to divorce. *Men's Studies Review, 8*(2), 17–21.

Kruk, E. (1992). Psychological and structural factors contributing to the disengagement of noncustodial fathers after divorce. *Family and Conciliation Courts Review, 30*(1), 81–101.

Kruk, E. (1993). *Divorce and disengagement: Patterns of fatherhood within and beyond marriage.* Halifax, Nova Scotia, Canada: Fernwood.

Kurdek, L. (1981). An integrated perspective on children's divorce adjustment. *American Psychologist, 36,* 856–866.

Kurkowski, K. P., Gordon, D. A., & Arbuthnot, J. (1993). Children caught in the middle: A brief educational intervention for divorced parents. *Journal of Divorce and Remarriage, 20,* 139–151.

Lamb, M. (1999). Non custodial fathers and their impact on children of divorce. In R. A. Thompson & P. R. Amato (Eds.), *The postdivorce family: Children, parenting and society* (pp. 105–125). Thousand Oaks, CA: Sage.

Lamb, S., Greenlick, M. R., & McCarty, D. (Eds.). (1998). *Bridging the gap between practice and research: Forging partnerships with community-based drug and alcohol treatment.* Washington, DC: National Academy Press.

Lambermon, M., & van Ijzendoorn, M. H. (1989). Influencing mother-infant interaction through videotaped or written instruction: Evaluation of a parent education program. *Early Childhood Research Quarterly, 4,* 449–458.

Leite, R. W., & McKenry, P. C. (2002). Aspects of father status and postdivorce father involvement with children. *Journal of Family Issues, 23*(5), 601–623.

Lund, M. (1987). The non-custodial father: Common challenges in parenting after divorce. In C. Lewis & M. O'Brien (Eds.), *Reassessing fatherhood: New observations on fathers and the modern family* (pp. 212–224). Thousand Oaks, CA: Sage.

Maccoby, E. E., Depner, C. E., & Mnookin, R. H. (1988). Custody of children following divorce, In E. M. Hetherington & J. D. Arasteh (Eds.), *Impact of divorce, single parenting, and stepparenting on children* (pp. 91–114). Hillsdale, NJ: Erlbaum.

Maccoby, E. E., & Mnookin, R. H. (1992). *Dividing the child: Social and legal dilemmas of custody.* Cambridge, MA: Harvard University Press.

Madden-Derdich, D. A., & Leonard, S. A. (2000). Parental role identity and fathers' involvement in coparental interaction after divorce: Fathers' perspectives. *Family Relations: Interdisciplinary Journal of Applied Family Studies, 49*(3), 311–318.

Madden-Derdich, D. A., & Leonard, S. A. (2002). Shared experiences, unique realities: Formerly married mothers' and fathers' perceptions of parenting and custody after divorce. *Family Relations: Interdisciplinary Journal of Applied Family Studies, 51*(1), 37–45.

Masheter, C. (1991). Postdivorce relations between ex-spouses: The roles of attachment and interpersonal conflict. *Journal of Marriage and the Family, 53,* 103–110.

Maton, K., Ledbetter, B., Schellenbach, C., & Solarz, A. (Eds.). (2004). *Investing in children, youth, families, and communities: Strengths based public policies.* Armonk, NY: American Psychological Association Press.

Mayadas, N. S., & Duehn, W. (1977). Stimulus modeling (SM) videotape for marital counseling: Methods and applications. *Journal of Marriage and Family Counseling, 35,* 75–88.

Mayer, G. S. (1994). *Divorced dad dilemma.* Scottsdale, AZ: Desert City.

McCleary, R. D., & Welsh, W. N. (1992). Philosophical and statistical foundations of time series experiments. In T. R. Kratochwill & J. R. Levin (Eds.), *Single case research design and analysis* (pp. 41–91). Hillsdale, NJ: Erlbaum.

McClure, F. D., & Saffer, J. B. (2000). *Wednesday evenings and every other weekend: From divorced dad to competent co-parent.* Charlottesville, VA: Van Doren.

McKenry, P. C., McKelvey, M. W., Leigh, D., & Wark, L. (1996). Nonresidential father involvement: A comparison of divorced, Separated, never married, and remarried fathers. *Journal of Divorce and Remarriage, 25*(3, 4), 1–13.

McKenry, P. C., Price, S. J., Fine, M. A., & Serovich, J. (1992). Predictors of single, noncustodial fathers' physical involvement with their children. *Journal of Genetic Psychology, 153*(3), 305–319.

McLanahan, S. S., & Sandefur, G. (1994). *Growing up with a single parent.* Cambridge, MA: Harvard University Press.

Meichenbaum, D. (1975). A self-instructional approach to stress management: A proposal for stress inoculation training. In C. Spilberger & I. Sarason (Eds.), *Stress and anxiety* (Vol. 2, pp. 237–264). New York: Wiley.

Meyer, D. R. (1999). Compliance with child support orders in paternity and divorce cases. In R. A. Thompson & P. R. Amato (Eds.), *The postdivorce family: Children, parenting and society* (pp. 127–157). Thousand Oaks, CA: Sage.

Meyer, D. R., & Garasky, S. (1993). Custodial fathers: Myths, realities, and child support policy. *Journal of Marriage and the Family, 55,* 73–89.

Minton, C., & Pasley, K. (1996). Fathers' parenting role identity and father involvement: A comparison of nondivorced and divorced, nonresident fathers. *Journal of Family Issues, 17*(1), 26–45.

Moon, J. R., & Eisler, R. M. (1983). Anger control: An experimental comparison of three behavioral treatments. *Behavior Therapy, 14,* 493–505.

National Advisory Mental Health Council (NAMHC). (2001). *Workgroup on child and adolescent mental health intervention development and deployment. Blueprint for change: Research on child and adolescent mental health.* Rockville, MD: The National Institute of Mental Health.

National Advisory Mental Health Council (NAMHC) Workgroup on Mental Disorders Prevention Research. (1998). *Priorities for prevention research at NIMH.* Rockville, MD: National Institutes of Health.

Nord, C. W., & Zill, N. (1996). *Non-custodial parents' participation in their children's lives: Evidence from the Survey of Income and Program Participation. Volume I. Summary of SIPP analysis.* Washington, DC: U.S. Department of Health and Human Services.

Novaco, R. W. (1977). Stress inoculation: A cognitive therapy for anger and its application to a case of depression. *Journal of Consulting and Clinical Psychology, 45,* 600–608.

Oakland, T. (1984). *Divorced fathers: Reconstructing a quality life.* New York: Human Sciences.

O'Dell, S. L., Krug, W. W., Patterson, J. N., & Faustman, W. (1980). An assessment of methods for training parents in the use of time-out. *Journal of Behavior Therapy and Experimental Psychiatry, 11,* 21–25.

O'Dell, S. L., Quinn, J. A., Alford, B. A., O'Briant, A. L., Bradlyne, A. S., & Gienbenhain, J. E. (1982). Predicting the acquisition of parenting skills via four training methods. *Behavior Therapy, 13,* 194–205.

Parke, R. D., & Brott, A. A. (1999). *Throwaway dads: The myths and barriers that keep men from being the fathers they want to be.* Boston: Houghton Mifflin.

Pasley, K., & Minton, C. (1997). Generative fathering after divorce and remarriage: Beyond the "disappearing dad." In A. J. Hawkins & D. C. Dollahite (Eds.), *Current issues in the family series: Vol. 3. Generative fathering: Beyond deficit perspectives* (pp. 118–133). Thousand Oaks, CA: Sage.

Patterson, G. R., Chamberlain, P., & Reid, J. B. (1982). A comparative evaluation of parent training procedures. *Behavior Therapy, 13,* 638–650

Pearson, J., & Thoennes, N. (1986). Will this divorced woman receive child support? *Minnesota Family Law Journal, 3,* 65–71.

Pearson, J., & Thoennes, N. P. (1988). Supporting children after divorce: The influence of custody on support levels and payments. *Family Law Quarterly, 22,* 319–339.

Peters, H. E., Argys, L. M., Maccoby, E. E., & Mnookin, R. H. (1993). Enforcing divorce settlements: Evidence from child support compliance and award modifications. *Demography, 30,* 499–517.

Peterson, J. L., & Nord, C. W. (1990). The regular receipt of child support: A multistep process. *Journal of Marriage and the Family, 52,* 539–551.

Pettit, E. J., & Bloom, B. L. (1984). Whose decision was it: The effects of initiator status on adjustment to marital disruption. *Journal of Marriage and the Family, 48,* 587–595.

Popenoe, D. (1996). *Life without father: Compelling new evidence that fatherhood and marriage are indispensable for the good of children and society.* New York: Free Press.

Prengel, S., & Yale, D. (1999). *Still a dad: The divorced father's journey.* New York: Mission Creative Energy.

Price, S. J., & McKenry, P. C. (1988). *Divorce.* Thousand Oaks, CA: Sage.

Reich, J. W., & Zautra, A. J. (1990). Dispositional control beliefs and the consequences of a control-enhancing intervention. *Journal of Gerontology, 45*(2), 46–51.

Rettig, K. D., Leichtentritt, R. D., & Stanton, L. M. (1999). Understanding noncustodial fathers' family and life satisfaction from resource theory perspective. *Journal of Family Issues, 20,* 507–538.

Riessman, C. K. (1990). *Divorce talk: Women and men make sense of personal relationships.* New Brunswick, NJ: Rutgers University Press.

Rosenthal, K. M., & Keshet, H. F. (1981). *Fathers without partners: A study of fathers and the family after marital separation.* New Jersey: Rowman & Littlefield.

Rothbaum, F., Weisz, J. R., & Snyder, S. (1982). Changing the world and changing the self: A two process model of perceived control. *Journal of Personality and Social Psychology, 42*(1), 5–37.

Rotheram-Borus, M. J., & Duan, N. (2003). Next generation of preventive interventions. *Journal of the American Academy of Child and Adolescent Psychiatry, 42*(5), 518–526.

Sandler, I. N., Coatsworth, J. D., Lengua, L. J., Fisher, J., Wolchik, S. A., Lustig, J., et al. (1992). *New Beginnings children of divorce program: Child coping-enhancement program manual.* Tempe: Arizona State University.

Sandler, I. N., Wolchik, S. A., Davis, C. H., Haine, R. A., & Ayers, T. S. (2003). Correlational and experimental study of resilience for children of divorce and parentally-bereaved children. In S. S. Luthar (Ed.), *Resilience and vulnerability: Adaptation in the context of childhood adversities* (pp. 213–240). New York: Cambridge University Press.

Schwartz, H. S. (2001). *The revolt of the primitive: An inquiry into the roots of political correctness.* Westport, CT: Praeger/Greenwood.

Seltzer, J. A. (1991). Relationships between fathers and children who live apart: The father's role after separation. *Journal of Marriage and Family, 53*(1), 79–101.

Seltzer, J. A. (1994). Consequences of marital dissolution for children. *Annual Review of Sociology, 2,* 235–266

Seltzer, J. A., Schaeffer, N. C., & Charng, H. (1989). Family ties after divorce: The relationship between visiting and paying child support. *Journal of Marriage and Family, 51,* 1013–1031.

Shiono, P. H., & Quinn, L. S. (1994). Epidemiology of divorce. *Future of Children, 4,* 15–28.

Simons, R. L., Whitbeck, L. B., & Beaman, J. (1994). The impact of mothers' parenting, involvement by nonresidential fathers, and parental conflict on the adjustment of adolescent children. *Journal of Marriage and the Family, 56,* 356–374.

Sorensen, E. (1997). A national profile of nonresident fathers and their ability to pay child support. *Journal of Marriage and the Family, 59*, 785–797.

Spaccarelli, S., Cotler, S., & Penman, D. (1992). Problem solving skills training as a supplement to behavioral parent training. *Cognitive Therapy and Research, 16*, 1–18.

Stewart, S. D. (1999). Disneyland dads, Disneyland moms? How nonresident parents spend time with absent children. *Journal of Family Issues, 20*, 539–556.

Stone, G., & McKenry, P. C. (1998). Nonresidential father involvement: a test of a mid-range theory. *The Journal of Genetic Psychology, 159*, 313–336.

Sweet, J. A., & Bumpass, L. L. (1996). *The National Survey of Families and Households—Waves 1 and 2: Data description and documentation.* Madison: University of Wisconsin/Madison.

Teachman, J. D., & Paasch, K. M. (1994). Financial impact of divorce on children and their families. *The Future of Children, 4*, 63–83.

Tepp, A. V. (1983). Divorced fathers: Predictors of continued paternal involvement. *American Journal of Psychiatry, 140*, 1465–1469.

Tropf, W. D. (1984). An exploratory examination of the effect of remarriage on child support and personal contacts. *Journal of Divorce, 7*, 57–73.

Tschann, J. M., Johnston, J. R., Kline, M., & Wallerstein, J. S. (1989). Family process and children's functioning during divorce. *Journal of Marriage and the Family, 51*, 431–444.

Umberson, D., & Williams, C. L. (1993) Divorced fathers: Parental role strain and psychological distress. *Journal of Family Stress, 14*, 378–400.

Wallerstein, J. S., & Blakeslee, S. (1989.). *Second chances: Men, women, and children a decade after divorce.* New York: Ticknor & Fields.

Wallerstein, J. S., & Corbin, S. B. (1986). Father-child relationships after divorce: Child support and educational opportunity. *Family Law Quarterly, 20*, 109–128.

Wallerstein, J. S., & Kelly, J.B. (1980) *Surviving the breakup.* New York: Basic Books.

Wasson, N. J., & Hefner, L. (2002). *Divorced dads: 101 ways to stay connected with your kids.* Pinson, AL: Adesso Press.

Webster-Stratton, C. (1984). Randomized trial of two parent-training programs for families with conduct disordered children. *Journal of Consulting and Clinical Psychology, 52*, 666–678.

Webster-Stratton, C., Hollinsworth, T., & Kolpacoff, M. (1989). The long-term effectiveness and clinical significance of three cost-effective training programs for families with conduct-problem children. *Journal of Consulting and Clinical Psychology, 57*, 550–553.

Webster-Stratton, C., Kolpacoff, M., & Hollinsworth, T. (1988). Self-administered videotape therapy for families with conduct problem children: Comparison with two cost-effective treatments and a control group. *Journal of Consulting and Clinical Psychology, 56*, 558–566.

Weiss, Y., & Willis, R. J. (1985). Children as collective goods and divorce settlements. *Journal of Labor Economics, 3*, 268–292.

Weitzstein, C. (2003, April 20). Jail time coming for deadbeat dads; but program helps make up arrears. *The Washington Times.*

Whiteside, M. F. (1998). The parental alliance following divorce: An overview. *Journal of Marital and Family Therapy, 24*(1), 3–24.

Wolchik, S. A., Braver, S. L., & Sandler, I. N. (1985). Maternal versus joint custody: Children's postseparation experiences and adjustment. *Journal of Clinical Child Psychology, 14,* 5–10.

Wolchik, S. A., Fenaughty, A. M., & Braver, S. L. (1996). Residential and nonresidential parents' perspectives on visitation problems. *Family Relations, 45,* 230–237.

Wolchik, S. A., Sandler, I. N., Millsap, R. E., Plummer, B. A., Greene, S. M., Anderson, E. R., et al. (2002). Six-year follow-up of preventive interventions for children of divorce: A randomized controlled trial. *Journal of the American Medical Association, 288*(15), 1874–1881.

Wolchik, S. A., West, S. G., Sandler, I. N., Tein, J.-Y., Coatsworth, D., Lengua, L., et al. (2000). An experimental evaluation of theory-based single-component and dual-component programs. *Journal of Consulting and Clinical Psychology, 68*(5), 843–856.

Wolchik, S. A, West, S. G., Westover, S., Sandler, I. N., Martin, A., Lustig, J., et al. (1993). The Children of Divorce Parenting Intervention: Outcome evaluation of an empirically based program. *American Journal of Community Psychology, 21*(3), 293–331.

Wortman, C. B., Hendricks, M., & Hillis, J. W. (1976). Factors affecting participant reactions to random assignment in ameliorative social programs. *Journal of Personality and Social Psychology, 33,* 256–266.

13

Fathers in African American Families: The Importance of Social and Cultural Context

Melvin N. Wilson, Anthony L. Chambers, and LaKeesha N. Woods

A family is influenced and facilitated by the opportunities and constraints of its social context. In order to ensure its own existence, a family adapts available resources to normal and abnormal transitional and crisis stress events. Family resources involve the ability of family members to contribute tangible help, such as material support, income, child care, and household maintenance, and nontangible aid, such as expressive interaction, emotional support, instruction, and social training and regulation. An important but not well-understood aspect of family life is the role that fathers play in the performance of familial activities and duties. In addition, fathers' involvement in family life is greatly influenced by the cultural context in which the family resides.

There is considerable variability in fathers' roles among different cultures. However, most research designs have failed to recognize this variability when studying the role of minority fathers in family life, relying on culture general approaches. The primary purpose of the current chapter is to delineate the influence of social and cultural context as it relates to diversity among African American fathers and to suggest methodological approaches to understanding the diversity.

■ Extant Methodological and Theoretical Approaches
to African American Families

Like most aspects of African American life, family research has assumed that the African American population is homogeneous. There is a paucity of research that examines the within-group variability among fathers in African American families. The majority of research conducted on African American fathers has focused on comparing Caucasian and African American fathers. Constructs developed for Caucasian Americans often are assumed to be equally applicable to African Americans. Moreover, measures developed for mothers are imposed on fathers. Although psychology is interested in investigating between-group differences, such comparisons only are meaningful once each group is well understood. Berry, Poortinga, Segall, and Dasen (1995) have advocated a culture-specific approach that allows the researcher to identify and appreciate the diversity among populations. The use of within-group methodologies can illuminate the variability that exists among African American fathers (Dallas & Chen, 1998; Hamer, 1997; Lindsay, Mize, & Pettit, 1997; Miller, 1994; Roy, 1999).

■ Understanding African American Fathers

The Role of Income, Race, and Father Involvement
in African American Families

The current research literature focuses heavily on the investigation of African American high-risk groups, such as teenage mothers, unemployed men, and the elderly. Although most are not poor, there always has been a higher proportion of African American families living below poverty levels than have Caucasian American families, with 22.7% of all African American families living in poverty, over twice the poverty rate for Caucasian families (U.S. Census Bureau [Census], 2002c). Persistent social and economic discrimination have produced a contextual circumstance that has shaped a unique family form within American society and contributed to alternate family structures, such as single-parent, extended, and cohabiting families.

The status of some African American families suggests that children are exposed to an alarmingly high level of instability in the family structure. For example, according to 2000 and 2002 statistics, 60.2% of African American parents are divorced, widowed, or never married (Census, 2002b); 68.7% of African American births were to unmarried mothers; and 19.8% of African American births were to adolescents (Martin, Hamilton, Ventura, Menacker, & Parks, 2002). From an African American child's perspective, there is a greater probability that the child will live in a single-parent family (53.3%) than in a dual-parent family (38.5%). Approximately 7% of African American children live with another relative (Census, 2002a). In fact, approximately 3 times as many African American children under the age of 18 live with a grandparent as Caucasian children (Census, 2001).

One problem in low-income African American communities is the lack of adequate adult resources in single-parent family units. In fact, the persistent and concentrated poverty among some African American families, especially single-parent African American families (43.5% classified as poor, Census, 2002d), is the primary factor correlated with extended family formation. The formation sometimes occurs by a viable family unit—nuclear, single parent, or childless couple—absorbing the less viable unit—single parent, dependent child, or adult. Alternately, a single-parent family unit may attach itself to the extended familial support system. Regardless of the method, once formed the extended family is multigenerational and extranuclear and embodies most of the family life span.

Single mothers, including those who are divorced, separated, widowed, or never married, account for 90% of African American single parents (Census, 2002a). When comparing single mothers on age, number of children, and income, mothers who are older and have greater numbers of children and higher incomes are more likely to live as single parents. Conversely, younger, never-married mothers are less likely to live as only adults in a household and are more likely to share the residence with their mothers. The age of the child and the education level of the mother also affect the nature of the single mother's living arrangements. For example, a single-parent family unit involving a young mother of limited education having few children and low income likely will share a residence with extended family members. Indeed, the most common composition of extended households involves a single-parent family structure that includes a mother, her children, and the mother's mother.

Father Involvement in Single-Parent Families. Although single-parent families commonly are composed of a mother and her children, it is inaccurate to assume that fathers are not involved in family life. It is becoming increasingly apparent that the visibility of fathers in the African American family varies. Two points should be noted about the availability of African American fathers in the family. First, although not always as active as the mother's role, the role of father/husband is very important in the African American family. Fathers' interactions with their children may reflect not only role flexibility in the family, but also the fact that many fathers desire to have a significant part in the development of their children. After the mother, the adult family members most likely to be involved in child care are the father and grandmother, respectively (Wilson, Tolson, Hinton, & Kiernan, 1990). A similar trend exists for financial support, with mothers being major contributors to the family's income and fathers sharing the responsibility for the family's economic and material comfort. In other words, African American families have depended on the wages of both parents. African American fathers also have a long history of participating in the nurturance and socialization of children. African American men, in fact, were expected by their wives to provide both material and emotional support to their children (Wilson et al., 1990).

Second, a significant portion of African American fathers experience chronic difficulty obtaining and maintaining stable and legitimate employment that adequately supports. The employment and economic instability of African American fathers causes a considerable amount of family stress and is a significant source of family vulnerability. Moreover, although divorce, desertion, separation, and extra-marital births reflect significant reasons for father/husband absence, joblessness, incarceration, and mortality are significant factors that influence the high disparity in the male to female ratio (Wilson, Woods, & Hijjawi, 2004).

The disparity in the male to female ratio in the African American community has been found to be a more significant predictor of marital status and economic well-being in the African American community than has the socioeconomic history of the family or individual (Wilson et al., 1995). Overall, low-income African American fathers are in an extremely vulnerable position; hence, they desire and need to be supported and active participants in their families. Poverty and unemployment, however, often lead to African American fathers' inability to contribute to the well-being of their family and an increased likelihood that they will receive family aid.

When discussing race and income in the context of research examining African American father involvement, the complexity of race versus social class effects becomes salient. Distinguishing race from social class effects quickly becomes a complex issue as the factors are socially confounded variables given that a disproportionate number of minority populations dwell in impoverished settings. Moreover, the effects of discrimination are similar for both race and socioeconomic status (SES). However, there are steps that can be taken to begin to tease the two factors apart.

Over the past 30 years, there has been a growing population of middle-class African Americans. However, middle-class African American families rarely are studied. Consistent with the principals of the scientific method, the sample is paramount to defining the limits of generalizability. Researchers, therefore, need to study the previously ignored population of middle-class African American fathers and their families. Specifically, research programs would benefit by delineating the within-group variability among middle-class fathers, the conditions under which normal father involvement occurs, the barriers that prevent father involvement, and the risk and protective factors relevant to middle-class African American fathers. That same process then needs to be repeated with low-income African American fathers, and the places where similarity occurs would be suggestive of race-related factors. Divergence may be indicative of SES-related factors. Although distinguishing race and SES influences is difficult, it is a worthwhile process, as the implications can impact policy as well as the efficacy of interventions.

Methodological Challenges and Father Involvement.   The first methodological challenge when studying the construct of father involvement lies in defining what that construct means. The challenge becomes salient, as changes in the social and political zeitgeist have forced us to reexamine what it means to be a father. Historically speaking, father involvement in the mid-20th century was simple. The father was the financial provider of the family, while the mother was the nurturer and "house manager". However, in the new millennium, fathers are expected to be more active in the child's life, participating in nurturing activities. Mothers are expected to contribute to the family income as well. In addition, with the increase of female-headed households, mothers often are taking on the roles of both mother and father. Hence, the parental roles may be developing some interchangeable aspects. From a research perspective, the similarity of roles suggests that researchers need to distinguish maternal and paternal involvement.

■ Issues Pertaining to the Mother-Father Relationship

Fathers and Marriage

Regarding the most traditional reason for family formation, African American women are similar to other ethnic women regarding marriage. Women want men who are employable and who can support a family economically, a basic criterion that is not met by many young African American men. The dearth of economically viable African American men has been linked to increases in the statuses divorced, single, and cohabiting (Lawson & Thompson, 1994; Taylor, Chatters, Tucker, & Lewis, 1990; Tucker & Taylor, 1989). Specifically, sociologists and psychologists have examined the impact of the mother-father relationship on father involvement. Allen and Doherty (1996) and Cervera (1991) found that adolescent fathers reported that a strained relationship with their children's mother was a major obstacle to their involvement with their children. Research suggests the development of the paternal role is strongly associated with the mother-father relationship (Belsky, Rovine, & Fish, 1989; Cervera, 1991; Westney, Cole, & Munford, 1986). Men who have a close relationship with their child's mother report a positive anticipation for fatherhood, a keen interest in the nutrition of the pregnant mother, and a willingness to care for the infant (Westney et al., 1986). Moreover, McAdoo (1986) suggested that such displays of paternal and marital affection are associated with positive self-esteem in the children.

Taylor and Johnson (1997) further explored the relationship between family roles and family dissatisfaction among African American men using the National Survey of Black Americans. African American husbands and fathers generally rated their performance in spousal and parental roles favorably and reported being very satisfied with their family life. Specifically, they reported that performing well in both husband and father roles was an important component of their lives. Indicators of family stress—family and marriage problems and problems with children—were the most consistent correlates of family role performance and family satisfaction, whereas marital happiness and good familial affective relations were related to overall perceptions of well-being. Such studies document the need for future research to examine the processes underlying the father's relationship with his child's mother and how the quality of the romantic relationship affects the children.

Research has documented that unemployment and underemployment among African American males are related directly to the decline in marriage rates among African American couples (Wilson, 1987). Stack (1974) examined how low-income, urban, African American families employed adaptive strategies, resourcefulness, and cooperation in order to cope with poverty and racism. Unemployment was the single largest factor that influenced relationships between men and women, along with a man's inability to secure employment. Specifically, losing a job or having a series of temporary jobs negatively affected the self-esteem and independence of men. Consequently, the men sacrificed their role as the financial provider of their families, terminating their romantic relationships by engaging in acts of infidelity. Although income-related difficulties could strain the mother-father relationship, not all couples respond similarly to the difficulties. For example, some men and childbearing women still are able to maintain long-term relationships, others are involved in multiple sexual relationships, and some marry. The lack of uniformity provides further evidence that low-income, minority couples display considerable within-group diversity.

Chadiha (1992) reports that an important factor in a couple's decision to marry is related to the man's ability to find a job and generate adequate family income. In general, low-income and limited educated African American men experienced difficulty in the labor market. African American men are disproportionately affected by financial strains. Poor prospects at earning a living make a person undesirable.

Stier and Tienda (1993) reported that marriage behavior clearly differed along ethnic and racial lines. They found that Mexican and European American fathers were more likely to marry than were their Puerto Rican and African American counterparts. African American men also were the most likely to enter fatherhood before marriage. Stier and Tienda highlighted the diversity among ethnic groups and bolstered the need to examine each group individually to understand the processes that influence the outcomes.

Factors Specific to Father-Mother Relationships. Researchers have attempted to examine the low marriage rates in low-income communities. Testa, Astone, Krogh, and Neckerman (1989) examined the influence of SES and race on fathers' likelihood of marrying the mother of their first child before or after the child's birth using data from the Urban Poverty and Family Structure Survey of 2490 inner-city residents in Chicago. Employed men were more likely than were jobless men to marry after the conception of their first child. Moreover, high school graduates were more likely to marry than were non–high school graduates, suggesting that both short-term economic realities and long-term prospects shape the marriage decisions of inner-city couples. In sum, neither employment nor education fully accounts for the racial and ethnic differences in rates of marriage for low-income fathers; thus, it is necessary to examine not only the mother-father relationship but also the relevant factors that affect the relationship.

Age is highly associated with the successful transition to fatherhood. Allen and Doherty (1996) and Cervera (1991) found that young fathers reported that a strained relationship with their children's mother was a major obstacle to their involvement with their children. Readiness is another potentially important factor that affects the quality of the mother-father relationship. Leathers and Kelley (2000) examined the consequences of unintended first pregnancy on the mental health of 124 cohabiting couples. Unintended pregnancy was partially related to the men's depressive symptoms, in that men who reported an unintended pregnancy also reported more symptoms of depression. Finally, relationship distress partly explained the associations between unintended pregnancy and the fathers' depressive symptoms. The quality of their relationships or difficulties with communication was linked to their perceptions of pregnancy intention with postpartum depressive symptoms. Particularly for men, the study revealed that difficulties in the couple's relationship and inadequate social support help explain the apparent negative effects of an unintended pregnancy, including postpartum depression.

Cohabitation and Culture

As with other types of romantic commitments, various factors influence a couple's decision to cohabit. Cohabitation primarily has been examined in the context of its effect on marital stability. Woods and Emery (2002) explored the nature of the relationship between cohabitation and marital dissolution to address the anomaly of inconclusive and, at times, contradictory findings in the cohabitation literature. The prospective study tested the selection hypothesis of cohabitation, postulating that personal attributes influence one's selection into cohabitation and subsequent divorce rather than cohabitation's directly contributing to divorce. The results of the study supported the selection hypothesis. Delinquency, which served as a proxy for personality, ethnicity, and cultural and individual beliefs, predicted divorce. Cohabitation had little effect on divorce after taking the selection factors into account. Personal attributes thus selected individuals into cohabitation and any subsequent marital dissolution, acting as mediators between cohabitation and divorce.

Strong evidence exists that ethnicity and culture influence marriage (e.g., Dickson, 1993), as well as divorce (e.g., Woods & Emery, 2002) and cohabitation (e.g., Manning & Landale, 1996; Woods & Emery, 2002). African Americans have a lower marriage rate than do European Americans (Raley, 1996). Impediments such as limited employment opportunities, incarceration, drug and alcohol abuse, and early mortality significantly decrease the number of African American men who are either physically available or considered eligible for marriage (Dickson, 1993). The increased economic and occupational opportunities of African American women decrease the financial incentive to marry and further enlarge the disparity between compatible African American men and women (Dickson, 1993; Wilson, 1987). African Americans have higher divorce rates than do European, Latino, and Asian Americans, which also may be related in part to the disparity between marriageable African American men and women (Dickson, 1993).

Whereas cohabitation has accelerated the transition to marriage among premarital pregnant Caucasian women, cohabitation has had no affect among African Americans (Manning & Landale, 1996; Raley, 1996). In the total population, Caucasians are more likely to have cohabited in their lifetime than are African Americans (Bumpass & Sweet, 1989). Never-married African Americans, however, are more likely to have cohabited than are never-married Caucasians (Bumpass, Sweet, & Cherlin, 1991), and compared to Caucasians, African Americans are almost twice as likely to cohabit in their first romantic union (Raley, 1996). Many African American cohabitors do not marry their partners (Schoen & Owens, 1992), and Manning and Landale (1996) found that cohabiting and single African American women have a similar likelihood of marriage. Cohabiting unions more quickly lead to marriage for Caucasians than for African Americans (Manning & Smock, 1996). Even among cohabiting unions, African Americans spend longer periods in less stable unions than do Caucasians (Raley, 1996).

Latino Americans' cultures affect their relationship decisions as well. Mexican Americans tend to favor marriage more than do Caucasians (Oropesa, 1996). Mexican Americans generally view marriage more positively than they do being single, and their marriage intentions increase their approval of cohabitation. Foreign-born Mexican Americans tend to adhere most strongly to the belief of marriage, but many other Mexican American women may prefer to cohabit in order to retain some of the freedom they potentially lose once married (Oropesa, 1996). Cohabitation has been found to have a profound negative effect among pregnant Puerto Rican women (Manning & Landale, 1996). Puerto Ricans are likely to cohabit, and cohabitation is more likely to serve as an alternative to marriage for Puerto Ricans than for Caucasians. Among Puerto Ricans, there is a historical prevalence of consensual unions and a higher level of acceptance of cohabitation (Manning & Landale, 1996). Puerto Ricans, in fact, are least disapproving of cohabitation in the absence of plans to marry, due considerably to their beliefs about nonmarital sex and childbearing.

The ethnic differences in cohabitation imply sociological factors, such as limited economic opportunities, incarceration, substance use, and mortality, which can affect the availability of romantic partners as well as relationship quality. The within-ethnic-group heterogeneity highlights the diversity that exists among a people. Within-group analyses thus reveal factors than can be masked when simply contrasting groups.

■ Family Structure Implications for Child Development

Limited research exists on the direct effects of the alternate family structures on child development. Extant research has found that various family practices and compositions can be adaptive for children as well as for the adult family members. For example, parenting styles considered maladaptive for middle-class and high-income families can be protective under certain circumstances. No-nonsense and even more authoritarian parenting styles, for example, have been found to be adaptive for many African American children and children living in dangerous environments (Brody & Flor, 1998; Peters, 1976, 1981).

Typically, research suggests that the presence of a responsive, sensitive grandmother seemed to safeguard infants against the deleterious influence of a single-parent family (e.g., Apfel & Seitz, 1996), that is, a single mother has an increased opportunity to improve her career options, participate in educational activities, and get gainful employment when she shares a residence with her mother. Furthermore, although adolescent mothers who are involved in some form of self-improvement are spending less time in child care tasks, the total amount of child care the infant receives is not reduced in 3-generation households. Several studies (Apfel & Seitz, 1996; Davis, 2002; Davis & Rhodes, 1994) indicate that an extended family's involvement with child care indirectly benefited the child of an adolescent mother by allowing her the opportunity to improve her situation. Adolescent mothers who remained in their mother's household were more likely to complete school and less likely to continue to receive public assistance than were adolescent mothers who established separate households. The mothers who continued to live at home spent a lower percentage of time engaging in child care tasks, were able to invest more time in self-improvement, and were more connected to their social networks than were the adolescent mothers who set up independent housing.

Low-income parents may have unrealistic educational aspirations for their children. The parents tend to have a relaxed attitude toward dropping out of school, and they often have little knowledge about how to enroll their children in college.

The parents also may have little or no knowledge about the academic discipline that is required of college students (Wilson, Pina, Chan, & Soberanis, 2000). These observations resulted in a consideration of how the parents' educational level could be relevant to reported parental influences on college attendance, assuming that the reported parental influence directly is associated with the parents' educational background.

Additional research on the impact of family interactions on child development is necessary to understand influences on normative and maladaptive development. Longitudinal research, for example, can help determine factors related to children's development and the direction of influence between variables. Longitudinal designs facilitate inferences about causality, thereby assisting in conclusions and implications of findings that can help promote positive development.

■ Empirical Perspectives

The importance of considering the cultural context of families is revealed in empirical explorations of relevant father characteristics. Using data from the Fragile Families study, the characteristics of fathers' social and psychological well-being that distinguish involved and noninvolved fathers are examined. The characteristics of interest include such social factors as race, age, last year's income, immigration status, and the number of children. Characteristics of psychological well-being include health, life satisfaction, sense of personal efficacy, depressive symptoms, substance use, and history of incarceration. Finally, cultural and religious factors are also considered. The descriptive analysis assumes that within a group of seemingly similar men, some characteristics will vary across the group. Given that the sample is screened for a demographic group of young, low-income women who are having their first or second child, it follows that the majority of the fathers are also young, low-income, and less educated. The analysis represents both a cross-sectional and longitudinal evaluation that examines the relationship between social and psychological characteristics and paternal behaviors. Unlike many studies that rely on mothers' reports of paternal activity, Fragile Families data contain the reports of both mothers and fathers. Hence, the Fragile Families sample represents an important opportunity to investigate a sample that represents a group of highly diverse low-income and working-class fathers.

Classification and regression tree technology (CART; Breitman, Freidman, Olshen, & Stone, 1997) represents an advanced actuarial approach to understanding variables and factors influencing father involvement. CART is employed to classify sample data as accurately and reliably as possible. The procedure permits a stepwise examination of the relationship between an outcome variable and multiple predictor variables (Steinberg & Colla, 1997).

CART analysis typically results in the categories of characteristics that are associated with the presence and absence of the primary outcome (Lewis, n.d.; Yohannes & Webb, 1999). Trees representing distinct classes of participants are created through a three-step process: recursive partitioning, pruning, and cross-validation.

Recursive partitioning allows for the best predictor variables to be selected by employing a binary decision tree as a classifier. It is a form of binary partitioning that splits the sample into binary subsamples. In addition, recursive partitioning involves a repetitive splitting of variables against the presence or absence of an outcome variable. All possible splits of the data are considered until further splitting is impossible, which occurs when only one case would remain in the node.

Pruning creates a sequence of smaller trees. Pruning occurs because the analysis produces more splits than are necessary to explain the relationships of variables to the criterion. CART determines the best tree by the testing of error rates. Additionally, the CART process includes a cross-validation step, which is a resampling technique that provides an unbiased estimate of the misclassification rates and identifies the tree that minimizes the misclassification rates. Cross-validation selects the optimal tree from the sequence of smaller trees created during the pruning process (Nelson, Bloch, Longstreth, & Shi, 1998). Calculating probabilities of group membership, or nodes, and the costs of misclassification is required.

CART allowed for the partitioning of all participants into categories of involved and noninvolved fathers. A decision tree was constructed by finding the single characteristic that provided the best split between the proportions of the men who were and were not actively involved with their children. The partitioning process continued until a decision tree was formed. The decision tree's various branches are subgroups that are characterized by questions relevant to the particular group of men.

Method

Procedures and Sample Recruitment.   The data were drawn from a larger study, referred to as the Fragile Families and Child Well-Being (FFCWB) Project (Garfinkel, McLanahan, Brooks-Gunn, & Tienda, 2000; McLanahan, Garfinkel, Brooks-Gunn, & Tienda, 2000). The FFCWB is a national study that is designed to examine the consequences of nonmarital childbearing in low-income families and the consequences of welfare reform and the role of fathers in unwed families.

A common data collection procedure was employed to recruit low-income, nonresident mothers and fathers in 20 U.S. cities. Within each city, participants were recruited from up to five hospitals to obtain a sample of nonmarital and marital births. All participants were parents (having their first or second child) and were selected based on welfare status and/or eligibility to receive public aid. Mothers and the majority of fathers were interviewed in the hospital within 24 hr after the birth of their child. Those fathers not interviewed in the hospital were interviewed shortly after the mother left the hospital. Data collection began in 1999, 3 years after the implementation of the Personal Responsibility and Reconciliation Act.

Social, Health, and Psychological Characteristics of Fathers.   Our analysis involved partitioning paternal characteristics into classifications associated with involved and noninvolved fathers. Table 13.1 contains a frequency distribution of all characteristics included in this analysis, and it includes social demographic characteristics such as

TABLE 13.1 *Fathers' Capacities and Well-Being in Twenty Cities: Definition of Variables in Analyses*

Characteristic	N	%
Race		
White	785	21
Black	1,789	47
Hispanic	1,048	28
Other	165	4
Relationship status		
No relations	72	2
Friends	195	5
On/off	200	5
Steady–no–living	602	16
Cohabiting	1,658	44
Married	1,076	28
Father's age (years)		
0–20	318	8
20–24	1,158	31
25–29	934	25
30–35	803	21
36+	584	15
Father's income ($)		
0–5,000	360	9
5,000–9,999	322	9
10,000–19,999	742	19
20,000–34,999	933	24
35,000–49,999	570	15
50,000–74,999	517	14
75,000+	386	10
Born in the United States		
Yes	3,076	80
No	746	20
Number of children		
One child	1,112	51
Two children	608	28
Three+ children	474	21
Health quality		
Poor	24	1
Fair	267	7
Good	785	21
Very good	1,433	37
Excellent	1,314	34

(*continued*)

TABLE 13.1 *Fathers' Capacities and Well-Being in Twenty Cities: Definition of Variables in Analyses* (continued)

Characteristic	N	%
Life satisfaction		
Yes	2,850	75
No	963	25
Feel pushed around		
Yes	564	15
No	3,247	85
Depressive symptoms		
No symptoms	616	16
Low endorsement	1,594	42
Moderate endorsement	938	25
High endorsement	635	17
Mental health problems		
Yes	258	7
No	3,395	93
Tobacco use		
Yes	1,493	39
No	2,327	61
Substance abuse problems		
Yes	252	7
No	3,390	93
Incarcerated		
Yes	1,186	29
No	2,905	71
Fathers regularly involved		
Never	510	14
Regular	3,067	86
Fathers live with child		
Nonresident	1,069	28
Resident	2,734	72

race, age, reported income, marital status, education, number of children, and immigration status. Health and psychological well-being characteristics involved perceived level of health, use of alcohol, drug, and tobacco products, and depressive symptom characteristics. Also, the men reported on their sense of life satisfaction and sense of personal control. Finally, incarceration history was recorded. The dependent measures are referred to as paternal involvement and were drawn from the 12-month follow-up questions that asked about fathers' involvement in child care activities, including behaviors directed toward caring for and playing with the child. In this analysis, fathers were given credit if they indicated ever having participated in child-rearing activities.

The social, health, and psychological characteristics were entered into a CART analysis as predictor variables. The variable father regularly involved was entered as the outcome variable. The CART analysis produced a 13-node tree with primary splits occurring on jail, immigrant status, being African American, and drug use. Figure 13.1 presents the output of the chart analysis.

Figure 13.1 outlines the various clusters of men. The deciding variables were substance use, incarceration, immigrant status, number of children, and being African American. Involved fathers were separated from uninvolved fathers by whether the fathers had ever been incarcerated and whether the fathers had a substance use problem. In addition, involved fathers were described as being immigrants and of Hispanic origin and having three or more children. Uninvolved fathers were described as being African American. Optimally, there were 14 different clusters of fathers. The clusters were evenly divided between involved and uninvolved fathers. The clusters were formed by first culling the sample for incarceration, substance problem, and immigration status, as those variables represent the base branches of the tree. Interestingly, ever incarcerated and immigration status were associated with being African American and Hispanic, respectively. Other predictors included depressive symptoms (asymptomatic), SES (not being poor), residential status (living with children), and age (older than 20 years).

The classification accuracy on this sample was 84% for predicting uninvolved fathers and 73% for predicting involved fathers. The cross-validation accuracy was similar, with 83% correctly classified as uninvolved and 73% classified as involved. Cross-validation tells us how accurately the tree would predict if applied to a new data set. Table 13.2 reports the terminal nodes and classifications characteristics. Splitters and characteristics indicate the specific variable and interacting variables, on which the data separated. Classification indicates the proportion of the split sample that had the characteristics, and probability represents their proportion within the whole sample.

Variable Importance

In addition to identifying the main predictor variables, CART identifies the relative importance for each of the independent. Variables are scored based on the improvement each variable makes to overall prediction of the outcome (see table 13.3). This allows for identification of variables that are important but whose significance is masked or hidden by other variables during the tree building process (Yohannes & Hoddinott, 1999). The characteristics *incarceration, substance use, immigration status,* and *race* were consistent predictors.

■ Discussion and Conclusions

Overall, the results indicate that fathers' involvement variables are associated with social characteristic variables in accordance with previous studies (Collins, 1986; Gove, 1972,

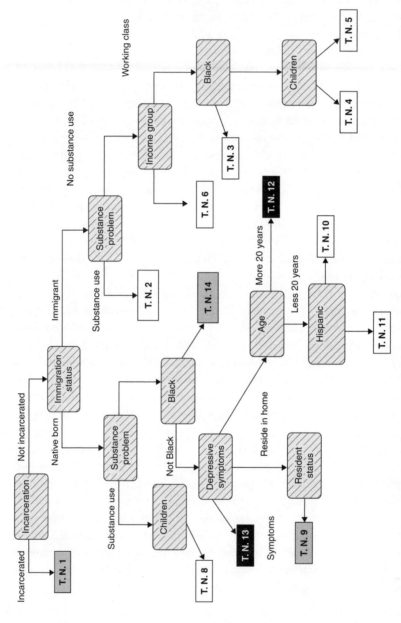

FIGURE 13.1 Complete classification tree with striped boxes representing parent nodes and small boxes representing terminal nodes. Gray terminal boxes indicate uninvolved fathers. Black terminal boxes indicate involved fathers.

TABLE 13.2 *Terminal Node Characteristics and Classification*

Terminal Node (Node Classification)	Splitters	Characteristics	Classification	Probability*
1 (N = 828) (uninvolved)	Incarceration	Incarcerated	46.4	.231
2 (N = 5) (uninvolved)	Incarceration Immigrant status Substance problem	Not incarcerated Immigrant Substance abuse	60.0	.001
3 (N = 328) (uninvolved)	Incarceration Immigrant status Substance problem Low SES Black	Not incarcerated Immigrant No substance abuse Not low SES Not black	60.7	.092
4 (N = 36) (uninvolved)	Incarceration Immigrant status Substance problem Low SES Black Children	Not incarcerated Immigrant No substance abuse Not low SES Black One child or three children	36.1	.010
5 (N = 20) (involved)	Incarceration Immigrant status Substance problem Low SES Black Children	Not incarcerated Immigrant No substance abuse Not low SES Black Two children	80.0	.005
6 (N = 40) (involved)	Incarceration Immigrant status Substance problem Low SES	Not incarcerated Immigrant No substance abuse Low SES	77.5	.011
7 (N = 34) (uninvolved)	Incarceration Immigrant status Substance problem Children	Not incarcerated Not immigrant Substance abuse Three children	50.0	.002
8 (N = 6) (involved)	Incarceration Immigrant status Substance problem Children	Not incarcerated Not immigrant Substance abuse One or two children	100.00	.002

(*continued*)

TABLE 13.2 *Terminal Node Characteristics and Classification* (*continued*)

Terminal Node (Node Classification)	Splitters	Characteristics	Classification	Probability*
9 (N = 96) (uninvolved)	Incarceration Immigrant status Substance problem Black Depressive symptoms Resident status	Not incarcerated Not immigrant No substance problem Not Black Depressive symptoms Not reside in home	39.6	.039
10 (N = 67) (uninvolved)	Incarceration Immigrant status Substance problem Black Depressive symptoms Resident status Age Hispanic	Not incarcerated Not immigrant No substance problem Not Black Depressive symptoms Reside in home Less than 20 years Hispanic	40.3	.020
11 (N = 55) (involved)	Incarceration Immigrant status Substance problem Black Depressive symptoms Resident status Age Hispanic	Not incarcerated Not immigrant No substance problem Not Black Depressive symptoms Reside in home Less than 20 years Not Hispanic	72.2	.016
12 (N = 418) (involved)	Incarceration Immigrant status Substance problem Black Depressive symptoms Reside with child Age	Not incarcerated Not immigrant No substance problem Not Black Asymptomatic Reside with child Greater than 20 years	72.2	.117
13 (N = 108) (involved)	Incarceration Immigrant status Substance problem Black Depressive symptoms	Not incarcerated Not immigrant No substance problem Not Black Depressive symptoms	34.4	.032
14 (N = 1536) (involved)	Incarceration Immigrant status Substance problem Black	Not incarcerated Not immigrant No substance problem Black	74.5	.430

*Probability of cases within each class at a specific node.

TABLE 13.3 *Variable Importance*

Variable	Relative Importance*
Incarceration[†]	100.00
Immigrant status[†]	31.02
Working socioeconomic status[†]	17.27
African American[†]	11.50
Substance problem[†]	11.12
Depressive symptoms[†]	10.84
Resident status[†]	7.93
Age less than 20 years[†]	7.24
Hispanic American	6.12
Children (number)	5.92
White American	3.53
Other American	3.35
Tobacco use	2.67
Satisfied with life	1.89
Self efficacy	0.000
Good health	0.000
Alcohol	0.000
Low socioeconomic status	0.000
Middle socioeconomic status	0.000

*Score based on improvement made as a surrogate to the primary splitting variable.
[†]Variables representing primary splitters.

1973; Umberson & Williams, 1993). That is, fathers who were married or cohabiting, working or middle-class, and perceived good health and no depressive symptoms were likely to be classified as involved fathers. On the other hand those fathers who had ever been incarcerated, abuse substance, very low income, symptoms of depression were classified as not involved with their children. In addition, being immigrant, participating in cultural and religious activities were associated with paternal involvement. The relationship between perceived health and life satisfaction, and race/ethnicity and reported income was consistent with previous literature (Collins, 1986; Gove, 1972, 1973; Umberson & Williams, 1993). Previous literature has suggested that divorced fathers experience an increased level of health problems and a diminished sense of life satisfaction that was associated with decreased contact with their children (Collins, 1986; Gove, 1972, 1973; Umberson & Williams, 1993). In addition, depressive symptoms strongly were associated with race/ethnicity. In particular, African American and Hispanic men expressed more symptoms than did Caucasian men (Radloff, 1977, 1991; Robins & Regier, 1991), but income was not a predictor.

In the past, family research that focused on parental involvement typically consisted of reports from mothers but not from fathers. However, research has longed suspect that children who had consistent paternal involvement fared better than those who do not have father involvement. The current study demonstrated that fathers are interested in their children well being. The results suggest that it is important to examine context as well as individual characteristics when investigating father involvement. For this particular analysis, a culture specific approach was employed to emphasize the within-group variation of low-income fathers.

Although research methodology consistent with the culture-specific approach is vital, there are logistical problems when conducting this type of research with African American fathers. Specifically, there is the problem of recruitment, which extends to identifying an appropriate setting for this research to occur. This problem is particularly salient when the researcher is from a different race given the historical events of African American subjects being mistreated (e.g., the Tuskegee Experiment). Hence, it is crucial for researchers to build connections and relationships with key members of the community in order to establish trust with that community, as trust with the community of interest is integral when performing cross cultural research (Berry et al., 1995).

In light of these methodological and conceptual issues, it is important that a culturally sound research agenda be set forth. Moreover, it is important that funding agencies become cognizant of inchoate state of research pertaining to African American and other minority fathers. It is important for funding agencies to set forth programmatic initiatives aimed at funding research projects that recognize the embryonic state of research on minority fathers and incorporate developmentally appropriate methodologies that will enhance and add to the extant literature on African American and other minority fathers.

In sum, our changing society warrants a need to reexamine paternal involvement, particularly African American paternal involvement. Fathers have become more involved with their children regardless of their residence status. Hence, research must begin to explore the multitude of ways and conditions in which fathers interact with their children.

■ References

Allen, W. D., & Doherty, W. J. (1996). The responsibilities of fatherhood as perceived by African American teenage fathers. *Families in Society, 77,* 142–155.

Apfel, N., & Seitz, V. (1996). African American mother adolescent mothers, their families, and their daughters: A longitudinal perspective over twelve years. In B. J. Ross Leadbeater and N. Way (Eds.), *Urban girls resisting stereotypes, creating identities* (pp. 149–170). New York: New York University Press.

Belsky, J., Rovine, M., & Fish, M. (1989). The developing family system. In M. R. Gunnar & E. Thelen (Eds.), *The Minnesota Symposia on Child Psychology: Vol. 22. Systems and development.* Hillsdale, NJ: Erlbaum.

Berry, J. W., Poortinga, Y. H., Segall, M. H., & Dasen, P. R. (1995). *Cross-cultural psychology.* New York: Cambridge University Press.

Breitman, L., Freidman, J., Olshen, R., & Stone, C. (1997). CART: Tree structured non parametric data analysis. San Diego, CA: Salford Systems.

Brody, G. H., & Flor, D. L. (1998). Maternal resources, parenting practices, and child competence in rural, single-parent African American families. *Child Development, 69*(3), 803–816.

Bumpass, L. L., & Sweet, J. A. (1989). National estimates of cohabitation. *Demography, 26,* 615–625.

Bumpass, L. L., Sweet, J. A., & Cherlin, A. (1991). The role of cohabitation in declining rates of marriage. *Journal of Marriage and the Family, 53,* 913–927.

Cervera, N. (1991). Unwed teenage pregnancy: Family relationships with the father of the baby. *Families in Society, 72,* 29–37.

Chadiha, L. A. (1992). Black husband's economic problems and resiliency during the transition to marriage. *Families in Society: Journal of Contemporary Human Services, 73,* 542–552.

Collins, P. H. (1986). The Afro-American work/family nexus: An exploratory analysis. *The Western Journal of Black Studies, 10*(3), 148–158.

Dallas, C. M., & Chen, S. P. C. (1998). Experiences of African American adolescent fathers. *Western Journal of Nursing Research, 20*(2), 210–222.

Davis, A. A. (2002). Younger and older African American adolescent mothers' relationship with their mothers and female peer. *Journal of Adolescent Research, 17*(5), 491–508.

Davis, A. A., & Rhodes, J. E. (1994). African American teenage mothers and their mothers: An analysis of supportive problematic interactions. *American Journal of Community Psychology 22*(1), 12–20.

Dickson, L. (1993). The future of marriage and family in black America. *Journal of Black Studies, 4,* 472–491.

Garfinkel, I., McLanahan, S., Brooks-Gunn, J., & Tienda, M. (2000). Fragile families and welfare reform: An introduction. *Children and Youth Services, 23,* 277–301.

Gove, W. R. (1972). The relationship between sex roles, marital status and mental illness. *Social Forces, 51,* 34–44.

Gove, W. R. (1973). Sex, marital status and morality. *American Journal of Sociology, 79,* 45–67.

Hamer, J. F. (1997). The fathers of "fatherless" black children. *Families in Society, 78*(6), 564–578.

Lawson, E., & Thompson, A. (1994). Historical and social correlates of African American Divorce: Review of the literature and implications for research. *The Western Journal of Black Studies, 18*(2), 91–103.

Leathers, S. L., & Kelley, M. A. (2000). Unintended pregnancy and depressive symptoms among first-time mothers and fathers. *American Journal of Orthopsychiatry, 70*(4), 523–531.

Lewis, R. J. (n.d.). *An introduction to classification and regression (CART) analysis.* Retrieved August 9, 2002, from http://www.saem.org/download/lewis1.pdf

Lindsay, E. W., Mize, J., & Pettit, G. S. (1997). Differential pay patterns of mothers and fathers of sons and daughters: Implications for children's gender role development. *Sex Roles, 37*(9, 10), 643–661.

Manning, W. D., & Landale, N. S. (1996). Racial and ethnic differences in the role of cohabitation in premarital childbearing. *Journal of Marriage and the Family, 58*(1), 63–77.

Manning, W. D., & Smock, P. J. (1996). Why marry? Race and the transition to marriage among cohabitors. *Demography, 32,* 509–520.

Martin, J. A., Hamilton, B. E., Ventura, S. J., Menacker, F., & Park, M. M. (2002). *Births: Finaldata for 2000. National vital statistics reports (Vol. 50, No. 5).* Hyattsville, MD: National Center for Health Statistics. Retrieved September 15, 2003, from http://www.cdc.gov/nchs/data/nvsr50/nvsr50_05.pdf

McAdoo, J. L. (1986). Black fathers' relationships with their preschool children and the children's ethnic identity. In R. A. Lewis & R. E. Salt (Eds.), *Men in families.* Newbury Park, CA: Sage.

McLanahan, S., Garfinkel, I., Brooks-Gunn, J., & Tienda, M. (2000). *The Fragile Families and Child Well-Being Study.* Retrieved August 9, 2002, from http://www.columbia.edu/cu/ssw/grants/indivproj/garf2.html

Miller, D. B. (1994). Influences of parental involvement of African American adolescent fathers. *Child and Adolescent Social Work Journal, 11*(5), 363–378.

Nelson, L. M., Bloch, D. A., Longstreth, W. T., & Shi, H. (1998). Recursive partitioning for the identification of disease risk subgroups: A case control study of subarachnoid hemorrhage. *Journal of Clinical Epidemiology, 51*(3), 199–209.

Oropesa, R. S. (1996). Normative beliefs about marriage and cohabitation: A comparison of non-Latino Whites, Mexican Americans, and Puerto Ricans. *Journal of Marriage and the Family, 58,* 49–62.

Peters, M. F. (1976). *Nine Black families: A study of household management and childrearing in Black families with working mothers.* Unpublished doctoral dissertation, Harvard University.

Peters, M. F. (1981). *Childrearing patterns in a sample of Black parents of children age 1 to 3.* Paper presented at Annual Meeting of the Society for Research in Child Development, Boston.

Radloff, L. S. (1977). The CES-D scale: A self-report depression scale for research in the general population. *Applied psychological measurement 1*(3), 385–401.

Radloff, L. S. (1991). The use of the Center for Epidemiologic Studies depression scale in adolescent and young adult. *Journal of Youth and Adolescence 20*(2), 149–166.

Raley, R. K. (1996). A shortage of marriageable men? A note on the role of cohabitation in Black-White differences in marriage rates. *American Sociological Review, 61,* 973–983.

Robins, L. N., & Regier, D. A. (1991). *Psychiatric disorders in America.* New York: Free Press.

Roy, K. (1999). Low-income single fathers in an African-American community and the requirements of welfare reform. *Journal of Family Issues, 20*(4), 432–457.

Schoen, R., & Owens, D. (1992). A further look at first marriages and first unions. In S. South & S. Tolney (Eds.), *The changing American: Sociological and demographic perspectives* (pp. 1090–1117). Boulder, CO: Westview.

Stack, C. B. (1974). *All our kin: Strategies for survival in a Black community.* New York: Harper & Row.

Steinberg, D., & Colla, P. (1997). *CART: Tree structured non-parametric data analysis.* San Diego, CA: Salford Systems.

Stier, H., & Tienda, M. (1993). Are men marginal to the family? Insights from Chicago's inner city. In J. Hood (Ed.), *Men, work, and family: Research on men and masculinities series* (Vol. 4, pp. 23–44). Newbury Park, CA: Sage.

Taylor, R. J., & Chatters, L. M., Tucker, M. B., & Lewis, E. (1990). Developments in research on black families: A decade in review. *Journal of Marriage and the Family, 52,* 993–1014.

Taylor, R. J., & Johnson, W. E., Jr. (1997). Family roles and family satisfaction among black men. In R. J. Taylor, J. S. Jackson, & L. M. Chatters (Eds.), *Family life in black America.* Thousand Oaks, CA: Sage.

Testa, M., Astone, N. M., Krogh, M., & Neckerman, K. M. (1989). Employment and marriage among inner-city fathers. *The Annals of The American Academy of Political and Social Science, 501,* 79–91.

Tucker, M. B., & Taylor, R. J. (1989). Demographic correlates of relationship status among Black Americans. *Journal of Marriage and the Family, 51,* 655–665.

Umberson, D., & Williams C. L. (1993). Divorced fathers: Parental role strain and psychological distress. *Journal of Family Issues, 14*(3), 378–400.

U.S. Census Bureau. (2002a). *Annual demographic supplement to March 2002 current population survey, current population reports, series P20-547, "Children's living arrangements and characteristics: March 2002."* Retrieved September 15, 2003, from http://www.census.gov/population/socdemo/hh-fam/tabCH-3.pdf

U.S. Census Bureau. (2002b). *Annual demographic supplement to March 2002 current population survey, current population reports, series P20-547, "Children's living arrangements and characteristics: March 2002."* Retrieved September 15, 2003, from http://www.census.gov/population/socdemo/hh-fam/tabMS-1.pdf

U.S. Census Bureau. (2002c). *Current population survey, 2001 and 2002 annual demographic supplements.* Retrieved September 15, 2003, from http://www.census.gov/hhes/poverty/poverty01/table1.pdf

U.S. Census Bureau. (2002d). *Living arrangements of child under 18 years and marital status of parents, by age, gender, race, and Hispanic origin of the child for all children: March 2002.* Retrieved September 15, 2003, from http://www.census.gov/population/socdemo/hh-fam/cps2002/tabC3-black.pdf

U.S. Census Bureau, Population Division, Fertility and Statistics Branch. (2001). *Children's living arrangements and characteristics: March 2001.* Retrieved September 15, 2003, from http://www.census.gov/population/wwww/socdemo/hh-fam/cps2001.html

Westney, O., Cole, O. J., & Munford, T. (1986). Adolescent unwed prospective fathers: Readiness for fatherhood and behaviors towards the mother and the expected infant. *Adolescence, 21*(84), 900–911.

Wilson, M. N., Lewis, J. B., Hinton, I. D., Kohn, L. P., Underwood, A., Kho Phoung Hogue, L., et al. (1995). Promotion of African American family life: African American families, poverty, and social programs. In M. N. Wilson (Issue Ed.) & W. Damon (Series Ed.), *New direction for child development: Vol. 68 African American family life: Its structural and ecological aspects.* San Francisco: Jossey-Bass.

Wilson, M. N., Pina, L. M. Chan, R., & Soberanis, D. D. (2000). Ethnic minority families and the majority educational systems: African American, Chinese American, Hispanic American and Native American families. In H. E. Fitzgerald, B. M. Lester, & B. S. Zuckerman (Eds.), *Children of color: Research, health and policy issues* (pp. 257–278). Ann Arbor, MI: SRCD.

Wilson, M. N., Tolson, T. F. J., Hinton, I., & Kiernan, M. (1990). Flexibility and sharing of childcare duties in Black families. *Sex Roles, 22,* 409–425.

Wilson, M. N., Woods, L. N., & Hijjawi, G. R. (2004). African American families in context: Internal and external phenomena. In J. E. Everett, S. S. Chipunga, & B. R. Leashore (Eds.), *Child welfare revisited: An Afrocentric perspective* (pp. 124–144). New Brunswick, NJ: Rutgers University Press.

Wilson, W. J. (1987). *The truly disadvantaged: The inner city, the underclass, and public policy.* Chicago: University of Chicago Press.

Woods, L. N., & Emery, R. E. (2002). The cohabitation effect on divorce: Selection or causation? *Journal of Divorce and Remarriage, 37,* 101–122.

Yohannes, Y., & Hoddinott, J. (1999). Classification and regression trees: An introduction. Washington, DC: International Food Policy Research Institute. Retrieved August 2002 from http://www.ifpri.org.

Yohannes, Y., & Webb, P. (1999). *Classification and regression trees, CART: A user manual for identifying indicators of vulnerability to famine and chronic food insecurity.* Washington, DC: International Food Policy Research Institute. Retrieved August 2002 from http://www.ifpri.org

14

Mothers in Transition: Model-Based Strategies for Effective Parenting

Bernadette Marie Bullock and Marion S. Forgatch

Divorce is a time of tremendous reorganization for every person in a family. Multiple transitions in family structure commonly occur, with most parents changing partners at least once if not several times. The family literature is replete with studies attesting to the negative outcomes of divorce on family members. While findings for remarriage are less consistent, a greater number of parental partner transitions are linked to increases in parent and child adjustment problems (Brody, Neubaum, & Forehand, 1988; Furstenberg & Spanier, 1984).

The sequelae of divorce can profoundly affect all members of the nuclear family system. Mothers typically experience increased stress and distress, disrupted social support, and socioeconomic decline (Amato, 2000). Children and adolescents tend to exhibit behavior problems, depression, anxiety, deteriorating academic performance, and poor peer relationships (Hetherington & Mekos, 1997). The sparse literature that exists regarding postdivorce adjustment for fathers and paternal parenting suggests that divorced men are more likely to participate in health-compromising acts than nondivorced men and to experience greater psychological distress than divorced mothers, particularly in the early stages of divorce (Bloom, Asher, & White, 1978; Jacobs, 1982). While the picture may appear grim for a significant subset of youngsters, long-term longitudinal studies indicate that many children of divorce develop normally (Amato, 2000). In the short run, however, most family members undergo turbulence and emotional upheaval.

Randomized experimental trials using theoretically based interventions are needed to better understand the mechanisms of family member adjustment following divorce and repartnering. The central aim of this chapter is to provide a contextual model of family structure transitions and to discuss the role of preventive interventions in mitigating the effects of divorce and repartnering on short- and long-term adjustment. We begin with a review of existing programs designed to improve family member adjustment following divorce. This is followed by an introduction of the social interaction learning (SIL) model and an examination of its relevance in explicating behavioral change within the context of household recon-stitution. A conceptual model of the dynamic cycle of family member transitions and its implications for family outcomes is then presented, followed by a discussion of prevention and intervention strategies for divorced families using the SIL model and related empirical findings. Last, cultural and ethnic considerations, ongoing efforts to implement these interventions in the community, and future directions for research are discussed.

■ Prevention and Intervention Programs for Divorcing Families

In spite of what is known regarding the negative impact of divorce on affected individuals, very few intervention programs exist that directly target the issues of individuals experiencing divorce (Forgatch, 1994; Forgatch & Marquez, 1993; Pedro-Carroll, 1985; Pedro-Carroll, Alpert-Gillis, & Sterling, 1987; Stolberg & Gar-rison, 1985; Wolchik et al., 1993). Most of these prevention efforts intervene directly with children at risk for developing psychosocial problems (Pedro-Carroll, 1985; Pedro-Carroll et al., 1987). Child-centered programs typically address issues per-taining to the development of constructive coping skills, increasing positive per-ceptions, clearing up misconceptions regarding the divorce process, and providing a supportive emotional venue to express divorce-related feelings and experiences. While there is evidence that these child-focused programs are effective in re-mediating children's divorce-related distress, they tend to ignore the extensive lit-erature that identifies parents as the most proximal and effective agents of change (Patterson, 1982; Patterson, Reid, & Dishion, 1992; and others).

A number of parent-centered programs have been developed to address parental adjustment issues following divorce. For two programs in which quasi-experimental designs were utilized, positive effects were obtained for parents' mental health as a function of participating in the interventions; however, these effects did not translate to improvements in child outcomes (Stolberg & Garrison, 1985; Warren, Grew, & Ilgen, 1984). Single-parenting skills were also not differentially affected in programs that emphasized a combination of support and skill building (Stolberg & Garrison, 1985). The absence of improvement in parenting domains and child adjustment may be due to a lack of emphasis on the putative mediators that have more recently been associated with child outcomes—in particular, parenting practices.

To date, the literature contains only two preventive interventions for divorced mothers that directly target parenting mechanisms (Forgatch, 1994; Wolchik et al., 1993). The New Beginnings Parenting Program for Divorced Mothers arose from the "small theory" approach (Lipsey, 1990). At the crux of this method is the identifi-cation of mechanisms that directly affect psychosocial outcomes—for example, the quality of the mother-child relationship is believed to directly impact child ad-justment (Wolchik et al., 1993). This is succeeded by the specification of proximal outcomes that are directly implicated by changes in the variables that are targeted for change in the intervention. To draw from the previous example, improving the quality of mother-child relationships should result in measurable reductions in child anxiety, depression, and conduct problems (Wolchik et al., 1993). These causal and mediational processes must be directly tested vis-à-vis experimental designs.

Wolchik and colleagues (1993) concentrated on five empirically supported environmental and interpersonal factors pertaining to divorcing families in their development of the New Beginnings program. These include the quality of a child's relationship with the custodial parent, parental discipline practices, the degree of contact between the child and the noncustodial parent (typically the father), exposure to divorce-related negative events, and social support from other adults. Intervention targets included improving positive mother-child interactions, developing more consistent and well-articulated discipline practices, reducing factors that may impede father-child contact, managing anger, and increasing successful listening skills. Great attention was paid to attaining high levels of treatment fidelity and to evaluation of the therapeutic process (Lustig, Wolchik, & Weiss, 1999).

Seventy families participated in a randomized prevention trial to test the efficacy of the New Beginnings program (Wolchik et al., 1993). The intervention consisted of 10 weekly group meetings and two individual sessions. An evaluation of the therapeutic process indicated high levels of attendance, treatment fidelity, participant approval of group leaders, and reports of changes in their utilization of parenting strategies. Analyses posttreatment, as well as 6 months and 6 years later, suggested that this preventive intervention was most beneficial for children who exhibited higher levels of psychological distress at baseline. Treatment gains were small for youngsters with few distinguishable problems preceding the intervention (Wolchik et al., 1993, 2000, 2002).

Unfortunately, it is difficult to ascertain from the data presented the extent to which these findings represent a regression toward the mean for this particular subgroup of highly distressed youth, as opposed to differential effectiveness of the intervention depending upon a child's initial status (Stoolmiller, Eddy, & Reid, 2000). Given that many children resume normal functioning postdivorce (Amato, 2000), it would be useful for these researchers to further unpack the nature of their treatment effects by presenting data from the high-risk subgroups of intervention and comparison children separately in their analyses.

■ Social Interaction Learning and Oregon Divorce Models

The SIL model also provides a sound developmental and theoretical basis for interventions designed for divorced and repartnered families. The model specifies that family structure transitions and their concomitants (e.g., stress, depression, decreased income) affect children to the extent that these adverse contexts increase coercive parenting and decrease effective parenting. Such relationships are documented in longitudinal studies that employ multiple-method assessment, including observations of family interactions (Anderson, Greene, Hetherington, & Clingempeel, 1999; Capaldi & Patterson, 1991; DeGarmo & Forgatch, 1999; Hetherington, Bridges, & Insabella, 1998; Hetherington & Clingempeel, 1992).

Within the SIL model, disruptions in parenting quality are posited to affect children's socioemotional development, leading to increases in maternal stress and depression. This hypothesis was supported in two independent single-mother data sets using multiple-method assessment and longitudinal modeling (DeGarmo, Patterson, & Forgatch, 2004; Forgatch, Patterson, & Ray, 1996). In sum, marital turmoil and dissolution provide the impetus for a cycle of disruption that presents systemwide challenges to the reorganizing family. This disruption usually takes the form of deteriorating parenting quality, which increases the risk for poor child adjustment.

Two child-rearing approaches mediate contextual disruptors and negative child outcomes in this model: coercive parenting and effective parenting. Interventions based on the SIL target parents as the primary agents of change and emphasize increases in effective parenting strategies and decreases in coercive behaviors. Experimental and passive longitudinal studies in which divorced and repartnered families are directly observed suggest that without intervention, positive practices deteriorate and coercive practices increase in families experiencing parental separation and divorce. This, in turn, undermines children's socioemotional development (Anderson, Lindner, & Bennion, 1992; DeGarmo et al., 2004; Forgatch & DeGarmo, 1999, Martinez & Forgatch, 2001; Shaw, Emery, & Tuer, 1993).

Coercive processes emphasize the role of escape and avoidance conditioning during family interactions in the development of aggressive and antisocial behavior. Key dimensions in coercion theory include negative reciprocity, escalation, and negative reinforcement. In particular, the reciprocal exchanges of aversive behavior in the context of family disagreements often lead to escalations in intensity until one person in the dispute yields, negatively reinforcing the other person for increasing hostility. These microsocial patterns of behavior become overlearned and generalize across settings, resulting in the instantiation of a coercive cycle for parents and their children. Coercion is a dynamic that is rooted within family conflict and negative affect and can travel into other social environments. While all families use coercion to some degree, the problem becomes serious when coercive processes outweigh positive interchanges.

With regard to effective parenting, five practices delineated in the SIL model represent positive parenting strategies that may reduce coercive interactions and promote healthy development for youngsters. These core components—effective discipline, skill encouragement, monitoring/supervision, problem solving, and positive involvement—are well defined for professionals and parents in a variety of books and media (Chamberlain, 1994; Dishion & Kavanagh, 2003; Forgatch & Patterson, 1989; Patterson & Forgatch, 1987; Reid & Eddy, 2002). Together, coercive and effective parenting practices are linked to both proximal and distal child adjustment in a number of studies with diverse populations (Dishion & Bullock, 2002; Dishion & Kavanagh, 2003; Forgatch & Knutson, 2002; Patterson et al., 1992; Reid, Patterson, & Snyder, 2002).

The Oregon divorce model (ODM) is based on the SIL framework and was developed during the course of iterative model refinement. The ODM specifies the mechanisms and consequences specifically related to divorce and repartnering based on the findings of the Oregon Divorce Study. In the ODM, maternal functioning is differentiated into two primary domains: mother as person and mother as parent. In the personal domain, the sequelae of divorce present numerous obstacles to mothers, including the challenge of single parenting (Forgatch & DeGarmo, 2002). Maternal depression, irritability, and other adjustment problems can arise in response to stress and disrupted social support, which in turn contribute to diminished parenting effectiveness. Consistent with the SIL model, the ODM is based on the assumptions that divorce and subsequent family transitions and their related stressors impact the parent-child relationship vis-à-vis increases in coercive parenting and decreases in effective parenting strategies. As such, both personal and parenting aspects of maternal functioning interact dynamically to elevate maternal distress and to precipitate a downward spiral of negative parent-child interactions.

Subsystems within the family are also viewed to continuously and reciprocally exert influence on each other (Bronfenbrenner, 1986). Changes in the dynamics of one subsystem (e.g., when a mother divorces or repartners) are presumed to shape processes within the entire system. For example, maternal stress during marital separation may increase a mother's depressed mood, which may disrupt her social support system and reduce her ability to effectively parent her child. Declines in parenting effectiveness may then lead to increasing child internalizing and externalizing problems, which may in turn exacerbate her depressed mood. Essentially, this negative process feeds back and carries forward.

Although *all* families operate in ever-changing contexts, the ODM and SIL model predict that such changes explain a good portion of the variability in how people interact with each other and how these dynamics impact adjustment. Contextual factors place youngsters at risk for problems when they interfere with practices in the parenting domain (Bank, Forgatch, Patterson, & Fetrow, 1993; Conger, Patterson, & Ge, 1995) and/or the marital domain (Biglan, Rothlind, Hops, & Sherman, 1989; Christensen, Jacobson, & Babcock, 1995; Emery, 1992). Some adults are at risk for adjustment problems because their personality traits (e.g., antisocial) or psychosocial difficulties (e.g., depression) interfere with relationships with their children, confidants, and intimate partners (Capaldi & Patterson, 1991; Forgatch & DeGarmo, 1997; Lahey et al., 1988). Such adults may vacillate between irritable and explosive reactions. Different contextual variables may identify which families are at increased risk for interpersonal problems. The relations are probabilistic ones; there is nothing inevitable about them.

Repartnering can present an entirely new set of challenges. Stepfamilies have more stress to manage than first-married families (Bray, Berger, Silverblatt, & Hollier, 1987; Lawton & Sanders, 1994). Much of this stress emerges from the struggles of reaching agreements on family rules and child-rearing issues, which may explain why problem-solving skills are so important. Effective parenting may ameliorate the effect of stressful circumstances on children's adjustment, but difficult children can challenge the best of parents.

Multiple family structure transitions are of particular interest because they increase the probability of declining parenting efficacy (Capaldi & Patterson, 1991; DeGarmo & Forgatch, 1999; Vuchinich, Vuchinich, & Wood, 1993). Divorced parents are likely to repartner about 75% of the time, and most reconstituted families break up (Bumpass, 1984; Bumpass & Sweet, 1989; Bumpass, Sweet, & Martin, 1990). Each change can alter the family context in ways that can amplify problems. Some parental characteristics, including younger maternal age, lower socioeconomic status, higher maternal depression, and parental arrests, are associated with an elevated frequency of such transitions (DeGarmo & Forgatch, 1999).

A number of studies show that the link between relationship transitions and child outcomes is fully mediated by the five core parenting practices identified in the SIL model. In a sample of families with mixed structures (two biological parents, single parents, first stepfamilies, and multiply reconstituted families), monitoring and positive involvement mediated the effect of family structure transitions on a construct measuring boys' academic performance, depression, and antisocial behavior (Capaldi & Patterson, 1991). For a group of separated/divorcing mothers, an observation-based measure of effective parenting fully mediated the relationship between family structure transitions and separate constructs assessing child acting-out behavior and emotional problems (Martinez & Forgatch, 2002). Thus, families characterized by effective parenting may be more resilient in the face of transitions than those in which parent behavior is chronically ineffective.

■ A Feed-Forward Model of the Cycle of Family Structure Transitions

Having outlined the ODM and SIL models and the impact of multiple structural transitions on family functioning, we now introduce a schema to provide a parsimonious framework for the discussion of new research in this area. Figure 14.1 illustrates a conceptual cycle of divorce, repartnering, and relationship problems that may or may not lead to further transitions and the effects of family reconstitution on maternal and child adjustment. Consistent with ODM, mothers are presented as both "person" and "parent," with difficulties in the person realm affecting parenting behavior and subsequent child adjustment. For example, maternal depression, which is a common accompaniment of divorce, is associated with more coercive and less effective parenting practices. Problematic parenting is a predictor of child adjustment problems, which in turn increases the likelihood of maternal depression. Thus, the family is a dynamic, interconnected system.

For mother as person, the sequelae of divorce frequently lead to increased stress and a decline in resources and support (Amato, 2000). Repartnering may provide greater access to financial resources and social support, as well as a reduction in a mother's depressed mood; however, relationship difficulties can compromise these gains, in that mothers may once again face another transition and its fellow travelers: depression and diminishing resources and social support. While the effects of stress have not been included in the model for the sake of simplicity, it is important to note that stress remains high in families characterized by multiple transitions.

The link between maternal depression, coercion, and parenting effectiveness is an important one. Longitudinal research suggests that maternal depression and the

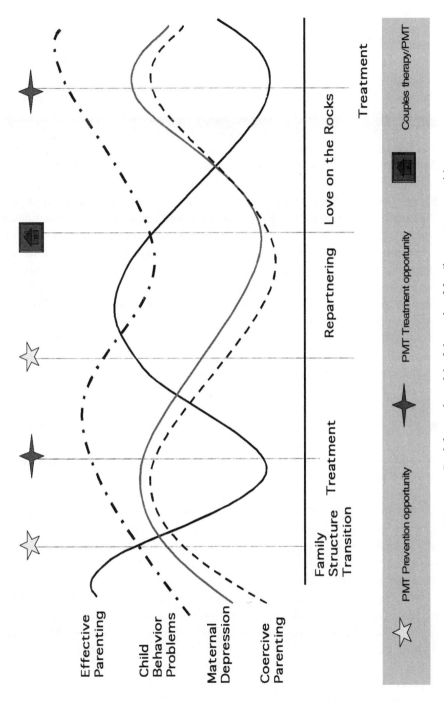

FIGURE 14.1 Feed-forward model of the cycle of family structure transitions.

stress associated with reductions in resources and supportive social networks can lead to increases in coercive behavior and an overall reduction in effective parenting (Forgatch et al., 1996; Patterson & Forgatch, 1990). Repartnering may provide access to social support and resources that are linked to reductions in maternal stress and coercion and to improved parenting practices. As a mother experiences stress and depression associated with relationship difficulties with her new partner, however, it is anticipated that her parenting skills will also decline. Increases in maternal coercion or deficits in parenting skills are anticipated to predict increases in child behavior problems throughout the cycle of transitions.

This evidence-based schema denotes opportunities in the cycle for prevention and treatment efforts. Prevention programs are designed to target maladaptive patterns of behavior before they emerge and to strengthen healthy patterns before they diminish. In this case, alleviating maternal depression and coercive behavior patterns and increasing prosocial behaviors and effective parenting skills prior to their decline can reduce the odds that mothers and children will fall into a downward spiral of coercion, depression, and child behavior problems. In the absence of a preventive intervention, mothers and their children are likely to slide down this slippery slope. Subsequent to the diagnosis of particular adjustment difficulties, treatment programs also emphasize coping with maternal depression, eliminating coercive exchanges, and instantiating more effective parenting practices. Programs using the parent management training (PMT) approach have proved particularly successful in remediating these problems (Dishion, Andrews, Kavanagh, & Soberman, 1996; Forehand, Wells, & Griest, 1980; Forgatch & DeGarmo, 1999; Patterson, Chamberlain, & Reid, 1982; Webster-Stratton & Taylor, 2001).

■ A Test of the ODM and SIL Model: The Oregon Divorce Study

We now turn to an evaluation of the research on which the "Cycle of Transitions" schema was based. The Oregon Divorce Study (ODS) began in 1984 with the goal of understanding divorce processes that enhance or detract from effective parenting. During the first phase (ODS-I), a sample of 197 single mothers and their sons was assessed within 1 year of separation and followed up for 4 years. The focus of this passive longitudinal design was to examine the processes that emerge during the separation and divorce process and to ascertain the extent to which these dynamics enhance or detract from effective parenting.

Findings from ODS-I provided strong correlational support for the ODM. Regarding the dimension of mother as person, the negativity of a maternal confidant predicted less observed confidant support and was directly associated with maternal distress, including depressed mood as well as family and financial stress (DeGarmo & Forgatch, 1997). Decreased income resulting from divorce was linked with decrements in parenting and later child academic problems (DeGarmo, Forgatch, & Martinez, 1999). Furthermore, child behavior problems also predicted future elevated maternal stress (Forgatch et al., 1996). Conversely, higher levels of observed support predicted improved maternal problem-solving outcomes, which in turn were associated with more effective parenting behavior even after controlling for confidant negativity, maternal distress, and child age (DeGarmo & Forgatch, 1997; Forgatch & DeGarmo, 1997).

Regarding the dimension of mother as a parent, higher levels of effective problem solving were associated with more successful parenting practices, which in turn predicted lower levels of child antisocial behavior. In sum, ODS-I results supported the ODM, in that mothers' distress, diminished resources, and disrupted social support predicted decrements in parenting quality, which, in turn, directly affected child outcomes. These data suggest a feedback loop of negative processes that carry forward to impact future developmental trajectories.

■ ODS-II Prevention Trial

Treatment and prevention trials afford experimental opportunities for model testing and for evaluation of the dynamic systems that emerge during divorce and repartnering. Such methods of theory building advance our understanding of the processes of divorce and facilitate the refinement and improvement of intervention programs. As the system feeds forward, an intervention can impact one level, which in turn can alter the trajectory of the entire system. Perhaps more important, randomized intervention trials provide evidence of a causal link between effective parenting and improved child and adolescent outcomes (Chamberlain, 1996; Dishion & Andrews, 1995; Forgatch, 1991; Forgatch & DeGarmo, 1999; Patterson, Dishion, & Chamberlain, 1993).

Several contextual variables are known to be malleable. Prevention research shows that income, stress, and depression can be manipulated through intervention (DeGarmo et al., 2004; Forgatch & DeGarmo, 1999, 2002; Martinez & Forgatch, 2001; Olds et al., 1997; Price, Van Ryn, & Vinokur, 1992). The prevention and treatment literature also indicates that PMT interventions that support parents' family management skills consistently produce reductions in child coercive actions and antisocial behavior (Dishion & Patterson, 1992; Dumas, 1989; Forgatch & DeGarmo, 1999; Kazdin, Esveldt-Dawson, French, & Unis, 1987; McMahon & Wells, 1989; Patterson & Forgatch, 1995; Wolchik et al., 1993).

The ODS-II prevention trial was designed to specifically test the ODM using a curriculum modified for divorced and repartnering mothers—Parenting Through Change (PTC; Forgatch, 1994). A sample of 238 single mothers with 6- to 10-year-old sons was randomly assigned to experimental or no-intervention control conditions. Based on the SIL model, previous intervention trials (Patterson et al., 1982; Patterson & Forgatch, 1995), and model testing from ODS-I, targets for intervention included effective discipline, skill encouragement, monitoring/supervision, problem solving, and positive involvement. Longitudinal analyses provide sound evidence that decrements in these parenting skills can lead to a wide variety of child adjustment problems, including depression, anxiety, delinquency, deviant peer affiliation, and antisocial behavior (Capaldi, 1992; Capaldi & Patterson, 1991; Conger et al., 1995; DeBaryshe, Patterson, & Capaldi, 1993; DeGarmo et al., 1999; Dishion & Andrews,

1995; Forgatch et al., 1996; Patterson, 1997). By randomly assigning families to either experimental or control groups, we were able to test the hypothesis that mothers receiving parent management and personal skills instruction would exhibit improved adjustment and increased parenting efficacy compared to no-intervention controls. Further, reductions in child adjustment problems would lead to improvements in maternal outcomes over time.

Treatment Design

The ODS-II intervention consisted of a series of 14 weekly parent group meetings. Group size ranged from 6 to 16 parents, with a mean of 9.5 mothers per group. The intervention is described fully in the PTC manual (Forgatch, 1994). In addition to group meetings, interventionists telephoned each mother during the week to provide additional support, including tailoring procedures to different family needs and troubleshooting difficulties with weekly home assignments. Mothers in the treatment condition attended an average of 8.5 group sessions ($SD = 5.7$, range $= 0–15$, 60.7%). A multiagent (parent, teacher, child, and coder observations), multimethod (observed laboratory interactions; questionnaires; in-person and telephone interviews; and school, motor vehicle, and criminal records) assessment strategy was employed to assess families at baseline and 6, 12, 18, and 30 months. The mean participation rate across all waves was 85.6% for the full sample (Forgatch & DeGarmo, 2002).

Mother-as-Person Effects

A linear group-by-time effect for depression was found, suggesting that mothers who received the intervention were less likely to be depressed 30 months following baseline than mothers who did not receive treatment. This effect decreased slightly after controlling for repartnering. It is interesting to note that mothers of older children were approximately 1.4 times more likely to be clinically depressed than those of younger children, and mothers who were rated as antisocial were nearly twice as likely to be depressed as their prosocial counterparts (Forgatch & DeGarmo, 2002).

Mothers who received the intervention also exhibited improvements in other domains, including fewer negative life events, less financial stress, and increased income, compared to those in the control group (Forgatch & DeGarmo, 2002). Furthermore, experimental mothers' gross annual and discretionary income increased and financial stress decreased relative to those of controls (Forgatch & DeGarmo, in preparation).

Mother-as-Parent Effects

Results indicated that mothers in the PTC intervention group maintained baseline levels of parenting effectiveness, while control mothers deteriorated. Mothers in the treatment group displayed significantly higher levels of effective parenting and less coercive behavior than controls. The trajectories of mothers in the experimental group displayed classic prevention patterns, with maintenance of baseline levels, whereas mothers in the control group showed increasing coercive parenting and decreasing effective parenting levels. These findings indicate that the PTC intervention produced significant benefits to parenting behavior (Forgatch & DeGarmo, 2002; Martinez & Forgatch, 2001).

Child Adjustment

Based on the SIL model, it was anticipated that changes in targeted parenting skills would result in better child outcomes. Significant improvements for boys in teacher-rated aggression and adaptive functioning at school, reading achievement (laboratory tests), and emotional distress (maternal report) were found for sons of mothers in the intervention group relative to controls. In addition, boys' self-report of their association with deviant peers indicated reduced contact with deviant friends for boys with mothers in the experimental group compared to controls (DeGarmo & Forgatch, 2000; Forgatch & DeGarmo, 2002).

When considering the results of prevention trials, it is important to bear in mind that these investigations differ from clinical trials in several important ways (Forgatch & DeGarmo, 1999). Clinical trials involve diagnostically homogeneous populations and treatment modalities that are designed to ameliorate specific symptoms related to the diagnosis in question (Kazdin, 1993). Prevention trials are typically conducted on a symptomatically heterogeneous population with the goal of alleviating presenting problems, preventing the development of new difficulties and the erosion of existing adaptive behaviors, and promoting future health and well-being (Coie et al., 1993). Due to the heterogeneity of prevention samples, larger sample sizes and longer follow-up periods are generally required, and effect sizes for distal variables tend to be smaller than those of clinical trials (Durlak & Wells, 1997; Goldklang, 1989). Consequently, for samples of divorced families in which parents and children experience a broad spectrum of adjustment difficulties across a variety of domains (e.g., diminished social support, reduced parenting effectiveness, emotional distress, child academic problems, peer difficulties, depression, and conduct problems), detecting and disentangling causal paths can be particularly challenging (DeGarmo et al., 2004; Forgatch & DeGarmo, 1999).

■ Longitudinal Treatment Effects

While the results of ODS-II are encouraging, they represent only the beginning of complex and fascinating longitudinal behavioral and emotional changes within these family systems. Our analyses revealed that intervention effects were not static and evolved gradually during the first 30 months (DeGarmo et al., 2004). Specifically, these data yielded evidence that changes in parenting behavior preceded better child outcomes, followed by improved maternal adjustment. Figure 14.2 describes changes in maternal and child outcomes for intervention and comparison groups by relative effect sizes over time for each respective outcome. Effect sizes are plotted using Cohen's *d* measured as differences in standard deviation

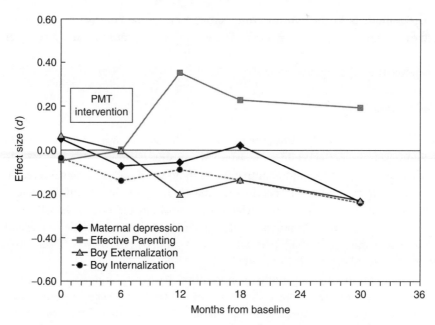

FIGURE 14.2 Univariate effect sizes of construct scores using Cohen's *d*.

between the intervention and control groups (Cohen, 1988). The univariate *d* for each of construct score is plotted as opposed to a multivariate D^2 for multiple indicators because the univariate *d* specifically represents outcomes employed in the latent growth models and it has directional interpretation of intervention influence, whereas D^2 does not (Stevens, 1992). Negative values on the *Y* axis represent greater reductions in behaviors associated with PMT, whereas more positive the effect sizes indicate increases in behaviors related to PMT.

It is important to note that the predictor and criterion variables are derived from different methods and/or agents. Observational data provide the most dynamic and objective measure of family processes. Teacher estimates are found to be conservative because educators are blind to treatment conditions at each wave of assessment. Child reports are particularly informative as, unlike maternal reports, children are not directly involved in the PTC intervention.

As illustrated in figure 14.2, the 14-week PMT intervention terminated by the 6-month follow-up, as indicated by the PMT Intervention box. The zero ordinate line for the *Y* axis represents no effect of the intervention. During the interval from 6 to 12 months, mothers' effective parenting showed the strongest increase, with a moderate effect size of *d* = 0.35. While this increased level of parenting effectiveness tended to wane during the next 24 months, a small intervention effect was still maintained at 30 months (*d* = 0.23 and 0.20, respectively). By and large, boys' internalizing and externalizing ratings exhibited a steady linear decline over time, with a moderate long-term effect for internalizing (*d* = −0.24) followed by a small long-term effect for externalizing (*d* = −0.23). Finally, maternal depression varied randomly around zero during the initial 18 months; however, at 30 months, significant intervention effects on mothers' depression emerged ($d = -0.24$). These findings suggest that treatment effects may unfold over time in a dynamic response to other changes in the family system (DeGarmo et al., 2004).

Indeed, these data illustrate a chronological "unpacking" of treatment effects. The plots suggest that differences in parenting effectiveness between the experimental and no-intervention groups were most pronounced at 12 months following baseline. These increases in effective family management preceded gradual decreases in boys' internalizing and externalizing behaviors, followed by changes in maternal depression. These experimental effects are consistent with the transitions schema (figure 14.1).

Latent growth modeling (LGM) provided a more formal test of this schema in that it permitted a rigorous test of both direct and indirect effects of the intervention on outcomes. Linear growth and initial status can be represented as latent variables by fixing growth factor loadings at 0, 1, 2, 3, and 5 to correspond to the respective assessment time line (refer to Muthen & Curran, 1997, and Stoolmiller, 1995, for a more comprehensive description of LGM).

LGM models indicated that the intervention effects on mothers' depression were mediated by changes in boys externalizing behavior—as boys' behavior problems decreased, mothers exhibited fewer depressive symptoms. Second, intervention effects on boys' externalizing were mediated by changes in boys' internalizing—boys' internalizing behaviors decreased followed by reductions in externalizing. Third, as anticipated, improved maternal parenting practices were predictive of reductions in boys' internalizing and externalizing; however, the intervention effect on internalizing was only partially mediated by increased parenting effectiveness (DeGarmo et al., 2004).

In sum, LGM analyses revealed that mothers in the intervention group exhibited improved parenting skills, which predicted a decline in boys' internalizing and externalizing behaviors. Fewer externalizing problems were associated with decreased maternal depression at 30 months. It is interesting to note that changes in boys' internalizing symptoms did not predict reductions in maternal depression. These data suggest a complex relation between mother as person and mother as parent and long-term adjustment for both mother and child. Replication and further experimental manipulations are needed to provide additional evidence that these outcomes evolve in any time-ordered pattern.

■ Divorce and Fathering—Where Do Dads Fit In?

To date, interventions designed to address the concerns of divorced fathers are conspicuously absent in the literature. There are few theoretical models or empirical studies that examine the role of fathers in the emergence of postdivorce family systems (Doherty, Kouneski, & Erickson, 1998) and even fewer preventive interventions that address the role of fathers in divorced or reconstituted families (Forgatch & Rains, 1997). In a recent ecologically oriented account of "responsible fathering," Doherty and colleagues (1998) suggest that "only an ecologically sensitive approach to parenting, which views the welfare of fathers, mothers, and children as intertwined and interdependent, can avoid a zero-sum approach to parenting in which fathers' gains become mothers' losses" (p. 277). Further, fathering is conceptualized as a multilateral process that comprises not only father-child relationships but also those with mothers, extended family members, and the broader social ecology.

Indeed, there is evidence that the relationship of children to their fathers can lead to improved behavioral outcomes for some children (Amato & Rezac, 1994). A number of studies, however, suggest that this finding is far from conclusive (Dishion, Owen, & Bullock, 2004; Hetherington, Cox, & Cox, 1982; Jaffee, Moffitt, Caspi, & Taylor, 2003; Kalter, Kloner, Schreier, & Okla, 1989). Consistent with a systemic or ecological framework, one of the most proximal indicators of the quality of father-child engagement following divorce is the coparental relationship (Doherty et al., 1998; Maccoby, Buchanan, Mnookin, & Dornbusch, 1993).

In the New Beginnings Parenting Program for divorced mothers (Wolchik et al., 1993), the father-child relationship and the remediation of interparental conflict were two of eight putative mediators targeted. Mothers who received the intervention did not exhibit increasingly greater negative attitudes toward their former husbands, as did comparisons; however, these differences decreased over time.

Without a doubt, a child's relationship with a noncustodial parent plays a significant role in the child's long-term developmental trajectory. Historically, family researchers have implicitly assumed that mothers are the custodial parents in their research designs. In recent decades, the role of fathers has become increasingly more active, with some studies reporting as many as 22% of children residing with their fathers following divorce (Lengua, Wolchik, & Braver, 1995). It is imperative that prevention scientists continue to develop and refine theoretical models and preventive interventions that account for the emerging role of fathers as well as the unique challenges that fathers face following divorce (Braver, Griffin, Cookston, Sandler, & Williams, 2002; Braver et al., 1993). In light of the fact that the preponderance of evidence suggests that children's involvement with their noncustodial fathers tends to decline following divorce (Amato & Rezac, 1994), it is important to develop programs to keep fathers engaged in the lives of their children following the dissolution of marriage.

■ Implications and Future Directions

In addition to considering the important role that fathers play in the socioemotional development of children, intervention scientists working with divorced and reconstituted families face other challenges. In the section below we address two aspects of prevention and intervention research that are necessary to consider: cultural influences and adaptation of efficacious programs to community environments.

The Role of Culture and Ethnicity in the Design of Prevention Programs

The term *culture* represents shared systems of meaning, patterns of ideas, and behavioral practices that both result from action and condition future action

(Kroeber & Kluckhohn, 1952). These patterns and social practices are ubiquitous and are related to behaviors within social relationships, emotional expression, and a host of other physical and psychosocial phenomena (Shore, 1996; Strauss, 1992). It is reasonable to assume that cultural and ethnic differences have bearing on child rearing and divorce. Doherty and colleagues (1998) proposed that "fathering may be more sensitive than mothering to contextual forces, forces that currently create more obstacles than bridges for fathers, but that potentially could be turned in a more supportive direction" (p. 278).

While some researchers question the practical significance of reported statistically significant differences between people of different cultures in a variety of social domains (Matsumoto, Grissom, & Dinnel, 2001), there is growing evidence that the structure and cross-generational involvement of adults in caregiving varies significantly across ethnic groups (Dishion & Bullock, 2002).

Given this understanding, consideration of cultural similarities and differences regarding parenting is central to the development of parent-centered prevention and intervention programs. In a recent adaptation of PMT for a nationwide implementation in Norway, we discovered that differences in cultural contexts regarding parenting called for extensive discussion and negotiation of the language regarding parenting behaviors addressed within the program (Forgatch, Bullock, & Patterson, 2004; Ogden, Forgatch, Bullock, Askeland, & Patterson, in preparation). At present, several researchers are involved in a modification of PMT principles for Latino families. Indeed, cultural sensitivity is necessary in all prevention and intervention programs, and working with adults regarding their parenting practices is no exception.

Implementing Prevention Programs in Community Settings

The ODS provides empirical support for the SIL and ODM perspectives, as well as the efficacy of the PTC program. The next important step in this research is to refine our conceptual models to ensure external validity, namely, to implement and test the effectiveness of PTC and other forms of the SIL model of PMT in community settings. Preliminary findings from the Norway implementation accentuate the importance of measuring and understanding the sociopolitical and organizational factors that facilitate or inhibit the adoption of research-based interventions in local communities.

At the organizational level of analysis, treatment fidelity and successful implementation may be affected by a number of factors inherent to agencies adopting PMT. Researchers in education, sociology, and organizational psychology propose several hypotheses regarding factors that facilitate or impede organization-wide adoption of new innovations. These characteristics include expertise of staff, access to necessary resources, perceived legitimacy of the organization, collective efficacy, social capital, openness to social innovation, effective communication, cohesion, adaptability of the system, and community readiness to accept change (Beebe, Harrison, Sharma, & Hedger, 2001; Morenoff, Sampson, & Raudenbush, 2001; Oetting et al., 1995; Price & Lorion, 1989; Provan & Milward, 2001; Sampson, Morenoff, & Earls, 1999).

To better understand the broader social ecology related to PMT adoption and treatment fidelity in Norway, we developed instruments to measure the underlying structural and dynamic features of mental health service providers at the level of the organization. We created four questionnaires to tap interventionist and agency leadership perceptions regarding their organization and PMT. The Community Readiness Questionnaire (Bullock, 2002a) was adapted from the Community Readiness Survey (Beebe et al., 2001). Items provide information regarding the prevalence of child, adolescent, and parent substance use and delinquency in the community, the extent to which prevailing norms support or discourage such conduct, and the level of involvement of community members in remediation of these problems.

The Organizational Structure Questionnaire (Bullock, 2002b) measures agency features believed to be central to successful PMT implementation, including availability of resources, legitimacy, collective efficacy,* social capital, social innovation, organizational cohesion, and communication. The Project Network Questionnaire (Bullock, 2002c) provides data regarding the degree to which each agency supports interventionists in their efforts to learn and implement PMT, as well as the extent to which they have benefited from involvement in the Norway implementation project.

Last, the Parent Management Training Organizational Implementation Survey (Bullock, 2002d) provides information regarding the adaptability of PMT to the current organizational framework, interventionists' willingness to adopt this treatment strategy, and client willingness to receive PMT versus traditional forms of therapy. These measures are currently being piloted in Oregon, Michigan, and selected regions of Norway.

■ Conclusions

Relationship transitions and the restructuring of family systems present formidable challenges to parents and children alike. While stress, depression, loss of social support, and socioeconomic decline are frequent visitors to mothers experiencing intimate partner transitions, and these obstacles can interfere with effective parenting, the picture is by no means unequivocal. The ODS and similar prevention programs that focus on buttressing mothers as people and parents prove effective in reducing maternal psychosocial adjustment problems, improving financial resources and social support, and strengthening parenting practices. Improvements in parenting effectiveness are, in turn, linked to more positive outcomes for children, which can lead to longitudinal improvement in maternal depression. Thus, the picture for mothers in transition may be more hopeful, particularly if appropriate interventions are provided early.

*The collective efficacy scale was adapted from the Goddard Teacher Collective Efficacy Scale (Goddard, 2002).

■ Acknowledgments

This research was supported by Grants R01 MH 38318 and R01 MH 54703 from the Prevention and Behavioral Research Branch, Division of Epidemiology and Services Research, NIMH, U.S. PHS, and by Grant R01 DA 16097 from the Prevention Research Branch, NIDA, U.S. PHS. Many thanks to the families who generously provided us with the data on which this research is based and to the research team for their dedication to these projects.

■ References

Amato, P. R. (2000). The consequences of divorce for adults and children. *Journal of Marriage and the Family, 62,* 1269–1287.

Amato, P. R., & Rezac, S. J. (1994). Contact with nonresident parents, interparental conflict, and children's behavior. *Journal of Family Issues, 15*(2), 191–207.

Anderson, E. R., Greene, S. M., Hetherington, E. M., & Clingempeel, W. G. (1999). The dynamics of parental remarriage: Adolescent, parent, and sibling influence. In E. M. Hetherington (Ed.), *Coping with divorce, single parenting, and remarriage: A risk and resiliency perspective* (pp. 295–319). Mahwah, NJ: Erlbaum.

Anderson, E. R., Lindner, M. S., & Bennion, L. D. (1992). The effect of family relationships on adolescent development during family reorganization. In E. M. Hetherington & W. G. Clingempeel (Eds.), *Coping with marital transitions: Monographs of the Society for Research in Child Development* (Vol. 57, pp. 178–200). Chicago: University of Chicago Press.

Bank, L., Forgatch, M. S., Patterson, G. R., & Fetrow, R. A. (1993). Parenting practices of single mothers: Mediators of negative contextual factors. *Journal of Marriage and Family, 55,* 371–384.

Beebe, T. J., Harrison, P. A., Sharma, A., & Hedger, S. (2001). The community readiness survey: Development and initial validation. *Evaluation Review, 25*(1), 55–71.

Biglan, A., Rothlind, J., Hops, H., & Sherman, L. (1989). Impact of distressed and aggressive behavior. *Journal of Abnormal Psychology, 98,* 218–228.

Bloom, B. L., Asher, S. J., & White, S. W. (1978). Marital disruption as a stressor: A review and analysis. *Psychological Bulletin, 85*(4), 867–894.

Braver, S. L., Griffin, W. A., Cookston, J. T., Sandler, I. N., & Williams, J. (2002, April). *Promoting better fathering among divorced nonresident fathers.* Paper presented at the APA Division 43 Research Conference, "Family Psychology: The Art of the Science," Evanston, IL.

Braver, S. L., Wolchik, S. A., Sandler, I. N., Sheets, V. L., Fogas, B., & Bay, R. C. (1993). A longitudinal study of noncustodial parents: Parents without children. *Journal of Family Psychology, 7*(1), 9–23.

Bray, J. H., Berger, S. H., Silverblatt, A. H., & Hollier, A. (1987). Family process and organization during early remarriage: A preliminary analysis. In J. P. Vincent (Ed.), *Advances in family intervention, assessment and theory* (Vol. 4, pp. 253–279). Greenwich, CT: JAI.

Brody, G. H., Neubaum, E., & Forehand, R. (1988). Serial marriage: A heuristic analysis of an emerging family form. *Psychological Bulletin, 103*(2), 211–222.

Bronfenbrenner, U. (1986). Ecology of the family as a context for human development: Research perspectives. *Developmental Psychology, 22,* 723–742.

Bullock, B. M. (2002a). *Community readiness questionnaire.* Eugene, OR: Oregon Social Learning Center. Unpublished instrument.

Bullock, B. M. (2002b). *Organizational structure questionnaire.* Eugene, OR: Oregon Social Learning Center. Unpublished instrument.

Bullock, B. M. (2002c). *Parent management training organizational implementation survey.* Eugene, OR: Oregon Social Learning Center. Unpublished instrument.

Bullock, B. M. (2002d). *Project network questionnaire.* Eugene, OR: Oregon Social Learning Center. Unpublished instrument.

Bumpass, L. L. (1984). Children and marital disruption: A replication and update. *Demography, 21*(1), 71–82.

Bumpass, L. L., & Sweet, J. A. (1989). National estimates of cohabitation. *Demography, 26*(4), 615–625.

Bumpass, L. L., Sweet, J., & Martin, T. C. (1990). Changing patterns of remarriage. *Journal of Marriage and Family, 52*(August), 747–756.

Capaldi, D. M. (1992). Co-occurrence of conduct problems and depressive symptoms in early adolescent boys: A 2-year follow-up at Grade 8. *Development and Psychopathology, 4,* 125–144.

Capaldi, D. M., & Patterson, G. R. (1991). Relation of parental transition to boys' adjustment problems: Mothers at risk for transitions and unskilled parenting. *Developmental Psychology, 27,* 489–504.

Chamberlain, P. (1994). *Family connections: A treatment foster care model for adolescents with delinquency* (Vol. 5). Eugene, OR: Castalia.

Chamberlain, P. (1996). Community-based residential treatment for adolescents with conduct disorder. In T. H. Ollendick & R. J. Prinz (Eds.), *Advances in clinical child psychology* (Vol. 18, pp. 63–90). New York: Plenum.

Christensen, A., Jacobson, N. S., & Babcock, J. C. (1995). Integrative behavioral couple therapy. In N. S. Jacobson & A. S. Gurman (Eds.), *Clinical handbook of marital therapy* (2nd ed., pp. 31–64). New York: Guilford Press.

Cohen, J. (1988). *Statistical power analysis for the social sciences* (2nd ed.). Hillsdale, NJ: Erlbaum.

Coie, J. D., Watt, N. F., West, S. G., Hawkins, J. D., Asarnow, J. R., Markman, H. J., et al. (1993). The science of prevention: A conceptual framework and some directions for a national research program. *American Psychologist, 48,* 1013–1022.

Conger, R. D., Patterson, G. R., & Ge, X. (1995). It takes two to replicate: A mediational model for the impact of parents' stress on adolescent adjustment. *Developmental Psychology, 66,* 80–97.

DeBaryshe, B. D., Patterson, G. R., & Capaldi, D. M. (1993). A performance model for academic achievement in early adolescent boys. *Developmental Psychology, 1993*(29), 795–804.

DeGarmo, D. S., & Forgatch, M. S. (1997). Confidant support and maternal distress: Predictors of parenting practices for divorced mothers. *Personal Relationships, 4,* 305–317.

DeGarmo, D. S., & Forgatch, M. S. (1999). Contexts as predictors of changing parenting practices in diverse family structures: A social interactional perspective to risk and resilience. In E. M. Hetherington (Ed.), *Coping with divorce, single parenting and remarriage: A risk and resiliency perspective* (pp. 227–252). Mahwah, NJ: Erlbaum.

DeGarmo, D. S., & Forgatch, M. S. (2000, November). *Preventing the "early start" within transitional divorce families: An experimental test of precursors influencing antisocial behavior and delinquency.* Paper presented at the American Society of Criminology Annual Meeting: Crime and Criminology in the Year 2000, San Francisco.

DeGarmo, D. S., Forgatch, M. S., & Martinez, C. R., Jr. (1999). Parenting of divorced mothers as a link between social status and boys' academic outcomes: Unpacking the effects of SES. *Child Development, 70,* 1231–1245.

DeGarmo, D. S., Patterson, G. R., & Forgatch, M. S. (2004). How do outcomes in a specified parent training intervention maintain or wane over time? *Prevention Science,* 5(2), 73–89.

Dishion, T. J., & Andrews, D. W. (1995). Preventing escalation in problem behaviors with high-risk young adolescents: Immediate and 1-year outcomes. *Journal of Consulting and Clinical Psychology, 63*(4), 538–548.

Dishion, T. J., Andrews, D. W., Kavanagh, K., & Soberman, L. H. (1996). Preventive interventions for high-risk youth: The Adolescent Transitions Program. In R. D. Peters & R. J. McMahon (Eds.), *Preventing childhood disorders, substance abuse, and delinquency* (pp. 184–214). Thousand Oaks, CA: Sage.

Dishion, T. J., & Bullock, B. M. (2002). Parenting and adolescent problem behavior: An ecological analysis of the nurturance hypothesis. In J. C. Borkowski, S. Landesman Ramey, & M. Bristol-Power (Eds.), *Parenting and the child's world. influences on academic, intellectual, and socio-emotional development* (pp. 231–249). Mahwah, NJ: Erlbaum.

Dishion, T. J., & Kavanagh, K. (2003). *Intervening on adolescent problem behavior: A family centered approach.* New York: Guilford Press.

Dishion, T. J., Owen, L. D., & Bullock, B. M. (2004). Like father, like son: Toward a developmental model for the transmission of male deviance across generations. *European Journal of Developmental Psychology, 1*(2), 105–126.

Dishion, T. J., & Patterson, G. R. (1992). Age effects in parent training outcome. *Behavior Therapy, 23*(4), 719–729.

Doherty, W. J., Kouneski, E. F., & Erickson, M. F. (1998). Responsible fathering: An overview and conceptual framework. *Journal of Marriage and Family, 60,* 277–292.

Dumas, J. E. (1989). Treating antisocial behavior in children: Child and family approaches. *Clinical Psychology Review, 9,* 197–222.

Durlak, J. A., & Wells, A. M. (1997). Primary prevention mental health programs for children and adolescents: A meta-analytic review. *American Journal of Community Psychology, 25*(2), 115–152.

Emery, R. E. (1992). Family conflicts and their developmental implications: A conceptual analysis of meanings for the structure of relationships. In C. U. Shantz & W. W. Hartup (Eds.), *Conflict in child and adolescent: Development* (pp. 1–49). New York: Cambridge University Press.

Forehand, R., Wells, K. C., & Griest, D. L. (1980). An examination of the social validity of a parent training program. *Behavior Therapy, 11,* 488–502.

Forgatch, M. S. (1991). The clinical science vortex: A developing theory of antisocial behavior. In D. Pepler & K. H. Rubin (Eds.), *The development and treatment of childhood aggression* (pp. 291–315). Hillsdale, NJ: Erlbaum.

Forgatch, M. S. (1994). *Parenting through change: A programmed intervention curriculum for groups of single mothers.* Eugene, OR: Oregon Social Learning Center.

Forgatch, M. S., Bullock, B. M., & Patterson, G. R. (2004). From theory to practice: Increasing effective parenting through role-play. The Oregon model of parent management training (PMTO). In H. Steiner (Ed.), *Handbook of mental health interventions in children and adolescents: An integrated developmental approach* (pp. 782–814). New Jersey: Jossey-Bass.

Forgatch, M. S., & DeGarmo, D. S. (1997). Adult problem solving: Contributor to parenting and child outcomes in divorced families. *Social Development, 6,* 238–254.

Forgatch, M. S., & DeGarmo, D. S. (1999). Parenting through change: An effective prevention program for single mothers. *Journal of Consulting and Clinical Psychology, 67,* 711–724.

Forgatch, M. S., & DeGarmo, D. S. (2002). Extending and testing the social interaction learning model with divorce samples. In J. B. Reid, G. R. Patterson, & J. Snyder (Eds.), *Antisocial behavior in children and adolescents: A developmental analysis and model for intervention* (pp. 235–256). Washington DC: American Psychological Association.

Forgatch, M. S., & DeGarmo, D. S. (in preparation). Accelerating recovery from poverty: Long-term prevention effects.

Forgatch, M. S., & Knutson, N. M. (2002). Linking basic and applied research in a prevention science process. In H. Liddle, G. Diamond, R. Levant, & J. Bray (Eds.), *Family psychology: Science-based interventions* (pp. 239–257). Washington, DC: American Psychological Association.

Forgatch, M. S., & Marquez, B. (1993). *The divorce workout* [Videotape]. Eugene, OR: Oregon Social Learning Center.

Forgatch, M. S., & Patterson, G. R. (1989). *Parents and adolescents living together: Vol. 2. Family problem solving.* Eugene, OR: Castalia.

Forgatch, M. S., Patterson, G. R., & Ray, J. A. (1996). Divorce and boys' adjustment problems: Two paths with a single model. In E. M. Hetherington & E. A. Blechman (Eds.), *Stress, coping, and resiliency in children and families* (pp. 67–105). Mahwah, NJ: Erlbaum.

Forgatch, M. S., & Rains, L. (1997). *MAPS: Marriage and parenting in stepfamilies* [parent training manual]. Eugene, OR: Oregon Social Learning Center.

Furstenberg, F. F., & Spanier, G. B. (1984). *Recycling the family: Remarriage after divorce.* Beverly Hills, CA: Sage.

Goddard, R. (2002). A theoretical and empirical analysis of the measurement of collective efficacy: The development of a short form. *Educational and Psychological Measurement 62*(1), 97–110.

Goldklang, D. S. (1989). Research workshop on prevention of depression with recommendations for future research. *Journal of Primary Prevention, 10*(1), 41–49.

Hetherington, E. M., Bridges, M., & Insabella, G. M. (1998). What matters? What does not? Five perspectives on the association between marital transitions and children's adjustment. *American Psychologist, 53*(2), 167–184.

Hetherington, E. M., & Clingempeel, G. (1992). *Coping with marital transitions* (Vol. 57). Chicago: University of Chicago Press.

Hetherington, E. M., Cox, M., & Cox, R. (1982). Effects of divorce on parents and children. In M. Lamb (Ed.), *Nontraditional families: Parenting and child development.* Hillsdale, NJ: Erlbaum.

Hetherington, E. M., & Mekos, D. (1997). Alterations in family life following divorce: Effects on children and adolescents. In J. Noshpitz & N. Alessi (Eds.), *Handbook of child and adolescent psychiatry. Vol. IV: Varieties of development* (pp. 99–111). New York: Wiley.

Jacobs, J. W. (1982). The effect of divorce on fathers: An overview of the literature. *American Journal of Psychiatry, 139*(10), 1235–1241.

Jaffee, S. R., Moffitt, T. E., Caspi, A., & Taylor, A. (2003). Life with (or without) father: The benefits of living with two biological parents depend on the fathers' antisocial behavior. *Child Development, 74*(1), 109–126.

Kalter, N., Kloner, A., Schreier, S., & Okla, K. (1989). Predictors of children's postdivorce adjustment. *American Journal of Orthopsychiatry, 59*, 605–618.

Kazdin, A. E. (1993). Psychotherapy for children and adolescents: Current progress and future research directions. *American Psychologist, 48*, 644–657.

Kazdin, A. E., Esveldt-Dawson, K., French, H. H., & Unis, A. S. (1987). Problem-solving skills training and relationship therapy in the treatment of antisocial child behavior. *Journal of Consulting and Clinical Psychology, 55*, 76–85.

Kroeber, A. L., & Kluckhohn, C. (1952). Culture: A critical review of concepts and definitions. *Papers. Peabody Museum of Archaeology and Ethnology, Harvard University, 47*(viii), 223.

Lahey, B. B., Hartdagen, S. E., Frick, P. J., McBurnett, K., Connor, R., & Hynd, G. W. (1988). Conduct disorder: Parsing the confounded relation to parental divorce and antisocial personality. *Journal of Abnormal Psychology, 97*(3), 334–337.

Lawton, J. M., & Sanders, M. R. (1994). Designing effective behavioral family interventions for stepfamilies. *Clinical Psychology Review, 14*(5), 463–496.

Lengua, L. J., Wolchik, S. A., & Braver, S. L. (1995). Understanding children's divorce adjustment from an ecological perspective. *Journal of Divorce and Remarriage, 22*(3, 4), 25–53.

Lipsey, M. W. (1990). *Design sensitivity: Statistical power for experimental research.* Newbury Park, CA: Sage.

Lustig, J. L., Wolchik, S. A., & Weiss, L. (1999). The New Beginnings parenting program for divorced mothers: Linking theory and intervention. In C. A. Essau & F. Petermann (Eds.), *Depressive disorders in children and adolescents: Epidemiology, risk factors, and treatment* (pp. 361–381). Northvale, NJ: Aronson.

Maccoby, E. E., Buchanan, C. M., Mnookin, R. H., & Dornbusch, S. M. (1993). Postdivorce roles of mothers and fathers in the lives of their children. *Journal of Family Psychology, 7*(1), 24–38.

Martinez, C. R., Jr., & Forgatch, M. S. (2001). Preventing problems with boys' noncompliance: Effects of a parent training intervention for divorcing mothers. *Journal of Consulting and Clinical Psychology, 69*, 416–428.

Martinez, C. R., Jr., & Forgatch, M. S. (2002). Adjusting to change: Linking family structure transitions with parenting and child adjustment. *Journal of Family Psychology, 16*(2), 107–117.

Matsumoto, D., Grissom, R. J., & Dinnel, D. L. (2001). Do between-culture differences really mean that people are different? A look at some measures of cultural effect sizes. *Journal of Cross-Cultural Psychology, 32*(4), 478–490.

McMahon, R. J., & Wells, K. C. (1989). Conduct disorders. In E. J. Mash & R. A. Barkley (Eds.), *Treatment of childhood disorders* (pp. 73–132). New York: Guilford Press.

Morenoff, J. D., Sampson, R. J., & Raudenbush, S. W. (2001). Neighborhood inequality, collective efficacy, and the spatial dynamics of urban violence. *Criminology, 39*(3), 517–559.

Muthen, B. O., & Curran, P. J. (1997). General longitudinal modeling of individual differences in experimental designs: A latent variable framework for analysis and power estimation. *Psychological Methods, 2*(4), 371–402.

Oetting, E. R., Donnermeyer, J. F., Plested, B. A., Edwards, R. W., Kelly, K., & Beauvals, F. (1995). Assessing community readiness for prevention. *The International Journal of the Addictions, 30*(6), 659–683.

Ogden, T., Forgatch, M. S., Bullock, B. M., Askeland, E., & Patterson, G. R. (in preparation). Large scale implementation of parent management training at the national level: The case of Norway.

Olds, D. L., Eckenrode, J., Henderson, C. R., Jr., Kitzman, H., Powers, J., Cole, R., et al. (1997). Long-term effects of home visitation on maternal life course and child abuse and neglect. *Journal of the American Medical Association, 278*(8), 637–643.

Patterson, G. R. (1982). *Coercive family process.* Eugene, OR: Castalia.

Patterson, G. R. (1997). Performance models for parenting: A social interactional perspective. In J. Grusec & L. Kuczynski (Eds.), *Parenting and the socialization of values: A handbook of contemporary theory* (pp. 193–235). New York: Wiley.

Patterson, G. R., Chamberlain, P., & Reid, J. B. (1982). A comparative evaluation of a parent-training program. *Behavior Therapy, 13*, 638–650.

Patterson, G. R., Dishion, T. J., & Chamberlain, P. (1993). Outcomes and methodological issues relating to treatment of antisocial children. In T. R. Giles (Ed.), *Effective psychotherapy: A handbook of comparative research* (pp. 43–88). New York: Plenum.

Patterson, G. R., & Forgatch, M. S. (1987). *Parents and adolescents living together: The basics* (Vol. I). Eugene, OR: Castalia.

Patterson, G. R., & Forgatch, M. S. (1990). Initiation and maintenance of process disrupting single-mother families. In G. R. Patterson (Ed.), *Depression and aggression in family interaction* (pp. 209–245). Hillsdale, NJ: Erlbaum.

Patterson, G. R., & Forgatch, M. S. (1995). Predicting future clinical adjustment from treatment outcome and process variables. *Psychological Assessment, 7*, 275–285.

Patterson, G. R., Reid, J. B., & Dishion, T. J. (1992). *Antisocial boys* (Vol. 4). Eugene, OR: Castalia.

Pedro-Carroll, J. (1985). *The Children of Divorce Intervention Program: Procedures manual.* Rochester, NY: University of Rochester.

Pedro-Carroll, J., Alpert-Gillis, L., & Sterling, S. (1987). *Children of Divorce Intervention Program: Procedures manual for conducting support groups with 2nd and 3rd grade children.* Rochester, NY: University of Rochester.

Price, R. H., & Lorion, R. P. (1989). Prevention programming as organizational reinvention: From research to implementation. In D. Shaffer, I. Philips, & N. B. Enzer (Eds.), *Prevention of mental disorders, alcohol and other drug use in children and adolescents* (pp. 97–123). (Prevention Monograph No. 2 [DHHS Publication No. ADM 89-1646]). Rockville, MD: Office of Substance Abuse Prevention and American Academy of Child Adolescent Psychiatry.

Price, R. H., Van Ryn, M., & Vinokur, A. D. (1992, June). Impact of a preventive job search intervention on the likelihood of depression among the unemployed. *Journal of Health and Social Behavior, 33*, 158–167.

Provan, K. G., & Milward, H. B. (2001). Do networks really work? A framework for evaluating public-sector organizational networks. *Public Administration Review, 61*(4), 414–423.

Reid, J. B., & Eddy, J. M. (2002). Preventive efforts during the elementary school years: The Linking the Interests of Families and Teachers project. In J. B. Reid, G. R. Patterson, & J. Snyder (Eds.), *Antisocial behavior in children and adolescents: A developmental analysis and model for intervention* (pp. 219–233). Washington DC: American Psychological Association.

Reid, J. B., Patterson, G. R., & Snyder, J. (Eds.). (2002). *Antisocial behavior in children and adolescents: A developmental analysis and model for intervention.* Washington, DC: American Psychological Association.

Sampson, R. J., Morenoff, J. D., & Earls, F. (1999). Beyond social capital: Spatial dynamics of collective efficacy for children. *American Sociological Review, 64*(5), 633–660.

Shaw, D. S., Emery, R. E., & Tuer, M. D. (1993). Parental functioning and children's adjustment in families of divorce: A prospective study. *Journal of Abnormal Child Psychology, 21*(1), 119–134

Shore, B. (1996). *Culture in mind: Cognition, culture, and the problem of meaning.* New York: Oxford University Press.

Stevens, J. (1992). *Applied multivariate statistics for the social sciences* (2nd ed.). Hillsdale, NJ: Erlbaum.

Stolberg, A. L., & Garrison, K. M. (1985). Evaluating a primary prevention program for children of divorce. *American Journal of Community Psychology, 13*(2), 111–124.

Stoolmiller, M. (1995). Using latent growth curve models to study developmental processes. In J. M. Gottman & G. Sackett (Eds.), *The analysis of change* (pp. 105–138). Hillsdale, NJ: Erlbaum.

Stoolmiller, M., Eddy, J. M., & Reid, J. B. (2000). Detecting and describing preventative intervention effects in a universal school-based randomized trial targeting delinquent and violent behavior. *Journal of Consulting and Clinical Psychology, 68*(2), 296–306.

Strauss, C. (1992). Models and motives. In R. DiAndrade & C. Strauss (Eds.), *Human motives and cultural models* (pp. 1–20). New York: Cambridge University Press.

Vuchinich, S., Vuchinich, R., & Wood, B. (1993). The interparental relationship and family problem solving with preadolescent males. *Child Development, 64*, 1389–1400.

Warren, N. J., Grew, R. S., & Ilgen, E. L. (1984). *Parenting after divorce: Preventive programs for divorcing families.* Paper presented at the National Institute of Mental Health, Washington, DC.

Webster-Stratton, C., & Taylor, T. (2001). Nipping early risk factors in the bud: Preventing substance abuse, delinquency, and violence in adolescence through interventions targeted at young children (0–8 years). *Prevention Science, 2*(3), 165–192.

Wolchik, S. A., Sandler, I. N., Millsap, R. E., Plummer, B. A., Greene, S. M., Anderson, E. R., et al. (2002). Six-year follow-up of preventive interventions for children of divorce: A randomized controlled trial. *Journal of the American Medical Association, 288*(15), 1874–1881.

Wolchik, S. A., West, S. G., Sandler, I. N., Tein, J.-Y., Coatsworth, D., Lengua, L., et al. (2000). An experimental evaluation of theory-based mother and mother-child programs for children of divorce. *Journal of Consulting and Clinical Psychology, 68*, 843–856.

Wolchik, S. A., West, S. G., Westover, S., Sandler, I. N., Martin, A., Lustig, J., et al. (1993). The children of divorce parenting intervention: Outcome evaluation of an empirically based program. *American Journal of Community Psychology, 21*(3), 293–331.

PART IV

FAMILIES AND DEPRESSION

This part focuses on the status of the science of family psychology in relation to the most frequently encountered depressive disorders: major affective disorder and dysthymic disorder. Although depression is often thought of as a disorder that only occurs within individuals (even to the point where it is viewed solely as a biological disorder), depression is a disorder with enormous relational meaning. As the authors in this part describe, depression becomes much more likely for adults in the context of distressed marriages and for children in the context of depressed parents. It also has a powerful ongoing impact on all those who are in the family of the depressed person. It therefore is no surprise that research has begun to accrue on couple and family therapies as stand-alone treatments for depression and/or as components of integrative treatments.

The family psychology research on depression takes many different forms and each of the chapters in this part probes deeply into the research in a specific domain. This part moves from a more general focus on family processes and depression to considering depression and relational processes in adults, adolescents, and children. Valerie E. Whiffen explores the complex task of disentangling causality between family processes and depression. Steven R. H. Beach and Maya E. Gupta focus on the set of interrelations between depression and marital difficulties, reviewing and critiquing the small body of extant efficacy and effectiveness research involving couple therapies. Joan Rosenbaum Asarnow, Martha C. Tompson, and Michele S. Berk examine treatment studies for adolescent depression and Nadine J. Kaslow, Claudia A. Jones, and Frances Palin look at the treatment research on depression in children. Guillermo Bernal and Emily Sáez-Santiago highlight the powerful cultural factors that have emerged in research, focusing particularly on the adolescent treatment literature as an example.

The chapters in this part illustrate the rich range of perspectives that family psychology can bring to bear on a specific disorder. They address a set of common issues: how to disentangle causal connections between family factors and the disorder; how couple and family interventions impact the disorder; how services can best be delivered to those with the disorder and at risk for it at various ages; and how culture interfaces with all these questions. For each kind of issue, a set of research methodologies is emerging. Family psychology research on depression, perhaps due to the high prevalence rates of depression, has evolved further than research on other disorders. Therefore, the kinds of issues raised in these chapters will also be relevant to family psychologists conducting research on other individual disorders.

These chapters clearly demonstrate that depression and family functioning are inextricably bound up with one another. They also clearly indicate that there are situations in which family intervention is more appropriate and others in which it is less helpful. For example, Beach and Gupta point to the beneficial role of marital therapies for those who are depressed and in distressed relationships, while couple therapy appears less beneficial and maybe even harmful for harmonious couples with depressed members. Now that the link between depression and family relationships has clearly been demonstrated, we look forward over the coming decades to a better elaboration of the causal pathways involved, as well as to specification of how and what forms of family and couple therapies are best incorporated in the treatment of depression.

15

Disentangling Causality in the Associations Between Couple and Family Processes and Depression

Valerie E. Whiffen

In this chapter I have the formidable task of reviewing the research literatures linking couple and family processes to depression. These comprise at least two separate literatures. The first assesses the impact of parental depression, particularly maternal depression, on children's risk for psychopathology. The second evaluates the role of marital distress in the etiology of adult depression or, less frequently, the impact of depression on the marital relationship. My goals are twofold: to paint a picture of the interpersonal context in which adult depression occurs and on which it has a reciprocal impact and to identify key research issues central to the problem of disentangling causality in both fields of research. Because of the scope of this chapter, I am not able to include research on family processes that are linked to child and adolescent depression.

■ The Nature of Depression

To understand the impact of depression on couples and families, as well as its origins within these systems, it is important to understand the nature of depression as an emotional problem. For most individuals, depression is chronic and/or recurring. The vast majority experience more than one episode; some have episodes so frequently that they essentially are chronically depressed. For instance, one prospective study followed a sample of patients receiving treatment for up to 12 years. On average, participants manifested symptoms during 59% of the follow-up weeks and spent 15% of the follow-up period in an episode of major depression (Judd et al., 1998). Thus, for most individuals and families, depression is not a one-shot disorder, which eventually remits; it is more like a chronic illness with periods of fluctuating, subclinical symptoms punctuated by full-blown episodes. The recurrent nature of depression presents real challenges to the researcher interested in disentangling causality. Most researchers take a snapshot at a specific point in time; the ambitious and well funded take two or three snap-shots. However, because of what we know about depression, we can predict that most of the depressed adults in research studies are experiencing recurrences rather than first episodes (Coyne & Benazon, 2001) and that most of their spouses and children already have experienced one or more episodes of depression with unknown consequences for the quality of these relationships. Thus, in the typi-cal cross-sectional study, depression and couple and family processes are con-founded.

The fact that most researchers do not appreciate the chronic and/or recurrent nature of depression is evident in their use of self-report questionnaires, which ask individuals to report on depressive symptoms experienced during the 1 or 2 weeks preceding the study. Couple and family processes are unlikely to be influenced by transient fluctuations in depressed mood. Thus, self-report questionnaires may underestimate or misrepresent the association between clinical depression and couple and family processes. In fact, studies using clinical depression versus self-reported mood may produce dissimilar results because the former often are based on a lifetime diagnosis and do not require that the individual be depressed presently. Lifetime diagnoses are problematic in that the episode may predate the marriage and/or the birth of children and therefore exert little influence on couple and family processes. Ideally, researchers need to select individuals who have experienced multiple episodes of depression during the marriage and/or children's lives. Un-fortunately, none of the studies reviewed in this chapter chose participants on this basis.

The core symptom of depression is negativity, directed toward oneself and toward others (Beck, Rush, Shaw, & Emery, 1979). Interpersonally, depressed people are characterized both by hostility (i.e., Gotlib & Whiffen, 1989) and by reassurance-seeking about their worthiness and lovability (Joiner, Alfano, & Me-talsky, 1992). Individuals who interact with depressed people feel more negative themselves (Joiner & Katz, 1999). Not surprisingly, people often reject depressed individuals, particularly in close relationships (Segrin & Dillard, 1991). This rejec-tion is likely to confirm the depressed person's negative views of self and others and to perpetuate both the depression and the disordered interpersonal context in which it thrives. Thus, perhaps more than other emotional disorders, depression is strongly tied to the interpersonal context, with implications both for its interper-sonal antecedents and for the impact that it is likely to have on couple and family relationships.

Finally, many depressed people also suffer from other emotional disorders, notably anxiety and personality disorders (Melartin & Isometsae, 2000). Estimates range as high as 92% for comorbidity with anxiety disorders and as high as 86% with personality disorders. Although there is reason to believe that individuals diag-nosed with pure depression differ significantly from those with comorbid anxiety (Wittchen, Kessler, Pfister, & Lieb, 2000), to date no attempt has been made to specify the links between these subtypes of depression and couple and family pro-cesses. More generally, no study has explored the role of comorbidity in explaining results apparently attributable to depression.

■ The Impact of Parental Depression on Children

There are several excellent narrative reviews of this literature, which show that maternal depression is associated with compromised child functioning, from infancy through adolescence (Downey & Coyne, 1990; Goodman & Gotlib, 1999; Murray & Cooper, 1997). Compared with the children of nondepressed mothers, the babies of depressed mothers are more temperamentally difficult; toddlers have greater difficulty controlling their negative emotions and self-soothing; school-aged children and adolescents are more emotionally distressed, they have more problems with peers and at school, and they have lower self-esteem (Goodman & Gotlib, 1999). The children of depressed mothers are at particular risk for internalizing symptoms and clinical depression (Downey & Coyne, 1990; Goodman & Gotlib, 1999). Girls are especially vulnerable; 43% of girls with one or more clinically depressed parents will experience an episode of major depression by the age of 19 (Wickramaratne & Weissman, 1998).

A recent meta-analysis quantified the association between parental depression and children's internalizing and externalizing symptoms and compared the relative impact of mothers and fathers (Connell & Goodman, 2002). Maternal depression was associated more strongly with children's internalizing disorders than was paternal depression, with relative effect sizes of 0.16 and 0.14. Consistent with the fact that mothers continue to be the primary caregivers to young children, the effect size for maternal depression was greater for younger than older children. The effect sizes associated with parental depression and externalizing symptoms were almost as strong, with relative values of 0.14 for mothers and 0.10 for fathers. Again, maternal depression was more strongly associated with externalizing symptoms in younger children, while paternal depression had a stronger association in older children. While the meta-analysis showed a consistent association, all of the effect sizes were small and accounted for less than 3% of the variance in children's symptoms. Thus, parental depression may be a less important factor in children's adjustment than is generally assumed. All of the studies also were cross-sectional, which introduces ambiguity about the direction of effects. While it is generally assumed that parental depression has an impact on children, longitudinal data from a small sample of clinically depressed mothers and their children showed that mothers' and children's episodes tended to overlap and that children's episodes could precipitate maternal episodes (Hammen, Burge, & Adrian, 1991). Thus, the association is likely to be reciprocal, a possibility that has received little empirical attention.

The children of depressed mothers may be at risk for internalizing symptoms and depression primarily because they carry the genetic vulnerability to depression. In addition, when mothers are depressed during pregnancy their infants' neurobiological development is compromised in ways that make these children more vulnerable to stress (Goodman & Gotlib, 1999). Animal analog studies show that stress that impedes the parents' ability to care for their newborns lowers the offspring's tolerance for stress later in life (Newport, Stowe, & Nemeroff, 2002). Women are at increased risk for depression during childbearing periods (Whiffen, 1992). Thus, the risk to children of having a depressed parent may derive substantially from genetic and/or neurobiological sources.

However, depressed mothers show distinctive patterns of interaction with their children, and researchers and reviewers have long speculated that negative maternal behaviors explain part of their children's difficulties. A meta-analysis of observational studies showed that, compared with nondepressed controls, depressed mothers were moderately more likely to show negative affect, such as hostility, particularly if their depression was current or recent (Lovejoy, Graczyk, O'Hare, & Neuman, 2000). However, even mothers with a lifetime history of depression were more negative with their children. In addition, depressed mothers were more disengaged or preoccupied. Finally, depressed mothers were somewhat less likely to show positive affect in the form of play, praise, and affection, although this effect may be an artifact of socioeconomic status (SES) and the setting in which the dyad was observed. Finally, the effect sizes did not differ for self-report versus diagnostic studies, which suggests that these interaction patterns are not specific to depression and can be expected in other distressed populations.

The first generation of research demonstrated conclusively that parental depression puts children at risk for emotional and behavioral problems. However, we have a very limited understanding of *why* and *under what conditions* parental depression is bad. Reviews of this literature repeatedly end with a call for researchers to move beyond documenting the negative impact of depression on children toward an understanding of the underlying mechanisms. Mechanisms of action or *mediators* explain why parental depression has a negative impact on children. For instance, negative interactions with depressed mothers may *mediate* or account for the association between depression and child psychopathology. Most reviewers also remark on the heterogeneity among the children of depressed parents. At best, parental depression accounts for less than 3% of the variance in children's emotional and behavioral problems. Thus, not all children of depressed parents are adversely affected. *Moderators* are variables that buffer or exacerbate the impact of parental depression, that is, they tell us about the conditions under which parental depression is more or less debilitating for the child.

Studies of Potential Mediators

In this section, I review studies testing the hypothesis that parental depression is linked to child outcomes through an impact on the family environment and parenting. The requirements for establishing mediation are both statistical and methodological. Baron and Kenny (1986) outlined a procedure for establishing mediation statistically. First, the researcher must show that depression is associated with children's maladjustment. This condition has been met repeatedly in the literature, but must also be met in individual studies testing for mediation. Second, a potential mediator must be associated both with parental depression and with child maladjustment. Finally, when both depression and the potential mediator are considered jointly as predictors of child maladjustment, the partial correlation between parental depression and child maladjustment should be lower than the zero order correlation between these variables. Full mediation requires that the statistical effect of depression disappears once the mediator is taken into account.

The second requirement is methodological. Most of the published research is cross-sectional; that is, data were collected from participants at only one point in time. Thus, parental depression, the potential mediator, and child adjustment were all measured at the same time. While cross-sectional studies are useful for pointing researchers in the direction of meaningful relationships, they are not conclusive because the independent variable (IV), dependent variable (DV), and mediator are confounded, and alternative links among the variables cannot be ruled out. For example, a child with behavioral problems may challenge parenting skills, which could have an adverse impact on the parent's mood. Ideally, longitudinal data are required to show mediation. Parental depression and the potential mediator at Time 1 are used to predict levels of child adjustment at Time 2. Few of the studies reviewed collected longitudinal data.

Contextual Adversity.   Parental depression is associated with a range of contextual variables, including low SES, marital conflict and breakdown, lack of cohesion, and family life stress (Billings & Moos, 1983; Fendrich, Warner, & Weissman, 1990; Hammen et al., 1987), any of which might account for the association between parental depression and child outcomes. Some researchers and reviewers consider these variables confounds or spurious variables that independently increase the risk of both parental depression and adverse child outcomes (Downey & Coyne, 1990; Fergusson & Lynsky, 1993) or moderators of parental depression (Billings & Moos, 1983). Others conceptualize them as potential mediators because of evidence that depressed persons generate life stress (Goodman & Gotlib, 1999).

When controlled, both divorce (Goodman, Brogan, Lynch, & Fielding, 1993) and chronic stress (Hammen et al., 1987) accounted for children's emotional and behavioral problems in cross-sectional studies of clinically depressed women. Fergusson and his colleagues (Fergusson, Horwood, & Lynskey, 1995; Fergusson & Lynskey, 1993) followed a large sample of mothers and children annually from the children's birth. At each assessment, the mothers reported on depressive symptoms experienced over the year. These reports were summed for the period when the children were 8 to 13 years old. Chronic maternal depressed mood was associated with children's externalizing symptoms at age 13 and with daughters' depressed mood at age 16. However, when contextual variables were controlled, these associations became nonsignificant. SES and marital breakdown accounted for the association with externalizing symptoms, while family life stress, marital conflict, and SES accounted for the daughters' depressed mood. The researchers also found that chronic depressed mood was predictive of subsequent family stress and marital conflict (Fergusson et al., 1995). Davies and Windle (1997) reported similar results. The link between chronic maternal depressed mood and daughters' depressive symptoms was accounted for by marital conflict, while the link with daughters' externalizing behaviors was accounted for by low family intimacy. Thus, these studies lend strong support to the hypothesis that parental depression poses a risk to children in part through contextual variables, such as SES, and in part through its impact on the marriage and family.

The findings for marital conflict replicate a cross-sectional study of the children of inpatients diagnosed with unipolar depression, in which teachers and peers rated children's behavior at school (Emery, Weintraub, & Neale, 1982). The association between unipolar depression and school problems, particularly externalizing problems like creating disturbances and being aggressive, was fully accounted for by marital discord. Miller, Cowan, Cowan, Hetherington, and Clingempeel (1993) extended this finding by hypothesizing that marital conflict has an impact on parenting, which then influences levels of externalizing behaviors. They found support for the model in the cross-sectional data provided by two samples of families, one with children aged 3.5 years and the other with children ranging in age from 9 to 13. In both samples, maternal depressed mood was associated with less warmth between the spouses and subsequently with less warmth toward the child, which was related to increased acting out by the children.

Attachment Insecurity. The jury is still out on whether maternal depression is associated with attachment insecurity. One meta-analysis showed that the infants of depressed mothers were less likely to be securely attached and more likely to be ambivalent (vanIjzendoorn, Schuengel, & Bakermans-Kranenberg, 1999). However, in a subsequent meta-analysis, maternal depression was moderately associated with attachment insecurity only in clinical samples (Atkinson et al., 2000). Even in clinical samples there was significant heterogeneity among the effect sizes, which suggests the presence of undetected moderators. Martins and Gaffan (2000) selected a subset of seven studies for meta-analysis, in which the mothers were diagnosed with clinical depression but there was no evidence of poverty, maltreatment, or marital breakdown. Even within this group of studies, they found significant heterogeneity. When two outlier studies were removed, the rates of attachment insecurity were not higher among the children of clinically depressed mothers. Thus, insecure attachment may be more strongly influenced by contextual factors than by maternal depression.

One cross-sectional study that set out to test for attachment insecurity as a mediator in a sample of 7- to 9-year-old children failed to find an association between maternal depressed mood and child attachment (Graham & Easterbrooks, 2000). In the absence of this association, attachment insecurity cannot be a mediator (Baron & Kenny, 1986). Murray and her colleagues (Murray, Sinclair, Cooper, Ducournau, & Turner, 1999) did find an association between postpartum depression and attachment insecurity at 18 months of age; however, 18-month attachment security did not mediate the link between postpartum depression and adjustment problems once the child started school. Thus, there is no evidence that attachment insecurity mediates the association between maternal depression and child maladjustment. However, there is some evidence that attachment security may moderate this association, as discussed in the section on moderators.

Impaired Parenting. Most of the mediation research has focused on the hypothesis that depressed parents are unable to adequately parent their children, which has a negative impact on their children's risk for emotional and behavioral problems. Unfortunately, researchers have assessed "parenting" with a range of variables, making it difficult to draw general conclusions.

A study of mother-infant dyads provided support for the general hypothesis that depressed mood disrupts parenting (Teti & Gelfand, 1991). The researchers examined mothers' behavioral competence in interactions with their infants and asked the mothers to report on their self-efficacy about parenting. Mediating analyses showed that more depressed mothers felt less efficacious, with negative consequences for their actual behavior. However, because of the ages of the infants, the researchers were unable to link maternal lack of competence to infant "psychopathology." Self-efficacy may be an interesting way of conceptualizing depressed parents' deficit because there is evidence that low self-efficacy is associated with many of the other behaviors that are shown by depressed parents, such as harsh and inconsistent discipline (Coleman & Karraker, 1997).

Another study observed the interactions of mothers with their 6.5-year-old children (Harnish, Dodge, & Valente, 1995). Mediating analyses showed that mothers with higher levels of depressed mood had less mutually positive interactions with their children, which predicted higher levels of their children's externalizing symptoms. Internalizing symptoms were not assessed. Interestingly, these associations did not hold for African American mothers, whose interactions did not appear to be influenced by depression levels. In addition, the strengths of these associations were reduced when SES was entered as a covariate, which suggests that much of the impact of depressed mood on interaction quality was attributable to low SES. In contrast, a study that compared clinically depressed parents of children aged 10 to 18 to nondepressed controls found few differences between the groups. Specifically, families with depressed fathers were less likely to respond positively (i.e., with agreement, approval, or humor) following positive communications by other family members (Jacob & Johnson, 2001). Families with depressed mothers did not show low levels of positivity, and families with depressed parents of either gender did not show higher levels of negativity. In addition, the failure to respond positively did not mediate the association between parental depression and child outcomes.

Two cross-sectional, self-report studies examined the hypothesis that parental anger mediates the association between parent and child symptoms (Renk, Phares, & Epps, 1999). The first study did not support the hypothesis, but it was limited by its design and sample. The second study asked parents of children aged 11 to 18 to report on their own anger and depression and their children's internalizing and externalizing symptoms. Mediating analyses showed that more depressed mothers expressed more anger, which was associated with increases in their sons' externalizing symptoms and their daughters' internalizing symptoms. Fathers' inward expression of anger mediated the link between their own depressed mood and their sons' internalizing and externalizing symptoms. It is important to note that the parents were not asked about anger expressed toward their children, only about their general tendency to express anger. However, these results are consistent with those from a cross-sectional study of rural seventh graders and their parents (Ge, Conger, Lorenz, & Simons, 1994), the data from which were compared with data from a smaller sample of urban boys in a subsequent publication (Conger, Patterson, & Ge, 1995). Although there were some differences between the patterns of association in the urban and rural samples, generally the studies supported the hypothesis that more depressed parents were more harsh and coercive with their children, particularly when disciplining them, which increased their children's depressed mood, externalizing symptoms, and antisocial behavior.

A within-subjects study by Snyder (1991) met both the statistical and methodological requirements for mediation. A small sample of single mothers and their preschool-aged sons were assessed repeatedly over a 1-month period. Previously, the mothers had reported that their sons had significant conduct problems. The mothers self-reported on their hassles and negative affect over the previous 2 days, and the dyads' interactions were observed. The researcher found evidence of both full and partial mediation. On days when mothers felt more stressed and distressed, they engaged in more reciprocally negative interactions with their sons and they were more likely to negatively reinforce their sons' aversive behaviors. Their sons showed more externalizing behaviors during these interactions and for the rest of the day. Because the children sampled were identified as having behavior problems, this study provides evidence that ineffective maternal discipline is implicated in the *maintenance* of sons' conduct problems. The evidence for partial mediation suggests either that mothers' negative affect has a direct effect on children's externalizing behaviors or that mediating variables not measured in the study also contribute to externalizing problems.

Summary of the Mediators Literature.   Most of the research on mediators has focused on parenting deficits that are assumed to accompany parental depression. There is consistent evidence from cross-sectional studies of nonclinical samples that higher levels of parental depressed mood are associated with lower parenting self-efficacy and competence, less positive interactions with children, more anger, and harsher discipline. In turn, these variables (with the exception of self-efficacy) fully or partially mediate the link between parental depressed mood and children's emotional difficulties. However, only one study demonstrated mediation over time. Most researchers do not seem to appreciate that these cross-sectional results also are consistent with the hypothesis that children's difficulties have a negative impact on parenting practices and parental mood. Children's negativity in interactions with their mothers does influence their mothers' depression (Hammen, Burge, & Stansbury, 1990). In addition, researchers need to determine that impairments in parenting arise from parental depression, rather than from such contextual variables as low SES, marital distress, and family stress, which, when they are controlled, account for the association between depression and child outcomes. In particular, researchers have paid astonishingly little attention to the role played by marital distress, in light of the emphasis given to it in a major and frequently cited review by Downey and Coyne (1990).

The single study that sampled parents with clinical depression did not find greater negativity in family interactions. Forehand, McCombs, and Brody (1987) suggested that mild levels of depression, produced by stressors such as marital conflict, may reduce temporarily parents' tolerance for their children's inappropriate behaviors. Ironically, clinically depressed parents may be more cognizant of the impact of their mood on perceptions of their children's behavior. There is a critical need for more studies assessing parenting as a mediator in samples of diagnosed depressed parents.

Finally, all of the research reviewed focused on children's internalizing and externalizing symptoms. There is a need for more research exploring the impact of depression on the acquisition of age appropriate skills and behaviors, which ultimately may contribute to the risk for depression among children (Goodman et al., 1993). Similarly, there is a need for better conceptual links between depression and normative parenting practices. If we are well informed about what parents typically do with children of a particular age, we will be better able to hypothesize how depression might interfere with these normal practices.

Studies of Potential Moderators

Baron and Kenny (1986) provided a relatively simple method for demonstrating moderation. Conceptually, the researcher examines the association between the IV (parental depression) and the DV (child outcome) at different levels of the moderator. Moderation is demonstrated if the association differs at high, medium, and low levels of the moderator. As was the case with mediators, cross-sectional studies are not conclusive because the IV, DV, and moderator are confounded.

The Nature of Parental Depression

Connell and Goodman's (2002) meta-analysis showed that maternal depression has a stronger association with younger than older children's symptoms, while paternal depression has a stronger association with older than younger children's externalizing symptoms. These findings indicate that the *timing* of parental depression is an important moderator of child outcome. Younger children probably are more affected by maternal depression because mothers provide most of the care to younger children. Developmentally, fathers become more salient as children mature. Unfortunately, the studies included in the meta-analysis were cross-sectional, so we do not know whether exposure to maternal depression at a younger age is associated with a greater *cumulative* impact, as proposed by Goodman and Gotlib (1999). Longitudinal studies that follow samples of children over the risk period are needed to answer this question.

Whether the parent's depression is chronic or delimited also may have an impact on children's functioning, with children exposed to more depression during their lifetimes being at greater risk. For instance, in the nonclinical study by Fergusson described previously (Fergusson & Lynskey, 1993), chronic depressed mood clearly had a greater impact on child outcomes than did the mother's current mood. Unfortunately, researchers rarely include chronicity as a variable.

A potential moderator that has not been examined at all by researchers is comorbidity. Parental depression tends to be comorbid with other Axis I and II disorders. We do not know if the effects that have been attributed to parental depression are in part or wholly influenced by the presence of these other problems.

The Nonindex Parent.   The potential moderator that is mentioned most frequently in the literature is the nonindex parent, typically the father. Reviewers hypothesize that having a warm and supportive father may buffer the effects of maternal depression, while having a father who has emotional problems of his own may increase the child's risk. This hypothesis is complicated by data showing that depressed individuals are likely to be partnered with people who either have psychiatric problems themselves or who have a family history of illness. For instance, Merikangas, Weissman, Prusoff, and John (1988) found that 41% of married depressed individuals had spouses with psychiatric disorders. Children whose parents both showed psychopathology were at increased risk for psychiatric problems of all kinds, compared with children having one affected parent. Similarly, Goodman et al. (1993) showed that, when paternal psychopathology and marital status were controlled, 5- to 10-year-old children of depressed mothers were at risk for very few difficulties in social and emotional development.

Only a handful of studies have considered the impact of both parents' psychopathology on child outcomes. When mothers' depressed mood was considered first, the addition of paternal depressed mood made a unique contribution to both girls' and boys' outcomes in a nonclinical sample of 11- to 15-year-olds (Thomas & Forehand, 1991). However, paternal and maternal depressed mood were not compared as predictors in this study. Carro, Grant, Gotlib, and Compas (1993) compared them in a nonclinical sample of parents of 2- to 3-year-old children. They found that paternal depressed mood did not contribute uniquely to the explained variance in children's internalizing or externalizing problems. However, a longitudinal analysis suggested that fathers' depressed mood contributed indirectly through an impact on the mother's mood.

The effects of paternal psychopathology are more striking when psychopathology is defined by diagnosis. Brennan, Hammen, Katz, and Le Brocque (2002) evaluated paternal depression and substance abuse as moderators of the association between maternal depression and child psychopathology in a large community sample of adolescents. They found few simple associations between paternal psychopathology and adolescents' emotional disorders. However, maternal and paternal depression interacted, such that when the father met lifetime criteria for depression, the mother's depression no longer contributed to the adolescent's risk for depression. Maternal depression also interacted with paternal substance abuse, such that only the combination was associated with increased risk for adolescent depression. Further analyses indicated that the combination of maternal depression and paternal substance abuse was associated with higher levels of chronic family stress and paternal expressed emotion (criticism and emotional overinvolvement with family members), both of which mediated the link between the interaction term and adolescent depression. Thus, this study suggests that the risk to adolescent children from clinically depressed mothers stems largely from comorbid paternal psychopathology and its impact on the family.

Only two studies specifically tested the hypothesis that a relationship with the father can buffer the impact of maternal depression on children. The simple presence of the father in the home did not moderate the effect of maternal depression in a small clinical sample of highly stressed children (Hammen et al., 1991). However, Tannenbaum and Forehand (1994) found support for this hypothesis in a nonclinical sample of 11- to 16-year-old children. When perceived communication with the father was good and levels of conflict low, maternal depressed mood was not associated with adolescent internalizing and externalizing problems. However, communication and conflict with the mother were not assessed, so we do not know if the father actually buffered the negative impact of the mother or if both parents were able to maintain good communication with their children despite the mothers' depressed mood.

Attachment Security.   Radke-Yarrow and her colleagues (1995) suggested that security in the child's attachment to the mother could buffer the effects of maternal depression. However, contrary to prediction and counterintuitively, the children of depressed mothers who were securely attached at 18 to 42 months had *more* emotional difficulties of all kinds at age 6. The interactions of these dyads were characterized by high levels of warmth and responsiveness on the mother's part and high levels of dependency on the child's part, which the researchers perceived as "engulfing" for the child. While this interaction pattern may have been optimal for the child as a preschooler and thus promoted attachment security, these depressed mothers may have been unable to foster their children's autonomy as they moved into the school-age years. Thus, this study raises the intriguing possibility that depressed parents have difficulty meeting the changing developmental needs of their children. Future researchers need to consider the possibility that subtypes of depressed mothers pose difficulties for their children at different developmental stages.

Summary of the Moderators Literature.   More attention has been paid to mediating than moderating variables, with the result that the latter research area lacks cohesion and is inconclusive. The timing of depression is an important factor in children's outcomes, with paternal depression playing a greater role as children mature. Paternal emotional disorders also interact with maternal depression in significant ways. The combination of a depressed mother and a father with substance abuse problems may be particularly detrimental to children's well-being, through the creation of chronic family stress and an emotionally charged family atmosphere. One study suggests that a good relationship with the father buffers the impact of maternal depressed mood. However, this hypothesis may be moot given the data on the clustering of maternal depression, paternal psychopathology, and family distress.

Aspects of the child's relationship with the depressed parent also may be important. Not all depressed parents behave similarly with their children. Variations in their relationships should be studied to understand how some of these children are resilient to the effects of parental depression.

■ Marital Distress and Depression

Depression is moderately correlated with marital distress. In a meta-analysis, Whisman (2001) reported effect sizes of 0.42 for women and 0.37 for men, which is a statistically significant difference. Thus, the link between marital distress and depression is slightly stronger for women than for men.

Consistent with the parental depression literature, this association appears to be bidirectional. There is strong evidence that marital distress increases the risk of an episode of depression and predicts relapse after recovery from an episode. For instance, using a large sample of married couples from the community, Whisman and Bruce (1999) showed that spouses who were maritally distressed but not depressed at baseline were nearly 3 times more likely to become clinically depressed over the subsequent year than were individuals who were neither maritally distressed nor depressed. In a separate study, Whisman (1999) showed that marital distress was uniquely related to the onset of major depression and posttraumatic stress disorder for women, and to dysthymia for men, which indicates that the association is specific. Hooley and Teasdale (1989) showed that the best predictor of relapse in a sample of recovered depressed patients was their perception that their spouses were critical of them. Thus, marital distress clearly can and does contribute to the onset or recurrence of depression.

However, there also is evidence that depressed mood has an impact on the quality of marital relations. The marital interactions of couples with a depressed spouse are characterized by hostility and negativity on the part of both partners (e.g., Gotlib & Whiffen, 1989). Karney (2001) showed that increases in either marital distress or depressive symptoms were associated with concomitant increases in the other variable. Interestingly, there was no difference in the two effect sizes, which suggests that marital distress is as likely to influence depression as vice versa.

Marital Distress Contributes to Depression

Longitudinal studies demonstrate that marital distress is implicated in the onset of depression. However, it is not clear *why* or *under what conditions* maritally distressed individuals are vulnerable. In this section, I review mediating and moderating studies of the association between marital distress and depression.

Mediating Studies.   In a large sample of disadvantaged Mexican American women, Vega, Kolody, and Valle (1988) examined the impact of marital strain on women's coping and self-esteem. *Marital strain* was defined as feeling unaccepted by the spouse, feeling that the relationship lacked reciprocity, and feeling frustrated with role expectations. Mediating analyses showed that women who saw their marriages as strained were less likely to "selectively ignore" their husbands' behavior and more likely to express anger. In addition, they were more self-denigrating and felt less efficacious. Collectively, these variables accounted for the association between marital strain and depressed mood. However, the self-esteem variables contributed much more to the final equation than did the coping variables. Thus, marital strain appears to have a particular impact on women's self-esteem, which increases their risk for depression. Culp and Beach (1998) reached a similar conclusion in their study of working, married individuals living in the community. They found that maritally distressed women reported lower self-esteem, which was associated with higher levels of depressed mood. In contrast, marital distress had a direct impact on depression for the men.

Jack (1991) proposed that women's self-esteem is more heavily invested in harmonious interpersonal relations than is men's self-esteem. She argued that when women find themselves in a distressed marriage, they "silence" themselves in order to preserve the illusion of harmony in the relationship. "Self-silencing" involves actively suppressing anger and thoughts or feelings that might threaten the relationship. While this strategy may benefit the relationship in the short term, self-silencing results in a loss of connection to the self that ultimately is responsible for depression. Thompson, Whiffen, and Aube (2001) tested this hypothesis in a community sample of men and women in committed relationships. Self-silencing fully mediated the association between perceived partner criticism and depressed mood; however, different aspects of silencing were identified as mediators for men and women. For the women, presenting a compliant facade while being angry mediated the link with depression, while for men judging oneself by harsh, external standards was the mediator. Thus, individuals who perceived their romantic partners as critical of them tended to fake compliance (women) or to judge themselves harshly (men), which was associated with increased depression.

In an earlier study, Whiffen and Aube (1999) examined the impact of spousal complaints and lack of intimacy on two personality variables known to be associated with depression, dependency and self-criticism. They argued that these personality variables are strongly influenced by the interpersonal context, such that a critical spouse increases self-criticism, while an emotionally distant one increases feelings of neediness. In a cross-sectional study of couples, they found support for both hypotheses. Men and women who were married to individuals who had many complaints about them were more self-critical, which subsequently was associated with increased levels of depressed mood. Similarly, women who were married to emotionally distant men were more needy, which increased their depression levels.

Recently, I proposed a model based on attachment theory to understand the link between marital distress and depression (Whiffen, in press). I hypothesized that marital distress interferes with the couple's ability to be sensitive and responsive to each other's emotional needs, which contributes to attachment insecurity and depression. The model was tested with data provided by a community sample of married or cohabiting couples who were followed over a three-month period. The results suggested that the model was supported for the husbands but not for the wives. Husbands who perceived their wives as unresponsive to them felt more insecurely attached and were more depressed at the follow-up. Wives who perceived their husbands as unresponsive to them were also more insecurely attached, but their attachment insecurity did not predict increases in their depressive symptoms over time. Women who are insecurely attached to their husbands may find other sources of emotional support that protect them from depression.

These studies are consistent with the hypothesis that marital distress has a negative impact on perceptions of the self. Interestingly, marital distress appears to influence men's levels of self-criticism specifically, but to influence women's self-esteem generally. Thus, the effects of marital distress on women may be more pervasive, which could explain why marital distress is more strongly associated with depression for women than men. Although consistent, all but one of the studies were cross-sectional, and none used clinical samples of couples or clinical diagnoses of depression. Thus, there is a need to extend these hypotheses to clinical populations and to test for mediation over time.

Moderating Studies. Marital distress and depression are even more closely associated when depression is defined by diagnosis, with a mean effect size of 1.75 according to a meta-analysis by Whisman (2001). Thus, individuals who are vulnerable to clinical depression may be particularly sensitive to the quality of their marital relations. Consistent with this hypothesis, Karney (2001) showed that marital distress was more likely to exacerbate depressive symptoms among women high in neuroticism than among those low on this trait.

Sensitivity to the quality of relationships may derive, in part, from negative childhood experiences that commonly are reported by depressed adults, such as childhood sexual abuse. A cross-sectional study by Whiffen, Judd, and Aube (1999) showed that women who were sexually abused during childhood were both better protected by marital relations and more prone to depressive symptoms when their relationships were of poor quality than were women without this history. Similarly, a cross-sectional study by Scott and Cordova (2002) showed that the link between marital distress and depressive symptoms was moderated by attachment insecurity in romantic relationships. Thus, individuals who are vulnerable to depression by virtue of an adverse interpersonal history also may be particularly sensitive to marital distress.

Katz, Beach, and Joiner (1998) hypothesized that a romantic partner who is devaluing would increase depression levels among individuals who tend to seek reassurance about their lovability. They tested this hypothesis in a longitudinal study of dating university couples. They found that partner devaluation was not generally associated with increased depressed mood over a 6-week period. However, it was associated with depressed mood among individuals who tended to seek reassurance about their lovability. Presumably, individuals who did not seek this confirmation were less aware of their partner's devaluation.

To summarize, the association between marital distress and depression appears to be moderated by neuroticism, a history of childhood sexual abuse, attachment insecurity, and reassurance-seeking. Marital distress may be especially problematic for individuals with a history of poor relationships. An attachment theory perspective on depression in couples is an emerging framework (Whiffen, in press; Whiffen, Kallos-Lilly, & MacDonald, 2001) that may prove useful as a way of consolidating apparently discrepant research findings. Again, however, all of the moderating studies used nonclinical samples of couples, and only one tested for moderation over time.

Depression Contributes to Marital Distress

Davila (2001) argued that negative cognitions and interaction behaviors that are associated with depression have an adverse impact on the quality of marital relations, which erodes marital satisfaction and maintains depression. She and her colleagues confirmed this hypothesis for wives in a longitudinal study of newly-weds followed over the first year of marriage (Davila, Bradbury, Cohan, & Tochluk, 1997). They found that wives' depressed mood predicted their expectation that their husbands would be negative and critical of them, which then predicted their tendency to behave negatively during a marital interaction. Over time, the wives' interaction behaviors predicted increases in both marital distress and depressed mood. Thus, this study suggests that depression can become self-perpetuating through its impact on marital relations.

Depression and marital distress also may be linked indirectly through the contagion of one partner's depressed mood to the other, with negative consequences for the quality of their marital relations. There is evidence that depressed mood is contagious even among strangers and roommates (Joiner & Katz, 1999); married or cohabiting couples should be especially vulnerable. If this hypothesis is correct, stronger covariation of depressed mood should occur in couples that are more intimate. In a large sample of married couples over the age of 65, Tower and Kasl (1995) showed that depressed mood was more strongly correlated in couples that were emotionally close. Katz, Beach, and Joiner (1999) found similar results in a sample of dating university couples, in that depressed mood was more strongly correlated with partner's mood for individuals who sought reassurance about their lovability. The authors speculated that individuals who feel depressed withdraw emotionally from their romantic partners, which is particularly distressing for partners who seek reassurance. Contagion effects are likely to be pronounced among women, who appear to be especially sensitive to their partners' marital distress and depressed mood (Thompson, Whiffen, & Blain, 1995; Whiffen & Gotlib, 1989).

To summarize, only one study tested a mediating hypothesis about the link between depression and marital distress. This study showed that, for women, depressed mood has a negative impact on the quality of marital interactions, which perpetuates marital distress and depression over time. Depressed mood is likely to have its greatest impact when partners are close or when they rely upon each other for reassurance. To date, no study has examined potential moderators of the link between depression and marital distress. Thus, we do not know the conditions under which depression is most likely to have an impact on marital relations.

■ Summary and Recommendations for Future Research

There is both good and bad news in this review of the literature. The good news is that research has advanced beyond documenting the simple association between depression and couple and family processes. Depression has a negative impact on marital relations and parenting, which can lead to emotional and behavioral problems in the children. This finding represents an important step in specifying the causal mechanisms that link parental depression to children's emotional difficulties. However, the strength of the association between parental depression and children's adjustment appears to be much weaker than is generally assumed. Thus, parental depression per se may be less important to children's well-being than its covariates and sequelae, such as poverty, marital conflict and divorce, and family stress. A small effect also suggests the presence of undetected moderators. The few studies that have examined moderators suggest that the presence of psychopathology in the nonindex spouse may be a critical determinant of children's outcomes.

Although the literature on marital distress and depression is less well developed, the trend toward second-generation research also is evident here. The results of mediating studies suggest that marital distress increases self-criticism and decreases self-esteem, which contributes to depression. Individuals who have an adverse interpersonal history are particularly vulnerable to marital distress, perhaps because their self-esteem is more tenuous. In both literatures, it is important to keep in mind that depression in one partner tends to be associated with depression or other types of psychopathology in the other, with implications for the overall health of the couple or family system. The importance of psychopathology in the nonindex spouse has not been explored at all in the marital distress literature, despite the fact that "dual psychopathology" couples are likely to be particularly prone to marital difficulties.

The bad news is that the strength of our conclusions must be tempered by the tendency to test hypotheses with inadequate methods and samples. I was able to locate only a handful of studies that tested potential mediators or moderators over time, and in all of these studies depression was measured by self-reported mood.

The measurement of psychopathology is problematic in both literatures. Researchers tend to use self-report measures of depressive symptoms and to be insensitive to the chronic, recurrent nature of clinical depression. While studies of self-reported distress are interesting in their own right, chronic or recurrent depression is likely to have a more dramatic impact on couple and family functioning and to be more closely tied to these systems etiologically. There is an urgent need for research that focuses on individuals with a history of clinical depression, particularly with episodes that occurred during the relationship of interest, whether that is the marriage or the child's lifetime. Careful tracking of the number and duration of episodes would enable us to assess what amount of depression is detrimental to couples and families and at what stage of the family life cycle adverse consequences are most likely. The use of structured interviews to determine the lifetime course of psychopathology also would permit researchers to identify the presence of comorbid disorders and to begin to compare couple and family processes in individuals who suffer from "pure" depression to those in individuals whose depression is comorbid with anxiety or personality disorders. This research would enable us to determine whether the apparent effects of depression are attributable to other commonly comorbid conditions. Finally, it is critical that future researchers not assume that one person's depression is the active ingredient, and assess psychopathology in all members of the system.

Both literatures also have overwhelmingly used cross-sectional research designs to test causal hypotheses. This practice is particularly dangerous when researchers are testing mediating hypotheses. Formal tests for mediation with cross-sectional data appear to give researchers false confidence in their results. Depression has an impact both on how relationships are perceived and on depressed persons' interactions with significant others. Thus, longitudinal studies are needed to distinguish the concomitants and consequences of depression from its antecedents (Barnett & Gotlib, 1988). Only longitudinal studies can demonstrate conclusively that a system variable has an impact on depression or vice versa. Longitudinal studies also enable researchers to evaluate the possibility of reciprocity in the relations between depressed persons and their interpersonal contexts. Studies are needed to assess the impact of children's behavior and emotional distress on parental depression, as well as the impact of the nonindex spouse on the course of the depressed person's episode. Finally, longitudinal studies are needed to follow families over salient risk periods. For instance, much could be learned about the impact of parental depression on children by following children through adolescence when the risk for depression emerges. Similarly, marital relations and depression should be followed through such relationship risk periods as the transition to parenthood.

■ Conclusions

At the broadest level, the research shows that adult depression occurs in a complex, interpersonal system that may include both spouses and children and that it both affects and is affected by characteristics of this system. Families that are identified because one of the adults is depressed are likely to experience multiple, co-occurring difficulties. The nonindex spouse and children may have emotional problems of their own, the marriage may be distressed, and parent-child relations may be compromised. These difficulties in turn likely perpetuate symptoms of depression. While these overlapping problem areas present challenges to the researcher interested in couple and family processes and depression, these challenges are not insurmountable.

It also may be useful to begin developing an organizing theory that helps researchers to understand the associations among the various parts of these systems. At the present time, only attachment theory is being applied to the problem of depression in this manner (Herring & Kaslow, 2002; Whiffen, in press; Whiffen et al., 2001). I hope to see other systemic theories emerge over the coming decade. Conceptualizing the marriages and families of depressed persons as systems that promulgate emotional distress may both guide our research efforts and help us to speculate about the mechanisms that link depression to couple and family processes.

■ References

Atkinson, L., Paglia, A., Coolbear, J., Niccols, A., Parker, K. C. H., & Guger, S. (2000). Attachment security: A meta-analysis of maternal mental health correlates. *Clinical Psychology Review, 20,* 1019–1040.

Barnett, P., & Gotlib, I. H. (1988). Psychosocial functioning and depression: Distinguishing among antecedents, concomitants, and consequences. *Psychological Bulletin, 104,* 97–126.

Baron, M. R., & Kenny, D. A. (1986). The moderator-mediator variable distinction in social psychological research: Conceptual, strategic, and statistical considerations. *Journal of Personality and Social Psychology, 51*(6), 1173–1182.

Beck, A. T., Rush, A. J., Shaw, B. F., & Emery, G. (1979). *Cognitive therapy of depression.* New York: Guilford Press.

Billings, A. G., & Moos, R. H. (1983). Comparisons of children of depressed and nondepressed parents: A social-environmental perspective. *Journal of Abnormal Child Psychology, 11,* 463–486.

Brennan, P. A., Hammen, C., Katz, A. R., & Le Brocque, R. M. (2002). Maternal depression, paternal psychopathology, and adolescent diagnostic outcomes. *Journal of Consulting and Clinical Psychology, 70,* 1075–1085.

Carro, M. G., Grant, K. E., Gotlib, I. H., & Compas, B. E. (1993). Postpartum depression and child development: An investigation of mothers and fathers as sources of risk and resilience. *Development and Psychopathology, 5,* 567–579.

Coleman, P. K., & Karraker, K. H. (1997). Self-efficacy and parenting quality: Findings and future applications. *Developmental Review, 18,* 47–85.

Conger, R. D., Patterson, G. R., & Ge, X. (1995). It takes two to replicate: A mediational model for the impact of parents' stress on adolescent adjustment. *Child Development, 66,* 80–97.

Connell, A. M., & Goodman, S. H. (2002). The association between psychopathology in fathers versus mothers and children's internalizing and externalizing behavior problems: A meta-analysis. *Psychological Bulletin, 128,* 746–773.

Coyne, J. C., & Benazon, N. R. (2001). Not agent blue: Effects of marital functioning on depression and implications for treatment. In S. R. H. Beach (Ed.), *Marital and family processes in depression.* Washington, DC: American Psychological Association.

Culp, L. N., & Beach, S. R. H. (1998). Marriage and depressive symptoms: The role and bases of self-esteem differ by gender. *Psychology of Women Quarterly, 22,* 647–663.

Davies, P. T., & Windle, M. (1997). Gender-specific pathways between maternal depressive symptoms, family discord, and adolescent adjustment. *Developmental Psychology, 33,* 657–668.

Davila, J. (2001). Paths to unhappiness: The overlapping courses of depression and romantic dysfunction. In S. R. H. Beach (Ed.), *Marital and family processes in depression.* Washington, DC: American Psychological Association.

Davila, J., Bradbury, T. N., Cohan, C. L., & Tochluk, S. (1997). Marital functioning and depressive symptoms: Evidence for a stress generation model. *Journal of Personality and Social Psychology, 73,* 849–861.

Downey, G., & Coyne, J. C. (1990). Children of depressed parents: An integrative review. *Psychological Bulletin, 108,* 50–76.

Emery, R., Weintraub, S., & Neale, J. M. (1982). Effects of marital discord on the school behavior of children of schizophrenic, affectively disordered, and normal parents. *Journal of Abnormal Child Psychology, 10,* 215–228.

Fendrich, M., Warner, V., & Weissman, M. M. (1990). Family risk factors, parental depression, and psychopathology in offspring. *Developmental Psychology, 26,* 40–50.

Fergusson, D. M., Horwood, L. J., & Lynskey, M. T. (1995). Maternal depressive symptoms and depressive symptoms in adolescents. *Journal of Child Psychology and Psychiatry and Allied Disciplines, 7,* 1161–1178.

Fergusson, D. M., & Lynskey, M. T. (1993). The effects of maternal depression on child conduct disorder and attention deficit behaviours. *Social Psychiatry and Psychiatric Epidemiology, 28,* 116–123.

Forehand, R., McCombs, A., & Brody, G. H. (1987). The relationship between parental depressive mood states and child functioning. *Advances in Behavior Research and Therapy, 9,* 1–20.

Ge, X., Conger, R. D., Lorenz, F. O., & Simons, R. L. (1994). Parents' stressful life events and adolescent depressed mood. *Journal of Health and Social Behavior, 35,* 28–44.

Goodman, S. H., Brogan, D., Lynch, M. E., & Fielding, B. (1993). Social and emotional competence in children of depressed mothers. *Child Development, 64,* 516–531.

Goodman, S. H., & Gotlib, I. H. (1999). Risk for psychopathology in the children of depressed mothers: A developmental model for understanding mechanisms of transmission. *Psychological Review, 106,* 458–490.

Gotlib, I. H., & Whiffen, V. E. (1989). Depression and marital functioning: An examination of specificity and gender differences. *Journal of Abnormal Psychology, 98,* 23–30.

Graham, C. A., & Easterbrooks, M. A. (2000). School-aged children's vulnerability to depressive symptomatology: The role of attachment security, maternal depressive symptomatology, and economic risk. *Development and Psychopathology, 12,* 201–213.

Hammen, C., Burge, D., & Adrian, C. (1991). Timing of mother and child depression in a longitudinal study of children at risk. *Journal of Consulting and Clinical Psychology, 59,* 341–345.

Hammen, C., Burge, D., & Stansbury, K. (1990). Relationship of mother and child variables to child outcomes in a high-risk sample: A causal modeling analysis. *Developmental Psychology, 26,* 24–30.

Hammen, C., Gordon, D., Burge, D., Adrian, C., Jaenicke, C., & Hiroto, D. (1987). Maternal affective disorders, illness, and stress: Risk for children's psychopathology. *American Journal of Psychiatry, 144,* 736–741.

Harnish, J. D., Dodge, K. A., & Valente, E. (1995). Mother–child interaction quality as a partial mediator of the roles of maternal depressive symptomatology and socioeconomic status in the development of child behavior problems. *Child Development, 66,* 739–753.

Herring, M., & Kaslow, N. J. (2002). Depression and attachment in families: A child-focused perspective. *Family Process, 41,* 494–518.

Hooley, J. M., & Teasdale, J. D. (1989). Predictors of relapse in unipolar depressives: Expressed emotion, marital distress, and perceived criticism. *Journal of Abnormal Psychology, 98*(3), 229–235.

Jack, D. C. (1991). *Silencing the self: Women and depression.* Cambridge, MA: Harvard University Press.

Jacob, T., & Johnson, S. L. (2001). Sequential interactions in the parent-child communications of depressed fathers and depressed mothers. *Journal of Family Psychology, 15,* 38–52.

Joiner, T. E., Alfano, M. S., & Metalsky, G. I. (1992). When depression breeds contempt: Reassurance-seeking, self esteem, and rejection of depressed college students by their roommates. *Journal of Abnormal Psychology, 101,* 165–173.

Joiner, T. E., & Katz, J. (1999). Contagion of depressive symptoms and mood: Meta-analytic review and explanations from cognitive, behavioral, and interpersonal viewpoints. *Clinical Psychology: Science and Practice, 6,* 149–164.

Judd, L. L., Akiskal, H. S., Maser, J. D., Zeller, P. J., Endicott, J., Coryell, W., et al. (1998). A prospective 12-year study of subsyndromal and syndromal depressive symptoms in unipolar major depressive disorders. *Archives of General Psychiatry, 55,* 694–700.

Karney, B. R. (2001). Depressive symptoms and marital satisfaction in the early years of marriage: Narrowing the gap between theory and research. In S. R. H. Beach (Ed.), *Marital and family processes in depression* (pp. 45–68). Washington, DC: American Psychological Association.

Katz, J., Beach, S. R. H., & Joiner, T. E. (1998). When does partner devaluation predict emotional distress? Prospective moderating effects of reassurance-seeking and self-esteem. *Personal Relationships, 5,* 409–421.

Katz, J., Beach, S. R. H., & Joiner, T. E. (1999). Contagious depression in dating couples. *Journal of Social and Clinical Psychology, 18,* 1–13.

Lovejoy, M. C., Graczyk, P. A., O'Hare, E., & Neuman, G. (2000). Maternal depression and parenting behavior: A meta-analytic review. *Clinical Psychology Review, 20,* 561–592.

Martins, C., & Gaffan, E. A. (2000). Effects of early maternal depression on patterns of infant–mother attachment: A meta-analytic investigation. *Journal of Child Psychology, Psychiatry and Allied Disciplines, 41,* 737–746.

Melartin, T., & Isometsae, E. (2000). Psychiatric comorbidity of major depressive disorder—a review. *Psychiatria Fennica, 31,* 87–100.

Merikangas, K. R., Weissman, M. M., Prusoff, B. A., & John, K. (1988). Assortative mating and affective disorders: Psychopathology in offspring. *Psychiatry, 51,* 48–57.

Miller, N. B., Cowan, P. A., Cowan, C. P., Hetherington, E. M., & Clingempeel, W. G. (1993). Externalizing in preschoolers and early adolescents: A cross-study replication of a family model. *Developmental Psychology, 29,* 3–18.

Murray, L., & Cooper, P. J. (1997). Postpartum depression and child development. *Psychological Medicine, 27,* 253–260.

Murray, L., Sinclair, D., Cooper, P., Ducournau, P., & Turner, P. (1999). The socio-emotional development of 5-year-old children of postnatally depressed mothers. *Journal of Child Psychology, Psychiatry, and Allied Disciplines, 40,* 1259–1271.

Newport, D. J., Stowe, Z. N., & Nemeroff, C. B. (2002). Parental depression: Animal models of an adverse life event. *American Journal of Psychiatry, 159,* 1265–1282.

Radke-Yarrow, M., McCann, K., DeMulder, E., Belmont, B., Martinez, P., & Richardson, D. T. (1995). Attachment in the context of high-risk conditions. *Development and Psychopathology, 7,* 247–265.

Renk, K., Phares, V., & Epps, J. (1999). The relationship between parental anger and behavior problems in children and adolescents. *Journal of Family Psychology, 13,* 209–227.

Scott, R. L., & Cordova, J. V. (2002). The influence of adult attachment styles on the association between marital adjustment and depressive symptoms. *Journal of Family Psychology, 16,* 199–208.

Segrin, C., & Dillard, J. P. (1991). The interactional theory of depression: A meta-analysis of the research literature. *Journal of Social and Clinical Psychology, 11,* 43–70.

Snyder, J. (1991). Discipline as a mediator of the impact of maternal stress and mood on child conduct problems. *Development and Psychopathology, 3,* 263–276.

Tannenbaum, L., & Forehand, R. (1994). Maternal depressive mood: The role of the father in preventing adolescent problem behaviors. *Behavior Research and Therapy, 32,* 321–325.

Teti, D. M., & Gelfand, D. M. (1991). Behavioral competence among mothers of infants in the first year: The mediational role of maternal self-efficacy. *Child Development, 62,* 918–929.

Thomas, A. M., & Forehand, R. (1991). The relationship between paternal depressive mood and early adolescent functioning. *Journal of Family Psychology, 4,* 260–271.

Thompson, J. M., Whiffen, V. E., & Aube, J. A. (2001). Does self-silencing link perceptions of care from parents and partners with depressive symptoms? *Journal of Social and Personal Relationships, 18,* 503–516.

Thompson, J. M., Whiffen, V. E., & Blain, M. D. (1995). Depressive symptoms, sex, and perception of intimate relationships. *Journal of Social and Personal Relationships, 12,* 49–66.

Tower, R. B., & Kasl, S. V. (1995). Depressive symptoms across older spouses and the moderating effect of marital closeness. *Psychology and Aging, 10,* 625–638.

vanIjzendoorn, M. H., Schuengel, C., & Bakermans-Kranenburg, M. J. (1999). Disorganized attachment in early childhood: Meta-analysis of precursors, concomitants, and sequelae. *Development and Psychopathology, 11,* 225–249.

Vega, W. A., Kolody, B., & Valle, R. (1988). Marital strain, coping, and depression among Mexican-American women. *Journal of Marriage and the Family, 50,* 391–403.

Whiffen, V. E. (1992). Is postpartum depression a distinct diagnosis? *Clinical Psychology Review, 12,* 485–508.

Whiffen, V. E. (in press). The role of partner characteristics in attachment insecurity and depressive symptoms. *Personal Relationships.*

Whiffen, V. E., & Aube, J. A. (1999). Personality, interpersonal context, and depression in couples. *Journal of Social and Personal Relationships, 16,* 369–383.

Whiffen, V. E., & Gotlib, I. H. (1989). Stress and coping in maritally distressed and nondistressed couples. *Journal of Social and Personal Relationships, 6,* 327–344.

Whiffen, V. E., Judd, M. E., & Aube, J. A. (1999). Intimate relationships moderate the association between childhood sexual abuse and depression. *Journal of Interpersonal Violence, 14,* 940–954.

Whiffen, V. E., Kallos-Lilly, A. V., & MacDonald, B. J. (2001). Depression and attachment in couples. *Cognitive Therapy and Research, 25,* 577–590.

Whisman, M. A. (1999). Marital dissatisfaction and psychiatric disorders: Results from the national comorbidity survey. *Journal of Abnormal Psychology, 108,* 701–706.

Whisman, M. A. (2001). The association between depression and marital dissatisfaction. In S. R. H. Beach (Ed.), *Marital and family processes in depression.* Washington, DC: American Psychological Association.

Whisman, M. A., & Bruce, M. L. (1999). Marital dissatisfaction and incidence of Major Depressive Episode in a community sample. *Journal of Abnormal Psychology, 108,* 674–678.

Wickramaratne, P., & Weissman, M. M. (1998). Onset of psychopathology in offspring by developmental phase and parental depression. *Journal of the American Academy of Child and Adolescent Psychiatry, 37,* 933–942.

Wittchen, H.-U., Kessler, R. C., Pfister, H., & Lieb, M. (2000). Why do people with anxiety disorders become depressed? A prospective-longitudinal community study. *Acta Psychiatrica Scandinavica, 102*(Suppl. 406), 14–23.

16

A Relational Perspective on Depressed Children: Family Patterns and Interventions

Nadine J. Kaslow, Claudia A. Jones, and Frances Palin

Childhood depression is a growing public health problem. Despite the fact that depressed children are overrepresented among high utilizers of health care services (Glied & Neufeld, 2001), few of these young people receive the appropriate mental health services (U.S. Department of Health and Human Services, 1999). Depressive symptoms and associated deficits in biological, cognitive, affective, and interpersonal functioning can skew normal development and may result in significant short- and long-term morbidity and mortality. Depression is on the increase among young people (Burke, Burke, Rae, & Regier, 1991), a finding attributable to an interaction of genetic and environmental factors (Gershon, Hamovit, Guroff, & Nurnberger, 1987). Changing familial and societal trends create increased stress on children and reduce available coping resources, thereby resulting in more depressions among children. As such, depression does not reflect a problem with the child, but rather is a disorder that is embedded within a social context. Not only does depression run in families, but family dynamics and adverse family environments may be associated particularly with the development and maintenance of depressive symptoms and disorders in prepubertal children (Duggal, Carlson, Sroufe, & Egeland, 2001; Harrington, Rutter, & Fombonne, 1996). In addition, a child's depression significantly impacts the family system. Further, protective factors within the family system can reduce a child's risk for depression and can be associated with a more positive course and prognosis for a depressed child. Thus, family interventions may be ideally suited for depressed youth and their families. Of course, these interventions must take into account contextual influences.

This chapter begins with a brief discussion of depression in children, focusing first on depression during infancy and early childhood and then on depression in middle childhood. A biopsychosocial framework is used to present information on both risk and protective factors for depressed youth. The next section of this chapter examines the link between childhood depression and family functioning. This section is organized in accord with the diagnostic criteria proposed for a relational diagnosis of childhood depression (Kaslow, Deering, & Ash, 1996). These two sections set the stage for the final focus of this chapter, namely, family interventions for depressed children. In closing, directions for future clinical research and practice with depressed children and their families are provided.

■ Depression in Children

Consistent with a developmental psychopathology framework in which the manifestations of depression are conceptualized in terms of a child's level of physiological, affective, cognitive, and social development (Cicchetti & Toth, 1998; Kaslow, Adamson, & Collins, 2000), we separately examine depression in infancy and early childhood and depression in middle childhood.

Infancy and Early Childhood

Little information is available on the epidemiology of depressive disorders in very young children. Point prevalence rates of major depressive disorder (MDD) in preschool children have been found to be about 1%. Although there are no data on the point prevalence rates of dysthymic disorder (DD) in preschoolers, there is evidence that DD does exist and can be diagnosed in these young children (Kashani, Allan, Beck, Bledsoe, & Reid, 1997). Diagnosis of depression in infants, toddlers, and preschoolers is compromised by these children's relative inability to verbally express emotional distress or depressive cognitions. Frequently, it is in the context of a depressed or absent mother that infants, toddlers, and preschoolers develop symptoms suggestive of depression. Core symptoms of depression in infants include withdrawal, sad face, apathy, irritability, sleep and eating disturbances, abnormal stranger reactions, fussiness, and tantrums. These behaviors indicate attachment disorders, which is consistent with the fact that maternal depression disrupts patterns of mother-infant interaction (Sexson, Glanville, & Kaslow, 2001).

Depression in toddlers often emerges in the context of maternal depression and disruptions or high levels of insecurity in parent-child attachment bonds (Cicchetti, Rogosch, & Toth, 1998; Sexson et al., 2001). Toddlers tend to exhibit negative affects consistent with depression in the face of mishaps and tend to respond with tension and frustration, as well as concerned reparation (Cole, Barrett, & Zahn-Waxler, 1992). Depression among toddlers is sometimes characterized by their style of peer interactions, in which these youngsters exhibit withdrawal, passivity, and behavioral inhibition during free play with a familiar peer (Rubin, Booth, Zahn-Waxler, Cummings, & Wilkinson, 1991). Similarly, displays of dysphoric affect in dyads in which one friend has an insecure attachment are more common than when both peers are securely attached (Park & Waters, 1989). Insecure attachment among preschoolers predicts internalizing problems (Anan & Barnett, 1999). This link is mediated by levels of perceived social support.

Middle Childhood

Depressive disorders in children are characterized by dysphoria and/or anhedonia, in conjunction with disturbances in sleep, appetite, concentration, motivation, and energy (American Psychiatric Association [APA], 1994). Although depressive disorders may be manifested differently in youth than adults (Kaufman, Martin, King, & Charney, 2001), our current standard diagnostic nomenclature applies the criteria associated with adult depression to children and largely ignores developmental considerations (Cicchetti & Toth, 1998). Estimates of the point prevalence of MDD and DD in children, respectively, range from 0.4 to 2.5% and from 0.6 to 1.7% (Birmaher, Ryan, & Williamson, 1996; Birmaher, Ryan, Williamson, et al., 1996). Depressive disorders occur at relatively similar rates among prepubertal males and females and depression may even be more common in prepubertal males than females (Angold, Costello, Erkanli, & Worthman, 1999). Rates of depressive symptoms in girls remain steady from 8 to 11 and then increase from 12 to 16, whereas boys' symptoms remain relatively stable across middle childhood and adolescence (Twenge & Nolen-Hoeksema, 2002). The possibility of higher rates of depression among prepubertal males than females is consistent with findings that young boys are less resilient in the face of stress (Reinherz, Giaconia, Hauf, Wasserman, & Silverman, 1999), that genetic factors play a more significant role in the development of depression in boys (Rice, Harold, & Thapar, 2002a), and that maternal prenatal depression is related to a greater biological susceptibility in boys with regard to emotional regulation (Carter, Garrity-Rokous, Chazan-Cohen, Little, & Briggs-Gowan, 2001).

Depressive disorders in young people tend to persist and reoccur and are often accompanied by academic problems, interpersonal difficulties, emotional maladjustment, maladaptive cognitive processing, and physical health problems (Kaslow, Croft, & Hatcher, 1999; Schwartz, Gladstone, & Kaslow, 1998). Even when these disorders remit, they often interfere with children's capacity to function competently. The maintenance or relapse of depression in children is related to intra- and extrafamilial social problems.

Depressive disorders during middle childhood often co-occur with other psychiatric disorders; 40–70% of depressed children develop an additional disorder, with 20–50% having two or more comorbid conditions. MDD and DD often co-occur (Kovacs, Akiskal, Gastonis, & Parrone, 1994). Commonly noted comorbid diagnoses include anxiety, disruptive, and substance use disorders. Comorbid conditions enhance the likelihood of a recurrence of depression and are associated with longer duration of an episode, a greater likelihood of a suicide attempts, more impaired functional outcomes, poorer response to treatment, and greater mental health services utilization (Birmaher, Ryan, & Williamson, 1996; Birmaher, Ryan, Williamson, et al., 1996; Cicchetti et al., 1998; Kovacs et al., 1994).

Recently, studies have begun to appear in the literature that examine children with prepubertal-onset MDD when they were grown up. This burgeoning body of work suggests that the clinical outcome in adulthood for individuals who were depressed as children is marked by a high risk of suicide attempts, substance abuse, disruptive behavior disorders, increased use of long-term mental health and health care services, and overall impaired functioning (Weissman et al., 1999). A study of children from Helsinki suggests that depression in children predicts depression, anxiety, aggression, and low self-esteem in young adulthood. In addition, childhood depression is related to poorer adaptive functioning in young adulthood, involving family relationships, friendships, jobs, and education (Aronen & Soininen, 2000).

Biopsychosocial Risk and Protective Factors

Over the years, increasing attention has been paid to risk factors for depression in young people and more recently to protective factors. A biopsychosocial framework can be useful in organizing these risk and protective factors (Engel, 1977).

Biological Factors.   Biological factors related to depression in children include genetic contributions, abnormalities in psychoneuroendocrinology and neurotransmitters, and functional and anatomical brain pathology (Garber & Horowitz, 2002). The only biological factor directly related to this chapter is genetics, and thus a few comments on the genetics of mood disorders in children are warranted. In terms of family history data, clinically referred depressed youth have higher familial rates of depression than do normal or psychiatric controls, a finding more true for children than adolescents or adults (Kovacs, Devlin, Pollock, Richards, & Mukerji, 1997; Moldin, Reich, & Rice, 1991; Puig-Antich et al., 1989; Todd, Newman, Geller, Fox, & Hickok, 1993). In addition, substance use disorders are more commonly reported in the relatives of mood-disordered children (Kovacs, 1997; Todd, Geller, Neuman, Fox, & Hickok, 1996).

There is a large body of work examining the offspring of depressed parents (Goodman & Gotlib, 2001; Radke-Yarrow, Martinez, Mayfield, & Ronsaville, 1998). Children of depressed parents are at high risk for MDD in childhood (Weissman, Warner, Wickramaratne, Moreau, & Olfson, 1997), attributable to both genetic factors and disruptions in the caregiving environment. Children of depressed mothers exhibit more reactive stress response systems, which may render them more vulnerable to difficulties when they encounter stress (Ashman, Dawson, Panagiotides, Yamada, & Wilkinson, 2002). In an investigation comparing middle-class, Caucasian, intact families with urban, single-parent, African American families, maternal depressive symptoms predicted both child depressive symptoms and the progression of these symptoms over time, suggesting the generalizability across racial groups of the family transmission of depressive symptoms (Jones, Forehand, & Neary, 2001).

Finally with regard to genetics, the limited data from twin studies reveals greater concordance of depression in monozygotic versus dizygotic twins, suggesting that depressive symptoms are significantly genetically influenced (Rice et al., 2002a), although the extent to which this is the case may depend on rater and measurement issues (Hudziak, Rudiger, Neale, Heath, & Todd, 2000; Rice, Harold, & Thapar, 2002b). Interestingly, adoption studies provide little evidence for the genetic contribution to depression in youth (Rice et al., 2002b). Although susceptibility to develop depression has a distinct genetic element, it is not evident what inherited factors are related to the increased risk for depression (Garber & Horowitz, 2002).

Psychological Factors.   Both affective and cognitive variables fall under the rubric of psychological factors that have been linked to a vulnerability to develop depressive symptoms (Garber & Horowitz, 2002). In terms of affective functioning, depressed youth manifest difficulties in the regulation of negative emotions, in terms of both the emergence and overexpression of dysphoria and difficulties experiencing positive feelings expressed as anhedonia (Cole & Kaslow, 1988). With regard to cognitive functioning, depressed children exhibit negative self-schemas and negative views of self; have faulty information processing, cognitive distortions, maladaptive attributional styles, and dysfunctional self-control cognitions; and negative expectancies about self (helplessness) and future (hopelessness) (Kaslow et al., 2000).

Social Factors.   A number of social factors are associated with increased risk for depression in young people, including family relationship patterns, stressful life events, peer relations, and community contexts. The family risk factors are discussed in more detail below and thus are not examined here. A clear link exists between stressful life events and depression in children (Compas, Grant, & Ey, 1994). This is true for single events, cumulative life events, hassles, and chronic stress. With regard to peer relations, depressed children have a negative view of their social relations with classmates and peers (Brendgen, Vitaro, Turgeon, & Poulin, 2002) and unpopularity is a precursor and correlate of depression (Reinherz et al., 1999). Teachers' reports of peer rejection in children are related to children's self-reported depressive symptoms (Rudolph, Hammen, & Burge, 1994).

A number of community-level risk factors are associated with depression in children. Several longitudinal and cross-sectional research studies indicate that exposure to economic difficulties is linked to negative psychological outcomes in children (Samaan, 2000). Children at high economic risk are more vulnerable to depression than those at low economic risk (Graham & Easterbrooks, 2000; Roberts, Roberts, & Chen, 1997), a finding that may be stronger for children of European American than African American descent (Costello, Keeler, & Angold, 2001). Consistent with this, the mothers of homeless and poor housed youth report higher levels of depressive symptoms in their children (Buckner, Bassuk, Weinreb, & Brooks, 1999). Although some studies suggest that lower socioeconomic status is related to increased risk for major depression development, this association is not consistently found (Reinherz et al., 1999; Twenge & Nolen-Hoeksema, 2002), a finding that may be due to the presence of protective factors. For example, low-income children with high levels of spirituality/religion and perceived social support, strong extended families, and mothers who use effective coping strategies appear to be protected from depression (Samaan, 2000).

Data from studies with ethnic minority youth reveal that the stress resulting from ethnic minority children's exposure to chronic levels of neighborhood violence often leads to depressive symptoms (Langrock, Compas, Keller, Merchant, & Copeland, 2002). Among low-income African American youth, although witnessing violence may not be related to depression, being a victim of violence from family and nonfamily members is related to greater levels of depression. This lack of depression in witnessing youth may reflect the use of protective coping mechanisms (Fitzpatrick, 1993).

Ethnicity appears somewhat related to depression in children. Some investigators find no differences in levels of depressive symptoms between European American and African American youth (Roberts et al., 1997; Twenge & Nolen-Hoeksema, 2002), whereas others note that rural European American youth have higher rates of depressive disorders than rural African American children (Angold et al., 2002). A number of studies reveal higher rates of depressive symptoms among Latino children compared to both European American and African American youth (Roberts et al., 1997; Twenge & Nolen-Hoeksema, 2002). Within the Latino community, preschool children whose parents emigrate from Central America are at greater risk for developing depression than those children with parents born in the United States (Weiss, Goebel, Page, Wilson, & Warda, 1999). The children's increased risk for depression is related to family functioning, cultural heritage, acclimation to the different culture, and poverty (Weiss et al., 1999). Although the causes of depressive symptoms are consistent across Asian and American children (Lee, Ottati, & Guo, 2002), rates of depressive symptoms and disorders appear to be quite low among Asian American children (Roberts et al., 1997). Similarly, relatively low rates of depression have been found among Native American children compared to their non-Native counterparts (Dion, Gotowiec, & Beiser, 1998).

Cumulative Risk Factors.   Recently, investigators have studied cumulative risk factors for depression. Of particular relevance is the emergence of numerous family factors in these cumulative risk factor models. Among school-aged children, the combination of attachment security, maternal depressive symptoms, and economic risk accounts for 47% of the variance in children's depression scores (Graham & Easterbrooks, 2000). In another study, depressive symptoms in children are accounted for by the cumulative effects of maternal depressive symptomatology, early care lacking in emotional supportiveness, abuse, and family stressors (Duggal et al., 2001).

A review of the literature on ethnic minority children from high-risk urban communities identified several crucially intertwined risk factors, such as economic destitution, exposure to traumatic life events, parenting styles, individual coping styles, and cognitive development, in the development of depression (Barreto & McManus, 1997). In a study of inner-city African American youth, the following variables emerged as predictors of depression: life stress, child maltreatment, lower levels of maternal education and high levels of maternal depression, and domestic violence experiences by the mother (Johnson & Kliewer, 1999). A second study of African American children showed that uninvolved parenting, racial discrimination, and criminal victimization predict depressive symptoms (Simons, Velma, & McLoyd, 2002). A third study of inner-city African American children found that depressive symptoms correlate cross-sectionally with mother-reported cognitive and social competence, aggressive behavior, and attention problems and longitudinally predict aggressive behavior, attention problems, poor grades, and mother-reported cognitive competence (Steele, Armistead, & Forehand, 2000). Finally, in a study of homeless families, depressive symptoms were found to correlate with significant housing instability and severe homelessness (Zima, Wells, Benjamin, & Duan, 1996). In addition, children with access to two or more social supports exhibited fewer depressive symptoms.

■ Family Patterns Associated With Depressive Disorders in Children

Historically, psychiatric diagnosis has been focused on the individual rather than on the individual in context. However, increasing attention has been paid to relational disorders, disorders that reflect that the bond among family members is disordered (First et al., 2002; Kaslow, 1996). Characteristics of relational disorders include that they have distinctive features for classification; cause severe emotional social, and occupational impairment; have a recognizable clinical course, recognizable patterns of comorbidity, patterns of family aggregation, and biological, psychological, and social etiological contributions; and that they respond to specific treatments and can be prevented (First et al., 2002).

Kaslow and colleagues presented criteria for a relational diagnosis of depression in youth (Kaslow et al., 1996). According to these criteria, the individual must be younger than 18 years of age and must meet criteria of the fourth edition of the *Diagnostic and Statistical Manual of Mental Disorders (DSM-IV;* APA, 1994) for at least one of these disorders: MDD, DD, adjustment with depressed mood/other adjustment subcategory that includes depression, reactive attachment, depressive personality, minor depression, recurrent brief depression, and mixed anxiety-depression. In addition, at least one of the following relational patterns must be present: attachment problems, low cohesion and low support, inappropriate levels of family control, high levels of family conflict and ineffective conflict resolution, family violence, affect regulation difficulties, transmission of depressive cognitions, and impaired communication patterns. Furthermore, a relationship pattern with peers, teachers, or other significant adults that continues over time and is characterized by social isolation, rejection, or criticism of the child and which is associated with low social self-esteem and/or difficulties in interpersonal problem solving is required. The following section is organized around the maladaptive family relational patterns as seen in the families of depressed children, as this is the focus of this chapter.

Attachment Problems

According to Bowlby (1969) attachment involves developing early intimate relationships and internalizing them as grounded cognitive representations of the connection of the self to significant others (Dadds & Barrett, 1996). One of the most significant protective factors against the development of depression in children is a secure attachment bond to parents (Samaan, 2000).

Interactions with a depressed mother can lead to insecure attachments in children, which in turn may lead to depression in children (Herring & Kaslow, 2002).

Children of depressed mothers are most likely to develop insecure attachments and become depressed themselves in the context of additional risk factors, such as co-morbid psychopathological conditions and life adversities (i.e., dangerous environments, poverty, family conflict, and single parenting) (Carter et al., 2001). However, a positive relationship with a nondepressed father can serve as a protective factor against insecure attachment (Herring & Kaslow, 2002).

Only a few studies have examined the attachment patterns of depressed children. Compared to nondepressed children, clinically referred depressed children and community samples of children with depressive symptoms report more attachment difficulties (Armsden, McCauley, Greenberg, Burke, & Mitchell, 1990; Stein et al., 2000). Children with MDD perceive their mothers and fathers as providing significantly less care, view their mothers as more overprotective, and report a more affectionless-control bonding than do nondepressed youth (Stein et al., 2000). These findings are particularly pronounced when the mother is depressed.

Low Cohesion and Support

Levels of family cohesion and support often reflect the nature and quality of the attachment bonds. Some studies reveal that low levels of cohesion are an influential family factor in the development of depression in children (Fendrich, Warner, & Weissman, 1990; Garrison, Jackson, Marstellar, McKeown, & Addy, 1990). Conversely, high levels of family cohesion and supportive mother-child relationships protect against the development of depression (Klein & Forehand, 2000; Reinherz et al., 1989). Consistent with this, parents' warm attitudes toward their children relate to lower levels of depression in the children; this is truer for mothers than fathers (Sugawara et al., 2002). There is some evidence that the impact of family cohesion and support on depression is stronger for boys than for girls (Cumsille & Epstein, 1994).

Inappropriate Levels of Family Control

Depressed children's parents tend to be controlling and authoritarian and are likely to employ forceful behavior by denying children's right to make decisions and express themselves openly (Amanat & Butler, 1984; Dadds, Sanders, Morrison, & Rebgetz, 1992; Friedrich, Reams, & Jacobs, 1988; Stark, Humphrey, Crook, & Lewis, 1990). This parenting style can create feelings of helplessness and incompetence in children (Amanat & Butler, 1984; Racusin & Kaslow, 1991). Alternatively, appropriate levels of parental monitoring are associated with lower levels of depressive symptoms (Klein & Forehand, 2000).

High Level of Family Conflict and Ineffective Conflict Resolution

Both family conflict (Burbach & Borduin, 1986; Forehand et al., 1988) and ineffective conflict resolution (Sanders, Dadds, Johnston, & Cash, 1992) typify numerous families of depressed children. Parent-child disagreements in older childhood predict the later emergence of depressive symptoms in both the short and longer terms (Fendrich et al., 1990; Rueter, Scaramella, Wallace, & Conger, 1999). Further, there is evidence that in inner-city African American families, increases in family conflict and decreases in parental monitoring are associated with increases in children's depressive symptoms over time (Sagrestano, Paikoff, Holmbeck, & Fendrich, 2003).

Family Violence

An extreme manifestation of inappropriate levels of control, family conflict, and ineffective conflict resolution is family violence. The literature indicates that a relationship exists between child maltreatment (physical and sexual abuse, neglect) and depressive symptoms in children. Specifically, 20–67% of abused preadolescents meet diagnostic criteria for MDD or experience symptoms consistent with a depression diagnosis (Kaufman & Charney, 2001). Follow-up studies of DD indicate that a history of sexual abuse is a major predictor variable (Durbin, Klein, & Schwartz, 2000). Moreover, among maltreated children, those with confused patterns of relatedness experience the highest levels of depression (Toth & Cicchetti, 1996).

Multiple factors may account for the association between childhood maltreatment and depression. Early life stress, including abuse, can alter brain structure and function in a manner that confers a neurobiological vulnerability for the development of later depressive disorders (Kaufman & Charney, 2001). Placement in foster care in which there are continued high levels of violence exposure can be associated with prolonged depressive symptoms (Stein et al., 2001). However, some factors can protect against depression in maltreated youth. These include high self-esteem and an internal locus of control for positive events (Moran & Eckenrode, 1992).

Another form of family violence is witnessing of intimate partner violence (i.e., domestic violence). Children of battered women are 2 to 4 times more likely than children from nonviolent homes to exhibit clinically significant emotional and behavioral problems, including depression (Grych, Jouriles, Swank, McDonald, & Norwood, 2000; Kolbo, Blakely, & Engleman, 1996; Marks, Glaser, Glass, & Horne, 2001; Somer & Braunstein, 1999). Among low-income African American youth, mother's psychological functioning, mother's intimate partner violence status, family cohesion and adaptability, and neighborhood disorder accounted for 38% of the variance in children's levels of internalizing distress, with two of the predictors being particularly significant, namely, mother's psychological functioning and intimate partner violence status (Kaslow et al., 2004). The effects of domestic violence on children are related to the strength and nature of domestic violence (child or partner), children's perceptions and appraisals of parental conflict, and the child outcome informant (mother, father, or child reports) (McClosky, Figueredo, & Koss, 1995; Sternberg et al., 1993).

Affect Regulation Difficulties

It has been argued that depression in young people reflects, in part, a failure to effectively regulate affective distress (Cole & Kaslow, 1988). Some authors have asserted that a family's need to constrict affect is a risk factor, whereas a family's ability to elaborate affect encourages relational resilience (Focht-Birkerts & Beardslee, 2000). However, the overexpression of negative affects, in the form of high levels of expressed emotion, is maladaptive. Thus, optimal family functioning entails the capacity to express negative affect in a modulated fashion.

A series of studies have explored the link between childhood depression and expressed emotion within the family, that is, elevated levels of critical comments, hostility, and emotional overinvolvement. Asarnow and colleagues have found that rates of expressed emotion are higher among families of depressed children than families of normal controls, children with schizophrenia spectrum disorders, and nondepressed youth with attention deficit hyperactivity disorder (Asarnow, Tompson, Hamilton, Goldstein, & Guthrie, 1994; Asarnow, Tompson, Woo, & Cantwell, 2001). High levels of expressed emotion are associated with a more insidious onset of MDD and a slower course of recovery (Asarnow, Goldstein, Thompson, & Guthrie, 1993) and serve as a risk factor for childhood depression beyond that accounted for by parental mood disorder (Schwartz, Dorer, Beardslee, Lavori, & Keller, 1990).

Family interaction data also suggest that children with mood disorders engage in a manner reflective of high levels of expressed emotion. Specifically, compared to nondepressed youth, depressed children are more prone to making guilt-inducing and critical statements (Hamilton, Asarnow, & Thompson, 1999). This finding mirrors the data with both depressed mothers who report more use of guilt induction with their children when compared to nondepressed mothers (Susman, Trickett, Iannotti, Hollenbeck, & Zahn-Waxler, 1985) and children of depressed mothers who exhibit more deviant themes of guilt expression than do children of normal controls (Zahn-Waxler, Kochanska, Krupnick, & McKnew, 1990). Thus, guilt induction may be a distinguishing characteristic of families with a depressed member (Hamilton et al., 1999).

Transmission of Depressive Cognitions

The data on similarities in the depressive cognitions of parents and their children are mixed. Some have found that a mother's attributional style for bad events and depressive symptoms correlates with her child's corresponding attributional style and depressive symptoms (Seligman, Peterson, Kaslow, Tanenbaum, & Abramson, 1984). In a related vein, mothers' but not fathers' cognitive triads (views of self, world, and future) have been found to relate to children's cognitive triads, and children's perceived parental messages associated with the cognitive triad predict children's cognitive triads and ratings of depression (Stark, Schmidt, & Joiner, 1996). Consistent with this, children's cognitive distortions are substantially related to both child and mother-reported depressive symptoms, even after accounting for both parent-rated and child-perceived competence (Epkins, 1998).

Impaired Communication Patterns

Both mothers and fathers of depressed children evidence lower levels of adaptive communication than do the parents of nondepressed or at-risk youth (Stein et al., 2000). Consistent with this, depressed children, compared to children with schizophrenia spectrum disorders, communicate with their mothers in less positive and more negative ways (Cook, Asarnow, Goldstein, Marshall, & Weber, 1990). Mothers of depressed children do not reciprocate their children's negative interactions; however, they do reciprocate their positiveness. Therefore, parents of depressed children do not respond to their children in less positive or reinforcing ways. However, depressed children do not reciprocate either maternal positiveness or negativeness (Cook et al., 1990).

■ Family Interventions for Depressed Children

To date, the bulk of interventions for depressed youth have focused on the individual child. Most of these interventions have been cognitive-behavior or psychopharmacological in nature, with some evidence for interpersonal and psychodynamic approaches as well (American Academy of Child and Adolescent Psychiatry, 1998; Asarnow, Jaycox, & Tompson, 2001; Compton, Burns, Egger, & Robertson, 2002; Curry, 2001; Gillham, Shatte, & Freres, 2000; Harrington, Whittaker, & Shoebridge, 1998; Kaslow, McClure, & Connell, 2002; Kaslow & Thompson, 1998; McClure, Kubiszyn, & Kaslow, 2002; Michael & Crowley, 2002; Reinecke, Ryan, & DuBois, 1998; Weisz & Jensen, 1999). In general, various forms of psychosocial interventions have produced moderate to large treatment gains that were clinically meaningful (Michael & Crowley, 2002). However, the evidence for pharmacological interventions is less compelling (Emslie & Mayes, 2001; Michael & Crowley, 2002).

Only recently have family interventions begun to appear in the literature. These family interventions can be divided into two categories, those that target children at risk for depression (primary and secondary preventive interventions) and those for children already depressed (tertiary preventive interventions). We limit our comments to studies that target children and do not include those efficacy and effectiveness studies that target depressed adolescents.

Family Interventions for At-Risk Children

Recently, there has been a burgeoning of efficacy and effectiveness family intervention studies for youth at risk for depression. In general, these programs offer hopeful directions for risk-reduction interventions.

Beardslee and his colleagues have been leaders in the development of interventions to protect children and strengthen families when a parent is depressed (Beardslee, 2002). In the early 1990s, Beardslee (Beardslee, 1990; Beardslee et al., 1993) developed two cognitive, psychoeducational prevention programs that presented the same information: (a) one that was clinician based—a short-term intensive program with long-term follow-up (6–10 sessions), in which the clinician worked with the parents to evaluate characteristics of risk and resilience in their children and held a family meeting aimed at increasing all members' knowledge about and experiences with mood disorders, and (b) one that was lecture only—lecture and group discussions presented to parents with mood disorders (two 1-hr lectures). Both programs have been found to be safe (Beardslee et al., 1992, 1993) and to have long-term benefits (Beardslee, Salt, et al., 1997; Beardslee, Wright, et al., 1997) with predominately Caucasian, middle-class families. In addition, qualitative analyses reveal that participation in the family intervention is associated with increases in parental responsiveness to their children and a greater openness among family members to the experience and expression of affect (Focht-Birkerts & Beardslee, 2000). Of note, however, compared to peers whose families were assigned randomly to the lecture-only condition, children in the clinician-based group evidenced more knowledge about their parents' mood disorder according to their own report and the feedback from raters and parents (Beardslee, Wright, et al., 1997). In addition, these young people manifested better adaptive functioning postintervention (Beardslee, Wright, et al., 1997).

More recently, Beardslee and coworkers developed the Family Depression Program, a videotape-based program for families with at least one depressed parent and a child aged 7–12 (Butler, Budman, & Beardslee, 2000). The program is designed to reduce risk in children and promote resiliency. The program consists of a videotape for the parents, one for children, and a parents' manual on using the tapes and on securing mental health services for the children. The 30-min parents' videotape, entitled *Depression: Helping Families Cope*, realistically portrays families in a documentary type film and outlines the effect that depression can have on families, especially on children. The 20-min-long children's tape recounts the experiences of a 12-year-old child whose family appears in the parents' tape. In the children's tape, the young boy learns about parental depression, how to gain support from other family members in the face of parental depression, the utility of treatment, and the importance of continuing with age-appropriate peer and educational activities. In the parents' manual, procedures are articulated regarding how to recognize depression in young people, ways to promote resiliency in children, and resources for depressed youth or those having difficulties coping effectively. In a study in which families were randomly assigned to either the Family Depression Program or a wait-list control group that subsequently received the intervention, results revealed the safety of the family prevention program, as well as a high degree of satisfaction with the program. In addition, the intervention was associated with a reduction in parental fears about the effects of depression on their children, a greater degree of communication among family members regarding the caregiver's mood disorder, and an increase in the support and understanding among the adults in the family. It should be noted that the generalizability of the effectiveness of this program for non-Caucasian ethnic groups has been questioned (Butler et al., 2000).

Family Interventions for Depressed Youth

Family Psychoeducation.   Fristad and her colleagues have developed and examined the impact of a multiple family psychoeducation program for families of mood-disordered children (Fristad, Arnett, & Gavazzi, 1998; Fristad, Gavazzi,

Centolella, & Soldano, 1996; Fristad, Gavazzi, & Soldano, 1998). This intervention program is designed as a means to lower the levels of expressed emotion found in families of depressed youth by means of education and support. It is designed to serve as an adjunct to the ongoing medication management and individual/family therapy a depressed child receives. One study investigated the impact of a 90-min psychoeducational workshop that addressed the symptom presentation, etiology, course, prognosis and treatment of childhood depression, and family factors (e.g., expressed emotion) that impact the outcome (Fristad, Arnett, et al., 1998). The workshop resulted in decreased levels of expressed emotion and increased understanding of mood disorders in the caregivers, most notably in fathers, both immediately upon the completion of the workshop and 4 months later.

Another investigation provided preliminary efficacy data for a six-session, manual driven, multifamily psychoeducation group intervention (Fristad, Gavazzi, et al., 1998). Findings indicated a high level of family satisfaction with the protocol. In addition, uncontrolled pilot data found that parents who attended the program believed that there was an overall improvement in the quality of the family climate following the intervention. In addition, this improvement was sustained over a 4-month period. Once again, fathers reported the most positive feedback and response. At 6-month follow-up, the majority of parents evidenced an attitudinal shift toward their child with a mood disorder; they reported more positive thinking about their child and his or her mood disorder, the family situation, and the educational and mental health care systems (Goldberg-Arnold, Fristad, & Gavazzi, 1999). Unfortunately, given that these families participated in multiple interventions simultaneously, it is difficult to ascertain the extent to which the improvements reported can be attributed to the multifamily psychoeducation group. Further, it should be noted that as the ethnic status of the samples in these studies is unknown, and the sample sizes are relatively small and predominantly middle and upper class, the generalizability of the findings from these family psychoeducational programs is questionable (Fristad, Arnett, et al., 1998).

A cognitive-behavioral family education intervention (Stress-Busters) for fourth- to sixth-grade, urban, private school, predominantly Caucasian children with depressive symptoms was found to be effective in reducing depressive symptoms, negative thoughts, and internalizing coping. This intervention was composed of a real world family education component to enhance supportive family environments, a videotaped cognitive-behavior therapy (CBT) session of the children, and the targeting of other symptoms associated with depression and other comorbid disorders (Asarnow, Scott, & Mintz, 2002). To date, no outcome data have been published on this program.

Behavioral and Strategic Child-Focused Family Interventions.   One study could be located that compared the effects of strategic and behavioral family therapies for depressive symptoms in youth (Steinberg, Sayger, & Szykula, 1997). The child-focused behavioral family therapy was brief, 8–12 weeks. The model focused on setting up for success, modeling, behavioral contracts, home token-economy incentive programs, social reinforcement, communication skills, and self-monitoring to increase prosocial behaviors. Families define specific problems that require remediation, identify contexts that trigger problem behaviors, and discuss prior strategies of problem management and resolution. The intervention was a non-manualized educational approach to teaching parenting skills and behavior self-control to the children. The child-focused strategic family therapy used strategic interviewing techniques to identify problem behavior sequences and problem resolution strategies, to offer reframes and suggestions of untried solutions, and to incorporate paradoxical interventions, benevolent doubt, and metaphorical storytelling. The two family modalities were equally effective in reducing parent-reported behavior problems and depressive symptoms in children. These interventions are not manualized and the children did not meet diagnostic criteria for depression.

Parental Involvement.   Some researchers have conducted child-focused interventions that have included a parental involvement component. For example, Stark and colleagues (Stark, Rouse, & Livingston, 1991) used one family meeting per month to supplement the cognitive-behavioral sessions for depressed elementary school children. During the monthly in-home family meetings, parents learned to support their children as they practiced new skills. Results showed greater reductions in depressive symptoms in children whose families had participated in the monthly meetings than in those whose families had not.

■ Future Directions

Clinical Implications

Future assessments and treatments for depressed children and their families need to incorporate a developmental psychopathology framework (Hammen, Rudolph, Weisz, Rao, & Burge, 1999; Zahn-Waxler, Klimes-Dougan, & Slattery, 2000) and need to be based on family systems approaches to treatment (Kaslow & Celano, 1995; Kaslow, Kaslow, & Farber, 1999). These interventions should target the family relational patterns described above as being salient to the development and maintenance of depressive disorders in children. These interventions are likely to be most beneficial if they incorporate already tested treatments for depressed youth, including cognitive-behavioral and interpersonal strategies. These interventions need to be designed in ways that are culturally competent (Griffith, Zucker, Bliss, Foster, & Kaslow, 2001; Lopez, Edwards, Pedrotti, Ito, & Rasmussen, 2002) and should be expanded for children and families of diverse cultures (Munoz, Penilla, & Urizar, 2002).

Sometimes it may be appropriate for family interventions to be conducted concurrently with, or sequential to, interventions with individual family members (Kaslow & Racusin, 1990; Racusin & Kaslow, 1994). When depression is present in both the child and one of the parents, the parent's depression needs to be targeted separately (American Academy of Child and Adolescent Psychiatry, 1998). Such interventions are likely to have a positive impact on the child. For example, there is some evidence that depressed mothers who receive psychotherapy are more able to accurately interpret their children's emotional expression, particularly vis-à-vis distressing affects, such as sadness and anger (Free, Alechina, & Zahn-Waxler, 1996). This is likely to result in more effective affect regulation within the family system, thereby reducing the child's risk for depression.

Based upon the extant empirical literature on family interventions with children (Carr, 2000) and the relevant literature on family interventions with depressed adolescents (Brent, Kolko, Birmaher, Baugher, & Bridge, 1999; Lewinsohn, Clarke, Hops, & Andrews, 1990; Lewinsohn, Clarke, Rhode, Hops, & Seeley, 1996), effective family interventions for depressed youth should decrease the family stress to which the child is exposed and enhance the availability of social support within the family system. These interventions should bolster attachment relationships, facilitate clear parent-child communication, promote systematic family-based problem solving, and disrupt negative parent-child interactions (Carr, 2000; Diamond & Siqueland, 1995; Herring & Kaslow, 2002; Sexson et al., 2001). Parents need to be taught to be aware of the depressogenic messages that they are communicating to their children; helped to communicate more positive and realistic messages to their children about themselves, the world, and the future; and engage in more positive reinforcement of their children's behavior (Stark, Swearer, Kurowski, Sommer, & Bowen, 1996).

The following is an example of an integrative approach to family therapy that includes elements of cognitive-behavioral, interpersonal, and culturally competent approaches (McClure, Connell, Zucker, Griffith, & Kaslow, in press). This approach was designed specifically for depressed, low-income, African American youth and their families. The flexibly manualized intervention integrates didactic and discussion segments in an effort to provide families with information and skills for coping with depression, as well as a time and place to address current concerns and questions. Therapists use a variety of tactics, such as games, role-playing, family discussions, and hand-outs, to facilitate dialogue and keep families engaged. The focus of the 12 sessions follows.

Session 1 focuses on joining, introducing the intervention, and formulating family goals collaboratively and building upon family strengths and protective factors. Attention is then paid to the topic of depression, which is introduced from a family perspective. The 2nd meeting revolves around continued joining with the family, education about child development, and discussion of African American identity development. Family members learn to use sheets to rate their mood, quality of family relationships, and positive events. In the 3rd session, therapists educate the family about the symptoms of depression, its causes and treatment. Basic strategies for coping with depression are examined, including seeking social support, using stress management techniques, and engaging in pleasant activities. The 4th session addresses depression management in greater depth. Information is offered on the effects of physical activity on mood, and relaxation exercises are taught. Emphasis is placed on increasing family cohesion while engaging in pleasurable activities. At the 5th meeting, family violence issues area addressed if an assessment indicates the presence of such concerns, and a family safety plan is discussed to prevent further abuse. During the 6th session, family discussions and games/activities focus on identifying, labeling, and appropriately expressing emotions. Active listening skills are taught to facilitate and reinforce appropriate emotional communication. In the 7th meeting, family members are taught about the associations among cognitions, emotions, and behavior. During the 8th session, a 5-step problem-solving model is introduced and practiced. Meeting 9 focuses on improving family communication. The 10th meeting helps the family better understand their interaction patterns and increase positive interactions among members. The 11th meeting revolves around social skills and ways in which family members can improve their peer interactions. In the final meeting, the therapists and family review previous meetings, progress that has been made, current functioning, and potential referrals. The need for continued family intervention is ascertained. It is hoped that this family approach will serve as a model for future family interventions for depressed youth.

Research Recommendations

Based upon this review of the literature, there are numerous recommendations that we have for research in this field that we highlight in this section. First, we suggest that more researchers assume a relational diagnostic perspective in assessing depressed youth and their families. This would entail the incorporation of informant and self-reports, as well as observational methodologies, with regard to the following family dynamics: attachment relationships, family cohesion and support, levels of family control, levels of family conflict and effectiveness of conflict resolution, family violence, affect regulation, transmission of depressive cognitions, and communication patterns. It would be useful for this work to compare and contrast depressed youth residing in different family constellations (e.g., single-parent homes, two-parent homes, blended families, families with and without siblings, extended families, foster families, adoptive families, etc.), youth from various ethnic and social class groups, youth of different ages, and males and females. This work would be strengthened by a focus on both risk and resilience relational processes (Focht-Birkerts & Beardslee, 2000). Understanding both family risks for depression and family factors that protect youngsters from succumbing to depression will provide useful information for family-oriented preventive intervention programs (Beardslee & Gladstone, 2001).

Second, despite the proliferation of research demonstrating the high rates of comorbidity of depression with other forms of psychopathology in children, there has been a relative dearth of empirical research designed to elucidate the phenomenology and etiology of comorbidity of depression in children. As noted by Avenevoli and coworkers (Avenevoli, Stolar, Li, Dierker, & Merikangas, 2001), family and twin study designs offer powerful methods for ascertaining the specificity of familial aggregation of comorbid and pure disorders. In addition, if family relational constructs were included in these designs, data could be gleaned on those family patterns associated with pure versus comorbid depression and with various forms of comorbidity.

Third, there is a need to conduct longitudinal studies and follow children with mood disorders and their families into adulthood (Kessler, Avenevoli, & Merikangas, 2001). Prospective longitudinal studies allow for the elucidation of both temporal sequencing and the stability of expression of depressive symptoms and family patterns over time and across development (Avenevoli et al., 2001). It would be advantageous for these studies to ascertain the ways in which changes in various family relational dynamics are associated with increases or reductions in depressive symptoms over time, as well as the manner in which changes in children's levels of depressive symptoms precede alterations in family dynamics. It is recommended that this line of work include caregiver report, child report, and observational measures. A good model of such research is the work of Sagrestano and colleagues (Sagrestano et al., 2003) with low-income, African American youth in transition from childhood to early adolescence. However, this group of investigators is one of the only teams taking a longitudinal perspective on the family dynamics that co-occur with depression in children.

Fourth, there is a need for both efficacy and effectiveness trials of family-oriented interventions with depressed youth (Hyman, 2001). Efficacy trials are critical in order to determine whether a specific family intervention protocol has intrinsic value. There are concerns, however, regarding the generalizability of findings from efficacy studies, which are typically conducted in academic health centers or university clinics, using short-term family interventions, with youth who are free of comorbid mental, substance use, or general medical disorders. Thus efficacy designs, which have high internal validity, have low external validity and thus must be supplemented by effectiveness studies with larger samples of depressed youth and their families, with fewer exclusion criteria, and in real world settings. Family intervention trials of longer duration are required, given the evidence that mood disorders in young people tend to persist and recur. In addition, these trials must focus not solely on symptom reduction and the child's functional status, but also on changes in the family context.

Fifth, there is a need to compare family interventions for depressed youth with other forms of psychotherapy, such as cognitive-behavioral or interpersonal treatments. While some efforts have been made to compare two different forms of psychotherapy with depressed adolescents (Brent et al., 1997, 1998, 1999; Kolko, Brent, Baugher, Bridge, & Birmaher, 2000; Rossello & Bernal, 1999), such a line of investigation is relatively nonexistent when the index person is a depressed child. Further, although some studies have begun to appear in the literature that compare family interventions with pharmacological interventions for depressed adolescents (Birmaher et al., 2000; Brent et al., 1997, 1998, 1999), no such studies could be located with depressed children. In addition to learning about the relative efficacy of family treatments versus other forms of psychosocial interventions or pharmacological treatments, it would be important to gather data on interventions administered alone versus in combined form. There is some evidence with depressed adults that the combination of specific forms of psychotherapy with antidepressant medications represents the maximally effective therapeutic modality (Keller et al., 2000; Pettit, Voelz, & Joiner, 2001).

Finally, it is our firm belief that it is imperative that all family-oriented research endeavors, whether focused on family patterns or family treatments, be conducted using a culturally competent framework (Griffith et al., 2001; McClure et al., in press). This entails attention to the following cultural variables within each family member and in the family unit as a whole: ethnic identity, race, gender and sexual orientation, age, religion, migration and country of origin, socioeconomic status, acculturation and acculturative processes, language, education, and disability status (Group for the Advancement of Psychiatry, 2002). Measures and observational methodologies that are specific to the cultural group being assessed and treated should be included when available. When such instruments or methodologies are not available, they may need to be designed by the researchers using a focus group approach to develop the relevant constructs to be assessed and the questions to be asked. In addition, culturally relevant norms need to be developed for commonly used measures and observations of family functioning, as normative practices in one cultural group may not be common in another. Further, while one approach to intervention research is to ascertain the efficacy and effectiveness of a given family approach with different cultural groups, a potentially more clinically meaningful and culturally sensitive strategy would be to develop, with the aid of individuals and families from the cultural group to be treated, culturally appropriate family-based intervention protocols, manuals, and intervention materials.

■ References

Amanat, E., & Butler, C. (1984). Oppressive behaviors in the families of depressed children. *Family Therapy, 11,* 65–75.

American Academy of Child and Adolescent Psychiatry. (1998). Practice parameters for the assessment and treatment of children and adolescents with depressive disorders. *Journal of the American Academy of Child and Adolescent Psychiatry, 37*(Suppl.), 63S–83S.

American Psychiatric Association. (1994). *Diagnostic and statistical manual of mental disorders* (4th ed.). Washington, DC: Author.

Anan, R. M., & Barnett, D. (1999). Perceived social support mediates between prior attachment and subsequent adjustment: A study of urban, African American children. *Developmental Psychology, 35,* 1210–1222.

Angold, A., Costello, E. J., Erkanli, A., & Worthman, C. M. (1999). Pubertal changes in hormone levels and depression in girls. *Psychological Medicine, 29,* 1043–1053.

Angold, A., Erkanli, A., Farmer, E. M. Z., Fairbank, J. A., Burns, B. J., Keeler, G., et al. (2002). Psychiatric disorder, impairment, and service use in rural African American and White youth. *Archives of General Psychiatry, 59,* 893–901.

Armsden, G. C., McCauley, E., Greenberg, M. T., Burke, P. M., & Mitchell, J. R. (1990). Parent and peer attachment in early adolescent depression. *Journal of Abnormal Child Psychology, 18,* 683–697.

Aronen, E. T., & Soininen, M. (2000). Childhood depressive symptoms predict psychiatric problems in young adults. *Canadian Journal of Psychiatry, 45,* 465–470.

Asarnow, J. R., Goldstein, M. J., Thompson, M., & Guthrie, D. (1993). One-year outcomes of depressive disorders in child psychiatric in-patients: Evaluation of the prognostic power of a brief measure of expressed emotion. *Journal of Child Psychology and Psychiatry, 34,* 129–137.

Asarnow, J. R., Jaycox, L. H., & Tompson, M. C. (2001). Depression in youth: Psychosocial interventions. *Journal of Clinical Child Psychology, 30,* 133–147.

Asarnow, J. R., Scott, C. V., & Mintz, J. (2002). A combined cognitive-behavioral family education intervention for depression in children: A treatment development study. *Cognitive Therapy and Research, 26,* 221–229.

Asarnow, J. R., Tompson, M., Hamilton, E. B., Goldstein, M. J., & Guthrie, D. (1994). Family expressed emotion, childhood-onset depression, and childhood-onset schizophrenia spectrum disorders: Is expressed emotion a nonspecific correlate of child psychopathology or a specific risk factor for depression? *Journal of Abnormal Child Psychology, 22,* 129–146.

Asarnow, J. R., Tompson, M., Woo, S., & Cantwell, D. P. (2001). Is expressed emotion a specific risk factor for depression or a nonspecific correlate of psychopathology. *Journal of Abnormal Child Psychology, 29,* 573–583.

Ashman, S. B., Dawson, G., Panagiotides, H., Yamada, E., & Wilkinson, C. W. (2002). Stress hormone levels of children of depressed mothers. *Development and Psychopathology, 14,* 333–349.

Avenevoli, S., Stolar, M., Li, J., Dierker, L., & Merikangas, K. R. (2001). Comorbidity of depression in children and adolescents: Models and evidence from a prospective high-risk family study. *Biological Psychiatry, 15,* 1071–1081.

Barreto, S., & McManus, M. (1997). Casting the net for "depression" among ethnic minority children for the high risk urban communities. *Clinical Psychology Review, 17,* 823–845.

Beardslee, W., Salt, P., Porterfield, K., Rothberg, P., Van de Velde, P., Swatling, S., et al. (1993). Comparison of preventive interventions for families with parental affective disorder. *Journal of the American Academy of Child and Adolescent Psychiatry, 32,* 254–263.

Beardslee, W. R. (1990). Development of a clinician-based preventive intervention for families with affective disorders. *Journal of Preventive Psychiatry and Allied Disciplines, 4,* 39-61.

Beardslee, W. R. (2002). *Out of the darkened room when a parent is depressed: Protecting the children and strengthening the family.* New York: Little, Brown, and Company.

Beardslee, W. R., & Gladstone, T. R. (2001). Prevention of childhood depression: Recent findings and future prospects. *Biological Psychiatry, 49,* 1101–1110.

Beardslee, W. R., Hoke, L., Wheelock, I., Rothberg, P. C., van de Velde, P., & Swatling, S. (1992). Initial findings on preventive intervention for families with parental affective disorders. *American Journal of Psychiatry, 149,* 1335–1340.

Beardslee, W. R., Salt, P., Versage, E. M., Gladstone, T. R. G., Wright, E. J., & Rothberg, P. C. (1997). Sustained change in parents receiving preventive interventions for families with depression. *American Journal of Psychiatry, 154,* 510–515.

Beardslee, W. R., Wright, E. J., Salt, P., Drezner, K., Gladstone, T. R., Versage, E. M., et al. (1997). Examination of children's responses to two preventive intervention strategies over time. *Journal of the American Academy of Child and Adolescent Psychiatry, 36,* 196–204.

Birmaher, B., Brent, D. A., Kolko, D., Baugher, M., Bridge, J., Holder, D., et al. (2000). Clinical outcome after short-term psychotherapy for adolescents with major depressive disorder. *Archives of General Psychiatry, 57,* 29–36.

Birmaher, B., Ryan, N. D., & Williamson, D. E. (1996). Depression in children and adolescents: Clinical features and pathogenesis. In K. I. Shulman, M. Tohen, & S. P. Kutcher (Eds.), *Mood disorders across the life span* (pp. 51–81). New York: Wiley.

Birmaher, B., Ryan, N. D., Williamson, D. E., Brent, D. A., Kaufman, J., Dahl, R. E., et al. (1996). Childhood and adolescent depression: A review of the past 10 years: Part I. *Journal of the American Academy of Child and Adolescent Psychiatry, 35,* 1427–1439.

Bowlby, J. (1969). *Attachment and loss: Attachment* (Vol. I). London: Hogarth.

Brendgen, M., Vitaro, F., Turgeon, L., & Poulin, F. (2002). Assessing aggressive and depressed children's social relations with classmates and friends: A matter of perspective. *Journal of Abnormal Child Psychology, 30,* 609–624.

Brent, D., Holder, D., Kolko, D., Birmaher, B., Baugher, M., Roth, C., et al. (1997). A clinical psychotherapy trial for adolescent depression comparing cognitive, family, and supportive therapy. *Archives of General Psychiatry, 54,* 877–885.

Brent, D. A., Kolko, D., Birmaher, B., Baugher, M., & Bridge, J. (1999). A clinical trial for adolescent depression: Predictors of additional treatment in the acute and follow-up phases of the trial. *Journal of the American Academy of Child and Adolescent Psychiatry, 38,* 263–269.

Brent, D. A., Kolko, D. J., Birmaher, B., Baugher, M., Bridge, J., Roth, C., et al. (1998). Predictors of treatment efficacy in a clinical trial of three psychosocial treatments for adolescent depression. *Journal of the American Academy of Child and Adolescent Psychiatry, 37,* 906–914.

Buckner, J. C., Bassuk, E. L., Weinreb, L. F., & Brooks, M. G. (1999). Homelessness and its relation to the mental health and behavior of low-income school-age children. *Developmental Psychology, 35,* 246–257.

Burbach, D. J., & Borduin, C. M. (1986). Parent–child relations and the etiology of depression: A review of methods and findings. *Clinical Psychology Review, 6,* 133–153.

Burke, K. C., Burke, J. D., Rae, D., & Regier, D. A. (1991). Comparing age at onset of major depression and other psychiatric disorders by birth cohorts in five U.S. community populations. *Archives of General Psychiatry, 48,* 789–795.

Butler, S. F., Budman, S. H., & Beardslee, W. R. (2000). Risk reduction in children from families with parental depression: A videotape psychoeducation program. *National Academies of Practice Forum, 2,* 267–276.

Carr, A. (2000). Evidence-based practice in family therapy and systemic consultation: I. Child-focused problems. *Journal of Family Therapy, 22,* 29–60.

Carter, A. S., Garrity-Rokous, F. E., Chazan-Cohen, R., Little, C., & Briggs-Gowan, M. J. (2001). Maternal depression and comorbidity: Predicting early parenting, attachment security, and toddler social-emotional problems and competencies. *Journal of the American Academy of Child and Adolescent Psychiatry, 40,* 18–26.

Cicchetti, D., Rogosch, F. A., & Toth, S. L. (1998). Maternal depressive disorder and contextual risk: Contributions to the development of attachment insecurity and behavior problems in toddlerhood. *Development and Psychopathology, 10,* 283–300.

Cicchetti, D., & Toth, S. L. (1998). The development of depression in children and adolescents. *American Psychologist, 53,* 221–241.

Cole, P. M., Barrett, K. C., & Zahn-Waxler, C. (1992). Emotion displays in two-year-olds during mishaps. *Child Development, 63,* 314–324.

Cole, P. M., & Kaslow, N. J. (1988). Interactional and cognitive strategies for affect regulation: Developmental perspective on childhood depression. In L. B. Alloy (Ed.), *Cognitive processes in depression* (pp. 310–341). New York: Guilford Press.

Compas, B. E., Grant, K. E., & Ey, S. (1994). Psychosocial stress and child and adolescent depression: Can we be more specific? In W. M. Reynolds & H. F. Johnston (Eds.), *Handbook of depression in children and adolescents* (pp. 509–523). New York: Plenum.

Compton, S. N., Burns, B. J., Egger, H. L., & Robertson, H. (2002). Review of the evidence base for treatment of childhood psychopathology: Internalizing disorders. *Journal of Consulting and Clinical Psychology, 70,* 1240–1266.

Cook, W. L., Asarnow, J. R., Goldstein, M. J., Marshall, V. G., & Weber, E. (1990). Mother-child dynamics in early-onset depression and childhood schizophrenia spectrum disorders. *Development and Psychopathology, 2,* 71–84.

Costello, E. J., Keeler, G. P., & Angold, A. (2001). Poverty, race/ethnicity, and psychiatric disorder: A study of rural children. *American Journal of Public Health, 91,* 1494–1498.

Cumsille, P. E., & Epstein, N. (1994). Family cohesion, family adaptability, social support, and adolescent depressive symptoms in outpatient clinic families. *Journal of Family Psychology, 8,* 202–214.

Curry, J. F. (2001). Specific psychotherapies for childhood and adolescent depression. *Biological Psychiatry, 49,* 1091–1100.

Dadds, M. R., & Barrett, P. M. (1996). Family processes in child and adolescent anxiety and depression. *Behaviour Change, 13,* 231–239.

Dadds, M. R., Sanders, M. R., Morrison, M., & Rebgetz, M. (1992). Childhood depression and conduct disorder: II. An analysis of family interaction patterns in the home. *Journal of Abnormal Psychology, 101,* 505–513.

Diamond, G., & Siqueland, L. (1995). Family therapy for the treatment of depressed adolescents. *Psychotherapy: Theory, Research, Practice, Training, 32,* 77–90.

Dion, R., Gotowiec, A., & Beiser, M. (1998). Depression and conduct disorder in Native and Non-Native children. *Journal of the American Academy of Child and Adolescent Psychiatry, 37,* 736–742.

Duggal, S., Carlson, E. A., Sroufe, L. A., & Egeland, B. (2001). Depressive symptomatology in childhood and adolescence. *Development and Psychopathology, 13,* 143–164.

Durbin, C. E., Klein, D. N., & Schwartz, J. E. (2000). Predicting the 2 1/2 year outcome of dysthymic disorder: The roles of childhood adversity and family history of psychopathology. *Journal of Consulting and Clinical Psychology, 68,* 57–63.

Emslie, G. J., & Mayes, T. L. (2001). Mood disorders in children and adolescents: Psychopharmacological treatment. *Biological Psychiatry, 49,* 1082–1090.

Engel, G. L. (1977). The need for a new medical model: A challenge for biomedicine. *Science, 196,* 129–136.

Epkins, C. C. (1998). Mother- and father-rated competence, child-perceived competence, and cognitive distortions: Unique relations with children's depressive symptoms. *Journal of Clinical Child Psychology, 27,* 442–451.

Fendrich, M., Warner, V., & Weissman, M. M. (1990). Family risk factors, parental depression, and psychopathology in offspring. *Developmental Psychology, 26,* 40–50.

First, M. B., Bell, C. C., Cuthbert, B., Krystal, J. H., Malison, R., Offord, D. R., et al. (2002). Personality disorders and relational disorders: A research agenda for addressing crucial gaps in DSM. In D. J. Kupfer, M. B. First, & D. A. Regier (Eds.), *A research agenda for DSM-V* (pp. 123–200). Washington, DC: American Psychiatric Press.

Fitzpatrick, K. M. (1993). Exposure to violence and presence of depression among low income, African-American youth. *Journal of Consulting and Clinical Psychology, 61,* 528–531.

Focht-Birkerts, L., & Beardslee, W. R. (2000). A child's experience of parental depression: Encouraging relational resilience in families with affective illness. *Family Process, 39,* 417–434.

Forehand, R., Brody, G. H., Slotkin, J., Fauber, R., McCombs, A., & Long, N. (1988). Young adolescents and maternal depression: Assessment, interrelations, and family predictors. *Journal of Consulting and Clinical Psychology, 56,* 422–426.

Free, K., Alechina, I., & Zahn-Waxler, C. (1996). Affective language between depression mothers and their children: The potential impact of psychotherapy. *Journal of the American Academy of Child and Adolescent Psychiatry, 35,* 783–790.

Friedrich, W. N., Reams, R., & Jacobs, J. (1988). Sex differences in depression in early adolescents. *Psychological Reports, 62,* 475–481.

Fristad, M. A., Arnett, M. M., & Gavazzi, S. M. (1998). The impact of psychoeducational workshops on families of mood-disordered children. *Family Therapy, 25,* 151–159.

Fristad, M. A., Gavazzi, S. M., Centolella, D. M., & Soldano, K. W. (1996). Psychoeducation: A promising intervention strategy for families of children and adolescents with mood disorders. *Contemporary Family Therapy, 18,* 371–383.

Fristad, M. A., Gavazzi, S. M., & Soldano, K. W. (1998). Multi-family psychoeducation groups for childhood mood disorders: A program description and preliminary efficacy data. *Contemporary Family Therapy, 20,* 385–402.

Garber, J., & Horowitz, J. L. (2002). Depression in children. In I. H. Gotlib & C. L. Hammen (Eds.), *Handbook of depression* (pp. 510–540). New York: Guilford Press.

Garrison, C. Z., Jackson, K. L., Marstellar, F., McKeown, R. E., & Addy, C. L. (1990). A longitudinal study of depressive symptomatology in young adolescents. *Journal of the American Academy of Child and Adolescent Psychiatry, 29,* 581–585.

Gershon, E. S., Hamovit, J. H., Guroff, J. J., & Nurnberger, J. I. (1987). Birth-cohort changes in manic and depressive disorders in relatives of bipolar and schizoaffective patients. *Archives of General Psychiatry, 44,* 314–319.

Gillham, J. E., Shatte, A. J., & Freres, D. R. (2000). Preventing depression: A review of cognitive-behavioral and family interventions. *Applied and Preventive Psychology, 9,* 63–88.

Glied, S., & Neufeld, A. (2001). Service system finance: Implications for children with depressed and manic depression. *Biological Psychiatry, 49,* 1128–1135.

Goldberg-Arnold, J. S., Fristad, M. A., & Gavazzi, S. M. (1999). Family psychoeducation: Giving caregivers what they want and need. *Family Relations, 48,* 1–7.

Goodman, S. H., & Gotlib, I. H. (Eds.). (2001). *Children of depressed parents: Mechanisms of risk and implications for treatment.* Washington, DC: American Psychological Association.

Graham, C. A., & Easterbrooks, M. A. (2000). School-aged children's vulnerability to depressive symptomatology: The role of attachment security, maternal depressive symptomatology, and economic risk. *Development and Psychopathology, 12,* 201–213.

Griffith, J., Zucker, M., Bliss, M., Foster, J., & Kaslow, N. (2001). Family interventions for depressed African American adolescent females. *Innovations in Clinical Practice, 19,* 159–173.

Group for the Advancement of Psychiatry. (2002). *Cultural assessment in clinical psychiatry.* Washington, DC: American Psychiatric Publishing, Inc.

Grych, J. H., Jouriles, E., Swank, P., McDonald, R., & Norwood, W. (2000). Patterns of adjustment among children of battered women. *Journal of Consulting and Clinical Psychology, 68,* 84–94.

Hamilton, E., Asarnow, J., & Thompson, M. (1999). Family interaction styles of children with depressive disorders, schizophrenia-spectrum disorders, and normal controls. *Family Process, 38,* 463–476.

Hammen, C. L., Rudolph, K. D., Weisz, J., Rao, U., & Burge, D. (1999). The context of depression in clinic-referred youth: Neglected areas in treatment. *Journal of the American Academy of Child and Adolescent Psychiatry, 38,* 64–71.

Harrington, R., Rutter, M., & Fombonne, E. (1996). Developmental pathways in depression: Multiple meanings, antecedents, and endpoints. *Journal of Development and Psychopathology, 8,* 601–616.

Harrington, R., Whittaker, J., & Shoebridge, P. (1998). Psychological treatment of depression in children and adolescents: A review of treatment research. *British Journal of Psychiatry, 173,* 291–298.

Herring, M., & Kaslow, N. J. (2002). Depression and attachment in families: A child-focused perspective. *Family Process, 41,* 494–518.

Hudziak, J. J., Rudiger, L. P., Neale, M. C., Heath, A. C., & Todd, R. D. (2000). A twin study of inattentive, aggressive, and anxious/depressed behaviors. *Journal of the American Academy of Child and Adolescent Psychiatry, 39,* 469–476.

Hyman, S. E. (2001). Mood disorders in children and adolescents: An NIMH perspective. *Biological Psychiatry, 49,* 962–969.

Johnson, P., & Kliewer, W. (1999). Family and contextual predictors of depressive symptoms in inner-city African American youth. *Journal of Child and Family Studies, 8,* 181–192.

Jones, J. D., Forehand, R., & Neary, E. M. (2001). Family transmission of depressive symptoms: Replication across Caucasian and African American mother–child dyads. *Behavior Therapy, 32,* 123–138.

Kashani, J., Allan, W. D., Beck, N. C., Bledsoe, Y., & Reid, J. C. (1997). Dysthymic disorder in clinically referred preschool children. *Journal of the American Academy of Child and Adolescent Psychiatry, 36,* 1426–1433.

Kaslow, F. W. (1996). *Handbook of relational diagnosis and dysfunctional family patterns.* New York: Wiley.

Kaslow, N. J., Adamson, L. B., & Collins, M. H. (2000). A developmental psychopathology perspective on the cognitive components of child and adolescent depression. In A. J. Sameroff, M. Lewis, & S. M. Miller (Eds.), *Handbook of developmental psychopathology* (2nd ed., pp. 491–510). New York: Kluwer Academic/Plenum.

Kaslow, N. J., & Celano, M. (1995). The family therapies. In A. S. Gurman & S. B. Messer (Eds.), *Essential psychotherapies: Theories and practice* (pp. 343–402). New York: Guilford Press.

Kaslow, N. J., Croft, S. S., & Hatcher, C. A. (1999). Depression and bipolar disorders in children and adolescents. In S. D. Netherton, D. Holmes, & C. E. Walker (Eds.), *Child and adolescent psychological disorders: A comprehensive textbook* (pp. 264–281). New York: Oxford University Press.

Kaslow, N. J., Deering, C., & Ash, P. (1996). Relational diagnosis of child and adolescent depression. In F. W. Kaslow (Ed.), *Handbook of relational diagnosis and dysfunctional family patterns* (pp. 171–185). New York: Wiley.

Kaslow, N. J., Heron, S., Roberts, D. K., Thompson, M., Guessous, O., & Jones, C. K. (2004). Family and community factors that predict internalizing and externalizing symptoms in low-income, African American children: A preliminary report. *New York Academy of Sciences, 1008,* 55–68.

Kaslow, N. J., Kaslow, F., & Farber, E. (1999). Theories and techniques of marital and family therapy. In M. B. Sussman, S. K. Steinmetz, & G. W. Peterson (Eds.), *Handbook of marriage and the family* (pp. 767–792). New York: Plenum.

Kaslow, N. J., McClure, E., & Connell, A. (2002). Treatment of depression in children and adolescents. In I. H. Gotlib & C. L. Hammen (Eds.), *Handbook of depression* (pp. 441–464). New York: Guilford Press.

Kaslow, N. J., & Racusin, G. (1990). Family therapy or child therapy: An open or shut case. *Journal of Family Psychology, 3,* 273–289.

Kaslow, N. J., & Thompson, M. (1998). Applying the criteria for empirically supported treatments to studies of psychosocial interventions for child and adolescent depression. *Journal of Clinical Child Psychology, 27,* 146–155.

Kaufman, J., & Charney, D. (2001). Effects of early stress on brain structure and function: Implications for understanding the relationship between child maltreatment and depression. *Development and Psychopathology, 13,* 451–471.

Kaufman, J., Martin, A., King, R. A., & Charney, D. (2001). Are child-, adolescent-, and adult-onset depression one and the same disorder? *Biological Psychiatry, 49,* 980–1001.

Keller, M. B., McCullough, J., Klein, D. N., Arnow, B., Dunner, D., Gelenberg, A. J., et al. (2000). A comparison of nefazodone, the cognitive behavioral-analysis system of psychotherapy, and their combination for the treatment of chronic depression. *New England Journal of Medicine, 342,* 1462–1470.

Kessler, R. C., Avenevoli, S., & Merikangas, K. R. (2001). Mood disorders in children and adolescents: An epidemiologic perspective. *Biological Psychiatry, 49,* 1002–1014.

Klein, K., & Forehand, R. (2000). Family processes as resources for African American children exposed to a constellation of sociodemographic risk factors. *Journal of Clinical Child Psychology, 29,* 53–65.

Kolbo, J. R., Blakely, E. H., & Engleman, D. (1996). Children who witness domestic violence: A review of empirical literature. *Journal of Interpersonal Violence, 11,* 281–293.

Kolko, D., Brent, D. A., Baugher, M., Bridge, J., & Birmaher, B. (2000). Cognitive and family therapies for adolescent depression. *Journal of Consulting and Clinical Psychology, 68,* 603–614.

Kovacs, M. (1997). Depressive disorders in childhood: An impressionistic landscape. *Journal of Child Psychology and Psychiatry, 38,* 287–298.

Kovacs, M., Akiskal, S., Gastonis, C., & Parrone, P. L. (1994). Childhood-onset dysthymic disorder: Clinical features and prospective naturalistic outcome. *Archives of General Psychiatry, 51,* 365–374.

Kovacs, M., Devlin, B., Pollock, M., Richards, C., & Mukerji, P. (1997). A controlled family history study of childhood-onset depressive disorder. *Archives of General Psychiatry, 54,* 613–623.

Langrock, A. M., Compas, B. E., Keller, G., Merchant, M. J., & Copeland, M. E. (2002). Coping with the stress of parental depression: Parents' reports of children's coping, emotional, and behavioral problems. *Journal of Clinical Child and Adolescent Psychology, 31,* 312–324.

Lee, Y.-T., Ottati, V., & Guo, D. (2002). Understanding and preventing depression among Mainland Chinese children. *Prevention & Treatment, 5.*

Lewinsohn, P., Clarke, G., Hops, H., & Andrews, J. (1990). Cognitive-behavioral treatment for depressed adolescents. *Behavior Therapy, 21,* 385–401.

Lewinsohn, P., Clarke, G., Rhode, P., Hops, H., & Seeley, J. (1996). A course in coping: A cognitive-behavioral approach to the treatment of adolescent depression. In

E. D. Hibbs & P. S. Jensen (Eds.), *Psychosocial treatments for child and adolescent disorders: Empirically based strategies for clinical practice* (pp. 109–135). Washington, DC: American Psychological Association.

Lopez, S. J., Edwards, L. M., Pedrotti, J. T., Ito, A., & Rasmussen, H. N. (2002). Culture counts: Examinations of recent applications of the Penn Resiliency Program or, toward a rubric for examining cultural appropriateness of prevention programming. *Prevention & Treatment, 5.*

Marks, C. R., Glaser, B. A., Glass, J. B., & Horne, A. M. (2001). Effects of witnessing severe marital discord on children's social competence and behavioral problems. *The Family Journal Counseling and Therapy for Couples and Families, 9,* 94–101.

McClosky, L. A., Figueredo, A. J., & Koss, M. P. (1995). The effects of systemic violence on children's mental health. *Child Development, 66,* 1239–1261.

McClure, E., Connell, A., Zucker, M., Griffith, J. R., & Kaslow, N. J. (in press). The Adolescent Depression Empowerment Project (ADEPT): A culturally sensitive family treatment for depressed, African American girls. In E. D. Hibbs & P. S. Jensen (Eds.), *Psychosocial treatments for child and adolescent disorders: Empirically based strategies for private practice* (2nd ed.). Washington, DC: American Psychological Association.

McClure, E. B., Kubiszyn, T., & Kaslow, N. J. (2002). Advances in the diagnosis and treatment of childhood mood disorders. *Professional Psychology: Research and Practice, 33,* 125–134.

Michael, K. D., & Crowley, S. L. (2002). How effective are treatments for child and adolescent depression? A meta-analytic review. *Clinical Psychology Review, 22,* 247–269.

Moldin, S. O., Reich, T., & Rice, J. P. (1991). Current perspectives on the genetics of unipolar depression. *Behavior Genetics, 21,* 211–242.

Moran, P. B., & Eckenrode, J. (1992). Protective personality characteristics among adolescent victims of maltreatment. *Child Abuse and Neglect, 16,* 743–754.

Munoz, R. F., Penilla, C., & Urizar, G. (2002). Expanding depression prevention research with children of diverse cultures. *Prevention & Treatment, 5.*

Park, K. A., & Waters, E. (1989). Security of attachment and preschool friendships. *Child Development, 60,* 1076–1081.

Pettit, J., Voelz, Z., & Joiner, T. (2001). Combined treatments for depression. In M. Sammons & N. B. Schmidt (Eds.), *Combined treatments for mental disorders* (pp. 131–160). Washington, DC: American Psychological Association.

Puig-Antich, J., Goetz, R., Davies, M., Kaplan, T., Davies, S. C., Ostrow, L., et al. (1989). A controlled family history study of prepubertal major depressive disorder. *Archives of General Psychiatry, 46,* 406–418.

Racusin, G. R., & Kaslow, N. J. (1991). Assessment and treatment of childhood depression. In P. A. Keller & S. R. Heyman (Eds.), *Innovations in clinical practice: A sourcebook* (Vol. 10, pp. 223–243). Sarasota, FL: Professional Resource Exchange.

Racusin, G. R., & Kaslow, N. J. (1994). Child and family therapy combined: Indications and implications. *American Journal of Family Therapy, 22,* 237–246.

Radke-Yarrow, M., Martinez, M., Mayfield, A., & Ronsaville, D. (Eds.). (1998). *Children of depressed mothers: From early childhood to maturity.* New York: Cambridge University Press.

Reinecke, M. A., Ryan, N. E., & DuBois, D. L. (1998). Cognitive behavioral therapy of depression and depressive symptoms during adolescence: A review and meta-analysis. *Journal of the American Academy of Child and Adolescent Psychiatry, 37,* 26–34.

Reinherz, H. Z., Giaconia, R. M., Hauf, A. M. C., Wasserman, M. S., & Silverman, A. B. (1999). Major depression in the transition to adulthood: Risks and impairments. *Journal of Abnormal Psychology, 108*, 500–510.

Reinherz, H. Z., Stewart-Barghauer, G., Pakiz, B., Frost, A. K., Moeykens, B. A., & Holmes, W. M. (1989). The relationship of early risk and current mediators to depressive symptomatology in adolescents. *Journal of the American Academy of Child and Adolescent Psychiatry, 28*, 942–947.

Rice, F., Harold, G. T., & Thapar, A. (2002a). Assessing the effects of age, sex, and shared environment on the genetic aetiology of depression in childhood and adolescence. *Journal of Child Psychology and Psychiatry and Allied Disciplines, 43*, 1039–1051.

Rice, F., Harold, G. T., & Thapar, A. (2002b). The genetic aetiology of childhood depression: A review. *Journal of Child Psychology and Psychiatry and Allied Disciplines, 43*, 65–79.

Roberts, R. E., Roberts, C. R., & Chen, Y. R. (1997). Ethnocultural differences in prevalence of adolescent depression. *American Journal of Community Psychology, 25*, 95–110.

Rossello, J., & Bernal, G. (1999). The efficacy of cognitive-behavioral and interpersonal treatments for depression in Puerto Rican adolescents. *Journal of Consulting and Clinical Psychology, 67*, 734–745.

Rubin, K., Booth, L., Zahn-Waxler, C., Cummings, E. M., & Wilkinson, M. (1991). Dyadic play behaviors of children of well and depressed mothers. *Development and Psychopathology, 3*, 243–251.

Rudolph, K., Hammen, C., & Burge, D. (1994). Interpersonal functioning and depressive symptoms in childhood: Addressing the issues of specificity and comorbidity. *Journal of Abnormal Child Psychology, 22*, 355–371.

Rueter, M. A., Scaramella, L., Wallace, L. E., & Conger, R. D. (1999). First onset of depressive or anxiety disorders predicted by the longitudinal course of internalizing symptoms and parent-adolescent disagreements. *Archives of General Psychiatry, 56*, 726–732.

Sagrestano, L., Paikoff, R. L., Holmbeck, G. N., & Fendrich, M. (2003). A longitudinal examination of familial risk factors for depression among inner-city African American adolescents. *Journal of Family Psychology, 17*, 108–120.

Samaan, R. A. (2000). The influences of race, ethnicity, and poverty on the mental health of children. *Journal of Health Care for the Poor and Underserved, 11*, 100–110.

Sanders, M. R., Dadds, M. R., Johnston, B. M., & Cash, R. (1992). Childhood depression and conduct disorder: I. Behavioral, affective, and cognitive aspects of family problem-solving interactions. *Journal of Abnormal Psychology, 101*, 495–504.

Schwartz, C. E., Dorer, D. J., Beardslee, W. R., Lavori, P. W., & Keller, M. B. (1990). Maternal expressed emotion and parental affective disorder: Risk for childhood depressive disorder, substance abuse, or conduct disorder. *Journal of Psychiatric Research, 24*, 231–250.

Schwartz, J. A. J., Gladstone, T. R., & Kaslow, N. J. (1998). Depressive disorders. In T. Ollendick & M. Hersen (Eds.), *Handbook of child psychopathology* (3rd ed., pp. 269–290). New York: Plenum.

Seligman, M. E. P., Peterson, C., Kaslow, N. J., Tanenbaum, R. L., & Abramson, L. Y. (1984). Attributional style and depressive symptoms among children. *Journal of Abnormal Psychology, 93*, 235–238.

Sexson, S. B., Glanville, D. N., & Kaslow, N. J. (2001). Attachment and depression: Implications for family therapy. *Child and Adolescent Psychiatric Clinics of North America, 10*, 465–486.

Simons, R. L., Velma, M., & McLoyd, V. (2002). Discrimination, crime, ethnic identity, and parenting as correlates of depressive symptoms among African American children: A multilevel analysis. *Development and Psychopathology, 14,* 371–393.

Somer, E., & Braunstein, A. (1999). Are children exposed to interparental violence being psychologically maltreated. *Aggression and Violent Behavior, 4,* 449–456.

Stark, K. D., Humphrey, L. L., Crook, K., & Lewis, K. (1990). Perceived family environments of depressed and anxious children: Child's and maternal figure's perspective. *Journal of Abnormal Child Psychology, 18,* 527–547.

Stark, K. D., Rouse, L., & Livingston, R. (1991). Treatment of depression during childhood and adolescence: Cognitive behavioral procedures for the individual and family. In P. Kendall (Ed.), *Child and adolescent therapy* (pp. 165–206). New York: Guilford Press.

Stark, K. D., Schmidt, K. L., & Joiner, T. E. (1996). Cognitive triad: Relationship to depressive symptoms, parents' cognitive triad, and perceived parental messages. *Journal of Abnormal Child Psychology, 24,* 615–631.

Stark, K. D., Swearer, S., Kurowski, C., Sommer, D., & Bowen, B. (1996). Targeting the child and the family: A holistic approach to treating child and adolescent depressive disorders. In E. D. Hibbs & P. S. Jensen (Eds.), *Psychosocial treatments for child and adolescent disorders: Empirically based strategies for clinical practice* (pp. 207–238). Washington, DC: American Psychological Association.

Steele, R. G., Armistead, L., & Forehand, R. (2000). Concurrent and longitudinal correlates of depressive symptoms among low-income, urban, African American children. *Journal of Clinical Child Psychology, 29,* 76–85.

Stein, B. D., Zima, B. T., Elliott, M. N., Burnam, M. A., Shahinfar, A., Fox, N. A., et al. (2001). Violence exposure among school-age children in foster care: Relationship to distress symptoms. *Journal of the American Academy of Child and Adolescent Psychiatry, 40,* 588–594.

Stein, D., Williamson, D. E., Birmaher, B., Brent, D. A., Kaufman, J., Dahl, R. E., et al. (2000). Parent-child bonding and family functioning in depressed children and children at high risk and low risk for future depression. *Journal of the American Academy of Child and Adolescent Psychiatry, 39,* 1387–1395.

Steinberg, E. B., Sayger, T. V., & Szykula, S. A. (1997). The effects of strategic and behavioral family therapies on child behavior and depression. *Contemporary Family Therapy, 19,* 537–551.

Sternberg, K., Lamb, M. E., Greenbaum, C., Cicchetti, D., Dawud, S., Cortes, R. M., et al. (1993). Effects of domestic violence on children's behavior problems and depression. *Developmental Psychology, 29,* 44–52.

Sugawara, M., Akiko, Y., Noriko, T., Tomoe, K., Haya, S., Kensuke, S., et al. (2002). Marital relations and depression in school-age children: Links with family functioning and parental attitudes toward child rearing. *Japanese Journal of Educational Psychology, 50,* 129–140.

Susman, E. J., Trickett, P. K., Iannotti, R. J., Hollenbeck, B. E., & Zahn-Waxler, C. (1985). Child-rearing patterns in depressed, abusive, and normal mothers. *American Journal of Orthopsychiatry, 55,* 237–251.

Todd, R., Newman, R., Geller, B., Fox, L., & Hickok, J. (1993). Genetic studies of affective disorders: Should we be starting with childhood onset probands? *Journal of the American Academy of Child and Adolescent Psychiatry, 32,* 1164–1171.

Todd, R. D., Geller, B., Neuman, R., Fox, L. W., & Hickok, J. (1996). Increased prevalence of alcoholism in relatives of depressed and bipolar children. *Journal of the American Academy of Child and Adolescent Psychiatry, 35,* 716–724.

Toth, S., & Cicchetti, D. (1996). Patterns of relatedness, depressive symptomatology, and perceived competence in maltreated children. *Journal of Consulting and Clinical Psychology, 64,* 32–41.

Twenge, J. M., & Nolen-Hoeksema, S. (2002). Age, gender, race, socioeconomic status, and birth cohort differences on the Children's Depression Inventory: A meta-analysis. *Journal of Abnormal Psychology, 111,* 578–588.

U.S. Department of Health and Human Services. (1999). *Mental health: A report of the Surgeon General.* Rockville, MD: U.S. Department of Health and Human Services, Substance Abuse and Mental Health Services Administration, Center for Mental Health Services, National Institutes of Health, National Institute of Mental Health.

Weiss, S. J., Goebel, P., Page, A., Wilson, P., & Warda, M. (1999). The impact of cultural and familial context on behavioral and emotional problems of preschool Latino children. *Child Psychiatry and Human Development, 29,* 287–301.

Weissman, M. M., Warner, V., Wickramaratne, P., Moreau, D., & Olfson, M. (1997). Offspring of depressed parents: 10 years later. *Archives of General Psychiatry, 54,* 932–940.

Weissman, M. M., Wolk, S., Wickramaratne, P., Goldstein, R. B., Adams, P., Greenwald, S., et al. (1999). Children with prepubertal-onset major depressive disorder and anxiety grown up. *Archives of General Psychiatry, 56,* 794–801.

Weisz, J. R., & Jensen, P. S. (1999). Efficacy and effectiveness of child and adolescent psychotherapy and pharmacotherapy. *Mental Health Services Research, 1,* 125–157.

Zahn-Waxler, C., Klimes-Dougan, B., & Slattery, M. J. (2000). Internalizing problems of childhood and adolescence: Prospects, pitfalls, and progress in understanding the development of anxiety and depression. *Development and Psychopathology, 12,* 443–466.

Zahn-Waxler, C., Kochanska, G., Krupnick, J., & McKnew, D. (1990). Patterns of guilt in children of depressed and well mothers. *Developmental Psychology, 26,* 51–59.

Zima, B. T., Wells, K. B., Benjamin, B., & Duan, N. (1996). Mental health problems among homeless mothers: Relationship to service use and child mental health problems. *Archives of General Psychiatry, 53,* 332–338.

17

Adolescent Depression: Family-Focused Treatment Strategies

Joan Rosenbaum Asarnow, Martha C. Tompson, and Michele S. Berk

Adolescence is a time of tension—youth pushing toward adulthood, parents awakening to changes in their child and the need to "let go" and convey trust, while shielding from dangers. Depression is a frequent complication of adolescence. National surveillance data indicate that 28.3% of high school students reported depressive symptoms that interfered with functioning for a period of at least 2 weeks during the year prior to the survey (Centers for Disease Control [CDC], 2001). Point prevalence for major depression among adolescents is roughly 6%, with lifetime prevalence ranging between 15 and 20% (Kessler, 2002; Lewinsohn & Essau, 2002). Prevalence among adolescents exceeds that for younger children (<1%) and adults (2–4% for adults). This age pattern, the shift from an equal gender ratio during childhood toward increased rates of depression among girls during adolescence, and data supporting a link between endocrinologic changes and depressive symptoms in girls suggest that pubertal changes contribute to the heightened risk for depression during adolescence, particularly for girls (Angold, Costello, Erkanli, & Worthman, 1999). Recent data also suggest that depression may be more common among younger age groups and that age of onset for depression may be decreasing, relative to prior generations (for review, Kessler, 2002), although it is possible that changes in reporting styles account for these patterns, with recent cohorts feeling more comfortable reporting depression and older cohorts forgetting prior histories of depression (Kessler, 2002).

Adolescent depression is not a benign condition and is associated with a high risk of recurrence, psychosocial and role impairments, delays in achieving critical developmental milestones, and a variety of negative sequelae, including drug and alcohol abuse, early parenthood, school failure and dropout, completed suicide and suicide attempts, and adult depression (American Academy of Child and Adolescent Psychiatry, 2000; Kandel & Davies, 1986; Kessler et al., 1997; Kessler, Foster, Saunders, & Stang, 1995; Rao et al., 1995). Although depression is associated with risk for negative sequelae, depression does not always lead to prolonged dysfunction and a sizable subgroup of adolescents who suffer from depression go on to become happy and well-functioning adults with no apparent scars from the pains of adolescence. Thus, while it is important to recognize the potential dangers of depression during adolescence, it is critical to maintain optimism and mobilize resources to address the disorder and mitigate against potential complications.

This chapter adopts a family perspective with respect to adolescent depression. We address the question of how best to help families negotiate the challenges of adolescence, prevent depression in adolescent children, and, if depression strikes, support their children in recovery and developmental progress. We begin with a brief overview of the current treatment literature, with an emphasis on those treatments with the strongest evidence base supporting efficacy. Next, we turn to a discussion of the rationale for adopting a family-focused treatment approach and review the relatively limited evidence on family interventions. We conclude with a discussion of the unique challenges of the adolescent period and recommendations for future clinical and research efforts.

■ The Treatment Literature: Where Do We Stand?

There is an accumulating research literature on the efficacy of different treatment strategies. Our goal here is to provide a brief overview for the purpose of clarifying the state of the evidence and its implications from the perspectives of families and family-focused interventions. Interested readers are referred to other more extensive reviews for additional detail (Asarnow, Jaycox, & Tompson, 2001; Kaslow, McClure, & Connell, 2002).

As shown in table 17.1, there is a modest literature supporting the efficacy of current treatments for depression among adolescents. Support is strongest for psychosocial treatment, with three different groups demonstrating an advantage of cognitive-behavior therapy (CBT) for the acute treatment of depressive disorders among adolescents, relative to control conditions. However, only one of these studies showed CBT to be more efficacious than alternative treatments (Brent et al., 1997). In the other studies, CBT was shown to be more effective than a wait-list control condition and therefore demonstrated only that CBT is associated with more improvement than time alone (Clarke, Rohde, Lewinsohn, Hops, & Seeley, 1999). Furthermore, results were mixed in the two studies with combined child and adolescent samples. The Wood et al. (Wood, Harrington, & Moore, 1996) study showed an advantage of CBT when compared to relaxation training at an immediate postintervention assessment, and the Vostanis (Vostanis, Feehan, Grattan, & Bickerton, 1996) study showed no advantage of CBT relative to an attention placebo condition. Support is also mixed for the value of social skills training in the treatment of adolescent depression (Fine, Forth, Gilbert, & Haley, 1991; Reed, 1994). Although the specific manuals employed in the CBT studies differed somewhat, they were all time-limited approaches that focused on enhancing strategies for responding to stresses and feelings with behaviors, thoughts, and problem-solving strategies that support improvements in mood and functioning.

TABLE 17.1 *Randomized Clinical Intervention Trials for Depressed Adolescents*

Reference	Subjects	Diagnoses/ Assessment	Family Component	Intervention Type(s)	Postintervention Assessment	Impact of Treatment
Brent et al. (1997)	Age 13–18 ($N = 107$)	MDD based on K-SADS; BDI $\geq$ 13	All participants received three sessions of family psychoeducation. Compares family treatment to other therapies.	Systemic behavioral family therapy vs. cognitive-behavioral therapy (CBT) vs. supportive therapy	Immediate	Compared to other groups, the CBT group had more rapid response, lower rates of MDD posttreatment, and fewer interviewer and self-reported depressive symptoms.
Clarke, Rohde, Lewinsohn, Hops, and Seeley (1999)	Age 14–18 ($N = 123$)	MDD or DD based on K-SADS	Compared an adolescent-only CBT intervention to one supplemented by a parent group	Adolescent coping with depression course (CWD-A) vs. CWD-A with nine-session parent group vs. wait-list control group (following treatment, youth randomized to three conditions: booster sessions and assessment every 4 months vs. assessments every 4 months vs. annual assessments	Immediate 12 months 24 months (half of treated youth were evaluated every 4 months, and half were evaluated every 12 months)	CBT was associated with higher depression recovery rates and greater reduction in self-reported depressive symptoms. Addition of the parent group had no significant effect. Following treatment, booster sessions were associated with accelerated recovery among youth who were still depressed, but did not reduce the rate of recurrence.

(continued)

TABLE 17.1 *Randomized Clinical Intervention Trials for Depressed Adolescents (continued)*

Reference	Subjects	Diagnoses/ Assessment	Family Component	Intervention Type(s)	Postintervention Assessment	Impact of Treatment
Diamond, Reis, Diamond, Siqueland, and Isaacs (2002)	Age 13–17 (N = 32)	MDD based on K-SADS	Specifically compared a family treatment to wait list	Attachment-based family therapy for depressed adolescents (ABFT) vs. wait list	Immediate 6 months	Compared to wait list, ABFT had a significantly higher rate of remission of depression, lower rates of self-reported suicidal thougths, hopelessness, and family conflict, and higher levels of attachment to mothers.
Fine, Forth, Gilbert, and Haley (1991)	Age 13–17 (N = 66) 83% female	Diagnosis of MDD or DD based on K-SADS interview	No family component	Therapeutic support group (TSG) vs. social skills group (SSG)	Immediate 9 Months	Although both improved, TSG was significantly more effective than SSG in reducing depression on K-SADS, with more subjects in nonclinical range. Group differences disappeared at follow-up.
Lewinsohn, Clarke, Hops, and Andrews (1990)	Age 14–18 (N = 59)	Major, minor, or intermittent depression based on K-SADS	Compared adolescent-only CBT intervention to adolescent plus parent CBT intervention	Adolescent-only cognitive-behavioral training group vs. adolescent-parent cognitive-behavioral training group vs. wait-list control	Immediate 1 month 6 months 12 months 24 months	Compared to wait list significantly fewer youths in the treatment groups met criteria for depressive disorders after treatment

Study	Age (N)	Diagnosis	Family component	Intervention	Timing	Results
						and at follow-up. Significantly improved on self-reported depression, anxiety, number of pleasant activities, and depressogenic thoughts. Trend for adolescent-parent condition to outperform adolescent-only group.
Mufson, Weissman, Moreau, and Garfinkel (1999)	Age 12–18 (N = 48)	Clinician diagnosis of MDD based on the HRSD	Parent contact and involvement included as part of IPT	Interpersonal psychotherapy for depressed adolescents (IPT) vs. clinical monitoring	Immediate	IPT patients reported greater decrease in depressive symptoms, improved social functioning, and improved problem-solving skills compared to controls; 74% recovered in the IPT-A condition, compared to 46% in the control condition.
Reed (1994)	Age 14–19 (N = 18)	Clinician diagnosis of MDD or DD	No family component	Social skills training vs. attention placebo control	Immediate 6–8 weeks	Skills group participants scored significantly higher than control group on clinician's rating of improvement. Male subjects improved, but female subjects deteriorated.

(continued)

TABLE 17.1 *Randomized Clinical Intervention Trials for Depressed Adolescents (continued)*

Reference	Subjects	Diagnoses/ Assessment	Family Component	Intervention Type(s)	Postintervention Assessment	Impact of Treatment
Rosello and Bernal (1999)	Age 13–18 (*N* = 71)	Diagnosis of MDD or DD	Family session included as part of CBT and IPT	Cognitive-behavioral (CBT) vs. IPT vs. wait-list control	Immediate 3 months	Both active treatments were associated with significant reductions in depression when compared to the wait-list condition. IPT was superior to CBT in enhancing social functioning and self esteem. The effect size for IPT was greater than that for CBT.
Sanford, Boyle, Offord, McCleary, and Steele (2002)	Adolescents (*N* = 31) at site where participants completed study	Met *DSM-IV* criteria for MDD in prior 6 months based on K-SADS	Intensive family psychoeducation plus usual care, 12 biweekly 90-min sessions conducted in-home plus 1 booster session during 3-month follow-up period	Family psychoeducation plus usual care vs. usual care	Mid-treatment, posttreatment, follow-up, 3 months (9 months after baseline)	At the site where families stayed in treatment, family treatment was associated with improvements in social and family functioning. There was a nonsignificant tendency for family treatment to be associated with higher remission rates and reduced depressive symptoms. At the other site, 8 of 10 participants withdrew.

Study	Sample	Diagnosis	Treatment notes	Comparison	Assessment	Results
Vostanis, Feehan, Grattan, and Bickerton (1996)	Age 8–17 (N = 56)	MDD, DD, or minor depression based on K-SADS	Includes parent contact, level of parent involvement determined on case by case basis	Depression treatment program vs. attention placebo	Immediate, 9 months	No difference in remission rates: remission rates were high in both groups.
Wood, Harrington, and Moore (1996)	Age 9–17 (N = 48)	MDD or minor depression based on K-SADS	Includes parent contact, level of parent involvement determined on case by case basic	Cognitive-behavioral vs. relaxation training	Immediate, 6 months	Posttest revealed greater reductions in both depressive symptoms and overall outcome in the cognitive-behavioral group. At 6 months group differences were attenuated.

Support has also accumulated for the efficacy of interpersonal psychotherapy (IPT) in the treatment of depressive disorders. Following an early demonstration that IPT was associated with improvements in depressed mood and social functioning (Mufson et al., 1994), a clinical trial was completed that showed that IPT was associated with greater reductions in depressive symptoms and more improvements in social functioning and adjustment, when compared to a clinical monitoring condition (Mufson, Weissman, Moreau, & Garfinkel, 1999). The efficacy of IPT was further supported in demonstrations by a second group, such that IPT was associated with more improvement in depression and social functioning than a wait-list control condition (Rosello & Bernal, 1999), a finding that was supported in a second study by this group (see Bernal and Sáez-Santiago, ch. 19 in this volume). As developed in each of these studies, IPT is a time-limited treatment that emphasizes improving interpersonal relationships through attending to interpersonal conflicts and losses, themes, and deficits (Moreau, Mufson, Weissman, & Klerman, 1991; Mufson, Moreau, Weissman, & Klerman, 1993).

There are also data supporting the efficacy of antidepressant medication for the treatment of depressive disorders in adolescents, particularly the selective serotonin reuptake inhibitors (SSRIs; e.g., Emslie et al., 1997, 2002). Although recent findings have highlighted a potential risk of suicidal thoughts and attempts for pediatric patients treated with certain antidepressant medications, the U.S. Food and Drug Administration (FDA) has approved fluoxetine for the treatment of pediatric major depression (FDA, 2003). Additionally, results from the study by Keller et al. (2001) indicated that youth treated with imipramine did not differ from those treated with placebo on any measure, suggesting that the older antidepressant medications may not be effective for the treatment of depression in youth.

Despite the promise of the overall findings on the treatment of adolescent depression, several caveats merit note. First, while current evidence suggests probably efficacious treatments, extant data most strongly support the advantages of current treatments in comparison to waiting, watchful waiting (clinical monitoring), or placebo. Only the Brent et al. (1997) study documented an advantage of the "specific treatment" (CBT) in comparison to other presumably active treatments (nondirective supportive therapy, systemic-behavioral family therapy). Second, evidence of sustained advantages for these treatments over extended follow-up is lacking, with the one study showing advantages for an "active" versus "presumably inactive" treatment showing no differences between treatment groups at a 24-month follow-up (Birmaher, Ryan, Williamson, Brent, & Kaufman, 1996; Brent et al., 1997). This may, however, be associated with the tendencies for depressive symptoms to resolve over time, and longer follow-up may have revealed differences in protection from relapse. Third, across treatment trials a substantial subgroup of roughly 40–50% of adolescents have not responded to treatment, and for many youth response has been incomplete, with full remission of symptoms an elusive but desired goal (Emslie, 1998; Emslie et al., 1997). Fourth, effectiveness trials that have attempted to improve access to evidence-based treatments within the real world of clinical practice have highlighted the importance of attending to treatment preferences and the wide range of barriers that can interfere with adherence to treatment recommendations. For example, preliminary data from our study of adolescent depression in primary care revealed that youth tended to prefer psychosocial as opposed to pharmacologic treatment, that youth and families confronted a wide range of barriers that interfered with treatment adherence, and that youth tended to receive fewer psychosocial treatment sessions than typically required in clinical trial protocols (Asarnow et al., 2005).

In conclusion, current data demonstrate both the promise and limitations of current treatment approaches. CBT, IPT, and pharmacotherapy with SSRIs have promise as first-line treatments for depressive disorder in adolescents. However, given the limitations in the existing data, careful monitoring is required with follow-up to ensure early detection of potential relapse or recurrence. Moreover, data evaluating combination treatments, algorithms for guiding decisions regarding the sequencing of treatment strategies, alternative treatment strategies, and service delivery strategies for typical practice conditions are desperately needed. Data from at least four current large multisite trials in the field will help provide these data: one comparing CBT, medication, and combined CBT plus medication (Treatment for Adolescents with Depression Study Team [TADS], 2003); one comparing different strategies for the treatment of depressions that have not responded to initial treatment with an SSRI (Treatment of Resistant Depression in Adolescents [TORDIA]) (TORDIA, n.d.); one evaluating the impact of adding a brief cognitive-behavior therapy as an adjunct to SSRIs within primary care settings (Clarke et al., 2000); and our study evaluating a collaborative care model for improving access to cognitive-behavior therapy and medication for depression within primary care settings (Youth Partners in Care) (Asarnow et al., 2005). These studies will clarify optimal treatment strategies for youth with depression, the value of combined psychosocial and pharmacologic treatment strategies, and begin to clarify optimal service delivery strategies for bringing evidence-based treatments into real-world clinical practice settings. However, there continues to be a need to search for treatment approaches with more robust and persistent effects that are feasible in the real world of clinical practice.

■ Why Adopt a Family-Focused Approach to Treatment?

A compelling case can be made for the need to adopt a family-focused approach to the treatment of depression in adolescents. The vast majority of adolescents live within families, are impacted by family characteristics, and impact family characteristics and patterns as well as the well-being of other family members. Among youth with depression, greater family stress has been found to be associated with a longer initial episode and lower social competence at 3-year follow-up (McCauley et al., 1993), and family factors predict treatment response among depressed youth (Asarnow, Goldstein, Tompson, & Guthrie, 1993; Birmaher et al., 2000). Additionally, parents of youth with depression tend to display high levels of critical expressed emotion compared to parents of never depressed community controls and children with some other forms of psychiatric disorder (Asarnow,

Tompson, Hamilton, Goldstein, & Guthrie, 1994; Asarnow, Tompson, Woo, & Cantwell, 2001), and negative parental attitudes and behaviors in parents appear to be part of a pattern of negative, reciprocal parent-child interactions in families with depressed youth (Hamilton, Asarnow, & Tompson, 1999). These data underscore the importance of promoting a positive, supportive, and noncritical family environment in the treatment of adolescents suffering from depression.

Another compelling reason to focus on the broader family unit when treating depression in adolescents is that parents of depressed youth are also likely to suffer from depression, relative to parents of controls with no mental illness (Klein, Lewinsohn, Seeley, & Rohde, 2001; Kovacs, Devlin, Pollock, Richards, & Mukerji, 1997; Mitchell, McCauley, Burke, Calderon, & Schloredt, 1989; Puig-Antich et al., 1989; Todd, Neuman, Geller, Fox, & Hickok, 1993; Wickramaratne, Greenwald, & Weissman, 2000; Williamson et al., 1995) and in some instances when compared to parents of youth with other forms of psychiatric disorder (Harrington et al., 1993; Klein et al., 2001; Kovacs et al., 1997). Moreover, maternal depression appears to be associated with poorer recovery among adolescents with depression, and depression in mothers and youth tends to be temporally linked such that symptoms in one member of the dyad potentiate symptoms in the other (Hammen, Burge, & Adrian, 1991; Kutcher & Marton, 1991; Rao et al., 1995). These data generally support an interactional model (Asarnow, Jaycox, et al., 2001; Coyne, Downey, & Boergers, 1994; Hammen et al., 1991; Keitner & Miller, 1990, 1994) in which parental depression and criticism, dysfunctional family interactional patterns, and family stress contribute to depression in adolescents, which in turn fuels family stress and dysfunction. Thus, regardless of their role in depression etiology, family factors likely impact depressive symptoms, and conversely, depression in adolescents and/or parents impacts the family system. Family-focused interventions have potential for decreasing the risk of depressive episodes across multiple family members (e.g., mother, children, father), for promoting recovery among multiple affected family members, and for promoting positive changes in the family climate.

■ Family Interventions: Is There Evidence for Efficacy?

Despite the clear importance of family environmental factors in adolescent depression, results of extant studies provide only limited support for the efficacy of family interventions as a single monotherapy for depressed adolescents. However, there have been very few completed evaluations of family interventions to date, and in-progress and future studies may support efficacy. Moreover, as shown in table 17.1, which provides an overview of completed randomized trials focusing on the treatment of adolescent depression, most completed trials included some family component as part of the intervention.

The most promising results supporting possible efficacy of a family intervention come from a small ($N = 32$) preliminary treatment development trial completed by Diamond and colleagues in a high-risk sample of primarily inner-city, low-income African American youth with depression. They tested an attachment-based family therapy model that focuses on building the bond between the adolescent and parents so the family can serve as a secure base from which the adolescent develops increasing autonomy. The therapeutic strategies include (a) a nonblaming reframing of the goals of treatment from a focus on the adolescent's symptoms to a focus on the quality of parent-adolescent relationships, (b) building alliances between the therapist and both the parent and adolescent, (c) promoting attachment between the parent(s) and the adolescent, and (d) building youth competencies (Diamond, Reis, Diamond, Siqueland, & Isaacs, 2002; Diamond & Siqueland, 1995, 1998). In this treatment development trial, patients receiving the family intervention showed significantly higher rates of remission (81%) than those in a wait-list group (47%). These gains were maintained at a 6-month follow-up.

Results from another small preliminary study conducted by Sanford and colleagues (Sanford, Boyle, Offord, McCleary, & Steele, 2002) provide some tentative support for the value of an intensive family psychoeducation intervention for adolescent major depression. The intervention involved 12 biweekly family sessions adapted from the Falloon et al. (Falloon, 1985) behavioral family intervention originally developed for adult schizophrenia, as well as a booster session during the 3-month period after acute treatment. The family psychoeducation intervention was added to usual care. Results indicate a nonsignificant trend toward decreased depressive symptoms and higher remission rates among adolescents in the family psychoeducation group compared to adolescents receiving usual care (79% vs. 50% in partial or full remission at posttreatment and 75% vs. 47% in partial or full remission at a 3-month follow-up). Additionally, growth curve analyses revealed that the family treatment group showed a significantly higher trajectory for improvement in global social functioning than the usual care group. An important caveat, however, is that this study was originally planned as a two-site study, and one site was eliminated because 80% of patients at that site withdrew from the study. This raises questions regarding the feasibility of this intervention across different service delivery systems and patient groups.

Results of two larger studies on the efficacy of extended family interventions for adolescent depression are less encouraging. However, it should be noted that both of these studies did include a family-focused component across all conditions. First, as shown in table 17.1, Brent et al. (1997) compared systemic-behavioral family therapy, individual CBT, and individual nondirective supportive therapy for adolescents with major depression. All groups in this study received a brief family psychoeducation intervention, however, which involved giving parents information about depression and its treatment and a psychoeducational manual and providing time to discuss this information and address questions and concerns. The systemic-behavioral family treatment utilized a combination of reframing and communication and problem-solving skills training to alter family interaction patterns. Results indicated that systemic-behavioral family therapy was significantly less effective than CBT and was comparable in efficacy to nondirective supportive therapy. Systemic-behavioral family therapy was, however, associated with a tendency for youth to have better relationships with parents when compared to the individual treatment conditions (i.e., CBT and nondirective supportive therapy).

Second, Lewinsohn and colleagues (Clarke et al., 1999; Lewinsohn, Clarke, Hops, & Andrews, 1990) compared adolescent-only group CBT, adolescent group CBT plus parallel parental group CBT, and a wait-list control condition. The overall goals of the parent intervention were to (a) provide information to parents regarding the skills being taught to the adolescents so that parents could support their adolescent's gains and (b) to teach parents the same negotiation, conflict resolution, and communication skills that were being taught to the adolescents and improve family communication and problem solving. The addition of the parental component offered no clear advantage over group CBT alone. However, it is important to note that the Lewinsohn et al. (1990) and Clarke et al. (1999) group CBT does focus on family interactions by teaching communication, negotiation, and conflict resolution skills for use with parents and peers, and it includes homework assignments practicing these skills with parents.

Although additional testing is needed to clarify the effects of family psychoeducation in the treatment of adolescent depression, there is accumulating evidence supporting the promise of this approach. Brent, Poling, McKain, and Baugher (1993) found that, after a 2-hr family psychoeducational intervention, participants showed greater knowledge about depression as well as fewer dysfunctional beliefs about depression and the treatment of depression. Participants almost uniformly rated the program as worthwhile (97%) and felt that they had learned a lot (98%). Additionally, as noted above, in perhaps the largest adolescent depression treatment study completed to date, Brent et al. (1997) added a brief family psychoeducation component across all treatment conditions as a means of minimizing dropout and promoting a family atmosphere that would support treatment gains. The impact of the family psychoeducational intervention on youth depression and functioning, however, remains to be evaluated.

Fristad and colleagues (Fristad, Gavazzi, & Soldano, 1998; Fristad, Goldberg-Arnold, & Gavazzi, 2003) developed a six-session multifamily psychoeducational group intervention (MFPG) for child and adolescent mood disorders. Psychoeducational group sessions begin and end with both the parents and youth; however, much of the material is presented in "break-out sessions" during which parallel parent and youth groups are conducted. Topics discussed in these groups include education about mood disorders, medication and medication side effects, interpersonal factors, communication skills, and stress reduction. During the child and adolescent groups, youth are able to meet others with similar problems, increase their knowledge of symptoms and symptom management, build their social skills, and discuss common developmental issues. In particular, adolescent sessions focus on identity development and concerns about dependency versus autonomy, handling interpersonal conflicts, interactions between drugs and alcohol and psychotropic medications, suicidality, and school performance. Results of an early uncontrolled trial evaluating this approach with children and adolescents showed a high level of satisfaction with the MFPG and reports of more positive family interactions (Fristad et al., 1998). In a subsequent small, randomized controlled trial ($n = 35$), Fristad et al. evaluated the impact of the MFPG as an adjunct to treatment as usual for 8- to 11-year-old children with mood disorders

(Fristad, Goldberg-Arnold, et al., 2003). Compared to wait-list controls, at 6-month follow-up, families who received the MFPG reported increases in parental knowledge of mood disorder symptoms, parental reports of positive family interactions, perception of parental support by children, and use of appropriate services by families. Anecdotal reports also indicated greater parental concordance in parenting styles, which could positively impact the home environment (Fristad, Gavazzi, & Mackinaw-Koons, 2003). The impact of the MFPG on symptom reduction still remains to be clarified.

Because family treatment is frequently associated with more problems with and barriers to treatment adherence (Brent et al., 1996; King, Hovey, Brand, & Wilson, 1997), there may be distinct advantages to brief family interventions that are combined with other forms of treatment. The importance of this issue is illustrated by our work with younger fourth- through sixth-grade children (Asarnow, Scott, & Mintz, 2002). With this sample, selected for the presence of depressive symptoms, we evaluated a combined cognitive-behavioral and family education intervention. A roughly 90-min family education session followed nine sessions of group CBT. The family education session was designed to promote generalization of skills to key environmental contexts (home, school, community), encourage parents to support the learning that was achieved through the group sessions, and foster positive attitudes toward the skills emphasized in the intervention. Consistent with Biemiller and Meichenbaum's (1998) emphasis on the importance of increasing levels of self-direction in moving from skill acquisition to mastery in CBT interventions, the intervention was designed to address the progression from skill acquisition, to skill consolidation (through practice), to assuming a consulting or teaching role. Intervention sessions were structured around the development of a videotape by the children that illustrated the treatment model and provided multiple opportunities for children to practice and consolidate the skills introduced in each CBT session. After a brief introduction to parents explaining their key role in promoting generalization of the CBT skills to real-world contexts and problems, parents and children were brought together for a multiple family meeting during which the children's video illustrating the treatment model was presented and children were given awards for their accomplishments. Each child then assumed the role of "consultant" as they taught their parents the skills emphasized in the group session. The session ended with the children presenting their parents with awards for their participation in the family session. Results indicated that the intervention was associated with greater reductions in depressive symptoms, reductions in negative automatic thoughts, and less internalizing coping, compared to a wait-list control group. Additionally, children and parents almost uniformly rated the intervention as enjoyable. When asked about the family component, all of the parents rated this intervention as useful and 60% indicated that despite its brevity more sessions were not needed. Thus, only 40% of the parents felt that a more extended family intervention would be helpful, underscoring the potential value of brief family interventions as well as the need to understand parent needs and preferences and develop interventions that will be acceptable and feasible for families.

Other promising treatment development work is also in progress. Tompson, Pierre, Asarnow, McNeil, and Fogler (2003) are currently testing a clinic-based family-focused intervention based on behavioral family management and cognitive-behavioral and family systems models for depressed youth aged 8 to 14. This approach provides expanded family psychoeducation and skills building within a family context. Goals of the intervention include: (a) educating family members about depression, focusing on its interpersonal nature, (b) teaching parents and children skills which will enable them to communicate and solve problems more effectively, (c) improving positive communication which may help family members to provide one another with more effective support, and (d) helping families to solve specific family problems. Results from a preliminary open trial support the value of this approach, with recovery rates of 67% at immediate posttest and 78% at 3-month follow-up. Recovery was defined as the youth's no longer meeting criteria for depressive disorder (Major Depression, Dysthymia, or Depression NOS; Tompson et al., 2003).

Additionally, Kaslow and colleagues have been strong advocates of including families in the treatment of adolescent depression and they have developed a sophisticated interpersonal family therapy model that integrates theory and techniques from family systems perspectives, cognitive-behavioral approaches, attachment theory, interpersonal therapy, and developmental psychopathology and adapted this approach to be culturally sensitive to the needs of African American girls and their families (Griffith, Zucker, Bliss, Foster, & Kaslow, in press; Kaslow & Racusin, 1994; Schwartz, Kaslow, Racusin, & Carton, 1998). This treatment attempts to focus on identifying and intervening in areas of particular need within each family with the goals of decreasing depressive symptomatology, changing maladaptive cognitive patterns, improving family affective communication, increasing adaptive behavior, and improving both interpersonal and family functioning. An evaluation of this approach is in progress and initial observations suggest that families find this approach acceptable and useful (Griffith et al., in press).

As noted previously, parental depression is a strong risk factor for depression in adolescents, with recent reports indicating an eightfold increase in youth depression among offspring of depressed parents (Wickramaratne & Weissman, 1998). Beardslee and colleagues have designed and tested a family-based preventive psychoeducational intervention for youth (aged 8 to 14) whose parents suffer from depression (Beardslee et al., 1992). This intervention provides an excellent example of how family interventions can be designed to address and prevent depression in both children and parents. The Beardslee et al. intervention began with a psychoeducation phase, during which parents were provided with information about youth depression, the impact of parental depression on youth, and factors that increase resiliency in youth. Parents then discussed how they would convey important information on their depression to their children. Second, in sessions with each child in the family, children were evaluated for depression and assisted in identifying questions and concerns for the parents to address. Finally, one or two family meetings were held to enable the parents and children to address these issues together. Compared to subjects in a lecture-only control group, parents in the family intervention group reported greater satisfaction and more behavior and attitude changes, including increased family communication about the mood disorder, and improved understanding of the child's experience. Children in the family intervention group reported greater understanding of the parent's mood disorder and improved family communication and showed greater adaptive functioning following the intervention.

There are also emerging data supporting the value of family interventions for adolescents who attempt suicide. Suicide is the most serious complication of adolescent depression and is the third leading cause of death in the United States for adolescents and young adults between 10 and 24 years of age (National Center for Health Statistics, 2000). Suicide attempts are also associated with depression in adolescents and are a strong predictor of completed suicide and subsequent suicide attempts in youth (for review, see American Academy of Child and Adolescent Psychiatry, 2000). Data indicating that family climate variables, such as family conflict, family structure, and impaired communication and support, are associated with suicidal behavior in adolescents (for review, see Miller & Glinski, 2000) have led to the development and testing of family-focused interventions for this population.

Rotheram-Borus and colleagues (Rotheram-Borus, Piacentini, Cantwell, Belin, & Song, 2000) evaluated a family intervention strategy for youth presenting to the emergency room (ER) with suicide attempts. The intervention included training of ER staff to implement standard protocols in the ER, patient and family education using a motivational "soap opera" video designed to highlight the seriousness of suicide attempts and motivate patients and parents to adhere to follow-up treatment, a structured family session conducted in the ER aimed at reframing the suicide attempt as a critical event requiring follow-up treatment, and linkage to a follow-up cognitive-behavioral family treatment designed to disrupt the cycle whereby increasing stress or family difficulties lead to escalating suicidal tendencies and behaviors. The follow-up treatment, Successful Negotiation Acting Positive (SNAP), focused on improving conflict resolution strategies, eliminating suicide attempts as a method of resolving future conflict, promoting more positive family interactions, and reframing the family's understanding of their problems. In the evaluation study all patients were offered the SNAP treatment and a quasi-experimental design was used to evaluate SNAP plus the ER intervention in comparison to SNAP alone. The quasi-experimental sequential assignment design involved a first time period during which patients were assigned to Usual ER Care and a second time period during which patients received the ER intervention. This design was required because the inclusion of a staff training component delivered to all staff within the ER in the ER intervention precluded a randomized design. Although the study design does not allow separation of the impact of the SNAP follow-up treatment from the ER intervention, or certainty that observed effects were not due to differences in the time periods during which the two intervention strategies were implemented, the combined ER plus SNAP intervention was associated with improved treatment adherence, reduced depression levels, and less severe suicidal ideation, with some gains maintained over an 18-month follow-up period. More specifically, the ER intervention was associated with greater adherence to follow-up treatment (95% attended first session vs. 82% in Usual ED Care, mean number of sessions attended was 5.7 in the ER intervention group vs. 4.7 in the Usual ER Care group.). At the postdischarge assessment, adolescents in the ER intervention condition reported significantly less suicidal ideation and depression. Similarly, mothers receiving the ER intervention reported lower levels of depression and less overall psychopathology, and they had more positive expectations toward treatment and toward family interactions. At 18 months, adolescents receiving the ER intervention were significantly less depressed and mothers reported higher family cohesion, when compared to the Usual ER Care group. Attempters with the most psychiatric symptoms in the ER intervention condition had mothers who reported the greatest improvements in depression and increased family cohesion 18 months later. These data highlight the promise of a cognitive-behavioral family treatment and call for further research to clarify the impact and active components of this multifaceted treatment.

Harrington and colleagues (1998) also examined the impact of a family intervention for adolescents who had attempted suicide, but restricted the sample to youth whose attempts had involved drug ingestion. In a randomized controlled trial, a brief, home-based family problem-solving intervention plus usual care led to a reduction in suicidal ideation at both 2- and 6-month follow-up, compared to usual care. Interestingly, this finding held only for those adolescents without major depression, suggesting that different or more intensive interventions are needed for depressed, suicidal youth. These findings underscore the importance of developing effective family-based intervention strategies for decreasing suicidality as well as depression in adolescents.

■ Developmental Considerations: Challenges of Adolescence

Adolescence is a distinct developmental phase during which youth confront the developmental challenge of transitioning from childhood to adulthood. Key developmental tasks during adolescence relate to this transition and include progressing through puberty and becoming mature sexually, developing intimate relationships outside of the family, and developing the educational and occupational skills required to move into the workforce and become financially independent (Burt, 2002). Family relationships and patterns can support the adolescent during this transitional period, or they can contribute to difficulties and dysfunction. A key reason for adopting a family perspective in the treatment of adolescent depression is to strengthen protective factors within the family that can contribute to successful negotiation of the developmental tasks of adolescence.

Parents of adolescents confront a complementary challenge: how to nurture growth and successful adaptation while protecting the youth from the dangers of this period. Despite the fact that adolescents as a group are generally healthy, the adolescent years are characterized by increasingly high rates of morbidity and mortality, mostly due to motor vehicle accidents, homicide, and suicide (for review, see Irwin, Burg, & Uhler Cart, 2002). Indeed, death rates triple between the ages of 10 and 14 years (mortality rate of 21.1/100,000) and 15 to 19 years (death rate of 69.8/ 100,000) and this represents the largest increase in death rates for any consecutive age cohort (CDC, 2002). Most deaths during this age period are also due to causes that can be prevented and are related to modifiable risk factors, such as risky driving; substance use and abuse; bad choices about where the youth goes, who the youth goes with, and who drives the car; and unsafe sexual practices (Irwin et al., 2002). Thus, parents struggle with the need to give the youth enough room to grow and the need to protect and nurture the youth through the dangers of this period.

The tensions that parents experience in guiding their children through adolescence are complicated by a number of societal factors. First, there has been an increase in single-parent families and mothers working out of the home, which means that parents are faced with multiple competing demands and may have less time for supervising and interacting with their children (Irwin et al., 2002). There are also gaps in care provided by other institutions and potential nurturing forces. For example, national trends for adolescents to be educated in larger more impersonal schools and for increased class size in high school suggest less teacher-student interaction and monitoring by school personnel (Irwin et al., 2002). Adolescents are also less likely than younger children to have health insurance, have the lowest rates of health care utilization of any age group, and are the least likely age group to seek health care in traditional office-based clinics (Irwin et al., 2002; Maternal and Child Health Bureau, 1998). Thus, during this challenging developmental period when rates of depression and high-risk behaviors increase, there appears to be a convergence of factors leading to decreased family and societal resources to monitor and care for adolescents.

Do the tensions of this period require a different approach to treatment, particularly family treatment? Although some adolescents may feel comfortable discussing issues openly with parents, others may prefer to be treated as "adults" and not have their parents in treatment sessions, and others may not trust any therapist who speaks to their parent alone because of concerns regarding confidentiality. Thus, a thorough assessment is required of the needs of each adolescent and family prior to selecting an optimal treatment approach. Moreover, in the real world of clinical practice, parents and youth choose the treatments that they prefer and effective strategies are needed for guiding families through available treatment options so that they can make informed decisions regarding available treatments. Algorithms for making decisions regarding the structure and type of family involvement and treatment, much like the algorithms that have been developed to guide medication choices and choices regarding which treatment modality to initiate (e.g., Asarnow et al., 2005; Asarnow et al., 2001; Depression Guideline Panel, 1993; Hughes et al., 1999; National Institute of Health, 1992), may be crucial for matching youth and families to a family intervention strategy that is most likely to be feasible, associated with treatment adherence, and lead to successful outcomes.

Research with adolescents also presents a number of key challenges. First, as noted previously, assessment data from different informants can conflict, leading to a desire to obtain evaluation data from multiple informants, such as the youth, parents, teachers, and clinicians, in order to obtain a full picture of youth functioning. This requires more time than assessments from a single informant, increases assessment burden, and can threaten participant compliance and the feasibility of the evaluation. Therefore, researchers must carefully weight feasibility and methodological needs in order to identify designs that are most appropriate for their research aims and lead to minimal attrition and rigorous methodological approaches. Second, the rapid developmental changes occurring during adolescence require consideration of key developmental milestones such as transitions from school to work, marriage, pregnancy, parenting, and the other specific issues of adolescence noted above. Although assessments of multiple domains of functioning such as depressive symptoms and disorders, comorbidities, social functioning and adjustment (e.g., family, school, work, peer, leisure time) are clearly desirable, again researchers will need to balance feasibility with the objectives of the research. Finally, because adolescents begin to leave their families of origin during late adolescence, longitudinal studies with adolescents require careful attention to strategies for maintaining contact with participants.

■ Conclusions: Where Do We Stand?

Much has been accomplished in the past few decades. Major advances have been achieved in treatments for adolescent depression and we now have support for the efficacy of two psychosocial intervention strategies (CBT and IPT) and pharmacotherapy. There are also accumulating data supporting the important role of the family in these disorders, a general consensus that effective treatment of adolescents living in families requires some intervention and guidance of parents, and promising examples in the field of family interventions that may prove to be effective. Based on the literature reviewed above, we offer the following conclusions and recommendations.

1. The collective clinical and treatment literatures highlight the crucial need for a family-focused perspective in the treatment of adolescent depression. Clearly, it is not possible to work with adolescents who live in families without obtaining the confidence of their parents, as parents play a critical role in paying for, providing transportation to, and facilitating treatment. Thus, with some exceptions (e.g., children removed from parent custody) some parent contact and information sharing is needed to obtain parent consent for treatment and parent support of the treatment process. For these reasons, adolescent treatment can be conceptualized as de facto "family context" therapy (Kazdin & Weisz, 1998).

2. Despite general acknowledgment of the importance of a family-focused perspective, additional research and treatment development work is needed to identify optimal family intervention strategies. As reviewed above, results of completed trials have not yet provided strong evidence supporting the efficacy of family treatment as a monotherapy or added benefits associated with adjunctive family treatment. Family treatments are also associated with

poorer attendance and more problems with treatment adherence, perhaps due to the combination of barriers to attendance for both parents and youth (Brent et al., 1996; King et al., 1997). That being said, there are a very limited number of completed trials evaluating family treatments on adolescent depressive disorders (Brent et al., 1997; Clarke et al., 1999; Diamond et al., 2002; Lewinsohn, Clarke, Rohde, Hops, & Seeley, 1996; Sanford et al., 2002), some promising examples of family interventions that are under development, and future research may well demonstrate the efficacy of family treatment strategies. At this point, whether or not family intervention is essential versus optional in treating adolescent depression remains a critical empirical question.

3. It is important to note that those psychosocial treatments that have demonstrated efficacy have included some components addressing family and interpersonal processes, such as family psychoeducation, family and interpersonal problem solving, and interpersonal and family issues. This attests to the recognition among clinical researchers and clinicians of the critical importance of a family-focused treatment perspective. Indeed, the dominant view within the field is that treatment is more likely to be successful if family concerns and issues are addressed and family members are supported in their efforts to steer their adolescents toward recovery. Moreover, two of the ongoing large multisite treatment studies of adolescent depression (TADS and TORDIA) include a "family component" as part of the treatment protocols. However, because in these studies family intervention occurs in combination with other treatments, the studies are not designed to measure the unique contribution of family treatment to symptom improvement.

4. A critical task for the future involves clarification of the degree to which adding a family component to treatments with demonstrated efficacy adds to treatment effects. This is particularly important because while current data support the efficacy of CBT, IPT, and pharmacotherapy with SSRIs, roughly 40–50% of youth have failed to show significant recovery or response as defined in these studies and response is frequently incomplete, with many youth showing continuing symptoms and psychosocial difficulties (Emslie et al., 1997). Therefore, there is substantial room to improve upon existing treatments. Given the identified links between family factors and treatment response, as well as demonstrations of positive responses to some family interventions, this would appear to be a particularly promising area for future treatment development work.

5. Another question requiring resolution involves identification of the optimal dose of family interventions and/or development of algorithms for matching families to the most beneficial doses and types of family interventions. Although the inclination can be to assume that more intensive interventions are likely to yield the strongest effects, it may be that brief interventions are more acceptable and effective with busy parents who are confronted with multiple demands (jobs, other children). A critical question requiring resolution is how to best match the needs of families to intervention types.

6. Given the issues detailed above, the next step is research that systematically varies the degree and type of family intervention, both alone and as an adjunct to other treatments (e.g., CBT, IPT, and medication), in order to determine the most effective doses and methods. As noted, such findings are likely to be affected by several adolescent and family-level variables, including the adolescent's degree of independence from parents and the desire to have them involved in his or her care, the severity of impairment, and comorbidity with other disorders, as well as various practical barriers to care for both teens and parents. Moreover, recent evidence showing that adolescent girls are more likely to have repeat depressive episodes than adolescent boys (Lewinsohn, Pettit, Joiner, & Seely, 2003) suggests that gender may affect treatment needs and impact. Cultural and other sociodemographic factors may also influence treatment efficacy and acceptability. Such variables need to be taken into account in the research in order to determine the specific treatment algorithms most likely to be successful in reducing depressive symptoms in teens.

7. The unique developmental challenges of the adolescent period need to be considered in developing optimal treatment strategies for this population. Strategies developed for adults or younger children may not yield comparable effects with adolescents and treatment strategies that attend to the developmental needs of adolescents and their families are likely to be the most beneficial.

8. Attention is needed to the question of optimal strategies for bringing family intervention strategies developed and tested in the laboratory into the real world of clinical practice. Information from observational studies and effectiveness trials on treatment preferences and service delivery strategies that are needed to enhance treatment adherence and effectiveness will be essential for guiding treatment development research and ensuring that developed treatments are feasible for use under real world practice conditions.

There is much promising ongoing work in the field. We optimistically await the next generation of family research to guide efforts to improve care and outcomes for adolescent depression.

■ Acknowledgments

Preparation of this paper was supported in part by Grant AHCPR HS09908 from the Agency for Healthcare Policy and Research. We thank John Lipson for his assistance in preparing the manuscript.

■ References

American Academy of Child and Adolescent Psychiatry. (2000). *Practice parameters for the assessment and treatment of children and adolescents with suicidal behavior.* Washington, DC: AACAP Communications Department.

Angold, A., Costello, E. J., Erkanli, A., & Worthman, C. M. (1999). Pubertal changes in hormone levels and depression in girls. *Psychological Medicine, 29*(5), 1043–1053.

Asarnow, J. R., Goldstein, M. J., Tompson, M., & Guthrie, D. (1993). One-year outcomes of depressive disorders in child psychiatric in-patients: Evaluation of the prognostic power of a brief measure of expressed emotion. *Journal of Child Psychology and Psychiatry, 34*(2), 129–137.

Asarnow, J. R., Jaycox, L. H., Duan, N., LaBorde, A. P., Rea, M. M., Murray, P., et al. (2005). Effectiveness of a quality improvement intervention for adolescent depression. *Journal of the American Medical Association, 293*, 311–319.

Asarnow, J. R., Jaycox, L. H., & Tompson, M. C. (2001). Depression in youth: Psychosocial inventions. *Journal of Clinical Child Psychology, 30*, 33–47.

Asarnow, J. R., Scott, C., & Mintz, J. (2002). A combined cognitive-behavioral family education intervention for depression in children: a treatment development study. *Cognitive Therapy and Research, 26*, 221–229.

Asarnow, J. R., Tompson, M., Hamilton, E. B., Goldstein, M. J., & Guthrie, D. (1994). Family-expressed emotion, childhood-onset depression, and childhood-onset schizophrenia spectrum disorders: Is expressed emotion a nonspecific correlate of child psychopathology or a specific risk factor for depression? *Journal of Abnormal Child Psychology, 22*(2), 129–146.

Asarnow, J. R., Tompson, M., Woo, S., & Cantwell, D. P. (2001). Is expressed emotion a specific risk factor for depression or a nonspecific correlate of psychopathology? *Journal of Abnormal Child Psychology, 29*(6), 573–583.

Beardslee, W. R., Hoke, L., Wheelock, I., Rothberg, P. C., van de Velde, P., & Swatling, S. (1992). Initial findings on preventive intervention for families with parental affective disorders. *American Journal of Psychiatry, 149*(10), 1335–1340.

Biemiller, A., & Meichenbaum, D. (1998). The consequences of negative scaffolding for students who learn slowly—a commentary on C. Addison Stone's *The metaphor of scaffolding: Its utility for the field of learning disabilities. Journal of Learning Disabilities, 31*(4), 365–369.

Birmaher, B., Brent, D. A., Kolko, D., Baugher, M., Bridge, J., Holder, D., et al. (2000). Clinical outcome after short-term psychotherapy for adolescents with major depressive disorder. *Archives of General Psychiatry, 57*(1), 29–36.

Birmaher, B., Ryan, N. D., Williamson, D. E., Brent, D. A., & Kaufman, J. (1996). Childhood and adolescent depression: A review of the past ten years. Part II. *Journal of the American Academy of Child and Adolescent Psychiatry, 35*, 1575–1583.

Brent, D. A., Holder, D., Kolko, D., Birmaher, B., Baugher, M., Roth, C., et al. (1997). A clinical psychotherapy trial for adolescent depression comparing cognitive, family and supportive therapy. *Archives of General Psychiatry, 54*, 877–885.

Brent, D. A., Poling, K., McKain, B., & Baugher, M. (1993). A psychoeducational program for families of affectively ill children and adolescents. *Journal of the American Academy of Child and Adolescent Psychiatry, 32*, 770–774.

Brent, D. A., Roth, C. M., Holder, D. P., Kolko, D. J., et al. (1996). Psychosocial interventions for treating adolescent suicidal depression: A comparison of three psychosocial interventions. In E. D. Hibbs & P. S. Jensen (Eds.), *Psychosocial treatments for child and adolescent disorders: Empirically based strategies for clinical practice.* (pp. 187–206). Washington, DC: American Psychological Association.

Burt, M. R. (2002). Reasons to invest in adolescents. *Journal of Adolescent Health, 31*(6, Suppl.), 136–152.

Centers for Disease Control. (2001). *2001 Youth Risk Behavior Survey.* Atlanta, GA: Author.

Centers for Disease Control. (2002). *Youth risk behavior surveillance—United States, 2001.* Retrieved from www.cdc.gov/mmwr/preview/mmwrhtml/ss5104a1.htm

Clarke, G. D. L., Lynch, F., Gale, J., Powell, J., Bennett, M., Herbert, S., et al. (2000). *CBT for depressed adolescents receiving SSRIs in HMO primary care.* Paper presented at the Annual Meeting of the American Academy of Child and Adolescent Psychiatry, New York.

Clarke, G. N., Rohde, P., Lewinsohn, P. M., Hops, H., & Seeley, J. R. (1999). Cognitive-behavioral treatment of adolescent depression: Efficacy of acute group treatment and booster sessions. *Journal of the American Academy of Child and Adolescent Psychiatry, 38,* 272–279.

Coyne, J. C., Downey, G., & Boergers, J. (1994). Depression in families: A systems perspective. In D. Cichetti & S.L. Toth (Eds.), *Developmental approaches to the affective disorders: Rochester Symposium on Developmental Psychopathology* (Vol. 4). Rochester, NY: University of Rochester.

Depression Guideline Panel. (1993). *Depression in primary care: Vol. II. Treatment of major depression. Clinical practice guideline No. 5* (AHCPR Publication No. 93-0551). Rockville, MD: Agency for Health Care Policy and Research.

Diamond, G., & Siqueland, L. (1995). Family therapy for the treatment of depressed adolescents. *Psychotherapy: Research and Practice, 32*(1), 77–90.

Diamond, G., & Siqueland, L. (1998). Emotions, attachment and the relational reframe: The first session. *Journal of Systemic Therapies, 17*(2), 36–50.

Diamond, G. S., Reis, B. F., Diamond G. M., Siqueland, L., & Isaacs, L. (2002). Attachment-based family therapy for depressed adolescents: A treatment development study. *Journal of the American Academy of Child and Adolescent Psychiatry, 41*(10), 1190–1196.

Emslie, G. J. (1998). Fluoxetine in child and adolescent depression: Acute and mainte-nance treatment. *Depression and Anxiety, 7,* 32–39.

Emslie, G. J., Heiligenstein, J. H., Wagner, K. D., Hoog, S. L., Ernest, D. E., Brown, E., et al. (2002). Fluoxetine for acute treatment of depression in children and adolescents: A placebo-controlled, randomized clinical trial. *Journal of the American Academy of Child and Adolescent Psychiatry, 10,* 1205–1215.

Emslie, G. J., Rush, J. A., Weinberg, W. A., Kowatch, R. A., Hughes, C. W., Carmody, T., et al. (1997). A double-blind, randomized, placebo-controlled trial of fluoxetine in children and adolescents with depression. *Archives of General Psychiatry, 54,* 1031–1037.

Falloon, I. R. H. (1985). *Family management of schizophrenia.* Baltimore, MD: Johns Hopkins University Press.

Fine, S., Forth, A., Gilbert, M., & Haley, G. (1991). Group therapy for adolescent depressive disorder: A comparison of social skills and therapeutic support. *Journal of the American Academy of Child and Adolescent Psychiatry, 30*(1), 79–85.

Fristad, M. A., Gavazzi, S. M., & Mackinaw-Koons, B. (2003). Family psychoeducation: An adjunctive intervention for children with bipolar disorder. *Biological Psychiatry, 53,* 1000–1008.

Fristad, M. A., Gavazzi, S. M., & Soldano, K. W. (1998). Multi-family psychoeducation groups for childhood mood disorders: A program description and preliminary efficacy data. *Contemporary Family Therapy, 20,* 385–402.

Fristad, M. A., Goldberg-Arnold, J. S., & Gavazzi, S. M. (2003). Multi-family psychoeducation groups in the treatment of children with mood disorders. *Journal of Marital and Family Therapy, 29,* 491–504.

Griffith, J., Zucker, M., Bliss, M., Foster, J., & Kaslow, N. (in press). Family intervention for depressed, low income, African American adolescent females with a history of childhood abuse. *Innovations in Clinical Practice.*

Hamilton, E. B., Asarnow, J. R., & Tompson, M. C. (1999). Family interaction styles of children with depressive disorders, schizophrenia-spectrum disorders, and normal controls. *Family Process, 38*(4), 463–476.

Hammen, C., Burge, K., & Adrian, C. (1991). Timing of mother and child depression in a longitudinal study of children at risk. *Journal of Consulting and Clinical Psychology, 59,* 341–345.

Harrington, R., Kerfoot, M., Dyer, E., McNiven, F., Gill, J., Harrington, V., et al. (1998). Randomized trial of a home-based family intervention for children who have deliberately poisoned themselves. *Journal of the American Academy of Child and Adolescent Psychiatry, 37,* 512–518.

Harrington, R. C., Fudge, H., Rutter, M. L., Bredenkamp, D., Groothues, C., & Pridham, J. (1993). Child and adult depression: A test of continuities with data from a family study. *British Journal of Psychiatry, 162,* 627–633.

Hughes, C. W., Emslie, G. J., Crimson, M. L., Wagner, K. D., Birmaher, B., Geller, B., et al. (1999). *The Texas Childhood Medication Algorithm Project: Report of the Texas Consensus Conference Panel on medication treatment of childhood major depressive disorder.*

Irwin, C. E., Jr., Burg, S. J., & Uhler Cart, C. (2002). America's adolescents: Where have we been, where are we going? *Journal of Adolescent Health, 31*(6, Suppl.), 91–121.

Kandel, D. B., & Davies, M. (1986). Adult sequelae of adolescent depressive symptoms. *Archives of General Psychiatry, 43*(3), 255–262.

Kaslow, N. J., McClure, E. B., & Connell, A. M. (2002). Treatment of depression in children and adolescents. In I. Gotlib & C. Hammen (Eds.), *Handbook of depression* (pp. 441–464). New York: Guilford Press.

Kaslow, N. J., & Racusin, G. R. (1994). Family therapy for depression in young people. In W. M. Reynolds & H. F. Johnston (Eds.), *Handbook of depression in children and adolescents* (pp. 345–364). New York: Plenum.

Kazdin, A. E., & Weisz, J. R. (1998). Identifying and developing empirically supported child and adolescent treatments. *Journal of Consulting and Clinical Psychology, 66*(1), 19–36.

Keitner, G. I., & Miller, I. W. (1990). Family functioning and major depression: An overview. *American Journal of Psychiatry, 147*(9), 1128–1137.

Keitner, G. I., & Miller, I. W. (1994). Family functioning and major depression. In G. P. Sholevar & L. Schwoeri (Eds.), *The transmission of depression in families and children.* Northvale, NJ: Jason Aronson.

Keller, M. B., Ryan, N. D., Strober, M., Klein, R. G., Kutcher, S. P., Birmaher, B., et al. (2001). Efficacy of paroxetine in the treatment of adolescent major depression: A randomized, controlled trial. *Journal of the American Academy of Child and Adolescent Psychiatry, 40*(7), 762–772.

Kessler, R. C. (2002). Epidemiology of depression. In I. Gotlib & C. Hammen (Eds.), *Handbook of depression* (pp. 23–42). New York: Guilford Press.

Kessler, R. C., Berglund, P. A., Foster, C. L., Saunders, W. B., Stang, P. E., & Walters, E. E. (1997). Social consequences of psychiatric disorders: II. Teenage parenthood. *American Journal of Psychiatry, 154*(10), 1405–1411.

Kessler, R. C., Foster, C. L., Saunders, W. B., & Stang, P. E. (1995). Social consequences of psychiatric disorders: I. Educational attainment. *American Journal of Psychiatry, 152*(7), 1026–1032.

King, C. A., Hovey, J. D., Brand, E., & Wilson, R. (1997). Suicidal adolescents after hospitalization: Parent and family impacts on treatment follow-through. *Journal of the American Academy of Child and Adolescent Psychiatry, 36*(1), 85–93.

Klein, D. N., Lewinsohn, P. M., Seeley, J. R., & Rohde, P. (2001). A family study of major depressive disorder in a community sample of adolescents. *Archives of General Psychiatry, 58*(1), 13-20.

Kovacs, M., Devlin, B., Pollock, M., Richards, C., & Mukerji, P. (1997). A controlled family history study of childhood-onset depressive disorder. *Archives of General Psychiatry, 54*(7), 613–623.

Kutcher, S., & Marton, P. (1991). Affective disorders in first-degree relatives of adolescent onset bipolars, unipolars, and normal controls. *Journal of the American Academy of Child and Adolescent Psychiatry, 30*(1), 75–78.

Lewinsohn, P., & Essau, C. A. (2002). Depression in adolescents. In I. Gotlib & C. Hammen (Eds.), *Handbook of depression* (pp. 541–553). New York: Guilford Press.

Lewinsohn, P. M., Clarke, G. N., Hops, H., & Andrews, J. (1990). Cognitive-behavioral treatment for depressed adolescents. *Behavior Therapy, 21,* 385–401.

Lewinsohn, P. M., Clarke, G. N., Rohde, P., Hops, H., & Seeley, J. R. (1996). A course in coping: A cognitive-behavioral approach to the treatment of adolescent depression. In Hibbs & Jensen (Eds.), *Psychosocial treatment for child and adolescent disorders* (pp. 109–135). Washington, DC: American Psychological Association.

Lewinsohn, P. M., Pettit, J. W., Joiner, T. E., & Seely, J. R. (2003). The symptomatic expression of major depressive disorder in adolescents and young adults. *Journal of Abnormal Psychology, 112,* 244–252.

Maternal and Child Health Bureau. (1998). *Child Health USA 1988.* Washington, DC: U.S. Department of Health and Human Services, Health Resources and Services Administration.

McCauley, E., Myers, K., Mitchell, J., Calderon, R., Schloredt, K., & Treder, R. (1993). Depression in young people: Initial presentation and clinical course. *Journal of the American Academy of Child and Adolescent Psychiatry, 32*(4), 714–722.

Miller, A. L., & Glinski, J. (2000). Youth suicidal behavior: assessment and intervention. *Journal of Clinical Psychology, 56*(9), 1131–1152.

Mitchell, J., McCauley, E., Burke, P., Calderon, R., & Schloredt, K. (1989). Psychopathology in parents of depressed children and adolescents. *Journal of the American Academy of Child and Adolescent Psychiatry, 28*(3), 352–357.

Moreau, D., Mufson, L., Weissman, M. M., & Klerman, G. L. (1991). Interpersonal psychotherapy for adolescent depression: Description of modification and preliminary application. *Journal of the American Academy of Child and Adolescent Psychiatry, 30*(4), 642–651.

Mufson, L., Moreau, D., Weissman, M. M., & Klerman, G. L. (1993). *Interpersonal psychotherapy for depressed adolescents.* New York: Guilford Press.

Mufson, L., Moreau, D., Weissman, M. M., Wickramaratne, P., Martin, J., & Samoilov, A. (1994). Modification of interpersonal psychotherapy with depressed adolescents (IPT-A): Phase I and II studies. *Journal of the American Academy of Child and Adolescent Psychiatry, 33*(5), 695–705.

Mufson, L., Weissman, M. M., Moreau, D., & Garfinkel, R. (1999). Efficacy of interpersonal psychotherapy for depressed adolescents. *Archives of General Psychiatry, 56,* 573–579.

National Center for Health Statistics. (2000). *Deaths: Final data for 1998* (Vol. 48). Retrieved November 22, 2002, from http://www.cdc.gov/nchs/data/nvsr/nvsr48/nvs48_11.pdf

National Institute of Health Consensus Development Panel on Depression in Late Life. (1992). Diagnosis and treatment of depression in late life. *Journal of the American Medical Association, 268,* 1018–1024.

Puig-Antich, J., Goetz, D., Davies, M., Kaplan, T., Davies, S., Ostrow, L., et al. (1989). A controlled family history study of prepubertal major depressive disorder. *Archives of General Psychiatry, 46*(5), 406–418.

Rao, U., Ryan, N. D., Birmaher, B., Dahl, R. E., Williamson, D. E., Kaufman, J., et al. (1995). Unipolar depression in adolescents: Clinical outcome in adulthood. *Journal of the American Academy of Child and Adolescent Psychiatry, 34*(5), 566–578.

Reed, M. K. (1994). Social skills training to reduce depression in adolescents. *Adolescence, 29*(114), 293–302.

Rosello, J., & Bernal, G. (1999). Treatment of depression in Puerto Rican adolescents: The efficacy of cognitive-behavioral and interpersonal treatments. *Journal of Consulting and Clinical Psychology, 67,* 734–745.

Rotheram-Borus, M. J., Piacentini, J., Cantwell, C., Belin, T. R., & Song, J. (2000). The 18-month impact of an emergency room intervention for adolescent suicide attempters. *Journal of Consulting and Clinical Psychology, 68,* 1081–1083.

Sanford, M., Boyle, M., Offord, D., McCleary, L., & Steele, M. (2002, October). *A controlled trial of adjunctive family psychoeducation in depressed adolescents.* Poster presented at the meetings of the American Academy of Child and Adolescent Psychiatry, San Francisco.

Schwartz, J. A. J., Kaslow, N. J., Racusin, G. R., & Carton, E. R. (1998). Interpersonal family therapy for childhood depression. In V. B. Van Hasselt & M. Hersen (Eds.), *Handbook of psychological treatment protocols for children and adolescents* (pp. 109–151). Mahwah, NJ: Erlbaum.

Todd, R. D., Neuman, R., Geller, B., Fox, L. W., & Hickok, J. (1993). Genetic studies of affective disorders: Should we be starting with childhood onset probands? *Journal of the American Academy of Child and Adolescent Psychiatry, 32*(6), 1164–1171.

Tompson, M. C., Pierre, C. B., Asarnow, J. R., McNeil, F. M., & Fogler, J. M. (2003, June). Adapting a family-based treatment for depressed preadolescents. Poster presented at the annual Conference of the International Society for Research in Child and Adolescent Psychopathology, Sydney, Australia.

TORDIA. *Treatment of Resistant Depression in Adolescents (TORDIA). Sponsored by the National Institute of Mental Health.* Retrieved November 22, 2004, from http://www.clinicaltrials.gov/ct/show/NCT00018902?order=1

Treatment for Adolescents with Depression Study Team. (2003). Treatment of Adolescents with Depression Study (TADS): Rationale, design, and methods. *Journal of the American Academy of Child and Adolescent Psychiatry, 42,* 531–542.

U.S. Food and Drug Administration. (2003). FDA public health advisory: Reports of suicidality in pediatric patients being treated with antidepressant medications for major depressive disorder (MDD). Retrieved November 23, 2004, from http://www.fda.gov/cder/drug/advisory/mdd.htm.

Vostanis, P., Feehan, C., Grattan, E., & Bickerton, W. L. (1996). A randomised controlled out-patient trial of cognitive–behavioural treatment for children and adolescents with depression: 9-month follow-up. *Journal of Affective Disorders, 40*(1, 2), 105–116.

Wickramaratne, P. J., Greenwald, S., & Weissman, M. M. (2000). Psychiatric disorders in the relatives of probands with prepubertal-onset or adolescent-onset major depression. *Journal of the American Academy of Child and Adolescent Psychiatry, 39*(11), 1396–1405.

Wickramaratne, P. J., & Weissman, M. M. (1998). Onset of psychopathology in offspring by developmental phase and parental depression. *Journal of the American Academy of Child and Adolescent Psychiatry, 37*(9), 933–942.

Williamson, D. E., Ryan, N. D., Birmaher, B., Dahl, R. E., Kaufman, J., Rao, U., et al. (1995). A case-control family history study of depression in adolescents. *Journal of the American Academy of Child and Adolescent Psychiatry, 34*(12), 1596–1607.

Wood, A., Harrington, R., & Moore, A. (1996). Controlled trial of a brief cognitive-behavioural intervention in adolescent patients with depressive disorders. *Journal of Child Psychology and Psychiatry and Allied Disciplines, 37*(6), 737–746.

18

Marital Discord in the Context of a Depressive Episode: Research on Efficacy and Effectiveness

Steven R. H. Beach and Maya E. Gupta

Couples in which one partner is diagnosable as depressed are encountered by virtually every marital therapist. In addition, couples in which one or both partners have significant levels of depressive symptoms are the norm rather than the exception in marital therapy. Similarly, therapists treating depressed clients individually often discover that marital distress is a major influence in many aspects of their clients' lives. In response to the apparent interconnection of marital discord and adult unipolar depression, the topic of marital therapy for depressed adults has become an important focus of research. Several questions have been partially answered: Do marital problems precede and predict continuation of depressive symptoms or episodes of depression? Does marital therapy for depression produce improvement in couple distress, in depression, or both? Can marital distress be treated while a depressive episode is ongoing or only after it is over? Would a successful individually focused intervention for a depressive episode cause marital stress to disappear? What specific culture, age, and gender features influence the relationship between marital distress and depression?

Our goal in the current chapter is to address these and other questions by presenting major findings in the literature to date and by summarizing them into a relatively simple argument as follows. Marital problems are often present for depressed persons; these problems are serious, and they carry unacceptable consequences for those depressed clients who suffer with them. There are a number of good treatments for marital discord and one approach already meets criteria to be designated efficacious and specific in relieving marital discord in the context of depression. Individual treatments for depression cannot be expected to relieve marital discord on average and for some couples may actually worsen marital discord. Accordingly, it is appropriate to redouble our efforts to ensure that marital discord occurring in the context of depression is treated with the seriousness it deserves. We conclude with a discussion of future research directions, including the need for research on treatment and prevention, the biobehavioral underpinnings of marital discord and its effects on mental health, an increased understanding of the basic structure of depression and marital discord, and the potential implications of relational diagnoses for ensuring adequate attention to marital discord in the context of depression.

■ Investigating the Relationship Between Marital Distress and Depression

Not all depressed persons are alike either in their symptom pattern or in the role that marital discord plays in their depression. Unipolar depression may occur as a single episode. However, current episodes of depression are much more likely to be recurrences than initial episodes (Coyne, Pepper, & Flynn, 1999), and because the average age at first episode has decreased dramatically over the past century (Weissman, Bruce, Leaf, Florio, & Holzer, 1991), current episodes are particularly likely to be recurrences when the client is old enough to be part of a married couple. At the same time, even those with recurrent depression are not actively "in episode" most of their lives (Judd et al., 1998). Accordingly, it is possible for clients to have marital problems that do not entirely overlap with their depressive illnesses. One can therefore ask research questions about the temporal patterning and development of particular episodes of depression in relation to development of marital discord.

Comorbidity Between Depression and Marital Discord

It is well known that marital distress is often present among depressed patients and that marital distress and depressive symptoms covary. In an exhaustive review of the quantitative marital literature, Whisman (2001) found that, across 26 cross-sectional studies, marital quality was negatively associated with depressive symptoms for both women ($r = -.42$) and men ($r = -.37$). Accordingly, there is a moderate relationship between global marital distress and depression and a significant, albeit small, gender difference in the magnitude of that relationship. This association suggests that marital discord and depression may be comorbid, but does not provide estimates of the rate of comorbidity. Because there is no commonly accepted criteria for "marital discord," at present our best estimates of comorbidity come from studies using cutoffs on standard, well-validated measures of marital distress.

What Percentage of Depressed Persons Exceeds Current Cutoffs for Marital Discord? Whisman (2001) examined the level of marital adjustment in published studies that examined both diagnostic status and level of marital dissatisfaction, excluding those in which participants had to be both depressed and maritally distressed. Based on the resulting sample of 493 depressed clients from 14 studies, Whisman reported that the average marital adjustment score of persons diagnosed with depression was in the distressed range and approximately 1.75 *SD* below the comparison sample, with an average Dyadic Adjustment Scale (DAS) (Spanier, 1976) score of 93. These statistics suggest that a need for relationship repair is associated with over half the cases of diagnosed depression. Thus, marital relationships are often distressed among depressed men and women, and rates of comorbidity between marital discord and depression may exceed 50% (see also Whiffen & Johnson, 1998, for a review of the postpartum literature).

However, marital adjustment scores provide only a cursory and impoverished assessment of marital problems, and one might wonder if a more detailed look would also suggest the presence of marital problems in need of marital therapy. Partially remedying this problem, Coyne, Thompson, and Palmer (2002) reported a study comparing 38 depressed outpatients and 35 depressed inpatients to a community sample. Replicating and extending the Whisman (2001) results, they found that approximately two thirds of the outpatients and approximately half of the inpatients scored in the distressed range of the DAS. They also provided an excellent level of clinical detail regarding the types of complaints and patterns of affection characteristic of couples with a depressed wife. Especially telling, 42% of the depressed outpatients compared to 0% of the comparison sample reported that their spouse did not fulfill their emotional needs, and more than 60% of both husbands and wives in the depressed outpatient sample reported difficulty discussing problems compared to 24 and 37% of community wives and husbands, respectively (see also Zlotnick, Kohn, Keitner, & Della Grotta, 2000). These data support the conclusion that comorbidity between depression and marital discord may approach the level of comorbidity between depression and other types of major psychopathology.

How Does Comorbidity Between Depression and Marital Discord Develop?   Illustrating the vicious cycle that links depressive symptoms and marital difficulties, Davila, Bradbury, Cohan, and Tochluk (1997) found that wives with more symptoms of depression were more negative in their supportive behaviors toward their husbands and in their expectations regarding partner support. These negative behaviors and expectations, in turn, were related to greater marital stress. Finally, closing the loop, level of marital stress predicted subsequent depressive symptoms (controlling for earlier symptoms). Likewise, in his review of self-propagating processes in depression, Joiner (2000) highlights the propensity for depressed persons to seek negative feedback, to engage in excessive reassurance-seeking, to avoid conflict by withdrawing, and to elicit changes in the partner's view of them. In each case, the behavior resulting from the individual's depression carries the potential to generate increased interpersonal stress or to shift the response of others in a negative direction. Consistent with a stress generation framework (Hammen, 1991), Joiner suggests that increased interpersonal negativity, in turn, helps maintain depressive symptoms.

At the same time, marital events have considerable potential to exacerbate depressive symptoms. Cano and O'Leary (2000), for example, found that humiliating events, such as partner infidelity and threats of marital dissolution, resulted in a sixfold increase in the diagnosis of depression and that this increased risk remained after controlling for family and personal history of depression. Further,

Whisman and Bruce (1999) examined the relationship between marital dissatis-faction at baseline and 12-month incidence of major depressive episode in the New Haven Epidemiological Catchment Area study among the 904 persons who did not meet criteria for a major depressive episode at baseline. Dissatisfied spouses were found to be nearly 3 times as likely as nondistressed spouses to develop an episode of depression during the year; the relationship remained significant after controlling for demographics and depression history, and the effect was not moderated by gender. Examining within-subject covariation between marital dissatisfaction and depressive symptoms, Karney (2001) showed that marital dissatisfaction was linked to depressive symptoms within individuals over time. Suggesting that the link may be causal, Whisman, Weinstock, and Uebelacker (2002) found that both marital distress and depression predicted greater reactivity to problem-solving discussions and so greater increases in depressive symptoms following attempts to discuss current marital difficulties. Further supporting the potential for marital distress to precede and aggravate depressive symptoms, Beach, Katz, Kim, and Brody (2003) found support for the general marital discord model (Beach, Sandeen, & O'Leary, 1990), with each partner's own marital satisfaction at time one predicting his or her own later depression, even after including the effect of time 1 depressive symptoms in the model.

The potential for marital discord to predict the onset of depressive symptoms, as well as the start of a new depressive episode, suggests the potential to prevent some relapses and new cases of depression by attending to marital problems. How many cases of depression might be prevented by providing successful marital in-tervention to the general population? In the Whisman and Bruce (1999) sample, 30% of new cases of depression during the year were attributable to baseline marital discord, suggesting the number of cases that could be prevented if marital discord could be prevented or alleviated prior to the onset of the depression. Further, between 30 and 45% of all new episodes were preceded by marital problems that were discernible in the absence of a depressive episode at baseline. These data suggest a potentially large population who might be benefited by the availability of marital therapy prior to the onset of a depressive episode. Unfortunately, to date, practical limitations have precluded the construction of large-scale, targeted in-terventions designed to reduce risk of depression among the maritally discordant. However, it has proven more feasible to design tests of the utility of marital therapy in helping treat an episode of depression after it has arisen in the context of marital discord.

Is There a Case for Intervention?

The potential for depression and marital discord to influence one another suggests the prudence of providing intervention for marital discord in some cases of de-pression. In order to break the vicious cycle maintaining the depression, it may be necessary to work with associated interpersonal problems. Even if intervention does not produce rapid reduction in depressive symptoms, a growing body of literature suggests that failure to address marital issues in therapy for depression may interfere with the recovery process and increase the risk for relapse (cf. Hooley & Gotlib, 2000; Hooley & Teasdale, 1989). Accordingly, marital relationships may be particularly useful targets of intervention for depressed individuals.

■ Current State of the Research on Marital Therapy for Depression

The Question of Efficacy

There are a number of well-specified approaches to marital therapy that are known to be efficacious or possibly efficacious, including behavioral marital therapy, cognitive-behavioral marital therapy, emotion-focused therapy, insight-oriented marital therapy, and strategic marital therapy (see Baucom, Shoam, Mueser, Daiuto, & Stickle, 1998). We have no strong a priori reason to expect differential efficacy of these different approaches when applied to marital discord occurring in the context of depression. However, because not all the approaches known to be efficacious treatments of marital discord have been tested in the context of depression, we are somewhat limited in the conclusions we can draw. Of the several studies that have examined the efficacy of marital therapy in reducing symptoms of depression and in enhancing marital satisfaction in couples with a depressed partner, three trials compared behavioral marital therapy to individual therapy (Beach & O'Leary, 1992; Emanuels-Zuurveen & Emmelkamp, 1996; Jacobson, Dobson, Fruzzetti, Schmaling, & Salusky, 1991), rendering this the best supported approach to treatment at present. Two trials involved adaptation of individual therapies for depression to a couples format (Emanuels-Zuurveen & Emmelkamp, 1997; Foley, Rounsaville, Weissman, Sholomskas, & Chevron, 1989). There has also been one trial of a cognitive couple therapy (Teichman, Bar-El, Shor, Sirota, & Elizur, 1995) and one trial comparing marital therapy to antidepressant medication (Leff et al., 2000). However, these latter two studies did not utilize empirically supported treatments for marital discord and did not examine change in marital satisfaction. Because of the importance of using empirically supported treatments as well as the value of assessing marital satisfaction, we first examine those studies that meet these criteria.

Three studies compared behavioral marital therapy to individual therapy, with similar results. Jacobson et al. (1991) randomly assigned 60 married, depressed women to behavioral marital therapy (BMT), individual cognitive therapy (CT), or a treatment combining BMT and CT. Couples were not selected for the presence of marital discord and so could be divided into those who were more and less maritally distressed. Beach and O'Leary (1992) randomly assigned 45 couples in which the wife was depressed to one of three conditions: (a) conjoint BMT, (b) individual CT, or (c) a 15-week waiting-list condition. To be included in the study, both partners had to score in the discordant range of the DAS and report ongoing marital discord. Emanuels-Zuurveen and Emmelkamp (1996) assigned 27 depressed outpatients to either individual cognitive-behavioral therapy or communication-focused marital therapy. They included both depressed husbands ($n = 13$) and depressed wives ($n = 14$). Consistently across the three studies, behavioral marital therapy and individual therapy yielded equivalent outcomes when the dependent variable was depressive symptoms and a better outcome in marital therapy than in individual therapy when the dependent variable was marital functioning. In addition, in one of the studies, marital therapy was found to be significantly better than a wait-list control group (Beach & O'Leary, 1992).

Foley et al. (1989) tested an individual therapy for depression adapted to a couples format. In their study, 18 depressed outpatients were randomly assigned to either individual interpersonal psychotherapy (IPT) or a newly developed, couple format version of IPT. Consistent with the findings of the studies comparing BMT with an individual approach, Foley et al. found that participants in the two treatments improved equally on symptoms of depression. Both interventions also produced equal enhancement of general interpersonal functioning. However, participants receiving couple IPT reported marginally higher marital satisfaction scores on the Locke-Wallace Short Marital Adjustment Test and scored significantly higher on one subscale of the DAS at session 16, indicating an advantage of a conjoint format with an explicit focus on communication relative to individually administered IPT.

Spouses have also been incorporated in the treatment of depression for persons not reporting marital distress. Spouse-aided cognitive therapy, as developed by Emanuels-Zuurveen and Emmelkamp (1997), was similar to individual cognitive therapy, except that the spouse attended all sessions, working with the depressed individual in developing strategies to cope with the depression. They found that spouse-aided cognitive therapy was equally as but not more effective than individual therapy in treating depression. Neither treatment had an effect on marital dissatisfaction.

Two of the studies reviewed above indicate that the effect of marital therapy on the level of symptoms of depression is mediated by changes in marital adjustment. Beach and O'Leary (1992) found that posttherapy marital satisfaction fully accounted for the effect of marital therapy on depression but posttherapy satisfaction did not mediate the effect of individual cognitive therapy on depression. Consistent with these results, Jacobson et al. (1991) found that changes in marital adjustment and depression covaried for depressed individuals who received marital therapy, but not for those who received cognitive therapy. Therefore, it appears that marital therapy influences depressive symptoms either by enhancing marital satisfaction or else by producing changes in the marital environment associated with enhanced satisfaction. Cognitive therapy appears to work through a different mechanism of change (i.e., cognitive change; see Whisman, 1993).

Two additional studies have examined nonempirically supported marital therapies in the treatment of depression. In both cases the studies do not provide an assessment of change in the level of marital satisfaction and have significant methodological flaws. Nonetheless, they provide some incremental support for the potential value of marital therapy in the treatment of depression. Teichman et al. (1995) compared cognitive marital therapy (CMT) to cognitive therapy and a no-treatment control group in a sample of 45 married, depressed individuals. CMT was superior to cognitive therapy and no treatment at posttherapy assessment. Leff et al. (2000) conducted a randomized control trial of antidepressants ($n = 37$) versus couple therapy ($n = 40$) in the treatment and maintenance of major depressive disorder. Depression improved as a function of therapy in both groups (but only on the Hamilton Rating Scale for Depression). At the same time, participants in the couple therapy condition demonstrated a significant advantage, both posttreatment and at a 2-year follow-up (but only on the Beck Depression Inventory).

It is clear that efficacious forms for marital therapy can be safely and usefully applied to a depressed population. Furthermore, BMT emerges as a specific and efficacious treatment for marital discord, even when the marital discord is occurring in the context of depression. That is, BMT has been shown in three independent studies to produce significant change in marital distress in a discordant and depressed population, and in each case it has outperformed a control group and/or an alternative intervention. Individual treatments for depression appear less able, on average, to provide relief from the symptoms of marital discord.

The research reviewed above suggests that marital therapy has the potential to help reduce depressive symptoms as well. By alleviating the marital stress that may be maintaining the episode, the marital therapist can help alleviate both the symptoms of depression and the salient marital problems that may be so distressing for the depressed individual.

The Question of Effectiveness

Incremental Utility of Marital Therapy.   One potential barrier to the widespread adoption of marital therapy approaches in the treatment of depression is the belief that few people have a better outcome with marital therapy approaches than with individual approaches to treatment that are already widely available. This is a question of efficacy. As described above, the current body of work comparing individual to dyadic approaches suggests that while depression outcome may be equivalent across approaches, marital therapy produces superior results in terms of marital functioning. Therefore, there appears to be sound evidence for the utility of disseminating marital treatments for depression in addition to those individual treatments that are already available. Other barriers to dissemination may be conceptualized as questions about the effectiveness of marital therapy for depression. Effectiveness refers to the extent to which a potentially efficacious treatment can be made available to potential consumers and the extent to which it will be accepted by them. Most simply, if no one will utilize an efficacious approach or if the side effects force most people to discontinue treatment prematurely, an "efficacious" treatment may be rendered "ineffective." Accordingly, issues related to effectiveness and the enhancement of effectiveness are conceptually dependent on treatment efficacy, but are of central importance in determining the overall utility of an intervention.

Will Partners Participate?   One potential barrier to the use of marital interventions in the research and treatment of adult depression is the possibility that the partner will refuse to participate in the therapy. This obstacle might appear in randomized trials as either refusal to be assigned to marital intervention or premature discontinuation of treatment. Although refusal of a partner to participate need not preclude a systemic focus, if it is quite common it may limit the advantages of marital interventions relative to widely available individual alternatives. For example, one might wonder why it is necessary to attempt marital therapy in an individual format when a well-developed alternative exists in the form of individually administered IPT. Currently, however, there is equivocal evidence regarding the degree to which refusal to participate represents a threat to the effectiveness of marital therapy for depression. On the one hand, an effectiveness study of marital therapy for depression conducted 25 years ago in a primary care setting failed when it proved impossible to enlist enough husbands to participate (McLean & Miles, 1975). On the other hand, the Leff et al. (2000) study reviewed above found much greater acceptance of marital therapy than cognitive therapy, and their marital therapy condition produced a significantly lower dropout rate than did their medication condition. As these considerations suggest, an important focus of research on marital interventions for depressed persons will be to examine consumer response to referrals for such treatments. Research that closely monitors the issues that render referral for marital treatment more and less acceptable to depressed persons and their partners seems particularly timely (for a discussion of general issues and directions in the relationship between efficacy and effectiveness research see Nathan, Stuart, & Dolan, 2000).

Need Partners Participate?   Backing up one step, we may ask ourselves whether partner satisfaction even matters. If the need for partner participation could be eliminated, this potential challenge to the effectiveness of marital approaches could be eliminated as well. A number of systemic approaches do not require spouse participation and yet retain a focus on the larger family system. Likewise, interpersonal therapy for depression has an explicit focus on various types of role disputes but does not require participation of the partner. Finally, recent innovations in marital therapy have focused on removing the requirement for spouses to participate in tandem (e.g., Halford, 1998) and for some time Coyne has suggested "shuttle diplomacy" as a model for marital therapy with depressed clients (e.g., Coyne & Benazon, 2001). If partner satisfaction is not consequential in predicting change in depressive symptoms, then it may make more sense to focus our therapeutic attention only on the depressed individual. In this way we would sidestep the potential problem of partner recruitment.

Suggesting caution in the use of non-conjoint formats in marital therapy for depression, however, is the research with IPT reviewed above. The Foley et al. (1989) study suggested that IPT provided to an individual was not as effective at dealing with marital problems as was conjoint-couple IPT, which included a focus on couple communication. Similarly suggesting the potential value of a conjoint format is the recent study we conducted (Beach et al., 2004). In addition to the primary finding of each partner's time 1 depressive symptoms predicting his or her time 2 depressive symptoms, we also found significant effects of each partner's satisfaction on the other's later depressive symptoms. These results suggest we should hesitate to move to individual-level interventions designed to enhance the marital satisfaction of depressed persons. If a partner's satisfaction cannot be enhanced without his or her presence in therapy, then effects on depression of an individual-level approach to relationship enhancement may be diminished.

Why might partner satisfaction be important? One possibility is that partner dissatisfaction is related to deficits in positive, supportive behavior that are important in the recovery process. An elaboration of this type of thinking can be found in work by Katz and Beach (1997), in which it was shown that having one's low self-esteem verified by a relative paucity of small positive supportive behaviors from the partner strengthened the effect of one's own low self-esteem on depressive symptoms. In addition to suggesting the importance of spouse involvement in marital therapy, this type of research indicates the potential benefit of increasing positive interactions even among the nondistressed depressed. In particular, there may be utility in efforts to establish better methods of increasing positive interactions among depressed inpatients for whom such interactions may have eroded considerably (Cordova & Gee, 2001; Coyne et al., 2002). This possibility invites contrasts with methods of spouse involvement that do not have a focus on decreasing negative exchanges and increasing positive exchanges, e.g., spouse education, which has produced mixed results in the treatment of unipolar depressed, adult inpatients using a psychoeducational framework (e.g., Clarkin et al., 1990).

As the results reviewed above suggest, there is room for differing opinions on the importance of retaining a conjoint format for marital therapy for depression. However, at present it is appropriate to view partner involvement as a necessary element of the marital approaches that have been demonstrated to be efficacious in the treatment of depression and that have been shown to be efficacious and specific in the treatment of marital discord in the context of depression. However, the evidence against non-conjoint formats is suggestive only.

The Question of Specificity

Do Any Depressed Clients Show a Uniquely Beneficial Response to Marital Therapy? O'Leary, Risso, and Beach (1990) found that for those depressed persons whose depressive episode followed a period of marital discord, marital therapy was uniquely beneficial compared to cognitive therapy. The effect was rather striking. When discordant and depressed couples whose marital problems preceded their depression were given marital therapy, their marital satisfaction improved just as it did for others receiving marital therapy. In contrast, when the depressed wives in these couples received individual cognitive therapy they showed deterioration in marital satisfaction over the course of therapy. Accordingly, there was an important and unique benefit to wives in this group of receiving marital therapy as the initial treatment for their depressive episode. Because the number of persons for whom marital problems preceded the current episode of depression is rather large (Whisman & Bruce, 1999), there is good reason to believe that many depressed patients could benefit uniquely from the provision of marital therapy early in the course of treatment, not just after symptomatic relief from depression has already been achieved.

In future outcome research on the use of marital interventions for depression it may be important to examine directly the moderating role of temporal precedence on response to marital therapy. It is possible that this distinction may prove important in determining when a conjoint approach to marital intervention is likely to fare better than a non-conjoint format. Alternatively, as suggested above, it may indicate when little or no direct attention to marital distress is necessary as part of the treatment process for depression.

Gender of the Depressed Partner.   In the studies reviewed above, the depressed partner has, as a rule, been the wife. In the Beach and O'Leary (1992) and the Jacobson et al. (1991) studies all the identified patients were wives. In the Foley et al. (1989) and the Emanuels-Zuurveen and Emmelkamp (1996) studies, the majority of identified patients were wives. Accordingly, although there has been no evidence to date of differential response to marital therapy by husbands and wives, it is not an issue that has received the close attention it deserves. Rates of major depressive disorder are approximately twice as high in women as in men (Kessler, McGonagle, Swartz, Blazer, & Nelson, 1993). Also, as determined by Whisman's (2001) review, the magnitude of the correlation between marital satisfaction and depression across studies was significantly, albeit only slightly, stronger for wives than for husbands. However, it appears that husbands also become depressed in an interpersonal context, that marital distress can precipitate depressive symptoms in husbands, and that husbands' depression can contribute to stress in a household (Beach et al., 2003; Fincham, Beach, Harold, & Osborne, 1997; Whisman & Bruce, 1999). Accordingly, there is no reason at present to assume that marital therapy is efficacious only for wives and so to restrict marital therapy to depressed wives. However, it may be that marital therapy for depressed husbands could be modified to render it more effective and acceptable to husbands, and this remains an important area for future empirical work.

Married Versus Unmarried Couples.   It should be noted that married couples have been the standard population sampled for the development and testing of the interventions described in this chapter. In recognition of this limitation of the database, we have used the term *marital therapy* to describe treatments for couples, envisioning the modal couple in treatment as a married one. However, increasing acceptance of cohabitation for unmarried partners may be leading to an increase in the number of unmarried couples entering marital therapy. In addition, there may be good clinical reasons for offering relationship therapy to persons who are not in marital relationships. For example, recent research suggests that difficulties in intimate relationships other than marital relationships may be relatively common among suicide attempters presenting for treatment in emergency room settings in urban centers (Kaslow, Twomey, Brooks, Thompson, & Reynolds, 2001). Accordingly, there has been a tendency to suggest that conjoint treatments developed for married couples should be readily generalizable to nonmarried couples. In the absence of research documenting the applicability of marital interventions to unmarried couples, our field has perhaps been too quick to assume that these two populations are fundamentally equivalent. To the contrary, sociological research has documented differences in attitudes toward the nature of relationships and partners' roles in those relationships, as well as a host of other variables potentially salient in therapy (Clarkberg, Stolzenberg, & Waite, 1995). Additionally, cohabiting couples exhibit higher rates of violence than married couples (Brownridge & Halli, 2002), and to the extent that the occurrence of either prior or ongoing intimate partner violence is a significant issue in conducting conjoint therapy or in the development of depressive symptoms (Beach et al., 2004), attention clearly needs to be paid to this phenomenon, as increasing numbers of cohabiting couples present for treatment.

Couples of Varying Ethnicities.   While other chapters in this volume more specifically address the influence of ethnicity on family distress processes and depression, we would be remiss in failing to acknowledge the importance of this topic here. Just as the modal sample in treatment research thus far has been married, these samples have had limited variability in demographics, using primarily White couples. Yet ethnicity (a person's identity in relation to race or other aspects of culture) is influential in relationship processes, as well as in the manifestation and perception of individual psychopathology, such as depression. Furthermore, even if efficacious treatments are developed based on non-White samples, these treatments may not be effective if utilization of psychological services is uncommon or stigmatized in the population to which they are offered. Accordingly, a substantial research effort is needed to examine the applicability of marital interventions to African American, Hispanic American, and Asian American married couples. It is likely that the effort to generalize results will be complicated by substantial within-group heterogeneity on such dimensions as acculturation, language, and cultural variation. Nonetheless, the utility of marital therapy for depression will need to be examined within these differing contexts to ensure its efficacy and effectiveness when applied beyond the populations already examined. One benefit of this examination is that as marital therapy for depression is offered to an increasingly diverse population of consumers, one might anticipate the development of important new insights regarding potential obstacles to be overcome as well as new promising techniques for delivering services. Accordingly, in addition to its importance in addressing issues of efficacy, application to a more diverse population is also likely to address issues of effectiveness.

Clinical Decision Making

The data for the efficacy of marital therapy for depression are compelling. The data for the efficacy of marital therapy in relieving the marital problems that so often trouble depressed persons are especially clear. As future research focuses on issues of effectiveness, efficiency, and application to a diverse range of potential consumers, it is important to begin to formalize guidelines for the application of marital therapy to marital discord occurring in the context of depression. Fortunately, given the current data, we can begin to formulate initial guidelines about who should be treated from a marital focus and who may be better served by an individual focus (cognitive therapy, interpersonal therapy, or pharmacotherapy).

When depressed individuals report no or mild marital distress, spouses often may be involved as helpful adjuncts to therapy (e.g., Emanuels-Zuurveen & Emmelkamp, 1997). Conversely, when depressed individuals report substantial difficulties in marital relationships, and indicate that the current episode of depression followed the onset of the relationship problems, an initial approach that focuses on systemic problems (e.g., marital therapy) may produce positive outcomes and provide benefits that are greater than those obtained from an individual focus (e.g., Beach & O'Leary, 1992). When depressed individuals report substantial relationship problems, but these emerged only after the onset of the depressive episode, an initial focus on either the individual and his or her symptoms of depression or an initial focus on the relational problems may be appropriate and useful. However, there is unlikely to be a unique benefit to an initial systemic focus relative to an individual focus (e.g., O'Leary et al., 1990).

■ Future Directions for Research

In addition to expanded treatment outcome studies and examination of clinical processes related to recruitment, retention, and efficiency of marital interventions to treat or prevent episodes of depression, it will also be important to focus on tests of basic theoretical propositions about the link between marital processes, biological processes, and depression. Of particular importance in this regard are potential changes in our understanding of the structure of depression and marital discord. Accordingly, after providing a broad outline of needed research, we provide a detailed overview of future directions for research on the basic structure of marital discord and depression. If we come to a new understanding of these constructs, it is clear that our discussion of the connection between the two constructs will need to be revised accordingly.

Intervention Research

Outcome Trials. Of primary importance for the health of the area is additional research on the efficacy of marital therapy for depression and its applicability to particular groups of individuals. Research designs that replicate the utility of marital therapy as a primary or adjunctive intervention for depression among persons whose marital problems preceded their current episode of depression will be particularly useful. Likewise, effectiveness research that demonstrates strategies to engage partners of depressed patients is sorely needed, and this is particularly true for research focused on community or cultural contexts in which marital therapy might be less familiar or less readily accepted. Similarly, it is time for research to go beyond efficacy and effectiveness and begin to focus as well on questions of efficiency. That is, it will be quite helpful for research to identify delivery methods that decrease the amount of time required by both therapists and participants. Likewise, it will be useful to focus on methods of delivery that overcome geographic barriers to participation, such as living in rural or underserved areas. In addition to the obvious implications for patient adherence and the potential to reach a larger population, more efficient approaches to marital therapy for depression also have the potential to render marital interventions available to the full spectrum of those who might benefit. This should greatly increase the appeal of using marital approaches as a primary and as an adjunctive treatment for depression.

Prevention Research.   Prevention trials raise a variety of methodological issues in addition to those associated with efficacy trials. Accordingly, evidence of clinical efficacy is not sufficient to demonstrate that an approach would be useful in preventing the onset of a particular problem. However, existing evidence of the value of marital therapy for many depressed persons provides a good foundation for hypothesizing that prevention work at the community level could have an impact as well. That is, it would be useful to examine the effects of increasing marital success rates in a community as a means of decreasing depression. Of particular importance in such trials would be to tailor interventions to fit the community context and to utilize methods that take full advantage of informal lines of communication within communities. Accordingly, research on prevention should focus on particular community contexts and attempt to change community norms at the same time that particular couples are helped to change their patterns of relating to one another.

Research on the Biobehavioral Foundations of Marital Discord

Relatively little is known about the biological foundations of the connection between marital discord and depression or the biological changes that may occur as a function of long-term marital discord. There are clues, however, that these changes may be substantial. In particular, hostile behaviors during conflict are related to alterations in immunological (Kiecolt-Glaser, Glaser, et al., 1997; Kiecolt-Glaser, Malarkey, et al., 1993), endocrine (Kiecolt-Glaser, Glaser, et al., 1997; Malarkey, Kiecolt-Glaser, Pearl, & Glaser, 1994), and cardiovascular (Ewart, Taylor, Kraemer, & Agras, 1991) functioning, and these effects appear to be mediated by chronic, negative emotional states (Kiecolt-Glaser, McGuire, & Robles, 2002). Although consequential for both husbands and wives, marital conflict has more pronounced health consequences for wives (Kiecolt-Glaser, Glaser, et al., 1997; Malarkey et al., 1994). These findings suggest that there may be an important but understudied biological cascade that eventually links marital discord to depression. Mapping the link between marital discord and depression in terms of intervening biological processes would undoubtedly lead to new ideas about both vulnerabilities and strategies for prevention and remediation.

Research on the Structure of Depression and Marital Discord

One recent development in the field of psychopathology has particular potential to lead to new applications and a new understanding of the connection between marital discord and depression. This important development is the introduction and spread of *taxometrics* as a tool for examining the "true structure" of constructs such as depressive symptomatology and marital satisfaction. A question that has plagued the literature on marriage and depression for many years is whether findings about the link between marital distress and depression at low levels of symptoms can be generalized to links that may exist at clinical levels of symptoms. Taxometrics provides a method for addressing this fundamental issue. Since much of our current understanding of the relationship between marital processes and depression is based on generalization from nonclinical levels of marital dissatisfaction and/or depressive symptomatology, the results of taxometric investigations have broad implications for our confidence about the generalizations typically drawn about this relationship.

First, it is important to give a brief review of the taxometric methods that have been introduced to the field of psychology by Paul Meehl (Waller & Meehl, 1998). In Meehl's MAXCOV procedure, two indicators of a construct are used to estimate the covariance between indicators at various levels of a third indicator. By repeating the analysis for all possible sets of item indicators, and averaging the results, it is possible to generate an average curve that represents the covariance among items at increasing symptom levels. If the curves resulting from the MAXCOV analyses display a prominent elevation and this elevation is relatively consistent in its placement, this indicates a taxonic solution. In addition, using the placement of the elevation, it is possible to generate base rate estimates for the taxon. As a result, using taxometric procedures one can determine both whether there is a distinct group that is qualitatively different and, if so, with what frequency membership in that group occurs.

Taxometrics of Depression.   Ruscio and Ruscio (2000) reported that commonly used indicators of depressive symptomatology behaved as a continuum and that there was no apparent "breaking point" at which depressive symptoms became qualitatively different. In this conclusion they were supported by earlier work with twins that also failed to find any clear boundaries between depressed and nondepressed states (e.g., Kendler & Gardner, 1998). This would be rather good news for the purposes of this chapter, as it would suggest that associations observed at any given level of symptoms may have implications for other symptom levels, whether in the clinical or subclinical range. For example, results from large-scale longitudinal research should be readily generalizable to relationships at the clinical end of the continuum.

However, there have been previous reports suggesting that the strength of the association between marital discord and depression may be greater for when the focus is on major depression rather than subclinical dysphoria (Whisman, 2001). Reopening the debate on continuity and discontinuity across different levels of depressive symptoms was a paper by Beach and Amir (2003). They found that a subset of depressive symptoms do show a breaking point and may identify qualitatively different experiences of depression. If future research supports the validity of their proposed distinction between "distress" and "homeostatic disruption," it will raise the question of whether marital interventions are differentially efficacious in the treatment of distress depending on the presence of this homeostatic disruption.

If some symptoms of depression form a continuum of distress, whereas others indicate a shift to a qualitatively different experience, much of what we think we know about the association between marital problems and depression may need to be revised (see Coyne & Benazon, 2001, for an elaboration of this view). At a minimum, much of what we currently believe we know may be based on measures of depression that conflate distress and homeostatic disruption. If these or other sets of symptoms should prove to function differently and are related differently to marital processes, this could lead to a very different understanding of the way marital processes come to be associated with depression. In turn, this may suggest novel approaches to treatment and prevention. However, the examination of the basic structure of depression is far from complete and so it would be premature to reformulate our conclusions at present. Accordingly, this is an area of research in psychopathology that requires the close attention of those interested in the link between marital discord and depression.

Taxometrics of Marital Conflict.   Just as taxometric research may lead to considerable changes in the way we view the fundamental nature of depression, our understanding of the nature of marital conflict could also change based on the results of future taxometric studies. In the existing literature, marital distress has primarily been treated as a continuum, as evidenced by the use of dimensional scoring systems on such instruments as the DAS. There have been calls to revise the dominant "bipolar" conceptualization of marital distress and to recognize its likely two-dimensional structure (Fincham, Beach, & Kemp-Fincham, 1997). In addition, it seems possible that some problems influencing reports of marital dissatisfaction may be relatively normative and may not require intervention to resolve. Recent work by Waite and Luo (2002) reported that nearly two thirds (62%) of unhappily married spouses who stayed married reported that their marriages were happy 5 years later (and 77% of unhappily married spouses remained married). Accordingly, it seems possible that some forms of distress may be transient and that such transient distress need not be a trigger for marital intervention. One might also suspect that such transient symptoms of marital distress have a relatively modest or perhaps even negligible association with depressive symptoms (but see Karney, 2001, for a demonstration of within-subject covariation). If there are, however, clusters of marital problems that are not transient and that indicate marital *discord* rather than marital *distress*, such problems might behave taxonically.

Identification of a cluster of marital problems that are taxonic and that can be shown to be associated with mental or physical health problems has the potential to provide a strong data-based foundation for a "diagnosis" of marital discord. In turn, identification of such diagnostic clusters would necessarily change the way recommendations for intervention are formulated and the way research on the connection between marital problems and depression is conducted. Most immediately, identification of such clusters of marital problems would be a strong impetus for the creation of a category of relational diagnoses in a fifth edition of the *Diagnostic and Statistical Manual for Mental Disorders* (*DSM-V*).

Relational Diagnoses

A preliminary case for relational diagnoses has been offered by Reiss and colleagues (First et al., 2002) in their recent discussion of the development of the *DSM-V*. They note that couples with marital disorders come to clinical attention for four primary reasons: (a) a couple recognizes their own dissatisfaction and comes for marital therapy, (b) there is serious violence in the marriage and an emergency room or legal authority makes a referral, (c) marital difficulties are noted as part of a comprehensive assessment of an Axis I or II disorder, or (d) marital difficulties are noted as part of a child evaluation. In each of these cases it is likely that there are multiple ongoing and interlocking problems confronting the couple and that both partners have some awareness of these troubles. In each case, one or both partners probably have come to the conclusion that they cannot solve all of the problems that need to be solved. As a result, they are likely to be pessimistic about their potential for change. Such couples are not likely to improve spontaneously. Indeed, in many cases, their efforts at solving their marital problems already have become part of the problem. Accordingly, such couples are likely to be in need of intervention in order to resolve their difficulties. In addition, such couples may be particularly likely to show adverse affects on the physical and mental health of one or both partners over time.

If we can reliably identify couples who are experiencing sustained, serious, and, from their perspective, hopeless conflict, this would be a great boon to the formulation of guidelines for marital therapy in general. In addition, it would provide a valuable research tool for better sorting out the effects of marital problems on depression. Indeed, if we follow Reiss's suggestions, we will consider a marital disorder present only when (a) there are clear, repeated, and fixed patterns of painful and destructive patterns, (b) the patterns are long-standing and not a response to a recent stressful event, and (c) the patterns are unresponsive to naturally occurring resources in the social environment. Under these circumstances the persons "diagnosed" would be at extremely high risk for continuing distress if left untreated, and at substantially elevated risk for an adverse impact of psychological, occupational, and physical functioning.

Stated differently, if we find that some marital problems behave taxonically we will have taken an important step toward distinguishing between marital distress and marital discord. This would indicate that some manifestations of marital difficulty cluster or aggregate in recognizable patterns in the same way that symptoms of individual disorder tend to cluster in recognizable patterns and that they can be considered "real" disorders in their own right, rather than merely inconvenient environmental complications.

If a category of Relational Disorders is included in some future version of the *DSM*, it will clearly influence the field of marital therapy. Treating marital distress as an Axis I psychopathological entity instead of a V code may well encourage reluctant researchers and clinicians to view some forms of marital distress as serious psychological problems in their own right rather than as distal variables to be justified by their effects on other conditions. Furthermore, an emphasis on disordered relationships rather than disordered individuals would certainly provide support for the argument that marital therapy is often indicated for the treatment of distressed persons, especially when an "individual-level" disorder such as depression can be shown to impinge upon the marital relationship. Accordingly, if the data support the creation of a diagnostic category related to marital discord, this will likely profoundly alter future research on the relationship between marital discord and depression.

■ Conclusions

In evaluating treatments for depression, as in any treatment selection process, careful consideration should be given to differentiating among those who would benefit most from an individual approach, those who would benefit most from a conjoint focus, and those for whom either approach would be equivalent. For now, however, it appears that the potential population that might experience unique benefit from marital therapy for depression is large. If those who might benefit from a focus on increased positive interaction with their partner are included, the population may include most depressed persons. At the same time, there are reasons to be cautious about attempting marital therapy in those cases in which the partner is unavailable for conjoint therapy. There is reason for concern that marital therapy without the partner could be compromised in its effectiveness and that important marital processes, such as low-level physical aggression, might be overlooked. Thus, although there is much to be done in elaborating the points of contact between marital discord and depression, the promise of marital therapy for depression appears well founded.

■ References

Baucom, D. H., Shoam, V., Mueser, K. T., Daiuto, A., & Stickle, T. R. (1998). Empirically supported couple and family interventions for marital distress and adult mental health problems. *Journal of Consulting and Clinical Psychology, 66*, 53–88.

Beach, S. R. H., & Amir, N. (2003). Is depression taxonic, dimensional, or both? *Journal of Abnormal Psychology, 112*, 228–236.

Beach, S. R. H., Katz, J., Kim, S., & Brody, G. H. (2003). Prospective effects of marital satisfaction on depressive symptoms in established marriages: A dyadic model. *Journal of Social and Personal Relationships, 20*, 355–371.

Beach, S. R. H., Kim, S., Cercone-Keeney, J., Gupta, M., Arias, I., & Brody, G. H. (2004). Physical aggression and depressive symptoms: Gender asymmetry in effects? *Journal of Social and Personal Relationships, 21,* 341–360.

Beach, S. R. H., & O'Leary, K. D. (1992). Treating depression in the context of marital discord: Outcome and predictors of response for marital therapy versus cognitive therapy. *Behavior Therapy, 23,* 507–258.

Beach, S. R. H., Sandeen, E. E., & O'Leary, K. D. (1990). *Depression in marriage: A model for etiology and treatment.* New York: Guilford Press.

Brownridge, D. A., & Halli, S. S. (2002). Understanding male partner violence against cohabiting and married women: An empirical investigation with a synthesized model. *Journal of Family Violence, 17,* 341–361.

Cano, A., & O'Leary, K. D. (2000). Infidelity and separations precipitate major depressive episodes and symptoms of non-specific depression and anxiety. *Journal of Consulting and Clinical Psychology, 68,* 774–781.

Clarkberg, M., Stolzenberg, R. M., & Waite, L. J. (1995). Attitudes, values, and entrance into cohabitational versus marital unions. *Social Forces, 74,* 609–632.

Clarkin, J. F., Glick, I. D., Haas, G. L., Spencer, J. H., Lewis, A. B., Peyser, J., et al. (1990). A randomized clinical trial of inpatient family intervention: V. Results for affective disorders. *Journal of Affective Disorders, 18,* 17–28.

Cordova, J. V., & Gee, C. B. (2001). Couples therapy for depression: Using healthy relationships to treat depression. In S. R. H. Beach (Ed.), *Marital and family processes in depression: A scientific foundation for clinical practice.* Washington, DC: American Psychological Association.

Coyne, J. C., & Benazon, N. R. (2001). Coming to terms with the nature of depression in marital research and treatment. In S. R. H. Beach (Ed.), *Marital and family processes in depression: A scientific foundation for clinical practice* (pp. 25–43). Washington, DC: American Psychological Association.

Coyne, J. C., Pepper, C. M., & Flynn, H. (1999). Significance of prior episodes of depression in two patient populations. *Journal of Consulting and Clinical Psychology, 67,* 76–81.

Coyne, J. C., Thompson, R., & Palmer, S. C. (2002). Marital quality, coping with conflict, marital complaints, and affection in couples with a depressed wife. *Journal of Family Psychology, 16,* 26–37.

Davila, J., Bradbury, T. N., Cohan, C. L., & Tochluk, S. (1997). Marital functioning and depressive symptoms: Evidence for a stress generation model. *Journal of Personality and Social Psychology, 73,* 849–861.

Emanuels-Zuurveen, L., & Emmelkamp, P. M. (1996). Individual behavioral-cognitive therapy vs. marital therapy for depression in maritally distressed couples. *British Journal of Psychiatry, 169,* 181–188.

Emanuels-Zuurveen, L., & Emmelkamp, P. M. (1997). Spouse-aided therapy with depressed patients. *Behavior Modification, 21,* 62–77.

Ewart, C. K., Taylor, C. B., Kraemer, H. C., & Agras, W. S. (1991). High blood pressure and marital discord: Not being nasty matters more than being nice. *Health Psychology, 10,* 155–163.

Fincham, F. D., Beach, S. R. H., Harold, G. T., & Osborne, L. N. (1997). Marital satisfaction and depression: Different causal relationships for men and women? *Psychological Science, 8,* 351–357.

Fincham, F. D., Beach, S. R. H., & Kemp-Fincham, S. I. (1997). Marital quality: A new theoretical perspective. In R.J. Sternberg & M. Hojjat (Eds.), *Satisfaction in close relationships* (pp. 275–304). New York: Guilford Press.

First, M. B., Bell, C. C., Cuthburt, B., Krystal, J. H., Malison, R., Offord, D. R., et al. (2002). Personality disorders and relational disorders: A research agenda for addressing crucial gaps in DSM. In D. J. Kupfer, M. B. First, & D. A. Regier (Eds.), *A research agenda for DSM-V*. Washington, DC: American Psychiatric Association.

Foley, S. H., Rounsaville, B. J., Weissman, M. M., Sholomskas, D., & Chevron, E. (1989). Individual versus conjoint interpersonal psychotherapy for depressed patients with marital disputes. *International Journal of Family Psychiatry, 10,* 29–42.

Halford, W. K. (1998). The ongoing evolution of behavioral couples therapy: Retrospect and prospect. *Clinical Psychology Review, 18,* 613–634.

Hammen, C. (1991). *Depression runs in families: The social context of risk and resilience in children of depressed mothers.* New York: Springer-Verlag.

Hooley, J. M., & Gotlib, I. H. (2000). A diathesis-stress conceptualization of expressed emotion and clinical outcome. *Applied and Preventive Psychology, 9,* 135–152.

Hooley, J. M., & Teasdale, J. D. (1989). Predictors of relapse in unipolar depressives: Expressed emotion, marital distress, and perceived criticism. *Journal of Abnormal Psychology, 98,* 229–235.

Jacobson, N. S., Dobson, K., Fruzzetti, A. E., Schmaling, K. B., & Salusky, S. (1991).Marital therapy as a treatment for depression. *Journal of Consulting and Clinical Psychology, 59,* 547–557.

Joiner, T. E. (2000). Depression's vicious scree: Self-propagating and erosive processes in depression chronicity. *Clinical Psychology: Science and Practice, 7,* 203–218.

Judd, L. L, Akiskal, H. S., Maser, J. D., Zeller, P. J., Endicott, J., Coryell, W., et al. (1998). A prospective 12-year study of subsyndromal and syndromal depressive symptoms in unipolar major depressive disorders. *Archives of General Psychiatry, 55,* 694–700.

Karney, B. R. (2001). Depressive symptoms and marital satisfaction in the early years of marriage: Narrowing the gap between theory and research. In S. R. H. Beach (Ed.), *Marital and family processes in depression: A scientific foundation for clinical practice.* Washington, DC: American Psychological Association.

Kaslow, N. J., Twomey, H., Brooks, A., Thompson, M., & Reynolds, B. (2001). Perceptions of family functioning of suicidal and non-suicidal African American women. In S. R. H. Beach (Ed.), *Marital and family processes in depression: A scientific foundation for clinical practice* (pp. 141–161). Washington, DC: American Psychological Association.

Katz, J., & Beach, S. R. H. (1997). Self-verification and depression in romantic relationships. *Journal of Marriage and the Family, 59,* 903–914.

Kendler, K. S, & Gardner, C. O., Jr. (1998). Boundaries of major depression: An evaluation of DSM-IV criteria. *American Journal of Psychiatry, 155,* 172–177.

Kessler, R. C., McGonagle, K. A., Swartz, M., Blazer, D. G., & Nelson, C. B. (1993). Sex and depression in the National Comorbidity Survey I: Lifetime prevalence, chronicity and recurrence. *Journal of Affective Disorders, 29,* 85–96.

Kiecolt-Glaser, J. K., Glaser, R., Cacioppo, J. T., MacCallum, R. C., Snydersmith, M., Kim, C., et al. (1997). Marital conflict in older adults: Endocrinological and immunological correlates. *Psychosomatic Medicine, 59,* 339–349.

Kiecolt-Glaser, J. K., Malarkey, W. B., Chee, M., Newton, T., Cacioppo, J. T., Mao, H., et al. (1993). Negative behavior during marital conflict is associated with immunological down-regulation. *Psychosomatic medicine, 55,* 395–409.

Kiecolt-Glaser, J. K., McGuire, L., & Robles, T. F. (2002). Emotions, morbidity, and mortality: New perspectives from psychoneuroimmunology. *Annual Review of Psychology, 53,* 83–107.

Leff, J., Vearnals, S., Brewin, C. R., Wolff, G., Alexander, B., Asen, E., et al. (2000). The London Depression Intervention Trial. *British Journal of Psychiatry, 177,* 95–100.

Malarkey, W., Kiecolt-Glaser, J. K., Pearl, D., & Glaser, R. (1994). Hostile behavior during marital conflict alters pituitary and adrenal hormones. *Psychosomatic Medicine, 56,* 41–51.

McLean, P. D., & Miles, J. E. (1975). Training family physicians in psychosocial care: An analysis of a program failure. *Journal of Medical Education, 50,* 900–902.

Nathan, P. E., Stuart, S. P., & Dolan, S. L. (2000). Research on psychotherapy efficacy and effectiveness: Between Scylla and Charybdis? *Psychological Bulletin, 126,* 964–981.

O'Leary, K. D., Risso, L., & Beach, S. R. H. (1990). Beliefs about the marital discord/depression link: Implications for outcome and treatment matching. *Behavior Therapy, 21,* 413–422.

Ruscio, J., & Ruscio, A. M. (2000). Informing the continuity controversy: A taxometric analysis of depression. *Journal of Abnormal Psychology, 109,* 473–487.

Spanier, G. B. (1976). Measuring dyadic adjustment: New scales for assessing the quality of marriage and similar dyads. *Journal of Marriage and the Family, 38,* 15–28.

Teichman, Y., Bar-El, Z., Shor, H., Sirota, P., & Elizur, A. (1995). A comparison of two modalities of cognitive therapy (individual and marital) in treating depression. *Psychiatry, 58,* 136–148.

Waite, L., & Luo, Y. (2002, August). *Marital happiness and marital stability: Consequences for psychological well-being.* Paper presented at the meetings of the American Sociological Association, Chicago.

Waller, N. G., & Meehl, P. E. (1998). *Multivariate taxometric procedures: Distinguishing types from continua.* Thousand Oaks, CA: Sage.

Weissman, M. M., Bruce, M. L., Leaf, P. J., Florio, L. P., & Holzer, C., III. (1991). Affective disorders. In L. N. Robbins & D. A. Reiger (Eds.), *Psychiatric disorders in America* (pp. 53–80). New York: Free Press.

Whiffen, V. E., & Johnson, S. M. (1998). An attachment theory framework for the treatment of childbearing depression. *Clinical Psychology: Science and Practice, 5,* 478–493.

Whisman, M. A. (1993). Mediators and moderators of change in cognitive therapy of depression. *Psychological Bulletin, 114,* 248–265.

Whisman, M. A. (2001). The association between depression and marital dissatisfaction. In S. R. H. Beach (Ed.), *Marital and family processes in depression: A scientific foundation for clinical practice* (pp. 3–24). Washington, DC: American Psychological Association.

Whisman, M. A., & Bruce, M. L. (1999). Marital distress and incidence of major depressive episode in a community sample. *Journal of Abnormal Psychology, 108,* 674–678.

Whisman, M. A., Weinstock, L. M., & Uebelaker, L. A. (2002). Mood reactivity to marital conflict: The influence of marital dissatisfaction and depression. *Behavior Therapy, 33,* 299–314.

Zlotnick, C., Kohn, R., Keitner, G., & Della Grotta, S. A. (2000). The relationship between quality of interpersonal relationships and major depressive disorder: Findings from the National Comorbidity Survey. *Journal of Affective Disorders, 59,* 205–215.

19

Toward Culturally Centered and Evidence-Based Treatments for Depressed Adolescents

Guillermo Bernal and Emily Sáez-Santiago

I n this chapter we discuss issues involved in considering culture and ethnicity in treatments. We present some of the recent developments in mental health within a framework that incorporates culturally sensitive criteria and aims to strengthen the ecological validity of treatment and intervention studies. Also, we discuss recent findings concerning depressed adolescents in Puerto Rico to reflect on the next steps in developing and evaluating culturally centered family interventions for this population. Our primary goal in this chapter is to contribute to the identification "of treatments that work for whom and under what circumstances, and why, to aid in improving mental health services and reducing disparities in mental health care" (p. 46), a recommendation of the recent National Institute of Mental Health (NIMH) report "Translating Behavioral Science into Action" (National Advisory Mental Health Council's Clinical Treatment and Services Research Workgroup, 2000).

To highlight the importance of the development of culturally sensitive interventions to ethnic minorities, this chapter begins with a brief description of the current situation of the mental health services use for this population. Then, we summarize several studies that have emphasized the need to consider culture and ethnicity in treatments. This section is followed by a discussion of essential concepts in the development of culturally sensitive treatments, such as ecological and external validity. Subsequently, we present a framework to inform culturally centered treatments; here we describe the eight dimensions that are part of this framework. We also present a summary of the Guidelines for Multicultural Practice, which support the proposed framework. Finally, we discuss findings of our research on Puerto Rican adolescents with depression in which we used culturally centered treatments. In the discussion of these studies, we emphasize the findings that point toward the importance of involving family members in the treatments of depression in adolescents, particularly in Puerto Ricans.

■ Mental Health Service Use by Ethnic Minorities

There is evidence suggesting that ethnic minorities in the United States are experiencing major mental health problems. Ethnic minorities often have less access to health care, and the care that is available is frequently of poorer quality than that available to the White population (U.S. Surgeon General, 2000). Ethnic minorities experience disproportionately higher poverty and social stressors associated with psychological and psychiatric conditions than do Whites (Mays & Albee, 1992). Even when controlling for environment and individual variables, such as socio-economic status, educational level, health and mental health history, and attitudes toward health-related issues, there are significant disparities in the use and quality of mental health services among and across ethnic, cultural, and racial communities (NIMH, 1999). These disparities in mental health services represent a major challenge to the field (U.S. Surgeon General, 2000), and the need to reduce them has lead to a number of important initiatives. Decreasing disparities between ethnic minority groups and White populations is currently a national effort spearheaded by the NIMH (1999).

To decrease the disparity in mental health, we must work to develop new studies. These studies should directly address disparities in access and in the knowledge base by using state-of-the-art research methods and the best practice treatment protocols that focus on mental health issues in the low-income, ethnic minority communities that are often overlooked by NIMH-funded research. In the absence of reliable information on the efficacy and effectiveness of mental health treatments for ethnic minorities, there is a need for research that can contribute to the knowledge base of what works and how it works. Thus, we must develop studies on the efficacy and effectiveness of treatments that are culturally sensitive or that use manuals that have been adapted to include important cultural considerations. There is a great need to produce or adapt treatment manuals and instruments and to test these manuals and instruments in preparation for efficacy trials with ethnic minority communities. In this manner, it may be possible to adequately respond to the NIMH's call for investigators to move toward more generalizable studies (National Advisory Mental Health Council's Clinical Treatment and Services Research Workgroup, 2000). Particularly necessary are studies that target underserved and under researched populations that approximate the types of cases seen in community mental health centers. If we conduct clinical trials that consider cultural and language issues integral to the treatment itself, we may be able to move more quickly from efficacy to effectiveness. Studies that consider ecological validity serve to bridge knowledge gaps and move the field toward translational and dissemination studies (National Advisory Mental Health Council's Clinical Treatment and Services Research Workgroup, 1999).

The Need to Consider Culture and Ethnicity in Treatments

There is increasing recognition of the importance of culture in both treatment and research. In fact, the American Psychological Association (APA) recently approved guidelines for multicultural counseling. These guidelines recommend that the domains of professional practice involve awareness, knowledge, and skills (APA, 2003) for clinical practice, research, and training. In addition, these guidelines suggest that investigators strive to increase their awareness of culture in research, acknowledging that contemporary research has a European American bias. The implication here is that multicultural issues and diversity must be incorporated in all aspects and phases of research, including the basic assumptions from which the theory is derived and the research is proposed.

There is an abundance of literature suggesting that treatment models need to consider the role of culture, ethnicity, and minority issues (Bernal, Bonilla, & Bellido, 1995; Lopez et al., 1989; McGoldrick, Pearce, & Giordano, 1982; Sue & Zane, 1987; Tharp, 1991). As we have noted elsewhere (Bernal & Scharron-del-Rio, 2001), there are multiple reasons that would lead one to include cultural factors into psychosocial treatments. First, psychotherapy is a cultural phenomenon, and culture plays an important role in treatment. Evidence from service utilization studies (Arroyo, Westerberg, & Tonigan, 1998; Cheung & Snowden, 1990; Flaskerud & Liu, 1991; McMiller & Weisz, 1996; Schacht, Tafoya, & Mirabla, 1989), treatment preferences (Aldous, 1994; Constantino, Malgady, & Rogler, 1994; Flaskerud & Hu, 1994; Flaskerud & Liu, 1991; Penn, Kar, Kramer, Skinner, & Zambrana, 1995; Schacht et al., 1989), and health beliefs (McMiller & Weisz, 1996; Penn et al., 1995) suggest that ethnic minorities tend to respond differently to treatment than do nonminorities.

Additionally, key concepts used in the treatment—such as independence, dependence, or interdependence—may have different meanings to different groups. As Nagayama Hall (2001) points out, there may be conflicts between cultural concepts and mainstream values used in conventional psychotherapies. For example, conventional treatment approaches tend to promote individualistic value systems (i.e., differentiation, individuation, etc.) over interdependent value systems (e.g., familialism) within which minority communities are often socialized. The role of spirituality in healing processes, which is being increasingly acknowledged in the realm of mental health care, has not traditionally been part of formal treatment approaches, and this too may have an important intra- and interpersonal role among ethnic minorities. Certainly, the intensity of the discrimination experienced has important implications for treatment. Poverty and lack of access to resources are too often part of the ethnic minority experience and it is essential to understand how ethnicity, culture, cultural values, discrimination, community resources, and socioeconomic status (SES) may impact a particular client or family. These dimensions can be considered in treatment protocols to work more effectively with ethnic minority groups.

Debate on Culturally Sensitive Treatments and Ecological Validity

A careful examination of the so-called empirically supported therapies (EST) list reveals that most of these studies include little formal consideration of the cultural, interpretative, population, ecological, and construct validity of the intervention. Cultural validity means the identification of specific "rules" that influence the behaviors of individuals, groups, and larger systems. Interpretative validity refers to how the motivations, backgrounds, goals, and methods of achieving the goals of the persons under study affect their actions. Population validity is defined as the degree to which one can generalize from a specific sample to the population and/or to other populations. Ecological validity may be defined as the degree of agreement between the perceived environment by the subject and the investigator. Construct validity integrates the ecological, population, interpretative, and cultural validities. Washington and McLoyd (1982) proposed that all of these dimensions need to be considered to ensure external validity in research involving minorities. While at the time these authors were referring to the developmental psychology literature, we believe that these are issues of relevance to psychosocial treatment research today.

To contribute to models that consider diversity, psychotherapy research with ethnic minorities is needed not only to address the problem of external validity but also because ethnic research is good science (Sue & Sue, 2003). The external validity of the so-called ESTs is simply not known. Most efficacy studies do not include minorities in their sample. The problem of generalization is central to this debate and may be addressed by culturally adapting treatments within a set of clinical trials on specific ethnic minority populations or by testing innovative culturally centered treatments with ethnic minority groups. Thus the development and testing of culturally sensitive therapies is critical to the field.

Toward a Framework of Culturally Centered Treatments

There is a growing movement toward the consideration of culture in psychotherapy, family therapy, and treatment research. Recently, a number of authors have argued in favor of *culturally centered* treatments in such a way that culture becomes the basis for understanding social interactions, behavior, and the meaning of actions (Casas, 1995; Lopez et al., 1989; McGoldrick et al., 1982; Pendersen, 2003; Rogler, 1989; Sue, 1998).

Lloyd Rogler (1989) called attention to the issues of cultural sensitivity and, later, cultural insensitivity (1999) in research. Rogler points out that cultural insentivity is persistence in research, which is manifested through the following procedural norms: "the expert-based, rational analysis model of content validity, which has been legitimized into a kind of orthodoxy through repetition in methodology texts; the unilateral elimination of the decentering process in translations, which stems from obedience to the well-known procedural norm of replicating the exact terms of standardized instruments; and . . . the tacit norm of an easy, uncritical transfer of concepts cross-culturally" (Rogler, 1999). Rogler proposed that research can be made culturally sensitive through careful attention to methodological issues that include the adaptations that consider culture. All aspects of the research process need to be considered (from the planning and design to instrumentation, analysis, and results) in light of changing cultural contexts. In this manner, culturally informed research is developed.

One of the early pioneers in building culturally informed research with Latinos is José Szapocznik, along with his colleagues (Szapocznik & Kurtines, 1993).

In addition to having developed culturally informed treatment studies with Latinos (Szapocznik, Santisteban, Kurtines, Perez-Vidal, & Hervis, 1984; Szapocznik et al., 1986, 1989), Szapocznik and colleagues proposed a contextual view in which the individual is embedded within a family context which, in turn, is embedded within cultural contexts. This view is based on the concept of contextualism that emphasizes that an individual needs to be understood in the context of his or her family and, at the same time, this family needs to be understood in the context of the culture in which it is immersed. This work is a result of a productive research program that focused on developing and testing treatments with Latino youth and their families living in the United States. Szapocznik has found that working with these Latino families, it is essential to pay attention to the increasingly multicultural and pluralistic context in which the family is embedded.

Our work is situated in a contextualist view of changing cultures and contexts. As a methodological tool for treatment research, Bernal and colleagues (1995) developed a framework for culturally sensitive interventions with ethnic minorities, in particular Latinos. The framework serves to culturally center an intervention (Pendersen, 2003). This framework includes eight elements or dimensions that need to be incorporated into a specific treatment to augment the ecological validity, and the overall external validity, of a treatment study. These centering elements are (a) language, (b) persons, (c) metaphors, (d) content, (e) concepts, (f) goals, (g) methods, and (h) context. In addition, this model emphasizes the consideration of developmental, technical, and theoretical issues. Table 19.1 presents the eight dimensions that are essential in the development of a culturally sensitive treatment.

The first dimension—*language*—is often a carrier of the culture; thus, treatments delivered in the native language of the target population assume an integration of culture. Regarding this idea, Sue and Zane (1987) have pointed out that knowledge of the language presumes greater cultural knowledge. Language is related not only to culture but also to the expression of emotional experiences. It is important to note that language appropriate interventions require more than the mere mechanical translation of a particular intervention. In contrast to a noncentered translation, a now common practice in cross-cultural research, the objective is to use culturally centered language as part of the intervention or treatment with the given ethnic group. The language used in an intervention must be culturally appropriate and syntonic, taking into consideration differences in inner-city, regional, or subcultural groups.

The dimension of *persons* refers to the client-therapist relationship during the intervention. A culturally centered intervention must consider the role of ethnic and racial similarities and differences in the client-therapist dyad. This dimension brings into focus the consideration of ethnic/race matching in the client-therapist dyad, as it may be important to acknowledge ethnic, racial, or cultural similarities and differences. To achieve this goal, these issues must be discussed and accepted/acknowledged during the treatment process.

The next dimension presented in our framework is the use of *metaphors* in interventions. This dimension refers to the symbols and concepts that are shared by a particular cultural group. Muñoz (1982) has recommended the incorporation

TABLE 19.1 *Culturally Sensitive Elements and the Dimensions of Treatment for Clinical Research Interventions With Latinos and Criteria for Evaluating Degree of Sensitivity*

Elements	Culturally Sensitive	Criteria
Language	Culturally appropriate, culturally syntonic language	Is the vocabulary of the treatment manual clear, understandable? Do patients understand language, idioms, and words used?
Persons	Role of ethnic/racial similarities and differences between client and therapist in shaping therapy relationship	Is patient comfortable with the therapy relationship? Is the patient comfortable with the similarity (or difference) in the ethnicity of the therapist?
Metaphors	Symbols and concepts shared with the populations; sayings or *dichos* in treatment	Are sayings, or *dichos*, common to Latinos part of the treatment manual? Are symbols associated with Latinos part of the treatment environment?
Content	Cultural knowledge: values, traditions; uniqueness of groups (social, economic, historical, and political)	Does the treatment manual use case examples that reflect common values and other issues presented by Latinos (e.g., *familismo*, respect, *personalismo*, gender roles)? Does the patient feel understood by the therapist? Does the patient feel that the therapist respects his/her cultural values?
Concepts	Treatment concepts consonant with culture and context, dependence vs. independence, emic vs. etic	Are treatment concepts framed within acceptable cultural values? Does the patient understand the problem and the reason for the treatment? Is the patient in agreement with the definition of the problem and the specific treatment?
Goals	Transmission of positive adaptive cultural values; support of adaptive values from culture of origin	Are treatment goals framed within adaptive cultural values of the patient? Are treatment goals consonant with cultural expectations of therapy? Does the patient agree with the goals of treatment?
Methods	Development and cultural adaptation of treatment methods	Are the treatment methods framed within adaptive cultural values of the patient? Does the patient agree with the methods of treatment?
Context	Consideration of changing contexts in assessment during treatment or intervention: acculturative stress, phase of migration, social supports and relationship to country of origin, economic and social context of intervention	Does the treatment manual consider contextual issues, such as migration and acculturation stress, social support, family relationships in country of origin, and barriers to treatment, common to Latinos? Are vouchers for transportation and reminders about sessions available to patients? Do patients view therapists as caring about their social and economic situation?

of objects and symbols of the client's culture in the office where the client will be received. This may make the client feel more comfortable and understood. On the other hand, Zuñiga (1992) points out that the use of *dichos*—sayings or idioms—is another way to incorporate metaphors into therapy, particularly with Latinos.

The dimension of *content* refers to cultural knowledge about values, customs, and traditions shared by ethnic and minority groups. Cultural and ethnic uniqueness should be integrated into all phases of a treatment process, including assessment and treatment planning. Thus, when working with ethnic minority communities, cultural content is an essential starting point for sharing experiences in a therapeutic context.

Concepts refer to the constructs of the theoretical model to be used in treatment. The way in which the presenting problem of a client is conceptualized and communicated to him or her is very important. In this process, the consonance between culture and context is critical for treatment efficacy. If this congruence is absent, the credibility of the therapist will be reduced, and as consequence the treatment efficacy may be threatened.

The sixth dimension—*goals*—implies the establishment of an agreement between the therapist and client as to the goals of treatment. The goals of treatment should reflect a cultural knowledge, since these goals need to be created taking into consideration the values, customs, and tradition of the client's culture.

The dimension of *methods* refers to the procedures to follow for the achievement of the treatment goals. As can be expected, the development of a culturally centered treatment should incorporate procedures that are congruent with the client's culture. An important methodological tool in treatment is the use of language.

Finally, the dimension of *context* refers to the consideration of the broader social, economic, and political contexts of the client. Additionally, it is important to consider cultural processes, such as acculturative stress, phases of migration, development stages, availability of social support, and the person's relationship to the country or culture of origin.

Guidelines for Multicultural Practice in Family Psychology Research

The framework of a culturally centered treatment as described above is consistent with the "Multicultural Guidelines" recently adopted by the American Psychological Association (2003). The general guidelines of this document state that "psychologists are encouraged to recognize that, as cultural beings, they may have attitudes and beliefs that can detrimentally influence their perceptions of, and interactions with, individuals who are ethnically and racially different from themselves" (p. 19) and to "recognize the importance of multicultural sensitivity/responsiveness, knowledge, and understanding about ethnically and racially different individuals" (p. 27). These guidelines for clinical practice emphasize that psychologists should focus the client within a cultural context. In this process the psychologist seeks to understand how some experiences, such as socialization, discrimination, and oppression, may relate to the client's presenting problem.

The guidelines bring attention to the importance of sociopolitical factors in the client's history (e.g., generational history, history of migration, citizenship or residency status, fluency in English and/or other languages, extent of family support, levels of community resources, and level of stress related to acculturation). These are issues that, within the proposed framework, are considered contextual or may be handled within specific cultural knowledge or unique aspects of a particular ethnic and minority group.

As noted in our discussion of the dimension of metaphors above, the multicultural guidelines encourage psychologists to be aware of the environment in which the client will be received. A recommendation was that the decoration in the waiting room should convey cultural and linguistic sensitivity. Another recommendation for psychologists in clinical practice is to have a broad repertoire of interventions. These interventions should reflect the different worldviews and cultural backgrounds of clients, incorporating clients' ethnic, linguistic, racial, and cultural background into therapy. In addition, the guidelines encourage therapists to examine the interventions used in traditional psychotherapies to determine their cultural appropriateness. Therapists are urged to expand these interventions to include multicultural awareness and culturally specific strategies.

Treatment for Puerto Rican Children and Adolescents

In an effort to develop a culturally centered therapy for the treatment of depressed adolescents, two clinical trials were carried out at the University of Puerto Rico by the *Centro Universitario de Servicios y Estudios Psicológicos* (University Center for Psychological Services and Research). These research projects evaluated the efficacy of the cognitive-behavioral therapy (CBT) and interpersonal therapy (IPT) models with Puerto Rican adolescents suffering from depression. Specific information about the treatment models, as well as the outcomes of these studies, have been presented in previous publications (Rosselló & Bernal, 1999, 2003). The results of both trials and preliminary findings are briefly presented below.

The First Controlled Clinical Trial: Adaptation and Testing of CBT and IPT.   The first clinical trial adapted and tested the efficacy of the CBT and IPT models with Puerto Rican adolescents with depression symptoms. The treatment manuals were adapted for Puerto Rican adolescents, using the framework of cultural sensitivity described earlier (Bernal et al., 1995; Rosselló & Bernal, 1996).

The inclusion criteria for this study included adolescents who scored over 11 on the Children's Depression Inventory (CDI; Kovacs, 1983) and who met *Diagnostic and Statistical Manual of Mental Disorders* (*DSM-III-R*) criteria for depression (DISC-2, parent and/or adolescent versions). Seventy-one adolescents between the ages of 13 and 17 years participated in the study. Of these, 54% were female and 46% were male.

A pretreatment, posttreatment, and follow-up design with three groups was used. Participants were randomly assigned either to treatment with the CBT model or the IPT model or to a wait-list control group. Adolescents and their parents were evaluated in interviews and tested at intake, at posttreatment, and at a 3-month follow-up using the following instruments: (a) CDI (Kovacs, 1992; Rosselló, Guisasola, Ralat, Martinez, & Nieves, 1992); (b) Piers–Harris Children's Self-Concept Scale (Piers, 1972); (c) Social Adjustment Measure (Beiser, 1990); (d) Child Behavior Checklist (Achenbach, 1983); and (e) Family Emotional Involvement and Criticism Scale (Shields, Franks, Harp, McDaniel, & Campbell, 1992).

The results showed a significant pre- to posttreatment change in all outcome measures across treatment conditions. Planned comparisons between the two treatment conditions and the wait-list control condition revealed that participants in CBT and IPT showed significantly lower depression scores when compared with participants in the wait-list control condition. No significant differences were found between IPT and CBT on the CDI. While self-esteem significantly increased for the IPT group when compared with the wait-list control group, no differences were found between IPT and CBT groups or between CBT and wait-list control groups for self-esteem or social adaptation. At posttreatment, 77% of the treated adolescents in IPT and 67% of the treated adolescents in CBT were better off than the adolescents in the control group.

At follow-up, attrition was high (52% for IPT, 44% for CBT), partly because some of the adolescents still needed additional treatment and had been referred to the appropriate resources, some had moved, and others did not attend their follow-up appointments. In light of ethical considerations, we discontinued the wait-list control group after the postevaluation and offered treatment to participants in this condition. Thus we did not have data on follow-up for the wait-list control. No significant differences were found at follow-up between IPT and CBT groups. Although not statistically significant, the CBT group appeared to continue to make gains in reduced symptoms of depression at follow-up.

Attrition has been a major concern in longitudinal studies. Burlew (2003) points out that although some studies have reported that retention rates are lower in ethnic minority groups, the evidence supporting this assumption is limited. Moreover, there are several studies that have had low attrition rates with ethnic minority samples. Burlew suggests that attrition may be related to lower socioeconomic status, such as lower home ownership rates, single parenthood, unstable employment patterns, and concentration in urban areas where contact with neighbors may be more limited. Given that many persons in ethnic minority communities are living under poverty levels, the retention issue might be a serious problem. In order to reduce the attrition when working with ethnic minorities, Cauce, Ryan, and Grove (1998) suggest the following strategies: (a) to collect accurate information, such as correct spelling of name, birth date, place of employment, and driver's license number, as well as information about a significant other who may know how to reach the family in case of moving; (b) to plan interim contacts, such as birthday and holiday greeting cards, to know early if the family has relocated; (c) to give incentives that increase in amount from the beginning to the end of the study; (d) to add staff to keep regular contact; and (e) to make the first experience especially pleasant so they will want to participate again. Others strategies to avoid high rates of attrition are to give refreshments during research activities, to use informal, personal approaches to recruit participants, and to provide logistical support, such as transportation and child care.

A Second Controlled Clinical Trial: Relative Efficacy of CBT and IPT.   The purpose of the second trial was to test the relative efficacy of CBT and IPT in group and individual formats for the treatment of depression in Puerto Rican adolescents with a larger sample size. The CBT and IPT interventions were adapted to a group format. The same procedure, criteria for inclusion, evaluations, and design were used.

The participants were 112 adolescents ranging from 12 to 18 years of age. The sample was 55.4% female and 44.6% male. Participants were randomly assigned to one of four treatment conditions: individual CBT, group CBT, individual IPT, or group IPT.

The results obtained in this trial showed that participants did not differ in treatment condition (CBT vs. IPT) in terms of age, gender, or SES. Similar results were obtained by treatment format (group vs. individual) for age and SES. The participants also did not differ in the severity of depressive symptoms at baseline or in other primary outcome measures. Intent-to-treat analyses showed that treatment format (group vs. individual) did not seem to have a significant effect on the primary outcome variables. However, the results obtained show that the CBT produced significantly greater decreases in depression symptoms, as measured by the CDI, as well as significant reductions in internalizing and externalizing behaviors in comparison to IPT.

Interestingly, a growth model estimated for this study showed that the effects of treatment condition (CBT and IPT) and treatment format (Group and Individual) were significant. For a participant in the CBT treatment condition our model estimated an additional decrease of 3.14 CDI units from baseline to follow-up. If the participant received therapy in an individual format our model estimated an additional decrease of 2.94 CDI units. The interaction effect between treatment condition and treatment format was nonsignificant. Therefore, for those patients receiving Individual CBT, the estimate of change from baseline to termination would be 12.30 fewer points on depressive symptoms. Also, the greatest degree of change occurred from baseline to the fourth session and from the fourth to the eighth sessions.

The findings of both clinical trials provide evidence on the relative efficacy of CBT and IPT for depressed adolescents in Puerto Rico. It is important to note that these studies followed the culturally informed procedures to ensure the ecological validity of the studies, which were described earlier in this chapter (Bernal et al., 1995). The culturally centered dimensions were applied in all phases of this research, beginning with the formulation of the research question itself and focusing on key aspects of the methodology, such as the translation, adaptation, and testing of instruments, as well as the adaptation of the treatment manuals. Thus our study serves as an example to those interested in conducting clinical trials with ethnic and/ or language minorities and other diverse populations. It also represents a contribution to developing a knowledge base on the external validity on the effects of psychosocial treatments beyond mainstream populations.

*Future Steps: Involving Family Members in the Treatment
of Depressed Adolescents*

The results from our clinical trials point toward the importance of the family in the manifestation of depression in Puerto Rican adolescents. The first clinical trial showed that 40% of the depressed adolescents considered their most frequent problem a family problem (Padilla, Dávila, & Rosselló, 2002), and 70% considered their most frequent interpersonal problem was with one or both parents (Rosselló & Rivera, 1999). Data from the second trial reveal a significant correlation between the primary caretaker parent (BDI score) and the adolescent son or daughter with depression (CDI score) at pretesting. At pos-testing, parents' depression measure (BDI) also correlated with the treated adolescents' BDI. Also, parents' depression scores at pretesting showed that 38% had no depressive symptoms, 32% had slight/low symptoms, 13% had moderate symptoms, and 20% had severe symptoms. An interesting unexpected outcome was a significant reduction in parents' depression symptoms (BDI) and other symptoms of psychiatric distress (SCL-36) scores when controlling for pretest scores. In other words, without targeting the depression and other symptoms of the parents, there was a significant reduction from pre- to posttreatment as a function of treating the adolescents.

Moreover, our research team has found a strong relationship between juvenile depression and family dysfunction (Martínez & Rosselló, 1995; Sáez & Rosselló, 1997, 2001). In one study, Martinez and Rosselló (1995) reported a correlation of .40 ($p > .01$) between depression and family dysfunction. The findings also showed that communication, emotional involvement, and accomplishment of tasks within the family were the areas with higher predictive value in the depressive symptoms of Puerto Rican children and adolescents. In a study on coping strategies and depression in adolescents (Velázquez, Sáez, & Rosselló, 1999), the investigators found that the coping strategies that strengthen family relationships and fit into the family lifestyle were those that best predict a change in depressive symptoms. These strategies include behaviors focused on open communication among family members, sharing activities, and following rules to keep family harmony, suggesting that the increased use of these coping strategies seems to reduce symptoms of depression in Puerto Rican adolescents. The findings of this study reflect a positive relationship between depressive symptoms in children and adolescents and family dysfunction. It is evident that family factors have a predictive value in adolescent depression, suggesting that while adolescents are in a process of becoming independent from their families, the perception of emotional involvement and acceptance from family members is important.

In another study conducted with this population, Sáez and Rosselló (1997) evaluated the relationship between the perception of family functioning, marital conflicts, and depression in adolescents. They found a positive, moderate, and statistically significant relationship between family dysfunction and depression in a community sample. In addition, they found a positive correlation between the perception of marital conflicts and depressive symptoms, though this correlation was low. This finding could be explained using the arguments of Cummings and

Davies (1994). They point out that the relationship between the perception of parental marital conflicts and depression in adolescents is significant when other stressors are present in the family, such as divorce (or separation) and depression in one or both parents, variables that were not measured in that study. Cummings and Davies highlighted that marital conflicts are mediators in the impact of several forms of family dysfunction—including parental depression or divorce. More recently, Sáez and Rosselló (2001) found a higher correlation between both variables in a study with a larger community sample. Additionally, in this study statistically significant correlations were reported between depression with family criticism and parental acceptance.

Sáez (2003) evaluated the relationship between family environment and symptoms of depression in Puerto Rican adolescents. This study included a community sample of 312 adolescents ages 12 to 19. The sample also included 104 parents (70 mothers and 34 fathers) of those adolescents. Family environment was evaluated through the following variables: family emotional overinvolvement, family negative criticism, parental acceptance, parental marital discord, and parental depressive symptoms. All of these family variables were significantly correlated with adolescents' depressive symptoms, with the exception of parental depressive symptoms. The family variable found to hold the strongest relationship with depressive symptoms was family negative criticism, with a significant and moderate correlation. The second variable with the highest significant correlation was parental acceptance. The variable of parental marital conflicts also had a significant and moderate correlation, while family emotional overinvolvement was the variable that showed the least relationship with symptoms of depression in adolescents. A multiple regression analysis indicated that the variables of family negative criticism, parental acceptance, and parental marital conflicts explained 36% of the variance in the adolescents' depressive symptoms. The variable with the best predictive value was parental acceptance, followed very closely by family negative criticism.

A number of other studies point to the role of family conflict, parental overinvolvement, and negative criticism as related to depression symptoms in adolescents (Asarnow, Goldstein, Tompson, & Guthrie, 1993; Caldwell, Antonucci, & Jackson, 1998; Jenkins & Karno, 1992; Mash & Terdal, 1997; Robin & Foster, 1989). The literature suggests that these processes may be potential moderators, and perhaps even mediators, of treatment with adolescents. Clinical trials that seek to improve family functioning are warranted, particularly in groups where the participation of parents and other family members would enhance treatment. Within the Puerto Rican culture, *familismo* (familialism) and personalism are values that organize patterns of behavior (Bernal & Flores-Ortiz, 1984; Comas-Díaz & Griffith, 1988; Sabogal, Marín, Otero-Sabogal, & Marín, 1987). Adjunct interventions that incorporate parents in the treatment of their children are likely to enhance the effects of treatment and strengthen the adolescents' commitment to a treatment program. Such studies would also shed light on the role of familial moderators and mediators, particularly in cultures and subgroups where the collective (in this case, family) is valued over the individual, as in less acculturated Latinos.

Although the relationship between family dysfunction and adolescent depression has been extensively documented, family therapy is a psychosocial treatment that warrants more investigation. Surprisingly few clinical trials for child and adolescent depression have incorporated a family focus. While two studies included parents (Clarke, Rohde, Lewinsohn, Hops, & Seeley, 1999; Lewinsohn, Clarke, Rohde, Hops, & Seeley, 1996), only Brent's study tested a family therapy model. This is especially striking in view of the call for more developmentally sensitive treatments (Kazdin, 1998). Further, increasing evidence suggests that family discord plays a critical role in the development, maintenance, and relapse of child and adolescent depression (Asarnow et al., 1993; Birmaher et al., 2000; Burbach & Borduin, 1986; Goodyer, 1995; Kovacs, 1997). These investigators and others have encouraged the development and testing of family treatments for this population (Jensen, Hibbs, & Pilkonis, 1996; Kazdin, 1991; Rutter, 1984).

However, the findings from the Brent et al. (1997) study with depressed adolescents would decrease one's enthusiasm for family therapy as a treatment of choice, given that CBT was quicker than family therapy in reducing symptoms of depression. It is worth noting that 60 to 70% of the adolescents in all three treatments demonstrated significant improvement on the Hamilton and on rates of remission of major depression disorder (MDD). The CBT and the family therapy condition showed similar reductions in suicidal ideation. CBT demonstrated quicker rates of symptom reduction, yet there were no significant differences between treatments at posttreatment or even at follow-up. While family therapy was slower than CBT in symptom reduction, in general it was as efficacious as family therapy in reducing depressive symptoms. An important consideration is that while there were essentially no differences in outcome for the three treatment conditions, family discord was the strongest predictor of relapse (Birmaher et al., 2000).

Based on the literature review and on our preliminary findings, including parents should be an important step in optimizing the efficacy of already effective treatments. Involving parents in the treatment of adolescents can help address treatment resistance, accelerate the treatment effects for the adolescent, and maintain therapeutic changes. A number of investigators recommend this avenue of research (Kazdin & Kendall, 1998; Sanford et al., 1995). After a review of the empirical and clinical focus of child and adolescent psychotherapy research, Kazdin, Bass, Ayers, and Rodgers (1990) established several priorities for treatment research. They noted the scant attention paid to parental influences that may moderate outcome and recommended research to determine whether parent involvement is critical in clinical work. Other investigators (Fauber & Long, 1991) recommend including parent involvement in treatment only if the initial assessment reveals that family processes are related to the adolescent's problems. Some family variables related to adolescent depression are parenting practices, parent depression, disciplinary methods, parent-adolescent conflict, inadequate supervision, criticism, hostility, overinvolvement, and communication difficulties. High emotional expressiveness in families has been related to difficulties in recovery and high relapse rates (Asarnow, Tompson, Hamilton, Goldstein, & Guthrie, 1994; Sanford et al., 1995). Also, Kovacs and Bastiaens (1995) recommend that empirical treatment studies of depressed youth should provide rationales for parental participation and guidelines for an optimal and healthy involvement in their children's treatment. This possible contribution to the field can be of great value for clinical practitioners. Finally, Kendall (1991) also argues for parental involvement when treating depressed children. He asserts that this facilitates changes in interaction patterns, communication, and family rules. It may help parents to identify the depressogenic thoughts and help their son or daughter restructure them. Parents can also learn the advantages of encouraging pleasant activities and those actions that will help their children attain self-improvement goals.

In summary, research findings have been consistent in reporting that parent-child conflicts and dysfunctional family environments are related to depressive symptoms in children and adolescents. The inclusion of parents and perhaps other family members may serve to address issues of negative cognitive styles, parent-child conflict, and communication that could enrich and maximize the treatment effects for adolescents with depression. Furthermore, the inclusion of parents may be a measure of culturally centering individually oriented treatments, such as CBT and IPT, when working with Latino adolescents. A next step in adolescent treatment research may be in exploring innovative ways in which parents can participate in the treatment of their depressed children.

■ Acknowledgments

The authors are grateful to María Sharron-del-Río who collaborated with the first author in developing a presentation on this material at the Family Psychology Research Conference held in Evanston, Illinois, in April 2002. Work on this manuscript was in part supported by a grant from the National Institute of Mental Health (R24-MH49368).

■ References

Achenbach, T. M. (1983). *Manual for the Child Behavior Checklist and Revised Child Behavior Profile*. Burlington: Department of Psychiatry, University of Vermont.

Aldous, J. L. (1994). Cross-cultural counseling and cross-cultural meanings: An exploration of Morita psychotherapy. *Canadian Journal of Counseling, 28,* 238–249.

American Psychological Association. (2003). Guidelines on multicultural education, training, research, practice, and organizational change for psychologists. *American Psychologist, 58,* 377–402

Arroyo, J. A., Westerberg, V. S., & Tonigan, J. S. (1998). Comparison of treatment utilization and outcome for Hispanics and non-Hispanic whites. *Journal of Studies on Alcohol, 59,* 286–291.

Asarnow, J. R., Goldstein, M. J., Tompson, M., & Guthrie, D. (1993). One-year outcomes of depressive disorders in child psychiatric in-patients: Evaluation of the prognostic power of a brief measure of expressed emotion. *Journal of Child Psychology & Psychiatry & Allied Disciplines, 34,* 129–137.

Asarnow, J. R., Tompson, M., Hamilton, E. B., Goldstein, M. J., & Guthrie, D. (1994). Family expressed emotion, childhood-onset depression and childhood-onset schizophrenia spectrum disorders: Is expressed emotion a nonspecific correlate of child psychopathology or a specific risk factor for depression. *Journal of Abnormal Psychology, 22,* 129–146.

Beiser, M. (1990). Final report submitted in fulfillment of requirements for the grants of the United States National Institute of Mental Health (5-R01-MH36678-04) and the Canada Health and Welfare National Health Research Directorate Program (NHRDP 6610-132-04). Unpublished manuscript. Toronto, ON, Canada.

Bernal, G., Bonilla, J., & Bellido, C. (1995). Ecological validity and cultural sensitivity for outcome research: Issues for the cultural adaptation and development of psychosocial treatments with Hispanics. *Journal of Abnormal Child Psychology, 23,* 67–82.

Bernal, G., & Flores-Ortiz, Y. (1984). *Latino families: Sociohistorical perspectives and cultural issues, Nueva Epoca.* Monograph published by the Bay Area Spanish Speaking Therapists Association, San Francisco.

Bernal, G., & Scharron-del-Rio, M. R. (2001). Are empirically supported treatments valid for ethnic minorities? Toward an alternative approach for treatment research. *Cultural Diversity and Ethnic Minority Psychology, 7,* 328–342.

Birmaher, B., Brent, D. A., Kolko, D., Baugher, M., Bridge, J., Holder, D., et al. (2000). Clinical outcome after short-term psychotherapy for adolescents with major depressive disorder. *Archives of General Psychiatry, 57,* 29–36.

Brent, D. A., Holder, D., Kolko, D., Brimaher, B., Baugher, M., Roth, C., et al. (1997). A clinical psychotherapy trial for adolescent depression comparing cognitive, family, and supportive treatments. *Archives of General Psychiatry, 54,* 877–885.

Burbach, D. J., & Borduin, C. M. (1986). Parent-child relations and the etiology of depression: A review of methods and findings. *Clinical Psychology Review, 6,* 133–153.

Burlew, A. K. (2003). Research with ethnic minorities. Conceptual, methodological, and analytical issues. In G. Bernal, J. E. Trimble, A. K. Burlew, & F. T. L. Leong (Eds.), *Handbook of racial and ethnic minority psychology* (pp. 179–197). Thousand Oaks, CA: Sage.

Caldwell, C. H., Antonucci, T. C., & Jackson, J. S. (1998). Supportive/conflictual family relations and depressive symptomatology: Teenage mother and grandmother perspectives. *Family Relations: Interdisciplinary Journal of Applied Family Studies, 47,* 395–402.

Casas, M. (1995). Counseling and psychotherapy with racial/ethnic minority groups in theory and practice. In V. Bongar & L. E. Buetler (Eds.), *Comprehensive textbook of psychotherapy: Theory and practice* (pp. 311–335). New York: Oxford University Press.

Cauce, A. M., Ryan, K., & Grove, K. (1998). Children and adolescents of color, where are you? Participation, selection, recruitment and retention in developmental research. In V. McLoyd & L. Steinberg (Eds.), *Studying minority adolescents* (pp. 147–166). Mahwah, NJ: Erlbaum.

Cheung, F. K., & Snowden, L. R. (1990). Community mental health and ethnic minority populations. *Community Mental Health Journal, 26,* 277–291.

Clarke, G. N., Rohde, P., Lewinsohn, P. M., Hops, H., & Seeley, J. R. (1999). Cognitive–behavioral treatment of adolescent depression: Efficacy of acute group treatment and booster sessions. *Journal of the American Academy of Child and Adolescent Psychiatry, 38,* 272–279.

Comas-Díaz, L., & Griffith, E. E. H. (Eds.). (1988). *Clinical guidelines in cross-cultural mental health.* New York: Wiley.

Constantino, G., Malgady, R. G., & Rogler, L. H. (1994). Storytelling through pictures: Culturally sensitive psychotherapy for Hispanic children and adolescent. *Journal of Clinical Child Psychology, 23,* 13–20.

Cummings, E. M., & Davies, P. (1994). Marital conflict and child development. In E. M. Cummings & P. Davies (Eds.), *Children and marital conflict. The impact of family dispute and resolution.* New York: Guilford Press.

Fauber, R. L., & Long, N. (1991). Children in context: The role of the family in child psychotherapy. *Journal of Consulting and Clinical Psychology, 59,* 813–820.

Flaskerud, J. H., & Hu, L. (1994). Participation in and outcome of treatment for major depression among low income Asian-Americans. *Psychiatry Research, 53,* 289–300.

Flaskerud, J. H., & Liu, P. Y. (1991). Effects of an Asian client-therapist language, ethnicity, and gender match on utilization and outcome of therapy. *Community Mental Health Journal, 27,* 31–42.

Goodyer, I. M. (1995). *The depressed child and adolescent: Developmental and clinical perspectives.* New York: Cambridge University Press.

Jenkins, J. H., & Karno, M. (1992). The meaning of expressed emotion: Theoretical issues raised by cross-cultural research. *American Journal of Psychiatry, 149,* 9–21.

Jensen, P. S., Hibbs, E. D., & Pilkonis, P. A. (1996). From ivory tower to clinical practice: Future directions for child and adolescent psychotherapy research. In E. D. Hibbs & P. S. Jensen (Eds.), *Psychosocial treatments for child and adolescent disorders: Empirically based strategies for clinical practice* (pp. 701–712). Washington, DC: American Psychological Association.

Kazdin, A., & Kendall, P. C. (1998). Current progress and future plans for developing effective treatments: Comments and perspectives. *Journal of Clinical Child Psychology, 27,* 217–226.

Kazdin, A. E. (1991). Effectiveness of psychotherapy with children and adolescents. *Journal of Consulting and Clinical Psychology, 59,* 785–798.

Kazdin, A. E. (1998). *Methodological issues and strategies in clinical research* (2nd ed.). Washington, DC: American Psychological Association.

Kazdin, A. E., Bass, D., Ayers, W. A., & Rodgers, A. (1990). Empirical and clinical focus of child and adolescent psychotherapy research. *Journal of Consulting and Clinical Psychology, 58,* 729–740.

Kendall, P. C. (1991). *Child and adolescent therapy: Cognitive-behavioral procedures.* New York: Guilford Press.

Kovacs, M. (1983). *The Children's Depression Inventory: A self-report depression scale for school-aged youngsters.* Pittsburgh, PA: University of Pittsburgh School of Medicine.

Kovacs, M. (1992). *Children's Depression Inventory (CDI) Manual.* New York: Multi-Health Systems.

Kovacs, M. (1997). First-episode of major depressive and dysthymic disorder in childhood: Clinical and sociodemographic factors in recovery. *Journal of the American Academy of Child and Adolescent Psychiatry, 36,* 777–784.

Kovacs, M., & Bastiaens, L. (1995). The psychotherapeutic management of major depressive and dysthymic disorders in childhood and adolescence: Issues and prospects. In I. M. Goodyear (Ed.), *The depressed child and adolescent developmental and clinical perspectives.* New York: Cambridge University Press.

Lewinsohn, P. M., Clarke, G. N., Rohde, P., Hops, H., & Seeley, J. (1996). A course in coping: A cognitive–behavioral approach to the treatment of adolescent depression. In P. S. Jensen (Ed.), *Psychosocial treatments for child and adolescent disorders: Empirically based strategies for clinical practice* (pp. 109–135). Washington, DC: American Psychological Association.

Lopez, S. R., Grover, K. P., Holland, D., Johnson, M. J., Kain, C. D., Kanel, K., et al. (1989). Development of culturally sensitive psychotherapists. *Professional Psychology: Research and Practice, 20,* 369–376.

Martínez, A., & Rosselló, J. (1995). Depresión y funcionamiento familiar en niños/as y adolescentes puertorriqueños/as. *Revista Puertorriqueña de Psicología, 10,* 215–245.

Mash, E. J., & Terdal, L. G. (1997). *Assessment of childhood disorders* (3rd ed.). New York: Guilford Press.

Mays, V. M., & Albee, G. W. (1992). Psychotherapy and ethnic minorities. In D. K. Freedheim & H. J. Freudenberger (Eds.), *History of psychotherapy: A century of change* (pp. 552–570). Washington, DC: American Psychological Association.

McGoldrick, N., Pearce, J. K., & Giordano, J. (1982). *Ethnicity and family therapy.* New York: Guilford Press.

McMiller, W. P., & Weisz, J. R. (1996). Help-seeking preceding mental health clinic intake among African-American, Latino, and Caucasian youths. *Journal of the American Academy of Child and Adolescent Psychiatry, 35,* 1086–1094.

Muñoz, R. F. (1982). The Spanish-speaking consumer and the community mental health center. In E. J. Jones & S. J. Korkin (Eds.), *Minority mental health* (pp. 362–398). New York: Praeger.

Nagayama Hall, G. (2001). Psychotherapy research with ethnic minorities: Empirical, ethical, and conceptual issues. *Journal of Consulting and Clinical Psychology, 69,* 502–510.

National Advisory Mental Health Council's Clinical Treatment and Services Research Workgroup. (1999). *Bridging science and service* (NIH Publication No. 99-4353). Rockville, MD: National Institute of Mental Health.

National Advisory Mental Health Council's Clinical Treatment and Services Research Workgroup. (2000). *Translating behavioral science into action* (NIH Publication No. 00-4699). Rockville, MD: National Institute of Mental Health.

National Institute of Mental Health. (1999). *Strategic plan on reducing health disparities.* Rockville, MD: Author.

Padilla, L., Dávila, E., & Rosselló, J. (2002). Problemas presentados por un grupo de adolescentes puertorriqueños/as con depresión y por sus padres. *Pedagogía, 36,* 80–91.

Pendersen, P. D. (2003). Cross-cultural counseling: Developing culture-centered interactions. In G. Bernal, J. E. Trimble, A. K. Burlew, & F. T. L. Leong (Eds.), *Handbook of racial and ethnic minority psychology* (pp. 487–503). Thousand Oaks, CA: Sage.

Penn, N. E., Kar, S., Kramer, J., Skinner, J., & Zambrana, R. (1995). Panel VI: Ethnic minorities, health care systems, and behavior. *Health Psychology, 14,* 641–646.

Piers, E. V. (1972). Prediction of children's self-concepts. *Journal of Consulting and Clinical Psychology, 38,* 428–433.

Robin, A. L., & Foster, S. L. (1989). *Negotiating parent-adolescent conflict: A behavioral-family systems approach.* New York: Guilford Press.

Rogler, L. H. (1989). The meaning of culturally sensitive research in mental health. *American Journal of Psychiatry, 146,* 296–303.

Rogler, L. H. (1999). Methodological sources of cultural insensitivity in mental health research. *American Psychologist, 54,* 424–433.

Rosselló, J., & Bernal, G. (1996). Cognitive-behavioral and interpersonal treatments for depressed Puerto Rican adolescents. In E. D. Hibbs & P. Jensen (Eds.), *Psychosocial treatments for children and adolescent disorders: Empirically based approaches* (pp. 152–187). Washington, DC: American Psychological Association.

Rosselló, J., & Bernal, G. (1999). The efficacy of cognitive-behavioral and interpersonal treatments for depression in Puerto Rican adolescents. *Journal of Consulting and Clinical Psychology, 67,* 734–745.

Rosselló, J., & Bernal, G. (2003). *A randomized trial of CBT and IPT in individual and group format for depression in Puerto Rican adolescents.* Unpublished manuscript, Rio Piedras, Puerto Rico.

Rosselló, J., Guisasola, E., Ralat, S., Martínez, S. & Nieves, A. (1992). La evaluación de la depresión en niños/as y adolescentes puertorriqueños. *Revista Puertorriqueña de Psicología, 8,* 155–162.

Rosselló, J., & Rivera, Z. (1999). Problemas interpersonales presentados por adolescentes puertorriqueños/as con depresión. *Revista Puertorriqueña de Psicología, 12,* 55–76.

Rutter, M. (1984). Family and school influences on behavioral development. *Journal of Child Psychology and Psychiatry, 26,* 349–367.

Sabogal, F., Marín, G., Otero-Sabogal, R., & Marín, B. (1987). Hispanic familism and acculturation: What changes and what doesn't? *Hispanic Journal of Behavioral Sciences, 9,* 397–412.

Sáez, E. (2003). *Influencia del ambiente familiar en los síntomas de la depresión y del desorden de conducta en adolescentes puertorriqueños/as.* Unpublished doctoral dissertation, University of Puerto Rico, Río Piedras.

Sáez, E., & Rosselló, J. (1997). Percepción sobre los conflictos maritales de los padres, ajuste familiar y sintomatología depresiva en adolescentes puertorriqueños/as. *Revista Interamericana de Psicología, 31,* 279–291.

Sáez, E., & Rosselló, J. (2001). Relación entre el ambiente familiar, los síntomas depresivos y los problemas de conducta en adolescentes puertorriqueños/as. *Revista Interamericana de Psicología, 35,* 113–125.

Sanford, M., Szatmari, P., Spinner, M., Monroe-Blum, H., Jamieson, E., Walsh, C., et al. (1995). Predicting the one-year course of adolescent major depression. *Journal of the American Academy of Child and Adolescent Psychiatry, 34,* 1618–1628.

Schacht, A. J., Tafoya, N., & Mirabla, K. (1989). Home-based therapy with American Indian families. *American Indian and Alaska Native Mental Health Research, 3,* 27–42.

Shields, C., Franks, P., Harp, J., McDaniel, S., & Campbell, T. (1992). Development of the Family Emotional Involvement and Criticism Scale (FEICS): A self-report scale to measure expressed emotion. *Journal of Marital and Family Therapy, 18,* 395–407.

Sue, S. (1998). In search of cultural competence in psychotherapy. *American Psychologist, 53,* 440–448.

Sue, S., & Sue, L. (2003). Ethnic research is good science. In G. Bernal, J. E. Trimble, A. K. Burlew, & F. T. L. Leong (Eds.), *Handbook of racial and ethnic minority psychology* (pp. 198–207). Thousand Oaks, CA: Sage.

Sue, S., & Zane, N. (1987). The role of culture and cultural techniques in psychotherapy: A critique and reformulation. *American Psychologist, 42,* 37–45.

Szapocznik, J., & Kurtines, W. M. (1993). Family psychology and cultural diversity: Opportunities for theory, research, and application. *American Psychologist, 48,* 400–407.

Szapocznik, J., Santisteban, D., Kurtines, W. M., Perez-Vidal, A., & Hervis, O. (1984). Bicultural effectiveness training: A treatment intervention for enhancing intercultural adjustment in Cuban American families. *Hispanic Journal of Behavioral Sciences, 6,* 317–344.

Szapocznik, J., Santisteban, D., Rio, A., Perez-Vidal, A., Kurtines, W. M., & Hervis, O. (1986). Bicultural effectiveness training (BET): An intervention modality for families experiencing intergenerational/intercultural conflict. *Hispanic Journal of Behavioral Sciences, 8,* 303–330.

Szapocznik, J., Santisteban, D., Rio, A., Perez-Vidal, A., Santisteban, D. A., & Kurtines, W. M. (1989). Family effectiveness training: An intervention to prevent drug abuse and problem behaviors in Hispanic youth. *Hispanic Journal of Behavioral Sciences, 1,* 4–27.

Tharp, R. G. (1991). Cultural diversity and treatment of children. *Journal of Consulting and Clinical Psychology, 11,* 101–106.

U.S. Surgeon General. (2000). *Supplement to "Mental health: A report of the Surgeon General." Disparities in mental health care for racial and ethnic minorities.* Washington, DC: Surgeon General of the U.S. Public Health Service.

Velázquez, M., Sáez, E., & Rosselló, J. (1999). Coping strategies and depression in Puerto Rican adolescents. *Cultural Diversity and Ethnic Minority Psychology, 5,* 65–75.

Washington, E. D., & McLoyd, V. (1982). The external validity of research involving American minorities. *Human Development, 25,* 324–339.

Zuñiga, M. E. (1992). Using metaphors in therapy: Dichos and Latino clients. *Social Work, 37,* 55–60.

PART V

FAMILIES AND HEALTH

From the perspective of the health care system, health and disease are individual issues. There are no items on medical reimbursement forms for anything having to do with family. Yet people do not become ill in isolation, and health and illness have profound effects on families. In the clinical literature, pioneers in family systems medicine, family psychology, and psychiatry, such as Don Bloch, Tom Campbell, Susan McDaniel, John Rolland, and Lyman Wynne, have focused attention on the need to address the family as being both affected by and affecting health outcomes and for collaboration between patients, families, and health care providers.

Yet we are only beginning to have a body of empirical research that assesses the relationships between families and physical illness, as well as interventions that might be brought to bear on those relationships. Perhaps this is a by-product of the biological focus of the medical establishment; or perhaps a function of the late arrival of systemic understandings into what traditionally has been an area of endeavor emphasizing simple, linear causal pathways; or perhaps a result of the lack of short-term financial payoff in attending to the psychosocial aspects of medical illnesses; or perhaps a function of all three and other factors as well. Nonetheless, as the authors in this part point out, a body of research is clearly emerging that establishes the importance of considering the family context in illness and the beneficial effects of interventions to support families in their reactions to the crises that often accompany these illnesses.

This part of our book provides a series of templates for considering current research and directions for future research, each through the lens of a distinct model of how families interface with health and illness. Beatrice L. Wood and Bruce D. Miller present a critical overview of the key issues in and strategies for research on the relationships between family variables and health, emphasizing the value of their biobehavioral family model as an overarching framework. Joän M. Patterson revisits the key questions that face researchers, focusing especially on her FAAR (family adjustment and adaptation response) model, which emphasizes the way in which families attribute meaning to themselves and the chronic illnesses that afflict their children. Lawrence Fisher delineates the need for specific, systemic, and practical family models to guide intervention research, reviews the current state of the art in regard to family models, recommends a number of "model enhancements" for the next stage of family and chronic disease intervention research, and illustrates the application of this enhanced model in research on families with members with type 2 diabetes. The level of theoretical and methodological rigor illustrated by the reflections and research programs of the authors of each of these chapters represent the finest and most rigorous discourse in this research domain.

As the authors suggest, innumerable questions await further research. When does family behavior affect health and illness and when not? What are the pathways for such effects? Under what circumstances are effects on family greater or less, and what mediates and moderates such effects? And, ultimately, what can family intervention offer to these families? The authors in this part define the theoretical and methodological landscape of this research domain, delineating key challenges, pathways, and strategies for the next stage of research.

20

Families, Health, and Illness: The Search for Pathways and Mechanisms of Effect

Beatrice L. Wood and Bruce D. Miller

■ The Systems Paradigm: Unique Assumptions and Valuable Features

Human beings and their families and social systems are complex and dynamic. Understanding families, health, and illness therefore requires an investigatory paradigm that can match that complexity. The systems paradigm meets this requirement because it assumes that biological, human, and social phenomena are multilevel, dynamic, and characterized by patterns of interactive and mutual influence. In considering mutual and reciprocal effects of family factors and health and illness, we find that for the most part the family and health models have focused on only one direction of effect at a time (i.e., the effect of family on health or the effect of health on the family). Although family models have addressed various aspects of the systemic paradigm, there is to date no fully comprehensive model, or even framework, that addresses health and illness in family and social contexts. It is a challenge for the future to examine whether one unified model is feasible, or whether a "family" of models will be required to cover the territory (see Fisher, ch. 22 in this volume). Regardless of whether one or several models are required, we submit that the most useful models will be multilevel, dynamic, and characterized by patterns of interactive and mutual influence, i.e., systems models.

Other chapters (Patterson, ch. 21, and Fisher, ch. 22) review models and research on the effect of illness on family function and on family coping and adaptation to illness. This chapter concentrates on models and research that focus on the influence of family functioning on an individual family member's physical well-being.

We make the case herein that establishing pathways, mechanisms, and directions of effect by which biopsychosocial factors influence physical well-being is essential in order to develop scientifically grounded and effectively targeted clinical intervention and prevention strategies. We orient the reader to research on behavioral pathways by which families influence the health of their family members, but we concentrate on direct psychobiologic pathways, which we believe have not been sufficiently studied. We review current family-relevant research that points to likely pathways and mechanisms by which family stress and emotions may influence physical well-being, and we present our own work to illustrate one way in which these advances in the stress literature may be applied to the family systems domain. Along the way, we underline various strengths and weaknesses in the literature and suggest directions for future research.

Are Family and Health Interrelated?

The social context with the most immediate effects on an individual, and that which is most immediately influenced by the individual, is the family. In our 21st century global context, *family* may be heuristically and practically defined as a constellation of at least two intimates, living in close proximity, having emotional bonds (positive and/or negative), a history, and an anticipated future. Thus defined, it is logical, and empirically validated, that family values, functioning, and relationships have important influence over a person's health, illness, and disease management and that illness has profound effects on family functioning and caregiver well-being. There are two excellent comprehensive reviews of families and health (Campbell, 2002; Weihs, Fisher, & Baird, 2002). Both report strong support for mutual effects of families and health. However, both note that the mediating factors and pathways transmitting these effects have not been adequately studied. Campbell (2002) suggests three potential pathways by which family can influence health: a direct biological one (such as shared genetic predispositions and shared infection risk), a health behavior pathway (including lifestyle behaviors and adherence to medical regimens), and direct psychophysiological pathways.

In conclusion, the family and health research to date permits the inference of a family-health association, yet it is limited in not being able to point to directions of effect and pathways. Later in this chapter, we illustrate one approach that takes a step in the direction of identifying direction of effects, focusing on direct psychophysiological pathways. However, first we review other potential pathways.

Is There Evidence for Family–Health Behavior Pathways?

One type of family–health behavior pathway is through lifestyle behaviors, such as exercise, diet, and smoking (Campbell, 2002). These behaviors are heavily influenced by family patterning and modeling (Doherty & Campbell, 1988). Changing negative health behaviors, such as smoking (Coppotelli & Orleans, 1985; Venters, Jacobs, Luepker, Maiman, & Gillum, 1984), and changing behavior relevant to nutrition and obesity are also influenced by family patterns (Doherty & Campbell, 1988). Family stress and dysfunction are likely to contribute directly to behaviors that undermine health and promote illness. Clearly, therefore, these lifestyle behaviors comprise one likely mediating pathway by which family stress and relational factors influence health and illness. Although there are many studies that demonstrate associations among these factors, there are too few studies directly testing these pathways. Specific knowledge about the nature of these pathways is essential in order to target interventions at multiple points in the pathways by which family stress influences health and illness.

Family Routine Adherence Pathways

One dramatically important family-health mediator is adherence to medical regimens. However, once again, while most of the relevant studies demonstrate associations between family factors and better or worse adherence, they do not elucidate pathways by which family stress and relational compromise may influence adherence.

One notable exception is Barbara Fiese's sophisticated and compelling model of pathways by which family routines and rituals influence coping and adherence in children with asthma. One important advantage of this model is that it not only focuses on family factors that compromise adherence, but also articulates how family routines and rituals may enhance adherence; thus the model has direct implications for intervention.

Fiese notes that adherence to medical regimens is in actuality a family affair. How well the family is organized around daily routines can contribute directly to the ease with which regimens are followed (Fiese & Wamboldt, 2001). In addition, the ways in which family members represent, or think about, their deliberate plan for routine care is directly related to rates of adherence (Fiese, Wamboldt, & Anbar, in press). The regular practice of routines and the creation of family beliefs transact with each other over time, providing guideposts for family behavior.

Fiese and colleagues (in press) propose four ways in which family routines may be preserved or disrupted in the context of chronic illness.

1. For some families, routines have been disrupted due to the illness. Family gatherings are postponed or canceled, bedtime routines may be altered to respond to emergent care, and family members not directly involved in care may be neglected. In this case, overall family functioning may be compromised and there is a need to redefine routines so that multiple members are involved and meaningful rituals created prior to diagnosis are preserved.

2. In other families, routines may be in place, but there are struggles with folding medical routines into daily life. In this instance, family functioning may be adequate but the individual's health is still compromised. An evaluation of existing routines may aid in identifying points in the day that could be targeted for disease management (e.g., bedtime, tooth brushing, leaving for school). In this way adherence becomes a part of preexisting routines and family functioning is preserved.

3. A third family pattern is one in which there is conflict among family members in terms of managing the illness. This is often found in families in which there is considerable conflict or there has been a divorce, and illness becomes yet another bone of contention. In this scenario one parent may ascribe to one set of routines in managing the illness and the other parent may deny that the child even has an illness. The child is thus exposed to two sets of beliefs, two sets of routines, and two sets of disease management strategies.

These pulls place the child at considerable health risk. In this instance, intervention is aimed at identifying the conflict and realigning routines into a coherent plan.

4. Finally, there are families in which life is more chaotic than organized, and there is not an appreciation of how routines may aid in reducing overall family stress. In this case, education efforts may be warranted to implement a few simple routines that can be paired with medication adherence (e.g., mealtime).

Although family routines have been found to be related to better physical and mental health, the pathways and mechanisms by which routines influence outcomes are not yet understood. Stable routines and accompanying belief systems likely support medical adherence, thus having a salutary effect on the illness. The stability and balance produced by family routines may also protect and buffer patients from stress, which may influence the disease process through more direct pathways and mechanisms. To date intervention research which would elucidate pathways and mechanisms is sparse, but this line of investigation holds promise for disentangling the relative contribution of family organization and beliefs in promoting medical adherence and reducing stress in families faced with the challenges of living with, and supporting, a family member with chronic illness.

Family Stress–Psychobiological Pathways

Although there is a robust literature demonstrating psychobiological pathways and mechanisms as mediating the effect of stress and emotions on health (Booth et al., 2001; Cohen et al., 1975; Salovey, Rothman, Detweiler, & Steward, 2000; also see Sternberg's 2000 book *The Balance Within: The Science Connecting Health and Emotions* for a scholarly but readable review), there is a paucity of literature addressing these pathways in the context of the effects of *family* stress and emotions on health and illness. The following section presents family stress models and identifies conceptual, theoretical, and methodological limitations which interfered with their application to physical illness.

There is a robust *family stress* literature (Boss, 1988, 2002; McCubbin & Boss, 1980) which has established that stressful family relations have significant impact on family members (Boss & Mulligan, 2003). This fact, along with the vast stress and mind-body literature, makes it surprising that direct psychobiological effects of stressful family relational patterns are the least studied, and most controversial, pathways of effect.

One obstacle to such research is the breadth, depth, and complexity of knowledge, research design, and methods required for systematic investigation of family-psyche-soma pathways. Second, until recently, there have been no compelling candidates for psychobiological mechanisms by which family relational process could impact an individual's physical well-being (this shortcoming is addressed in a later section).

In addition, there are two related major methodological challenges to empirically identifying such pathways. It is clear that mere association between family relational patterns and disease activity gives no clue regarding direction of effect, nor does such association indicate specific pathways by which such effects could influence health and illness. Experimental manipulation to demonstrate direction of effect of family on disease outcomes by manipulation of family relational patterns, holding constant behavioral mediators of the effects (e.g., health behavior and adherence behaviors), is likely impossible. Theoretically, one might study direct psychobiological pathways by finding families in which health behavior and adherence are adequate, but in which there are emotionally negative or stressful relational patterns. However, data indicate that emotionally stressful family relational patterns are also typically associated with compromised health behavior and adherence, thus making it very difficult to disentangle stress-biological pathways from stress-behavior/adherence pathways. Longitudinal designs, frequently touted as the solution to interpreting causality and pathways of effect, are subject to the same limitations. Path analysis and other complex statistical approaches also cannot solve this problem, although they are frequently treated as if they do. We submit that the most tractable approach is to study family relational patterns in a laboratory context that allows structured elicitation of stressful relational patterns along with concurrent assessment of physiological responses which reflect disease-specific mediating pathways and mechanisms. But these are enormously complex and expensive studies and one should ask what rationale and data suggest that such investigations could yield clinically significant findings. Are such endeavors really justified? Or are they expensive wild goose chases? We believe that the following lines of research suggest that such endeavors are indeed well justified and that they promise fruitful avenues for cross-fertilization with family systems and health research.

Lines of Research Converging on Family-Psychobiologic Pathways

In recent years there have been several lines of research that compel consideration of how family relationships, emotions, and stress may influence disease through psychobiologic mechanisms. First, it is widely accepted, and scientifically supported, that social isolation predicts morbidity, mortality, and health, with effect sizes comparable to those of smoking, blood pressure, blood lipids, obesity, and physical activity, even after being corrected for these and other traditional risk factors (House, Landis, & Umberson, 1988). One seminal study was conducted 22 years ago in which 6,928 adults reported social ties (i.e., marriage, contacts with friends and relatives, organizational membership, and church membership) in 1965. Nine years later the mortality risk comparing the most isolated to the most social ranged from 2.3 for men and 2.8 for women. The association was independent of self-reported physical health status at baseline, year of death, socioeconomic status, and health practices, such as smoking, alcohol consumption, obesity, physical activity, and the use of health services (Berkman & Syme, 1979).

There is also a robust literature substantiating the connection between emotions (and stress) and physical health (Salovey et al., 2000). Salovey and his colleagues (2000) review findings that suggest a direct effect of emotions on disease-relevant physiology. They also review the health-relevant information value of emotions, the ways in which mood can motivate health-relevant behaviors, and how emotions can elicit social support, which is associated with positive health effects. Salovey et al. also emphasize the potential importance of positive emotions, although there is much less research in this domain. All of the research on the effect of emotions and stress on physiology and disease beg to be investigated in the context of one of the most emotion-rich and influential interpersonal contexts: the family.

Other examples of family-relevant findings demonstrate that the perception of warmth and caring by others predicts health and well-being (Berkman, 1995; Shumaker & Czajkowski, 1994; Uchino, Cacioppo, & Kiecolt-Glaser, 1996). One of the most compelling and provocative studies specifically relevant to family is a 35-year follow-up to the Harvard Mastery of Stress study (Funkenstein, King, & Drolette, 1957), in which Russek and Schwartz (1994, 1996, 1997a, 1997b) asked whether perceptions of parental love and caring, obtained in college, would predict the occurrence of physical disease in midlife. The 126 students were recruited because they were in excellent physical and psychiatric health. Subjects rated a series of 14 word pairs separately for their mothers and fathers, using a 1 to 19 Likert scale. Items included *loving-rejection, brutal-kind,* and *just-unjust.* On follow-up 116 individuals were evaluated by interview, and medical records independently reviewed by an academic physician. Of those students who rated both parents as high in love and caring (35 years prior to follow-up), 25% had diagnoses of physical disease in midlife, whereas students who rated both their mothers and fathers as low in loving had 87% diagnosed disease. These findings were independent of family history of disease, death and/or divorce history of parents, smoking history of subjects, and marital history of subjects. These studies compel family investigators and clinicians to take seriously the importance of family relations and emotions in health outcome. The emotional component, considered in the context of the robust emotion/stress psychobiologic literature cited above, strongly suggests a direct emotion-physiological connection. Nonetheless, the design of the research studies precludes inference of psychobiological causal effect. For example, it is possible that the students' degree of positive versus negative reports of their loving parents were shaped by their own negative affectivity or lack of optimism, both of which have been associated with negative health outcomes, and both of which may be heritable characteristics. However, it is also possible that the students' characteristic level of negative affectivity and optimism might have been partially engendered by parental love or lack thereof, and thus negativity/ optimism may mediate the family relational effect. Indeed, negative affectivity and optimism may be mediators (i.e., one pathway) of the effect of a gene-environment interaction, which together dispose to health or illness. But what is the proximal mechanism by which negative affectivity and optimism affect health; is it a direct psychobiologic pathway, a health-behavior pathway, or both? Yet another possibility is that loving parents might have set good examples and assisted in health maintaining behavior patterns and good adherence to such behavior. Clearly there are several possible family-health pathways and mechanisms that require investigation, each of which would dictate quite different intervention strategies were they to be substantiated.

*What Are the Potential Psychobiologic Pathways and Mechanisms
by Which Family Relations Could Impact Physical Well-Being?*

It is known that strong emotions and stress produce physiological changes in the body. It is also known that these changes are orchestrated by tightly interlinked mutually regulatory afferent and efferent pathways of the autonomic nervous system (ANS; parasympathetic and sympathetic nervous systems), hypothalamic-pituitary-adrenal axis (HPA), and immune system (Sternberg, 2000). The specifics of the linkages have not been elucidated. However, one of the most useful organizing models for integrated study of these systems is McEwen's model of allostasis and allostatic load (McEwen, 1998). When presented by an internal or external environmental challenge (physical, stressful, or emotional) requiring active response, the ANS, HPA, and immune system are activated in a coordinated fashion to ready the organism (allostasis) for adaptive response. The bodily requirements for response elicit psychobiologic changes which place a load on these systems in the organism (allostatic load). In the face of chronic unrelieved or repeated acute challenge or stress, the load may produce ANS/HPA/immune changes, including physiological imbalances and dysregulation, that may render the organism susceptible to disease or physiological dysregulation (Beauchaine, 2001). Many diseases, including heart disease, arthritis, asthma, inflammatory bowel disease, cancer, etc., have been associated with these changes. Recent scientific advances in the realm of psychoneuroimmunology (Cohen et al., 1998; Cohen & Herbert, 1996; Herbert & Cohen, 1993; McCabe, Schneiderman, Field, & Skyler, 1991), psycho-neuroendocrinology (Campeau, Day, Helmreich, Kollack-Walker, & Watson, 1998; Ryan, 1998), and psychophysiology substantiate these systems as potential pathways by which highly emotional or stressful interpersonal relations may influence physical well-being within the family. A key consideration in the investigation of the impact of family stress and emotions on disease is to make certain to choose for investigation mechanisms and pathways that are relevant to the pathophysiology of the disease under consideration.

■ The Biobehavioral Continuum of Disease: A Systems Framework

There is now full recognition and documentation of *psychosomatic* phenomena, which are currently referred to as stress-related illnesses or psychophysiological disorders. It is noteworthy that the research in this area renders obsolete the placement of organic and psychological/psychiatric illness in dichotomous relation to one another. Nonetheless, the current literature still appears to linger in a unidirectional linear paradigm. It is noteworthy that in the early 1950s conceptualizations of psychosomatic illness were systemic, proposing reciprocal influence between psychological and physiological/disease processes (Alexander, 1950). Subsequently, theory and research drifted into an essentially linear paradigm. We propose that a more valid perspective follows from the systems paradigm, which assumes mutual influence of social, psychological, and physical factors in all aspects

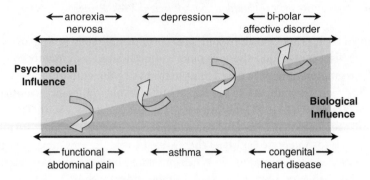

FIGURE 20.1 Biobehavioral continuum of psychological and physical influences on disease.

of health and illness. Within this framework we propose a continuum of emotional and physical disease that varies according to the relative proportions of psychosocial and physical influences on the disease (see figure 20.1).

At one extreme are diseases with relatively strong psychosocial influence, such as functional abdominal pain. At the other extreme would be diseases such as congenital heart disease. Diseases such as asthma and diabetes range in between, depending on the relative contribution of psychosocial and biological factors in the course of illness for a particular patient, at a particular period in his or her development. For example, a given individual with asthma may have disease that is equally influenced by psychosocial and emotional factors. However, if family conflict becomes intense and prolonged and involves the individual, then psychosocial factors might assume greater proportional influence on the disease process, thus shifting the disease toward the psychosocial end of the continuum. This recognition of relative influences on the disease is crucial for effective intervention. In the situation just described, giving more medication might not have the desired ameliorative effect. Intervention to decrease conflict might "treat" the asthma more successfully.

Current findings in psychiatry indicate that diseases previously considered due to psychosocial and psychological factors (e.g., bipolar affective disorder, schizophrenia, autism) are also due to biological factors, indicating a comparable convergence of psychological and biological factors in mental illness (Bellack & Morrison, 1987). Thus, physical *and* emotional illnesses can be conceptualized in the same biobehavioral continuum. The curved arrows in the diagram represent the interaction of psychosocial/psychological and biological factors as they influence a given disease. They represent mechanisms or pathways of biobehavioral influence. The Biobehavioral Family Model (BBFM; Wood, 1993; Wood, Klebba, & Miller, 2000), described in a later section, specifies some of these pathways and hypothesizes how family relational process may play a pivotal role in health and illness.

The advantage of conceptualizing disease in this manner is that it organizes a more sophisticated approach to investigating factors influencing illness, and it supports an integrated biopsychosocial approach to the understanding and treatment of both physically and behaviorally or emotionally manifested illness. Before articulating the BBFM, which is a specific model informed by the concept of a biobehavioral continuum of disease, we revisit a pioneer model that broke the ground for a systemic vision of family process and physical disease.

The Psychosomatic Family Model: A Pioneer
Systems Theory of Families and Health

Minuchin and colleagues (1975) developed a groundbreaking model of how family and illness interrelate in ways to exacerbate disease activity in ill children. This open systems model, called the *Psychosomatic Family Model,* comprises a constellation of family relational patterns plus somatic patterns of disease activity and illness behavior in children. The model evolved from the study of children with diabetes mellitus who were experiencing recurrent episodes of ketoacidosis and/or chronic acetonuria, despite adequate diabetic management and diet. These children had families who displayed characteristic patterns of interaction: enmeshment, over-protection, rigidity, poor conflict resolution and/or conflict avoidance, and triangulation of the patient in family conflict. The disease and illness interact with family relational patterns so as to maintain this particular family organization. Conversely it was proposed that these family relational patterns trigger physiological processes in the child patient, which then exacerbate the disease process. In turn, the child's increased illness reinforces these family patterns, establishing a reverberating and escalating process. Although the model was developed in the context of pediatric illness, the principles and dimensions apply appropriately to illness at any developmental stage, with appropriate adaptation.

What was new and heuristically provocative about the model was its basis in the systems paradigm. As an open systems model, the model permitted focused evaluation of bidirectional influences between biological and social (family) levels of illness. Plus it proposed a direct psychobiological effect of family relational process on the child's disease process (i.e., the stress of the diabetic child's exposure to the problematic family patterns of relational process elicited physiological changes that potentiates the disease process). Although the psychosomatic family model was originally conceptualized as a model of mutual influence between the child's illness and family patterns of interaction, there was a subsequent focus on examining the family's potential influence on the child's disease process, and theoreticians, researchers, and clinicians lost touch with the mutual influence aspect of the model. The model was misquoted and misapplied in ways that resulted in too narrow an application of the model's principles. Furthermore, the model was accepted as validated prematurely, resulting in unwise assumptions that if a patient was having difficulty controlling a chronic illness it was due to dysfunctional family patterns. This inappropriate application of the model has been corrected by subsequent critiques and by the development of related family models (Campbell, 1986; Coyne & Anderson, 1988, 1989; Wood, 1993; Wood et al., 1989).

The results of research testing this model have been mixed, in part because of limitations in the design of the studies purporting to test the model (see Coyne & Anderson, 1988, 1989; Wood et al., 1989; and Wood, 1993, for reviews and commentary). There has been no decisive study testing all aspects of the model. Wood and colleagues (1989) addressed some of the limitations in a laboratory-based study of children with inflammatory bowel disease and functional abdominal pain. Results indicated that the five characteristics of the psychosomatic family configuration were highly correlated with one another, supporting the idea that they mutually reinforce one another and form a genuine complex. However, only marital discord and triangulation were associated with a physiological index of disease activity. Furthermore, there was some indication that enmeshment, overprotection, conflict avoidance, and rigidity may be adaptive for some of the patients (Wood et al., 1989). In the course of clinical experience with chronically ill children from disadvantaged homes and communities, it became clear that the psychosomatic family model was focusing on only one end of the dimension of involvement (enmeshment) and protection (overprotection) (Celano, personal communication). It was Celano's contention that neglect and lack of protection have similar effects on disease in children with asthma. Other conceptual and theoretical limitations became apparent. For example, there was no systematic consideration of the emotional climate in these families, which has subsequently been shown to be an important factor in both physical and emotional illness (Langfitt, Wood, Brand, Brand, & Erba, 1999; Wood et al., 2000). Also, there was no consideration of the individual biological characteristics (i.e., temperament) of the child that may contribute to vulnerability to illness, as well as to the shaping of family relational patterns. Finally, there was no conceptualization of how parent-child dyadic relationships (e.g., attachment security) might mediate or moderate the impact of stressful family relations on the child's emotional and physical well-being. There is now a vast literature on how a child's development in the realm of attachment relationships influences emotional, behavioral, and physical outcomes and evidence that insecure attachment is associated with emotional and physiological dysregulation, both of which would likely exacerbate the influence of stress upon a disease process (Cassidy & Shaver, 1999; Cicchetti, 2001; Wood, 2002; Wood et al., 2000). Taken together these considerations led to a reconceptualization and reformulation of the Psychosomatic Family Model (Wood, 1993, 2001; Wood & Miller, 2002; Wood et al., 2000). The reformulation, called the BBFM, concentrates upon the family-illness direction of effect, but is consistent with mutual influence of illness and family factors.

The Biobehavioral Family Model: A Prototype for Investigation of Family-Psychobiologic Pathways and Mechanisms

In an attempt to systematically examine pathways by which family relations may influence disease in children, Wood has developed and tested a heuristic model, the BBFM. The BBFM posits that particular family relational patterns influence

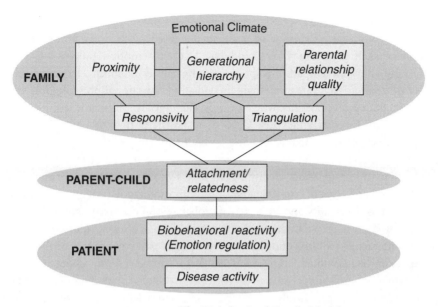

FIGURE 20.2   The Biobehavioral Family Model.

and are influenced by the psychological and physiological processes of individual family members (Wood, 1993) (see figure 20.2). Specifically, the BBFM proposes that emotional climate, family proximity, generational hierarchy, parental relationship, triangulation, and interpersonal responsivity are processes that influence one another and interact with individual (family member) psychological and emotional processes in ways which either buffer or exacerbate biological processes relevant to disease activity in children. It is also posited that individual psychological and emotional processes, in turn, influence and shape the specific family patterns. Parent-child attachment is proposed as a potential moderating or mediating factor influencing the impact of stressful family relational process (or life events) on disease-related psychological and physiological processes in children (Wood et al., 2000). Although the BBFM has been developed in the context of pediatric illness, it is applicable, with appropriate adaptation, to any developmental stage. The BBFM is currently conceptualized as *a family relational stress model of disease,* in keeping with the more current scientific advances concerning the psychobiological effects of stress on emotional and physical functioning in individuals.

Proximity is defined as the extent to which family members share personal space, private information, and emotions. *Generational hierarchy* refers to the extent to which caregivers are in charge of the children by providing nurturance and limits through strong parental alliance and absence of cross-generational coalitions. *Parental relationship quality* refers to caregiver interactions with one another, which include mutual support, understanding, and adaptive disagreement (respectful and resolving) versus hostility, rejection, and conflict. *Triangulation* refers to involving a child in the parental conflictual process in ways which render the child responsible, blamed, scapegoated, or in loyalty conflict. *Responsivity* refers to the extent to which family members are behaviorally, emotionally, and physiologically reactive to one another. Responsivity depends, in part, on the *biobehavioral* (i.e., emotional) *reactivity* of each family member. Moderate levels of emotional/physiological responsivity allow for empathic response among family members. Extremely high levels of responsivity can exacerbate maladaptive emotional/physiological resonance in the family, possibly worsening psychologically influenced emotional or physical disorders. Extremely low levels of responsivity may be part of a general pattern of neglect or avoidance, leaving family members unbuffered from internal, familial, or environmental stressors. Levels of responsivity reflect family-level patterns of emotion regulation, stemming, in part, from the confluence of individual family members' ways of regulating emotion. Emotion regulation or dysregulation is reflected in the quality and intensity of biobehavioral reactivity (defined below). The negativity versus positivity of the family *emotional climate* colors the characteristic interactive patterns and thus determines, in part, the impact of the family patterns on the individual family members. For example, a family characterized by high proximity and high responsivity with positive emotional climate might be a passionate, lively happy family, whereas one characterized by high proximity, high responsivity, but with negative emotional climate is likely to be a stressful family in which to live.

Biobehavioral reactivity, the pivotal construct that links psychological to biological processes in the BBFM, is conceptualized as the degree or intensity with which an individual family member responds physiologically, emotionally, and behaviorally to emotional stimuli (Boyce, Barr, & Zeltzer, 1992; Jemerin & Boyce, 1990, 1992; Wood, 1993). Biobehavioral reactivity reflects the ability of the individual to self-regulate emotions and physiological processes. Biobehavioral reactivity/emotion regulation is presumed to be influenced both by temperament (Kagan, Reznick, & Snidman, 1988; Suomi, 1987) and by external influences, particularly by patterns of caregiving (Calkins, 1994; Cassidy, 1994; Field, 1994). Depending on which physiological processes are activated or deactivated by particular patterns of emotion dysregulation, such processes may influence specific psychological or physical diseases, depending upon the presence of a pathogenic pathway. Different configurations of proximity and hierarchy structure maintain, contain, or magnify the mutual influence which patterns of parental relationship, triangulation, responsivity, and individual biobehavioral reactivity have on one another (see Wood, 1993, 2001, and 2002, and Wood et al., 2000, for further explication of the BBFM with clinical application).

The Scope of the BBFM.   To date the BBFM has concentrated on physiological processes and physical illness in children. However, the model, in principle, could be focused to address the processes affecting *any* family member (adult or child) suffering from physically and/or psychologically manifested disease. This broad developmental application is justified by the ill person's likely dependence upon, and high levels of involvement with, the family, regardless of age or developmental status. The broad interpretation of "disease" is justified by research developments which increasingly demonstrate the mutual contribution of psychological and biological factors to both physically and psychologically manifested disease. It is also consistent with the biobehavioral continuum of disease presented above.

To date no study has tested the BBFM in toto, but several studies reviewed below address links in the model.

Negative Family Emotional Climate and Emotional and Physical Illness.   The BBFM defines negative family emotional climate as a preponderance of negative versus positive emotional interchanges. Using this definition Wood found negative family climate to be associated with epilepsy outcome (Langfitt et al., 1999) and vagal activation in children with asthma (Wood et al., 2000). Other studies have shown that related constructs of low family cohesion and high conflict are implicated in child depression and hopelessness in physically well (Garrison et al., 1997; Marton & Maharaj, 1993; Olsson, Nordstrom, Arinell, & von Knorring, 1999) and in chronically ill children (Grey, Boland, Yu, Sullivan-Bolyai, & Tamborlane, 1998; Mengel et al., 1992; Wyllie, Glazer, Benbadis, Kotagal, & Wolgamuth, 1999). Criticism and hostility have been associated with ANS activation (Tarrier, 1989; Valone, Norton, Goldstein, & Doane, 1984) and worsening of many illnesses (Hahlweg et al., 1989; Miklowitz, Goldstein, Nuechterlein, Snyder, & Mintz, 1988), including childhood depression (Cook, Strachan, Goldstein, & Miklowitz, 1989) and childhood asthma (Hermanns, Florin, Dietrich, Rieger, & Hahlweg, 1989; Schobinger, Florin, Zimmer, Lindemann, & Winter, 1992).

Parental Conflict, Child Depression, and Physiological Dysregulation.   Parental discord not only contributes to negative family emotional climate, but also has direct effects on children's emotional functioning (Davies & Cummings, 1994; Emery, 1982; Reid & Crisafulli, 1990), including childhood depression (Seligman, Reivich, Jaycox, & Gillham, 1995). Davies and Cummings demonstrated that marital discord predicted internalizing disorders more robustly than externalizing disorders and that emotional security mediated the link (Davies & Cummings, 1998). Parental conflict is accompanied by physiologic stress responses in the exposed child. El-Sheikh (1994) found that girls from high- versus low-conflict homes exhibited increased, and boys decreased, heart rate reactivity in response to an argument between two adults in a laboratory setting. Gottman and Katz (1989) found marital conflict associated with children's increased levels of catecholamines.

Triangulation of the Child Patient and Disease Activity.   Findings on triadic involvement of the child in parent conflict are mixed with respect to positive versus negative outcomes for the child (Davies & Cummings, 1994; Vuchinich, Emery, & Cassidy, 1988), and the construct needs further specification. The BBFM construct of *triangulation* refers to the child's being involved in parental conflictual process in ways that render the child responsible, blamed, scapegoated, or in loyalty conflict regarding the conflict. Triangulation of a child in parental conflict has been associated with poor course of physical illness in children (Minuchin et al., 1975; Wood et al., 1989), with increased disease activity in child inflammatory bowel disease

(Wood et al., 1989), and with hopelessness and vagal activation child asthma (Wood et al., 2000).

Attachment Security as a Moderator.   Disruption in animal maternal-offspring relationship can lead to depression, hopelessness, and emotional and physiological dysregulation (Field, 1994, 1996; Gunnar, Brodersen, Nachmias, Buss, & Rigatuso, 1996; Hofer, 1996; Schore, 1996). Field and others have shown that such disruptions have significant effects on emotional and physiological regulation in humans (Field, 1994, 1996; Fox & Card, 1999; Gunnar et al., 1996; Schore, 1996). In addition, compromised attachment has been found to be related to child and adolescent depression (Armsden, McCauley, Greenberg, Burke, & Mitchell, 1990; Kobak, Sudler, & Gamble, 1991) and hopelessness (Strang & Orlofsky, 1990). On the other hand, there is also evidence that *secure attachment may buffer* a child from difficult life events (Masten, Best, & Garmezy, 1990) and stress (Gunnar et al., 1996). More specifically, Nachmias and colleagues have demonstrated that attachment security moderates the cortisol response to stress (Nachmias, Gunnar, Mangelsdorf, Parritz, & Buss, 1996). These findings suggest a moderating role for security of parent-child relationship vis-à-vis the effect of stressful family relations on child illness.

Taken together these findings are consistent with the BBFM. However, what is missing in all these studies is the link to the disease process itself in terms of the identification of plausible pathways and mechanisms. Asthma is a condition in which stress and emotions are believed to play important roles (Busse et al., 1995; Lehrer, Feldman, Giardino, Song, & Schmaling, 2002; Wright, Rodriguez, & Cohen, 1998). Our testing of the BBFM is currently focusing on asthma, an illness for which Miller (coauthor) has developed a psychophysiological model of mechanism which provides a potential testable pathway for the influence of family relational stress on asthma.

The Missing Link: ANS Dysregulation

Although the research reviewed above is consistent with stressful family relations having an impact on disease activity, neither the research nor the BBFM itself suggests specific psychobiologic pathways or mechanisms. Without specifying a potential link there can be no direct test of the direction of effect. However, the ANS Dysregulation Model of the Influence of Emotions in Asthma (Miller, 1987; Miller & Wood, 1995) provides a heuristic model of specific pathways (see figure 20.3). The two mechanisms of airway constriction in asthma (immune/inflammatory and ANS/vagal) point to two possible psychobiologic pathways by which emotions may influence airway function: (a) psychoneuroimmunologic (PNI) and (b) ANS/vagal. The fact that both the ANS and immune system play crucial roles in both the regulation of stress and emotions *and* in airway constriction in asthma makes them likely candidates as psychobiologic pathways mediating the effect of family relational stress/emotions on asthma.

In the asthma realm, Miller and Strunk (1989) found that family turmoil, extreme sensitivity to separation and loss, and hopelessness and despair characterized

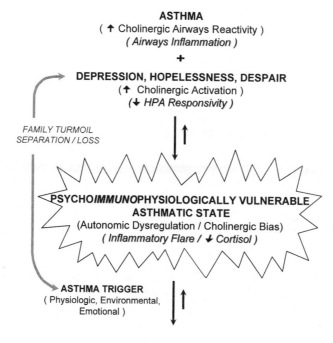

FIGURE 20.3   An autonomic and immunologic dysregulation model of emotional influence on asthma.

asthmatic children who died from, compared to those who survived, a life-
threatening asthma attack. Furthermore, disruptions in parent-child attachment
have also been associated with depression/hopelessness, along with increased vagal
activation and poor emotional and physical outcomes. Based on these research
connections, Miller developed the ANS Dysregulation Model of the Influence of
Emotions in Asthma (Miller, 1987).

This model proposes that depressed, despairing, or hopeless (burnout) emotional states are associated with an ANS dysregulation which potentiates vagally
mediated airway constriction, giving rise to a destabilized asthmatic state. Support
for the ANS model rests upon three laboratory-based studies (Miller & Wood,
1994, 1997; Wood et al., 2000). In addition, research indicates that ANS pathways
may mediate the effect of stress and depression on airways (Lehrer et al., 2002; Ritz,
Steptoe, DeWilde, & Costa, 2000). Recently, PNI findings suggest that distressed
asthmatics may be in a hyperstable proinflammatory state (Coe, 1994). Since the
ANS and immune system are closely interconnected, the ANS model can subsume
both pathways. It should be noted that this model is not limited to emotional
triggering, but rather also encompasses the sustained effects of emotional/physi-
ological conditions as they physiologically potentiate chronic airway compromise,
thus giving rise to a state of vulnerability to asthma triggers, physical as well as

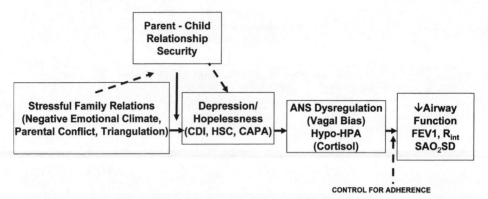

FIGURE 20.4   A conceptual model guiding hypothesis testing that integrates the BBFM and ANS dysregulation models.

emotional. Taken together the BBFM and the ANS models suggest that ANS and immune dysregulation may mediate the effect of the BBFM-predicted stressful family relations on airway function in asthma, as pictured above (see figure 20.4). But how would one test this conjoined model?

A Laboratory-Based Method for Testing Family-Psychobiological Pathways and Mechanisms

Miller has tested the ANS model in children with asthma. He developed a controlled laboratory protocol in which children viewed an emotionally challenging movie, *E.T.—The Extra-Terrestrial,* while having specific ANS functions measured in synchrony with the movie. Pulmonary function tests were performed before and after the movie. Pulmonary compromise was associated with ANS and emotional reactivity to the movie, particularly in the death scene (Miller & Wood, 1994, 1997). Wood conducted an analogous laboratory protocol, using a structured set of emotionally challenging family interaction tasks in synchrony with ANS measures. Triangulation and hopelessness were associated with insecure father-child related-ness, all of which were associated with vagal activation. The child's perception of parental conflict showed trends of association with triangulation and insecure father-child relatedness. Insecure mother-child relatedness was correlated only with hopelessness (Wood et al., 2000).

In follow-up investigations of 300 children with asthma presenting to the emergency room, Miller and Wood will extend the measures to include both sympathetic and vagal branches of ANS, salivary cortisol, and pulmonary function tests during both the movie and family interaction tasks, the latter of which will be scored by the Iowa Family Interaction Rating Scale (Melby & Conger, 2001). This will permit synchronous assessment of stressful family interactions, mediating psychobiologic mechanisms (ANS and cortisol) and disease activity (pulmonary function). Structural equation modeling will be used to assess the complex configuration of hypotheses: (a) negative family emotional climate, parental conflict, and triangulation of a child in conflict predict depression/hopelessness in the child; (b) the family-depression effect is moderated by parent-child relationship security; and (c) depression predicts airway compromise, which is mediated by vagal bias and/or hypo-HPA function. Adherence will also be assessed in this same study in order to disentangle family adherence–disease pathways from family psychobiologic–disease pathways in childhood asthma.

This is a prototype methodology that could be applied to virtually any disease in which stress- or emotion-induced psychobiologic pathways may be implicated in the pathogenesis of the disease under investigation. Another related approach to studying the potential influence of couples relations on disease is presented next.

Psychobiological Pathways of Disease in Couples: The Case
For PNI, HPA, and ANS

Recent data suggest that immune dysregulation may be one core mechanism for a spectrum of illnesses, including cardiovascular disease, osteoporosis, arthritis, diabetes, certain cancers, inflammatory bowel disease, asthma, and frailty and functional decline. Production of proinflammatory cytokines that influence these and other conditions can be stimulated directly by negative emotion. Thus, immunological alterations provide one likely physiological pathway by which stressful family relational processes may influence health and illness. Indeed, the link between personal relationships and immune function is one of the most robust findings in the PNI literature (Kiecolt-Glaser, McGuire, Robles, & Glaser, 2002a, 2002b; Uchino et al., 1996). Age, race, gender, and social economic status contribute effects as well (Kiecolt-Glaser et al., 2002a) and thus must be factored into the investigation of psychobiological mediation of the effects of relational stress on health and illness.

The quality of marital and couple relationships is associated with immune and endocrine function (Kiecolt-Glaser & Newton, 2001). For example, women with rheumatoid arthritis were followed for 12 weeks. Although both immune function and clinician's ratings changed during a week of increased interpersonal stress, women who reported more positive spousal interaction patterns and less spousal criticism or negativity did not show as large an increase in clinical symptoms (Zautra et al., 1998). When close relationships are discordant, they can also be associated with depression and immune dysregulation. Both syndromal depression and depressive symptoms have been strongly associated with marital discord (Fincham & Beach, 1999).

Most of the research on the relationship between quality of relationships and health have been self-report in nature. In contrast, Kiecolt-Glaser and her colleagues have developed a rigorous laboratory-based program of research that is a model for researchers committed to investigating mechanisms and pathways by which stressful relational interaction may influence disease-relevant immune, endocrine, HPA, and ANS processes. In this laboratory paradigm physiological changes are assessed during and following couples' discussion of relationship problems. The topics are chosen by the experimenter, based on each spouse's ratings of common relationship problems. Pervasive differences in endocrine and immune function were reliably associated with hostile behaviors during marital conflict among diverse samples that included newlyweds selected on the basis of stringent mental and physical health criteria, as well as couples married an average of 42 years (Kiecolt-Glaser, Glaser, Cacioppo, & MacCallum, 1997; Kiecolt-Glaser et al., 1993; Malarkey, Kiecolt-Glaser, Pearl, & Glaser, 1994). Kiecolt-Glaser notes that the endocrine system serves as one central gateway for psychological influences on health; stress and depression can provoke the release of pituitary and adrenal hormones that have multiple effects on immune function (Rabin, 1999). For example, social stressors can substantially elevate key stress hormones, including catecholamines and cortisol, and these hormones have multiple immunomodulatory effects on immune function (Glaser & Kiecolt-Glaser, 1994). In addition the autonomic nervous system, particularly the sympathetic branch, plays an active role in modulating immune function (Kiecolt-Glaser et al., 2002b). The endocrine, ANS, HPA, and immune systems are all tightly intertwined in mutual orchestration of physiological response to stress and emotional challenge. Furthermore, it is these systems that are implicated in the phenomenon conceptualized as allostatic load, the cumulative long-tern effects of physiological responses to stress (McEwen, 1998). (For a comprehensive review of pathways leading from the marital relationship to physical health see (Kiecolt-Glaser & Newton, 2001.)

Shortcomings of the Models to Date

Goals of the Model.   Most models are not clear about, or have not explicitly specified, the goal for which they were developed. For example, some models seem well suited to discovering information that will support the best treatment intervention for the physical well-being of the patient. Others seem better suited to investigating factors affecting the patient's quality of life. Still others appear to privilege the overall function of the family. Models cannot likely be "all things to all people," but they should at least be clear about their goals (see Fisher, ch. 22, for further discussion of these issues).

Definition of Family and Ethnocultural Considerations.   Systematic investigation of families and health is further compromised because the concept family is not well or consistently defined, conceptualized, and operationalized within and across studies. For example, studying African American, Latino, and other ethnic groups requires a conceptualization of family that includes fictive as well as biological family. Until recently, most studies confined themselves to middle-class, two-parent White families, a group that is actually in the minority when considering the vast diversity of ethnic and socioeconomic status factors that affect family configuration. Such narrow investigation precludes finding differential relationships, based on ethnicity and class, among beliefs, values, expectations, motivations, and family relational patterns, on one hand, and health behaviors and outcomes on the other hand. Such differences could include salutary effects of particular ethnically based adaptations to stressful life conditions, including illness. We propose adopting a definition of family similar to one proposed in Weihs and Fisher's review article (Weihs et al.,

2002), i.e., "a constellation of at least two intimates, living in close proximity, having some sort of emotional bonds (positive and/or negative), a history and an antici- pated future." We think this is a useful definition, but operationalizing this defi- nition in studies is an awesome challenge. A related limitation of current models is the lack of systematic consideration of the influence of race, gender, ethnicity, and social class as main or moderating factors. A useful investigatory strategy might be to seek to identify factors that apply across race, gender, ethnicity, and social class, while distinguishing those that are specific to group.

"Health" is not the opposite of "illness" and the factors that lead to health may be different from those that lead to the absence of illness, or to healing or dimin- ishing of illness. There is a paucity of models and research concentrating on family factors affecting and affected by health (see Future Directions below for expansion of this idea).

Level of Specificity.   Another shortcoming of current models is that most of them were shaped based on a particular disease and age group, thus precluding gener- alization to other illnesses and developmental stages. It is an open question, so far, whether the most productive approach would be to have separate models for each disease, specific for major developmental stage, family type, ethnic group, and SES of the patient. This approach might more readily yield clinically significant findings that can be immediately applied to that particular disease. On the other hand, such an approach precludes potentially important theoretical advances, such as learning what factors apply across disease, age, and other demographic variables. We contend that these more elusive and long-term scientific advances would ultimately yield a more complete knowledge, and one which could lead to more comprehensive and efficient health care prevention, intervention, and policy.

Importance of Pathways and Mechanisms for All Models

One goal of this chapter is to demonstrate why it is important to identify mecha- nisms and pathways by which family factors and health and illness influence one another. We concentrate, in our work and in this chapter, on direct psychobio- logical pathways by which stressful family relations may influence a family mem- ber's physical well-being because we believe that the vast literature on stress, emotions, and disease argues that such pathways are of great clinical significance. However, we wish to emphasize that the importance of identifying mechanisms and pathways is not limited to psychobiological factors in health and illness. It is equally important to identify the specific pathways underlying other robust family-health/ illness associations. We contend that it is essential to move beyond mere association to the identification of causal effects. Understanding causal effects and their mech- anisms allows targeted intervention and prevents misplaced intervention, which can occur if an intervention mistakenly targets the wrong predictor. For example, it has been found that marital conflict predicts cardiovascular outcomes. But what if marital conflict is an epiphenomenon of the patient's personal trait of hostility, which not only gives rise to high levels of marital conflict, but itself has been shown to contribute to poor cardiovascular outcomes by way of allostatic load? It could be wasteful, ineffective, and even potentially iatrogenic to try to change marital interaction with therapy, rather than helping the individual with his or her own tendency to hostile arousal by using behavioral, biofeedback, or pharmacological interventions. Thus, knowledge of the mechanisms and pathways can guide more accurate intervention and prevention. We propose that this is true not only for psychobiologic factors but also for behavioral factors in health, including adherence, and for the families' response and adaptation or maladaptation to illness. For example, if family-level meaning-making helps the physical and emotional function of the chronically ill child and the family, we need to know exactly what is meant by *meaning-making* and exactly *the pathway or means by which* meaning is constructed, in order to intervene in knowledgeable and targeted ways. Furthermore, we would argue that models of intervention also need to consider pathways and mechanisms for the same reasons outlined above.

It should also be cautioned that models, such as ours, which focus on a particular set of pathways and mechanisms, i.e., psychobiological, should allow for alternative equally plausible pathways that are not built into the model. Ideally researchers would build more than one potential pathway/mechanism into their heuristic model.

Shortcomings of Methods to Date

Blind Empiricism.   Research is often not guided by well articulated models and is subject to what we would label *blind empiricism.* The current PNI research suffers from this shortcoming, despite the vast size of the literature in this realm. The result is that there is a collection of findings, many of which are contradictory. It is likely that the findings are contradictory for a reason, and models might facilitate a systematic appraisal of how, for example, specific demographic, disease, and stress characteristics might influence disease-related psychobiologic function relevant to particular diseases.

Problems With Measurement.   The lack of heuristic models also results in use of outcome measures that are not thoughtfully or wisely chosen, well defined, or tightly linked to a reasonable interpretation. For the same reason, the measures of biologic disease activity/outcome are often faulty, limited, or confounded. Furthermore, most family and individual psychological and emotional measures were developed within a particular ethnic and social class (White, middle class) and are *not* well suited, even if psychometrically sound, with other groups. Most family and individual measures used are either self-report or observational, each of which alone poses limitations. Self-report fails to capture behavioral or relational patterns that are not easily available to self-reflection and report. On the other hand, observational measures are limited in not capturing the individual's internal experience of the relationships in the family. Moreover, the meaning of a set of relational interactions is not always apparent to the observer, particularly when there are demographic differences between the family and the observer/rater. The solution is to use a multimethod approach to measurement.

■ Conclusions and Future Directions: "Subvert the Dominant Paradigm"?

We contend that the complexity and multidimensional nature of relations among family function health and illness require a paradigm that can match that complexity, and we propose that the systems paradigm meets this requirement. The knowledge required in the relevant domains of biology, physiology, psychology, development, family relations, and sociocultural realms requires multidisciplinary inquiry. A systems paradigm has the virtue of facilitating, if not requiring, cross-discipline fertilization and collaboration. Systems theory crosses disciplines in its assumptions, principles, and methods and thus can be a bridge to productive collaboration. For these reasons, to the extent that the systems paradigm is *not* dominant we declare "subvert the dominant paradigm" (quote from a 60's bumper sticker).

A recent example of an ongoing effort to subvert the dominant paradigm is the paradigm shift reflected in the field of developmental psychopathology as conceived by Dante Cicchetti (2001). Developmental psychopathology is a developmental transactional systems paradigm that integrates biological, psychological, and environmental/social levels of mutual influence. It challenges categorical notions and assumptions underlying the conceptualization of psychopathology and proposes psychopathology as a deviation from normal developmental trajectory that is caused by the interaction of biological, psychological, and environmental factors. It embraces the notions of equifinality of cause and effect and focuses on understanding pathways, processes, and mechanisms by which these effects occur. The innovative implications of this paradigm for the investigation of pathways and mechanisms are of enormous significance for understanding health and illness (psychological *and* biological). Most recently this paradigm has been applied to stress (see Cicchetti & Nurcombe, 2003). There is stunning evidence presented in this special issue that points to long-term neurobiological changes in the brain, brought about by deviations in normal parenting in infancy, that affect susceptibility to stress and consequent psychological and biological outcomes. Attachment processes have also been importantly implicated as impacting disease-related neurobiological processes (Schore, 1994, 1996; Siegel, 1999). This line of research has tremendous implications bearing upon directions that family research could usefully take, particularly research focusing on family relational processes as they relate to biological and psychological development and outcomes.

Another attempt to "subvert the dominant paradigm" is the movement called *positive psychology* initiated by M. E. P. Seligman when he was president of the American Psychological Association. The position underlying this movement is that psychological inquiry has too long been dominated by the focus on deviance and dysfunction and that there needs to be a shift toward investigating how to make the lives of all people more fulfilling and to identifying and nurturing high talent. The definition of positive psychology is the scientific study of optimal human functioning (Seligman & Csikszentmihalyi, 2000). Positive psychology seeks to understand and encourage factors that allow individuals, communities, and societies to flourish. The alteration in perspective that this paradigm shift suggests has great potential significance for family research as a whole, including the field of families and health. To be specific, this new paradigm may help identify aspects of biological, psychological, and social life that engender individual and family health, rather than to just concentrate on illness, which has been the focus to date. One line of research consistent with positive psychology is Gary Schwartz and Linda Russek's research on love (reviewed above), which is long overdue and which has tremendous application and implication for all of family systems research, and not limited to research in the health realm.

The lines of family-relevant health research reviewed in the main body of this chapter, and presented in this "subversion section," suggest many unexplored fertile and exciting avenues for future research. Whatever directions are taken, it is clear that a systems paradigm is essential. Furthermore, in the realm of families and health/illness, the necessity for simultaneous investigation of biological, psychological, and social levels of mutual influence demands a depth and breadth of knowledge that can be obtained only by interdisciplinary collaboration and integrated multilevel models.

■ Acknowledgments

This work was supported by NIMH Grants R01 MH064154 (Wood, P.I.) and R01 MH058761 (Miller, P.I.).

We thank William Pinsof and Jay Lebow who convened the special APA conference on Family Psychology: The Art of the Science, and those who participated in this conference. The collegial conversations engendered in this exchange stimulated significant changes and development in our perspectives. We also thank Tressa Wagner and William Tallmadge for technical assistance in preparation of the manuscript.

■ References

Alexander, F. (1950). *Psychosomatic medicine: Its principles and applications.* New York: Norton.

Armsden, G. C., McCauley, E., Greenberg, M. T., Burke, P. M., & Mitchell, J. R. (1990). Parent and peer attachment in early adolescent depression. *Journal of Abnormal Child Psychology, 18,* 683–697.

Beauchaine, T. (2001). Vagal tone, development, and Gray's motivational theory: Toward an integrated model of autonomic nervous system functioning in psychopathology. *Development and Psychopathology, 13,* 183–214.

Bellack, A. S., & Morrison, R. L. (1987). Physical and psychological dysfunction: An integrative perspective. In R. L. Morrison, A. S. Bellack, et al. (Eds.), *Medical factors and psychological disorders: A handbook for psychologists* (pp. 3–17). New York: Plenum.

Berkman, L. F. (1995). The role of social relations in health promotion. [Review]. *Psychosomatic Medicine, 57,* 245.

Berkman, L. F., & Syme, S. L. (1979). Social networks, host resistance, and mortality: A nine-year follow-up study of Alameda County residents. *American Journal of Epidemiology, 109*, 186–204.

Booth, R. J., Cohen, S., Cunningham, A., Dossey, L., Dreher, H., Kiecolt-Glaser, J. K., et al. (2001). The state of the science: The best evidence for the involvement of thoughts and feelings in physical health. *Advances, 17*, 2–59.

Boss, P. (1988). *Family stress management.* Newbury Park, CA: Sage.

Boss, P. (2002). *Family stress management : A contextual approach* (2nd ed.) Thousand Oaks, CA: Sage.

Boss, P. E., & Mulligan, C. E. (2003). *Family stress: Classic and contemporary readings.* Thousand Oaks, CA: Sage.

Boyce, W. T., Barr, R. G., & Zeltzer, L. K. (1992). Temperament and the psychobiology of childhood stress. *Pediatrics, 90*(3), 483–486.

Busse, W. W., Kiecolt-Glaser, J. K., Coe, C., Martin, R. J., Weiss, S. T., & Parker, S. R. (1995). Stress and asthma. *American Journal of Respiratory and Critical Care Medicine, 151*, 249–252.

Calkins, S. D. (1994). Origins and outcomes of individual differences in emotion regulation. *Monographs of the Society for Research in Child Development, 240*, 53–72.

Campbell, T. L. (1986). Family's impact on health: A critical review. *Family Systems Medicine, 4*, 135–328.

Campbell, T. L. (2002). *Family interventions for physical disorders.* Manuscript prepared for the AAMFT conference on Marriage and Family Therapy Effectiveness.

Campeau, S., Day, H. E., Helmreich, D. L., Kollack-Walker, S., & Watson, S. J. (1998). Principles of psychoneuroendocrinology. *Psychiatric Clinics of North America, 21*, 259–276.

Cassidy, J. (1994). Emotion regulation: Influences of attachment relationships. *Monographs of the Society for Research in Child Development, 59*, 228–249.

Cassidy, J. E., & Shaver, P. R. E. (1999). *Handbook of attachment: Theory, research, and clinical applications.* New York: Guilford Press.

Cicchetti, D., & Nurcombe (Eds.). (2003). Stress and development: Biological and psychological consequences. *Development and Psychopathology* (Special Issue).

Cicchetti, D. E. (2001). Stress and development: Biological and psychological consequences. [Monograph]. *Development and Psychopathology* (Serial No. 13).

Coe, C. L. (1994). Implications of psychoneuroimmunology for allergy and asthma. In E. Middleton, Jr., C. E. Reed, E. F. Ellis, N. F. Adkinson, Jr., J. W. Yunginger, & W. W. Busse (Eds.), *Update 19: Allergy principles and practice* (4th ed.). St. Louis, MO: Mosby Yearbook.

Cohen, H. D., Goodenough, D. R., Witkin, H. A., Oltman, P., Gould, H., & Shulman, E. (1975). The effects of stress on components of the respiration cycle. *Psychophysiology, 12*, 377–380.

Cohen, S., Frank, E., Doyle, W. J., Skoner, D. P., Rabin, B. S., & Gwaltney, J. M. J. (1998). Types of stressors that increase susceptibility to the common cold in healthy adults. *Health Psychology, 17*, 214–223.

Cohen, S., & Herbert, T. B. (1996). Health psychology: Psychological factors and physical disease from the perspective of human psychoneuroimmunology. *Annual Review of Psychology, 47*, 113–142.

Cook, W. L., Strachan, A. M., Goldstein, M. J., & Miklowitz, D. J. (1989). Expressed emotion and reciprocal affective relationships in families of disturbed adolescents. *Family Process, 28*, 337–348.

Coppotelli, H. C., & Orleans, C. T. (1985). Partner support and other determinants of smoking cessation maintenance among women. *Journal of Consulting and Clinical Psychology, 53,* 455–460.

Coyne, J. C., & Anderson, B. J. (1988). The "psychosomatic family" reconsidered: Diabetes in context. *Journal of Marital and Family Therapy, 14,* 113–123.

Coyne, J. C., & Anderson, B. J. (1989). The "psychosomatic family" reconsidered: II. Recalling a defective model and looking ahead. *Journal of Marital and Family Therapy, 15,* 139–148.

Davies, P. T., & Cummings, E. M. (1994). Marital conflict and child adjustment: An emotional security hypothesis. *Psychological Bulletin, 116,* 387–411.

Davies, P. T., & Cummings, E. M. (1998). Exploring children's emotional security as a mediator of the link between marital relations and child adjustment. *Child Development, 69,* 124–139.

Doherty, W. A., & Campbell, T. L. (1988). *Families and health.* Beverly Hills, CA: Sage.

El-Sheikh, M. (1994). Children's emotional and physiological responses to interadult angry behavior: The role of history of interparental hostility. *Journal of Abnormal Child Psychology, 22,* 661–678.

Emery, R. E. (1982). Interparental conflict and the children of discord and divorce. *Psychological Bulletin, 92,* 310–330.

Field, T. (1994). The effects of mother's physical and emotional unavailability on emotion regulation. *Monographs of the Society for Research in Child Development, 59,* 208–227.

Field, T. (1996). Attachment and separation in young children. *Annual Review of Psychology, 47,* 541–561.

Fiese, B. H., & Wamboldt, F. S. (2001). Family routines, rituals, and asthma management: A proposal for family based strategies to increase treatment adherence. *Families, Systems, and Health, 18,* 405–418.

Fiese, B. H., Wamboldt, F. S., & Anbar, R. D. (in press). Family asthma management routines: Connections to medical adherence and quality of life. *Journal of Pediatrics.*

Fincham, F. D., & Beach, S. R. H. (1999). Conflict in marriage: Implications for working with couples. *Annual Review of Psychology, 50,* 47–77.

Fox, N., & Card, J. A. (1999). Psychophysiological measures in the study of attachment. In J. Cassidy & P. R. Shaver (Eds.), *Handbook of attachment: Theory, research, and clinical application* (pp. 226–245). New York: Guilford Press.

Funkenstein, D. H., King, S. H., & Drolette, M. E. (1957). *Mastery of stress.* Cambridge, MA: Harvard University Press.

Garrison, C. Z., Waller, J. L., Cuffe, S. P., McKeown, R. E., Addy, C. L., & Jackson, K. L. (1997). Incidence of major depressive disorder and dysthymia in young adolescents. *Journal of the American Academy of Child and Adolescent Psychiatry, 36,* 458–465.

Glaser, R., & Kiecolt-Glaser, J. K. (1994). *Handbook of human stress and immunity.* San Diego, CA: Academic Press.

Gottman, J. M., & Katz, L. F. (1989). Effects of marital discord on young children's peer interaction and health. *Developmental Psychology, 25,* 373–381.

Grey, M., Boland, E. A., Yu, C., Sullivan-Bolyai, S., & Tamborlane, W. V. (1998). Personal and family factors associated with quality of life in adolescents with diabetes. *Diabetes Care, 21,* 909–914.

Gunnar, M. R., Brodersen, L., Nachmias, M., Buss, K., & Rigatuso, J. (1996). Stress reactivity and attachment security. *Developmental Psychobiology, 29,* 191–204.

Hahlweg, K., Goldstein, M. J., Nuechterlein, K. H., Magana, A. B., Doane, J. A., Miklowitz, D. J., et al. (1989). Expressed emotions and patient–relative interaction in families of recent onset schizophrenics. *Journal of Consulting and Clinical Psychology, 57*, 11–18.

Herbert, T. B., & Cohen, S. (1993). Depression and immunity: A meta-analytic review. *Psychological Bulletin, 113*, 472–486.

Hermanns, J., Florin, I., Dietrich, M., Rieger, C., & Hahlweg, K. (1989). Maternal criticism, mother–child interaction and bronchial asthma. *Journal of Psychosomatic Research, 33*, 469–476.

Hofer, M. A. (1996). On the nature and consequences of early loss. *Psychosomatic Medicine, 58*, 570–581.

House, J. S., Landis, K. R., & Umberson, D. (1988). Social relationships and health. *Science, 241*, 540–545.

Jemerin, J. M., & Boyce, W. T. (1990). Psychobiological differences in childhood stress response: II. Cardiovascular markers of vulnerability. *Journal of Developmental and Behavioral Pediatrics, 11*, 140–150.

Jemerin, J. M., & Boyce, W. T. (1992). Cardiovascular markers of biobehavioral reactivity. *Developmental and Behavioral Pediatrics, 13*(1), 46–49.

Kagan, J., Reznick, J. S., & Snidman, N. (1988). Biological basis of childhood shyness. *Science, 240*, 167–171.

Kiecolt-Glaser, J. K., Glaser, R., Cacioppo, J. T., & MacCallum, R. C. (1997). Marital conflict in older adults: Endocrinological and immunological correlates. *Psychosomatic Medicine, 59*, 339–349.

Kiecolt-Glaser, J. K., Malarkey, W. B., Chee, M., Newton, T., Cacioppo J. T., Mao, H. Y., et al. (1993). Negative behavior during marital conflict is associated with immunological down-regulation. *Psychosomatic Medicine, 55*, 395–409.

Kiecolt-Glaser, J. K., McGuire, L., Robles, T. F., & Glaser, R. (2002a). Emotions, morbidity, and mortality: New perspectives from psychoneuroimmunology. *Annual Review of Psychology, 53*, 83–107.

Kiecolt-Glaser, J. K., McGuire, L., Robles, T. F., & Glaser, R. (2002b). Psychoneuroimmunology: Psychological influences on immune function and health. *Journal of Consulting and Clinical Psychology, 70*, 537–547.

Kiecolt-Glaser, J. K., & Newton, T. L. (2001). Marriage and health: His and hers. *Psychological Bulletin, 127*, 472–503.

Kobak, R. R., Sudler, N., & Gamble, W. (1991). Attachment and depressive symptoms during adolescence: A developmental pathways analysis. *Development and Psychopathology, 3*, 474.

Langfitt, J. T., Wood, B. L., Brand, K. L., Brand, J., & Erba, G. (1999). Family interactions as targets for intervention to improve social adjustment after epilepsy surgery. *Epilepsia, 40*, 735–744.

Lehrer, P., Feldman, J., Giardino, N., Song, H. S., & Schmaling, K. (2002). Psychological aspects of asthma. *Journal of Consulting and Clinical Psychology, 70*, 691–711.

Malarkey, W. B., Kiecolt-Glaser, J. K., Pearl, D., & Glaser, R. (1994). Hostile behavior during marital conflict alters pituitary and adrenal hormones. *Psychosomatic Medicine, 56*, 41–51.

Marton, P., & Maharaj, S. (1993). Family factors in adolescent unipolar depression. *Canadian Journal of Psychiatry—Revue Canadienne de Psychiatrie, 38*, 373–382.

Masten, A. S., Best, K. M., & Garmezy, N. (1990). Resilience and development: Contributions from the study of children who overcome adversity. *Development and Psychopathology, 2,* 425–444.

McCabe, P. M., Schneiderman, N., Field, T. M., & Skyler, J. S. (1991). *Stress, coping, and disease.* Hillsdale, NJ: Erlbaum.

McCubbin, H. I., & Boss, P. G. (1980). *Family stress, coping, and adaptation.* Minneapolis, MN: National Council on Family Relations.

McEwen, B. S. (1998). Protective and damaging effects of stress mediators. *New England Journal of Medicine, 338,* 171–179.

Melby, J. N., & Conger, R. D. (2001). The Iowa Family Interaction Rating Scales: Instrument summary. In P. K. Kerig & K. M. Lindahl (Eds.), *Family observational coding systems: Resources for systemic research.* Mahwah, NJ: Erlbaum.

Mengel, M. B., Lawler, M. K., Volk, R. J., Viviani, N. J., Dees, M. S., & Davis, A. B. (1992). Parental stress response within a family context: Association with diabetic control in adolescents with IDDM. *Family Systems Medicine, 10,* 395–404.

Miklowitz, D. J., Goldstein, M. J., Nuechterlein, K. H., Snyder, K. S., & Mintz, J. (1988). Family factors and the course of bipolar affective disorder. *Archives of General Psychiatry, 45,* 225–231.

Miller, B. D. (1987). Depression and asthma: A potentially lethal mixture. *Journal of Allergy and Clinical Immunology, 80,* 481–486.

Miller, B. D., & Strunk, R. C. (1989). Circumstances surrounding the deaths of children due to asthma. *American Journal of Diseases of Children, 143,* 1294–1299.

Miller, B. D., & Wood, B. L. (1994). Psychophysiologic reactivity in asthmatic children: A cholinergically mediated confluence of pathways. *Journal of the American Academy of Child and Adolescent Psychiatry, 33,* 1236–1245.

Miller, B. D., & Wood, B. L. (1995). "Psychophysiologic reactivity" in asthmatic children: A new perspective on emotionally triggered asthma. *Pediatric Asthma Allergy and Immunology, 9,* 133–142.

Miller, B. D., & Wood, B. L. (1997). Influence of specific emotional states on autonomic reactivity and pulmonary function in asthmatic children. *Journal of the American Academy of Child and Adolescent Psychiatry, 36*(5), 669–677.

Minuchin, S., Baker, L., Rosman, B. L., Liebman, R., Milman, L., & Todd, T. C. A. (1975). A conceptual model of psychosomatic illness in children: Family organization and family therapy. *Archives of General Psychiatry, 32,* 1031–1038.

Nachmias, M., Gunnar, M. R., Mangelsdorf, S., Parritz, R., & Buss, K. (1996). Behavioral inhibition and stress reactivity: The moderating role of attachment security. *Child Development, 67,* 508–522.

Olsson, G. I., Nordstrom, M. L., Arinell, H., & von Knorring, A. L. (1999). Adolescent depression: Social network and family climate—a case-control study. *Journal of Child Psychology and Psychiatry and Allied Disciplines, 40,* 227–237.

Rabin, B. S. (1999). *Stress, immune function, and health: The connection.* New York: Wiley-Liss.

Reid, W. J., & Crisafulli, A. (1990). Marital discord and child behavior problems: A meta-analysis. *Journal of Abnormal Child Psychology, 18,* 105–117.

Ritz, T., Steptoe, A., DeWilde, S., & Costa, M. (2000). Emotions and stress increase respiratory resistance in asthma. *Psychosomatic Medicine, 62,* 401–412.

Russek, L. G., & Schwartz, G. E. (1994). Interpersonal heart–brain registration and the perception of parental love: A 42-year follow-up of the Harvard Mastery of Stress study. *Subtle Energies, 5,* 195–208.

Russek, L. G., & Schwartz, G. E. (1996). The heart, dynamic energy, and integrated medicine. *Advances, 12,* 36–45.

Russek, L. G., & Schwartz, G. E. (1997a). Feelings of parental caring predict health status in midlife: A 35-year follow-up of the Harvard Mastery of Stress Study. *Journal of Behavioral Medicine, 20,* 1–13.

Russek, L. G., & Schwartz, G. E. (1997b). "Perceptions of parental caring predict health status in midlife: A 35-year follow-up of the Harvard Mastery of Stress Study": Reply. *Psychosomatic Medicine, 59,* 558–559.

Ryan, N. D. (1998). Psychoneuroendocrinology of children and adolescents. *Psychiatric Clinics of North America, 21,* 435–441.

Salovey, P., Rothman, A. J., Detweiler, J. B., & Steward, W. T. (2000). Emotional states and physical health. *American Psychologist, 55,* 110–121.

Schobinger, R., Florin, I., Zimmer, C., Lindemann, H., & Winter, H. (1992). Childhood asthma: Paternal critical attitude and father-child interaction. *Journal of Psychosomatic Research, 36,* 743–750.

Schore, A. N. (1994). *Affect regulation and the origin of the self: The neurobiology of emotional development.* Hillsdale, NJ: Erlbaum.

Schore, A. N. (1996). The experience-dependent maturation of a regulatory system in the orbital prefrontal cortex and the origin of developmental psychopathology. *Development and Psychopathology, 8,* 59–87.

Seligman, M. E. P., & Csikszentmihalyi, M. (2000). Positive psychology: An introduction. *American Psychologist, 55,* 5–14.

Seligman, M. E. P., Reivich, K., Jaycox, L., & Gillham, J. (1995). *The optimistic child.* Boston: Houghton Mifflin.

Shumaker, S. A., & Czajkowski, S. M. (1994). *Social support and cardiovascular disease.* New York: Plenum.

Siegel, D. J. (1999). *The developing mind.* New York: Guilford Press.

Sternberg, E. M. (2000). *The balance within: The science connecting health and emotions.* New York: Freeman.

Strang, S. P., & Orlofsky, J. L. (1990). Factors underlying suicidal ideation among college students: A test of Teicher and Jacobs' model. *Journal of Adolescence, 13,* 39–52.

Suomi, S. J. (1987). Genetic and maternal contributions to individual differences in rhesus monkey behavioral development. In N. A. Krasnegor, E. M. Blass, & M. A. Hofer (Eds.), *Perinatal development: A psychobiological perspective* (pp. 397–419). Orlando, FL: Academic Press.

Tarrier, N. (1989). Electrodermal activity, expressed emotion, and outcome in schizophrenia. *British Journal of Psychiatry, 155,* 174–178.

Uchino, B. N., Cacioppo, J. T., & Kiecolt-Glaser, J. K. (1996). The relationship between social support and physiological processes: A review with emphasis on underlying mechanisms and implications for health. *Psychological Bulletin, 119,* 488–531.

Valone, K., Norton, J. P., Goldstein, M. J., & Doane, J. A. (1984). Parental expressed emotion and physiological reactivity in an adolescent sample at risk for schizophrenia spectrum disorders. *Journal of Abnormal Psychology, 93,* 448–457.

Venters, M. H., Jacobs, D. R., Jr., Luepker, R. V., Maiman, L. A., & Gillum, R. F. (1984). Spouse concordance of smoking patterns: The Minnesota Heart Survey. *American Journal of Epidemiology, 120,* 608–616.

Vuchinich, S., Emery, R. E., & Cassidy, J. (1988). Family members and third parties in dyadic family conflict: Strategies, alliances and outcomes. *Child Development, 59,* 1293–1302.

Weihs, K., Fisher, L., & Baird, M. (2002). Families, health, and behavior: A section of the commissioned report by the Committee on Health and Behavior: Research, Practice, and Policy Division of Neuroscience and Behavioral Health and Division of Health Promotion and Disease Prevention Institute of Medicine, National Academy of Sciences. *Families, Systems and Health, 20,* 7–46.

Wood, B. L. (1993). Beyond the "psychosomatic family": A biobehavioral family model of pediatric illness. *Family Process, 32,* 261–278.

Wood, B. L. (2001). Physically manifested illness in children and adolescents: A biobehavioral family approach. *Child and Adolescent Psychiatric Clinics of North America, 10,* 543–562.

Wood, B. L. (2002). Attachment and family systems. [Monograph]. *Family Process* (Special Issue, Serial No. 41).

Wood, B. L., Klebba, K. B., & Miller, B. D. (2000). Evolving the biobehavioral family model: The fit of attachment. *Family Process, 39,* 319–344.

Wood, B. L., & Miller, B. D. (2002). A biopsychosocial approach to child health. In F. W. Kaslow (Ed.), *Comprehensive handbook of psychotherapy* (4th ed., pp. 59–80). New York: Wiley.

Wood, B. L., Watkins, J. B., Boyle, J. T., Nogueira, J., Zimand, E., & Carroll, L. (1989). The "psychosomatic family": A theoretical and empirical analysis. *Family Process, 28,* 399–417.

Wright, R. J., Rodriguez, M., & Cohen, S. (1998). Review of psychosocial stress and asthma: An integrated biopsychosocial approach. *Thorax, 53,* 1066–1074.

Wyllie, E., Glazer, J. P., Benbadis, S., Kotagal, P., & Wolgamuth, B. (1999). Psychiatric features of children and adolescents with pseudoseizures. *Archives of Pediatrics and Adolescent Medicine, 153,* 244–248.

Zautra, A. J., Hoffman, J. M., Matt, K. S., Yocum, D., Potter, P. T., Castro, W. L., et al. (1998). An examination of individual differences in the relationship between interpersonal stress and disease activity among women with rheumatoid arthritis. *Arthritis Care and Research, 11,* 271–279.

21

Weaving Gold Out of Straw: Meaning-Making in Families Who Have Children With Chronic Illnesses

Joän M. Patterson

Meanings communicated by illness can amplify or dampen symptoms, exaggerate or lessen disability, impede or facilitate treatment... however, these understandings often remain unexamined, silent emblems of a covert reality that is usually dealt with either indirectly or not at all.

—A. KLEINMAN, 1988

When a family member has a chronic health condition, the family as a group is drawn into an ongoing set of challenges that can inextricably change their life course and affect the health and well-being of all members. In the past, the primary focus in published research was on how chronic conditions negatively affect functioning—in the person with the condition, in other family members, and in family system functioning and structure. An equally important set of research questions, to which investigators are increasingly turning their attention, includes the following: Why and how do some families successfully adapt to this chronic source of stress? What accounts for the observation that many of these families actually appear to function better than relevant comparison groups who are not living with a chronic condition?

In this chapter, my focus is primarily on these latter two questions—what do we know from family research about successful or adaptive family processes and outcomes when a child in the family has a chronic illness or disability? I organize my observations of family research about childhood chronic conditions using a family stress theoretical model, the family adjustment and adaptation response (FAAR) model (Patterson, 1988). This model is particularly relevant to the "what accounts for successful adaptation" question because the outcomes of interest are individual and family adaptation (which can range from positive to negative) when a family is confronted with stressful conditions, such as a chronic illness. I give particular emphasis to one component of the FAAR model, the construct of family meanings, focusing on the question, What is the role of family meanings in adaptation to chronic illness?

■ The Family Adjustment and Adaptation Response Model

The FAAR model (Patterson, 1988) is an extension of the classic ABCX model (Hill, 1949) and the double ABCX model (McCubbin & Patterson, 1983a). Emphasized in the FAAR model are the active processes families engage in to balance *family demands* with *family capabilities* as these interact with *family meanings* to arrive at a level of *family adjustment* or *adaptation* (see figure 21.1). The concept of family

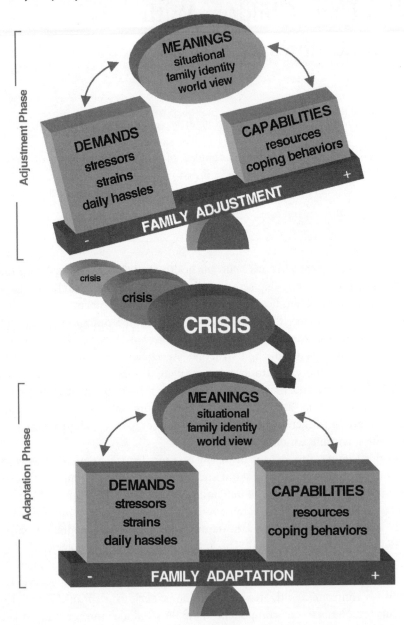

FIGURE 21.1 The family adjustment and adaptation response (FAAR) model.

demands emphasizes the pileup of multiple sources of stress for a family: normative and nonnormative stressors (discrete events of change), ongoing family strains (unresolved, insidious tensions), and daily hassles (minor disruptions of day-to-day life). The diagnosis of chronic illness is clearly a nonnormative stressor that carries with it many ongoing strains and hassles. Family capabilities include tangible and psychosocial resources (what a family *has*) and coping behaviors (what a family *does*). Both demands and capabilities can emerge from individual family members, from a family unit, or from various community contexts. Theoretically, what is important for family adaptation is not simply the magnitude of demands, but the ratio of capabilities to demands—does the family have or can they acquire the needed resources and coping behaviors for managing their ongoing demands? An important issue for researchers studying chronic health conditions is understanding the processes by which families achieve balance, that is, how families acquire needed resources for the demands they are experiencing and/or reduce actual or perceived demands.

In the FAAR model, three levels of family meanings are emphasized as important mediators or moderators of demands and capabilities relative to family adjustment or adaptation: (a) family definitions of their current demands and capabilities, (b) their identity as a family (how they see themselves internally as a unit), and (c) their world view (how they see their family in relationship to systems outside of their family) (Patterson & Garwick, 1994). As discussed later in this chapter, the process of achieving adaptation when living with chronic illness appears to be strongly influenced by "meaning-making" and how families make meaning out of adversity raises important research questions.

There are two phases emphasized in the FAAR model: adjustment and adaptation. On a day-to-day basis, families engage in relatively stable patterns of interacting as they juggle the demands they face with their existing capabilities, to achieve a level of family adjustment. However, there are times when family demands significantly exceed their capabilities and when this imbalance persists, families experience *crisis*, which is a period of significant disequilibrium, disorganization, and disruptiveness in the family. A crisis is very often a turning point for a family, leading to major change in their structure and/or functioning patterns. A crisis, characterized by discontinuity in the family's trajectory of functioning, can be in the direction of either improved functioning or poorer functioning. This turning point is similar to the developmental discontinuities noted by Rutter (1987), Cowan, Cowan, and Schulz (1996), and others; when the discontinuity is in the direction of improved functioning, the family is showing resilience. With the onset of a chronic illness, a family would move into crisis because of the need to reorganize their functioning to accommodate the challenges of the illness. Crisis should not be interpreted pejoratively as an indication that a family has in any way failed or is dysfunctional. Empirical evidence for these distinct phases would require a longitudinal study design in which individual or family functioning would be assessed at the time of diagnosis and then repeatedly over time to examine changes in functioning.

The process by which families restore balance (reducing demands, increasing capabilities, and/or changing meanings) is called adaptation. Adaptation is the master process as White (1974) pointed out; it is more than just coping. Adaptation also can be viewed as an outcome, which can be observed on a continuum from good adaptation to poor adaptation. Good outcomes are reflected in the (a) positive physical and mental health of individual members, (b) optimal role functioning of individual members, and (c) maintenance of a family unit that can accomplish its life cycle tasks.

The trajectory of any given family outcome is not necessarily stable or linear. As noted above, there can be additional major discontinuities as families experience new or accumulated stressors. In other words, over time, a family likely experiences repeated cycles of adjustment-crisis-adaptation. For families living with chronic illnesses, changes in the course of the illness or, when a child has the illness, the interaction of the chronic illness demands with new developmental tasks can push some families beyond their capabilities and lead to another crisis. Adolescence is one such developmental phase that has been noted by many investigators as particularly challenging and often associated with declines in adolescent and family functioning (for reviews, see Patterson, 1991; Patterson & Garwick, 1998).

Applying the FAAR Model to Chronic Illness Research

A review of family research on child, parent, and family functioning when a child has a chronic illness or disability reveals a range of outcomes, as well as a range of individual, family, and community risk and protective factors associated with these outcomes. Most studies of family adaptation to childhood chronic illness have focused on one chronic condition or, in comparative studies, on two or three conditions. However, as several investigators have pointed out, the psychosocial impact of childhood chronic health conditions on children and families is more similar across conditions than different (Perrin et al., 1993; Stein, Bauman, Westbrook, Coupey, & Ireys, 1993; Stein & Jessop, 1989), suggesting the utility of a noncategorical approach in studying psychosocial impact. In fact, these investigators have encouraged researchers to focus on measuring characteristics of chronic conditions, such as prognosis (normal vs. shortened or uncertain life expectancy), illness course (stable vs. declining or relapsing), type and degree of impairment (cognitive, motor, sensory, physiological), etc., as a more useful way to examine differential impacts of chronic illness on families, rather than focusing on differences by virtue of diagnosis alone. Further support for a noncategorical approach emphasizing condition characteristics derives from the variability that exists within specific diagnoses. For example, in the case of cerebral palsy, a child may or may not have motor impairment, or cognitive impairment, or restricted ability to communicate.

Any characteristic of a chronic condition that creates uncertainty for the family is hypothesized to increase distress for the family and adversely affect child and/or family functioning. For example, rating 98 different childhood chronic conditions as invisible (normal appearance) versus visible, Jessop and Stein (1985) reported that invisible chronic conditions more negatively affected child dependency, mother psychological functioning, and family/social relationships than visible conditions. They linked this counterintuitive finding to the increased uncertainty the child and family confront in whether to acknowledge and accommodate the chronic condition in day-to-day life, particularly with others outside the family. Similar to their findings, we found that uncertainty associated with unpredictable symptoms of young children's chronic conditions was associated with greater distress in mothers' and fathers' reports of family/social relationships (Dodgson et al., 2000). In a similar analysis for adolescents with chronic conditions, two aspects of uncertainty were associated with more parental distress: unpredictable symptoms and uncertain life expectancy (Garwick, Patterson, Meschke, Bennett, & Blum, 2002). In these latter two studies, we operationalized over 20 different characteristics of chronic conditions with a parent report measure, Characteristics of Chronic Conditions, which is described in the two published papers. Researchers should carefully consider their research questions in deciding whether their study design is best served by diagnosis-specific sampling or whether assessing specific characteristics of a broad range of conditions will yield more useful program and policy information.

Implied in studies of child or family adaptation to chronic illnesses is recognition that a chronic health condition creates added stress in a family, which, if the family cannot manage it, will negatively affect functioning. Thus an important research issue is how to measure variability in the amount of stress a condition places on families. Severity of the condition is one way to conceptualize this variability, although it is important to recognize there are different kinds of condition severity. For example, physiological severity is specific to a given disease, such as pulmonary function capacity in a child with cystic fibrosis or asthma. Because it is disease specific, physiological severity is less useful for studies using a non-categorical approach. However, functional severity, which is the amount of assistance needed by the affected person to perform age-expected tasks of daily living (such as toileting, dressing, bathing, etc.) could be applied noncategorically. The Wee-FIM (Uniform Data System for Medical Rehabilitation, 1993) and the Functional Status Measure (Stein et al., 1987) are two standardized scales for assessing a child's functional status.

A third way that severity has been defined is in terms of the burden experienced by the family in caring for the person with the condition (Stein et al., 1987). Asking the caregivers to report the number of hours/minutes a day needed to provide care is one objective way to assess this caregiving burden, although it is important to note that many families resist the notion that providing care is in any way a "burden." Burden of the illness is a good example of how a family's subjective definition of the situation (first level of family meanings) interacts with the presence of the condition to determine the amount of stress associated with a condition. Stein and Riessman (1980) developed the Impact on Family Scales as a way to quantify perceived burden of a child's chronic condition in three domains: financial, personal (emotional), and family/social relationships. These scales have been used by many investigators to measure impact of an illness on the family, primarily as an outcome rather than as a way to quantify the amount of stress or burden associated with a condition. As conceptualized, I do not think the Impact on Family Scales are a good indicator of family adaptation; rather, I think they are a good indicator of subjective burden of the condition—a part of the pileup of demands in the FAAR model—which may be useful in trying to explain individual or family adaptive functioning.

In addition to considering variability in characteristics of the chronic condition or subjective burden of the chronic condition as part of the pileup of demands, other aspects of family demands should also be considered in trying to understand child, parent, and/or family functioning outcomes. For example, family structural characteristics, such as single-parent status, young age of the parent(s), or large family size, have been associated with poorer adaptation to a child's illness (Gortmaker, Walker, Weitzman, & Sobol, 1990; Thompson, Auslander, & White, 2001). When a parent has mental health or alcohol problems, occurring either before or after the diagnosis of the child's chronic condition, child and family adaptation are compromised (Silver, Stein, & Bauman, 1999; Williamson, Walters, & Shaffer, 2002). Unresolved marital or family conflict is probably the most toxic family process that has been studied as a predictor of poor child and family outcomes when a member has a chronic health condition (see Weihs, Fisher, & Baird, 2002, for a review of the literature). Because continuity in functioning is more expectable than discontinuity, the best predictor of family adaptation to a child's chronic condition is the quality of family functioning *before* the onset of the condition. Unfortunately, in most studies we do not have the advantage of assessing precondition functioning since we identify our sample based on the presence of a condition.

It is important to keep in mind that deciding whether an individual or family factor is a predictor (independent variable) or an outcome (dependent variable) can vary. In the FAAR model, I have conceptualized outcomes—indicators of adaptation—as feedback to the system that become part of demands if the outcome is negative or, conversely, become part of capabilities if the outcome is positive. Obviously, this differentiation requires studying families over time. Conflict (for example) at time 1 is probably a major predictor of conflict at time 2, even though other variables may occur during this time interval that could either moderate or mediate this association.

On the capabilities side of the FAAR equation, numerous family resources have been identified as protective factors associated with positive adaptation. The following are some examples: (a) family cohesiveness (Martin, Miller-Johnson, Kitzmann, & Emery, 1998; Skinner & Hampson, 1998); (b) family organization, especially when the illness requires carrying out a home treatment regimen (Patterson, 1985); and (c) communication skills, both instrumental and affective (Jacobson et al., 1994). Families who are able to work effectively with health, education, and social service systems to get their children's needs met also show better adaptation (Stein & Jessop, 1984). The ability to obtain social support from extended family and friends also has been associated with better child and family functioning (Hamlett, Pellegrini, & Katz, 1992; Ievers, Brown, Lambert, Hsu, & Eckman, 1998).

Generally, the procedures used to assess these resources or protective factors are standardized self-report measures completed by parents of children with chronic conditions. Frequently used instruments include the Family Environment Scale (Moos & Moos, 1981), Family Assessment Device (Epstein, Baldwin, & Bishop,

1983), Family Assessment Measure (Skinner, Santa-Barbara, & Steinhauer, 1983), and Family Adaptability and Cohesion Evaluation Scales (Olson, Portner, & Bell, 1982). None of these measures are specific to children with chronic conditions. Since there are normative data for these measures, comparative data are available for studies lacking a comparison group. In most of the published studies, mothers have been the informants about the child and family. Presumably, this is because they are more readily accessible through clinics where study participants often are recruited. Less attention has been given to collecting data from fathers, which is a still a major gap and need in this research. Even less attention has been given to meaningful ways to combine mother and father reports to obtain a dyadic or family score for these variables.

Just as families are faced with increased demands, many families responding to their child's chronic condition show the development of new protective factors. There is not yet sufficient evidence in the literature to determine whether more families acquire or strengthen their protective factors versus develop added risk factors. The dynamic nature of adapting to new demands and crisis frequently leads to new risks begetting more risks or, conversely, having resources seems to be associated with acquiring more of them. Families who are already resource poor and live with multiple stressors are expectably more at risk when a child is diagnosed with a chronic condition (Gortmaker et al., 1990; White, Kolman, Wexler, Polin, & Winter, 1984). Families lacking adequate income, health insurance, and education, perhaps facing unstable employment, experiencing substandard housing and residential mobility, etc. will have a harder time managing their child's chronic condition. This may then be associated with more medical emergencies, the declining health status of their child, school absences, behavioral problems, etc. In other words, more risks emerge—what Rutter (1987) refers to as a cascade of risks, which is why multiproblem families continue to be likely to show adverse outcomes in multiple domains. As noted, each negative outcome is feedback to the family system, increasing their pileup of demands (Patterson, 1988). It is when their downward trajectory of functioning becomes discontinuous and things begin to improve that we see evidence of resilience. It is absolutely crucial in research on families with children with chronic conditions that a family's demographic and social context be assessed in examining individual or family functioning. Not only does context affect potential resources available or potential sources of other demands, but families' expectations regarding outcomes for their children and families vary by such contextual factors.

Let me offer two examples. A pediatrician caring for inner-city youth with chronic illnesses described a situation that occurred with several adolescents being treated for juvenile rheumatoid arthritis (JRA). These very poor, minority kids, like their peers, were doing poorly in school, skipping school, getting into fights, and sometimes in trouble with juvenile authorities. They began an intensive treatment program for their JRA that involved consistent, sustained contact with health providers at the inner-city clinic who, using an empowerment model, worked with them on strategies to minimize and manage their pain. Not only were these youth able to discover ways to manage their JRA more effectively, but they started going to school regularly, getting better grades, staying out of trouble, and getting along with their families better. What happened? The pediatrician's explanation was that, in addition to reducing their pain, these kids acquired new psychological resources, especially self-efficacy and self-esteem, which generalized to other areas of their life—school and home (A. Kohrman, 1991, personal communication). Cases like this can generate hypotheses that could be tested in a research design with pre-post measures of relevant variables or, ideally, in a randomized intervention design to see if youth functioning can be altered by empowering youth to take charge of their chronic health conditions.

Another example comes from our study of parents caring for medically fragile children at home. The parents in this study came from diverse socioeconomic backgrounds. When their children were released from the hospital to home care, they were entitled to extensive home health provider services—as much as 24 hr a day for some of them. There is a lot of stress associated with caring for such sick children plus having non-family members in the home on a regular basis. In 75% of these families, one or both of the parents scored in the psychiatric case range on a standardized symptom inventory. The only parents who did not show such high scores were single-parent families with low incomes (Leonard, Brust, & Patterson, 1991). It was our interpretation that the latter group of parents were getting important new resources—in-home care for their sick child, a new source of tangible aid support, and perhaps emotional support and help with their other children, hence reducing overall parental distress. In other words, the chronic condition was a ticket to resources many of these mothers may not have had otherwise.

A different kind of scenario plays out among families who already have a pool of family resources at the time of diagnosis of their child's chronic illness. Many are able to use their existing resources to acquire additional resources—again, in a kind of cascade of protective factors. When parents have more education, good health insurance and services, and supportive contacts in their community, they acquire expertise about the chronic condition, learn behaviors for managing it, and, for many, they develop strong new advocacy skills to ensure that their children's educational rights are met and that they get high quality health services (Patterson, Holm, & Gurney, 2004; Patterson & Leonard, 1994).

In one study with families who had a child with a chronic condition, we observed higher than average scores on standardized measures of child and family functioning (such as the Family Assessment Measure), suggesting that some families were stronger from living with a chronic condition (Patterson, Blum, Stinchfield, & Garwick, 1994). However, this sample of families was not representative of all families living with a chronic illness. Most of the children lived in two-parent families with middle-class family incomes and higher levels of parental education. Furthermore, because we did not have prediagnosis assessments of these families, we do not know if they were above average in family functioning before the diagnosis (a selection bias) or if they became stronger following the diagnosis.

When stressors bring out greater (than average) strengths in families, this represents the inoculation or challenge model of resilience (Zimmerman & Arunkumar, 1994). Improved functioning or growth occurs when a system is challenged just enough to encourage the development of new capabilities but not so much that the system is overwhelmed by the demands, believes them to be beyond the family's ability to manage, and gives up trying. However, to know whether the new stressor actually improved functioning, a baseline measure of individual or family functioning would be needed—data that are seldom available since a study sample is usually identified *after* the diagnosis of a chronic condition has occurred.

Included in the *processes of adaptation* are the ways that families cope with the added strains of a chronic health condition. As already noted, in the FAAR model, coping is viewed as what families *do* in contrast to what they *have* (resources). Coping may function to (a) reduce demands (e.g., quitting a job or reducing hours at work to care for a chronically ill child); (b) increase resources (e.g., finding good health services); (c) maintain resources (e.g., finding new sources of social support); (d) manage tension from unresolved demands (e.g., meditating, exercising); and/or (e) change the way a situation is appraised (Patterson, 1988). With regard to the latter coping strategy, appraisals are made about stressors and strains (called primary appraisal) or about the resources for managing them (called secondary appraisal) (Lazarus & Folkman, 1984). These primary and secondary appraisals are referred to as "situational" meanings in the FAAR model and are critically important in shaping family adaptation.

■ Family Meanings and Adaptation to Chronic Illness

As we have sought to understand why some families successfully adapt to their child's chronic illness and others do not, family beliefs and meanings have emerged as a critical aspect of the family adaptation process. These cognitive factors include the definitions a family gives to the chronic illness event, its related hardships, and their resources for managing them. But these cognitive constructions go beyond the situational level. In open-ended interviews with families living with chronic health conditions, they often talk about how they have changed as a family—how they see themselves differently, compared to the time before the diagnosis or compared to other families. They often talk about focusing on different priorities in life and developing a new sense of what is important—again comparing themselves to the way they used to be or to other families. These data from the qualitative aspects of our studies led to the emergence of three levels of meaning in the FAAR model: (a) situational meanings, (b) family identity, and (c) family world view (Patterson, 1993; Patterson & Garwick, 1994).

The importance of meanings for individuals adapting to illness and loss also has emerged from the work of other psychologists (Folkman & Moskowitz, 2000; Park & Folkman, 1997; Taylor, 1983; Thompson, 1991). However, their work focused on individual-level and not on *family-level* meanings. Conceptualizing a cognitive factor at the group level needs clarification.

What Are Family-Level Meanings?

Family meanings are not the sum of individually held meanings, nor are they consensus on meanings held by individual family members. Drawing from the work of Reiss (1981) and Wamboldt and Wolin (1989), Ann Garwick and I defined family meanings as interpretations, images, and views that have been collectively constructed by family members as they interact with each other; as they share time, space, and life experience; and as they talk with each other and dialogue about these experiences (Patterson & Garwick, 1994). Family meanings are a family's social constructions, the product of their interactions. They belong to no one member, but to a family as a whole unit. Berger and Luckmann (1966) and Bruner (1990), among others, emphasize that language creates the reality we perceive and that all meanings are created and maintained through social interaction. A family is the most proximate context for social interaction for most of us, and hence it is a major context for creating meanings.

Within a family, shared meanings help to organize and maintain group process by reducing ambiguity and uncertainty about a complex array of stimuli, thereby making coordination of responses among group members possible (Reiss, 1981). Furthermore, this coordination of responses contributes to group stability and helps establish an identity for the group.

One family member's report about the family's meanings can be viewed as his or her story, what Wamboldt and Wolin (1989) call the "family myth," or what Reiss (1989) calls the "represented family." It is what the individual has internalized and can recall from his or her immersion in family experiences. When a family member completes a self-report questionnaire about his or her family process, the respondent is providing a subjective account of his or her family—a family myth. The notion of consensus or disagreement between individual subjective accounts would be relevant. However, these individual self-reports should be differentiated from what actually happens when family members are engaged with each other, what Reiss (1989) calls the "practicing family" and what Wamboldt and Wolin (1989) call "family reality." Following this line of reasoning, we could only know about family-level meanings if we assessed a family's language and behavior as it emerges from their interaction together, in other words, observed them conjointly. What evidence do we have for these three levels of family meaning in the context of family adaptation to a child's chronic health condition?

Situational Meanings

In open-ended interviews with mothers and fathers with a child who was medically fragile, many parents described the positive aspects of having a child with intense medical needs: the child's warmth and responsiveness; the tenacity and perseverance of the child to endure that made the parents want to invest more of their effort; the closeness felt in the family unit by pulling together to manage; the assertiveness and skills that they as parents developed in response to caring for the child as well as learning to deal with multiple home health providers and payers of these services; and the growth in empathy and kindness in their other children (Patterson & Leonard, 1994). In other words, parents selectively attended to many positive aspects of their child's personality and behaviors, while minimizing the limitations or health problems. In addition, many parents emphasized their own personal growth and development or their family's added strengths in response to the challenges. In that study, interviews were conducted separately with mothers and fathers, audiotaped, analyzed separately, and then analyzed as a family unit. These analyses are an example of consensus of two family members' "myths" about the represented family as defined above.

More recently, using focus group methodology with couples of children who have survived treatment for cancer, the above results were corroborated with parents reporting many of the same strengths in their children, themselves, and their families emerging from the stress of having their child diagnosed and treated for cancer (Patterson et al., 2004).

In addition to situational meanings that increase the family's perceived resources and competencies, other investigators have reported that when parents have more positive appraisals and attitudes about the chronic illness and its demands, such as for epilepsy (Austin & McDermott, 1988) or autism (Bristol, 1987), they are able to adapt more effectively to their situations. It is not uncommon that a family will compare their child's chronic illness to another type of chronic health condition and conclude that they are lucky they don't have the challenges associated with other chronic illnesses (Affleck & Tennen, 1993; Behr & Murphy, 1993; Brown, 1993). This kind of "downward social comparison" is yet another example of how situational meanings are used by families to reduce perceived demands.

When the occurrence of a situation cannot be prevented (primary control), situational meanings that minimize the negative and accentuate the positive are an example of secondary control or accommodating to existing realities by maximizing perceived benefits of things that cannot be changed (Weisz, Rothbaum, & Blackburn, 1984). In the FAAR model, these efforts would be considered a way of using meanings to balance demands and capabilities.

Measuring Situational Meanings.   Self-report measures are the most widely used method in studies of families living with chronic health conditions. Built into many stress scales assessing the accumulation of demands experienced by a family in a specified time period is a weighting scheme for rating how stressful each experienced event was. This method is an example of primary appraisal of demands by the respondent. While it is possible to ask family members to complete a paper and pencil stress measure together as a way to obtain their shared view of family demands, this procedure is seldom used. Out of convenience, investigators often rely on one family member's report, and this is usually the mother in childhood chronic illness research. Using the Family Inventory of Life Events and Changes (McCubbin, Patterson, & Wilson, 1980), a strategy for combining individual self-reports about experienced demands is to sum items (or subjective ratings) that are checked by any family member. If all family members checked an item, it is still counted just once, or if subjective weights have been given, the highest or average weight can be used for that item (McCubbin & Patterson, 1983b). The premise underlying this procedure is based on family systems theory. If any one family member perceives a source of stress, it has an effect on the whole family.

Within a stress and coping paradigm, family member self-report about family resources is the second component of situational meanings. As already noted, the Family Environment Scale (Moos & Moos, 1981), the Family Cohesion and Adaptability Evaluation Scales (Olson et al., 1982), etc., are examples of myriad scales for assessing family functioning resources, such as cohesiveness, organization, expressiveness, etc. These scale scores can be used to construct latent variables by combining two or more family members' individual self-reports in a structural equation model as a way of controlling for shared error variance and approximating a family-level assessment of the family resource.

In addition to resources, the capabilities construct of the FAAR model also includes coping, which is integral to understanding situational meanings. Coping is defined as what individuals and families *do*. In addition to actual behaviors, coping can involve ways of perceiving. Lazarus and Folkman (1984) and others refer to the latter as appraisal-focused coping. Evidence of the important role of appraisal-focused coping emerged in our study of parents with a child who had survived cancer for at least 1 year. In the qualitative analysis of focus group results, 89% of the parents described at least one appraisal-focused coping behavior, such as being positive and maintaining hope, making positive comparisons, believing/trusting in God, focusing on the present, etc. (Patterson et al., 2004).

Self-report coping inventories usually include items to assess directly the degree to which the respondent uses cognitive coping strategies to manage stressful situations. For example, the Coping Health Inventory for Parents (CHIP; McCubbin, McCubbin, Nevin, & Cauble, 1979), which was developed specifically to assess coping when parents have a child with a chronic illness, includes several cognitive coping items. It is important to note that cognitive coping is not equivalent to meaning-making as discussed in this chapter. It is only one component of the more encompassing process of meaning-making.

Family Identity

At the next level of family meanings, families have implicit ways of knowing what makes them a distinct system, separate from the larger context in which they live. Walsh (1998) emphasized that a family's shared beliefs are fundamental to their identity as a group and are particularly powerful in shaping how a family responds to challenges, such as chronic illness.

Family identity emerges from the stories that family members tell about themselves, both to each other and to those outside the family, and from the spoken and unspoken rules of relationship that guide family members in how they are to relate to each other. Through day-to-day repeated patterns of interaction, family identity is developed and maintained. The construct of family identity is more abstract than situational meanings, and if asked, family members would probably be unable to articulate their identity per se. However, by listening to a family's stories/narratives, and by observing a family's patterned interactions, it is possible to gain insight into a family's identity. The family identity construct builds on the work of several family scholars who have examined the role of family routines and rituals in maintaining a family's sense of itself as a collective whole, in establishing shared rules, attitudes, and ways of relating, as well as maintaining continuity and stability in family functioning over time (Bennett, Wolin, & McAvity, 1988; Bossard & Boll, 1950; Fiese et al., 2002; Fiese & Wamboldt, 2000; Steinglass, Bennett, Wolin, & Reiss, 1987; Walsh, 1998; Wolin & Bennett, 1984). Family rituals, more than routines, are usually symbolic and imbued with meanings, values, and beliefs that a family shares, thereby fostering group identity (Fiese et al., 2002).

Families vary in their commitment to rituals and there is some evidence that under-ritualized families may experience more dysfunction (Imber-Black, Roberts, & Whiting, 1988). Rituals are often used therapeutically to help families establish boundaries, mark transitions, or develop a clear sense of their own identity. This process facilitates adaptation by reducing strains associated with uncertainty. Markson and Fiese (2000) found that in families who had meaningful routines and rituals, their children with asthma showed significantly less anxiety. Fiese and Wamboldt (2000) have proposed that encouraging families to develop routines and rituals surrounding their children's asthma management would significantly improve asthma treatment adherence. They are currently investigating such interventions.

Included in the many types of family rituals are rituals for family boundary changes, such as when a child is born, when someone gets married, or when a family member dies. When family boundaries are *not* clear, the family identity is challenged. This usually increases strain and adds to the pileup of demands in the family. Boss's (1999, 2002) work on boundary ambiguity is particularly relevant to this second level of family meanings. When there is incongruence between a family member's physical presence and psychological presence, the resultant ambiguity increases family stress because the boundary about who is "in" the family and who is "out" is unclear. Families experiencing chronic illness are particularly vulnerable to this kind of boundary ambiguity. For example, the birth of a premature infant who spends many months in a neonatal intensive care unit is an example of psychological presence in the family system but with physical absence, which may be exacerbated even further by uncertainty about the infant's survival. Another example, related to disabilities, is a person who has a severe cognitive impairment. Is a person who is physically present but psychologically absent in or out of the family system? Boundary ambiguity and uncertainty may partially account for the findings that childhood chronic conditions characterized by brain involvement are associated with poorer child and family adaptation (Bresleau, 1993; Howe, Feinstein, Reiss, Molock, & Berger, 1993). Chronic illness or disability can and usually does have a significant impact on a family's identity, challenging an old identity and calling for something new.

Rituals and routines provide some sense of stability as well as an identity for a family, which can serve to provide a kind of anchoring point and a sense of balance when stressful events call for changes in the family system. Steinglass and his colleagues (Gonzalez, Steinglass, & Reiss, 1989; Reiss, Steinglass, & Howe, 1993; Steinglass & Horan, 1987) have emphasized how chronic illness can disrupt normal family regulatory processes, such as routines and rituals. In an effort to meet the demands associated with the chronic illness, such as a different diet, home therapies, activity restrictions, etc., valued aspects of family life may be altered significantly or even given up. For example, families who have children with cystic fibrosis are asked to follow a daily routine of aerosol treatments, bronchial drainage treatments, exercise, special diet, and medications, which can require as much as 2 to 4 hr a day to accomplish. Such demands have a way of taking over the family and in so doing giving the family an identity as a "cystic fibrosis family." This kind of family reorganization around an illness often has negative implications for the course of development of all family members, including the child with the illness, as well as the course of development of the family unit (Reiss et al., 1993). Can a child, for example, whose family's organization and identity are based primarily on his or her illness ever leave home?

The metaphor Gonzalez et al. (1989) use for family reorganization following diagnosis of chronic illness is, "finding a place for the illness in the family and keeping the illness in its place." Even though a family may give less attention to the chronic illness than is prescribed by medical providers, maintaining some balance in family life may be associated with better psychosocial outcomes in the long run. In studies of children with diabetes, the *best* metabolic control (i.e., rigid adherence) and the *poorest* metabolic control were associated with psychological and family problems, whereas *moderate* control was associated with better psychosocial outcomes (Evans & Hughes, 1987; Smith, Mauseth, Palmer, Pecoraro, & Wenet, 1991). These findings suggest that disproportionate attention to treatment regimens at the expense of other family needs may lead to psychosocial problems.

Additional support for this observation was found in our analysis of family factors associated with a 10-year trend in pulmonary function among children with cystic fibrosis. Parents' available time (measured as the inverse of the total number of paid work hours of the parent[s]) and balanced parental coping were associated with less decline in pulmonary function over time (Patterson, Budd, Goetz, & Warwick, 1993). Balanced parental coping was assessed as the highest score for either mother or father on three coping scales: attending to family needs, personal support needs, and the child's medical condition. Each parent independently completed a self-report coping inventory (CHIP; McCubbin et al., 1979) and using the lowest scale score for one (single-parent families) or both parents provided a meaningful way to create a family-level coping score that emphasized the importance of simultaneously attending to family needs, personal needs, and the child's chronic illness needs. This is another example of creating a family-level score from individual parent self-reports.

Measuring Family Identity.   Because the family identity construct is both more abstract and more encompassing than situational meanings, assessing it is more challenging. In all of our studies that have employed qualitative analyses of parents' narratives of various aspects of the chronic illness experience, there is invariably a description of how the family has changed as a unit through their experiences. It is in the aftermath of the health crisis these families have lived through that many are able to reflect and articulate their family's patterned responses, suggestive of a new style of interaction.

As described above, many scholars suggest that observing or knowing about a family's routines and rituals provides a window for understanding a family's identity as a unit. As Fiese et al. (2002) point out, many family routines and rituals are likely to involve the whole family, rather than just a family dyad. Routines are usually defined as recurring day-to-day activity patterns. Hence, they provide a sense of organization and stability, which may be especially important when families are struggling to understand who they are becoming when a chronic illness invades their lives. Family rituals, on the other hand, are much more symbolic and full of meaning, often linking families across many generations and linking them to a cultural or religious tradition. Hence, they help create an identity for a family that both differentiates them from and aligns them with other families in their context. Rituals also help to solidify beliefs and values related to a family's world view.

Several self-report inventories for assessing family routines and family rituals have been developed (Eaker & Walters, 2002; Fiese & Kline, 1993; Jenson, James, Boyce, & Hartnett, 1983; Klapp, 1959). Generally speaking, these inventories have been used in studies showing how the presence of routines and/or rituals is protective for families and children under varying stressful circumstances. For example, the Family Ritual Questionnaire (Fiese & Kline, 1993) is a self-report instrument from which two summary scores can be derived, a ritual routine score and a ritual meaning score. Mothers' ritual meaning score and fathers' ritual routine score were protective against anxiety in children with asthma (Markson & Fiese, 2000).

Analysis of family stories and narratives is another way to assess family identity. Qualitative analysis as described above can be used to reveal a family's sense of itself. When family members conjointly tell their stories, it is more defensible to consider the family as the unit of analysis. One limiting feature, however, is that all family members are not always equally involved in telling the story and tacit agreement does not necessarily indicate the level to which the story/identity is genuinely shared. Silence could mean disagreement or it could mean "I agree with what is being said and have nothing to add."

A methodology for quantitatively coding family narratives has been developed by Fiese et al. (1999). Three dimensions are included: (a) narrative coherence, which codes each individual's story in terms of its internal consistency, organization, flexibility, and congruence of affect and content; (b) narrative interaction, which refers to how well the couple or family work together in putting together their story (codes for couple narrative style, coordination, and confirmation/disconfirmation); and (c) relationship beliefs, which focuses on the trustworthiness of the social world and expectations for rewarding relationships (codes for relationship expectations and interviewer intimacy). This coding system captures more than a family's identity, with the first dimension emphasizing individual psychological functioning, the second providing a window into relationship functioning—closest to family identity—and the third providing more of a world view. The studies that have been published using this system have not yet focused on family adaptation to chronic illness, however.

Another possible way of thinking about family identity would be in terms of family types, where a set of core family process dimensions are assessed by self-report or observational coding and scores are used to create a typology of families. Using the family paradigm dimensions of configuration, coordination, and closure, Reiss (1981) differentiated two family types: consensus-sensitive versus distance-sensitive families. Olson et al. (1982) proposed 16 family types based on scores for cohesion and flexibility from the Family Adaptability and Cohesion Scales (FACES) measure. Fisher and Ransom (1995) used cluster analysis with 11 family and couple variables to identify four family types: balanced, traditional, disconnected, and emotionally strained, which discriminated adult family members on self-reported health measures. Typologies may be a useful strategy for examining family adaptation to chronic illnesses, albeit somewhat removed from the idiosyncratic ways families might describe their family identity.

Family World View

At the third level of family meanings, the focus is on the family's orientation toward the world, how they interpret reality, what their core assumptions are about their environment, as well as their more enduring existential beliefs, such as the family's purpose in life. This is the most abstract of the three levels of meaning and most families probably would not be able to directly report their world view if asked. Because the focus is on a *family world view,* an orientation and meanings that the family shares as a collective are emphasized.

David Reiss and his colleagues have written extensively about the family's conception of their social world, which they call the family paradigm (Reiss, 1981; Reiss et al., 1993). Their emphasis is on the *collective* family's world view as opposed to any one individual's report about the family's world view. His group has reported that individuals engage in different problem-solving strategies (indicative of their paradigm) if they are interacting together with family members compared to circumstances when they are alone (Reiss, Oliveri, & Curd, 1983). Reiss identified three dimensions of the family paradigm: (a) configuration or a sense of mastery, (b) coordination of effort with other family members, and (c) closure or the degree of openness to new information.

Reiss's (1981) method for operationalizing a family's paradigm is to have family members simultaneously engage in a laboratory problem-solving task. Based on the way they approach and try to solve the task, scores are derived for configuration (the degree to which a family perseveres and is tenacious thereby suggesting a belief that they can discover a solution), coordination (based on how well they work together as a group), and closure (based on their openness to new information at different phases of the task).

Using this laboratory task to study families of patients with end-stage renal disease, Reiss, Gonzalez, and Kramer (1986) examined how the world view of the patient's family shaped their response to the chronic illness. They expected that family paradigms characterized by high configuration, high coordination, and delayed closure would be associated with better emotional adjustment in the family and with a more benign course of the illness. Their most striking finding was that high coordination (a shared perception of the family as a highly integrated group) predicted early death. The three family paradigm dimensions, together with family accomplishment (education and income) and family intactness (duration of marriage), perfectly predicted death or survival of renal patients at 36 months. Paradoxically, strict patient adherence to the renal dialysis regimen also predicted early death. The investigators interpreted these findings as follows: (a) as a patient's medical needs increased, the most integrated, cohesive families became increasingly vulnerable because their responsiveness to the medical needs threatened their ability to meet other family needs and stay strong; (b) this led to an implicit understanding between patient and family that in order to protect the family unit from disintegration, the terminally ill patient and his family needed to disengage from each other; and (c) as the patient withdrew from his family, he sought social integration with the staff of the hospital dialysis unit by more willingly adhering to their prescribed medical regimen, even though he had now resigned himself to death. All of the families in their study were African American.

When a description of the FAAR model was first published (Patterson, 1988), five dimensions of world view were described: (a) shared purpose, indicating that the family shared an ideology; (b) collectivity, which was viewing one's family as part of something larger than itself; (c) frameability, which reflected family optimism grounded in reality; (d) relativism, which involved a focus on living in the present; and (e) shared control, which involved balancing internal control with trust in others. Each dimension was viewed as a continuum along which a family could vary from low to high. Support for these five dimensions of world view has been reported based on the qualitative analysis of interviews with parents who have a child that is medically fragile (Patterson, 1993). These families reported a greater commitment to life and to working for the needs of those with disabilities (shared purpose). They felt stronger connections within the family unit and with the health team and people in their community as they managed their child's needs (collectivity). They developed a new outlook on life, valuing their strengths and what they had (frameability). They lived more in the present and were more flexible (relativism). They realized they had less control over life than they thought and they learned to let go and trust others and became more aware of a higher power (shared control). At the same time, parents talked about taking responsibility for managing their child's care and for teaching him or her how to take age-appropriate responsibility for his or her own care.

A family's world view has its roots in the culture and social conditions of which a family is part. For example, the dimension I have called "shared control" varies considerably among different cultural groups. European Americans value taking charge, being independent, and having a high sense of being able to personally control life circumstances. This orientation is associated with self-efficacy and mastery. Hence, a belief and value of taking charge is part of the world view of many middle- and upper-class American families. In contrast, among lower social classes in the United States and in less developed countries where social conditions preclude the same kind of opportunities, families may be more fatalistic and have a passive orientation to life and less of an internal locus of control.

Family therapists working with families living with chronic health conditions have emphasized the importance of the type or content of families' beliefs as they affect family adaptation. Wright, Watson, and Bell (1996) describe enabling beliefs (in contrast to constraining beliefs) as key to a family's ability to adapt to the changed circumstances of living with a chronic illness. In a similar vein, Walsh (1998) views family belief systems as the core of family resilience. She emphasizes coherence, affiliative values and sharing the challenge with others, positive appraisals and outlook, and a spiritual orientation, which can transform families, as beliefs that lead to successful adaptation.

Measuring Family World View.   The Reiss Card Sort Procedure described above for measuring the world view dimensions of configuration, coordination, and closure is the only method of which I am aware that assesses the "practicing family's" world view. More commonly, specific beliefs or values about life and/or illness are assessed for individuals in the family and then various methods for combining individual self-reports are used. Consensus-disagreement on which views are shared or the degree to which there is shared variance in their self-reports through construction of latent variables may be applied.

One example of the consensus approach is from the work of Antonovsky and Sourani (1988) related to the life orientation called "sense of coherence." A sense of coherence is "the pervasive, enduring, though dynamic feeling of confidence that internal and external environments are predictable and there is a high probability that things will work out as well as can reasonably be expected" (Antonovsky, 1979). Three dimensions underlie a sense of coherence: meaningfulness, manageability, and comprehensibility (Antonovsky, 1987). Adapting the Life Orientation Questionnaire to the family level, Antonovsky and Sourani (1988) defined family coherence as the degree to which the family unit (as well as the rest of the world) is seen as coherent and the degree to which family members share this orientation, i.e., their degree of consensus.

Another method for arriving at a family world view score was described by Ransom, Fisher, and Terry (1992). Eight dimensions of world view were included in their individual self-report assessment: optimism, religiousness, life engagement, child-adult separateness, child centeredness, chance locus of control, powerful others locus of control, and internal locus of control. Focusing on the husband-wife dyad as the unit of analysis and using both spouses' self-report scores in an inter-battery factor analysis, they created four family world view scales: child-adult separateness, family optimism, family chance locus of control, and family religiousness. Partial validity for these scales was shown through associations with adult health status.

■ The Process of Making Family Meanings

Meaning-making is a dynamic process that emerges over time as families search for meaning in a life that has been seriously disrupted, sometimes shattered, by the diagnosis/onset of a chronic health condition, with its added demands, multiple losses, changed routines, roles, and expectations. The implicit and explicit meanings a family may have held in the past, at any of the three levels, will be affected and, most likely, reconstructed. This meaning-making process is at the core of family adaptation. To date, it is primarily through qualitative research methods that we are beginning to understand the process of meaning-making.

From our studies and those of others described throughout this chapter, it appears that a family unit is not only *the* critical social context where this search for meaning occurs, but in many families, the family itself is transformed. In our qualitative analysis of parents' stories about learning to live with their infants' chronic conditions, many parents described how their expectations for themselves, their children, and their futures changed (Garwick, Patterson, Bennett, & Blum, 1995). Some parents were shocked to learn that their newborn had a chronic condition, especially when there was no family history of the disease and the pregnancy had been uneventful. Parents whose world view included a mastery orientation had taken measures to provide for a healthy birth (e.g., through prenatal care and avoiding risks such as cigarettes, drugs, and alcohol); now they struggled to find a "just" reason for their child's disability. A loss of a personal sense of control can lead family members to join more closely with each other. Steinglass and Horan (1987) report that families confronted with chronic illness often pull together—giving up individual world views for a shared one.

On the other hand, some families may grow further apart. In trying to coordinate their responses to a new set of challenges, greater explicit awareness of the degree to which they do or do not have shared understandings may be triggered. Crises, by definition, are characterized by disorganization and disruptiveness. The patterns holding the family identity together may seem to become unglued. Adult family members may begin to question whether they want to invest the energy in accommodating to other members' needs and perspectives. In essence, the family's identity is challenged in terms of membership. In fact, the dissolution of a family unit in the aftermath of crisis may imply that the reconstruction of new shared meanings has not occurred.

The interconnections between meanings, behaviors, and emotions stimulate the meaning-making process. Existing beliefs do not always fit with the new reality. For example doctors can't always cure disease and parents can't always protect their children from harm. As families engage in new behaviors to learn about the chronic condition, actively manage it, and then witness improvements in their children as a result of their efforts, new understandings emerge about the chronicity of illness and disability, what a child is, what a parent is, work roles, relationships, and what matters in life. From our study of families with medically fragile children, there would be too much cognitive dissonance for parents to spend the time and energy caring for their children's intense needs while viewing them as undesirable or even their circumstances as something bad (Patterson & Leonard, 1994). Rather, parents did what Venters (1981) described in families of children with cystic fibrosis: they "endowed the situation with meaning."

Families whose children survived treatment for cancer talked about experiencing a roller coaster of emotions, including anger, sadness, fear, and worry, as well as gratitude and joy (Patterson et al., 2004). These emotions shaped both behaviors and meanings. Worrying parents sometimes did not trust medical staff and when errors were made, they became angry. They took on roles of advocating vigorously to assure their children were getting the best possible care and in so doing, came to see themselves in a new light. From many studies, mothers especially report surprise at their assertiveness and forthrightness in talking to authority figures about their children's rights. It is not uncommon that parents join together with other parents around the country to advocate for their children's rights—in the educational system, with public and private payers of health care, and so on. They take on a new purpose in life, and they adjust expectations for their own life course. In another study, many families described the stigmatizing reactions of other people to their children's conditions, which changed their view about people, who their friends were, their values, and what matters in life (Patterson, Garwick, Bennett, & Blum, 1997).

The behavior of telling and retelling the story of the family's experiences, within the family and to others outside the family, contributes to generating new meanings and a new family identity, especially when the stories are co-constructed by family members together. Relaying illness-related information happens repeatedly in multiple contexts—between immediate family members with regard to day-to-day management; with health providers, school personnel, and other professionals providing services; with friends, relatives, and acquaintances who inquire about child and family well-being; and so on. Family stories and narratives often include a strong affective component, which contributes to their significance for the family.

■ Conclusions and Implications for Future Research

Many of the published studies of individual and family adaptation to chronic illness and disability have not been guided by any theoretical orientation. Future studies of child and family adaptation to chronic health conditions would benefit from developing hypotheses and conceptualizing variables using a family theoretical framework. In this chapter, I have emphasized the FAAR model as one useful family theoretical orientation because of the emphasis on chronic stress, resources, coping, and meanings as critical factors affecting family adaptation (all of which are relevant to chronic illness) and because there is an emphasis on positive as well as negative functioning as the outcomes. We need more studies focusing on why and how families succeed. On the one hand, the broad constructs of the FAAR model may seem too generic to be useful in generating hypotheses; on the other hand, the inclusion of individual, family, and community sources of demands and resources and the emphasis on meanings allow for selecting variables specific to diverse ecological contexts, particularly taking into account cultural and ethnic diversity.

In addition, several relevant self-report measures for assessing various aspects of the FAAR model already exist, making tests of the FAAR model possible. However, research using self-report measures of various aspects of family functioning could be strengthened by obtaining reports from more than one family member and by using structural equation modeling to more closely approximate a family systems assessment of family factors. Alternatively, methods for creating family-level scores from more than one self-report, such as those discussed in this chapter for stress and coping, could be employed. In addition to more family-level assessment, it is important that more data be collected from fathers of children with chronic conditions since their perspective is often quite different than that of mothers, who have been the informants in the majority of studies to date.

Given the growing number of valid and reliable coding systems for assessing family processes (see Kerig & Lindahl, 2001), there is a clear need to incorporate multiple methods for measuring family variables in future studies. For example, a measure of expressed emotion derived from a 5-minute speech sample has been associated with more severe asthma symptoms and poorer treatment adherence in youth with asthma (Wamboldt, Wamboldt, Gavin, Roesler, & Brugman, 1995).

As described throughout this chapter, methods for assessing family beliefs and meanings and particularly for examining the process of family meaning-making are in their infancy. Clearly, there is a need for more empirical studies to provide support for the presence of levels of family meanings and then to understand their contribution to adaptation, particularly with families of diverse cultural, ethnic, and racial backgrounds. Much of this research will call for qualitative methods because of the subjective nature of meanings and meaning-making. It is still unclear whether there are a relatively limited set of meanings that constitute family identity and family world view or whether fairly idiosyncratic beliefs held by a particular family are what make meaning-making so important to adaptation. The commonalities of meaning content across so many qualitative studies would suggest that the contents of meanings are not unique to each family. Classifying the quality of meanings or beliefs, such as whether they are constraining versus enabling, is yet another approach that may offer additional insight into family adaptation (Wright et al., 1996).

However, it may be that the content of beliefs is less important than the process of arriving at shared meanings in a family. What remains unclear is why some families engage in a process of meaning-making, which has been described across so many qualitative studies, and why other families do not. The evidence for this process seems to have emerged from families who have adapted relatively well to living with a chronic condition. Does meaning-making contribute to more adaptive functioning or do well-adapted families naturally engage in this process more readily? Since meanings in general emerge through social interaction, future studies need to examine what social contexts beyond the family contribute to the meaning-making process. For example, other families living with chronic conditions and church groups are two important sources of support frequently identified by families. How is giving and receiving support related to meaning-making?

We need more longitudinal studies in which the natural processes by which families change meanings in response to the diagnosis and presence of chronic conditions can be understood, as well as how the different levels of meanings are related. In addition, studies of the relationship between meanings at the different levels and outcomes of interest need to be expanded.

While qualitative methods that involve observations or open-ended interviews with one family member at a time can provide some insight about family meanings, it is whole family narratives, interviews, and observations that are particularly recommended if we are to capture family *reality* versus family myths (as described above).

Some attention needs to be given to the development of standardized measures for assessing family meanings so that the relationship of family meanings to health outcomes and other outcomes of interest can be assessed with large samples. While self-report measures intrinsically capture perceptions of the existence of demands and resources, they do not usually ascertain the valence or importance of these variables, which would more closely approximate situational meanings. Similarly, quantitative self-report or observational measures of implicit or explicit beliefs about family relationships (identity) and more existential issues (world view) are possible when the content of these beliefs is decided a priori by the investigator in choosing what assessment instrument to use. One advantage of using these structured measures is that they can be repeated over time and hence change can be assessed, giving insight into the dynamic nature of changing meanings and the adaptation process.

We need more longitudinal studies in which the natural processes by which families adapt over time to developmental changes or changes in the chronic condition can be understood. Longitudinal studies emphasizing the interplay between biological (illness) factors, psychological functioning of individual family members, and family and other social relationship factors would allow us to more fully understand the direction of effects linking these different domains.

Most of the published research related to families and chronic health conditions has remained at the descriptive and analytic levels. There are very few intervention studies that have been designed to promote the development of resources and coping behaviors identified from these descriptive/analytic studies in families living with a child's chronic health condition. Intervention studies are, of course, the ultimate test of our theories and, for applied researchers, the primary reason for doing research in the first place. Intervention studies designed to support families in the development of meanings that contribute to healthy adaptation to chronic illness are needed. For example, the protocol developed by Gonzalez et al. (1989) for a multiple family discussion group where maintenance of a family's chosen identity is emphasized needs to be tested in clinical trials to determine its efficacy.

Families are complex social units that vary widely in their adaptive capacities. One of the challenges social scientists face is to extend our understanding by describing the range of this variability. One of the most interesting questions still facing us is why some families are able to "weave gold out of straw" and develop positive, adaptive beliefs and meanings and others are not. Further studies are needed to understand how families share and construct meanings about illness and disability. In addition to contributing to family stress theory, such findings would contribute to improved practices in working with families who are adapting to chronic stress, particularly the presence of disability or chronic illness.

■ Acknowledgment

I would like to thank Diane Hovey, Director of the Family Institute for Creative Well-Being and parent of a child with severe disabilities, who coined the phrase "Creating Gold Out of Straw" and allowed me to use it in the title of this chapter.

■ References

Affleck, G., & Tennen, H. (1993). Cognitive adaptation to adversity: Insights from parents of medically fragile infants. In A. P. Turnbull, J. M. Patterson, S. K. Behr, D. L. Murphy, J. G. Marquis, & M. J. Bue-Banning (Eds.), *Cognitive coping research and developmental disabilities* (pp. 135–150). Baltimore, MD: Paul Brookes.

Antonovsky, A. (1979). *Health, stress, and coping.* San Francisco: Jossey-Bass.

Antonovsky, A. (1987). *Unraveling the mystery of health. How people manage stress and stay well.* San Francisco: Jossey-Bass.

Antonovsky, A., & Sourani, T. (1988). Family sense of coherence and family adaptation. *Journal of Marriage and the Family, 50,* 79–92.

Austin, J., & McDermott, N. (1988). Parental attitude and coping behaviors in families of children with epilepsy. *Journal of Neuroscience Nursing, 20,* 174–179.

Behr, S., & Murphy, D. (1993). Research progress and promise: The role of perceptions in cognitive adaptation to disability. In A. P. Turnbull, J. M. Patterson, S. K. Behr, D. L. Murphy, J. G. Marquis, & M. J. Bue-Banning (Eds.), *Cognitive coping research and developmental disabilities* (pp. 151–163). Baltimore, MD: Paul Brookes.

Bennett, L., Wolin, S., & McAvity, K. (1988). Family identity, ritual and myth. A cultural perspective on life cycle transitions. In K. Falicov (Ed.), *Family transitions* (pp. 211–234). New York: Guilford Press.

Berger, P. L., & Luckmann, T. (1966). *The social construction of reality.* New York: Doubleday.

Boss, P. (1999). *Ambiguous loss. Learning to live with unresolved grief.* Cambridge, MA: Harvard University Press.

Boss, P. (2002). *Family stress management. A contextual approach.* Thousand Oaks, CA: Sage.

Bossard, J., & Boll, E. (1950). *Ritual in family living,* Philadelphia: University of Pennsylvania Press.

Bresleau, N. (1993). Psychiatric sequelae of brain dysfunction in children: The role of family environment. In R. Cole & D. Reiss (Eds.), *How do families cope with chronic illness?* Hillsdale, NJ: Erlbaum.

Bristol, M. M. (1987). Mothers of children with autism or communication disorders: Successful adaptation and the double ABCVX model. *Journal of Autism and Developmental Disorders, 17,* 469–486.

Brown, J. (1993). Coping with stress: The beneficial role of positive illusions. In A. P. Turnbull, J. M. Patterson, S. K. Behr, D. L. Murphy, J. G. Marquis, & M. J. Bue-Banning (Eds.), *Cognitive coping research and developmental disabilities* (pp. 123–133). Baltimore, MD: Paul Brookes.

Bruner, J. (1990). *Acts of meaning.* Cambridge, MA: Harvard University Press.

Cowan, P. A., Cowan, C. P., & Schulz, M. S. (1996). Thinking about risk and resilience in families. In E. M. Hetherington & E. A. Blechman (Eds.), *Stress, coping, and resiliency in children and families* (pp. 1–38). Mahwah, NJ: Erlbaum.

Dodgson, J., Garwick, A., Blozis, S., Patterson, J., Bennett, F., & Blum, R. (2000). Uncertainty in childhood chronic conditions and distress in families of young children. *Journal of Family Nursing,* 6(3), 252–266.

Eaker, D. G., & Walters, L. H. (2002). Adolescent satisfaction in family rituals and psychosocial development: A developmental systems theory perspective. *Journal of Family Psychology,* 16(4), 406–414.

Epstein, N. B., Baldwin, L. M., & Bishop, D. S. (1983). The McMaster Family Assessment Device. *Journal of Marital and Family Therapy,* 9, 171–180.

Evans, C., & Hughes, I. (1987). The relationship between diabetic control and individual and family characteristics. *Journal of Psychosomatic Research,* 31(3), 367–374.

Fiese, B. H., & Kline, C. A. (1993). Development of the Family Ritual Questionnaire: Initial reliability and validation studies. *Journal of Family Psychology,* 6(3), 290–299.

Fiese, B. H., Sameroff, A. J., Grotevant, H. D., Wamboldt, F. S., Dickstein, S., & Fravel, D. L. (1999). The stories that families tell: Narrative coherence, narrative interaction, and relationship beliefs. *Monograph of the Society for Research in Child Development,* 64(2, Series No. 257).

Fiese, B. H., Tomcho, T. J., Doublas, M., Josephs, K., Poltrock, S., & Baker, T. (2002). A review of 50 years of research on naturally occurring family routines and rituals: Cause for celebration? *Journal of Family Psychology,* 16(4), 381–390.

Fiese, B. H., & Wamboldt, F. S. (2000). Family routines, rituals, and asthma management: A proposal for family-based strategies to increase treatment adherence. *Families, Systems and Health,* 18(4), 405–418.

Fisher, L., & Ransom. D. C. (1995). An empirically derived typology of families: 1. Relationships with adult health. *Family Process,* 34, 161–182.

Folkman, S., & Moskowitz, J. T. (2000). Positive affect and the other side of coping. *American Psychologist,* 55(6), 647–654.

Garwick, A. W., Patterson, J. M., Bennett, F., & Blum, R. (1995). Breaking the news: How families first learn about their child's chronic condition. *Archives of Pediatrics and Adolescent Medicine,* 149, 991–997.

Garwick, A. W., Patterson, J. M., Meschke, L. L., Bennett, F. C., & Blum, R. W. (2002). The uncertainty of preadolescents' chronic health conditions and family distress. *Journal of Family Nursing,* 8(1), 11–31.

Gonzalez, S., Steinglass, P., & Reiss, D. (1989). Putting the illness in its place: Discussion groups for families with chronic medical illnesses. *Family Process,* 28, 69–87.

Gortmaker, S. L., Walker, D. K., Weitzman, M., & Sobol, A. M. (1990). Chronic conditions, socioeconomic risks, and behavioral problems in children and adolescents. *Pediatrics,* 85(3), 267–276.

Hamlett, K. W., Pellegrini, D. S., & Katz, K. S. (1992). Childhood chronic illness as a family stressor. *Journal of Pediatric Psychology,* 17, 33–47.

Hill, R. (1949). *Families under stress.* New York: Harper.

Howe, G. W., Feinstein, C., Reiss, D., Molock, S., & Berger, K. (1993). Adolescent adjustment to chronic physical disorders: I. Comparing neurological and non-neurological conditions. *Journal of Child Psychology and Psychiatry and Allied Disciplines,* 34(7), 1153–1171.

Ievers, C. E., Brown, R. T., Lambert, R. G., Hsu, L., & Eckman, J. R. (1998). Family functioning and social support in the adaptation of caregivers of children with sickle cell syndromes. *Journal of Pediatric Psychology,* 23, 377–388.

Imber-Black, E., Roberts, J., & Whiting, R. (Eds.). (1988). *Rituals and family therapy.* New York: Norton.

Jacobson, A., Hauser, S., Lavori, P., Willett, J., Cole, C., Wolfsdorf, J., et al. (1994). Family environment and glycemic control: A four-year prospective study of children and adolescents with insulin-dependent diabetes mellitus. *Psychosomatic Medicine, 56,* 401–409.

Jenson, E. W., James, S. A., Boyce, W. T., & Hartnett, S. A. (1983). The Family Routines Inventory: Development and validation. *Social Science and Medicine, 17,* 201–211.

Jessop, D., & Stein, R. (1985). Uncertainty and its relation to the psychological and social correlates of chronic illness in children. *Social Science and Medicine, 20*(10), 993–999.

Kerig, P. K., & Lindahl, K. M. (2001). *Family observational coding systems: Resources for systemic research.* Mahwah, NJ: Erlbaum.

Klapp, O. E. (1959). Ritual and family solidarity. *Social Forces, 37,* 212–214.

Kleinman, A. (1988). *The illness narratives: Suffering, healing, and the human condition.* New York: Basic Books.

Lazarus, R. S., & Folkman, S. (1984). *Stress, appraisal and coping.* New York: Springer.

Leonard, B. J., Brust, J. D., & Patterson, J. M. (1991). Home-care reimbursement for technology-dependent children: It's impact on parental distress. *Lifestyles: Family and Economic Issues, 12*(1), 63–76.

Markson, S., & Fiese, B. H. (2000). Family rituals as a protective factor for children with asthma. *Journal of Pediatric Psychology, 25*(7), 471–480.

Martin, M., Miller-Johnson, S., Kitzmann, K., & Emery, R. (1998). Parent–child relationships and insulin-dependent diabetes mellitus: Observational ratings of clinically relevant dimensions. *Journal of Family Psychology, 12,* 102–111.

McCubbin, H. I., McCubbin, M. A., Nevin, R. S., & Cauble, E. (1979). *CHIP—Coping Health Inventory for Parents.* St. Paul: University of Minnesota, Family Social Science.

McCubbin, H. I., & Patterson, J. M. (1983a). The family stress process: The double ABCX model of family adjustment and adaptation. *Marriage and Family Review, 6*(1, 2), 7–37.

McCubbin, H. I., & Patterson, J. M. (1983b). Stress: The family inventory of life events and changes. In E. E. Finsinger (Ed.), *Marriage and family assessment* (pp. 275–297). Beverly Hills, CA: Sage.

McCubbin, H. I., Patterson, J. M., & Wilson, L. (1980). *Family Inventory of Life Events and Changes (FILE).* St. Paul: University of Minnesota, Family Social Science.

Moos, R. H., & Moos, B. S. (1981). *Family Environment Scale (FES).* Palo Alto, CA: CPP/ Consulting Psychologists.

Olson, D. H., Portner, J., & Bell, R. (1982). *Family Adaptability and Cohesion Evaluation Scales (FACES).* St. Paul: University of Minnesota, Family Social Science.

Park, C. L., & Folkman, S. (1997). Meaning in the context of stress and coping. *Review of General Psychology, 1*(2), 115–144.

Patterson, J. M. (1985). Critical factors affecting family compliance with cystic fibrosis. *Family Relations, 34,* 79–89.

Patterson, J. M. (1988). Families experiencing stress: The family adjustment and adaptation response model. *Family Systems Medicine, 5*(2), 202–237.

Patterson, J. M. (1991). A family systems perspective for working with youth with disability. *Pediatrician, 18,* 129–141.

Patterson, J. M. (1993). The role of family meanings in adaptation to chronic illness and disability. In A. P. Turnbull, J. M. Patterson, S. K. Behr, D. L. Murphy, J. G. Marquis, &

M. J. Bue-Banning (Eds.), *Cognitive coping research and developmental disabilities* (pp. 221–238). Baltimore, MD: Paul Brookes.

Patterson, J. M., Blum, R., Stinchfield, R., & Garwick, A. (1994, November). *Understanding resilience in families of children with chronic conditions.* Symposium presentation at the Annual Meeting of the National Council on Family Relations, Minneapolis, MN.

Patterson, J. M., Budd, J., Goetz, D., & Warwick, W. (1993). Family correlates of a ten-year pulmonary health trend in cystic fibrosis. *Pediatrics, 91,* 383–389.

Patterson, J. M., & Garwick, A. W. (1994). Levels of family meaning in family stress theory. *Family Process, 33,* 287–304.

Patterson, J. M., & Garwick, A. W. (1998). Coping with chronic illness: A family systems perspective on living with diabetes. In G. Werther & J. Court (Eds.), *Diabetes and the adolescent* (pp. 3–34). Victoria, Australia: Miranova.

Patterson, J. M., Garwick, A., Bennett, F., & Blum, R. (1997). Social support in families with children with chronic conditions. *Journal of Developmental and Behavioral Pediatrics, 18*(6), 383–391.

Patterson, J. M., Holm, K. E., & Gurney, J. G. (2004). Family impact of childhood cancer: A qualitative analysis of strains, resources, and coping behaviors. *Psycho-Oncology, 13*(6), 390–407.

Patterson, J. M., & Leonard, B. J. (1994). Caregiving and children. In E. Kahana, D. Biegel, & M. Wykel (Eds.), *Family caregiving across the lifespan* (pp. 133–158). Newbury Park, CA: Sage.

Perrin, E. C., Newacheck, P., Pless, I. B., Drotar, D., Gortmaker, S. L., Leventhal, J., et al. (1993). Issues involved in the definition and classification of chronic health conditions. *Pediatrics, 91*(4), 787–793.

Ransom, D. C., Fisher, L., & Terry, H. E. (1992). Family world view and adult health. *Family Process, 31*(3), 251–267.

Reiss, D. (1981). *The family's construction of reality.* Cambridge, MA: Harvard University Press.

Reiss, D. (1989). The represented and practicing family: contrasting visions of family continuity. In A. Sameroff & R. Emde (Eds.), *Relationship disturbances in early childhood. A developmental approach* (pp. 191–220). New York: Basic Books.

Reiss, D., Gonzalez, S., & Kramer, N. (1986). Family process, chronic illness and death. *Archives of General Psychiatry, 43,* 795–804.

Reiss, D., Steinglass, P., & Howe, G. (1993). The family's organization around the illness. In R. Cole & D. Reiss (Eds.), *How do families cope with chronic illness?* Hillsdale, NJ: Erlbaum.

Reiss, R., Oliveri, M., & Curd, K. (1983). Family paradigm and adolescent social behavior. In H. Grotevant & C. Cooper (Eds.), *Adolescent development in the family: New directions for child development* (p. 22). San Francisco: Jossey-Bass.

Rutter, M. (1987). Psychosocial resilience and protective mechanisms. *American Journal of Orthopsychiatry, 57,* 316–331.

Silver, E. J., Stein, R. E., & Bauman, L. J. (1999). Sociodemographic and condition-related characteristics associated with conduct problems in school-aged children with chronic health conditions. *Archives of Pediatrics and Adolescent Medicine, 153*(8), 815–820.

Skinner, H. A., Santa-Barbara, J., & Steinhauer, P. D. (1983). The family assessment measure. *Canadian Journal of Community Mental Health, 2,* 91–105.

Skinner, T., & Hampson, S. (1998). Social support and personal models of diabetes in relation to self-care and well-being. *Journal of Adolescence, 21,* 703–715.

Smith, M. S., Mauseth, R., Palmer, J. P., Pecoraro, R., & Wenet, G. (1991). Glycosylated hemoglobin and psychological adjustment in adolescents with diabetes. *Adolescence, 26*(101), 31–40.

Stein, R., Gortmaker, S., Perrin, E., Perrin, J., Pless, I., Walker, D., et al. (1987). Severity of illness: Concepts and measurements. *Lancet, December 26,* 1–8.

Stein, R. E., Bauman, L. J., Westbrook, L. E., Coupey, S. M., & Ireys, H. T. (1993). Framework for identifying children who have chronic conditions: The case for a new definition. *Journal of Pediatrics, 122*(3), 342–347.

Stein, R. E., & Jessop, D. J. (1984). Does pediatric home care make a difference for children with chronic illness? Findings from the pediatric ambulatory care treatment study. *Pediatrics, 73,* 845–853.

Stein, R. E., & Jessop, D. J. (1989). What diagnosis does not tell: The case for a noncategorical approach to chronic illness in childhood. *Social Science and Medicine, 29,* 769–778.

Stein, R. E., & Riessman, C. K. (1980). The development of an Impact-on-Family Scale: Preliminary findings. *Medical Care, 19,* 465–472.

Steinglass, P., Bennett, L., Wolin, S., & Reiss, D. (1987). *The alcoholic family.* New York: Basic Books.

Steinglass, P., & Horan, M. (1987). Families and chronic medical illness. *Journal of Psychopathology and the Family, 3,* 127–142.

Taylor, S. (1983). Adjustment to threatening events: A theory of cognitive adaptation. *American Psychologist, 38,* 624–630.

Thompson, S. C. (1991). The search for meaning following a stroke. *Basic and Applied Social Psychology, 12,* 81–96.

Thompson, S. J., Auslander, W. F., & White, N. H. (2001). Comparison of single-mother and two-parent families on metabolic control of children with diabetes. *Diabetes Care, 24*(2), 234–238.

Uniform Data System for Medical Rehabilitation. (1993). *Guide for the Uniform Data Set for Medical Rehabilitation for Children (Wee-FIM), Version 4—Community/Outpatient.* Buffalo, NY: Author.

Venters, M. (1981). Familial coping with chronic and severe childhood illness: The case of cystic fibrosis. *Social Science and Medicine, 15A,* 289–297.

Walsh, F. (1998). *Strengthening family resilience.* New York: Guilford Press.

Wamboldt, F., & Wolin, S. (1989). Reality and myth in family life: Changes across generations. *Journal of Psychotherapy and the Family, 4,* 141–165.

Wamboldt, F. S., Wamboldt, M. Z., Gavin, L. A., Roesler, T. A., & Brugman, S. M. (1995). Parental criticism and treatment outcome in adolescents hospitalized for severe, chronic asthma. *Journal of Psychosomatic Research, 39*(8), 95–105.

Weihs, K., Fisher, L., & Baird, M. (2002). Families, health, and behavior. *Families, Systems and Health, 20*(1), 7–46.

Weisz, J. R., Rothbaum, F. M., & Blackburn, T. C. (1984). Standing out and standing in: The psychology of control in America and Japan. *American Psychologist, 39*(9), 955–969.

White, K., Kolman, M. L., Wexler, P., Polin, G., & Winter, R. J. (1984). Unstable diabetes and unstable families: A psychosocial evaluation of diabetic children with recurrent ketoacidosis. *Pediatrics, 73,* 749–755.

White, R. W. (1974). Strategies of adaptation. An attempt at systematic description. In G. V. Coelho, D. Hamburg, & J. E. Adams (Eds.), *Coping and adaptation* (pp. 17–32). New York: Basic Books.

Williamson, G. M., Walters, A. S., & Shaffer, D. R. (2002). Caregiver models of self and others, coping, and depression: Predictors of depression in children with chronic pain. *Health Psychology, 21*(4), 405–410.

Wolin, S., & Bennett, L. (1984). Family rituals. *Family Process, 23,* 401–420.

Wright, L. M., Watson, W. L., & Bell, J. M. (1996). *Beliefs: The heart of healing in families and illness.* New York: Basic Books.

Zimmerman, M. A., & Arunkumar, R. (1994). Resiliency research: Implications for schools and policy. *Social Policy Report: Society for Research in Child Development, 8*(4), 1–17.

22

Using Family Models in Health Research: A Framework for Family Intervention in Chronic Disease

Lawrence Fisher

Chronic diseases, such as diabetes, cardiovascular disease, asthma/chronic obstructive pulmonary disease, and depression, continue to exact a staggering toll on the nation's health care system. It is estimated that about 80 cents of every health care dollar is spent on services related to chronic disease and its management. Despite considerable progress in the development of effective biological treatments and the prevention of associated comorbidities for many chronic diseases, the day-to-day management of these diseases is tedious, repetitive, and at times invasive for both patients and family members. Changes in lifestyle, leisure activities, work and daily routines, and family relationships are required on a continuing basis, and the disease often becomes a major new component of personal and family life.

There is considerable variation in the ways in which patients and families respond to disease and how effective they are in dealing with the management demands of the disease over time. For example, studies have shown that between 47 and 93% of patients with diabetes deviate substantially from disease management recommendations at least weekly (Clement, 1995; Glasgow, 1991). Variations in disease management among patients and families have been associated with four major categories of influence (Fisher et al., 1998). First, there is a vast literature linking a large number of personal traits, coping styles, attitudes, beliefs, and sentiments to disease management over time. These include, for example, self-efficacy, beliefs about the cause and outcome of the disease, and beliefs about the effectiveness of treatment (Anderson et al., 1995; Kleinman, Eisenberg, & Good, 1978; Scheier & Bridges, 1995; Toobert & Glasgow, 1994). Second is the varying intensity of extra disease-related stresses that are experienced by patients and families. These often include economic, work, parental, and extended family problems. Stress has been shown to affect disease management through at least two pathways. Stress has direct physiologic linkages to the endocrine system, thus influencing the body's homeostatic and allostatic systems via the physiologic stress response (McEwen, 1998; Sapolsky & Krey, 1986). Stress also leads to direct behavioral outcomes by disrupting routine and consistent disease management behaviors (Demers, Neale, Wenzloff, Gronsman, & Jaber, 1989; Fiscella, Franks, & Shields, 1997). Third, the content and quality of interactions between patients and their health care providers are potent influences of disease management. In general, interactions characterized by a high degree of patient involvement, control, information seeking, trust, and expression of emotion have been linked to high patient satisfaction and positive clinical outcomes (Charles, Gafni, & Whelan, 1997; Golin, DiMatteo, & Gelberg, 1996; Greenfield, Kaplan, Ware, Yanko, & Frank, 1988; Kaplan, Greenfield, & Ware, 1989).

The fourth influence on disease management reflects an ecological or social systems perspective. It places the individual with chronic disease within his or her primary social context and observes how the patient and other influential members of that context operate together to be affected by and to affect disease outcomes (Weihs, Fisher, & Baird, 2002). The social context with the most powerful and immediate effects on disease management is the family, broadly defined. Most research in chronic disease considers the family only as part of the unitary construct of social support (Cox & Gonder-Frederick, 1992; Goodall & Halford, 1992). A social systems perspective, however, targets the family as unique because the specific bonds that tie family members together reflect greater levels of emotional intensity, attachment, and duration than most other sets of social relationships (Franks, Campbell, & Shields, 1992; Primono, Yates, & Woods, 1990). This orientation also expands disease outcomes beyond the patient with the chronic disease, by examining the effects of disease management on the health and well-being of all family members and not just the patient.

Despite the increasing interest in recent years in research on chronic disease and its management, studies of the family context of care have increased at a far slower rate than research that addresses other potential influences, i.e., personal characteristics of patients, stress, and patient–health system relationships. By and large, most family-based studies in the recent literature cluster around diseases of children and adolescents and among diseases of the elderly. There are relatively fewer studies of the family context of care that address diseases of adulthood (Weihs et al., 2002), the age range that contains a large percentage of the U.S. population that is chronically ill.

This notable gap in the terrain of chronic disease research became particularly apparent as our research group began to address a program of intervention for patients with type 2 diabetes and their families. For the past 10 years our group has been studying how personal, family, and other social context factors influence the management of patients with diabetes and their partners. Our findings have implications not only for diabetes, but also for other major chronic diseases that require ongoing changes to patient and family lifestyle and health behavior. Type 2 diabetes provides a useful set of management requirements and biological markers for study. Findings from diabetes research can be generalized easily to other chronic diseases of adulthood that require similar lifestyle changes. We have collected data on approximately 500 patients and their partners. The sample is composed of male and female patients from four ethnic groups: European Americans, Latinos, Chinese

Americans, and African Americans. This has enabled us to focus on the major crosscutting themes of patient gender and ethnicity throughout our analyses. Our task in recent years has been to make use of our comprehensive family data set to develop interventions that target for change specific aspects of family or relationship life that have empirically demonstrated links to disease management. These may include, for example, family conflict resolution, directness of communication, emotional expressiveness, beliefs about the disease, and problem solving. Thus, we are now looking at family and health research from an applications or intervention perspective, rather than from a more theoretical, descriptive orientation.

This change in research perspective has identified a number of glaring problems facing family health psychology in our efforts to translate family models to templates for effective family-based interventions in the clinical setting. Underlying these problems is the need to develop well-specified, systematic, and practical family models that provide the conceptual foundation for intervention research. In the first section of this chapter I pose three questions to guide a review of the current state of the art with respect to family and health models. These questions establish a structure to review and classify current family models and highlight where development needs to occur. In the second section I list a number of model enhancements that need to occur in the next generation of family and chronic disease intervention research. In the last section, I illustrate these enhancements by proposing a family intervention framework for use in type 2 diabetes.

■ Current Family and Health Models: Questions About the State of the Art

1. What aspects of family life should be targeted for change in chronic disease interventions, and how are they dynamically related? Interventionists design programs that target specific behaviors for change. Using a family perspective, what family or relationship behaviors should be targeted for change in a program to improve the management of chronic disease? Furthermore, what are the dynamic pathways through which behavioral change in one area of family life affects behavior in another? For example, does an interventionist need to design specific programs to address both family beliefs about the disease and family problem solving, or can it be hypothesized that changes in family beliefs will lead directly to changes in family problem-solving behavior?

These questions highlight the need to identify crucial family qualities for intervention and to identify the order of their influence on outcomes. For example, Fisher, Ransom, and Terry (1993) ran a series of global analyses of family variables from four domains of family life taken together that previously had been linked individually to family member health and well-being in a community-based sample of families. The four domains were family Structure/Organization, World View (beliefs), Emotion Management, and Problem Solving. Using cross-sectional data, they found that the domains of family World View and Emotion Management maintained their linkages to health status variables when placed in the context of the other two family domains, whereas the variables in the other two domains (Structure/Organization, Problem Solving) did not. This suggested, at its most simplistic level, that family beliefs (World View) and family emotional regulation (Emotion Management) may "drive" how family structures and problem-solving skills are formed in relationship to the health status of family members. This suggested further that programs of intervention might focus initially on family beliefs and emotional regulation as a prelude to focusing on family structures and problem-solving skills. Thus, a dynamically structured ordering effect among the family variables suggested a plan for intervention.

2. *What do current family and health models tell us about applying family programs of intervention to different kinds of families?* This question addresses the issue of qualifying variables and conditional effects. How should programs vary as a function of the gender of the patient with the diagnosed disease (Kiecolt-Glaser & Newton, 2001) or the ethnicity of the family (Fisher, Chesla, Skaff, Gilliss, Mullan, et al., 2000)? For example, Fisher, Gundmundsdottir, et al. (2000) showed that European American couples with diabetes displayed patterns of patient-partner verbal exchange around disease-related problems that were considerably different than those of Latino couples. The pace of problem resolution, the directness of the discussion, and the task focus of the couples varied considerably between the two ethnic groups. Does this mean that separate programs with couples of different ethnicities should be developed, or can single programs accommodate couples from different ethnic settings?

3. *What do family models tell us about when family programs of intervention are most and least efficacious in health care settings?* Even though many family and health practitioners adhere to the view that a family perspective in the health arena is useful, most also admit that a family-focused intervention may not be necessary in all cases. One size does not fit all! If so, when is a family oriented program most and least efficacious?

■ A Classification of Family Models in Health Research

An indication of how well existing family and health models address these three questions can be obtained by a selective overview of some of the most often used approaches. These have been classified in table 22.1. The first group of models is typified by the pioneering work of John Rolland (1987, 1994), who presents an overarching and orienting family framework. This family frame sets the stage for intervention by identifying some of the key precepts of family theory as applied to disease: the variability of family boundaries across different family developmental levels and how disease often forces a reversal of developmentally expected changes; how disease management can become a dominating force in the family, undermining developmentally appropriate changes; and how disease may force changes in long-standing role behaviors, which can force a renegotiation of power and decision making in the family. Furthermore, Rolland calls attention to the characteristics of the disease itself, the so-called demand aspects of the disease: is the onset acute or

TABLE 22.1   *A Classification of Selected Family Models in Health Research*

Type	Author	Variables	Outcome
Orienting models	Rolland (1994)	The interface between family and disease	Family adaptation
Operational models	FAAR; Patterson and Garwick (1994)	Balance between demands and family resources, a family stress and coping approach	Family adaptation
	BBFM; Wood and Miller (in press)	Ordered sequence: proximity, generational hierarchy, parental relationship quality, emotional climate, triangulation, responsivity	Disease activity
Multidimensional models	Reiss (1981)	Communication, coordination, closure	Problem solving
	Fisher, Ransom, and Terry (1993)	World view, problem solving	Family member health and well-being
Unidimensional model	Shields, Franks, Harp, McDaniel, and Campbell (1992)	Expressed emotion: criticalness	Disease relapse, reoccurrence
	Antonovsky and Sourani (1988)	Family coherence	Family member health

gradual; is the course progressive, constant, or relapsing; does the course lead to progressive incapacity or to stability in functioning; is the course predictable or uncertain; are the symptoms visible or hidden; are there genetic implications for other family members or is the genetic risk to other generations inconsequential? All of these disease qualities have profound effects on family behavior and they shape clinical intervention.

A second group of family models is labeled *operational.* These identify a number of crucial family characteristics as targets for change, and they suggest, in a relatively circumscribed way, the paths through which these characteristics might affect behavior. The family adjustment and adaptation response (FAAR) model (Patterson, 1988; Patterson & Garwick, 1994) and the biobehavioral family model (BBFM) (Wood, 1993; Wood & Miller, in press) are good examples. Both list potential family targets and an ordering of their effects. The FAAR model is based on a stress and coping paradigm in which a pileup of disease- and non-disease-related demands on the family are offset by personal and family resources that enhance resilience

(Patterson, 2002). Family resources include clarity of rules and expectations, family routines, clear generational boundaries, parental hierarchy, mutual support, intimacy, and satisfaction. In a recent iteration of the FAAR model, outlined in chapter 21 in this book, Joän Patterson emphasizes family meanings and interpretations as crucial family resources that shape the response to the disease. Based primarily on the systems notion of boundary, the BBFM evolved from structural family therapy in an initial attempt to link family and personal variables to disease activity, relapse, or severity (Wood, 1993; Wood & Miller, in press). In the BBFM, Wood suggested that the effects of general stress, triangulation, and quality of the parental relationship are contained or exacerbated by family proximity (closeness) and hierarchy (boundary). The outcome of this process challenges the child's biobehavioral reactivity, which, in turn, affects the frequency and/or intensity of disease activity.

Although evolving from different research traditions, both the FAAR and BBFM approaches are similar in several respects: they both include family-level, in contrast to person-level, variables; they both identify several family constructs as important in understanding a family's reaction to the disease and their ability to manage the disease over time (many of the targets are similar in the two approaches); they both imply an ordering to the components of the model (FAAR—family qualities in a response to the stress of the disease; BBFM—proximity, generational hierarchy, and responsivity lead to biobehavioral reactivity, which leads to disease activity); and they both focus on change to the psychosocial interior of the family. They also share a few limitations: both focus primarily on diseases of childhood and adolescence—at least both have been applied almost exclusively to ill family members of this age range; both include only selected qualifying variables, such as socioeconomic status (SES), to help identify potential variations among populations of families; and both employ family variables with different degrees of specificity and theoretical justification (this is particularly true of the FAAR model, in which family variables are listed primarily as potential resources).

The third group of family models is labeled *multidimensional.* These models are for the most part drawn from empirical findings, rather than from more complex theoretical underpinnings, and they provide a list of family dimensions as targets for change, although they frequently do not provide much direction in terms of how the dimensions are ordered. For example, Reiss (1981) described three family attributes that emerged from a series of studies in which families engaged in a card sorting task. These qualities described the processes and structures that the families used to solve the card sort problem: configuration, coordination, and closure. Similarly, Fisher, Ransom, Terry, Lipkin, and Weiss (1992) identified from the literature four domains of family life with documented links to health status (World View, Structure/Organization, Emotion Management, Problem Solving). They showed how various descriptors of each domain were linked individually and together to different aspects of health and well-being among adults and adolescents. Unlike operational models, these multidimensional models provide lists of characteristics of family life that display documented linkages to health status. They tell us very little, however, about how these family variables interrelate with each other in a coherent way.

The last group of family models is labeled *unidimensional*. These focus on a single aspect of family life as crucial to health, although they rarely imply that other aspects are unimportant. For example, the expressed emotion literature emphasizes family criticalness (Shields, Franks, Harp, McDaniel, & Campbell, 1992) and Antonovsky and Sourani (1988) address primarily family coherence. Each construct is a single dimension with family relevance, but each has limited applicability when a variety of other important family dimensions are considered.

This brief and admittedly nonexhaustive overview of current family and health models or approaches provides a sampling of family models to address the three questions posed at the outset: how well do family models direct programs of intervention to target areas for family change, what kinds of qualifying variables have been considered, and what do family models tell us about the efficiency of family based interventions? With respect to the first question, all four groups of models identify crucial family attributes with respect to health and disease management, and they suggest, or at least outline, what specific aspects of the family might be identified for change. Only the operational models suggest a dynamic ordering among the family variables with some conceptual justification. Although Rolland's writings guide the interventionist, in general the models, as a group, remain relatively unspecified, which reduces their applicability across diseases and across family developmental levels. Most seem relevant to diseases of children and adolescents; far fewer have been applied to diseases of adulthood.

With respect to the second question, with the exception of Rolland's writings and to some extent the FAAR approach, the models do not directly address how application needs to be modified for different kinds of families, except in the most general terms. Clearly, future efficiency research that addresses the impact of patient gender, SES, and ethnicity will need to be incorporated into the next generation of family and health models to increase their applicability to different disease and family settings.

Last, the models provide little guidance concerning when to apply and when not to apply a family approach to intervention. As reviewed, issues of efficiency are rarely addressed.

With full acknowledgment of the considerable research already devoted to current models of family and health, it is not too surprising that only moderate levels of theoretical development have been achieved. This is a relatively new field of study and the complexities of the family and the diversity of disease place great demands on any family model. In addition, most thinking about the family from a clinical perspective has evolved from couple and family psychotherapy, which deals more with behavioral and relational psychopathology than with the management of acute or chronic disease. As a result, models that have evolved over time, such as those reviewed above, have used bits and pieces of family theory that were developed for use in other family settings. It is important to recognize that many of these approaches assume the kinds of pathological family processes that are found among psychologically or relationally disturbed or conflicted families. Yet most families dealing with physical disease are not psychologically disturbed; they are usually valiantly struggling under very difficult circumstances. Thus, much of general family theory is not easily translatable to the physical disease setting.

This state of affairs can lead to considerable confusion about what a family approach to intervention in chronic disease really is. Without a clear set of theoretical guidelines and directions, the probability of misapplying a family perspective to the health arena increases. For example, some "family" interventionists talk about a family program when what they are really doing is telling the spouses of patients with a chronic disease to be more understanding or encouraging patients to bring spouses to a brief educational session for "support." These are not family-based interventions in the sense of the family models reviewed above.

■ Enhancing Family Models in Health Research

The dynamic issues underlying current family and health models, especially those applied to diseases of adulthood, require greater specificity in their description and objectives for practical application. To guide discussion, an elaborated outline of the general processes involved is presented in figure 22.1. The family intervention framework is composed of five columns of constructs: general contextual factors, family and individual targets of the intervention, moderator variables, behavioral and relationship outcomes, and biological outcomes. The sequence of constructs within the framework suggests that contextual factors set the stage for intervention, selected family and personal behaviors are identified as objects for intervention, the effects of the intervention on outcomes are conditioned by the moderator variables, and behavioral change is documented at both the family and personal levels. In most cases the intervention is exclusively behavioral, for example, focusing on disease education, improved problem solving, changes in disease beliefs, etc. It is then assumed that the resulting behavioral and relationship changes will lead directly to biological change, which for people with diabetes usually means improved metabolic control, weight loss, and reduced or limited comorbidities over time.

Taking the family models described above as a start and using the family intervention framework as a guide, a list of six model enhancements is suggested in this section to advance current thinking to the next generation of family models for use in health research.

1. A clear specification of the outcomes: What does the intervention seek to change? A review of the fourth column of table 22.1 suggests that the outcomes among the family models vary considerably. What was considered a uniform list of family and health models at the outset, upon review yields approaches that predict important but very different kinds of health behaviors and conditions. For example, the FAAR model focuses on how well a family adapts to the multiple stresses and strains that result from disease- and non-disease-related stresses. Alternatively, the BBFM approach predicts disease activity, which can be taken to mean exacerbations of disease, such as increases in frequency or severity of asthma attacks. Other terms, such as level of family member health and well-being, rate of disease relapse, and level of general personal adaptation, suggest that these models predict qualitatively different kinds of outcomes at different levels of assessment: some at the general family level, some at the individual family member well-being level, and some at the disease severity level.

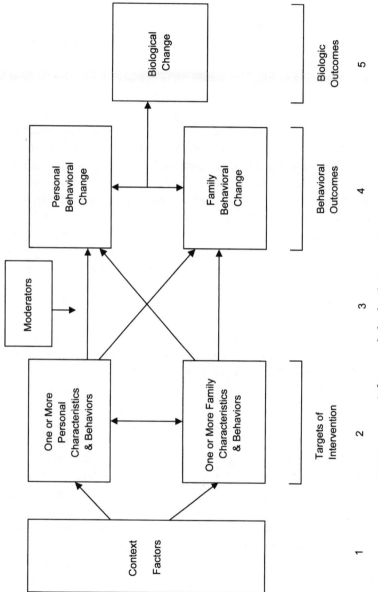

FIGURE 22.1 A framework for family intervention in chronic disease.

Two problems emerge with respect to a specification of outcomes in chronic physical diseases like type 2 diabetes. The first concerns the sheer volume of potential outcomes that can be assessed: person variables, relationship variables, specific disease management behaviors, attitudes and beliefs about the disease, quality of life, satisfaction, stress, depression, biological variables, comorbidities. Many intervention studies employ a relatively simplistic outcome assessment framework, which increases the probability of type 2 error. In this scenario, one concludes that the intervention did not yield the desired effect when in fact it did. The effect was not detected simply because a relevant measure was not included in the outcome assessment protocol. However, time demands force selective outcomes assessment and a rationale needs to be considered concerning what specific behaviors and conditions are expected to change as a direct result of the constructs targeted for change in the intervention. Thus, a conceptual link between intervention and outcome needs to be included in the intervention framework.

The second problem regarding the specification of outcomes concerns the relationship between behavioral and biological outcomes, as outlined in columns four and five in figure 22.1. Since most of the interventions under discussion focus on behavioral or relationship change, can we assume that changes in these behaviors will lead to measurable changes among relevant biological variables over time? The findings from studies of type 2 diabetes and similar diseases are relatively clear: the correlation between changes in disease management behavior and corresponding changes in metabolic control are significant and clinically meaningful, but they are far lower than unity, and they vary considerably from patient to patient (Goodall & Halford, 1992). Levels of biological variables, like hemoglobin A1C in diabetes, a measure of glycemic control over a 3-month period, are a function of many factors in addition to behavioral management, e.g., genetics, body type, and medication regimen. Yet in many studies, changes among biological markers are viewed as the exclusive gold standard, since it is argued by some that the foremost goal of health related interventions is enhancement of biological health.

A rationale for the importance of behavioral and relationship change, however, in the context of chronic disease, irrespective of biological change, has been made by Kaplan (1990) and by Wolbert and Anderson (2001). Kaplan suggested that behavioral change, and by extension relationship change, has value in its own right because in addition to its less than one-to-one relationship with specific biological variables, it improves quality of life, enhances general physical health, has indirect effects on biological outcomes, and reduces stresses that can have biological implications. Furthermore, programs of intervention that have only biological variables as outcomes set up patients, families, and programs for failure, since there is no guarantee that major behavioral change will lead, in a one-to-one fashion, to major biological change. Thus, the specification of outcome variables is a complicated process that is complicated even further by family-based interventions, since the family is often viewed as one step removed from the linkages between personal health behaviors and biological change. Issues include the number and type of outcomes selected, on whom they are collected, how they are linked rationally to the targets of intervention, whether they are at the level of the person or the relationship, and the assumptions underlying the relationship between behavioral change and biological change as a function of intervention. Thus, family models must be used with clear linkages to behavioral and biological outcomes.

2. A clear specification of which characteristics of the family or couple relationship are to be targeted for change. No single intervention can address all of the complexities of personal, family, and relationship life with a time-limited protocol. What is the theoretical or empirical justification for the selection of specific family characteristics that will lead to change in a set of associated dependent variables? For example, one might suggest that an improvement in patient-partner collaboration caused by enhanced couple conflict resolution skills might lead to better general disease management. Family models must identify specific relationship targets for change.

3. A clear outline of the pathways and mechanisms through which the selected family characteristics targeted for intervention operate together to affect change in the outcomes. It is important for family models to employ a rationale that suggests that some crucial family characteristics will affect others through a defined path of influence. Following the last example, improved conflict resolution might lead to greater relationship harmony, which, in turn, might lead to higher marital satisfaction and less family stress, thus improving general quality of life.

4. A determination if characteristics of the individuals in the family will be included in the model. Personal traits of family members influence family relationships and vice versa in a mutually reinforcing, circular pattern. Should selective trait characteristics of individuals be included in the model, and, if so, which are the most important with respect to a given outcome? For example, data suggest that the personality traits of conscientiousness and neuroticism, as defined by the five-factor model of personality (Digman, 1990), influence chronic disease outcomes (Christensen et al., 2002). Since these are generally considered trait characteristics and are more than likely not themselves targets for change in a family intervention, should they be included in the model as potentially important moderator variables? Likewise, should trait characteristics of other family members be included? Family models cannot be so focused on relationships that they exclude or neglect the characteristics, styles, and traits of the individuals involved.

5. Including contextual, mediating, or moderating variables in the intervention framework. Are the contextual variables (e.g., SES, gender, ethnicity, disease status) mediated by the personal and family variables and do the moderating variables condition the impact of the intervention on the outcomes? Mediating and moderating processes add complexity to the framework, but they lead to a greater understanding of the underlying dynamics, permit clearer hypothesis testing, and provide greater efficacy and efficiency than omitting them.

6. A clear decision concerning for whom the intervention is intended and in whom will change occur. Can the intervention be operationalized by working only with individual family members or does the intervention require that both the patient and the partner attend? For example, Mittelman, Ferris, Shulman, Steinberg, and Levin (1996) developed a highly effective program of intervention for individual family members of elderly dementing patients to deal not only with the personal stresses of dealing with the disease, but also for improving their skills in dealing with other members of the family, anticipating family conflicts, and defusing potential family crises. Although emphasizing a family perspective, the intervention was directed at individuals and in most cases only one member of each family attended. Their intervention decreased reported family stress and led to a delay in institutionalization of the patient. Other family programs have included entire family units (Steinglass, 1998), adult couples (Family Heart Study Group, 1994), or a parent and an adolescent (Anderson, Brackett, Ho, & Laffel, 1999).

A parallel question involves how to measure change following the intervention: does measurement need to occur at the individual self-report level or at the couple or family interactional level, especially when relationship change is a focus of the intervention? For example, Wysocki et al. (1999) assessed interaction via videotape in families with an adolescent with type 1 diabetes both before and after an extensive and highly structured family-level program to improve communication and problem-solving skills. Changes in observational codes over time documented the effects of the intervention. In contrast, Anderson et al. (1999) used parental self-report measures to assess change in levels of parental-adolescent conflict following an office-based intervention for adolescents with type 1 diabetes and their parents. Even though in both of these examples the object of change was the same family-level variable, communication and problem solving, in the first example assessment of change occurred at the interactional level, whereas in the second example assessment of change occurred at the personal level.

The last issue concerns who is included in the outcome assessment protocol: patient, partner, other family member. Most family and health research addressing diseases of adulthood rarely includes family members other than the patient in the outcomes assessment protocol. The focus of the intervention is to improve the health status of the patient and changes in the health status of the partner or other family members are rarely documented. Yet we know that chronic disease in one family member affects others as well (Fisher, Chesla, Skaff, Mullan, & Kanter, 2002; Lieberman & Fisher, 1995) and it is not a great leap of faith to suggest that a family intervention for a patient with chronic disease will have health implications for other family members. Many of these health-related changes go undetected, leaving a significant proportion of the effects of the intervention undocumented. With the exception of disease-specific biological variables, a case can be made to include the partner or other family members in the assessment of the same variables as those collected on the patient. Lifestyle factors (diet, exercise), affective status, disease-related stress, quality of life, etc. operate throughout the family system and interventions that address these factors have implications beyond the patient with the chronic disease.

■   A Family Intervention Framework for Type 2 Diabetes

To illustrate how a family intervention framework might take shape in a specific disease setting, figure 22.2 and table 22.2 expand the outline presented in table 22.1

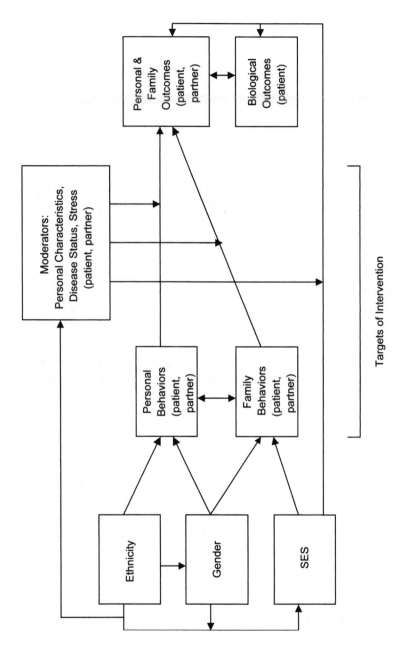

FIGURE 22.2. A framework for family intervention in type 2 diabetes.

TABLE 22.2   *Variables for Each Construct in the Intervention Framework*

Constructs	Variables
Contextual variables	Ethnicity: self-identified
	Gender: self-identified
	SES: education, income, access to care
Personal behaviors	Self-efficacy, disease knowledge
Family behaviors	Beliefs and emotion regulation → conflict resolution → problem solving
Moderators	Personal characteristics: neuroticism, conscientiousness
	Disease status: time since diagnosis, number of comorbidities
	Stress: economic, job, extended family, events
Behavioral and family outcomes	General health and functional status, emotional tone, quality of life, behavioral, relationship
Biological outcomes	HbA1C, lipids, BMI

for a couple intervention in which one member of the dyad has type 2 diabetes. The conceptual framework is presented graphically in figure 22.2 and a list of variables associated with each construct in the framework is presented in table 22.2. The framework includes three contextual constructs (ethnicity, patient gender, SES), personal and family behavioral targets for intervention, three sets of moderator variables (personal characteristics, disease status, extra disease stress), and personal, family, and biological outcomes. Note also that the paths of influence among the constructs are specified.

Several aspects of the framework should be highlighted. First, the three contextual variables directly influence all four remaining groups of constructs in the path-ordered framework: the intervention targets, the moderators, and the personal, relationship, and biological outcomes. For example, ethnicity can directly affect family beliefs and expectations for role behavior, and SES can have a direct effect on outcomes, especially through access to care. Likewise, gender can affect the family targets directly because of differences in gender-related behavioral roles, and gender also can affect the moderators because of gender-related variations in stress. Second, the moderators condition the effects of the intervention on outcomes. For example, the linkages between change in partner self-efficacy, a personal target of intervention, and change in behavioral outcomes can be limited by the severity of the patient's disease, the level of neuroticism, and the amount of external stress. Third, as noted at the bottom of the diagram, the moderators also can be targets of intervention in and of themselves. For example, a portion of the intervention can be directed at improving the management of extra disease stress in patient and partner. Fourth, the personal and family targets of intervention are mutually reinforcing, since each occurs in the presence of the other. Thus, it may be difficult to tease apart the independent contributions of each on outcomes. Fifth, the intervention is directed at patients and partners, rather than singling out the patient alone. Sixth, partners and patients receive the same assessment protocol, including assessment of moderators, contextual variables, relationship and personal factors, and outcomes, excluding the disease-specific biological outcome variables. Interestingly, we have experimented with assessing body mass index (BMI) and lipids in partners as well as patients because both of these measures can be considered biological risk indicators for each member of the dyad. Since our goal was to improve health-related lifestyle, we reasoned that improvements in partner biological markers are as important as improvements in patient biological markers. Also, focusing on health-related behavioral and biological change among both patients and partners levels the playing field and fosters greater mutual empathy between spouses regarding the difficulty of behavioral change. Thus, the framework carefully lays out an ordered sequence of constructs and paths of influence to link intervention to outcome within sets of contextual and mediating influences. The framework also helps guide hypothesis testing regarding the relevance of each variable and it helps determine for whom the intervention works best and under what circumstances, thus addressing issues of efficiency raised earlier.

Contextual Variables

The variables listed in table 22.2 specify the constructs. Ethnicity and gender are self-identified. Education and income define social class, and access to care is included as a crucial contextual variable with direct links to outcome, regardless of intervention. Good medical care is a prerequisite to good diabetes management, irrespective of behavioral intervention.

Personal Behaviors

Within the personal behavioral construct, we elected to include patient and partner disease self-efficacy and disease knowledge. Both have important implications for changing disease management behaviors (Anderson et al., 1995).

Family Behaviors

The family constructs were drawn from an extensive review of family characteristics that are linked to health outcomes across different diseases (Weihs et al., 2002). As indicated by arrows in the family behavior row of table 22.2, the model targets family beliefs and family emotion regulation as primary family constructs from which changes in patient-partner collaboration in problem solving and conflict resolution emerge.

Beliefs (meanings) and feelings establish interpersonal expectations regarding appraisals of significant others, they shape behavioral responses, and they create the context in which new experiences and problems are interpreted and understood. Hence, they create the perceptual and cognitive frame for how marital partners respond to each other in the face of chronic disease and its management over time. Improvements in patient-partner disease-related collaboration cannot easily take place without addressing the beliefs and expectations that underlie patient-partner behavior. For example, the chances of success in teaching methods for direct, open communication about planning a diet for a multiday trip when one partner has diabetes are limited when one partner is appraised by the other as angry, intrusive, and controlling, and the second partner is expected by the first partner to withdraw at the first sign of disagreement or conflict.

Several literatures suggest that beliefs and expectations drive behavior in relationship settings, especially as it relates to health and disease (Rolland, 1994; Wright, Watson, & Bell, 1996). Examples include meaning-making (Patterson), the health belief model (Rosenstock, 1974), the theory of reasoned action and planned behavior (Prochaska & DiClemente, 1983), attribution theory (Weiner, 1979), self-determination theory (Williams, Freedman, & Deci, 1998), and the transtheoretical model (Marshall & Biddle, 2001). Personal and family beliefs and expectations can be based on the broad cultural context of the multigeneration family (Chesla, Skaff, Bartz, Mullan, & Fisher, 2000; Kleinman et al., 1978) and through individual family experience over time (Hampson, Glasgow, & Foster, 1995).

The importance of the emotional context of the family has not been neglected in current research. Studies of expressed emotion (Hooley, 1985), attachment theory (Scheier & Bridges, 1995; Uchino, Cacioppo, & Kiecolt-Glaser, 1996), and depression (Fisher et al., 2002; Whisman, 2001) are but a few areas in which affective themes have played a prominent role. It is also interesting to note that emotion and emotion-related constructs underlie the vast majority of programs of family and couple research described in this volume. These include attachment (Wood, Johnson), safety theory (Markman), sound relationship house theory (Gottman, Ryan), depression (Whiffen, Bernal, Asarnow, Beach, Kaslow), and vulnerability coping (Wilson). These programs of research and intervention address relationship satisfaction, emotional tone, emotion management, or emotion regulation and dysregulation as primary family or relationship constructs.

Underlying beliefs and feelings can create roadblocks to successful collaboration because they prevent the partners from dealing directly with underlying negative and disruptive affect, they limit the learning of alternative adaptive responses and behaviors, and they prevent patients and partners from reconciling differences in beliefs and perspectives that characterize their understandings and approaches to the disease and its management. Thus, beliefs, meanings, and expectations, plus the tone and management of affect that surrounds the relationship, can be viewed as primary family constructs that help shape couple problem solving and conflict resolution in diabetes management.

Moderators

The three sets of moderators included in the framework play particularly important roles in the management of type 2 diabetes, in which repetitive, ongoing, and often invasive lifestyle changes have to be initiated and maintained over long periods of time. Disease severity can place limits on biological outcomes and can limit the effects of improvements in diabetes self-efficacy on outcomes (Anderson, Funnell, Fitzgerald, & Marrero, 2000). Likewise, high levels of extra disease-related stress can offset the effects of even the most constructive intervention (Demers et al., 1989). And the personal traits of neuroticism can disrupt the effect of intervention, whereas conscientiousness can enhance the systematic and repetitive behaviors advocated in intervention programs for patients and partners (Christensen et al., 2002).

Outcomes

The groups of outcome variables outlined in the last two rows of table 22.2 are based on a framework of outcome assessment in diabetes developed by Fisher, Chesla, Skaff, Gilliss, Kanter, et al. (2000). The various groups of outcomes listed tap into the major areas of disease management required by the disease and the comorbidities that frequently accompany them.

■ Models and Methods

Given the issues raised above, it may be useful to address briefly what remains a set of ongoing methodological problems in family and health research. These problems can be summarized to some extent by posing three questions: how to develop and test alternative models and strategies of the family in health research; how to address the ongoing problems of family measurement within the context of health research; and what are the most important contextual variables that need to be addressed in the next generation of studies?

How to adopt an effective and practical model of family and health research remains problematic and defies an easy solution. Two specific issues are worthy of note. First, the search to document clear differences between one or more experimental and control conditions in a family intervention design often tells us little about the process underlying variations in outcomes and the importance of specific moderators and mediators. These aspects of the research are part of the efficiency of the intervention and addressing them advances the application of the intervention to the health care setting. In this sense, frequently testing articulated models of change, such as the example presented in figure 22.2, tells us not only if change occurred, but what contributed to change and what qualified change. Statistical methods, such as structural equation modeling in conjunction with confirmatory factor analysis and random regression, are now available to help document paths of influence among variables over time and to identify subsets of families that display different patterns of relations among the variables. The key question concerns not if change occurred at all, but for whom it occurred and what explains the differences between the subgroup of families that changed and the subgroup of families that did not change.

The second, related, issue regarding strategies of family intervention research is frequently overlooked: do we really expect families to change in some very definable way as a function of the intervention, or are we simply considering the family as a very important moderator variable? That is, are we trying to enhance change in an important and measurable aspect of family functioning that is related to the disease, or, alternatively, do we think that the effects of an intervention will be different for different kinds of families? In my view, most family interventions portray themselves as undertaking the former, when in fact they are entertaining the latter. Families are inherently stable and many resist change with enthusiasm. Is it realistic to assume that a very brief, although important, clinical intervention will change a fundamental aspect of the family structure or system of beliefs? Is it not more realistic to assume that some families will be able to make more use of this type of intervention than others and to document for which families this occurs, suggesting that other, perhaps more intense, interventions be reserved for these newly identified families? Again, this attends to the need for efficiency in family and health research.

Second, family measurement issues remain particularly problematic in health research because of their complexity and time requirements, the variety of windows into the family that are possible, and the lack of agreement among different family members when several are assessed on the same family variables. Although there are no universal solutions to the complexity of family assessment, several guidelines may prove helpful. First, the complexity of the assessment framework probably should parallel the complexity of the intervention. The literature is replete with studies that employ an extensive intervention framework and then assess its effectiveness with overly simplistic, generic family measures that most likely were not constructed with sufficient sensitivity to detect the hoped-for change or were unrelated conceptually to what the interventionists elected to target for change. Detecting change, however, forces the developer of the intervention to define the targets of change clearly and to measure them carefully with the same level of sophistication that was devoted to the development and implementation of the intervention itself. Second, questionnaire, personal structured interview, interaction, and unobtrusive measures can be used in reasonable and balanced ways to document different kinds of change efficiently and to increase the breadth and scope of assessment. For example, one spouse can be asked to complete a questionnaire while the second spouse is interviewed, an interaction task can be audio- or videotaped while the couple waits for a physical exam or a blood draw, and unobtrusive measures of health care visits, costs of family health care, searches on the internet for additional information, family logs, etc. can be collected with minimal cost in time and resources. Third, combining qualitative and quantitative measurement strategies in the same study increases the richness of the research geometrically. Qualitative approaches can be directed at selected subsamples to make the method cost-efficient, and they can inform broader quantitative approaches by providing greater depth and focus. Comprehensive yet targeted assessment using as many methods as are sensible and practical provides for elegant designs that enhance the field.

A final issue concerns the attention paid to contextual variables. Family ethnicity and patient gender remain crucial but often neglected areas of study with far reaching implications. Ethnicity, for example, is acknowledged by most as a powerful influence, such that all would agree that programs of intervention need to be ethnically relevant and unbiased. How ethnicity is handled in the design, however, often leaves much to be desired. Adopting the banner of inclusion, many studies include a mix of ethnicities but then have too few of any one ethnic group to undertake a within-ethnic group analysis. The mix reduces precision and increases the risk of type 1 error. For example, we showed that patterns and styles of couple conflict resolution around diabetes management were different between Latinos and Euro-Americans (Fisher et al., 2000): Latino couples tended to dance around the issue delicately, never confronting directly, whereas Euro-American couples often were blunt and direct. Latino couples, therefore, took much longer to address their differences than Euro-American couples, suggesting that stylistic differences led to differences in process, although, notably, not necessarily differences in outcome. Using the same criteria for success in the task with a mixed group sample, rather than separate samples, would have hidden the effect and not added to our understanding of these process differences, differences that are crucial when applying the method to large patient groups. Thus, attention to ethnicity requires a design that permits evaluation of ethnic differences and similarities using measures that are sensitive to the variables under study.

Few can argue against the importance of gender, yet despite the arguments, it is infrequent to find family and health studies that address the fact that patient gender colors the entire course of disease in the family. For example, in a recent paper we reported that the spouses of patients with type 2 diabetes had rates of depressive affect that were significantly higher than community levels, suggesting that diabetes placed spouses at increased risk for depression and its consequences (Fisher et al., 2002). Interestingly, when analyzed separately by spouse gender, we found that the effect held almost entirely for female spouses of male patients and that their levels of depressive affect were as high as or in many cases even higher than the already elevated levels of depressive affect among patients. The level of male spouse depressive affect was relatively low. Why this is the case and how the differences in beliefs, roles, and expectations between male and female spouses of patients with diabetes influences couple dynamics provides rich information into the behavioral management of the disease. This means that we need not only to observe gender differences in level and dispersion among the crucial variables of the study, but we also need a sufficient sample size for each gender to observe differences in the patterns and relationships among variables on which the model is based. This information, however, is only available when gender is viewed not as a control variable but as an underlying moderator that shapes the underlying research questions and the subsequent analyses.

■ Conclusions

The major goal of this chapter has been to review the current state of development of family models in health research and to suggest directions for the future. The overview identified six areas for future development, which were called model enhancements. A conceptual framework for incorporating these enhancements into intervention programs was presented and illustrated using type 2 diabetes.

Applying a family perspective to interventions in chronic disease poses a number of unique challenges: integrating family and personal variables into the same protocol, including more than one individual from the same family in the intervention, selecting relevant family and relationship targets for change, adopting a sensible and comprehensive outcome assessment protocol, and selecting sets of contextual and moderating variables that will provide important information about the efficacy and efficiency of the intervention.

The complexity of these processes is notable. The conceptual diagrams reveal the number of variables that must be considered and they suggest the complicated dynamics of the interrelationships among the constructs and the paths of influence that need to be included. Family approaches to clinical phenomena are inherently complex and family clinicians have over the years rarely shied away from or over-simplified this complexity. Yet the family-based conceptual approaches that have been applied to the health arena, and many of the interventions that have emerged from them, have been limited in scope relative to the object of study. The health care setting is ripe for cost-efficient, innovative, family-based programs of care. To document its potential, however, family and health researchers and practitioners must expand current models and intervention frameworks to account for the complexities of families, diseases, and interventions.

■ Acknowledgments

This work was supported by Grants DK-49816 and DK-53203 from the National Institute of Diabetes, Digestive, and Kidney Disease and by a grant from the American Diabetes Association. Appreciation is expressed to Catherine A. Chesla, R.N., D.N.Sc., for her helpful comments on an earlier draft of this chapter.

■ References

Anderson, B. J., Brackett, J., Ho, J., & Laffel, L. M. (1999). An office-based intervention to maintain parent adolescent teamwork in diabetes management. *Diabetes Care, 22*, 713–721.

Anderson, R. M., Funnell, M. M., Butler, P. M., Arnold, M. S., Fitzgerald, J. T., & Feste, C. C. (1995). Patient empowerment: Results of a randomized controlled trial. *Diabetes Care, 18*, 943–949.

Anderson, R. M., Funnell, M. M., Fitzgerald, J. T., & Marrero, D. G. (2000). The diabetes empowerment scale: A measure of diabetes self-efficacy. *Diabetes Care, 23*, 739–743.

Antonovsky, A., & Sourani, T. (1988). Family sense of coherence and family adaptation. *Journal of Marriage and the Family, 50*, 79–82.

Charles, C., Gafni, A., & Whelan, T. (1997). Shared decision-making in the medical encounter: What does it mean? *Social Science and Medicine, 44*, 681–692.

Chesla, C. A., Skaff, M. M., Bartz, R. J., Mullan, J. T., & Fisher, L. (2000). Differences in personal models among Latinos and European-Americans: Implications for clinical care. *Diabetes Care, 23,* 1780–1785.

Christensen, A. J., Ehlers, S. L., Wiebe, J. S., Moran, P. J., Raichle, K., Ferneyhough, K., et al. (2002). Patient personality and mortality: A 4-year prospective examination of chronic renal insufficiency. *Health Psychology, 21,* 315–320.

Clement, S. (1995). Diabetes self-management education. *Diabetes Care, 18,* 1204–1214.

Cox, D. J., & Gonder-Frederick, L. (1992). Major developments in behavioral diabetes research. *Journal of Consulting and Clinical Psychology, 60,* 628–638.

Demers, R. Y., Neale, A. V., Wenzloff, N. J., Gronsman, K. J., & Jaber, L. A. (1989). Glycosylated hemoglobin levels and self-reported stress in adults with diabetes. *Behavioral Medicine, 15,* 167–172.

Digman, J. M. (1990). Personality structure: Emergence of the five-factor model. *Annual Review of Psychology, 41,* 417–440.

Family Heart Study Group. (1994). Randomized controlled trial evaluating cardiovascular screening and intervention in general practice: Principal results of British family heart study. *British Medical Journal, 308,* 313–320.

Fiscella, K., Franks, P., & Shields, C. G. (1997). Perceived family criticism and primary care utilization: Psychosocial and biomedical pathways. *Family Process, 36,* 25–41.

Fisher, L., Chesla, C. A., Bartz, R. J., Gilliss, C., Skaff, M. A., Sabogal, F., et al. (1998). The family and type 2 diabetes: A framework for intervention. *Diabetes Educator, 24,* 599–607.

Fisher, L., Chesla, C. A., Skaff, M. A., Gilliss, C., Kanter, R., Lutz, C. P., et al. (2000). Disease management status: A typology of Latino and Euro-American patients with type 2 diabetes. *Behavioral Medicine, 26,* 53–66.

Fisher, L., Chesla, C. A., Skaff, M. M., Gilliss, C., Mullan, J. T., Bartz, R. J., et al. (2000). The family and disease management in Latino and Euro-American patients with type 2 diabetes. *Diabetes Care, 23,* 267–272.

Fisher, L., Chesla, C., Skaff, M. A., Mullan, J., & Kanter, R. (2002). Depression and anxiety among partners of European-American and Latino patients with type 2 diabetes. *Diabetes Care, 25,* 1564–1570.

Fisher, L., Gudmundsdottir, M., Gilliss, C., Skaff, M. A., Mullan, J., Kanter, R., et al. (2000). Resolving disease management problems in European-American and Latino couples with type 2 diabetes: The effects of ethnicity and patient gender. *Family Process, 39,* 403–416.

Fisher, L., Ransom, D. C., & Terry, H. L. (1993). The California Family Health Project: VI. Multi-domain analyses. *Family Process, 32,* 49–68.

Fisher, L., Ransom, D. C., Terry, H. E., Lipkin, M., & Weiss, R. (1992). The California Family Health Project: I. Introduction and a description of adult health. *Family Process, 31,* 231–250.

Franks, P., Campbell, T. L., & Shields, C. G. (1992). Social relationships and health: The relative roles of family functioning and social support. *Social Science and Medicine, 34,* 779–788.

Glasgow, R. E. (1991). Compliance to diabetes regimens: Conceptualization and complexity. In J. A. Kramer & B. Spiker (Eds.), *Patient compliance in medical practice and clinical trials.* (pp. 209–221). New Orleans, LA: Raven Press.

Golin, C. E., DiMatteo, M. R., & Gelberg, L. (1996). The role of patient participation in the doctor visit. *Diabetes Care, 19,* 1153–1164.

Goodall, T., & Halford, W. (1992). Self-management of diabetes mellitus: A critical review. *Health Psychology, 10,* 1–8.

Greenfield, S., Kaplan, S. H., Ware, J. E., Yanko, E. M., & Frank, H. J. (1988). Patients' participation in medical care: Effects on blood sugar control and quality of life in diabetes. *Journal of General Internal Medicine, 3,* 448–457.

Hampson, S. E., Glasgow, R. E., & Foster, L. S. (1995). Personal models of diabetes among older adults: Relationship to self-management and other variables. *The Diabetes Educator, 21,* 300–307.

Hooley, J. M. (1985). Expressed emotion: A critical review of the literature. *Clinical. Psychology Review, 5,* 119–139.

Kaplan, R. M. (1990). Behavior as the central outcome in health care. *American Psychologist, 45*(11), 1211–1220.

Kaplan, S. H., Greenfield, S., & Ware, J. E. (1989). Assessing the effects of physician–patient interactions on the outcomes of chronic disease. *Medical Care, 27,* S110–S127.

Kiecolt-Glaser, J. K., & Newton, T. L. (2001). Marriage and health: His and hers. *Psychological Bulletin, 127,* 472–503.

Kleinman, A., Eisenberg, L., & Good, B. (1978). Culture, illness and care: Clinical lessons from anthropologic and cross-cultural research. *Annals of Internal Medicine, 88,* 251–258.

Lieberman, M. A., & Fisher, L. (1995). The impact of chronic illness on the health and well-being of family members. *The Gerontologist, 35,* 94–102.

Marshall, S. J., & Biddle, S. J. (2001). The transtheoretical model of behavior change: A meta analysis of applications to physical activity and exercise. *Annals of Behavior Medicine, 23,* 229–246.

McEwen, B. (1998). Protective and damaging effects of stress mediators. *New England Journal of Medicine, 338,* 171–179.

Mittelman, M. S., Ferris, S. H., Shulman, E., Steinberg, G., & Levin, B. (1996). A family intervention to delay nursing home placement of patients with Alzheimer's disease: A randomized controlled trial. *Journal of the American Medical Association, 276,* 1725–1731.

Patterson, J. (1988). Families experiencing stress: I. The Family Adjustment and Adaptation Response Model; II. Applying the FAAR model to health-related issues for intervention and research. *Family Systems Medicine, 6,* 202–237.

Patterson, J. M. (2002). Integrating family resilience and family stress theory. *Journal of Marriage and the Family, 64,* 349–360.

Patterson, J. M., & Garwick, A. W. (1994). The impact of chronic disease on families: A family systems perspective. *Annals of Behavioral Medicine, 16,* 131–142.

Primono, J., Yates, B. C., & Woods, N. F. (1990). Social support for women during chronic illness: The relationship between sources and types of adjustment. *Research in Nursing and Health, 13,* 153–161.

Prochaska, J. O., & DiClemente, C. C. (1983). Stages and processes of self-change of smoking: Toward an integrative model of change. *Journal of Consulting and Clinical Psychology, 51,* 390–395.

Reiss, D. (1981). *The family's construction of reality.* Cambridge, MA: Harvard University Press.

Rolland, J. S. (1987). Chronic illness and the life cycle: A conceptual framework. *Family Process, 26,* 203–221.

Rolland, J. S. (1994). *Families, illness, and disability.* New York: Basic Books.

Rosenstock, I. (1974). The health belief model and preventative behavior. *Health Education Monographs, 2*, 345–386.

Sapolsky, R. L., & Krey, L. (1986). The neuroendocrinology of stress and aging: The glucocorticoid cascade hypothesis. *Endocrinology Review, 7*, 284–301.

Scheier, M. F., & Bridges, M. W. (1995). Person variables and health: Personality dispositions and acute psychological states as shared determinants for disease. *Psychosomatic Medicine, 57*, 255–268.

Shields, G. C., Franks, P., Harp, J. J., McDaniel, S. H., & Campbell, T. L. (1992). Development of the family emotional involvement and criticism scales: A self-report scale to measure expressed emotion. *Journal of Marital and Family Therapy, 18*, 395–407.

Steinglass, P. (1998). Multiple family discussion groups for patients with chronic medical illness. *Families, Systems, and Health, 16*, 55–70.

Toobert, D. J., & Glasgow, R. E. (1994). Problem-solving and diabetes self-care. *Journal of Behavioral Medicine, 14*, 71–86.

Uchino, B. N., Cacioppo, J. T., & Kiecolt-Glaser, J. K. (1996). Relationship between social support and physiological processes: A review with emphasis on underlying mechanisms. *Psychological Bulletin, 119*, 488–531.

Weihs, K., Fisher, L., & Baird, M. (2002). Families, health, and behavior—a section of the commissioned report by the Committee on Health and Behavior: Research, Practice, and Policy, Division of Neuroscience and Behavioral Health and Division of Health Promotion and Disease Prevention, Institute of Medicine, National Academy of Sciences. *Families Systems, and Health, 20*, 7–46.

Weiner, B. (1979). A theory of motivation for some classroom experience. *Journal of Educational Psychology, 6*, 160–170.

Whisman, M. A. (2001). The association between depression and marital dissatisfaction. In S. R. Beach (Ed.), *Marital and family processes in depression* (pp. 3–25). Washington, DC: American Psychological Association.

Williams, G. C., Freedman, Z. R., & Deci, E. L. (1998). Supporting autonomy to motivate patients with diabetes for glucose control. *Diabetes Care, 21*, 1644–1651.

Wolbert, H. A., & Anderson, B. J. (2001). Management of diabetes: are doctors framing the benefits from the wrong perspective? *British Medical Journal, 323*, 994–996.

Wood, B. L. (1993). Beyond the "psychosomatic family": A bio behavioral family model of pediatric illness. *Family Process, 32*, 261–278.

Wood, B. L., & Miller, B. D. (in press). A biobehavioral family approach to the treatment of physically manifested illness in children and adolescents. In F. Kaslow (Ed.), *Comprehensive handbook of psychotherapy* (Vol. 4, pp. 31–80). New York: Wiley & Sons.

Wright, L. M., Watson, W. L., & Bell, J. M. (1996). *Beliefs: The heart of healing in families and illness.* New York: Basic Books.

Wysocki, T., Miller, K. M., Greco, P., Harris, M. A., Harvey, L. M., Taylor, A., et al. (1999). Behavior therapy for families of adolescents with diabetes: Effects on directly observed family interactions. *Behavior Therapy, 30*, 507–525.

Index

Abuse during pregnancy, women and partner violence, 194–195
Acceptance, couple therapy, 35
Accommodation, satisfaction, 35–36
Action priming, emotion, 94
Adaptation phase, family adjustment and adaptation response model, 522, 523–524
Adaptive processes, marital stability, 31
Addictions, getting help, 131–132
Adjustment
    children and divorce, 359
    family adjustment and adaptation response model, 522, 523
    marital satisfaction, 26
Adolescent depression. *See also* Culture and depressed adolescents
    antidepressant medication like selective serotonin reuptake inhibitors (SSRIs), 432, 433
    behavioral family management, 438
    challenges of adolescence, 440–442
    cognitive-behavior therapy (CBT), 426, 433
    developmental considerations, 440–442
    family conflict and, 482–483
    family education session, 437
    family-focused approach to treatment, 433–434
    family interventions, 434–440
    family systems model, 438
    interpersonal family therapy model, 438
    interpersonal psychotherapy (IPT), 432, 433
    involving family members in treatment, 481–484
    multifamily psychoeducational group intervention (MFPG), 436–437
    parental depression, 438–439
    pharmacotherapy with SSRIs, 432, 433
    potential dangers, 425–426
    prevalence, 425
    psychoeducation intervention, 435–436
    randomized clinical intervention trials, 427–431
    recommendations, 442–444

Successful Negotiation Acting Positive (SNAP), 439
    suicide, 439–440
    treatment literature, 426, 432–433
Adolescents, adjustment in stepfamilies, 274–275
Adult love, attachment theory, 97–99
Advocacy. *See also* Domestic violence advocacy
    domestic violence, 196–199
Affect regulation difficulties, depressed children, 405–406
Affective disorders, assortative partnering, 155
Affective functioning, depression in children, 401
Affective systems, partner violence and children, 234–235
African American children, depression, 402–403
African American families. *See also* Fathers in African American families
    adjustment in stepfamilies, 275–276
    children and family structure, 328
    exposure to partner violence, 230
    father involvement, 343–344
    marriage crisis, 14, 128
    single mothers, 329
Age
    father-mother relationships, 332
    fathers' capacities and well-being, 337
    prevalence of physical aggression, 142–143
Aggression. *See also* Partner aggression; Physical aggression; Psychosocial interventions for aggression
    challenges in understanding couples', 141, 151–152
    cross-sectional vs. longitudinal designs, 148–149
    definitional issues, 147–148
    peer socialization, 154
Aggressors, female perpetrators of partner violence, 209–210
Alcohol abuse, treatment, 252–253
Allegiance effect, 45–46
Ambience-salience dialectic, self-reported relationship satisfaction, 28–29